Taking
SIDES

Clashing Views on
Controversial
Legal Issues

Sixth Edition

Taking SIDES

Clashing Views on
Controversial
Legal Issues

Sixth Edition

Edited, Selected, and with Introductions by

M. Ethan Katsh

University of Massachusetts–Amherst

The Dushkin Publishing Group, Inc.

To Beverly

Photo Acknowledgments

Part 1   Families/DPG
Part 2   Transportation/DPG
Part 3   United Nations/John Robaton

Cover Art Acknowledgment

Charles Vitelli

Library of Congress Cataloging-in-Publication Data

Main entry under title:
  Taking sides: clashing views on controversial legal issues/edited, selected, and with introductions by M. Ethan Katsh.—6th ed.
    Includes bibliographical references and index.
    1. Justice, Administration of—United States. 2. United States—Constitutional law. 3. Political questions and judicial power—United States. 4. Law—Social aspects—United States. I. Katsh, M. Ethan, *comp.*
      KF384.A2T33   340′.115′0973—dc20
      1-56134-323-4   94-32837

Printed on Recycled Paper

The Dushkin Publishing Group, Inc.

PREFACE

The study of law should be introduced as part of a liberal education, to train and enrich the mind.... I am convinced that, like history, economics, and meta-physics—and perhaps even to a greater degree than these—the law could be advantageously studied with a view to the general development of the mind.

—Justice Louis D. Brandeis

The general study of law in colleges, universities, and even high schools has grown rapidly during the last 10 years. Accompanying this development has been the publication of new curriculum materials that go beyond the analysis of legal cases and doctrines that make up much of professional law study in law schools. This book is part of the effort to view and study law as an institution that continuously interacts with other social institutions. Law should be examined from an interdisciplinary perspective and be accessible to all students.

This book focuses on a series of controversial issues involving law and the legal system. It is, I believe, an appropriate starting point for law study since controversy and conflict are inherent in law. Law is based on an adversary approach to conflict resolution, in which two advocates representing opposing sides are pitted against each other. Judicial decisions often contain both majority and dissenting opinions, which reveal some of the arguments that went on in the judges' chambers. Perhaps most relevant to a discussion of the place of controversy in the legal system is the First Amendment guarantee of freedom of speech and press, which presumes that we all benefit by a vigorous debate of important issues.

Since many of the issues in *Taking Sides* are often in the news, you probably already have opinions on them. What you should remember, however, is that there is usually more to learn about any given issue, and the topics discussed here are best approached with an open mind. You should not be surprised if your views change as you read the selections.

Changes to this edition   This sixth edition represents a considerable re-vision. There are seven completely new issues: *Does Mediation in Divorce Cases Hurt Women?* (Issue 2); *Are School Districts Created for Religious Reasons a Violation of the Constitution?* (Issue 5); *Should Affirmative Action Policies Be Con-tinued?* (Issue 8); *Can Courts Restrict the Picketing of Abortion Clinics?* (Issue 11); *Will Waiting Periods Control Gun Purchases?* (Issue 15); *Does the Clipper Chip Give the Government Too Much Control Over Citizens' Privacy?* (Issue 16); and *Should Drug Use Be Legalized?* (Issue 18). I have also revised Issue 12, *Should the Death Penalty Be Abolished?* so completely that I feel I should count it as brand new. In all, there are 16 new selections in this edition.

i

A word to the instructor   An *Instructor's Manual With Test Questions* (multiple-choice and essay) is available through the publisher for the instructor using *Taking Sides* in the classroom. And a general guidebook, *Using Taking Sides in the Classroom,* which discusses methods and techniques for integrating the pro-con approach into any classroom setting, is also available.

Acknowledgments   I received helpful comments and suggestions from the many users of *Taking Sides* across the United States and Canada. Their suggestions have markedly enhanced the quality of this edition of the book and are reflected in the seven totally new issues and the updated selection.

Special thanks go to those who responded with specific suggestions for the sixth edition:

John Baker
Indiana University,
    Bloomington

Sherry L. Blakey
University of
    Nebraska–Lincoln

Murray Comarow
American University

Phil Finney
Southeast Missouri State
    University

David B. Fletcher
Wheaton College

Michael A. Foley
Marywood College

Sheryl J. Grana
University of
    Minnesota–Duluth

Robin Hoffmann
Salve Regina University

Louis M. Holscher
San Jose State University

Radha Jhappan
Carleton University

Wayne A. Moss
University of Maine–Augusta

Jana Nestlerode
West Chester University

James M. Pleszewski
Rowan-Cabarrus Community
    College

Jack Rossotti
American University

Malcom D. Schlusberg
Syracuse University

Douglas W. Scott
Troy State University

Rachel Smith
Indiana University,
    Bloomington

Richard Stempien
Syracuse University

Susan Thomas
Oakland University

Anthony Walsh
Boise State University

William J. Zanardi
St. Edwards University

A note on case citations Throughout this book you will see references to judicial opinions. The judge's opinion or decision refers to the written statement of reasons the judge provides when making an interpretation of law or deciding a case. These opinions are printed and distributed in books called *reporters*, which can be found in law libraries and many university libraries. There are separate reporters for federal and state cases. When you see a reference to a case such as *Brown v. Board of Education*, 347 U.S. 483 (1954), it means that the case with that name can be found in volume 347 of the *United States Reports* on page 483 and that the case was decided in 1954. When you see a legal citation with a series of numbers and words, the first number is always the volume number and the last number is the page number.

M. Ethan Katsh
University of Massachusetts–Amherst

CONTENTS IN BRIEF

CONTENTS

Professor of law Harry I. Subin argues that greater responsibility should be placed on lawyers not to pervert the truth to help their clients. Attorney John B. Mitchell disputes the contention that the goal of the criminal justice process is to seek the truth and argues that it is essential that there be independent defense attorneys to provide protection against government oppression.

Penelope Bryan, a professor in the School of Law at the University of Denver, asserts that the process of mediation in divorce cases works more to the benefit of men than women. Stephen Erickson, a practicing divorce mediator, argues that all parties benefit from a process that is less adversarial, namely, mediation, and which is not controlled by lawyers.

Professor of philosophy Kenneth Kipnis argues that plea bargaining often subverts the cause of justice. District Attorney Nick Schweitzer finds that plea bargaining is fair, useful, desirable, necessary, and practical.

Supreme Court justice Antonin Scalia finds that the St. Paul ordinance punishing "hate speech" cannot be constitutional because it regulates speech depending on the subject the speech addresses. Justice John Paul Stevens argues that this particular ordinance is perhaps simply overbroad.

Justice David H. Souter maintains that a New York statute that established a school serving only a single religious community violates the Establishment Clause of the First Amendment. Justice Antonin Scalia argues that the school is secular in nature and does not violate the First Amendment.

Supreme Court justice Sandra Day O'Connor upholds a woman's constitutional right to abortion under most circumstances. Chief Justice William

H. Rehnquist argues that Pennsylvania regulations on abortion should be upheld and that it is appropriate to overrule *Roe v. Wade*.

Judge Sarah Evans Barker argues that the ordinances banning pornography are unconstitutional infringements on freedom of speech. Author Andrea Dworkin maintains that pornography should not be constitutionally protected because it is destructive, abusive, and detrimental to women.

William Taylor, a lawyer, and Susan Liss, the deputy assistant attorney general of the U.S. Department of Justice, believe that affirmative action policies have been very effective in providing new opportunities for education and economic advancement. Wm. Bradford Reynolds, a senior litigation partner, argues that any preference provided on the basis of race, gender, religion, or national origin is inconsistent with the ideal of equality.

Supreme Court chief justice William H. Rehnquist recognizes that a competent individual may refuse medical treatment but believes a showing of clear and convincing proof of the individual's wishes is required before allowing the termination of feeding to an incompetent person. Justice William J. Brennan, Jr., argues that the Court is erecting too high a standard for allowing an individual's wishes to be followed.

Judge Hewitt P. Tomlin, Jr., argues that an award of child custody to a homosexual parent cannot be in the best interests of the child. Justice Melvin P. Antell refuses to allow one parent's homosexuality to be a deciding factor in the custody decision of the court.

Chief Justice William H. Rehnquist found that a set of restrictions on persons protesting at abortion clinics did not violate the First Amendment. Justice Antonin Scalia, in dissent, maintains that a 36-foot buffer zone limiting how a group may protest is inconsistent with the First Amendment.

Former Supreme Court justice Harry Blackmun argues that the application of the death penalty has been arbitrary and discriminatory. Attorney James Anders argues that the death penalty is the appropriate punishment for some crimes and that it should not be abolished.

U.S. Court of Appeals judge Malcolm Richard Wilkey raises objections to the
exclusionary rule on the grounds that it may suppress evidence and allow the
guilty to go free. Professor of law Yale Kamisar argues that the exclusionary
rule is necessary to prevent abuses by police and to protect citizens' rights.

Justice Burley B. Mitchell, Jr., is unwilling to recognize "battered wife syndrome" as meeting the standards needed for a self-defense claim in a homicide case. Justice Harry C. Martin believes that the wife's behavior can be
viewed in such a way as to meet the standards of self-defense.

Sarah Brady, head of a citizens' lobby for gun control, argues that a waiting
period for purchasing a weapon does not change who is lawfully allowed to
buy a gun and that it would prevent many crimes. James Jay Baker, director of
federal affairs for the National Rifle Association, claims that waiting periods
do not work, that criminals would still be able to obtain weapons, and that
an additional burden would be placed on law enforcement authorities.

Computer scientist Whitfield Diffie argues that a governmental program to permit government to unlock encrypted communications will violate privacy. Attorney Stewart Baker believes that the Clipper Chip proposal contains adequate safeguards to protect privacy and that the proposal does no more than preserve the power that law enforcement agencies have today.

Editor Jonathan Rowe examines the insanity defense as it is now administered and finds that its application is unfair and leads to unjust results. Professor of law Richard Bonnie argues that the abolition of the insanity defense would be immoral and would leave no alternative for those who are not responsible for their actions.

James Ostrowski, a policy analyst, asserts that drug prohibition increases crime, raises medical and economic costs, and fails to deter people from using illicit drugs. Steven Brill, lawyer and founder of *The American Lawyer* magazine, maintains that government should not abdicate its responsibility and that legalization would make the drug problem worse.

INTRODUCTION

The Role of Law

M. Ethan Katsh

Two hundred years ago, Edmund Burke, the influential British statesman and orator, commented that "in no other country perhaps in the world, is the law so general a study as it is in the United States." Today, in America, general knowledge about law is at a disappointing level. One study conducted several years ago concluded that "the general public's knowledge of and direct experience with courts is low."[1] Three out of four persons surveyed admitted that they knew either very little or nothing at all about state and local courts. More than half believed that the burden of proving innocence in a criminal trial is on the accused, and 72 percent thought that every decision made by a state could be reviewed by the Supreme Court. In a 1990 study, 59 percent could not name at least one current justice of the Supreme Court.

One purpose of this volume is to provide information about some specific and important legal issues. In your local newspaper today, there is probably at least one story concerning an issue in this book. The quality of your life will be directly affected by how many of these issues are resolved. But gun control (Issue 15), the insanity defense (Issue 17), drug legalization (Issue 18), abortion (Issue 6), legal ethics (Issue 1), and other issues in this book are often the subject of superficial, misleading, or inaccurate statements. *Taking Sides* is designed to encourage you to become involved in the public debate on these issues and to raise the level of the discussion on them.

The issues that are debated in this book represent some of the most important challenges our society faces. How they are dealt with will influence what kind of society we will have in the future. While it is important to look at and study them separately, it is equally necessary to think about their relationship to each other and about the fact that there is a tool called "law," which is being called upon to solve a series of difficult conflicts. The study of discrete legal issues should enable you to gain insight into some broad theoretical questions about law. This introduction, therefore, will focus on several basic characteristics of law and the legal process that you should keep in mind as you read this book.

THE NATURE OF LAW

The eminent legal anthropologist E. Adamson Hoebel once noted that the search for a definition of law is as difficult as the search for the Holy Grail. Law is certainly complicated, and trying to define it precisely can be frustrating. What follows, therefore, is not a definition of law but a framework or perspective for looking at and understanding law.

Law as a Body of Rules

One of the common incorrect assumptions about law is that it is merely a body of rules invoked by those who need them and then applied by a judge. Under this view, the judge is essentially a machine whose task is simply to find and apply the right rule to the dispute in question. This perspective makes the mistake of equating law with the rules of law. It is sometimes even assumed that there exists somewhere in the libraries of lawyers and judges one book with all the rules or laws in it, which can be consulted to answer legal questions. As may already be apparent, such a book could not exist. Rules alone do not supply the solutions to many legal problems. The late Supreme Court justice William O. Douglas once wrote, "The law is not a series of calculating machines where definitions and answers come tumbling out when the right levers are pushed." As you read the debates about the issues in this book, you will see that much more goes into a legal argument than the recitation of rules.

Law as a Process

A more meaningful way of thinking about law is to look at it as a process or system, keeping in mind that legal rules are one of the elements in the process. This approach requires a considerably broader vision of law: to think not only of the written rules, but also of the judges, the lawyers, the police, and all the other people in the system. It requires an even further consideration of all the things that influence these people, such as their values and economic status.

"Law," one legal commentator has stated, "is very like an iceberg; only one-tenth of its substance appears above the social surface in the explicit form of documents, institutions, and professions, while the nine-tenths of its substance that supports its visible fragment leads a sub-aquatic existence, living in the habits, attitudes, emotions and aspirations of men."[2]

In reading the discussions of controversial issues in this book, try to identify what forces are influencing the content of the rules and the position of the writers. Three of the most important influences on the nature of law are economics, moral values, and public opinion.

Law and Economics

Laws that talk about equality, such as the Fourteenth Amendment, which guarantees that no state shall "deny to any person... equal protection of the laws," suggest that economic status is irrelevant in the making and application of the law. As Anatole France, the nineteenth-century French satirist, once wrote, however, "The law, in its majestic equality, forbids the rich as well as the poor to sleep under bridges, to beg in streets, and to steal bread." Sometimes the purpose and effect of the law cannot be determined merely from the words of the law.

Marxist critics of law in capitalistic societies assert that poverty results from the manipulation of the law by the wealthy and powerful. It is possible to look at several issues in this book and make some tentative judgments about the influence of economic power on law. For example, what role does economics play in the debate over drug legalization (Issue 18)? Is the controversy over the fight against drugs one of social concerns or one of economics, in that it costs the government billions of dollars each year? In considering whether or not pornography should be protected (Issue 7), is the controversy purely over morality and values, or is it related to the enormous growth of the pornographic videotape industry? Plea bargaining (Issue 3), which mostly affects poor persons who cannot afford bail, also involves the question of whether or not the law is responsible for or perpetuates poverty and economic classes.

Law and Values

The relationship between law and values has been a frequent theme of legal writers and a frequent source of debate. Clearly, there is in most societies some relationship between law and morality. One writer has summarized the relationship as follows:

1. *There is a moral order in society.* Out of the many different and often conflicting values of the individuals and institutions that make up society may emerge a dominant moral position, a "core" of the moral order. The position of this core is dynamic, and as it changes, the moral order of society moves in the direction of that change.
2. *There is a moral content to the law.* The moral content of law also changes over time, and as it changes, the law moves in the direction of that change.
3. *The moral content of the law and moral order in society are seldom identical.*
4. *A natural and necessary affinity exists between the two "bodies" of law and moral order.*
5. *When there is a gap between the moral order of society and the law, some movement to close the gap is likely.* The law will move closer to the moral order of society, or the moral order will move closer to the law, or each will move toward the other. The likelihood of the movement to close the gap between law and moral order depends upon the size of the gap between the two bodies and the perceived significance of the subject matter concerning which the gap exists.[3]

Law and morality will not be identical in a pluralistic society, but there will also be attempts by dominant groups to insert their views of what is right into the legal code. The First Amendment prohibition against establishment of religion and the guarantee of freedom of religion are designed to protect those whose beliefs are different. Yet there have also been many historical examples of legal restrictions or limitations being imposed on minorities or of laws being ineffective because of the resistance of powerful groups. Prayers in the public schools, for example, which have been forbidden since the early 1960s, are still said in a few local communities.

Of the topics in this book, the insertion of morality into legal discussions has occurred most frequently in the abortion and capital punishment debates

(Issues 6 and 12). It is probably fair to say that these issues remain high on the agenda of public debate because they involve strongly held values and beliefs. The nature of the debates is also colored by strong feelings that are held by the parties. Although empirical evidence about public health and abortion or about deterrence and capital punishment does exist, the debates are generally more emotional than objective.

Public Opinion and the Law

It is often claimed that the judicial process is insulated from public pressures. Judges are elected or appointed for long terms or for life, and the theory is that they will, therefore, be less subject to the force of public opinion. As a result, the law should be uniformly applied in different places, regardless of the nature of the community. It is fair to say that the judicial process is less responsive to public sentiment than is the political process, but that is not really saying much. What is important is that the legal process is not totally immune from public pressure. The force of public opinion is not applied directly through lobbying, but it would be naive to think that the force of what large numbers of people believe and desire never gets reflected in what happens in court. The most obvious examples are trials in which individuals are tried as much for their dissident beliefs as for their actions. Less obvious is the fact that the outcomes of cases may be determined in some measure by popular will. Judicial complicity in slavery or the internment of Japanese Americans during World War II are blatant examples of this.

Many of the issues selected for this volume are controversial because a large group is opposed to some practice sanctioned by the courts. Does this mean that the judges have taken a courageous stand and ignored public opinion? Not necessarily. Only in a few of the issues have courts adopted an uncompromising position. In most of the other issues, the trend of court decisions reflects a middle-of-the-road approach that could be interpreted as trying to satisfy everyone but those at the extremes. For example, in capital punishment (Issue 12), the original decision declaring the death penalty statutes unconstitutional was followed by the passing of new state laws, which were then upheld and which have led to a growing number of executions. Similarly, in affirmative action (Issue 8), the *Bakke* decision, while generally approving of affirmative action, was actually won by Bakke and led to the abolition of all such programs that contained rigid quotas.

ASSESSING INFLUENCES ON THE LAW

This summary of what can influence legal decisions is not meant to suggest that judges consciously ask what the public desires when interpretations of law are made. Rather, as members of society and as individuals who read newspapers and magazines and form opinions on political issues, there are subtle forces at work on judges that may not be obvious in any particular opinion but that can be discerned in a line of cases over a period of time.

This may be explicitly denied by judges, such as in the statement by Justice Harry A. Blackmun in his majority opinion for the landmark *Roe v. Wade* abortion case, "Our task, of course, is to resolve the issue by constitutional measurement, free of emotion and predilection." However, a reading of that opinion raises the question of whether or not Blackmun succeeds in being totally objective in his interpretation of law and history.

Do these external and internal influences corrupt the system, create injustice, inject bias and discrimination, and pervert the law? Or, do these influences enable judges to be flexible, to treat individual circumstances, and to fulfill the spirit of the law? Both of these ends are possible and do occur. What is important to realize is that there are so many points in the legal system where discretion is employed that it is hopeless to think that we could be governed by rules alone. "A government of laws, not men," aside from the sexism of the language, is not a realistic possibility, and it is not an alternative that many would find satisfying either.

On the other hand, it is also fair to say that the law, in striving to get the public to trust in it, must persuade citizens that it is more than the whim of those who are in power. While it cannot be denied that the law may be used in self-serving ways, there are also mechanisms at work that are designed to limit abuses of discretionary power. One quality of law that is relevant to this problem is that the legal process is fundamentally a conservative institution, which is, by nature, resistant to radical change. Lawyers are trained to give primary consideration in legal arguments to precedent, previous cases involving similar facts. As attention is focused on how the present case is similar to or different from past cases, some pressure is exerted on new decisions to be consistent with old ones and on the law to be stable. Thus, the way in which a legal argument is constructed tends to reduce the influence of currently popular psychological, sociological, philosophical, or anthropological theories. Prior decisions will reflect ideologies, economic considerations, and ethical values that were influential when these decisions were made and, if no great change has occurred in the interim, the law will tend to preserve the status quo, both perpetuating old injustices and protecting traditional freedoms.

LEGAL PROCEDURE

The law's great concern with the procedure of decision making is one of its more basic and important characteristics. Any discussion of the law that did not note the importance of procedure would be inadequate. Legal standards are often phrased not in terms of results but in terms of procedure. For example, it is not unlawful to convict the innocent if the right procedures are used (and it is unlawful to convict the guilty if the wrong procedures are followed). The law feels that it cannot guarantee that the right result will always be reached and that only the guilty will be caught, so it minimizes the risk of reaching the wrong result or convicting the innocent by specifying procedural steps to be followed. Lawyers, more than most people, are satisfied if the right procedures are followed even if there is something disturbing about the outcome. Law, therefore, has virtually eliminated the word *justice* from its vocabulary and has substituted the phrase *due process*, meaning that the proper procedures, such as right to counsel, right to a public trial, and right to cross-examine witnesses, have been followed. This concern with method is one of the pillars upon which law is based. It is one of the characteristics of law that distinguishes it from nonlegal methods of dispute resolution, where the atmosphere will be more informal and there may be no set procedures. It is a trait of the law that is illustrated in Issue 1 (*Should Lawyers Be Prohibited from Presenting a False Case?*).

CONCLUSION

There is an often-told anecdote about a client who walks into a lawyer's office and asks the receptionist if the firm has a one-armed lawyer. The receptionist asks why in the world anyone would have such a preference. The client responds that he has already visited several lawyers to discuss his problem but could not get a definite answer from any of them. Their stock reply to his question of whether or not he would win his case began, "On the one hand this could happen and on the other hand. . . ."

You may feel similarly frustrated as you examine the issues in this book. The subjects are not simple or amenable to simple solutions. The legal approach to problem solving is usually methodical and often slow. We frequently become frustrated with this process and, in fact, it may be an inappropriate way to deal with some problems. For the issues in this book, however, an approach that pays careful attention to the many different aspects of these topics will be the most rewarding. Many of the readings provide historical, economic, and sociological data as well as information about law. The issues examined in *Taking Sides* involve basic cultural institutions such as religion, schools, and the family as well as basic cultural values such as privacy, individualism, and equality. While the law takes a narrow approach to problems, reading these issues should broaden your outlook on the problems discussed and, perhaps, encourage you to do further reading on those topics that are of particular interest to you.

NOTES

1. Yankelovich, Skelly, and White, Inc., *The Public Image of Courts* (National Center for State Courts, 1978).

2. Iredell Jenkins, *Social Order and the Limits of Law* (Princeton University Press, 1980), p. xi.

3. Wardle, "The Gap Between Law and Moral Order: An Examination of the Legitimacy of the Supreme Court Abortion Decisions," *Brigham Young University Law Review* (1980), pp. 811–835.

PART 1

The Operation of Legal Institutions

According to much of what appears in the mass media, the public is increasingly disenchanted with many of the institutions that are part of the legal process. Critics complain about the proliferation of needless lawsuits, about lawyers and their tactics, and about courts that seem too lenient in their sentencing of serious criminals.

In this section we examine issues that involve our legal institutions, and the picture that emerges from these debates will reveal realities with which you may not be familiar.

- Should Lawyers Be Prohibited from Presenting a False Case?

- Does Mediation in Divorce Cases Hurt Women?

- Should Plea Bargaining Be Abolished?

1

ISSUE 1

Should Lawyers Be Prohibited from Presenting a False Case?

YES: Harry I. Subin, from "The Criminal Lawyer's 'Different Mission': Reflections on the 'Right' to Present a False Case," *Georgetown Journal of Legal Ethics* (vol. 1, 1987)

NO: John B. Mitchell, from "Reasonable Doubts Are Where You Find Them: A Response to Professor Subin's Position on the Criminal Lawyer's 'Different Mission,'" *Georgetown Journal of Legal Ethics* (vol. 1, 1987)

ISSUE SUMMARY

YES: Professor of law Harry I. Subin examines the ethical responsibilities of criminal defense lawyers and argues that greater responsibility should be placed on lawyers not to pervert the truth to help their clients.

NO: Attorney John B. Mitchell disputes the contention that the goal of the criminal justice process is to seek the truth and argues that it is essential that there be independent defense attorneys to provide protection against government oppression.

In 1732, Georgia was founded as a colony that was to have no lawyers. This was done with the goal of having a "happy, flourishing colony... free from that pest and scourge of mankind called lawyers." While there are no serious efforts to abolish the legal profession today, public opinion surveys reveal that lawyers still are not held in the highest esteem. The public today may feel a little more positive about lawyers than did citizens of colonial America, and large numbers of students aspire to become lawyers, but hostility and criticism of what lawyers are and what they do are still common.

Part of the reason for the public's ambivalent attitude about lawyers concerns the adversary system and the lawyer's role in it. The adversary system requires that the lawyer's main responsibility be to the client. Except in rare instances, the lawyer is not to consider whether the client's cause is right or wrong and is not to allow societal or public needs to affect the manner in which the client is represented. The adversary system assumes that someone other than the client's lawyer is responsible for determining truth and guaranteeing justice.

The code of ethics of the legal profession instructs lawyers not to lie. However, it is permissible to mislead opponents—indeed, to do anything short of lying, if done to benefit the client. We have a system of "legal ethics" because some things lawyers are obligated to do for their clients would violate traditional standards of ethical behavior. As one legal scholar has written, "Where the attorney-client relationship exists, it is often appropriate and many times even obligatory for the attorney to do things that, all other things being equal, an ordinary person need not, and should not, do" (Richard W. Wasserstrom, "Lawyers as Professionals: Some Moral Issues," 5 *Human Rights* 1 [1975]).

In a highly publicized case that occurred a few years ago, two criminal defense lawyers learned from their client that, in addition to the crimes he was charged with, the client had murdered two girls who were missing. The lawyers discovered where the bodies were but refused to provide the parents of the missing children with any of this information. There was a public outcry when it was later discovered what the lawyers had done, but their position was generally felt to be consistent with standards of legal ethics.

Why do we have a legal system that allows truth to be concealed? Is a diminished concern with truth necessary in order to preserve the status and security of the individual? What should be the limits as to how one-sided legal representation should be? Would it be desirable to require lawyers to be more concerned with truth, so that they would be prohibited from putting forward positions they know are false? In the following articles, Harry I. Subin and John B. Mitchell debate whether or not increasing the attorney's "truth" function would be both desirable and feasible. As you read the articles, determine whether Subin's suggestion is a dangerous first step toward a more powerful state and less protection for the individual or whether it would increase public respect toward the legal system and the legal profession with little cost.

At the heart of the adversary system's attention to the relationship between client and counsel is the belief that there is something more important than discovering truth in every case. Finding the guilty and punishing them is not the sole goal of the criminal justice process. We rely on the criminal process, particularly trials, to remind us that our liberty depends on placing restrictions on the power of the state. The argument on behalf of the adversary model is that increasing the power of the state to find truth in one case may hurt all of us in the future. As you read the following articles, it will be difficult not to be troubled by the lawyer's dilemma; you may wonder if there is any acceptable middle ground when state power and individual rights clash.

YES
Harry I. Subin

THE CRIMINAL LAWYER'S "DIFFERENT MISSION": REFLECTIONS ON THE "RIGHT" TO PRESENT A FALSE CASE

I. THE INQUIRY

Should the criminal lawyer be permitted to represent a client by putting forward a defense the lawyer knows is false?...

Presenting a "false defense," as used here, means attempting to convince the judge or jury that facts established by the state and known to the attorney to be true are not true, or that facts known to the attorney to be false are true. While this can be done by criminal means—e.g., perjury, introduction of forged documents, and the like—I exclude these acts from the definition of false defense used here. I am not concerned with them because such blatant criminal acts are relatively uninteresting ethically, and both the courts and bar have rejected their use.[1]

My concern, instead, is with the presently legal means for the attorney to reach favorable verdict even if it is completely at odds with the facts. The permissible techniques include: (1) cross-examination of truthful government witnesses to undermine their testimony or their credibility; (2) direct presentation of testimony, not itself false, but used to discredit the truthful evidence adduced by the government, or to accredit a false theory; and (3) argument to the jury based on any of these acts. One looks in vain in ethical codes or case law for a definition of "perjury" or "false evidence" that includes these acts, although they are also inconsistent with the goal of assuring a truthful verdict.

To the extent that these techniques of legal truth-subversion have been addressed at all, most authorities have approved them. The American Bar Association's *Standards for Criminal Justice*,[2] for example, advises the criminal defense attorney that it is proper to destroy a truthful government witness when essential to provide the defendant with a defense, and that failure to do so would violate the lawyer's duty under the *Model Code of Professional*

Responsibility to represent the client zealously.[3] The *Standards for Criminal Justice* cite as authority for this proposition an opinion by Justice White in *United States v. Wade*,[4] which, in the most emphatic form, is to the same effect. In *Wade*, the Court held that in order to assure the reliability of the pretrial line-up, the right to counsel must be extended to the defendant compelled to participate in one.[5] Justice White warned that the presence of counsel would not necessarily assure that the identification procedure would be more accurate than if the police were left to conduct it themselves. The passage dealing with this issue, which includes the phrase that inspired the title of this piece, is worth repeating at length:

> Law enforcement officers have the obligation to convict the guilty and to make sure they do not convict the innocent. They must be dedicated to making the criminal trial a procedure for the ascertainment of the true facts surrounding the commission of the crime. To this extent, our so-called adversary system is not adversary at all; nor should it be. But defense counsel has no comparable obligation to ascertain or present the truth. Our system assigns him a different mission. He must be and is interested in preventing the conviction of the innocent, but... we also insist that he defend his client whether he is innocent or guilty. The State has the obligation to present evidence. Defense counsel need present nothing, even if he knows what the truth is. He need not furnish any witnesses to the police, or reveal any confidences of his client, or furnish any other information to help the prosecution's case. If he can confuse a witness, even a truthful one, or make him appear at a disadvantage, unsure or indecisive, that will be his normal course. Our interest in not convicting the innocent permits counsel to put the State to its proof, to put the State's case in the worst possible light, regardless of what he thinks or knows to be the truth. Undoubtedly there are some limits which defense counsel must observe but more often than not, defense counsel will cross-examine a prosecution witness, and impeach him if he can, even if he thinks the witness is telling the truth, just as he will attempt to destroy a witness who he thinks is lying. In this respect, as part of our modified adversary system and as part of the duty imposed on the most honorable defense counsel, we countenance or require conduct which in many instances has little, if any, relation to the search for truth.[6]

... The article begins with a description of a case I handled some years ago, one that I believe is a good illustration of the false defense problem. I next address the threshold question of the attorney's knowledge. It has been argued that the attorney cannot "know" what the truth is, and therefore is free to present any available defense theory. I attempt to demonstrate that the attorney can, in fact, know the truth, and I propose a process to determine when the truth is known.

I then analyze the arguments that have been advanced in support of the "different mission" theory: that the defense attorney, even if he or she knows the truth, remains free to disregard it in presenting a defense. I argue that neither the right to a defense nor the needs of the adversary system justify the presentation of a false defense. Finally, I describe a new standard that explicitly prohibits the defense attorney from asserting a false defense. I conclude with some thoughts as to why this rule would produce a generally more just system.

II. TRUTH SUBVERSION IN ACTION: THE PROBLEM ILLUSTRATED

A. The Accusation

About fifteen years ago I represented a man charged with rape and robbery. The victim's account was as follows: Returning from work in the early morning hours, she was accosted by a man who pointed a gun at her and took a watch from her wrist. He told her to go with him to a nearby lot, where he ordered her to lie down on the ground and disrobe. When she complained that the ground was hurting her, he took her to his apartment, located across the street. During the next hour there, he had intercourse with her. Ultimately, he said that they had to leave to avoid being discovered by the woman with whom he lived.[7] The complainant responded that since he had gotten what he wanted, he should give her back her watch. He said that he would.

As the two left the apartment, he said he was going to get a car. Before leaving the building, however, he went to the apartment next door, leaving her to wait in the hallway. When asked why she waited, she said that she was still hoping for the return of her watch, which was a valued gift, apparently from her boyfriend.

She never did get the watch. When they left the building, the man told her to wait on the street while he got the car. At that point she went to a nearby police precinct and reported the incident. She gave a full description of the assailant that matched my client. She also accurately described the inside of his apartment. Later, in response to a note left at his apartment by the police, my client came to the precinct, and the complainant identified him. My client was released at that time but was arrested soon thereafter at his apartment, where a gun was found.[8] No watch was recovered.

My client was formally charged, at which point I entered the case. At our initial interview and those that followed it, he insisted that he had nothing whatever to do with the crime and he had never seen the woman before.[9] He stated that he had been in several places during the night in question: visiting his aunt earlier in the evening, then traveling to a bar in New Jersey, where he was during the critical hours. He gave the name of a man there who would corroborate this. He said that he arrived home early the next morning and met a friend. He stated that he had no idea how this woman had come to know things about him such as what the apartment looked like, that he lived with a woman, and that he was a musician, or how she could identify him. He said that he had no reason to rape anyone, since he already had a woman, and that in any event he was recovering from surgery for an old gun shot wound and could not engage in intercourse. He said he would not be so stupid as to bring a woman he had robbed and was going to rape into his own apartment.

I felt that there was some strength to these arguments, and that there were questionable aspects to the complainant's story. In particular, it seemed strange that a man intending rape would be as solicitous of the victim's comfort as the woman said her assailant was at the playground. It also seemed that a person who had just been raped would flee when she had the chance to, and in any case would not be primarily concerned with the return of her watch. On balance, however, I suspected that my client was not telling me the truth. I thought the complaining witness could not possibly have known what she knew about him and his apartment, if she had not had any contact with him. True, someone else could have posed as him, and used his apartment. My client, however, could suggest no one who could have done so.[10] Moreover, that hypothesis did not explain the complainant's accurate description of him to the police. Although the identification procedure used by the police, a one person "show up," was suggestive,[11] the woman had ample opportunity to observe her assailant during the extended incident. I could not believe that the complainant had selected my client randomly to accuse falsely of rape. By both her and my client's admission, the two had not had any previous association.

That my client was probably lying to me had two possible explanations. First, he might have been lying because he was guilty and did not see any particular advantage to himself in admitting it to me. It is embarrassing to admit that one has committed a crime, particularly one of this nature. Moreover, my client might well have feared to tell me the truth. He might have believed that I would tell others what he said, or, at the very least, that I might not be enthusiastic about representing him.

He also might have lied not because he was guilty of the offense, but because he thought the concocted story was the best one under the circumstances. The sexual encounter may have taken place voluntarily, but the woman complained to the police because she was angry at my client for refusing to return the valued wrist watch, perhaps not stolen, but left, in my client's apartment. My client may not have been able to admit this, because he had other needs that took precedence over the particular legal one

that brought him to me. For example, the client might have felt compelled to deny any involvement in the incident because to admit to having had a sexual encounter might have jeopardized his relationship with the woman with whom he lived. Likewise, he might have decided to "play lawyer," and put forward what he believed to be his best defense. Not understanding the heavy burden of proof on the state in criminal cases, he might have thought that any version of the facts that showed that he had contact with the woman would be fatal because it would simply be a case of her word against his.

I discussed all of these matters with the client on several occasions. Judging him a man of intelligence, with no signs of mental abnormality, I became convinced that he understood both the seriousness of his situation, and that his exculpation did not depend upon maintaining his initial story. In ensuring that he did understand that, in fact, I came close enough to suggesting the "right" answers to make me a little nervous about the line between subornation of perjury and careful witness preparation, known in the trade as "horseshedding."[12] In the end, however, he held to his original account.

B. The Investigation

At this point the case was in equipoise for me. I had my suspicions about both the complainant's and the client's version of what had occurred, and I supposed a jury would as well. That problem was theirs, however, not mine. All I had to do was present my client's version of what occurred in the best way that I could.

Or was that all that was required? Committed to the adversarial spirit reflected in Justice White's observations about my role, I decided that it was not. The "different mission" took me beyond the task of presenting my client's position in a legally correct and persuasive manner, to trying to untrack the state's case in any lawful way that occurred to me, regardless of the facts.

With that mission in mind, I concluded that it would be too risky to have the defendant simply take the stand and tell his story, even if it were true. Unless we could create an iron-clad alibi, which seemed unlikely given the strength of the complainant's identification, I thought it was much safer to attack the complainant's story, even if it were true. I felt, however, that since my client had persisted in his original story I was obligated to investigate the alibi defense, although I was fairly certain that I would not use it. My students and I therefore interviewed everyone he mentioned, traveled and timed the route he said he had followed, and attempted to find witnesses who may have seen someone else at the apartment. We discovered nothing helpful. The witness my client identified as being at the bar in New Jersey could not corroborate the client's presence there. The times the client gave were consistent with his presence at the place of the crime when the victim claimed it took place. The client's aunt verified that he had been with her, but much earlier in the evening.

Because the alibi defense was apparently hopeless, I returned to the original strategy of attempting to undermine the complainant's version of the facts. I demanded a preliminary hearing, in which the complainant would have to testify under oath to the events in question. Her version was precisely as I have described it, and she told it in an objective manner that, far from seeming contrived, convinced me that she was telling the truth. She seemed a person who, if not at home with the meanness of the streets, was re-signed to it. To me that explained why she was able to react in what I perceived to be a nonstereotypical manner to the ugly events in which she had been involved.

I explained to my client that we had failed to corroborate his alibi, and that the complainant appeared to be a credible witness. I said that in my view the jury would not believe the alibi, and that if we could not obtain any other information, it might be appropriate to think about a guilty plea, which would at least limit his exposure to punishment. The case, then in the middle of the aimless drift towards resolution that typifies New York's criminal justice system, was left at that.

Some time later, however, my client called me and told me that he had new evidence; his aunt, he said, would testify that he had been with her at the time in question. I was incredulous. I reminded him that at no time during our earlier conversations had he indicated what was plainly a crucial piece of information, despite my not too subtle explanation of an alibi defense. I told him that when the aunt was initially interviewed with great care on this point, she stated that he was not with her at the time of the crime. Ultimately, I told him that I thought he was lying, and that in my view even if the jury heard the aunt's testimony, they would not believe it.

Whether it was during that session or later that the client admitted his guilt I do not recall. I do recall wondering whether, now that I knew the truth, that should make a difference in the way in which the case was handled. I certainly wished that I did not know it and began to understand, psychologically if not ethically, lawyers who do not want to know their clients' stories.[13]

I did not pause very long to ponder the problem, however, because I concluded that knowing the truth in fact did not make a difference to my defense strategy, other than to put me on notice as to when I might be suborning perjury. Because the mission of the defense attorney was to defeat the prosecution's case, what I knew actually happened was not important otherwise. What did matter was whether a version of the "facts" could be presented that would make a jury doubt the client's guilt.

Viewed in this way, my problem was not that my client's story was false, but that it was not credible, and could not be made to appear so by legal means. To win, we would therefore have to come up with a better theory than the alibi, avoiding perjury in the process. Thus, the defense would have to be made out without the client testifying, since it would be a crime for him to assert a fabricated exculpatory theory under oath.[14] This was not a serious problem, however, because it would not only be possible to prevail without the defendant's testimony, but it would probably be easier to do so. Not everyone is capable of lying successfully on the witness stand, and I did not have the sense that my client would be very good at it.

There were two possible defenses that could be fabricated. The first was mistaken identity. We could argue that the opportunity of the victim to observe the defendant at the time of the original encounter was limited, since it had occurred on a dark street. The woman could be made out to have been in great emotional distress during the incident.[15] Expert testimony would have to be adduced to show the hazards of eyewitness identification.[16] We could demonstrate that an unreliable identification procedure had been used at the precinct.[17] On the other hand, given that the complainant had spent considerable time with the assailant and had led the police back to the defendant's apartment, it seemed doubtful that the mistaken identification ploy would be successful.

The second alternative, consent, was clearly preferable. It would negate the charge of rape and undermine the robbery case.[18] To prevail, all we would have to do would be to raise a reasonable doubt as to whether he had compelled the woman to have sex with him. The doubt would be based on the scenario that the woman and the defendant met, and she voluntarily returned to his apartment. Her watch, the subject of the alleged robbery, was either left there by mistake or, perhaps better, was never there at all.

The consent defense could be made out entirely through cross-examination of the complainant, coupled with the argument to the jury about her lack of credibility on the issue of force. I could emphasize the parts of her story that sounded the most curious, such as the defendant's solicitude in taking his victim back to his apartment, and her waiting for her watch when she could have gone immediately to the nearby precinct that she went to later. I could point to her inability to identify the gun she claimed was used (although it was the one actually used), that the allegedly stolen watch was never found, there was no sign of physical violence, and no one heard screaming or any other signs of a struggle. I could also argue as my client had that even if he were reckless enough to rob and rape a woman across the street from his apartment, he would not be so foolish as to bring the victim there. I considered investigating the complainant's background, to take advantage of the right, unencumbered at the time, to impeach her on the basis of her prior unchastity.[19] I did not pursue this, however, because to me this device, although lawful, was fundamentally wrong. No doubt in that respect I lacked zeal, perhaps punishably so.

Even without assassinating this woman's character, however, I could argue that this was simply a case of a casual tryst that went awry. The defendant would not have to prove whether the complainant made the false charge to account for her whereabouts that evening, or to explain what happened to her missing watch. If the jury had reason to doubt the complainant's charges it would be bound to acquit the defendant.

How all of this would have played out at trial cannot be known. Predictably, the case dragged on so long that the prosecutor was forced to offer the unrefusable plea of possession of a gun.[20] As I look back, however, I wonder how I could justify doing what I was planning to do had the case been tried. I was prepared to stand before the jury posing as an officer of the court in search of the truth, while trying to fool the jurors into believing a wholly fabricated story, i.e., that the woman had consented, when in fact she had been forced at gunpoint to have sex with the defendant. I was also prepared to demand an acquittal because the state had not met its burden of proof when, if it had not, it would have been because I made the truth look like a lie. If there is any redeeming social value in permitting an attorney to do such things, I frankly cannot discern it....

III. CAN LAWYERS "KNOW" THE TRUTH?

A. "The Adversary System" Excuse[21]
A principle argument in favor of the propriety of asserting a "false" defense

is that there is, for the lawyer, no such thing. The "truth," insofar as it is relevant to the lawyer, is what the trier of the fact determines it to be.[22] The role of the lawyer in the adversary system is not to interpose his or her own belief about what the facts are.[23] Instead, the truth will emerge through a dialectical process, in which the vigorous advocacy of thesis and antithesis will equip the neutral arbiter to synthesize the data and reach a conclusion....

Suppose, for example, that I had interviewed the neighbor into whose apartment the defendant had gone following the rape—and who was unknown to the police. Suppose that he had told me that at the time of the incident he heard screams, and the sound of a struggle, and that my client had made incriminating remarks to him about what had occurred. It may be that there are reasons of policy that permit me to conceal these facts from the prosecution. It is ludicrous to assert, however, that because I can conceal them I do not know them. It is also ludicrous to suggest that if in addition I use my advocacy skills—and rights—to advance the thesis that there were no witnesses to the crime, I have engaged in a truth finding process.[24]

The argument that the attorney cannot know the truth until a court decides it fails. Either it is sophistry, designed to simplify the moral life of the attorney,[25] or it rests on a confusion between "factual truth" and "legal truth." The former relates to historical fact. The latter relates to the principle that a fact cannot be acted upon by the legal system until it is proven in accordance with legal rules. Plainly one can know the factual truth, for example, that one's client forced a woman to have sex with him, without or before knowing the legal truth that he is punishable for the crime of rape. The question is not whether an attorney can know the truth, but what standards should be applied in determining what the truth is. . . .

IV. DOES THE TRUTH MATTER? APPRAISING THE DIFFERENT MISSION

We confront at last the "Different Mission" argument we set out initially to examine. It is that the defense attorney has a broader function than protecting the innocent against wrongful conviction. Equally important is the task of protecting the factually guilty individual against overreaching by the state. The defense attorney may well be able to know the truth, but can be indifferent to it because it is the state's case, not the client's with which he or she is concerned. Professor Freedman puts it this way:

> The point . . . is not that the lawyer cannot know the truth, or that the lawyer refuses to recognize the truth, but rather that the lawyer is told: "You, personally, may very well know the truth, but your personal knowledge is irrelevant. In your capacity as an advocate (and, if you will, as an officer of the court) you are forbidden to act upon your personal knowledge of the truth, as you might want to do as a private person, because the adversary system could not function properly if lawyers did so."

The adversary system must function because it is our basic protection against governmental overreaching. The danger of such overreaching is so great, moreover, that we must allow the defense attorney broad latitude in disrupting that case, even by presenting a spurious defense.

Two principal arguments have been advanced to explain why the needs of the adversary system permit the attorney to assert a defense not founded upon the truth. The first is that a false defense may have to be asserted to protect the defendant's right in a particular case right to have a defense at all. The second argument is that it may be necessary to subvert the truth in a particular case as a way of demonstrating the supremacy of the autonomous individual in the face of the powerful forces of organized society.

A. Subverting the Truth to Protect the Defendant's Right to a Defense

The most commonly offered justification for a right to undermine a truthful case is that if there were no such right, the guilty defendant would effectively be deprived of a defense. All defendants, it is asserted, are entitled to have the state prove the case against them, whether they are factually innocent or guilty. If the spurious defense were not allowed it would be impossible to represent persons who had confessed their guilt to their lawyers, or who, in accordance with rules of the sort I advanced in the last section, were "found" guilty by them. The trial, if there were one at all, would not be an occasion to test the government's case, but a kind of elaborate plea of guilty. I believe that this argument fails for two reasons: first, because it proves too much, and second, because it is based on an erroneous assumption as to what the defendant's rights are.

If it were true that a false defense must be allowed to assure that the guilty defendant has a defense, it would seem to follow that presently established constraints on the defense attorney representing the guilty person, let alone an innocent person against whom the state had incriminating evidence, should be removed. An exception to the criminal laws prohibiting the deliberate introduction of false evidence would have to be adopted. Some have argued that a criminal defendant has a right to commit perjury, and that the defense attorney has a concomitant duty not to interfere with such testimony, or for that matter with even more extraordinary means of prevailing at trial.

The notion of a right to commit perjury, however, has been forcefully rejected by the courts[26] and by the organized bar, albeit less forcefully.[27] I suggest, however, that it cannot logically be rejected by those who espouse the Different Mission theory in defense of subverting the truth. If the right to mount a defense is paramount, and if the only conceivable defense which the guilty defendant can mount involves the defendant, or his or her witnesses committing perjury, and the defense attorney arguing that that perjury is true, then it follows that the restraints of the penal law should not be conceded to be applicable.[28] ...

The extravagant notion of the right to put on a defense is the second fallacy in the argument supporting a right to assert a false defense. Again, a moment's reflection on prevailing penal law limitations on advocacy will demonstrate that the defendant is not entitled to gain an acquittal by any available means.[29] Unless we abandon completely the notion that verdicts should be based upon the truth, we must accept the fact that there may simply be no version of the facts favorable to the defense worthy of assertion in a court. In such cases, the role of the defense attorney should be limited to assuring that the state adduces sufficient legally competent evidence to sustain its burden of proof....

Subverting the Truth to Preserve Individual Autonomy Against Encroachment by the State

The second prong of the "different mission" theory is that the truth must be sacrificed in individual cases as a kind of symbolic act designed to reaffirm our belief in the supremacy of the individual. This theory in turn is argued in several different ways.

The false defense may be necessary to preserve the individual's access to the legal system.

This argument is based on the proposition that because the legal system is so complex, meaningful access requires representation by an attorney. An attorney cannot perform his or her function unless the client provides the facts. The client will not do that if the facts will be used against the client, as, in this context, by not providing an available false defense. Thus it is necessary to permit the attorney to conceal harmful information obtained from the client and to act as if it did not exist.

As I have argued elsewhere, the importance of confidentiality to the performance of the lawyer's role has been greatly overstated. Even conceding its value, it does not seem to me that permitting the attorney to achieve the client's ends by subverting the truth advances the cause of individual autonomy. The legitimate concern of those who advance the autonomy argument is that the government must be prevented from interfering wrongfully or unnecessarily with individual freedom, not that there should be no interference with individual liberty at all. Here we are positing that the government has behaved reasonably, and the lawyer knows it. In my view, permitting such a case to be undermined by false evidence glorifies winning, but has very little to do with assuring justice.[30]

A false defense may be necessary to preserve the rigorous process by which guilt is determined.

Those taking this view see the criminal process not as a truth-seeking one, but a "screening system" designed to assure the utmost certainty before the criminal sanction is imposed. Only by permitting the defense attorney to use all of the tools which we have described here can we be certain that the prosecution will be put to its proof in all cases. The argument seems to be that if the prosecutor knows that the defense attorney will attempt to demolish the government's case, the prosecutor will in a sense be kept on his or her toes, and will seek the strongest evidence possible.[31]

This position is difficult to understand. In the situation under discussion here the prosecution has presented the strongest case possible, i.e., the truthful testimony of the victim of a crime. In any case, it is one thing to attack a weak government case by pointing out its weakness. It is another to attack a strong government case by confusing the jury with falsehoods. Finally, as a proponent of this "screening theory" concedes, there may be a danger that if the prosecutor sees that the truth alone is inadequate, he or she may be inspired to embellish it. That, of course, is not likely to make the screening mechanism work better.

For others, the desirability of prevailing against the state seems to be seen not as a means to assure that the prosecution will strive for high standards of proof, but as a positive good in its own right. The goal, as Professor Schwartz has put it, is to prevent the "behemoth" state from becoming a "juggernaut."[32] Schwartz states

that "[c]ross-examination to give the impression that [witnesses] are telling falsehoods may be justified as a way of keeping the state from overreaching,"[33] but we are not told what precise danger this will avert, or how it will do so. I cannot discern these, either, unless one takes the view that the exercise of a particular state power is inherently wrong, justifying resistance by any means. Otherwise, it would seem sufficient to insure that the defendant had a right to make a good faith challenge to the state's allegations.

V. ACCOMPLISHING THE DEFENSE ATTORNEY'S DIFFERENT MISSION—MORALLY

I propose a system in which the defense attorney would operate not with the right to assert defenses known to be untrue, but under the following rule:

> It shall be improper for an attorney who knows beyond a reasonable doubt the truth of a fact established in the state's case to attempt to refute that fact through the introduction of evidence, impeachment of evidence, or argument.

In the face of this rule, the attorney who knew there were no facts to contest would be limited to the "monitoring" role. Assuming that a defendant in my client's situation wanted to assert his right to contest the evidence against him, the attorney would work to assure that all of the elements of the crime were proven beyond a reasonable doubt, on the basis of competent and admissible evidence. This would include enforcing the defendant's rights to have privileged or illegally obtained evidence excluded: The goal sought here is not the elimination of all rules that result in the suppression of truth, but only those not supported by sound policy. It would also be appropriate for the attorney to argue to the jury that the available evidence is not sufficient to sustain the burden of proof. It would not, however, be proper for the attorney to use any of the presently available devices to refute testimony known to be truthful. I wish to make clear, however, that this rule would not prevent the attorney from challenging *inaccurate* testimony, even though the attorney knew that the defendant was guilty. Again, the truth-seeking goal is not applicable when a valid policy reason exists for ignoring it. Forcing the state to prove its case is such a reason.[34]

Applying these principles to my rape case, I would engage fully in the process of testing the admissibility of the state's evidence, moving to suppress testimony concerning the suggestive "show-up" identification at the precinct, and the gun found in the defendant's apartment after a warrantless search, should the state attempt to offer either piece of evidence. At the trial, I would be present to assure that the complainant testified in accordance with the rules of evidence.

Assuming that she testified at trial as she had at the preliminary hearing, however, I would not cross-examine her, because I would have no good faith basis for impeaching either her testimony or her character, since I "knew" that she was providing an accurate account of what had occurred.[35] Nor would I put on a defense case. I would limit my representation at that stage to putting forth the strongest argument I could that the facts presented by the state did not sustain its burden. In these ways, the defendant would receive the services of an attorney in subjecting the state's case to the final stage of the screening process provided by the system to insure against unjust convictions. That, however, would be all that the defense attorney could do....

VI. CONCLUSION

...If this proposal seems radical, consider that it is essentially an adaptation of what today is the principal function of the defense attorney in every criminal justice system of significance in this nation. That function is not to create defenses out of whole cloth to present to juries, but to guide the defendant through a process that will usually end in a guilty plea. It will so end, at least when competent counsel are involved, very frequently because the defense attorney has concluded after thorough analysis that there is no answer to the state's case. If that role can be played in out of court resolution of the matter there seems to be no reason why it cannot be played in court, when the defendant insists upon his right to a trial. The important point is that the right to a trial does not embody the right to present to the tribunal any evidence at all, no matter how fictitious it is.

NOTES

1. *Nix v. Whiteside*, 106 S. Ct. 988 (1986) (criminal defendant not denied effective assistance of counsel when attorney refused to allow him to present perjured testimony); ...

2. Standard 4-7.6 (2d ed. 1980 & Supp. 1986). The ABA apparently has had a complete reversal in its view of this matter. *See* ABA STANDARDS RELATING TO THE ADMINISTRATION OF CRIMINAL JUSTICE, Compilation, at 132 (1974). Standard 4-7.6 states that the lawyer "should not misuse the power of cross-examination or impeachment by employing it to discredit or undermine a witness if he knows the witness is testifying truthfully."

3. MODEL CODE DR 7-101(A)(1) and EC 7-1. DR 7-102 appears on its face to be to the contrary, prohibiting lawyers from, *inter alia*, conducting a defense merely to harass another (subd. (1));

knowingly using false evidence (subd. (3)); making a false statement of fact (subd. (5)); creating or preserving false evidence (subd. (6)); or assisting the client in fraudulent conduct (subd. (7)). None of the noncriminal acts with which this article is concerned, however, have, to the author's knowledge, been cited by the bar as coming within the proscription of DR 7-102.

A similar conclusion can be reached with respect to the *Model Rules*. Rule 3.3 is an adaptation of DR 7-102, *see* rule 3.3, model code comparison. Rule 3.1 suggests that the drafters approved of the precise conduct under discussion here, at least for criminal lawyers. The rule prohibits assertion or controversion of an issue at trial unless there is a reasonable basis for doing so, except in criminal cases. The criminal case exception is based upon the drafter's conclusion, mistaken in my view, that the constitutional requirement that the state shoulder the burden of proof requires that the defense attorney be permitted to "put the prosecution to its proof even if there is no 'reasonable basis' for the defense." MODEL RULES Rule 3.1 model code comparison.

4. 388 U.S. 218, 250 (1967) (White, J., joined by Harlan and Stewart, J.J., dissenting in part and concurring in part).

5. *Id.* at 236–37.

6. *Id.* at 256–58 (footnotes omitted).

7. She also said that he told her that he was a musician. The significance of this remark will appear shortly.

8. The woman was not able to make a positive identification of the gun as the weapon used in the incident.

9. A student working on the case with me photographed the complainant on the street. My client stated that he could not identify her.

10. The woman had indicated that her assailant opened the door with a key. There was no evidence of a forced entry.

11. *Cf. Stovall v. Denno*, 338 U.S. 293 (1967) (identification in which murder suspect shown alone to and positively identified by bedridden, hospitalized victim not unnecessarily suggestive and therefore did not deny defendant due process).

12. The dilemma faced by the lawyer is whether, in explaining to the client the legal implications of conduct, he or she is shaping the client's version of the facts. The issue was put dramatically in R. TRAVER, ANATOMY OF A MURDER (1958), in which the attorney explained the facts needed to establish an insanity defense to an apparently normal person accused of murder. *Id.* at 44–47. Whether I was quite as blatant I frankly cannot remember, but it is clear that I did more than simply listen to what the client said. I explained how one would make out an alibi defense, and I made sure that he understood both that consent was a defense to rape,

and that corroboration was necessary to support a rape conviction.

13. *See* Mitchell, *The Ethics of the Criminal Defense Attorney—New Answers to Old Questions*, 32 STAN L. REV. 293 n. 12 (1980) (author properly analogizes lawyer's preference not to know of the client's guilt to the doctrine of "conscious avoidance," which constitutes "knowledge" under criminal law).

14. The notion that the defendant in a criminal case has a right to commit perjury was finally put to rest in *Nix v. Whiteside*, 106 S. Ct. 988 (1986) (criminal defendant not denied effective assistance of counsel when attorney refused to allow him to present perjured testimony).

15. This would be one of those safe areas in cross-examination, where the witness was damned no matter what she answered. If she testified that she was distressed, it would make my point that she was making an unreliable identification; if she testified that she was calm, no one would believe her. Perhaps this is why cross-examination has been touted as "beyond any doubt the greatest legal engine ever invented for the discovery of truth." 5 J. WIGMORE, EVIDENCE § 1367 (J. Chadbourn rev. ed. 1974). Another commentator makes similar claims for his art, and while he acknowledges in passing that witnesses might tell the truth, he at no point suggests what the cross-examiner should do when faced with such a situation. F. WELLMAN, THE ART OF CROSS-EXAMINATION 7 (4th ed. 1936). The cross-examiner's world, rather, seems to be divided into two types of witnesses: those whose testimony is harmless and those whose testimony must be destroyed on pain of abandoning "all hope for a jury verdict." *Id.* at 9.

16. On the dangers of misidentification, *see, e.g., United States v. Wade*, 388 U.S. 218 (1967). The use of experts to explain the misidentification problem to the jury is well established. *See generally* E. LOFTUS, EYEWITNESS TESTIMONY 191–203 (1979) (discussing ways expert testimony on eye witness testimony can be used and problems arising from its use).

17. *See Watkins v. Sowders*, 499 U.S. 341 (1981) (identification problems properly attacked during cross-examination at trial; no per se rule compelling judicial determination outside presence of jury concerning admissibility of identification evidence).

18. Consent is a defense to a charge of rape. *E.g.*, N.Y. PENAL LAW § 130.05 (McKinney 1975 & Supp. 1987). While consent is not a defense to a robbery charge, N.Y. PENAL LAW § § 160.00–15 (McKinney 1975 & Supp. 1987), if the complainant could be made out to be a liar about the rape, there was a good chance that the jury would not believe her about the stolen watch either.

19. When this case arose it was common practice to impeach the complainant in rape cases by eliciting details of her prior sexual activities. Subsequently the rules of evidence were amended

to require a specific showing of relevance to the facts of the case. N.Y. CRIM. PROC. LAW § 60.42 (McKinney 1981 & Supp. 1987).

20. The client, who had spent time in jail awaiting trial, was not given an additional prison sentence.

21. The phrase is the title of David Luban's essay, *The Adversary System Excuse*, in THE GOOD LAWYER: LAWYERS' ROLES AND LAWYERS' ETHICS 83 (D. Luban ed. 1983).

22. *See* M. FRANKEL, PARTISAN JUSTICE, *supra* note 43, at 24. Judge Frankel, who is critical of this theory, quotes the famous answer of Samuel Johnson to the question how he can represent a bad cause: "Sir, you do not know it to be good or bad till the judge determines it." *Id.* (quoting J. BOSWELL, THE LIFE OF SAMUEL JOHNSON 366 (1925)).

23. MODEL CODE DR 7-106©(4) provides in part that a lawyer shall not "[a]ssert his personal opinion as to the justness of a cause, as to the credibility of a witness... or as to the guilt or innocence of an accused...."

24. My "proof" that there were no witnesses to the crime would come in the form of an "accrediting" cross-examination of the complainant and/or a police officer who testified. I could inquire of both concerning whether they saw or otherwise became aware of the presence of any witnesses, and then argue to the jury that their negative answers established that there were none.

25. As all lawyers who are honest with themselves know, occasions arise when doubts about a client turn into suspicion and then moral certainty that a client is lying. Although his professional role may require a lawyer to take a detached attitude of unbelief, the law of lawyering does not permit a lawyer to escape all accountability by suspending his intelligence and common sense. A lawyer may try to persuade himself that he is not absolutely sure whether his client is committing perjury.... But all authorities agree... that there comes a point when only brute rationalization, moral irresponsibility, and pure sophistry can support the contention that the lawyer does not "know" what the situation is.

G. HAZARD & W. HODES, THE LAW OF LAWYERING: A HANDBOOK ON THE MODEL RULES OF PROFESSIONAL CONDUCT 343 (1985) (citing M. FREEDMAN, *supra* note 6, at 52–55, 71–76 (1975)).

26. *Nix v. Whiteside*, 106 S. Ct. 988 (1986) (criminal defendant not denied effective assistance of counsel when attorney refused to permit him to present perjured testimony).

27. The *Model Code* prohibits the knowing introduction of perjured testimony or false evidence. MODEL CODE DR 7-102(A)(4). The *Model Code* essentially eliminates, however, the duty of the attorney to disclose the client's attempt to commit these crimes, by prohibiting such disclosure if it would reveal a protected privileged communication. MODEL CODE DR 7-102(B)(1). The *Model Rules*, however, prohibit the introduction of false testimony, and appear to modify the restriction on disclosure of client misconduct in this area. The *Model Rules* require the attorney to disclose to the court that false evidence has been introduced. MODEL RULES Rule 3.3. The disclosure requirement ends, however, if the criminal conduct of the client is not discovered until after the proceeding has ended.

28. For example, if in my rape case there were incontrovertible evidence that force had been used on the complainant, the consent defense would have been impossible. I would then have had to revert to the mistaken identification defense. Given the strength of the complainant's identification testimony, the defendant's or his aunt's perjurious testimony might have been necessary to provide a defense at all.

29. In addition to the laws against perjury, there are laws, for example, against tampering with witnesses, 18 U.S.C. § § 1512–14 (1982 & Supp. 1985) and bribery, 18 U.S.C. § 201 (1982).

30. It is ironic that some who have supported the right to put on a false defense do so as part of the argument that defending the guilty teaches a lesson to the defendant, especially the indigent defendant, that the system is fair.... Again, the problem is the failure to distinguish between the right to a defense and the right to a false defense. Commenting on the criminal justice system in general, Jonathan Casper has observed that it "not only fails to teach [defendants] moral lessons, but reinforces the idea that the system has no moral content." Casper, *Did You Have A Lawyer When You Went to Court? No, I Had A Public Defender*, 1 YALE REV. L. & SOC. ACTION 4, 9 (1971). The same could very well be said of a method of representation in which the defendant sees the lawyer, an official of the system, attempting to win by engaging in conduct similar to that which may have brought the defendant to court.

31. The cross-examination of the "truthful" witness is justified... [because] [w]eaknesses in the witness' testimony brought out on cross-examination will make the prosecution understand the range in "quality" of evidence for subsequent cases so that in the future he or she will recognize and seek the best evidence possible.

Mitchell, *supra* note 34, at 312 n.67.

32. Schwartz, *The Zeal of the Civil Advocate*, 1983 AM. B. FOUND. RES. J. 543, 554.

33. *Id.*

34. My colleague Stephen Gillers, for whose thoughtful criticism of my view I am indebted, called my attention to this illustrative case, ruled

on by the Michigan State Bar Committee on Professional and Judicial Ethics:

A defendant is charged with armed robbery. The victim testifies that the defendant robbed him at 1:00 p.m. The defendant has confessed to his lawyer. In fact, the robbery took place at 1:30 p.m. The victim is in error about the time. The defendant has a solid and truthful alibi witness who will testify that the defendant was with the witness at 1:00 p.m.

The question presented was whether the defense could call the alibi witness. The Bar Committee answered affirmatively. Michigan State Bar Committee of Professional and Judicial Ethics Op. CI-1164, Jan. 23, 1987, *reported in* 3 LAWYER'S MANUAL ON PROFESSIONAL CONDUCT (ABA/BNA) No. 3, at 44 (March 4, 1987). I would agree. The state's proof of the time of the crime was incorrect, and therefore subject to impeachment. I would not, however, permit the defense to offer evidence that the crime occurred at 1:00 p.m. if the victim correctly testified that it occurred at 1:30 p.m.

35. I recently made an informal presentation of this position to a group of my colleagues, who beseiged me with hypotheticals, the most provocative of which were these: (A) A witness not wearing her glasses, identifies my client as having been at a certain place. If my client were in fact at that place, could I cross-examine the witness on the grounds that she was not wearing her glasses? The answer is yes: The witness' ability to perceive affects the quality of the state's proof, and the fact that she happened to be correct is irrelevant. (B) In the same situation, except here I knew that the witness was wearing her glasses. Could I cross-examine the witness in an effort to show that she was not? The answer is no: The state had adduced reliable evidence, and that is all that it was required to do.

I was also asked whether I would apply the same truth based rule and refuse, in the situation described in (B), to impeach the witness if I knew that my client were innocent. My first response was something of a dodge: If I knew that, it was difficult for me to see why I would have to impeach this witness. Ultimately (albeit tentatively) I would conclude that it was too dangerous to adopt the notion that even these ends justified subverting the truth, and I would not cross-examine on that point.

NO

John B. Mitchell

REASONABLE DOUBTS ARE WHERE YOU FIND THEM: A RESPONSE TO PROFESSOR SUBIN'S POSITION ON THE CRIMINAL LAWYER'S "DIFFERENT MISSION"

I. INTRODUCTION

In *A Criminal Lawyer's "Different Mission": Reflections on the "Right" to Present a False Case*,[1] Professor Harry I. Subin attempts to draw what he considers to be the line between attorney as advocate, and attorney as officer of the court. Specifically, he "attempts to define the limits on the methods a lawyer should be willing to use when his client's goals are inconsistent with truth."[2] This is no peripheral theme in professional responsibility. Quite the contrary, Professor Subin has chosen a difficult issue which touches upon the very nature of our criminal justice system, the role of the attorney in that system, the relationship of the individual to the state, and the Constitution. Further, Professor Subin takes a tough and controversial stand on this issue and, although I disagree with him, I respect his position....

II. PROFESSOR SUBIN'S ASSUMPTIONS

Professor Subin rests his entire analysis on two basic premises: (1) the principle goal of the criminal justice system is "truth"; and (2) it is contrary to the goal of "truth" to permit a criminal defense attorney to put on a "false defense." In Subin's terms, a false defense is an attempt to "convince the judge or jury that facts established by the state and known to the attorney to be true are not true, or that the facts known to the attorney to be false are true." Such a defense is put on by: "... (1) cross-examination of truthful government witnesses to undermine their testimony or their credibility; (2) direct presentation of testimony, not in itself false, but used to discredit the truthful evidence adduced by the government, or to accredit a false theory; and, (3) argument to the jury based on any of these acts." I take exception to both of these premises, as set out below.[3]

A. The Principal Concern of the Criminal Justice System Is Not "Truth"

The idea that the focus of the criminal justice system is not "truth" may initially sound shocking. I have valued truth throughout my life and do not condone lying in our legal system. But the job of our criminal justice system is simply other than determining "truth." ...

A system focused on truth would first collect all information relevant to the inquiry. In our system, the defendant is generally the best source of information in the dispute, but he is not available unless he so chooses. The police may not question him. He may not be called to the stand with his own lawyer beside him and with a judge controlling questioning under the rules of evidence. The prosecutor may not even comment to the jury about the defendant's failure to testify, even though fair inferences may be drawn from the refusal to respond to serious accusations.

A system focused on truth would have the factfinder look at all the information and then decide what it believed had occurred. In our system, the inquiry is dramatically skewed against finding guilt. "Beyond a reasonable doubt" expresses the deep cultural value that "it is better to let ten guilty men go than convict one innocent man." It is a system where, after rendering a verdict of not guilty, jurors routinely approach defense counsel and say, "I thought your guy was guilty, but that prosecutor did not prove it to me beyond a reasonable doubt." What I have just described is not a "truth system" in any sense in which one could reasonably understand that term.[4] Truth may play a role, but it is not a dominant role; there is something else afoot.[5] The criminal defense attorney does not have a "different mission";[6] the system itself has a "different mission." ...

Put directly, the criminal justice system protects the individual from the police power of the executive branch of government. Between the individual citizen and the enormous governmental power residing in the executive stands a panel of that individual's peers—a jury. Through them, the executive must pass. Only if it proves its case "beyond a reasonable doubt," thereby establishing legal guilt, may the executive then legitimately intrude into the individual citizen's life. Thus, "factual" guilt or innocence, or what Professor Subin would call "truth," is not the principle issue in the system. Our concern is with the legitimate use of the prosecutor's power as embodied in the concept of "legal guilt." ...

B. A Defense Attorney Acting in a Manner Meeting with Subin's Disapproval Is Not Putting on a "False Defense"

When placed in the "reasonable doubt" context, Professor Subin's implicit distinction between "true" and "false" defenses misportrays both how a defense attorney may actually function in a case, and the very nature of evidence in that case. His categories are too imprecise to capture the subtle middle ground of a pure reasonable doubt defense, in which counsel presents the jury with alternative possibilities that counsel knows are false, without asserting the truth of those alternatives.

For example, imagine I am defending a young woman accused of shoplifting a star one places on top of Christmas trees. I interview the store manager and find that he stopped my client when he saw her walk straight through the store, star in hand, and out the door. When he stopped her and asked why she had taken the star without paying, she made no reply and burst into tears. He was then about to take her inside to the security office when an employee called out, "There's a fire!" The manager rushed inside and dealt with a small blaze in the camera section. Five minutes later he came out to find my client sitting where he had left her. He then took her back to the security room and asked if she would be willing to empty her pockets so that he could see if she had taken anything else. Without a word, she complied. She had a few items not belonging to the store and a ten-dollar bill. The star was priced at $1.79.

In an interview with my client, she admitted trying to steal the star: "It was so pretty, and would have looked so nice on the tree. I would have bought it, but I also wanted to make a special Christmas dinner for Mama and didn't have enough money to do both. I've been saving for that dinner and I know it will make her so happy. But that star.... I could just see the look in Mama's eyes if she saw that lovely thing on our tree."

At trial, the manager tells the same story he told me, except he *leaves out* the part about her waiting during the fire and having a ten-dollar bill. If I bring out these two facts on cross-examination and argue for an acquittal based upon my client "accidentally" walking out of the store with the star, surely Professor Subin will accuse me of raising a "false defense." I have brought out testimony, not itself false, to accredit a false theory and have argued to the jury based on this act. But I am not really arguing a false theory in Professor Subin's sense.

My defense is not that the defendant accidentally walked out, but rather that the prosecution cannot prove the element of intent to permanently deprive beyond a reasonable doubt. Through this theory, I am raising "doubt" in the prosecution's case, and therefore questioning the legitimacy of the government's lawsuit for control over the defendant. In my effort to carry out this legal theory, I will *not assert* that facts known by me to be true are false or those known to be false are true. As a defense attorney, I do not have to prove what *in fact* happened. That is an advantage in the process I would not willingly give up. Under our constitutional system, I do not need to try to convince the factfinder about the truth of any factual propositions. I need only try to convince the factfinder that the prosecution has not met its burden. Again, I will not argue that particular facts are true or false. Thus, in this case I will not claim that my client walked out of the store with innocent intent (a fact which I know is false); rather, I will argue:

The prosecution claims my client stole an ornament for a Christmas tree. The prosecution further claims that when my client walked out of that store she intended to keep it without paying. Now, maybe she did. None of us were there. On the other hand, she had $10.00 in her pocket, which was plenty of money with which to pay for the ornament without the risk of getting caught stealing. Also, she didn't try to conceal what she was doing. She walked right out of the store holding it in her hand. Most of us have come close to innocently doing the same thing. So, maybe she didn't. But then she cried the minute she was stopped. She might have been feeling guilty. So, maybe she did. On the other hand, she might just have been scared when she realized what had happened. After all, she didn't run away when she was left alone even though she knew the manager was going to be occupied with the fire inside. So, maybe she didn't. The point is that, looking at all the evidence, you're left with "maybe she intended to steal, maybe she didn't." But, you knew that before the first witness was even sworn. The prosecution has the burden, and he simply can't carry any burden let alone "beyond a reasonable doubt" with a maybe she did, maybe she didn't case....

Is this a "false defense" for Professor Subin? Admittedly, I am trying to raise a doubt by persuading the jury to appreciate "possibilities" other than my client's guilt. Perhaps Professor Subin would say it is "false" because I know the possibilities are untrue. But if that is so, Professor Subin will have taken a leap from defining "false defense" as the assertion that true things are false and false things are true, for I am doing neither of those things here. The fact that one cannot know how Subin would reach this "pure" reasonable doubt case only reinforces my initial statement that Professor Subin's categories are imprecise.

Another perspective from which to look at the function of a defense attorney involves understanding that function in the context of the nature of evidence at trial. Professor Subin speaks of facts and the impropriety of trying to make "true facts" look false and "false facts" look true. But in a trial there are no such things as facts. There is only information, lack of information, and chains of inferences therefrom. In the courtroom there will be no crime, no store, no young girl with a star in her hand. All there will be is a collection of witnesses who are strangers to the jury, giving information which may include physical evidence and documents. For example, most people would acknowledge the existence of eyewitness identifications; however, in

an evidentiary sense they do not exist. Rather, a particular person with particular perceptual abilities and motives and biases will recount an observation made under particular circumstances and utter particular words on the witness stand (e.g., "That's the man"). From this mass of information, the prosecution will argue, in story form, in favor of the inference that the defendant is their man (e.g., "The victim was on her way home, when...."). The defense will not then argue that the defendant is the wrong man in a *factual sense*, but instead will attack the persuasiveness of the criminal inference and resulting story (e.g., "The sun was in the witness' eyes; she was on drugs").

In our shoplifting example, the prosecution will elicit that the defendant burst into tears when stopped by the manager. From this information will run a chain of inferences: defendant burst into tears, people without a guilty conscience would explain their innocence, not cry; defendant has a guilty conscience; her guilty conscience is likely motivated by having committed a theft. Conversely, if the defense brings out that the manager was shaking a lead pipe in his hand when he stopped the defendant, defense counsel is *not asserting* that defendant did not have a guilty conscience when stopped. Counsel is merely *weakening* the persuasiveness of the prosecution's inference by raising the "possibility" that she was crying not from guilt, but from fear. By raising such "possibilities," the defense is making arguments against the ability of the prosecution's inferences to meet their burden of "beyond a reasonable doubt." The defense is not arguing what are true or false facts (i.e., that the tears were from fear as opposed to guilt). Whatever Professor Subin cares to call it, this commentary on the prosecution's case, complete with raising possibilities which weaken the persuasiveness of central inferences in that case, is in no ethical sense a "false case." "False case" is plainly a misnomer. In a system where factual guilt is not at issue, Professor Subin's "falsehoods" are, in fact, "reasonable doubts."

C. Even If Criminal Defense Attorneys Do Raise a "False Defense," the Role of the Defense Attorney in the Criminal Justice System Permits Such a Defense

Professor Subin does not seek to eliminate all impediments to truth, just those based upon sound policy. In failing to appreciate fully the institutional role of the defense attorney, he glosses over a major countervailing policy: even if the attorney is putting forth what Subin would term "false defense," this defense is the side effect, not the goal or function of the defense attorney's role in the criminal justice system.

Subin apparently believes that the principal position he must overcome from his opponents who seek leeway with the "truth" is that such leeway is necessary to protect the adversary system, and the adversary system, in turn, is necessary to protect the factually guilty from "overreaching by the state."[7] My position, however, does not rest on these ideas. Though the adversary system serves to protect the factually guilty from state overreaching, my position is principally based upon the criminal justice system—a system with rationales different from the general adversary system, including the protection of the factually innocent.[8]

Our criminal justice system is more appropriately defined as a screening system than as a truth-seeking one.[9] The ultimate objective of this screening system is to determine who are the proper subjects of

criminal sanction. The process goes on continually. Someone notices a window which looks pried open or a suspicious-looking stranger. Neighbor talks to neighbor, and information filters to the police. The police comb the streets gathering information, focusing upon those whose behavior warrants special attention. Those selected by the police for special attention are then placed in the hands of prosecutors, courts, and juries who constantly sift through this "residue" to make final determinations about who is to be subjected to criminal sanction.

The criminal justice system is itself composed of a series of "screens," of which trial is but one. These screens help keep innocents out of the process and, at the same time, limit the intrusion of the state into people's lives. Each of these screens functions to protect the values of human dignity and autonomy, while enforcing our criminal laws. Further, to ensure that the intrusion of the state into the individual's life will be halted at the soonest possible juncture, our system provides a separate screen at each of the several stages of the criminal process. At any screen, the individual may be taken out of the criminal process and returned to society with as little disruption as possible.

By pushing hard in every case (whether the client is factually guilty or not) and thereby raising "reasonable doubts" in the prosecution's case whenever possible, the defense attorney helps "make the screens work" and thus protects the interests of the factually innocent.[10]...

III. PROFESSOR SUBIN'S APPROACH

... My analysis in this section will focus upon Professor Subin's basic approach to "defin[ing] the limits on the methods a lawyer should be willing to use when his or her client's goals are inconsistent with the truth"; i.e., distinguishing between the role of what Subin calls a "monitor" and the more familiar role of "advocate." . . .

To illustrate, imagine I am representing a defendant accused of robbery. I have seen the victim at a preliminary hearing, and based upon the circumstances of the identification and my overall impression of the witness, I am certain that he is truthful and accurate. My client has confessed his factual guilt. And therefore I "know" (in Professor Subin's sense) beyond a reasonable doubt that my client has been accurately identified.

In his direct examination, the victim states, "The defendant had this big, silvery automatic pistol right up near my face the whole time he was asking for money." In accordance with Professor Subin's view that defense counsel can "persuade the jury that there are legitimate reasons to doubt the state's evidence," may I raise the general vagaries of eyewitness identification?

> All of us have had some stranger come up to us, call us by an unfamiliar name, and indicate they thought we were someone they knew. We have been with a friend who points to someone a few tables over exclaiming, "Isn't she an exact double of Sue Smith? Could be her twin," and we think to ourselves that other than the hair color, there is no resemblance at all.

Perhaps Subin would say I cannot make the misidentification argument. He might argue that the "legitimacy" of reasons to doubt the state's evidence is not to be judged from the perspective of a reasonable juror hearing the prosecution's evidence but from my subjective knowledge. Since I "know" that there was no difficulty with the identification, I cannot put forward a "legitimate" reason to doubt. If this is Professor Subin's meaning, I, as monitor, am left with the following closing argument: "Ladies and gentlemen, thank you for your attention to this case. Remember, the prosecution must prove each element beyond a reasonable doubt. Thank you." The Constitution aside (and in my view this would be putting the Constitution aside), it is hard to imagine this is Subin's intended result.

"Legitimate reason" to doubt must refer to a reasonable juror's perception of the state's evidence, not to the defense attorney's private knowledge. Bringing out reasonable doubts in the state's evidence concerning the identification therefore must be legitimate, and yet this would seem to raise a "false defense" (i.e., mistaken identification). Presumably, Subin would permit this defense because of a greater policy than "truth," i.e., the right to have the state prove guilt beyond a reasonable doubt. If this is permissible in Subin's view, it is difficult to understand why it would not be permissible to call an expert on eyewitness identification to testify.

In the hypothetical case described above, I should also be permitted to bring specific evidence about the gun into my closing argument because it offers a "legitimate" reason to doubt the accuracy of the identification (e.g., "The eyewitness was not someone sitting calmly in a restaurant looking at someone else a few tables away. Here, the eyewitness had a gun in his face.") Of course, if I can bring the gun into my closing, I presumably can do it in a manner I believe most effective; for I don't believe Professor Subin's position is that you are permitted to do it, but not very well:

> And did he notice that gun? Was he staring at that big... silvery... automatic? Wouldn't you? Not knowing if this assailant was going to beat or kill you. Wouldn't your mind turn inward? Inward to that gun, to calming your fear of death, to not provoking this spectre who could end your life in a moment? Would you be thinking "Let me see. His eyes are hazel... I want to get a good look at him so I can identify him later"? Would you want to do anything to make that person with a big... silvery... automatic gun in your face think you could identify him?...

What then is Subin really saying? Subin could not mean by his reference to the "state's evidence" that I can use evidence of the gun to raise a reasonable doubt in aid of the "false defense" of misidentification if the information is elicited on *the state's direct examination*, but that I am not permitted to bring out the information through cross-examination or defense witnesses. He could not mean that information I thus actively elicit is not "legitimate" for raising doubts. Yet, the only mechanisms he lists for putting on a "false defense" are defense cross-examination, defense witnesses, and arguments therefrom. If this distinction between information elicited by the prosecution and that elicited by the defense is really what he intends to divine the legitimate from the illegitimate, it is a strange structure upon which to rest a principle of ethical guidance, especially given the nature of the trial process. As a practical matter, this structure would allow conviction or acquittal to rest on such fortuitous circumstances as whether, when asked on direct examination if he saw a weapon in the hands of the robber, the witness in our hypothetical answered:

> — "Yes."
> — "Yes. Pointing at me."
> — "Yes. Pointing at my face."
> — "Yes. A big, silvery, automatic pointing at my face."

Much of cross-examination emphasizes points elicited in the direct examination (e.g., "Now, this gun was pointing at you?") and expands upon helpful points made during the direct (e.g., "You said on direct the gun was pointing at you. Where exactly was it pointing?"). If Professor Subin would not let me aid the "false defense" of mistaken identification by this type of cross-examination, then my client's chances for acquittal will vary with which of these responses happens to flow from the witness' mouth during direct examination on the day of trial.

Statements, however, do not just, "flow from" witnesses' mouths on direct examination. Witnesses are often coached regarding their testimony. That reality is at the core of my next point. If the content of the prosecution's direct examination limits the range of my ethical behavior, then my adversary controls my client's fate by deciding what to ask in the direct examination (e.g., "When I ask you in your direct examination about the gun, be certain you *do not* mention that it was directly pointed at you, and especially *do not* say it was pointed at your face."). Is this prosecutorial manipulation, in conjunction with the serendipity of answers proffered on the prosecution's direct examination, the basis for Professor Subin's ethical standards for criminal defense? If not, and if I may fully cross-examine in support of my "false defense" of misidentification, then it is difficult to see Professor Subin's point.

It is possible Subin was thinking about a situation where a defense attorney argues that the crime did not occur at all. For example, assume that when asked by the prosecution where he was going with a wallet full of money, the robbery victim's testimony is that he was going to get his wife a gift because she was angry at him for wasting his paycheck gambling the previous week. In closing, the defense argues an alternative explanation for the information the prosecution has presented, one based on the possibility that the victim had created the entire robbery story to cover up further gambling losses. While this would be a "false defense," there appears no real difference between a "false defense" that seeks acquittal by raising doubts that the defendant committed the crime (questioning identification evidence), which Professor Subin would seem to sanction, and one which raises doubts, as in this example, that the crime occurred at all. The former more closely tracks the prosecution's theory that there *was* a robbery, but this is a distinction of no apparent significance. In both examples, the defense counsel takes information in the case and arranges it differently than the prosecution to present alternative "possibilities" which resonate with reasonable doubts. Both are equally "false" in Subin's sense. Once Subin allows the defense attorney to argue reasonable doubts in support of a "false" defense, the line between the permissible and the impermissible is blurred and is definable only in terms of the false dichotomy between evidence brought in by the prosecution and evidence elicited by the defense.

Another indication that Subin would not adhere to the "stark" definition of lawyer as monitor is that he would allow the defense to demonstrate the inaccuracy of information that may be harmful to its case. Imagine that the robbery victim in my hypothetical testifies that Bloogan's Department Store, directly across the street from where the nighttime robbery occurred, had all of its lights on at the time of the robbery. In fact, I find out in investigation that Bloogan's was closed for remodeling that evening. Subin would undoubtedly allow me to bring this out. What, after all, would a "truth" theory be if I were not permitted to confront "lies" and "misperceptions." If Professor Subin permits me to bring out this "inaccuracy" on cross-examination and/or through other witnesses, he must also allow me to use it in closing or my initial access to this information would be meaningless. In closing, my only real use for this information would be in support of my "false defense" of mistaken identification. The line between advocate and monitor is again blurred.

Another example of the unworkability of his distinction between advocate and monitor is reflected in the defense lawyer's use of inaccurate information brought out in the prosecution's case that is helpful to the defense. The victim of the robbery now testifies that the robbery took place at 10 p.m. My client has a strong alibi for 10 p.m. I "know," however, that the robbery actually took place at 10:30 p.m. May I put on my alibi in support of my "false defense," raising doubts that my client was the robber? Subin would say yes. In a similar set of circumstances Subin stated: "The state's proof of the time of the crime was incorrect, and therefore subject to impeachment." This, however, is not "impeachment." The probative value of the information is not being questioned. Quite the contrary, the incorrect information is being embraced as true. A prosecution witness has simply made a "mistake" and Professor Subin allows the defense attorney to take advantage of it, furthering a "false defense." Without some analysis tied to the rationales for the advocate-monitor distinction in the first place, the distinction seems to depend on ad hoc judgments....

A. A Reevaluation of a Monitor's Role in Subin's Rape Case

To summarize, our monitor may bring in information and draw inferences which support "false defense" if the information or inferences fall within any one of six categories: (1) quality, (2) reliability, (3) mistakes in the prosecution's case, (4) adequacy, (5) inaccuracy, or (6) legitimate reasons to doubt. These broad, imprecise categories are not very confining for a profession which makes its living developing plausible positions for filing things into categories. It is instructive focusing on Subin's principal example, the rape case in which he "knows" his client is factually guilty, with these categories in mind.

In that case, two principal pieces of information emerged which were potentially helpful for the defense: 1) the victim stated that the defendant took her to his apartment; and 2) the victim was left alone for a time in a hallway after the rape but did not try to flee. Professor Subin recognized the significance of these and other miscellaneous pieces of information for the defense:

I could emphasize the parts of her story that sounded the most curious, such as the defendant's solicitude in taking his victim back to his apartment, and her waiting for her watch when she could have gone immediately to the nearby

precinct that she went to later. I could point to her inability to identify the gun she claimed was used (although it was the one actually used), that the allegedly stolen watch was never found, that there was no sign of physical violence, and no one heard screaming or any other signs of a struggle. I could also argue as my client had that even if he were reckless enough to rob and rape a woman across the street from his apartment, he would not be so foolish as to bring the victim there.

However, Subin is unclear as to what he would have done with this information. He claims he would have had no right to raise the "false defense" of consent. He would not have cross-examined the victim or put on defense witnesses. Instead, Subin would "limit my representation at that stage to putting forth the strongest argument I could that the facts presented by the state did not sustain its burden." Assuming sufficient information was elicited on the victim's direct examination to make the two helpful points above, what "strong argument" would defense counsel Subin make? Without using any of the information helpful to the defense, his argument could not have been other than: "Thank you, the prosecution has the burden."

Imagine instead he had taken the information and argued as follows:

This just doesn't make sense. If he took her to his apartment, he'd have to know he'd be identified within hours. There's no evidence he blindfolded her or in any other way made an effort to conceal the identity and location of the apartment. And here she'd just been raped at gunpoint by a man who, for all she knew, might now kill her, and she was alone in the hallway, neighbors around, a staircase 10 feet away leading to the outside and safety. Yet her testimony is

NO John B. Mitchell / 27

she just sat there and waited for the defendant. None of this makes sense, and the prosecution cannot carry its burden if the story it is presenting does not make sense.

Would this have been a "false defense" for Professor Subin? The argument raises "legitimate" doubts. The fact that the prosecution's underlying story does not make sense goes to the quality, reliability, and adequacy of the prosecution's case. Maybe the line would have been crossed if as defense counsel he had added:

Who knows from this evidence what really happened? Maybe she consented and then felt guilty—afraid to acknowledge the truth to herself and her boyfriend. Who knows? All we know is that the story does not make sense.

Does even mentioning the possibility of consent really cross Subin's line between the ethical and unethical? One major shortcoming in Subin's presentation is his failure to illustrate what a monitor in this rape case *may* do. He tells us what he would do, but does not show us what his "monitor's" closing argument would really look like.

Subin has left us in a quandary. The "stark" definition of monitor may have been at odds with the nature of the criminal justice system and the Constitution, but at least it was consistent with an unmitigated desire for truth. This current wavering line between advocates and monitors, based as it is on permissible versus impermissible information and inferences, is somewhat more in step with the Constitution and the justice system, but hopelessly vague and uncertain.

B. Bigger Problems: Constitutional Concerns and Jeopardizing an Independent Defense Bar

If Professor Subin's approach is more than a statement of his own private ethics, the vagueness and uncertainty of the line which divides the advocate from the monitor presents a serious problem. First, constitutional concerns additional to those already expressed may arise. Criminal defense representation touches significant interests: 1) protection of the individual from the state; 2) the freedom of the defendant in a nation which values liberty; and 3) significant constitutional rights (fourth, fifth, sixth, eighth, and fourteenth amendments). It is within these areas that the impreciseness in Professor Subin's categories comes to the fore. To the extent defense attorneys are guided by ethical rules which are vague about what conduct is proper, the representation of the clients is hampered. Counsel, uncertain as to appropriate behavior, may fall into a "conflict" between pushing the client's interests as far as is legitimate and protecting himself against charges of unethical conduct. Attorneys' decisions may then tend to fall on the self-protective side, raising constitutional concerns regarding zealous representation.

Second, if Subin's approach were enforced as a rule of professional conduct, the independent defense bar would be seriously jeopardized. Professor Subin may or may not be correct that the public and the bar have a low view of the criminal defense bar. Nonetheless, the independence of that bar has provided all citizens with significant protection against government oppression.[11] With Professor Subin's approach, however, if an acquittal were gained by a defense attorney who was a thorn in the government's side, the prosecutor's office might be tempted to file an ethical complaint stating that defense counsel should have known he put on a "false defense." Subin's position now becomes a weapon of repression in the hands of the government. Even if vindication follows upon a disciplinary hearing, time, expense, and public humiliation might ensue. This will deliver a powerful message to defense attorneys. Don't risk fighting, plead your clients guilty.

IV. CONCLUSION

Discussions of "monitors," "advocates," and "false defenses," while interesting, are premature. If the legal profession is ever to develop meaningful guidelines for criminal and civil attorneys, the focus must be on certain basic premises. Specifically, we must consider: What is the relationship between our criminal and civil systems, and what is the implication of that relationship for those practicing in the two systems? Is the criminal justice system primarily a truth system? Is it primarily a screening system intended as a check on governmental power? It seems to me that here is where we must begin.

NOTES

1. Subin, *The Criminal Lawyer's "Different Mission": Reflections on the "Right" to Present a False Case*, 1 GEO. J. LEGAL ETHICS 125 (1987).
2. Subin, *supra* note 1, at 125.
3. For a very well-thought out recent discussion which generally takes the position that the defense attorney's knowledge of the client's guilt should have no bearing upon that attorney's representation, *see* Kaplan, *Defending Guilty People*, 7 U. BRIDGEPORT L. REV. 223 (1986).
4. Mitchell, *supra* note 3, at 300–01.
5. For an interesting discussion of various justifications for the truth-dysfunctional nature of the criminal trial which implicitly leads one to conclude that Professor Subin's quest for factual truth is the least of what is going on, *see* Goodpaster, *On the Theory of American Adversary Criminal Trials*, 78 J. CRIM. L. & CRIMINOLOGY 118 (1987).
6. Subin, *supra* note 1, at 127–29, 143. As the title presages, Professor Subin makes this concept of a "different mission" the metaphorical focus of his article.
7. Subin, *supra* note 1, at 143.
8. For a defense of the lawyer's position as an "amoral" actor on behalf of a client which does not rely on the adversary system rationale, *see* Pepper, *The Lawyer's Amoral Ethical Role: A Defense, A Problem, and Some Possibilities*, A.B.A. RESEARCH J. 613 (1986).
9. Mitchell, *supra* note 3, at 299–302.
10. *Id.* at 302–21.
11. They did after all defend strikers in the early labor movement, were present during the McCarthy hearings and the Smith Act prosecutions and defended those voicing objections to the government's policies in Vietnam. Most of us take comfort in thinking they will be there in the future. *Cf.* Babcock, *Defending the Guilty*, 32 CLEV. ST. L. REV. 175 (1983–84) (discussing reasons to defend a person one knows is guilty).

POSTSCRIPT

Should Lawyers Be Prohibited from Presenting a False Case?

During the last 30 years, the legal profession has experienced unprecedented change. The most frequently publicized development of this period has been the great increase in the size of the profession. The United States now has almost 1,000,000 lawyers, nearly triple the number in 1970.

In addition to larger numbers of lawyers, recent years have seen the following significant changes take place: (1) A decline in the number of lawyers practicing independently or in firms and an increase in the number of lawyers employed by corporations and institutions. As a result, "a profession that was 85 percent self-employed in 1948 and about 60 percent self-employed in 1980 soon may be more than half employees." (2) Elimination of some anticompetitive practices previously enjoyed by the profession, such as minimum fee schedules and restrictions on advertising. (3) An increase in the size of law firms. The largest firms now have hundreds of lawyers with offices in many states. (4) Increasing heterogeneity of the legal profession. Due to the recent growth of the bar, members of the profession are younger, with more women and minorities. There are more fields of specialization and types of practice. (5) Increases in the number and use of paraprofessionals.

Clearly, the legal profession is not as stable as it once was. The work that lawyers do and where and how they do it is changing. This may have an impact on the ethical standards of lawyers. One of the characteristics of a "profession" is that it sets its own standards. But what happens when, because of changes in the makeup of the profession, it becomes harder to do this? What happens when there is less and less agreement in the profession about what the standards should be? What happens when there are increasing challenges from outside the profession to the traditional standards?

For further insight into the role and nature of the legal profession and of legal ethics, see Peter Joy, "What We Talk About When We Talk About Professionalism," 7 *Georgetown Journal of Legal Ethics* 987 (Spring 1994); Elliston and van Schaick, *Legal Ethics: An Annotated Bibliography and Research Guide* (Fred Rothman, 1984); R. Abel, *American Lawyers* (Oxford University Press, 1989); and Hazard and Rhode, eds., *The Legal Profession: Responsibility and Regulation,* 2d ed. (The Foundation Press, 1988). Recent cases involving the ethical practices of lawyers are *Shapero v. Kentucky Bar Association,* 108 S. Ct. 1916 (1988), allowing lawyers to use mailing lists to advertise their services to potential clients, and *Nix v. Whiteside,* 106 S. Ct. 988 (1986), which held that it is not a violation of the right to counsel for an attorney to threaten to resign if the client insists on lying while testifying.

ISSUE 2

Does Mediation in Divorce Cases Hurt Women?

YES: Penelope E. Bryan, from "Killing Us Softly: Divorce Mediation and the Politics of Power," *Buffalo Law Review* (vol. 40, 1992)

NO: Stephen K. Erickson, from "ADR and Family Law," *Hamline Journal of Public Law and Policy* (Spring 1991)

ISSUE SUMMARY

YES: Penelope Bryan, a professor in the School of Law at the University of Denver, asserts that the process of mediation in divorce cases works more to the benefit of men than women and preserves a dominant position for husbands.

NO: Stephen Erickson, a practicing divorce mediator, argues that all parties benefit from a process that is less adversarial, namely, mediation, and which is not controlled by lawyers.

Mediation is a method of resolving disputes and conflicts and is being used increasingly in the United States. Unlike the adversary process, where a lawyer's only aim is to help his or her client win, mediation stresses compromise and agreement between the parties. In mediation, all parties to a dispute are given the opportunity to actively participate in the settlement of their problems without being involved in a formal judicial proceeding.

Mediation is one of several techniques for settling disputes that are alternatives to litigation; collectively, these techniques are known as alternative dispute resolution (or ADR). Supporters of ADR consider litigation to be a costly and time-consuming process, which typically ends with one party the winner and the other the loser, and which often makes the parties more hostile to each other at the end than they were at the beginning.

There was extraordinary growth in the use of alternatives to litigation in the 1980s. There are thousands of mediation programs in the United States today, as compared to only a handful that existed in the late 1970s. The most common ADR processes are negotiation, arbitration, and mediation. These processes differ from litigation in a number of ways.

1. They are more informal than litigation. Lawyers are often not present and rules of evidence do not have to be followed. Cases are settled more quickly and more cheaply.

2. The are generally held in private and the proceedings are confidential.
3. They are often voluntary, with the parties coming together because of a desire to settle the dispute out of court.
4. There is usually no appeal from a settlement reached through ADR.

There are also significant differences among the various ADR techniques, some of which are as different from each other as they are from litigation. Some ADR methods, for example, have some of the features of litigation and others do not. Negotiation is the ADR process that is least like litigation. There is no third party present to assist in the resolution of the problem and the parties are free to leave and break off negotiations at any time. Arbitration, on the other hand, is an ADR process that has some qualities in common with litigation. The parties agree ahead of time that the arbitrator has the authority to issue rulings and decide the case. Lawyers are often involved in presenting the case to the arbitrator. Typically, arbitration will still be quicker than litigation and proceed in a less legalistic fashion.

Mediation differs from arbitration in that a mediator does not have the power to issue rulings. Like negotiation, mediation works only when the settlement that is reached is acceptable to the parties. If any party is dissatisfied, there will be no settlement. Mediators will have different styles and some are more comfortable than others in making suggestions and indicating to the parties what they feel is fair. But what is most important in increasing the likelihood that any settlement will last and that the parties will walk away pleased with the outcome is for the parties in conflict to believe that they have contributed to the nature of the settlement. The best settlements are those where the parties come to understand the motives and needs of their opponents and have worked out a solution that benefits all sides. The mediator is much more interested than a judge in promoting communication, understanding, and a complete airing of the circumstances that contributed to the dispute.

Should more cases be resolved through mediation and fewer through the court system? Would anything be lost if cases that might have been resolved through litigation are instead diverted to a mediation project? What kinds of cases are best handled through mediation and what kinds should be litigated? The following articles focus on the use of mediation in family law cases. The use of mediation has been heavily promoted in divorce cases since it has been assumed that mediation would lead to more creative problem solving and there would be less hostility during the process of distributing assets and arranging custody. In the first selection, however, law professor Penelope Bryan argues that mediation places women at a distinct disadvantage. The appropriateness of ADR is defended by Stephen Erickson, a practicing divorce mediator, in the second reading.

YES

Penelope E. Bryan

KILLING US SOFTLY: DIVORCE MEDIATION AND THE POLITICS OF POWER

Divorce mediation's seductive marketing rhetoric masks a political agenda: entrenchment. Recently reformed divorce law confers greater economic rights upon divorcing women. Custody law also favors women. Negotiating lawyers rely upon these legal entitlements and craft divorce agreements reflecting them, thereby loosening the control men traditionally wield over economic resources and the socialization of children. While mediation proponents employ the obscuring rhetoric of relatedness, mediation unobtrusively reduces this threat to patriarchy by returning men to their former dominant position. This article explains how mediation accomplishes this feat....

DISTRIBUTION OF POWER BETWEEN HUSBANDS AND WIVES

During negotiation the parties explore their relative power and reach agreements reflecting their strengths and weaknesses. Since the husband and wife negotiate directly with each other in divorce mediation, absent active mediator intervention, outcomes should reflect power differences between them....

Throughout this article, the mediation model I contemplate offers an informal conflict resolution process in which a neutral mediator helps the husband and wife negotiate the disputed issues in their divorce. The mediator guards the process, while the parties determine the substance of the divorce agreement. Substantive law does not control the divorce settlement's terms. Rather the mediator encourages the couple to design an agreement that reflects their particular needs and interests. While some variation exists, this model captures most divorce mediation. Moreover, because most divorce mediation occurs in court affiliated programs and most divorce mediators have mental health backgrounds, this article anticipates a mediation program with these characteristics....

Tangible Resources

The spouse with greater income has several advantages in negotiation. He more easily can hire experts to advise him on how to negotiate or how to structure an agreement to maximize his, and minimize the other party's, interests. Moreover, due to greater self-sufficiency, he more credibly can threaten to terminate or extend the length of negotiations if the other party fails to meet his demands. Income disparity between negotiating spouses then affects their negotiating strength.

In the United States men earn much more than women. The wage gap between husbands and wives is even wider than between men and women generally. Approximately fifty percent of married women and married women with children in the home earn no income because they do not participate in the paid labor force. Even when married women work outside the home, they average less than half the income of married men. More specifically, in 1980 wives' earnings, on the average, accounted for only twenty-six percent of total family income, and the median contribution to the total family income of wives with full-time, year round employment was only thirty-eight percent. Wives with children whose births are spaced over many years and wives with many children have the lowest wages of all wives. While certainly some spouses will have equivalent incomes and a few wives' incomes will exceed that of their husbands, most marriages will reflect the pattern these statistics reveal: the wife, if employed at all, will earn much less than her husband. The husband thus is better able to purchase expert advice and to threaten termination or extension of negotiations....

Educational superiority also can create negotiating power. The individual with more education may have important knowledge, such as the tax consequences of property distribution, that enables him to negotiate an agreement more favorable to him than the other spouse suspects. Advanced education also might provide training in negotiation skills. Moreover, the better educated individual can control outcomes because his exposure to a wider range of ideas helps him generate more alternatives during negotiation. Higher education, too, implies a superior ability to understand what occurs in mediation. Tellingly, in one custody mediation program, only the women with graduate educations and/or women over forty-five years of age failed to complain of jumbled and confused thoughts during negotiations with their husbands.

In the United States men and women tend to marry those of similar educational levels. However, where a difference exists, women more than men marry people with higher educational attainment. When this occurs the husband has further advantages in divorce mediation. One's occupation also can increase one's negotiating strength by providing training or information relevant to divorce issues. If the husband is an attorney or a corporate financial officer, his occupation provides him knowledge of legal rights and finances. Moreover, some occupations require negotiation skills. A construction foreman, for instance, must negotiate....

Effects of Tangible Resource Power on Mediated Outcomes

... Research on marital negotiations shows that the greater income and education and the higher occupational level of husbands, compared to wives, confers upon husbands greater power over routine decisions and decisions on issues over which the couple frequently disagrees. Moreover, husbands believe they control decisions over important financial issues, whereas they perceive as shared or wife-dominated less important financial decisions or mundane decisions requiring time to implement. That employed wives have more decisional power relative to their husbands than unemployed wives, further illustrates the importance of tangible resources to marital negotiating power.

Tangible resources probably create more power for the husband in divorce negotiations than marital decisionmaking research indicates. Spouses inevitably develop psychological and emotional interdependencies. A wife then has some power over her husband during marriage because of his dependence on her for emotional and psychological support, as well as sexual gratification. At divorce these sources of power evaporate. Thus, tangible resources probably have even more influence in divorce than in marital negotiations.

In summary, marital decisionmaking research suggests that, unless the mediator intervenes, the husband's greater tangible resources will grant him the lion's share of power in divorce negotiations, particularly over critical financial issues. Differences in possession of tangible resources, however, are only one source of inequality between spouses. Intangible factors such as status, dominance, depression, self esteem, reward expectation and fear of achievement further empower the husband during divorce mediation. . . .

Mediator Coercion on Child Issues

In divorce mediation the wife confronts a mental health mediator surrounded by an aura of professional expertise regarding the children's best interests. Mediators claim expert authority by describing their training and experience to the couple and by sharing their allegedly expert knowledge on children's developmental needs. The wife's legitimate authority over the children pales in the shadow of the professional's expert authority.

If the expert mediator remained neutral, the wife still could use her child-centered power in direct negotiation with her husband. Or, if the formal law that recognized the caretaking mother's superior right to children remained relevant in mediation, it might enhance the wife's power over child issues. But formal law does not dictate mediated outcomes and mental health mediators do not remain neutral. Emboldened and legitimated by their professional expertise, divorce mediators abandon their prescribed neutrality and zealously intervene to protect defenseless children from the custody and visitation decisions of their allegedly destructive parents. Mediator intervention results in custody arrangements more favorable to fathers than fathers could obtain in direct negotiations with their authoritative wives.

Divorce mediators have a strong bias in favor of joint custody and coerce divorcing mothers into this arrangement. Irving and Benjamin unwittingly provide an illustrative case. At mediation's beginning, the mother requested sole custody of the couple's two girls, aged ten and six. The case report nowhere indicates the mother's unfitness. The mother, however, did raise some question about the quality of the father's prior involvement with the girls. During the course of the mediation, the mediators convinced the mother that, irrespective of the father's past behavior, the children "needed" and "loved" their father and suggested the mother should behave in accordance with the children's best interests. In seeking to persuade the mother, the mediators engaged the children in the mediation as well as the maternal grandmother who, at the outset, had insisted the girls' mother should have sole custody. At mediation's end, the agreement reflected a joint physical custody arrangement with the girls spending weekdays with their mother and weekends with their father. The couple, however, continued having difficulty and returned for follow-up mediation. With the mediator's assistance, the couple arrived at a new custody arrangement: the girls would stay with their father two evenings per week as well as the weekends, leaving them with their mother only three days per week.

Only the mother's resistance offers to control a biased mediator's imposition of joint custody. However, the mother's insistence upon sole custody or her threat to walk out of mediation seems unlikely because of the mental health professional's expert authority and because the mother's sex role socialization makes her susceptible to manipulation by the mediator. Her belief in her responsibility to maintain familial relationships predisposes her to joint custody because mediators present that arrangement as the one best designed to preserve the children's relationship with their father. Moreover, as the above case illustrates, mediators appeal to the traditional mother's care orientation by emphasizing the father's emotional importance to the children. The traditional mother then falls victim to a skillful mediator armed with such rhetoric. Unsurprisingly, mediation produces a significantly greater percentage of joint custody arrangements than any other process of custody dispute resolution.

The joint custody agreements reached in mediation, however, more commonly seem to reflect joint legal, rather than joint physical, custody. In contrast to joint physical custody where the child spends extended periods of time living with each parent, joint legal custody requires the parents only to share control over important child related decisions. Because this form of custody superficially seems less threatening to mothers, its subtle political implications frequently go unnoticed. Joint legal custody often perpetuates the preexisting patriarchal family structure by allocating the day-to-day care of the children to the mother, while solidifying the ex-husband's power over important child related decisions. The mother can make decisions as long as they reflect her ex-husband's wishes. The moment, however, her opinion differs from his, he has veto power. This veto power, or the threat of its use, invades the ex-wife's consciousness and makes her ex-husband, and the male control he represents, an ever-present force with which to contend. The message is clear: she may escape the marriage but will remain subject to male domination. This implicit, yet powerful, message keeps women aware of their required submissiveness and thus strengthens patriarchy.

The effect joint legal or physical custody has on the children of divorce also reinforces existing hierarchy between men and women. The father's absence from the family unit interferes with socialization of the children into patriarchal patterns. How, for instance, does a little girl learn proper submissiveness to male authority in the absence of a powerful male figure and in the presence of an independently decisive mother. Likewise, how can a little boy learn proper domination of women if he lacks his father's modeling, his mother dominates the household, and he observes his mother operating as an autonomous adult. While certainly children's exposure to patriarchal patterns in other areas of life will influence them, the absence of these patterns in their homes makes their socialization less effective. Joint legal and joint physical custody reintroduce male power into the post-divorce family and ensure that children remain aware of male dominance. The significant increase in joint custody, whether physical or legal, generated by mediation thus reflects a corresponding increase in the male dominance characteristic of patriarchy.

Not only does mediator bias in favor of joint custody reinforce patriarchy through custody arrangements, it also further weakens the wife's already precarious financial position in divorce mediation by eliminating the wife's ability to use her child-centered power during negotiations over financial issues. Moreover, a mother intent upon sole custody despite mediator coercion might attempt to circumvent the mediator and appeal directly to the father by offering to accept a grossly inequitable financial arrangement in exchange for sole custody. While those working in family law recognize that fathers frequently threaten to dispute custody in order to strengthen their financial position, the mediator's advocacy of joint custody enhances the father's coercive power.

Considering the foregoing, women's highly ambivalent response to custody mediation causes no surprise:

Although a complete analysis is not available, there is reason to think that women are significantly more likely to regard mediation as threatening and balanced against them than are men. While women did report that mediation helped them in understanding themselves and their spouses, they were also far more likely than men to report a sense of being pressured into agreement, a lack of comfort in expressing their feelings, anger during mediation sessions, and a sense that mediators essentially dictated the terms of the agreement.

In conclusion, traditional sex role ideology enhances the husband's power over financial issues and, when coupled with mediator bias for joint custody, strengthens the father's position in custody matters as well....

PROTECTION FOR THE DISADVANTAGED WIFE

Balancing the Power: A Rhetorical Smokescreen

Mediator Self-Interested Ignorance on Power Issues. Given the importance of power balancing, divorce mediation literature carefully should explain the factors that create power, how those factors normally are distributed among husbands and wives, and methods for detecting these factors as well as techniques for correcting power disparities rooted in different factors. As I mentioned earlier, however, the literature proves insensitive to power issues. Characteristically, a recent book on divorce mediation devotes only sixteen of over four hundred pages to power imbalances. In those sixteen pages the authors deny the existence of power imbalances or suggest that if they exist they do not affect mediation.

Divorce mediation training programs show equivalent insensitivity to power issues. The better divorce mediation training programs require trainees to devote a maximum of forty hours, usually over a five day period, to becoming a mediator. In that short time the program director attempts to instill in the trainees an expertise in basic mediation skills, the psychology of divorce, child psychology, and the complex financial and legal issues presented in divorce. During this ambitious agenda, power issues remain unacknowledged or receive scant attention.

Because mediation literature and training fail to address and explain power adequately, mediators can avoid acknowledging the seriousness of unequal power between divorcing spouses and the need for mediator intervention. Moreover, because of insufficient training, even those who do recognize the need to power balance have knowledge and skills inadequate to the task. Deficient in both skills and awareness, mediators lack the motivation and the ability to power balance.

More importantly, the mediation profession cannot be expected to correct its inadequate response to power issues: their ignorance serves their purposes. Candid exposition of the depth, breadth, and tenacity of power disparities between spouses threatens the survival of this budding profession because it suggests the impossibility of power balancing. In order to alter a power disparity, a mediator must first be able to detect its existence. Yet diagnosis of a disparity based on intangible power factors or sex role ideology proves difficult. For instance, if a highly educated professional wife earns a high income and the husband does not make obvious his greater power during mediation by dominating conversation, the mediator has little reason to suspect an imbalance. This wife, however, may agree to her husband's inadequate financial proposal because her adherence to traditional sex role ideology, her depression, and her low self-esteem override her more obvious tangible power bases. The mediator, insensitive to the wife's low power based on intangible factors, will assure the wife freely has chosen to accept her husband's proposal and will see no need to power balance. Because many of the bases for power disparity remain elusive, the need to power balance frequently will go unrecognized. Without this recognition power balancing cannot occur.

Moreover, the severity and complexity of power disparities between most spouses suggest that power balancing requires skills most mediators do not and cannot have. It defies imagination to think of the skill and knowledge required to empower a depressed wife with low self-esteem who believes in traditional sex role ideology, fears confronting her husband, and has no occupation outside the home. Certainly the mediator cannot alter the wife's occupation during mediation. Nor can the mediator significantly improve the wife's psychological and emotional state. Even if the mediator has knowledge of counseling psychology, mediation focuses on the task of reaching agreement, rather than on therapy for troubled spouses. The extensive therapy required to balance a power disparity grounded in a wife's low self-esteem, depression, fear of confrontation, and traditional sex role ideology would require a mediator willing to redefine mediation and develop complex skills.

Even if a sufficiently talented mediator was willing to assume this task, the efficiency rationale justifying court affiliated mediation programs makes therapy a practical impossibility. The efficiency focus of these programs pressures the mediator to produce agreements quickly. For instance, studies indicate that custody mediation in court affiliated programs takes an average of four hours. In contrast, two therapeutic mediators in a private mediation program acknowledged that "detection" of the twenty percent of their clients who were totally inappropriate for mediation and the other fifty percent who needed a therapeutic "premediation" stage to prepare them for mediation, required an approximately six hour assessment stage. Mediator power balancing through extensive therapy thus proves a practical impossibility.

In summary, full exploration of power issues by mediation proponents would require the corresponding admission that detection difficulties, lack of skill, and program constraints make power balancing impossible for most, if not all, mediators. With power balancing no longer available as a rhetorical safeguard, judicial administrators and the public would understand mediation for what it is: an informal process that places the low powered spouse, usually the wife, fully at the mercy of her more powerful husband. This recognition might cause the demise of this new profession. Mediation proponents thus have a vested interest in remaining ignorant of power issues.

THE COMPARATIVE EFFECTIVENESS OF LAWYER NEGOTIATION

Divorce agreements negotiated by lawyers will be more favorable to wives than mediated agreements for several reasons. While mediators must remain substantively neutral, lawyers have a professional obligation to pursue and protect the client's interests during negotiations. The lawyer advocate also insulates the disadvantaged wife from her husband and prevents the tangible, intangible, and sex role differences between them from dictating the terms of the agreement. By forcing the husband and wife to deal directly with one another, mediation, in contrast, sharpens the wife's disadvantages. Even lawyers who might compromise their clients' concerns in order to fulfill their own interests have an advocacy role and professional ethic to constrain their self-interested behaviors. The mediator, as a neutral, has no counterbalancing role or ethical prescription to mitigate the mediator's interest in obtaining an agreement irrespective of its substance. The lawyer's advocacy role thus differs markedly from mediator neutrality and offers far greater protection for a low power spouse.

Market factors provide the lawyer additional motivation to protect the low powered wife's interests. An attorney's ability to generate business turns upon whether professional peers and clients see her as competent in protecting client interests. To remain in business the mediator in a court affiliated program, on the other hand, need only produce many agreements quickly. Market factors suggest then that negotiating lawyers will provide much more protection for client interests than will mediators.

In addition to role and market factors, liability for professional malpractice helps motivate the lawyer to seek legally defined client interests during negotiations. The possibility of a malpractice claim for failure to secure the wife's legal entitlement to part of her husband's pension plan, for instance, motivates the lawyer to negotiate assertively to secure that right in the divorce settlement. In contrast, the mediator, who lacks accountability for the mediated agreement's substance, will have less difficulty allowing the wife to relinquish her right to a portion of the pension plan.

The above observation invites recognition of the importance of legal rights in determining the substance of a lawyer negotiated, as opposed to a mediated, divorce agreement. Women's ability to avoid substantive law in mediation might seem attractive to a group these laws consistently have treated unfairly. However, as argued throughout this article, movement out of a dispute resolution system in which law is relevant into an informal system where it is not limits law's ability to constrain power abuses and ensures that preexisting power disparities, rather than law, will dictate the divorce agreement's terms. In contrast, substantive legal norms form the expectations of negotiating lawyers and create a foundation from which they can begin to judge the acceptability of the negotiated agreement. Thus, while formal substantive law may not reflect true distributive justice for divorcing women, because of power disparities and the lack of meaningful safeguards in mediation women will obtain more advantageous outcomes when negotiating lawyers rely on law than when mediators rely on vague and biased equity norms.

CONCLUSION

Today custody law still favors women and recent reforms in family law create new economic rights for divorcing women. Lawyers negotiating divorce settlements concern themselves with implementing these legal entitlements. Mediation proponents believe the lawyer's focus on rights generates hostility among divorcing parties and unnecessarily infringes upon the couple's right to order their post divorce lives. In contrast they maintain mediation preserves relationships, empowers the parties, and generates good feelings. Legal rights fade into the shadows of informality.

This shift in focus from rights to relatedness, however, endangers divorcing women and reinforces male dominance. Mediation proponents seductively appeal to women's socialized values by speaking softly of relatedness. Yet mediation exploits wives by denigrating their legal entitlements, stripping them of authority, encouraging unwarranted compromise, isolating them from needed support, and placing them across the table from their more powerful husbands and demanding that they fend for themselves. The process thus perpetuates patriarchy by freeing men to use their power to gain greater control over children, to implant more awareness of male dominance into women's consciousness, and to retain more of the marital financial assets than men would obtain if lawyers negotiated divorce agreements.

The insidious nature of mediation for divorcing women, though, remains hidden beneath its carefully crafted marketing rhetoric. This article looks beneath that rhetoric. The effects upon women of the political agenda disclosed should inspire critical debate on the propriety of divorce mediation. At the very least those who structure court affiliated programs, as well as mediators, now should recognize their complicity in the continued oppression of women and their dependent children.

NO

Stephen K. Erickson

ADR AND FAMILY LAW

INTRODUCTION

Shakespeare's oft-quoted phrase, "First thing, let's kill all the lawyers," commits the cardinal sin by attacking the person rather than the problem. Mediators argue that it is necessary to attack the problem, rather than the person; therefore, if Shakespeare really wanted to find a solution, he should have said: "First thing, let's kill the system and design something that protects the parties, is less costly and works better." Mediators would say "You don't have to kill the system; let's just learn to live side by side in harmony."

...The purpose of this article is to attempt to show how mediation creates different ground rules and an entirely different environment so that settlement can occur more easily. These new rules permit the professional to avoid getting caught up in the couple's battle, focusing rather on how to end the battle in a constructive manner....

MEDIATION DEFINED

Jay Folberg, Dean of the San Francisco University Law School, attempts to define mediation as:

> An alternative to violence, self-help, or litigation that differs from the processes of counseling, negotiation, and arbitration. It can be defined as the process by which the participants, together with the assistance of a neutral person or persons, systematically isolate disputed issues in order to develop options, consider alternatives, and reach a consensual settlement that will accommodate their needs. Mediation is a process that emphasizes the participants' own responsibility for making decisions that affect their lives.

Folberg continues by pointing out that a competitive process of conflict resolution focuses on the parties' differences, while a mediation process focuses on the parties' similarities.

Mediation is best thought of as a process of conflict resolution whereby the parties are encouraged to find the best result they can for themselves by using cooperative negotiation rules rather than a competitive or adversarial

From Stephen K. Erickson, "ADR and Family Law," *Hamline Journal of Public Law and Policy* (Spring 1991). Copyright © 1991 by Stephen K. Erickson. Reprinted by permission. Notes omitted.

process. One of the main points of the co-operative mediation process is an effort to resolve the underlying aspects of the divorce dispute through focusing on the things couples really want, rather than focusing on who is more powerful or who is right. William Ury's recent book, *Getting Disputes Resolved*, suggests that there are three methods people have traditionally used to resolve conflict: power, rights, and interests. A power-based system of conflict resolution focuses on who has the most power. A rights-based system focuses on who is right and who is wrong using certain relevant standards or guideposts for a fair outcome. However, the parties may also choose to resolve disputes by trying to reconcile their underlying interests. Ury argues that a system that reconciles people's underlying interests, while not invariably better than focusing on rights and power, "simply means that it tends to result in lower transaction costs, greater satisfaction with outcomes, less strain on the relationship and less recurrence of disputes."

Perhaps influenced by Fisher and Ury's 1981 book, *Getting to Yes*, mediators in this country have tended to use an interest based approach to conflict resolution. This makes sense, because most couples have already failed at power-based negotiations within the relationship, and most couples lack the ability to understand and apply the complex legal principles of divorce law (rights). By focusing on the underlying interests of the couple, mediators have created a conceptual framework that attempts to reconcile both parties' need to have a good relationship with their children, the need to obtain some measure of financial security after the divorce, and the need to create a fair division of the accumulated property of the marriage relationship.

ACCEPTANCE OF MEDIATION BY THE PUBLIC AND THE JUDICIARY

The ABA Standing Committee on Dispute Resolution reports there are approximately 4,500 jurisdictions requiring mediation in family custody and visitation disputes, whereas no such requirement existed in any jurisdiction in 1977. The Academy of Family Mediators, founded in 1981 as a non-profit Minnesota corporation, now has 1,400 practicing members nationwide and in Canada. Most popular magazines have run articles about divorce mediation and in 1984, ABC Television News' *Nightline* featured live interviews with two Minneapolis couples telling Sam Donaldson about their wonderful experiences in mediation....

HOW COOPERATION IS ACHIEVED IN THE MEDIATION ROOM

Mediators do not have the power to wave a magic wand and suddenly people begin to cooperate. However, mediators do have the ability to influence what goes on in the room in a number of powerful ways.

Asking Different Questions

It has been said that the person who defines the problem has a great deal of power over the resolution of the problem. This is nowhere more evident than in custody battles. If you really think about it only the adversarial system asks the question "Who will have custody of the minor children?" This question, by its very nature, creates a competitive battle for "ownership" of the minor children.

Just the words "custody" and "visitation" also create problems. The only other place in our language where "custody" is frequently used is in prisons. The word "visitation" is also used in connection with funerals. The words and the questions asked create a situation where parties fight over who will get the children. Mediators can reduce the fighting by simply asking a different question: Not who is a better or worse parent, but when will each of you care for the children.

The Idaho Supreme Court, in the case of *Stockwell v. Stockwell*, recognized this concept. Justice Robert Huntley, writing for the Idaho Supreme Court, described the child custody case as "unusually acrimonious and expensive," and directed the parties to participate under the auspices of the district court, in "a mediation process wherein all concerned focus on seeking the interests of the children."

With regard to mediation, the court stated:

> It is obvious that the parties have expended thousands of dollars in attorney fees, travel expenses, and loss of time from employment, while pursuing interests other than those which might be expected to be in the best interests of the child as distinguished from the best interests of the parents and their respective families. It is a case where all might benefit if they were to cooperate in seeking a mutually satisfactory resolution through a mediation process wherein all concerned focus on seeking the best interests of the children.

The court directed the trial court, prior to conducting further custody hearings, to require the parties to "undergo a mediation process under the auspices of the district court before a qualified mediator."

Justice Johnson, concurring, referred the trial court and the parties to J. Folberg and A. Milne, *Divorce Mediation: Theory and Practice*. He also quoted at some length from on of the articles in that volume, S. Erickson, "The Legal Dimension of Divorce Mediation." Justice Johnson quoted in part:

> The legal adversarial system asks, "Who will be awarded custody of the minor children?" ...
>
> ... A more appropriate question to ask the divorcing couple is, "What future parenting arrangements can you agree to, so that each of you can continue to be involved, loving parents?" This version of the custody question creates a different focus and a very different outcome. First, the question is mutual, and answering it requires cooperation. Asking "Who shall have custody?" creates a competitive focus and is likely to produce an adversarial or fighting response, but asking the couple to agree to certain parenting arrangements requires collaborative discussions and mutual planning.
>
> Second, the question is future oriented. Mediation pushes couples to look more to the future because it can be controlled and changed.

Couples can usually discuss future parenting arrangements with little conflict because they are prevented from fighting over who was a more faulty parent in the past. This becomes easier to accomplish when a different question is asked.

Focusing on the Future

Divorce trials, by their very nature, focus on information about the past. Some time must be spent establishing factual data about incomes, expenses, and the nature of marital assets. However, once this is accomplished, the real focus must then be on the future. An interest-based approach to conflict resolution deals primarily with solving future problems. In divorce, these problems are always: 1) How will both of you be able to act as good, loving parents in the future, even though you are living separately? 2) How will it be possible to achieve some measure of economic security for both of you, given the fact that it now costs more money to live in two separate residences? 3) How can the property be fairly divided in order to meet your future needs for housing, transportation, and financial security? A rights-based approach, with its requirements of applying legal standards of fairness, tends to keep people in the past. An interest-based approach tends to focus people on the future, thereby eliminating a good measure of blaming and fault-finding, because the future can be shaped and controlled hundreds of different ways, and the past can only be fought about.

Discourage Blaming and Fault Finding
Conflict tends to escalate when parties seek to fix blame over some past events. Cooperation is easier to achieve when parties are told by the mediator: "No one in this room has the power to change the past; therefore, it is important to avoid using time and effort trying to determine who was more at fault for your present problems. Rather, let's try to turn past problems into an opportunity to find solutions that will prevent these problems from occurring again." This is a difficult task to accomplish with an angry, highly conflicted couple, but it creates a much better environment for cooperative problem solving.

Avoiding Positional Bargaining
When a parent in mediation states: "I want custody of the minor children,"

that person's underlying interest is in trying to avoid losing the children. More important, it is a positional statement that says, "My position is that I don't want to lose my relationship with the children; therefore, my solution is to demand custody." Positions can only be met in one way—either custody is won, or it is lost. By moving the couple to talk about their real underlying interest in remaining good, loving parents, the mediator can explore a range of options and eventually find some way to achieve resolution. A positional statement can only be solved in one way. An interest statement can be solved in hundreds of different ways. Therefore, opening statements are avoided and the future needs of the parties, rather than the past problems are stressed, and options, rather than positions, are discussed.

CONCLUSION

The exciting aspect of mediation is that it allow professionals to avoid getting bruised in acrimonious family law battles. To represent couples in mediation, or to act as a neutral in cooperation with the parties' attorneys, requires understanding of the underlying principles of mediation. Different rules, different questions, and effective control of the process make mediation more than another hoop to jump through for the attorney who hears the judge order a client into mediation. It presents a better opportunity for the client than could be obtained in litigation, especially when the financial and emotional cost of the contested trial are considered.

POSTSCRIPT

Does Mediation in Divorce Cases Hurt Women?

These articles raise a question on legal ethics—namely, what are the goals of the legal process? The attractiveness of mediation is that it does such an excellent job of fostering communication between hostile parties and of allowing them to work through their differences. But, as Bryan argues, law is designed to do more than help the particular disputants in a case. The resolution of disputes through law sends a message to all of us indicating what the norms of our society are and should be, what is acceptable behavior and what is not. When disputes are mediated privately, as occurs with most ADR processes, the public is left out. Having read the preceding articles, consider whether this is a problem that is insurmountable or whether there are ways to determine which kinds of problems should be settled in court and which might be resolved through ADR.

Several decades ago, a common rallying cry was the phrase "law and order." The solution to disorder and to conflict was to have more law. It would have been inconceivable for many to believe that one could have more order with less law. Since that time, we have become more skeptical about the power of our institutions. We are also more knowledgeable about the strengths and weaknesses of the law. The growth of ADR reflects this increased level of both skepticism and knowledge. The increased use of ADR presents us with more choices in how disputes may be settled. It also provides us with a more complicated system of dispute resolution, since we no longer automatically run to court to solve a problem but instead ask which of several available methods is most appropriate.

Modern life is characterized by increased options and choices. Our range of alternatives in both ideas and material goods has been expanded, and making choices is not easy. We are no longer able to react to some social problem or dispute with the attitude of "there ought to be a law." We are more sensitive today to the limits of the law and to the strengths of some alternatives to law. We also have to be very careful to know when it is appropriate to use some alternative in lieu of law and when it is not.

Further information about the practice and theory of ADR can be found in Jonathan Shailor, *Empowerment in Dispute Resolution* (1994); Deborah Kolb, *When Talk Works: Profiles of Mediators* (1993); Goldberg, Green, and Sander, *Dispute Resolution* (1985); Auerbach, *Justice Without Law* (1983); and Fisher and Ury, *Getting to Yes* (1981). Family mediation is discussed in Robert Dingwall and John Eekelaar, *Divorce Mediation and the Legal Process* (1988) and Jay Folberg and Ann Milne, eds, *Divorce Mediation: Theory and Practice* (1988).

ISSUE 3

Should Plea Bargaining Be Abolished?

YES: Kenneth Kipnis, from "Criminal Justice and the Negotiated Plea," *Ethics* (vol. 86, 1976)

NO: Nick Schweitzer, from "Plea Bargaining: A Prosecutor's View," *Wisconsin Bar Bulletin* (October 1988)

ISSUE SUMMARY

YES: Professor of philosophy Kenneth Kipnis makes the case that justice cannot be traded on the open market and that plea bargaining often subverts the cause of justice.

NO: District Attorney Nick Schweitzer finds that plea bargaining is fair, useful, desirable, necessary, and practical.

One of the most common myths fostered by television programs about lawyers concerns the place of the trial in the American legal system. The television lawyer, who is invariably a criminal trial lawyer, defends an innocent individual and, at a particularly dramatic point in the trial, achieves vindication for the client. One can now watch "Court TV," a cable channel, and see trials at almost any hour. As this book is being completed during the summer of 1994, the O.J. Simpson trial is scheduled to begin in September and will undoubtedly attract huge audiences.

If you visit a courthouse, you may be able to find a trial being held that resembles what you have seen on television. The lawyer may be less dramatic, the judge less dour, and the defendant less appealing, but the main elements of the television version of justice, such as cross-examination of witnesses, opening and closing arguments, and, perhaps, a jury verdict, will be present. What is important to understand, however, is that of the cases processed by the criminal justice system, only a handful are disposed of in this manner. Instead, as many as 90 percent of the cases are resolved through plea bargaining.

Plea bargaining is a method of avoiding trials by securing guilty pleas from defendants. It occurs primarily because trials are expensive and time consuming. In plea bargaining, the defendant agrees to plead guilty in exchange for an agreement by the prosecutor to reduce the charges or recommend a lenient sentence. The defendant essentially has a choice between going to trial and possibly being found guilty on a more serious charge or pleading guilty now and suffering less severe consequences.

This is a difficult choice for any defendant, and at the center of the debate over the legitimacy of plea bargaining is the question of whether or not the defendant, in these circumstances, is making a voluntary choice. In the following articles, Kenneth Kipnis argues that there is too much coercion involved for the choice to be considered voluntary, that the process is inherently unjust, and that innocent individuals may be coerced into pleading guilty. District attorney Nick Schweitzer believes that the system is not at fault and that if the standard legal procedures are followed, plea bargaining is not only indispensable but also just and desirable.

Plea bargaining has been upheld by the Supreme Court, but only when the Court was persuaded that the plea was made voluntarily. Yet it is rare for a convicted defendant to make a successful challenge to the voluntariness of a guilty plea because the defendant must admit in open court, prior to making the plea, that it is being made voluntarily. In every courtroom in which plea bargaining occurs, the judge asks the defendant the following questions:

1. Do you understand the charges against you and the maximum penalties authorized by law?
2. Are you, in fact, guilty of the charge you are pleading guilty to?
3. Are you pleading guilty voluntarily?
4. Do you understand that you have the right to a trial by jury and that you are waiving that right?

The judge will not accept a plea unless the defendant answers yes to all of these questions. For a plea of guilty to be challenged later, therefore, the defendant must persuade a higher court that he was coerced into lying when he was asked these questions.

Another important issue in the controversy over plea bargaining is the fact that plea bargaining is mainly a poor person's problem. The reason for this is that the greatest incentive to plead guilty exists for those persons who are in jail awaiting trial and cannot afford bail. Their choice is to plead guilty now and get out of jail immediately, or at some definite future date, or to insist on a trial, stay in jail until the trial occurs, and risk a long sentence if convicted. As you read the following articles, you should consider how important this factor is in making a decision about whether or not plea bargaining should be abolished.

YES

Kenneth Kipnis

CRIMINAL JUSTICE AND THE NEGOTIATED PLEA

In recent years it has become apparent to many that, in practice, the criminal justice system in the United States does not operate as we thought it did. The conviction secured through jury trial, so familiar in countless novels, films, and television programs, is beginning to be seen as the aberration it has become. What has replaced the jury's verdict is the negotiated plea. In these "plea bargains" the defendant agrees to plead guilty in exchange for discretionary consideration on the part of the state. Generally, this consideration amounts to some kind of assurance of a minimal sentence. The well-publicized convictions of Spiro Agnew and Clifford Irving were secured through such plea bargains. In 1974 in New York City, 80 percent of all felony cases were settled as misdemeanors through plea bargains.[1] Only 2 percent of all felony arrests resulted in a trial.[2] It is at present a commonplace that plea bargaining could not be eliminated without substantial alterations in our criminal justice system.

Plea bargaining involves negotiations between the defendant (through an attorney in the standard case) and the prosecutor as to the conditions under which the defendant will enter a guilty plea.[3] Both sides have bargaining power in these negotiations. The prosecutor is ordinarily burdened with cases and does not have the wherewithal to bring more than a fraction of them to trial. Often there is not sufficient evidence to ensure a jury's conviction. Most important, the prosecutor is typically under administrative and political pressure to dispose of cases and to secure convictions as efficiently as possible. If the defendant exercises the constitutional right to a jury trial, the prosecutor must decide whether to drop the charges entirely or to expend scarce resources to bring the case to trial. Since neither prospect is attractive, prosecutors typically exercise their broad discretion to induce defendants to waive trial and to plead guilty.

From the defendant's point of view, such prosecutorial discretion has two aspects; it darkens the prospect of going to trial as it brightens the prospect of pleading guilty. Before negotiating, a prosecutor may improve his bargaining position by "overcharging" defendants[4] or by developing a reputation for

From Kenneth Kipnis, "Criminal Justice and the Negotiated Plea," *Ethics*, vol. 86 (1976). Copyright © 1976 by The University of Chicago. Reprinted by permission of University of Chicago Press as publisher.

severity in the sentences he recommends to judges. Such steps greatly increase the punishment that the defendant must expect if convicted at trial. On the other hand, the state may offer to reduce or to drop some charges, or to recommend leniency to the judge if the defendant agrees to plead guilty. These steps minimize the punishment that will result from a guilty plea. Though the exercise of prosecutorial discretion to secure pleas of guilty may differ somewhat in certain jurisdictions and in particular cases, the broad outlines are as described.

Of course a defendant can always reject any offer of concessions and challenge the state to prove its case. A skilled defense attorney can do much to force the prosecutor to expend resources in bringing a case to trial.[5] But the trial route is rarely taken by defendants. Apart from prosecutorial pressure, other factors may contribute to a defendant's willingness to plead guilty: feelings of guilt which may or may not be connected with the charged crime; the discomforts of the pretrial lockup as against the comparatively better facilities of a penitentiary; the costs of going to trial as against the often cheaper option of consenting to a plea; a willingness or unwillingness to lie; and the delays which are almost always present in awaiting trial, delays which the defendant may sit out in jail in a kind of preconviction imprisonment which may not be credited to a postconviction sentence. It is not surprising that the right to a trial by jury is rarely exercised.

If one examines the statistics published annually by the Administrative Office of the U.S. Courts,[6] one can appreciate both the size of the concessions gained by agreeing to plead guilty and (what is the same thing) the size of the additional burdens imposed upon those convicted without so agreeing. According to the 1970 report, among all convicted defendants, those pleading guilty at arraignment received average sentences of probation and/or under one year of imprisonment. Those going to a jury trial received average sentences of three to four years in prison.[7] If one looks just at those convicted of Marijuana Tax Act violations with no prior record, one finds that those pleading guilty at arraignment received average sentences of probation and/or six months or less of imprisonment while those going to trial received average sentences more than eight times as severe: four to five years in prison.[8] Among all Marijuana Tax Act convictions, defendants pleading guilty at the outset had a 76 percent chance of being let off without imprisonment, while those who had gone to trial had only an 11 percent chance.[9] These last two sets of figures do not reflect advantages gained by charge reduction, nor do they reflect advantages gained by electing a bench trial as opposed to a jury trial. What these figures do suggest is that the sentences given to convicted defendants who have exercised their constitutional right to trial are many times as severe as the sentences given to those who do not. In *United States v. Wiley*[10] Chief Judge Campbell laid to rest any tendency to conjecture that these discrepancies in sentences might have explanations not involving plea bargains.

... I believe, and it is generally accepted by trial judges throughout the United States, that it is entirely proper and logical to grant some defendants some degree of leniency in exchange for a plea of guilty. If then, a trial judge grants leniency in exchange for a plea of guilty, it follows, as the reverse side of the same coin, that he must necessarily forego leniency, generally speaking, where the defendant stands trial and is found guilty.

... I might make general reference to a "standing policy" not to consider probation where a defendant stands trial even though I do not in fact strictly adhere to such a policy.

No deliberative body ever decided that we would have a system in which the disposition of criminal cases is typically the result of negotiations between the prosecutor and the defendant's attorney on the conditions under which the defendant would waive trial and plead guilty to a mutually acceptable charge. No legislature ever voted to adopt a procedure in which defendants who are convicted after trial typically receive sentences far greater than those received by defendants charged with similar offenses but pleading guilty. The practice of plea bargaining has evolved in the unregulated interstices of our criminal justice system. Its development has not gone unnoticed. There is now a substantial literature on the legality and propriety of plea bargaining.[11] But though philosophers do not often treat issues arising in the area of criminal procedure, there are problems here that cry for our attention. In the preceding pages I have been concerned to sketch the institution of plea bargaining. In what follows I will raise some serious questions about it that should concern us. I will first discuss generally the intrinsic fairness of plea bargains and then, in the final section, I will examine critically the place of such bargains in the criminal justice system.

I

As one goes through the literature on plea bargaining one gets the impression that market forces are at work in this unlikely context. The terms "bargain" and "nego-tiation" suggest this. One can see the law of supply and demand operating in that, other things being equal, if there are too many defendants who want to go to trial, prosecutors will have to concede more in order to get the guilty pleas that they need to clear their case load. And if the number of prosecutors and courts goes up, prosecutors will be able to concede less. Against this background it is not surprising to find one commentator noting:[12] "In some places a 'going rate' is established under which a given charge will automatically be broken down to a given lesser offense with the recommendation of a given lesser sentence." Prosecutors, like retailers before them, have begun to appreciate the efficiency of the fixed-price approach.

The plea bargain in the economy of criminal justice has many of the important features of the contract in commercial transactions. In both institutions offers are made and accepted, entitlements are given up and obtained, and the notion of an exchange, ideally a fair one, is presented to both parties. Indeed one detects something of the color of consumer protection law in a few of the decisions on plea bargaining. In *Baily v. MacDougal*[13] the court held that "a guilty plea cannot be accepted unless the defendant understands its consequences." And in *Santo Bello v. New York*[14] the court secured a defendant's entitlement to a prosecutorial concession when a second prosecutor replaced the one who had made the promise. Rule 11 of the Federal Rules of Criminal Procedure requires that "if a plea agreement has been reached by the parties which contemplates entry of a plea of guilty or nolo contendere in the expectation that a specific sentence will be imposed or that other charges before the court will be dismissed, the court shall require the disclosure of the agreement in open court at the time the plea is offered." These procedures all have analogues in contract law. Though plea bargains may not be seen as contracts by the parties, agreements like them are the stuff of contract case law. While I will not argue that plea bargains are contracts (or even that they should be treated as such), I do think it proper to look to contract law for help in evaluating the justice of such agreements.

The law of contracts serves to give legal effect to certain bargain-promises. In particular, it specifies conditions that must be satisfied by bargain-promises before the law will recognize and enforce them as contracts. As an example, we could look at that part of the law of contracts which treats duress. Where one party wrongfully compels another to consent to the terms of an agreement the resulting bargain has no legal effect. Dan B. Dobbs, a commentator on the law in this area, describes the elements of duress as follows: "The defendant's act must be wrongful in some attenuated sense; it must operate coercively upon the will of the plaintiff, judged subjectively, and the plaintiff must have no adequate remedy to avoid the coercion except to give in. . . . The earlier requirement that the coercion must have been the kind that would coerce a reasonable man, or even a brave one, is now generally dispensed with, and it is enough if it in fact coerced a spineless plaintiff."[15] Coercion is not the same as fraud, nor is it confined to cases in which a defendant is physically compelled to assent. In Dobb's words: "The victim of duress knows the facts but is forced by hard choices to act against his will." The paradigm case of duress is the agreement made at gunpoint. Facing a mortal threat, one readily agrees to hand over the cash. But despite such consent, the rules of duress work to void the effects of such

agreements. There is no legal obligation to hand over the cash and, having given it over, entitlement to the money is not lost. The gunman has no legal right to retain possession even if he adheres to his end of the bargain and scraps his murderous plans.

Judges have long been required to see to it that guilty pleas are entered voluntarily. And one would expect that, if duress is present in the plea-bargaining situation, then, just as the handing over of cash to the gunman is void of legal effect (as far as entitlement to the money is concerned), so no legal consequences should flow from the plea of guilty which is the product of duress. However, Rule 11 of the Federal Rules of Criminal Procedure requires the court to insure that a plea of guilty (or nolo contendere) is voluntary by "addressing the defendant personally in open court, determining that the plea is voluntary and not the result of force or promises *apart from a plea agreement*" (emphasis added). In two important cases *(North Carolina v. Alford* and *Brady v. United States)*[16] defendants agreed to plead guilty in order to avoid probable death sentences. Both accepted very long prison sentences. In both cases the Supreme Court decided that guilty pleas so entered were voluntary (through Brennan, Douglas, and Marshall dissented). In his dissent in *Alford*, Brennan writes: " . . . the facts set out in the majority opinion demonstrate that Alford was 'so gripped by fear of the death penalty' that his decision to plead guilty was not voluntary but was the 'product of duress as much so as choice reflecting physical constraint.' " In footnote 2 of the *Alford* opinion, the Court sets out the defendant's testimony given at the time of the entry of his plea of guilty before the trial court. That testimony deserves examination: "I pleaded guilty on second degree murder because they said there is too much evidence, but I ain't shot no man, but I take the fault for the other man. We never had an argument in our life and I just pleaded guilty because they said if I didn't they would gas me for it, and that is all." The rule to be followed in such cases is set out in *Brady:* "A plea of guilty entered by one fully aware of the direct consequences, including the actual value of any commitments made to him by the court, prosecutor or his own counsel, must stand unless induced by threats (or promises to discontinue improper harassment), misrepresentation (including unfilled or unfillable promises), or perhaps by promises that are by their very nature improper as having no proper relationship to the prosecutor's business (e.g. bribes)." Case law and the Federal Rules both hold that the standard exercise of prosecutorial discretion in order to secure a plea of guilty cannot be used to prove that such a plea is involuntary. Even where the defendant enters a guilty plea in order to avert his death at the hands of the state, as in *Alford*, the Court has not seen involuntariness. Nevertheless, it may be true that some guilty pleas are involuntary in virtue of prosecutorial inducement considered proper by the Supreme Court.

Regarding the elements of duress, let us compare the gunman situation with an example of plea bargaining in order to examine the voluntariness of the latter. Albert W. Alschuler, author of one of the most thorough studies of plea bargaining, describes an actual case:

> San Francisco defense attorney Benjamin M. Davis recently represented a man charged with kidnapping and forcible rape. The defendant was innocent, Davis says, and after investigating the case Davis was confident of an acquittal. The prosecutor, who seems to have shared the defense attorney's opinion on this point, offered to permit a guilty plea to simple battery. Conviction on this charge would not have led to a greater sentence than thirty days' imprisonment, and there was every likelihood that the defendant would be granted probation. When Davis informed his client of this offer, he emphasized that conviction at trial seemed highly improbable. The defendant's reply was simple: "I can't take the chance."[17]

Both the gunman and the prosecutor require persons to make hard choices between a very certain smaller imposition and an uncertain greater imposition. In the gunman situation I must choose between the very certain loss of my money and the difficult-to-assess probability that my assailant is willing and able to kill me if I resist. As a defendant I am forced to choose between a very certain smaller punishment and a substantially greater punishment with a difficult-to-assess probability. As the size of the certain smaller imposition comes down and as the magnitude and probability of the larger imposition increases, it becomes more and more reasonable to choose the former. This is what seems to be occurring in Alschuler's example: "Davis reports that he is uncomfortable when he permits innocent defendants to plead guilty; but in this case it would have been playing God to stand in the defendant's way. The attorney's assessment of the outcome at trial can always be wrong, and it is hard to tell a defendant that 'professional ethics' require a course that may ruin his life." Davis's client must decide whether to accept a very certain, very minor punishment or to chance a ruined life. Of course the gunman's victim can try to overpower his assailant and the defendant can attempt to clear himself at trial. But the same considerations that will drive reasonable people to give in to the gunman compel one to accept the prosecutor's offer. Applying the second and third elements of duress, one can see that, like the gunman's act, the acts of the prosecutor can "operate coercively upon the will of the plaintiff, judged subjectively," and both the gunman's victim and the defendant may "have no adequate remedy to avoid the coercion except to give in." In both cases reasonable persons might well conclude (after considering the gunman's lethal weapon or the gas chamber) "I can't take the chance." A spineless person would not need to deliberate.

That prosecutors could exercise such duress apparently seemed plain to the authors of the *Restatement of Contracts*.[18] Their summarization of the law of contracts, adopted in 1932 by the American Law Institute, contained the following: "A threat of criminal prosecution... ordinarily is a threat of imprisonment and also... a threat of bringing disgrace upon the accused. Threats of this sort may be of such compelling force that acts done under their influence are coerced, and the better foundation there is for the prosecution, the greater is the coercion." While it is always true that even in the most desperate circumstances persons are free to reject the terms offered and risk the consequences, as Morris Raphael Cohen put it: "such choice is surely the very opposite of what men value as freedom."[19]

Indeed if one had to choose between being in the position of Davis's client and facing a fair-minded gunman, I think that it would be reasonable to prefer the latter. While the law permits one to recover money upon adverting to the forced choice of the gunman, it does not permit one to retract a guilty plea upon adverting to the forced choice of the prosecutor. This is the impact of *Brady* and Rule 11.

Note that the duress is not eliminated by providing defendants with counsel. While a good attorney may get better concessions and may help in the evaluation of options, in the end the defendant will still have to decide whether to settle for the smaller penalty or to risk a much heavier sentence. One does not eliminate the injustice in the gunman situation by providing victims with better advice.

Nor does it help matters to insure that promises of prosecutorial concessions are kept. The gunman who violates his part of the bargain—murdering his victims after they give over their money—has compounded his wrongdoing. Reputations for righteousness are not established by honoring such bargains.

Nor is it legitimate to distinguish the prosecutor from the gunman by saying that, while the gunman is threatening harm unless you hand over the cash, the prosecutor is merely promising benefits if you enter a guilty plea. For, in the proper context, threats and promises may be intertranslatable. Brandishing his pistol, the holdup man may promise to leave me unharmed if I hand over the cash. Similarly, the prosecutor may threaten to "throw the book" at me if I do not plead guilty to a lesser charge. In the proper context, one may be compelled to act by either form of words.

One might argue that not all "hard choices" are examples of duress. A doctor could offer to sell vital treatment for a large sum. After the patient has been cured it will hardly do for her to claim that she has been the victim of duress. The doctor may have forced the patient to choose between a certain financial loss and the risk of death. But surely doctors are not like gunmen.

Two important points need to be made in response to this objection. First, the doctor is not, one assumes, responsible for the diseased condition of the patient. The patient would be facing death even if she had never met the doctor. But this is not true in the case of the gunman, where both impositions are his work. And in this respect the prosecutor offering a plea bargain in a criminal case is like the gunman rather than like the doctor. For the state forces a choice between adverse consequences that it imposes. And, of course, one cannot say that in the defendant's wrongdoing he has brought his dreadful dilemma upon himself. To do so would be to ignore the good reasons there are for the presumption of innocence in dispositive criminal proceedings.

Second, our laws do not prohibit doctors from applying their healing skills to maximize their own wealth. They are free to contract to perform services in return for a fee. But our laws do severely restrict the state in its prosecution of criminal defendants. Those who framed our constitution were well aware of the great potential for abuse that the criminal law affords. Much of the constitution (especially the Bill of Rights) checks the activity of the state in this area. In particular, the Fifth Amendment provides that no person "shall be compelled in any criminal case to be a witness against himself." If I am right in judging that defendants like Alford and Davis's client do not act freely in pleading guilty to the facts of their cases, that the forced choice of the prosecutor may be as coercive as the forced choice of the gunman, that a defendant may be compelled to speak against himself (or herself) by a prosecutor's discretion inducing him to plead

guilty, then, given the apparent constitutional prohibition of such compulsion, the prosecutor acts wrongfully in compelling such pleas. And in this manner it may be that the last element of duress, wrongfulness, can be established. But it is not my purpose here to establish the unconstitutionality of plea bargaining, for it is not necessary to reach unconstitutionality to grasp the wrongfulness of that institution. One need only reflect upon what justice amounts to in our system of criminal law. This is the task I will take up in the final section of this paper.

II

Not too long ago plea bargaining was an officially prohibited practice. Court procedures were followed to ensure that no concessions had been given to defendants in exchange for guilty pleas. But gradually it became widely known that these procedures had become charades of perjury, shysterism, and bad faith involving judges, prosecutors, defense attorneys and defendants. This was scandalous. But rather than cleaning up the practice in order to square it with the rules, the rules were changed in order to bring them in line with the practice. There was a time when it apparently seemed plain that the old rules were the right rules. One finds in the *Restatement of Contracts*:[20] " . . . even if the accused is guilty and the process valid, so that as against the State the imprisonment is lawful, it is a wrongful means of inducing the accused to enter into a transaction. To overcome the will of another for the prosecutor's advantage is *an abuse of the criminal law which was made for another purpose*" (emphasis added). The authors of the *Restatement* do not tell us what they were thinking when they spoke of the purpose of the criminal law. Nonetheless it is instructive to conjecture and to inquire along the lines suggested by the *Restatement.*

Without going deeply into detail, I believe that it can be asserted without controversy that the liberal-democratic approach to criminal justice—and in particular the American criminal justice system—is an institutionalization of two principles. The first principle refers to the intrinsic point of systems of criminal justice.

A. Those (and only those) individuals who are clearly guilty of certain serious specified wrongdoings deserve an officially administered punishment which is proportional to their wrongdoing.

In the United States it is possible to see this principle underlying the activities of legislators specifying and grading wrongdoings which are serious enough to warrant criminalization and, further, determining the punishment appropriate to each offense; the activities of policemen and prosecutors bringing to trial those who are suspected of having committed such wrongdoings; the activities of jurors determining if defendants are guilty beyond a reasonable doubt; the activities of defense attorneys insuring that relevant facts in the defendant's favor are brought out at trial; the activities of judges seeing to it that proceedings are fair and that those who are convicted receive the punishment they deserve; and the activities of probation officers, parole officers, and prison personnel executing the sentences of the courts. All of these people play a part in bringing the guilty to justice.

But in liberal-democratic societies not everything is done to accomplish this end. A second principle makes reference to the limits placed upon the power of the state to identify and punish the guilty.

B. Certain basic liberties shall not be violated in bringing the guilty to justice.

This second principle can be seen to underlie the constellation of the constitutional checks on the activities of virtually every person playing a role in the administration of the criminal justice system.

Each of these principles is related to a distinctive type of injustice that can occur in the context of criminal law. An injustice can occur in the outcome of the criminal justice procedure. That is, an innocent defendant may be convicted and punished, or a guilty defendant may be acquitted or, if convicted, he or she may receive more or less punishment than is deserved. Because these injustices occur in the meting out of punishment to defendants who are being processed by the system, we can refer to them as internal injustices. They are violations of the first principle. On the other hand, there is a type of injustice which occurs when basic liberties are violated in the operation of the criminal justice system. It may be true that Star Chamber proceedings, torture, hostages, bills of attainder, dragnet arrests, unchecked searches, *ex post facto* laws, unlimited invasions of privacy, and an arsenal of other measures could be employed to bring more of the guilty to justice. But these steps lead to a dystopia where our most terrifying nightmares can come true. However we limit the activity of the criminal justice system in the interest of basic liberty, that limit can be overstepped. We can call such infringements upon basic liberties external injustices. They are violations of the second principle. If, for example, what I have suggested in the previous section is correct, then plea bargaining can bring about an external injustice with respect to a basic liberty secured by the Fifth Amendment. The remainder of this section will be concerned with internal injustice or violations of the first principle.

It is necessary to draw a further distinction between aberrational and systemic injustice. It may very well be that in the best criminal justice system that we are capable of devising human limitations will result in some aberrational injustice. Judges, jurors, lawyers, and legislators with the best of intentions may make errors in judgment that result in mistakes in the administration of punishment. But despite the knowledge that an unknown percentage of all dispositions of criminal cases are, to some extent, miscarriages of justice, it may still be reasonable to believe that a certain system of criminal justice is well calculated to avoid such results within the limits referred to by the second principle.[21] We can refer to these incorrect outcomes of a sound system of criminal justice as instances of aberrational injustice. In contrast, instances of systemic injustice are those that result from structural flaws in the criminal justice system itself. Here incorrect outcomes in the operations of the system are not the result of human error. Rather, the system itself is not well calculated to avoid injustice. What would be instances of aberrational injustice in a sound system are not aberrations in an unsound system: they are a standard result.

This distinction has an analogy in the area of quality control. Two vials of antibiotic may be equally contaminated. But depending upon the process used to produce each, the contamination may be aberrational or systemic. The first sample may come from a factory where every conceivable step is taken to insure that such contamination will not take place. The second vial may come from a company which uses a cheap manufacturing process offering no protection against contamination. There is an element of tragedy if death results when all possible precautions have been taken: there just are limits to human capability at our present level of understanding. But where vital precautions are dropped in the name of expediency, the contamination that results is much more serious if only because we knew it would take place and we knew what could be done to prevent it. While we have every reason to believe that the first sample is pure, we have no reason to believe that the second sample is uncontaminated. Indeed, one cannot call the latter contamination accidental as one can in the first case. It would be more correct to call it an accident if contamination did not take place in the total absence of precaution.

Likewise, systematic injustice in the context of criminal law is a much more serious matter than aberrational injustice. It should not be forgotten that the criminal sanction is the most severe imposition that the state can visit upon one of its citizens. While it is possible to tolerate occasional error in a sound system, systematic carelessness in the administration of punishment is negligence of the highest order.

With this framework in mind, let us look at a particular instance of plea bargaining recently described by a legal aid defense attorney.[22] Ted Alston has been charged with armed robbery. Let us assume that persons who have committed armed robbery (in the way Alston is accused of having committed it) deserve five to seven years of prison. Alston's attorney sets out the options for him: "I told Alston it was possible, perhaps even probable, that if he went to trial he would be convicted and get a prison term of perhaps five to seven years. On the other hand, if he agreed to plead guilty to a low-grade felony, he would get a probationary sentence and not go to prison. The choice was his." Let us assume that Alston accepts the terms of the bargain and pleads guilty to a lesser offense. If Alston did commit the armed robbery, there is a violation of the first principle in that he receives far less punishment than he deserves. On the other hand, if Alston did not commit the armed robbery, there is still a violation of the first principle in that he is both convicted of and punished for a crime that he did not commit, a crime that no one seriously believes to be his distinctive wrongdoing. It is of course possible that while Alston did not commit the armed robbery, he did commit the lesser offense. But though justice would be done here, it would be an accident. Such a serendipitous result is a certain sign that what we have here is systemic injustice.

If we assume that legislatures approximate the correct range of punishment for each offense, that judges fairly sentence those who are convicted by juries, and that prosecutors reasonably charge defendants, then, barring accidents, justice will *never* be the outcome of the plea-bargaining procedure: the defendant who "cops a plea" will never receive the punishment which is deserved. Of course legislatures can set punishments too high, judges can oversentence those who are convicted by juries, and prosecutors can overcharge defendants. In these cases the guilty can receive the punishment they deserve through plea bargaining. But in these cases we compensate for one injustice by introducing others that unfairly jeopardize the innocent and those that demand trials.

In contrast to plea bargaining, the disposition of criminal cases by jury trial seems well calculated to avoid internal injustices even if these may sometimes occur. Where participants take their responsibilities seriously we have good reason to believe that the outcome is just, even when this may not be so. In contrast, with plea bargaining we have no reason to believe that the outcome is just even when it is.

I think that the appeal that plea bargaining has is rooted in our attitude toward bargains in general. Where both parties are satisfied with the terms of an agreement, it is improper to interfere. Generally speaking, prosecutors and defendants are pleased with the advantages they gain by negotiating a plea. And courts, which gain as well, are reluctant to vacate negotiated pleas where only "proper" inducements have been applied and where promises have been understood and kept. Such judicial neutrality may be commendable where entitlements are being exchanged. But the criminal justice system is not such a context. Rather it is one in which persons are justly given, not what they have bargained for, but what they deserve, irrespective of their bargaining position.

To appreciate this, let us consider another context in which desert plays a familiar role; the assignment of grades in an academic setting. Imagine a "grade bargain" negotiated between a grade-conscious student and a harried instructor. A term paper has been submitted and, after glancing at the first page, the instructor says that if he were to read the paper carefully, applying his usually rigid standards, he would probably decide to give the paper a grade of D. But if the student were to waive his right to a careful reading and conscientious critique, the instructor would agree to a grade of B. The grade-point average being more important to him than either education or justice in grading, the student happily accepts the B, and the instructor enjoys a reduced workload.

One strains to imagine legislators and administrators commending the practice of grade bargaining because it permits more students to be processed by fewer instructors. Teachers can be freed from the burden of having to read and to criticize every paper. One struggles to envision academicians arguing for grade bargaining in the way that jurists have defended plea bargaining, suggesting that a quick assignment of a grade is a more effective influence on the behavior of students, urging that grade bargaining is necessary to the efficient functioning of the schools. There can be no doubt that students who have negotiated a grade are more likely to accept and to understand the verdict of the instructor. Moreover, in recognition of a student's help to the school (by waiving both the reading and the critique), it is proper for the instructor to be lenient. Finally, a quickly assigned grade enables the guidance personnel and the registrar to respond rapidly and appropriately to the student's situation.

What makes all of this laughable is what makes plea bargaining outrageous. For grades, like punishments, should be deserved. Justice in retribution, like justice in grading, does not require that the end result be acceptable to the parties. To reason that because the parties are satisfied the bargain should stand is to be seriously confused. For bargains are out of place in contexts where persons are to receive what they deserve. And the American courtroom, like the American classroom, should be such a context.

In this section, until now I have been attempting to show that plea bargaining is not well calculated to insure that those guilty of wrongdoing will receive the punishment they deserve. But a further point needs to be made. While the conviction of the innocent would be a problem in any system we might devise, it appears to be a greater problem under plea bargaining. With the jury system the guilt of the defendant must be established in an adversary proceeding and it must be established beyond a reasonable doubt to each of the twelve jurors. This is very staunch protection against an aberrational conviction. But under plea bargaining the foundation for conviction need only include a factual basis for the plea (in the opinion of the judge) and the guilty plea itself. Considering the coercive nature of the circumstances surrounding the plea, it would be a mistake to attach much reliability to it. Indeed, as we have seen in *Alford*, guilty pleas are acceptable even when accompanied by a denial of guilt. And in a study of 724 defendants who had pleaded guilty, only 13.1 percent admitted guilt to an interviewer, while 51.6 percent asserted their innocence.[23] This leaves only the factual basis for the plea to serve as the foundation for conviction. Now it is one thing to show a judge that there are facts which support a plea of guilty and quite another to prove to twelve jurors in an adversary proceeding guilt beyond a reasonable doubt. Plea bargaining substantially erodes the standards for guilt and it is reasonable to assume that the sloppier we are in establishing guilt, the more likely it is that innocent persons will be convicted. So apart from having no reason whatever to believe that the guilty are receiving the punishment they deserve, we have far less reason to believe that the convicted are guilty in the first place than we would after a trial.

In its coercion of criminal defendants, in its abandonment of desert as the measure of punishment, and in its relaxation of the standards for conviction, plea bargaining falls short of the justice we expect of our legal system. I have no doubt that substantial changes will have to be made if the institution of plea bargaining is to be obliterated or even removed from its central position in the criminal justice system. No doubt we need more courts and more prosecutors. Perhaps ways can be found to streamline the jury trial procedure without sacrificing its virtues.[24] Certainly it would help to decriminalize the host of victimless crimes —drunkenness and other drug offenses, illicit sex, gambling and so on—in order to free resources for dealing with more serious wrongdoings. And perhaps crime itself can be reduced if we begin to attack seriously those social and economic injustices that have for too long sent their victims to our prisons in disproportionate numbers. In any case, if we are to expect our citizenry to respect the law, we must take care to insure that our legal institutions are worthy of that respect. I have tried to show that plea bargaining is not worthy, that we must seek a better way. Bargain justice does not become us.

NOTES

1. Marcia Chambers, "80% of City Felony Cases Settled by Plea Bargaining," *New York Times* (February 11, 1975), p. 1.

2. Tom Goldstein, "Backlog of Felonies Rose Sharply Here Despite Court Drive," *New York Times* (February 12, 1975), p. 1.

3. Often the judge will play an important role in these discussions, being called upon, for example, to indicate a willingness to go along with a bargain involving a reduction in sentence. A crowded calendar will make the bench an interested party.

4. In California, for example, armed robbers are technically guilty of kidnapping if they point a gun at their victim and tell him to back up. Thus,

beyond the charge of armed robbery, they may face a charge of kidnapping which will be dropped upon entry of a guilty plea (see Albert W. Alschuler, "The Prosecutor's Role in Plea Bargaining," *University of Chicago Law Review* 36 (Fall 1968): 88).

5. Arthur Rosett, "The Negotiated Guilty Plea," *Annals of the American Academy of Political and Social Science* 374 (November 1967): 72.

6. Administrative Office of the United States Courts, *Federal Offenders in the United States District Courts* (Washington, D.C. 1970).

7. Ibid., pp. 57, 59.

8. Ibid., pp. 57, 65.

9. Ibid., p. 60.

10. 184 F. Supp. 679 (N.D. Ill. 1960).

11. Some of the most significant treatments of plea bargaining are Alschuler; Arnold Enker, "Perspectives on Plea Bargaining," in *Task Force Report: The Courts*, by the President's Commission on Law Enforcement and Administration of Justice (Washington, D.C., 1967), p. 108; "The Unconstitutionality of Plea Bargaining," *Harvard Law Review* 83 (April 1970); 1387; Donald J. Newman, *Conviction: The Determination of Guilt or Innocence without Trial* (Boston, 1966); Abraham S. Blumberg, *Criminal Justice* (Chicago, 1967); National Advisory Commission on Criminal Justice Standards and Goals, *Task Force Report: The Courts* (Washington, D.C., 1973): American Bar Association Project on Minimum Standards for Criminal Justice, *Standards Relating to Pleas of Guilty, Approved Draft* (New York, 1968).

12. Rosett, p. 71.

13. 392 F.2d 155 (1968).

14. 404 U.S. 257 (1971).

15. Dan B. Dobbs, *Handbook on the Law of Remedies* (Saint Paul, 1973), p. 658.

16. 400 U.S. 25 (1970) and 397 U.S. 742 (1970), respectively.

17. Alschuler, p. 61.

18. American Law Institute, *Restatement of Contracts* (Saint Paul, 1933), p. 652.

19. Morris Raphael Cohen, "The Basis of Contract," in *Law and the Social Order* (New York, 1933), p. 86.

20. American Law Institute, p. 652.

21. My discussion here owes much to John Rawls's treatment of "imperfect procedural justice" in his *A Theory of Justice* (Cambridge, 1971), pp. 85–86.

22. Robert Hermann, "The Case of the Jamaican Accent," *New York Times Magazine* (December 1, 1974), p. 93 (© The New York Times Company).

23. Blumberg, p. 91.

24. John Langbein has suggested that we look to the German legal system to see how this might be done. See his "Controlling Prosecutorial Discretion in Germany," *University of Chicago Law Review* 41 (Spring 1974): 439.

NO
Nick Schweitzer

PLEA BARGAINING:
A PROSECUTOR'S VIEW

More than nine out of every ten cases I handle are disposed of by plea bargaining. And, to the best of my knowledge, except for Marco Polo-like reports from exotic foreign jurisdictions like Alaska and New Orleans, that ratio holds true for all prosecutors. Yet, despite the pervasiveness of the practice, plea bargaining often is criticized as improper—a conspiracy to emasculate the criminal justice system.

Plea bargaining is a useful, nay vital, tool. It is a response to a court system that never could accord the luxury of a trial to every criminal charge and civil suit brought before it. It is a practical way to dispose of matters that do not require the full solemnity of legal procedure. Plea bargaining in criminal cases is the equivalent of negotiation and mediation in civil cases. While the latter are praised and encouraged, the former is frequently condemned. Why?

At one level, academicians and other legal thinkers disapprove of prosecutors' unbridled discretion as not fitting into an orderly scheme. But, I see the criticism more often arising out of dissatisfaction with a particular case and expanding to the generalization that plea bargaining is bad. I find two basic reasons for such criticism. The first is that a particular plea-bargain genuinely may be "bad," which means that an offender is offered either a charge reduction or a sentence concession, or both, which is unmerited by the offender and unjustified by any necessity. Experience shows that such "bad" plea-bargains do occur in a small number of cases—generally for expedience, as explained later. The second source of criticism is much more common. This is where an interested party is dissatisfied with the outcome, finding it wholly inadequate to salve his or her injured feelings. I find that this is as likely to occur with a "good" plea-bargain, which is reasoned, conscientious and practical, as it is with a "bad" one.

The reason, I believe, lies in the differing expectations held by experienced criminal attorneys and the general public. Experienced attorneys know the inherent constraints and time-honored practices of our criminal justice system, which imposed practical limits on the punishment of an offender even if she or he were convicted at trial. However, if the case happens to be disposed of by a negotiated plea, critics may ascribe all their frustrations and disappointments to the plea-bargain.

LOOKING AHEAD TO SENTENCING

Strange as it sounds, and despite all the criticism, an essential aspect of plea bargaining is the need to be fair. Plea negotiations, like the sentencing discretion of judges, reflect the need to individualize justice. Only the most naive person would think that a single determinate sentence awaits the end of any particular prosecution. For any given defendant, on any given charge, there is a range of penalties. Most criminal statutes carry a maximum penalty, and some a minimum penalty. However, all Wisconsin statutes, except that for first-degree murder, permit a range. In addition, sentencing options may include community service and probation as well as conditions on probation such as counseling, restitution, jail time and alcohol and drug treatment. Except in certain categories of cases for which sentencing guidelines have been set,[1] sentencing is a human decision. At some stage, some person must decide what sentence will deter future acts by this offender and by other potential offenders without being unduly harsh and at the same time sufficiently assuage the victim.

The sentencing decision is not the function of a trial. A trial is held to determine facts and the essential facts are truly at issue in only a small fraction of criminal cases. The majority of people charged with crimes are guilty and know it, but before they plead guilty or no contest, they want to know what punishment they face. Often, the only argument is over one or more mitigating

factors that do not rise to the level of legal defenses, so a trial in most criminal cases would be a waste of time. Sentencing is the bottom line for most defendants. If they can live with the sentence, most defendants are happy to save the court system and themselves the trouble of a trial. Generally, a bargain can be struck when the advantage to the defendant of an acceptable, known, sentence meets the advantage to the prosecutor of concluding the case for what it realistically is worth.

THE PROSECUTOR'S ROLE

The responsibility for sentencing ultimately lies with a judge. However, no judge has the time to check into the details of every felony, misdemeanor and ordinance that comes before the court. Court calendars being what they are, most judges want a recommendation from someone who already has taken the time to investigate the offense, the situation of any victims and the background of the defendant. A judge can accomplish this by ordering the local probation office to conduct a presentence investigation, but resources limit this option to only the more serious cases.

The prosecution and defense attorneys are in a position to review the offense, check the defendant's record and character, contact any victims and recommend an appropriate sentence. The prosecuting attorney knows the details of the offense and the defendant's prior record. The defense attorney knows the defendant and any mitigating factors. In most routine cases, these two lawyers are in the best position early on to discuss the merits of the case and are best able to find the time to negotiate before trial. If these two sides can reach agreement, the judge's decision can reasonably be reduced to review and ratification.

Another important reason for negotiation to take place at this level is the prosecutor's exclusive discretion to reduce or amend charges. A charge may be totally dismissed only with the court's approval.[2] However, the judge has no mandate to amend or reduce a charge. The discretion to amend charges is vested in the prosecutor to cover those rare cases where the wrong charge is issued.[3] This authority turns out to be even more useful in the frequent cases where some penalty is inappropriate. As an example, cooperative first offenders usually are offered some alternative, such as a county ordinance, that allows them to avoid a criminal record. This discretion to amend adds a second dimension to plea negotiations; the parties can consider not only the range of penalties associated with the original charge, but also the ranges associated with all related charges.

There are other reasons for a prosecutor to make concessions in return for a guilty or no contest plea. More often than not, a prosecutor will dismiss or read in one or more offenses for a defendant facing multiple charges. Usually, the prosecutor still will insist on a sentence consistent with the total number of offenses, but there is a general belief that reducing the number of convictions on the defendant's record will induce the defendant not to tie up the court system by trying all the cases. There also are cases in which the prosecutor faces some obstacle to conviction, other than the defendant's innocence, such as an unavailable witness or a witness who would be compromised or traumatized by having to testify. In such cases, any conviction, even on a reduced charge, generally is seen as better than a dismissal, an acquittal or a Pyrrhic conviction. Then, there are the infrequent cases in which a concession is necessary to secure a defendant's testimony against a co-defendant in an unrelated case. Plea bargaining also can be used to expedite cases that would drag on for months or years. A prosecutor may agree to a charge or sentence concession in return for a speedy disposition that benefits a victim or quickly takes an offender out of circulation.

THE QUALITY OF THE BARGAIN

For all the above reasons, cases will continue to be settled at the trial attorneys' level. The real issue is the quality of the decisions made. Plea bargaining is a tool and its mark largely depends on the skill and care of the crafter. If the product is flawed, the fault lies less with the tool than with the user. The quality of the plea-bargain depends on the values, interests and abilities of the attorneys. If both sides are interested in finding a "just" sentence, the result is as likely to be "good" as that made by a conscientious judge. But if one or both sides are mainly interested in expedience, primarily want to "win" or have priorities unrelated to the merits of the defendant and the case, then the bargain may well be "bad." Unfortunately, it is true that prosecutors and defense attorneys make some "bad" plea-bargains. It also is true that judges can make sentencing decisions that are injudicious. Since the majority of cases are disposed of by negotiated plea, the opportunity for a "bad" decision by prosecutors is that much greater.

Two weaknesses exist in the plea bargaining process. First, it can become routine and thereby an end rather than a means. As stated earlier, very few cases crossing a prosecutor's desk deserve a trial. The majority of cases do settle and prosecutors develop a strong work habit of managing their caseload that way. As a result, a holdout case may be seen as a nuisance, causing plea bargaining to deteriorate into coercion, concession and compromise without regard for the merits of the case. The indiscriminate use of plea bargaining to clear court calendars justly has been condemned. But under pressure, a prosecutor's definition of a "reasonable" plea-bargain has an unfortunate tendency to expand.

Second, plea bargaining does not encourage participation by the victim. The criminal justice system historically has treated victims cavalierly. It is only with the recent development of victim/witness programs that victims' involvement is being encouraged.

Most victims want to have a voice in the outcome of a case, but this very seldom happens when cases are plea-bargained. Victims generally are left out because negotiations often are informal and unscheduled and talking to victims can be time-consuming and painful, as a victim's viewpoint often is very different from that of an experienced criminal attorney. Victims have difficulty accepting the concept of "what a case is worth" in criminal justice terms and understanding the realistic limitations on punishment. The prosecutor risks becoming the focus of the victim's anger, disappointment and abuse.

SUGGESTIONS

There are no standards or checks imposed on plea bargaining by statute or case law. In fact, courts strictly have avoided involvement in the process.[4] Whether to subject plea-bargaining to some degree of quality control is a policy decision balancing discretion and accountability. However, I offer a few suggestions to district attorneys and judges.

First, have set guidelines as have some D.A. offices. Well-understood policies for reductions and sentencing recommendations can limit very effectively the possibilities for poor judgment. Guidelines could be developed statewide, similar to the sentencing guidelines for judges, which set standard dispositions yet allow departure from the standards for good reason.

Second, plea-bargains could be reduced to writing and reviewed within the D.A.'s office before final agreement. Although this would add a step or two to the process, it would go a long way toward establishing uniformity, avoiding bad decisions and, if part of the policy, assuring that victims' views are considered.

Finally, any judge who is concerned about the quality of the plea-bargains brought before the court could develop questions for accepting a plea bargain, similar to those for the taking of a guilty plea. This allows the judge to play a more active role, or at least to signal that certain aspects of plea bargaining are open to scrutiny, without taking part in the actual negotiations. One question might ask the attorneys for justification of any reduction or sentencing recommendation. Another might ask whether a victim was involved and, if so, whether the victim has been consulted.

CONCLUSION

Despite my reservations about the potential and occasional weaknesses of plea bargaining, I defend the practice as a practical solution to some of the needs and pressures of today's criminal justice system. Plea bargaining is a vital part of the complex system of powers and responsibilities that has evolved in our efforts to make justice as equal, fair and efficient as resources permit. Without it, other parts of the system would have to absorb increased stress. Specifically, if we wanted judges to make all the decisions (even assuming that their decisions would uniformly be better), we would need more judges, more courtrooms, more jurors and more trials. This is not because defendants want trials but largely because most defendants will "plead in" only if they know ahead of time what sentence is likely to be imposed. Plea bargaining is essential until society decides to allocate sufficient resources to these ends. When exercised with a due regard to the case, the victim and the defendant, plea-bargains can result in outcomes as "just" as any available in our current system.

NOTES

1. State of Wisconsin Sentencing Commission, "Wisconsin Sentencing Guidelines Manual," (1985).

2. *State v. Kenyon,* 85 Wis. 2d 36, 270 N.W.2d 160 (1978).

3. Wis. Stat. § 971.29.

4. See *In the Matter of the Amendment of Rules of Civil & Criminal Procedure: Sections 971.07 & 971.08, Stats.,* 128 Wis. 2d 422, 383 N.W.2d 496 (1986); *State v. Erickson,* 53 Wis. 2d 474, 192 N.W.2d 872 (1972); *Rahhal v. State,* 52 Wis. 2d 144, 187 N.W.2d 800 (1971); *State v. Wolfe,* 46 Wis. 2d 478, 175 N.W.2d 216 (1970).

POSTSCRIPT

Should Plea Bargaining Be Abolished?

Plea bargaining, former Supreme Court chief justice Warren E. Burger has stated, "is an essential component of the administration of criminal justice." What is more debatable is another statement by Burger that "properly administered, it is to be encouraged." We do not know how many innocent persons have pleaded guilty in order to avoid a trial. On the other hand, abolitionists have difficulty describing what a workable replacement for plea bargaining would be like.

Interesting experiments to reform or abolish plea bargaining have taken place in Texas, as seen in Weninger, "The Abolition of Plea Bargaining: A Case Study of El Paso County, Texas," 35 *UCLA Law Review* 265 (1987) and Callan, "An Experiment in Justice Without Plea Negotiation," 13 *Law and Society Review*, pp. 327–347 (1979); Alaska, as seen in Carns, "Alaska's Ban on Plea Bargaining Reevaluated," 75 *Judicature* 310 (1992) and Rubinstein and White, "Plea Bargaining: Can Alaska Live Without It?" *Judicature* (December–January, 1979); and Arizona, as seen in Berger, "The Case Against Plea Bargaining," *ABA Journal*, p. 621 (1976). These and other alternatives to the plea bargaining system are examined in Alschuler, "Implementing the Criminal Defendant's Right to Trial: Alternatives to the Plea Bargaining System," 50 *University of Chicago Law Review* 931 (1983); Cohen and Doob, "Public Attitudes to Plea Bargaining," 32 *Criminal Law Quarterly* 85 (1989); "The Victim's Veto: A Way to Increase Victim Impact on Criminal Case Dispositions," 77 *California Law Review* 417 (1989); Fine, "Plea Bargaining: An Unnecessary Evil," 70 *Marquette Law Review* 615 (1987); Schulhofer, "Plea Bargaining as Disaster," 101 *Yale Law Journal* 1979 (1992); and Note, "Constitutional Alternatives to Plea Bargaining: A New Waive," 132 *University of Pennsylvania Law Review* 327 (1984).

Plea bargaining has been the subject of a considerable number of Supreme Court cases. Among the most noteworthy are *Boykin v. Alabama,* 395 U.S. 238 (1969); *Brady v. U.S.,* 397 U.S. 742 (1970); *North Carolina v. Alford,* 400 U.S. 25 (1970); *Santobello v. New York,* 404 U.S. 257 (1971); and *Bordenkircher v. Hayes,* 434 U.S. 357 (1978). Each of these cases describes the plight of a particular defendant, but probably the most vivid account of the plea bargaining process is a journalist's description. See Mills, "I Have Nothing To Do With Justice," *Life* (March 12, 1971), reprinted in Bonsignore et al., *Before the Law: An Introduction to the Legal Process* (Houghton Mifflin, 1979).

PART 2

Law and Social Values

In any democratic society, the laws must reflect some consensus concerning the values of that society. Some of these values are clearly and easily determined. Laws against murder and theft, for example, command respect and acceptance and reflect widely held values.

In an increasingly complex, diverse, and technologically advanced society, however, questions of how best to protect individual rights of minorities and those with unpopular views inspire intense emotional debate, as evidenced by the issues in this section.

- Is "Hate Speech" Fully Protected by the Constitution?

- Are School Districts Created for Religious Reasons a Violation of the Constitution?

- Is Abortion Protected by the Constitution?

- Should Pornography Be Protected by the First Amendment?

- Should Affirmative Action Policies Be Continued?

- Can States Restrict the Right to Die?

- Should Homosexuality Bar a Parent from Being Awarded Custody of a Child?

- Can Courts Restrict the Picketing of Abortion Clinics?

ISSUE 4

Is "Hate Speech" Fully Protected by the Constitution?

YES: Antonin Scalia, from Majority Opinion, *R. A. V. v. City of St. Paul, Minnesota,* U.S. Supreme Court (1992)

NO: John Paul Stevens, from Concurring Opinion, *R. A. V. v. City of St. Paul, Minnesota,* U.S. Supreme Court (1992)

ISSUE SUMMARY

YES: Supreme Court justice Antonin Scalia finds that the St. Paul ordinance punishing "hate speech" cannot be constitutional because it regulates speech depending on the subject the speech addresses.

NO: Justice John Paul Stevens concurs that this particular ordinance is not constitutional, but he argues that it is perhaps simply overbroad.

> There are certain well-defined and narrowly limited classes of speech, the prevention and punishment of which have never been thought to raise any Constitutional problem. These include the lewd and obscene, the profane, the libelous, and the insulting or "fighting" words—those which by their very utterance inflict injury or tend to incite an immediate breach of the peace. It has been well observed that such utterances are no essential part of any exposition of ideas, and are of such slight social value as a step to truth that any benefit that may be derived from them is clearly outweighed by the social interest in order and morality.
>
> —*Chaplinsky v. New Hampshire*

Seven hundred and eighty-three hate crimes were recorded in Los Angeles County in 1993, more than a hundred more than in 1991. For the first time since 1980, when the county began tracking hate crimes, gay men supplanted African Americans as the primary target. Jews constitute only 5% of the Los Angeles County population but account for 89.5% of all victims of religious hate crimes. According to the F.B.I., 7,684 hate crimes were reported to law enforcement agencies in the United States in 1993. Even that figure is low, since police agencies contributing to the study represented only 56 percent of the population. Klanwatch, a project of the Southern Poverty Law Center in Montgomery, Alabama, reported a record number of white supremacist groups—346—actively operating in 1991 and a doubling of reported incidents of cross burnings, from 50 in 1990 to 101 in 1991.

We do not live in particularly tranquil, quiet, or harmonious times. Even on college campuses, controversies over courses of study or "political correctness" seem to have a more strident tone than they used to. In 1990 Congress enacted the "Hate Crimes Statistics Act," which requires the FBI to compile data tracking the frequency of hate crimes. And cities and universities have dealt with situations where speech is racist or sexist or denigrating and offensive to someone or some group by enacting regulations that punish such speech.

Typical of hate speech codes at universities is the excerpt below, which was enacted at the University of Wisconsin and then declared unconstitutional by a court.

The university may discipline a student in nonacademic matters in the following situations:

(2)(a) For racist or discriminatory comments, epithets or other expressive behavior directed at an individual or on separate occasions at different individuals, or for physical conduct, if such comments, epithets or other expressive behavior or physical conduct intentionally:

1. Demean the race, sex, religion, color, creed, disability, sexual orientation, national origin, ancestry or age of the individual or individuals and
2. Create an intimidating, hostile or demeaning environment for education, university-related work, or other university-authorized activity.

Current First Amendment law allows regulation over a very limited class of expressions, among them obscenity, fighting words, and libel. Advocates of hate speech codes argue that hate speech causes deep and permanent injury, that words can at times injure as much as sticks and stones. Opponents argue that the best antidote for hate speech is not to punish speech, but to produce more speech. As Benno Schmidt, former president of Yale University, has stated, "It is precisely societies that are diverse, pluralistic, and contentious that most urgently need freedom of speech." In addition, opponents claim that it is not really possible to distinguish the worst hate speech from that which is moderately disagreeable and offensive.

Are there other avenues for institutions to confront racism, sexism, anti-Semitism and homophobia? Would hate speech codes lead us down the slippery slope toward uniformity of thought? Or is the dehumanization that occurs with such speech too harmful to tolerate? The following opinions constitute a fairly strong warning to state and local governmental bodies and institutions to be extremely careful in trying to restrict speech. The majority opinion, by Justice Antonin Scalia, indicates that it is unlikely that any hate speech codes could be found to be constitutional in the future. The concurring opinion, by Justice John Paul Stevens, agrees with the result in this particular case; however, he suggests that a more narrowly drawn code might be approved.

YES

Antonin Scalia

MAJORITY OPINION

R. A. V. *v.* ST. PAUL

JUSTICE SCALIA delivered the opinion of the Court.

In the predawn hours of June 21, 1990, petitioner and several other teen-agers allegedly assembled a crudely-made cross by taping together broken chair legs. They then allegedly burned the cross inside the fenced yard of a black family that lived across the street from the house where petitioner was staying. Although this conduct could have been punished under any of a number of laws, one of the two provisions under which respondent city of St. Paul chose to charge petitioner (then a juvenile) was the St. Paul Bias-Motivated Crime Ordinance, St. Paul, Minn. Legis. Code Sec. 292.02 (1990), which provides:

> "Whoever places on public or private property a symbol, object, appellation, characterization or graffiti, including, but not limited to, a burning cross or Nazi swastika, which one knows or has reasonable grounds to know arouses anger, alarm or resentment in others on the basis of race, color, creed, religion or gender commits disorderly conduct and shall be guilty of a misdemeanor." ...

I

In construing the St. Paul ordinance, we are bound by the construction given to it by the Minnesota court. *Posadas de Puerto Rico Associates v. Tourism Co. of Puerto Rico*, 478 U.S. 328, 339 (1986); *New York v. Ferber*, 458 U.S. 747, 769, n. 24 (1982); *Terminiello v. Chicago*, 337 U.S. 1, 4 (1949). Accordingly, we accept the Minnesota Supreme Court's authoritative statement that the ordinance reaches only those expressions that constitute "fighting words" within the meaning of *Chaplinsky*. 464 N. W. 2d, at 510–511. Petitioner and his *amici* urge us to modify the scope of the Chaplinsky formulation, thereby invalidating the ordinance as "substantially overbroad," *Broadrick v. Oklahoma*, 413 U.S. 601, 610 (1973). We find it unnecessary to consider this issue. Assuming, *arguendo*, that all of the expression reached by the ordinance is proscrib-able under the "fighting words" doctrine, we nonetheless conclude that the

From *R. A. V. v. City of St. Paul, Minnesota*, 60 L.W. 4667 (1992). Notes and some case citations omitted.

ordinance is facially unconstitutional in that it prohibits otherwise permitted speech solely on the basis of the subjects the speech addresses.

The First Amendment generally prevents government from proscribing speech, or even expressive conduct, because of disapproval of the ideas expressed. Content-based regulations are presumptively invalid. From 1791 to the present, however, our society, like other free but civilized societies, has permitted restrictions upon the content of speech in a few limited areas, which are "of such slight social value as a step to truth that any benefit that may be derived from them is clearly outweighed by the social interest in order and morality." *Chaplinsky, supra,* at 572. We have recognized that "the freedom of speech" referred to by the First Amendment does not include a freedom to disregard these traditional limitations. See, e.g., *Roth v. United States,* 354 U.S. 476 (1957) (obscenity); *Beauharnais v. Illinois,* 343 U.S. 250 (1952) (defamation); *Chaplinsky v. New Hampshire, supra,* ("fighting words"); see generally *Simon & Schuster, supra,* at _____ (KENNEDY, J., concurring in judgment) (slip op., at 4). Our decisions since the 1960's have narrowed the scope of the traditional categorical exceptions for defamation, see *New York Times Co. v. Sullivan,* 376 U.S. 254 (1964); *Gertz v. Robert Welch, Inc.,* 418 U.S. 323 (1974); see generally *Milkovich v. Lorain Journal Co.,* 497 U.S. 1, 13–17 (1990), and for obscenity, see *Miller v. California,* 413 U.S. 15 (1973), but a limited categorical approach has remained an important part of our First Amendment jurisprudence.

We have sometimes said that these categories of expression are "not within the area of constitutionally protected speech," or that the "protection of the First Amendment does not extend" to them. Such statements must be taken in context, however, and are no more literally true than is the occasionally repeated shorthand characterizing obscenity "as not being speech at all," Sunstein, Pornography and the First Amendment, 1986 Duke L. J. 589, 615, n. 146. What they mean is that these areas of speech can, consistently with the First Amendment, be regulated *because of their constitutionally proscribable content* (obscenity, defamation, etc.)—not that they are categories of speech entirely invisible to the Constitution, so that they may be made the vehicles for content discrimination unrelated to their distinctively proscribable content. Thus, the government may proscribe libel; but it may not make the further content discrimination of proscribing only libel critical of the government. We recently acknowledged this distinction in *Ferber,* 458 U.S., at 763, where, in upholding New York's child pornography law, we expressly recognized that there was no "question here of censoring a particular literary theme...."

Our cases surely do not establish the proposition that the First Amendment imposes no obstacle whatsoever to regulation of particular instances of such proscribable expression, so that the government "may regulate [them] freely," *post,* at 4 (WHITE, J., concurring in judgment). That would mean that a city council could enact an ordinance prohibiting only those legally obscene works that contain criticism of the city government or, indeed, that do not include endorsement of the city government. Such a simplistic, all-or-nothing-at-all approach to First Amendment protection is at odds with common sense and with our jurisprudence as well. It is not true that "fighting words" have at most a "de minimis" expressive content, *ibid.*, or that their content is *in all respects* "worthless and undeserving of constitutional protection"; sometimes they are quite expressive indeed. We have not said that they constitute "*no* part of the expression of ideas," but only that they constitute "no *essential* part of any exposition of ideas." *Chaplinsky*, 315 U.S., at 572 (emphasis added).

The proposition that a particular instance of speech can be proscribable on the basis of one feature (e.g., obscenity) but not on the basis of another (e.g., opposition to the city government) is commonplace, and has found application in many contexts. We have long held, for example, that nonverbal expressive activity can be banned because of the action it entails, but not because of the ideas it expresses—so that burning a flag in violation of an ordinance against outdoor fires could be punishable, whereas burning a flag in violation of an ordinance against dishonoring the flag is not. See *Johnson*, 491 U.S., at 406–407. Similarly, we have upheld reasonable "time, place, or manner" restrictions, but only if they are "justified without reference to the content of the regulated speech." *Ward v. Rock Against Racism*, 491 U.S. 781, 791 (1989); see also *Clark v. Community for Creative Non-Violence*, 468 U.S. 288, 298 (1984) (noting that the *O'Brien* test differs little from the standard applied to time, place, or manner restrictions). And just as the power to proscribe particular speech on the basis of a noncontent element (e.g., noise) does not entail the power to proscribe the same speech on the basis of a content element; so also, the power to proscribe it on the basis of *one* content element (e.g., obscenity) does not entail the power to proscribe it on the basis of *other* content elements.

In other words, the exclusion of "fighting words" from the scope of the First Amendment simply means that, for purposes of that Amendment, the unprotected features of the words are, despite their verbal character, essentially a "non-speech" element of communication. Fighting words are thus analogous to a noisy sound truck: Each is, as Justice Frankfurter recognized, a "mode of speech," *Niemotko v. Maryland,* 340 U.S. 268, 282 (1951) (Frankfurter, J., concurring in result); both can be used to convey an idea; but neither has, in and of itself, a claim upon the First Amendment. As with the sound truck, however, so also with fighting words: The government may not regulate use based on hostility—or favoritism—towards the underlying message expressed. Compare *Frisby v. Schultz,* 487 U.S. 474 (1988) (upholding, against facial challenge, a content-neutral ban on targeted residential picketing) with *Carey v. Brown,* 447 U.S. 455 (1980) (invalidating a ban on residential picketing that exempted labor picketing)....

When the basis for the content discrimination consists entirely of the very reason the entire class of speech at issue is proscribable, no significant danger of idea or viewpoint discrimination exists. Such a reason, having been adjudged neutral enough to support exclusion of the entire class of speech from First Amendment protection, is also neutral enough to form the basis of distinction within the class. To illustrate: A State might choose to prohibit only that obscenity which is the most patently offensive *in its prurience*—i.e., that which involves the most lascivious displays of sexual activity. But it may not prohibit, for example, only that obscenity which includes offensive *political* messages. And the Federal Government can criminalize only those threats of violence that are directed against the President, see 18 U.S.C. sec. 871—since the reasons why threats of violence are outside the First Amendment (protecting individuals from the fear of violence, from the disruption that fear engenders, and from the possibility that the threatened violence will occur) have special force when applied to the person of the President. See *Watts v. United States*, 394 U.S. 705, 707 (1969) (upholding the facial validity of § 871 because of the "overwhelmin[g] interest in protecting the safety of [the] Chief Executive and in allowing him to perform his duties without interference from threats of physical violence"). But the Federal Government may not criminalize only those threats against the President that mention his policy on aid to inner cities. And to take a final example (one mentioned by Justice Stevens, *post*, at 6–7), a State may choose to regulate price advertising in one industry but not in others, because the risk of fraud (one of the characteristics of commercial speech that justifies depriving it of full First Amendment protection, see *Virginia Pharmacy Bd. v. Virginia Citizens Consumer Council, Inc.*, 425 U.S. 748, 771–772 (1976)) is in its view greater there. But a State may not prohibit only that commercial advertising that depicts men in a demeaning fashion.

Another valid basis for according differential treatment to even a content-defined subclass of proscribable speech is that the subclass happens to be associated with particular "secondary effects" of the speech, so that the regulation is "justified without reference to the content of the... speech," *Renton v. Playtime Theatres, Inc.*, 475 U.S. 41, 48 (1986). A State could, for example, permit all obscene live performances except

those involving minors. Moreover, since words can in some circumstances violate laws directed not against speech but against conduct (a law against treason, for example, is violated by telling the enemy the nation's defense secrets), a particular content-based subcategory of a proscribable class of speech can be swept up incidentally within the reach of a statute directed at conduct rather than speech. Thus, for example, sexually derogatory "fighting words," among other words, may produce a violation of Title VII's general prohibition against sexual discrimination in employment practices, 42 U.S.C. § 2000e-2; 29 CFR § 1604.11 (1991). See also 18 U.S.C. § 242; 42 U.S.C. § 1981, 1982. Where the government does not target conduct on the basis of its expressive content, acts are not shielded from regulation merely because they express a discriminatory idea or philosophy.

These bases for distinction refute the proposition that the selectivity of the restriction is "even arguably 'conditioned upon the sovereign's agreement with what a speaker may intend to say.'" *Metromedia, Inc. v. San Diego*, 453 U.S. 490, 555 (1981) (STEVENS, J., dissenting in part) (citation omitted). There may be other such bases as well. Indeed, to validate such selectivity (where totally proscribable speech is at issue) it may not even be necessary to identify any particular "neutral" basis, so long as the nature of the content discrimination is such that there is no realistic possibility that official suppression of ideas is afoot. (We cannot think of any First Amendment interest that would stand in the way of a State's prohibiting only those obscene motion pictures with blue-eyed actresses.) Save for that limitation, the regulation of "fighting words," like the regulation of noisy speech, may address some offensive instances and leave other, equally offensive, instances alone.

II

Applying these principles to the St. Paul ordinance, we conclude that, even as narrowly construed by the Minnesota Supreme Court, the ordinance is facially unconstitutional. Although the phrase in the ordinance, "arouses anger, alarm or resentment in others," has been limited by the Minnesota Supreme Court's construction to reach only those symbols or displays that amount to "fighting words," the remaining, unmodified terms make clear that the ordinance applies only to "fighting words" that insult, or provoke violence, "on the basis of race, color, creed, religion or gender." Displays containing abusive invective, no matter how vicious or severe, are permissible unless they are addressed to one of the specified disfavored topics. Those who wish to use "fighting words" in connection with other ideas—to express hostility, for example, on the basis of political affiliation, union membership, or homosexuality—are not covered. The First Amendment does not permit St. Paul to impose special prohibitions on those speakers who express views on disfavored subjects.

In its practical operation, moreover, the ordinance goes even beyond mere content discrimination, to actual viewpoint discrimination. Displays containing some words—odious racial epithets, for example—would be prohibited to proponents of all views. But "fighting words" that do not themselves invoke race, color, creed, religion, or gender—aspersions upon a person's mother, for example—would seemingly be usable ad libitum in the placards of those arguing in favor of racial, color, etc., tolerance and equality, but could not be used by that speaker's opponents. One could hold up a sign saying, for example, that all "anti-Catholic bigots" are misbegotten; but not that all "papists" are, for that would insult and provoke violence "on the basis of religion." St. Paul has no such authority to license one side of a debate to fight freestyle, while requiring the other to follow Marquis of Queensbury Rules.

What we have here, it must be emphasized, is not a prohibition of fighting words that are directed at certain persons or groups (which would be facially valid if it met the requirements of the Equal Protection Clause); but rather, a prohibition of fighting words that contain (as the Minnesota Supreme Court repeatedly emphasized) messages of "bias-motivated" hatred and in particular, as applied to this case, messages "based on virulent notions of racial supremacy." 464 N. W. 2d, at 508, 511. One must wholeheartedly agree with the Minnesota Supreme Court that "[i]t is the responsibility, even the obligation, of diverse communities to confront such notions in whatever form they appear," ibid., but the manner of that confrontation cannot consist of selective limitations upon speech. St. Paul's brief asserts that a general "fighting words" law would not meet the city's needs because only a content-specific measure can communicate to minority groups that the "group hatred" aspect of such speech "is not condoned by the majority." Brief for Respondent 25. The point of the First Amendment is that majority preferences must be expressed in some fashion other than silencing speech on the basis of its content.

Despite the fact that the Minnesota Supreme Court and St. Paul acknowledge that the ordinance is directed at expression of group hatred, Justice Stevens suggests that this "fundamentally misreads" the ordinance. It is directed, he claims, not to speech of a particular content, but to particular "injur[ies]" that are "qualitatively different" from other injuries. This is word-play. What makes the anger, fear, sense of dishonor, etc. produced by violation of this ordinance distinct from the anger, fear, sense of dishonor, etc. produced by other fighting words is nothing other than the fact that it is caused by a distinctive idea, conveyed by a distinctive message. The First Amendment cannot be evaded that easily. It is obvious that the symbols which will arouse "anger, alarm or resentment in others on the basis of race, color, creed, religion or gender" are those symbols that communicate a message of hostility based on one of these characteristics. St. Paul concedes in its brief that the ordinance applies only to "racial, religious, or gender-specific symbols" such as "a burning cross, Nazi swastika or other instrumentality of like import." Brief for Respondent 8. Indeed, St. Paul argued in the Juvenile Court that "[t]he burning of a cross does express a message and it is, in fact, the content of that message which the St. Paul Ordinance attempts to legislate." Memorandum from the Ramsey County Attorney to the Honorable Charles A. Flinn, Jr., dated July 13, 1990, in *In re Welfare of R. A. V.*, No. 89-D-1231 (Ramsey Cty. Juvenile Ct.), p. 1, reprinted in App. to Brief for Petitioner C-1.

The content-based discrimination reflected in the St. Paul ordinance comes within neither any of the specific exceptions to the First Amendment prohibition we discussed earlier, nor within a more general exception for content discrimination that does not threaten censorship of ideas. It assuredly does not fall within the exception for content discrimination based on the very reasons why the particular class of speech at issue (here, fighting words) is proscribable. As explained earlier, the reason why fighting words are categorically excluded from the protection of the First Amendment is not that their content communicates any particular idea, but that their content embodies a particularly intolerable (and socially unnecessary) *mode* of expressing *whatever* idea the speaker wishes to convey. St. Paul has not singled out an especially offensive mode of expression—it has not, for example, selected for prohibition only those fighting words that communicate ideas in a threatening (as opposed to a merely obnoxious) manner. Rather, it has proscribed fighting words of whatever manner that communicate messages of racial, gender, or religious intolerance. Selectivity of this sort creates the possibility that the city is seeking to handicap the expression of particular ideas. That possibility would alone be enough to render the ordinance presumptively invalid, but St. Paul's comments and concessions in this case elevate the possibility to a certainty.

St. Paul argues that the ordinance comes within another of the specific exceptions we mentioned, the one that allows content discrimination aimed only at the "secondary effects" of the speech. According to St. Paul, the ordinance is intended, "not to impact on [sic] the right of free expression of the accused," but rather to "protect against the victimization of a person or persons who are particularly vulnerable because of their membership in a group that historically has been discriminated against." Brief for Respondent 28. Even assuming that an ordinance that completely proscribes, rather than merely regulates, a specified category of speech can ever be considered to be directed only to the secondary effects of such speech, it is clear that the St. Paul ordinance is not directed to secondary effects within the meaning of *Renton*. As we said in *Boos v. Barry*, 485 U.S. 312 (1988), "listeners' reactions to speech are not the type of 'secondary effects' we referred to in *Renton*." *Id.*, at 321. "The emotive impact of speech on its audience is not a 'secondary effect.'"

It hardly needs discussion that the ordinance does not fall within some more general exception permitting *all* selectivity that for any reason is beyond the suspicion of official suppression of ideas. The statements of St. Paul in this very case afford ample basis for, if not full confirmation of, that suspicion.

Finally, St. Paul and its *amici* defend the conclusion of the Minnesota Supreme Court that, even if the ordinance regulates expression based on hostility towards its protected ideological content, this discrimination is nonetheless justified because it is narrowly tailored to serve compelling state interests. Specifically, they assert that the ordinance helps to ensure the basic human rights of members of groups that have historically been subjected to discrimination, including the right of such group members to live in peace where they wish. We do not doubt that these interests are compelling, and that the ordinance can be said to promote them. But the "danger of censorship" presented by a facially content-based statute requires that that weapon be employed only where it is "*necessary* to serve the asserted [compelling] interest," (emphasis added). The existence of adequate content-neutral alternatives thus "undercut[s] significantly" any defense of such a statute, casting considerable doubt on the government's protestations that "the asserted justification is in fact an accurate description of the purpose and effect of the law." The dispositive question in this case, therefore, is whether content discrimination is reasonably necessary to achieve St. Paul's compelling interests; it plainly is not. An ordinance not limited to the favored topics, for example, would have precisely the same beneficial effect. In fact the only interest distinctively served by the content limitation is that of displaying the city council's special hostility towards the particular biases thus singled out. That is precisely what the First Amendment forbids. The politicians of St. Paul are entitled to express that hostility—but not through the means of imposing unique limitations upon speakers who (however benightedly) disagree.

Let there be no mistake about our belief that burning a cross in someone's front yard is reprehensible. But St. Paul has sufficient means at its disposal to prevent such behavior without adding the First Amendment to the fire.

The judgment of the Minnesota Supreme Court is reversed, and the case is remanded for proceedings not inconsistent with this opinion.

It is so ordered.

NO

John Paul Stevens

OPINION OF JOHN PAUL STEVENS

Concurring opinion by Justice Stevens:

Conduct that creates special risks or causes special harms may be prohibited by special rules. Lighting a fire near an ammunition dump or a gasoline storage tank is especially dangerous; such behavior may be punished more severely than burning trash in a vacant lot. Threatening someone because of her race or religious beliefs may cause particularly severe trauma or touch off a riot, and threatening a high public official may cause substantial social disruption; such threats may be punished more severely than threats against someone based on, say, his support of a particular athletic team. There are legitimate, reasonable, and neutral justifications for such special rules.

This case involves the constitutionality of one such ordinance. Because the regulated conduct has some communicative content—a message of racial, religious or gender hostility—the ordinance raises two quite different First Amendment questions. Is the ordinance "overbroad" because it prohibits too much speech? If not, is it "underbroad" because it does not prohibit enough speech? ...

I

Fifty years ago, the Court articulated a categorical approach to First Amendment jurisprudence.

> "There are certain well-defined and narrowly limited classes of speech, the prevention and punishment of which have never been thought to raise any Constitutional problem.... It has been well observed that such utterances are no essential part of any exposition of ideas, and are of such slight social value as a step to truth that any benefit that may be derived from them is clearly outweighed by the social interest in order and morality." *Chaplinsky v. New Hampshire,* 315 U.S. 568, 571-572 (1942).

We have, as Justice White observes, often described such categories of expression as "not within the area of constitutionally protected speech." *Roth v. United States,* 354 U.S. 476, 483 (1957).

From *R. A. V. v. City of St. Paul, Minnesota,* 60 L.W. 4667 (1992). Some notes and case citations omitted.

The Court today revises this categorical approach. It is not, the Court rules, that certain "categories" of expression are "unprotected," but rather that certain "elements" of expression are wholly "proscribable." To the Court, an expressive act, like a chemical compound, consists of more than one element. Although the act may be regulated because it contains a proscribable element, it may not be regulated on the basis of another (nonproscribable) element it also contains. Thus, obscene antigovernment speech may be regulated because it is obscene, but not because it is antigovernment. It is this revision of the categorical approach that allows the Court to assume that the St. Paul ordinance proscribes *only* fighting words, while at the same time concluding that the ordinance is invalid because it imposes a content-based regulation on expressive activity.

As an initial matter, the Court's revision of the categorical approach seems to me something of an adventure in a doctrinal wonderland, for the concept of "obscene antigovernment" speech is fantastical. The category of the obscene is very narrow; to be obscene, expression must be found by the trier of fact to "appea[l] to the prurient interest, ... depic[t] or describ[e], in a patently offensive way, sexual conduct, [and] taken as a whole, *lac[k] serious literary, artistic, political or scientific value.*" *Miller v. California*, 413 U.S. 15, 24 (1973) (emphasis added). "Obscene antigovernment" speech, then, is a contradiction in terms: If expression is antigovernment, it does not "lac[k] serious... political... value" and cannot be obscene.

The Court attempts to bolster its argument by likening its novel analysis to that applied to restrictions on the time, place, or manner of expression or on expressive conduct. It is true that loud speech in favor of the Republican Party can be regulated because it is loud, but not because it is pro-Republican; and it is true that the public burning of the American flag can be regulated because it involves public burning and not because it involves the flag. But these analogies are inapposite. In each of these examples, the two elements (e.g., loudness and pro-Republican orientation) can coexist; in the case of "obscene antigovernment" speech, however, the presence of one element ("obscenity") by definition means the absence of the other. To my mind, it is unwise and unsound to craft a new doctrine based on such highly speculative hypotheticals.

I am, however, even more troubled by the second step of the Court's analysis—namely, its conclusion that the St. Paul ordinance is an unconstitutional content-based regulation of speech. Drawing on broadly worded *dicta*, the Court establishes a near-absolute ban on content-based regulations of expression and holds that the First Amendment prohibits the regulation of fighting words by subject matter. Thus, while the Court rejects the "all-or-nothing-at-all" nature of the categorical approach, it promptly embraces an absolutism of its own: within a particular "proscribable" category of expression, the Court holds, a government must either proscribe *all* speech or no speech at all. This aspect of the Court's ruling fundamentally misunderstands the role and constitutional status of content-based regulations on speech, conflicts with the very nature of First Amendment jurisprudence, and disrupts well-settled principles of First Amendment law.

Although the Court has, on occasion, declared that content-based regulations of speech are "never permitted," *Police*

Dept. of Chicago v. Mosley, 408 U.S. 92, 99 (1972), such claims are overstated. Indeed, in *Mosley* itself, the Court indicated that Chicago's selective proscription of nonlabor picketing was not *per se* unconstitutional, but rather could be upheld if the City demonstrated that nonlabor picketing was "clearly more disruptive than [labor] picketing." *Id.,* at 100. Contrary to the broad *dicta* in *Mosley* and elsewhere, our decisions demonstrate that content-based distinctions, far from being presumptively invalid, are an inevitable and indispensable aspect of a coherent understanding of the First Amendment.

This is true at every level of First Amendment law. In broadest terms, our entire First Amendment jurisprudence creates a regime based on the content of speech. The scope of the First Amendment is determined by the content of expressive activity: Although the First Amendment broadly protects "speech," it does not protect the right to "fix prices, breach contracts, make false warranties, place bets with bookies, threaten, [or] extort." Schauer, Categories and the First Amendment: A Play in Three Acts, 34 Vand. L. Rev. 265, 270 (1981). Whether an agreement among competitors is a violation of the Sherman Act or protected activity under the *Noerr-Pennington* doctrine hinges upon the content of the agreement. Similarly, "the line between permissible advocacy and impermissible incitation to crime or violence depends, not merely on the setting in which the speech occurs, but also on exactly what the speaker had to say." *Young v. American Mini Theatres, Inc.,* 427 U.S. 50, 66 (1976) (plurality opinion).

Likewise, whether speech falls within one of the categories of "unprotected" or "proscribable" expression is determined,

in part, by its content. Whether a magazine is obscene, a gesture a fighting word, or a photograph child pornography is determined, in part, by its content. Even within categories of protected expression, the First Amendment status of speech is fixed by its content. *New York Times Co. v. Sullivan,* 376 U.S. 254 (1964), and *Dun & Bradstreet, Inc. v. Greenmoss Builders, Inc.,* 472 U.S. 749 (1985), establish that the level of protection given to speech depends upon its subject matter: speech about public officials or matters of public concern receives greater protection than speech about other topics. It can, therefore, scarcely be said that the regulation of expressive activity cannot be predicated on its content: much of our First Amendment jurisprudence is premised on the assumption that content makes a difference.

Consistent with this general premise, we have frequently upheld content-based regulations of speech. For example, in *Young v. American Mini Theatres,* the Court upheld zoning ordinances that regulated movie theaters based on the content of the films shown. In *FCC v. Pacifica Foundation,* 438 U.S. 726 (1978) (plurality opinion), we upheld a restriction on the broadcast of *specific* indecent words. In *Lehman v. City of Shaker Heights,* 418 U.S. 298 (1974) (plurality opinion), we upheld a city law that permitted commercial advertising, but prohibited political advertising, on city buses. In *Broadrick v. Oklahoma,* 413 U.S. 601 (1973), we upheld a state law that restricted the speech of state employees, but only as concerned partisan political matters. We have long recognized the power of the Federal Trade Commission to regulate misleading advertising and labeling, and the National Labor Relations Board's power to regulate an employer's election-related speech on the basis of its content. It is also beyond question that the Government may choose to limit advertisements for cigarettes, see 15 U.S.C. § 1331–1340, but not for cigars; choose to regulate airline advertising, but not bus advertising; or choose to monitor solicitation by lawyers, see *Ohralik v. Ohio State Bar Assn.*, 436 U.S. 447 (1978), but not by doctors.

All of these cases involved the selective regulation of speech based on content— precisely the sort of regulation the Court invalidates today. Such selective regulations are unavoidably content based, but they are not, in my opinion, "presumptively invalid." As these many decisions and examples demonstrate, the prohibition on content-based regulations is not nearly as total as the *Mosley* dictum suggests.

Disregarding this vast body of case law, the Court today goes beyond even the overstatement in *Mosley* and applies the prohibition on content-based regulation to speech that the Court had until today considered wholly "unprotected" by the First Amendment—namely, fighting words. This new absolutism in the prohibition of content-based regulations severely contorts the fabric of settled First Amendment law.

Our First Amendment decisions have created a rough hierarchy in the constitutional protection of speech. Core political speech occupies the highest, most protected position; commercial speech and nonobscene, sexually explicit speech are regarded as a sort of second-class expression; obscenity and fighting words receive the least protection of all. Assuming that the Court is correct that this last class of speech is not wholly "unprotected," it certainly does not follow that fighting words and obscenity receive the *same* sort of protection afforded core political speech. Yet in ruling that proscribable speech cannot be regulated based on subject matter, the Court does just that. Perversely, this gives fighting words *greater* protection than is afforded commercial speech. If Congress can prohibit false advertising directed at airline passengers without also prohibiting false advertising directed at bus passengers and if a city can prohibit political advertisements in its buses while allowing other advertisements, it is ironic to hold that a city cannot regulate fighting words based on "race, color, creed, religion or gender" while leaving unregulated fighting words based on "union membership or homosexuality." The Court today turns First Amendment law on its head: Communication that was once entirely unprotected (and that still can be wholly proscribed) is now entitled to greater protection than commercial speech—and possibly greater protection than core political speech.

Perhaps because the Court recognizes these perversities, it quickly offers some ad hoc limitations on its newly extended prohibition on content-based regulations. First, the Court states that a content-based regulation is valid "[w]hen the content discrimination is based upon the very reason the entire class of speech... is proscribable." In a pivotal passage, the Court writes

"the Federal Government can criminalize only those physical threats that are directed against the President, see 18 U.S.C. § 871—since the reasons why threats of violence are outside the First Amendment (protecting individuals from the fear of violence, from the disruption that fear engenders, and from the possibility that the threatened violence will occur) have special force when applied to the... President."

As I understand this opaque passage, Congress may choose from the set of unprotected speech (all threats) to proscribe only a subset (threats against the President) because those threats are particularly likely to cause "fear of violence," "disruption," and actual "violence."

Precisely this same reasoning, however, compels the conclusion that St. Paul's ordinance is constitutional. Just as Congress may determine that threats against the President entail more severe consequences than other threats, so St. Paul's City Council may determine that threats based on the target's race, religion, or gender cause more severe harm to both the target and to society than other threats. This latter judgment—that harms caused by racial, religious, and gender-based invective are qualitatively different from that caused by other fighting words —seems to me eminently reasonable and realistic.

Next, the Court recognizes that a State may regulate advertising in one industry but not another because "the risk of fraud (one of the characteristics that justifies depriving [commercial speech] of full First Amendment protection...)" in the regulated industry is "greater" than in other industries. Again, the same reasoning demonstrates the constitutionality of St. Paul's ordinance. "[O]ne of the characteristics that justifies" the constitutional status of fighting words is that such words "by their very utterance inflict injury or tend to incite an immediate breach of the peace." *Chaplinsky*, 315 U.S., at 572. Certainly a legislature that may determine that the risk of fraud is greater in the legal trade than in the medical trade may determine that the risk of injury or breach of peace created by race-based threats is greater than that created by other threats....

In sum, the central premise of the Court's ruling—that "[c]ontent-based regulations are presumptively invalid"— has simplistic appeal, but lacks support in our First Amendment jurisprudence. To make matters worse, the Court today extends this overstated claim to reach categories of hitherto unprotected speech and, in doing so, wreaks havoc in an area of settled law. Finally, although the Court recognizes exceptions to its new principle, those exceptions undermine its very conclusion that the St. Paul ordinance is unconstitutional. Stated directly, the majority's position cannot withstand scrutiny....

III

As the foregoing suggests, I disagree with both the Court's and part of Justice White's analysis of the constitutionality [of the] St. Paul ordinance. Unlike the Court, I do not believe that all content-based regulations are equally infirm and presumptively invalid; unlike Justice White, I do not believe that fighting words are wholly unprotected by the First Amendment. To the contrary, I believe our decisions establish a more complex and subtle analysis, one that considers the content and context of the regulated speech, and the nature and scope of the restriction on speech. Applying this analysis and assuming *arguendo* (as the Court does) that the St. Paul ordinance is *not* overbroad, I conclude that such a selective, subject-matter regulation on proscribable speech is constitutional.

Not all content-based regulations are alike; our decisions clearly recognize that some content-based restrictions raise more constitutional questions than others. Although the Court's analysis of content-based regulations cannot be reduced to a simple formula, we have considered a number of factors in determining the validity of such regulations.

First, as suggested above, the scope of protection provided expressive activity depends in part upon its content and character. We have long recognized that when government regulates political speech or "the expression of editorial opinion on matters of public importance," *FCC v. League of Women Voters of California*, 468 U.S. 364, 375–376 (1984), "First Amendment protectio[n] is 'at its zenith.'" *Meyer v. Grant*, 486 U.S. 414, 425 (1988). In comparison, we have recognized that "commercial speech receives a limited form of First Amendment protection," *Posadas de Puerto Rico Associates v. Tourism Co. of Puerto Rico*, 478 U.S. 328, 340 (1986), and that "society's interest in protecting [sexually explicit films] is of a wholly different, and lesser magnitude than [its] interest in untrammeled political debate." *Young v. American Mini Theatres*, 427 U.S., at 70; see also *FCC v. Pacifica Foundation*, 438 U.S. 726 (1978). The character of expressive activity also weighs in our consideration of its constitutional status. As we have frequently noted, "the government generally has a freer hand in restricting expressive conduct than it has in restricting the written or spoken word." *Texas v. Johnson*, 491 U.S. 397, 406 (1989); see also *United States v. O'Brien*, 391 U.S. 367 (1968).

The protection afforded expression turns as well on the context of the regulated speech. We have noted, for example, that "[a]ny assessment of the precise scope of employer expression, of course, must be made in the context of its labor relations setting... [and]

must take into account the economic dependence of the employees on their employers." *NLRB v. Gissel Packing Co.*, 395 U.S., at 617. Similarly, the distinctive character of a university environment or a secondary school environment, see *Hazelwood School Dist. v. Kuhlmeier*, 484 U.S. 260 (1988), influences our First Amendment analysis. The same is true of the presence of a "'captive audience, [one] there as a matter of necessity, not of choice.'" *Lehman v. City of Shaker Heights*, 418 U.S., at 302 (citation omitted). Perhaps the most familiar embodiment of the relevance of context is our "fora" jurisprudence, differentiating the levels of protection afforded speech in different locations.

The nature of a contested restriction of speech also informs our evaluation of its constitutionality. Thus, for example, "[a]ny system of prior restraints of expression comes to this Court bearing a heavy presumption against its constitutional validity." *Bantam Books, Inc. v. Sullivan*, 372 U.S. 58, 70 (1963). More particularly to the matter of content-based regulations, we have implicitly distinguished between restrictions on expression based on *subject matter* and restrictions based on *viewpoint*, indicating that the latter are particularly pernicious. "If there is a bedrock principle underlying the First Amendment, it is that the Government may not prohibit the expression of an idea simply because society finds the idea itself offensive or disagreeable." *Texas v. Johnson*, 491 U.S., at 414. "Viewpoint discrimination is censorship in its purest form," *Perry Education Assn. v. Perry Local Educators' Assn.*, 460 U.S. 37, 62 (1983) (Brennan, J., dissenting), and requires particular scrutiny, in part because such regulation often indicates a legislative effort to skew public debate on an issue. See, e.g., *Schacht v. United States*, 398 U.S. 58, 63 (1970). "Especially where . . . the legislature's suppression of speech suggests an attempt to give one side of a debatable public question an advantage in expressing its views to the people, the First Amendment is plainly offended." *First National Bank of Boston v. Bellotti*, 435 U.S. 765, 785–786 (1978). Thus, although a regulation that on its face regulates speech by subject matter may in some instances effectively suppress particular viewpoints, in general, viewpoint-based restrictions on expression require greater scrutiny than subject-matter based restrictions.

Finally, in considering the validity of content-based regulations we have also looked more broadly at the scope of the restrictions. For example, in *Young v. American Mini Theatres*, 427 U.S., at 71, we found significant the fact that "what [was] ultimately at stake [was] nothing more than a limitation on the place where adult films may be exhibited." Similarly, in *FCC v. Pacifica Foundation*, the Court emphasized two dimensions of the limited scope of the FCC ruling. First, the ruling concerned only broadcast material which presents particular problems because it "confronts the citizen . . . in the privacy of the home"; second, the ruling was not a complete ban on the use of selected offensive words, but rather merely a limitation on the times such speech could be broadcast. 438 U.S., at 748–750.

All of these factors play some role in our evaluation of content-based regulations on expression. Such a multi-faceted analysis cannot be conflated into two dimensions. Whatever the allure of absolute doctrines, it is just too simple to declare expression "protected" or "un-protected" or to proclaim a regulation "content-based" or "content-neutral."

In applying this analysis to the St. Paul ordinance, I assume *arguendo*—as the Court does—that the ordinance regulates *only* fighting words and therefore is *not* overbroad. Looking to the content and character of the regulated activity, two things are clear. First, by hypothesis the ordinance bars only low-value speech, namely, fighting words. By definition such expression constitutes "no essential part of any exposition of ideas, and [is] of such slight social value as a step to truth that any benefit that may be derived from [it] is clearly outweighed by the social interest in order and morality." *Chaplinsky*, 315 U.S., at 572. Second, the ordinance regulates "expressive conduct [rather] than . . . the written or spoken word." *Texas v. Johnson*, 491 U.S., at 406.

Looking to the context of the regulated activity, it is again significant that the statute (by hypothesis) regulates *only* fighting words. Whether words are fighting words is determined in part by their context. Fighting words are not words that merely cause offense; fighting words must be directed at individuals so as to "by their very utterance inflict injury." By hypothesis, then, the St. Paul ordinance restricts speech in confrontational and potentially violent situations. The case at hand is illustrative. The cross-burning in this case—directed as it was to a single African-American family trapped in their home—was nothing more than a crude form of physical intimidation. That this cross-burning sends a message of racial hostility does not automatically endow it with complete constitutional protection.

Significantly, the St. Paul ordinance regulates speech not on the basis of its subject matter or the viewpoint expressed, but rather on the basis of the *harm* the speech causes. In this regard, the Court fundamentally misreads the St. Paul ordinance. The Court describes the St. Paul ordinance as regulating expression "addressed to one of [several] specified disfavored *topics*," as policing "disfavored *subjects*," and as "prohibit[ing] ... speech solely on the basis of the *subjects* the speech addresses" (emphasis supplied). Contrary to the Court's suggestion, the ordinance regulates only a subcategory of expression that causes *injuries based* on race, color, creed, religion or gender," not a subcategory that involves discussions that concern those characteristics.[1] The ordinance, as construed by the Court, criminalizes expression that "one knows ... [by its very utterance inflicts injury on] others on the basis of race, color, creed, religion or gender." In this regard, the ordinance resembles the child pornography law at issue in *Ferber*, which in effect singled out child pornography because those publications caused far greater harms than pornography involving adults.

Moreover, even if the St. Paul ordinance did regulate fighting words based on its subject matter, such a regulation would, in my opinion, be constitutional. As noted above, subject-matter based regulations on commercial speech are widespread and largely unproblematic. As we have long recognized, subject-matter regulations generally do not raise the same concerns of government censorship and the distortion of public discourse presented by viewpoint regulations. Thus, in upholding subject-matter regulations we have carefully noted that viewpoint-based discrimination was not implicated. ... Indeed, some subject-matter restrictions are a functional necessity in contemporary governance: "The

First Amendment does not require States to regulate for problems that do not exist."

Contrary to the suggestion of the majority, the St. Paul ordinance does *not* regulate expression based on viewpoint. The Court contends that the ordinance requires proponents of racial intolerance to "follow the Marquis of Queensbury Rules" while allowing advocates of racial tolerance to "fight freestyle." The law does no such thing.

The Court writes:

> "One could hold up a sign saying, for example, that all 'anti-Catholic bigots' are misbegotten; but not that all 'papists' are, for that would insult and provoke violence 'on the basis of religion.'"

This may be true, but it hardly proves the Court's point. The Court's reasoning is asymmetrical. The response to a sign saying that "all [religious] bigots are misbegotten" is a sign saying that "all advocates of religious tolerance are misbegotten." Assuming such signs could be fighting words (which seems to me extremely unlikely), neither sign would be banned by the ordinance for the attacks were not "based on ... religion" but rather on one's beliefs about tolerance. Conversely (and again assuming such signs are fighting words), just as the ordinance would prohibit a Muslim from hoisting a sign claiming that all Catholics were misbegotten, so the ordinance would bar a Catholic from hoisting a similar sign attacking Muslims.

The St. Paul ordinance is evenhanded. In a battle between advocates of tolerance and advocates of intolerance, the ordinance does not prevent either side from hurling fighting words at the other on the basis of their conflicting ideas, but it does bar *both* sides from hurling such words on the basis of the target's "race, color, creed, religion or gender." To extend the Court's pugilistic metaphor, the St. Paul ordinance simply bans punches "below the belt"—*by either party.* It does not, therefore, favor one side of any debate.

Finally, it is noteworthy that the St. Paul ordinance is, as construed by the Court today, quite narrow. The St. Paul ordinance does not ban all "hate speech," nor does it ban, say, all cross-burnings or all swastika displays. Rather it only bans a subcategory of the already narrow category of fighting words. Such a limited ordinance leaves open and protected a vast range of expression on the subjects of racial, religious, and gender equality. As construed by the Court today, the ordinance certainly does not " 'raise the specter that the Government may effectively drive certain ideas or viewpoints from the marketplace.' " Petitioner is free to burn a cross to announce a rally or to express his views about racial supremacy, he may do so on private property or public land, at day or at night, so long as the burning is not so threatening and so directed at an individual as to "by its very [execution] inflict injury." Such a limited proscription scarcely offends the First Amendment.

In sum, the St. Paul ordinance (as construed by the Court) regulates expressive activity that is wholly proscribable and does so not on the basis of viewpoint, but rather in recognition of the different harms caused by such activity. Taken together, these several considerations persuade me that the St. Paul ordinance is not an unconstitutional content-based regulation of speech. Thus, were the ordinance not overbroad, I would vote to uphold it.

NOTES

1. The Court contends that this distinction is "wordplay," reasoning that "[w]hat makes [the harms caused by race-based threats] distinct from [the harms] produced by other fighting words is... the fact that [the former are] caused by a *distinctive idea*" (emphasis added). In this way, the Court concludes that regulating speech based on the injury it causes is no different from regulating speech based on its subject matter. This analysis fundamentally miscomprehends the role of "race, color, creed, religion [and] gender" in contemporary American society. One need look no further than the recent social unrest in the Nation's cities to see that race-based threats may cause more harm to society and to individuals than other threats. Just as the statute prohibiting threats against the President is justifiable because of the place of the President in our social and political order, so a statute prohibiting race-based threats is justifiable because of the place of race in our social and political order. Although it is regrettable that race occupies such a place and is so incendiary an issue, until the Nation matures beyond that condition, laws such as St. Paul's ordinance will remain reasonable and justifiable.

POSTSCRIPT

Is "Hate Speech" Fully Protected by the Constitution?

Law professor Rodney Smolla has inquired, "Should an open culture tolerate speech designed to spread intolerance? This may be the hardest free speech question of all, because an open culture is largely built on the ethos of tolerance." Smolla's question becomes even more significant because the principal arena where hate speech codes have been put into place has been college campuses, arguably the institution in our society that is most tolerant of deviant speech.

When the Supreme Court in 1989 ruled that state laws to punish flag burning were unconstitutional, the outcry was fairly brief. Many disagreed with the decision, but instances of flag burning are not very numerous. Racist speech, sexist speech, homophobic speech, and anti-Semitic speech, however, touch many on a daily basis. Hundreds of college campuses had hate speech codes in place at the time of the *R. A. V.* decision. A 1993 study showed that 36 percent of 384 colleges surveyed still had hate speech rules, many of which were probably unconstitutional. The challenge in drafting codes is to distinguish between actions and conduct, such as hate crimes, which are not protected by the First Amendment, and speech, which is protected.

The Supreme Court decision in *R. A. V.* was not all that surprising, given the breadth of the St. Paul statute. Judges have more experience with First Amendment theory than do campus administrators or politicians. They are more likely to have a clearer historical perspective, and they are certainly removed from the pressures facing those who have enacted such codes. The traditional answer of the courts to disturbing speech has been that the antidote is more speech and counterprotests that will educate the public and not simply punish those who have caused anger and hurt. Whether or not this is an appropriate response to hate speech, which degrades and injures and which seems to be on the increase, will, in spite of the opinions you have just read, continue to challenge us.

A recent case allowing stiffer sentences in cases of hate crimes is *Wisconsin v. Todd Mitchell*, 113 S. Ct. 2194 (1993). The case declaring flag burning constitutionally protected is *Texas v. Johnson*, 109 S. Ct. 2533 (1989). The University of Wisconsin code was declared unconstitutional in *UWM Post v. Regents*, 774 F. Supp. 1163 (1991). Readings that discuss hate speech include R. Smolla, *Free Speech in an Open Society* (Alfred A. Knopf, 1992); L. Bollinger, *The Tolerant Society* (Oxford University Press, 1986); Matsuda, "Public Response to Racist Speech: Considering the Victim's Story," 87 *Michigan Law Review* 2320 (1989); and Minow, "Speaking and Writing Against Hate," 11 *Cardozo Law Review*

1393 (1990). A famous case involving a plan by a Nazi group to march in the largely Jewish community of Skokie, Illinois, is recounted in D. Downs, *Nazis in Skokie* (University of Notre Dame Press, 1985), and in *Skokie v. National Socialist Party of America*, 373 N.E.2d 21 (1978) and *Collin v. Smith*, 578 F.2d 1197 (7th Cir. 1978). Also see the Hate Crime Statistics Act, 28 U.S.C.S. § 534. The impact of computers and electronic communication on the First Amendment is discussed in E. Katsh, *The Electronic Media and the Transformation of Law* (Oxford University Press, 1989).

ISSUE 5

Are School Districts Created for Religious Reasons a Violation of the Constitution?

YES: David H. Souter, from Majority Opinion, *Board of Education of Kiryas Joel Village School District v. Louis Grumet et al.*, U.S. Supreme Court (1994)

NO: Antonin Scalia, from Dissenting Opinion, *Board of Education of Kiryas Joel Village School District v. Louis Grumet et al.*, U.S. Supreme Court (1994)

ISSUE SUMMARY

YES: Justice David H. Souter maintains that a New York statute that established a school serving only a single religious community violates the Establishment Clause of the First Amendment.

NO: Justice Antonin Scalia argues that the New York public school, run by a local school district, is secular in nature and does not violate the First Amendment.

An Easter egg hunt on the White House lawn. Christmas as a national holiday. Prayers opening legislative sessions of state legislatures. If you were a judge and the above practices were challenged as being unconstitutional, how would you rule?

The First Amendment to the Constitution states that "Congress shall make no law respecting an establishment of religion, or prohibiting the free exercise thereof." Interpreting these words and applying them in particular cases has been exceedingly difficult for the courts. What, for example, does "respecting an establishment of religion" mean? Is any governmental involvement or support for religion, direct or indirect, small or great, barred by this phrase?

While the courts have struggled to keep church and state separate, they have also recognized that it would be impossible to have an absolute prohibition on the celebration of religious values and holidays. Cases continue to be brought, therefore, challenging the courts to determine how the words of the Constitution and the standards of prior cases should be applied to the facts of the new case.

The clearest and most well known of the establishment of religion cases are the school prayer decisions. In 1963, in *School District of Abington Township, Pennsylvania v. Schempp*, 374 U.S. 203, the Supreme Court ruled that it was unconstitutional to require students to open the school day by reading biblical passages and reciting the Lord's Prayer. A year earlier, in *Engel v. Vitale*, 370 U.S. 421 (1962), the Supreme Court had ruled that recitation of the New York Regent's Prayer was unconstitutional. This prayer read, "Almighty God, we acknowledge our dependence upon Thee, and we beg thy blessings upon us, our parents, our teachers, and our country."

The Supreme Court has attempted to make its decisions in this area appear less subjective by considering the following three questions:

1. Does the statute have a secular legislative purpose?
2. Does its principal effect advance or inhibit religion?
3. Does the statute foster an excessive governmental entanglement with religion?

Using this standard, the courts have upheld some questionable practices, such as blue laws (regulating business on Sundays) and the loaning of secular textbooks to parochial schools. However, they have struck down other statutes, such as the Kentucky law that required posting the Ten Commandments in the classroom (see *Stone v. Graham*, 101 S. Ct. 192, 1980). More generally, the Supreme Court has upheld prayers at the beginning of a legislative session, the existence of after-school religious clubs, and tuition tax credits for parochial schools. Yet, using the same test, it has held unconstitutional a statute requiring a moment of silence in public schools, remedial programs for parochial schools, and a law requiring the teaching of "creation science" whenever evolution was taught.

The many cases involving religion that have been considered by the Supreme Court in the past 25 years indicate that the task of defining precisely what role religion should have in government-sponsored activities is extraordinarily difficult. Religion has not been banned from public life. "In God We Trust" appears on our coins, prayers are said at presidential inaugurations, Christmas is a national holiday, the lighting of the national Christmas tree at the White House is a newsworthy event, and tax exemptions are given to religious institutions. As a Supreme Court justice once wrote, "We are a religious people whose institutions presuppose a Supreme Being." It is also true, however, that many religious activities may not be sponsored by the government.

The following case is the most recent Supreme Court decision to consider what "establishment of religion" means. Some observers had predicted that the court might abandon the three-part test mentioned above. It did not do so, and more religion cases, probably involving schools in some way, can be expected to come before the Court.

YES

David H. Souter

MAJORITY OPINION

BOARD OF EDUCATION *v.* GRUMET

SOUTER, J., announced the judgment of the Court and delivered the opinion of the Court...

The Village of Kiryas Joel in Orange County, New York, is a religious enclave of Satmar Hasidim, practitioners of a strict form of Judaism. The village fell within the Monroe-Woodbury Central School District until a special state statute passed in 1989 carved out a separate district, following village lines, to serve this distinctive population. The question is whether the Act creating the separate school district violates the Establishment Clause of the First Amendment, binding on the States through the Fourteenth Amendment. Because this unusual act is tantamount to an allocation of political power on a religious criterion and neither presupposes nor requires governmental impartiality toward religion, we hold that it violates the prohibition against establishment.

I

The Satmar Hasidic sect takes its name from the town near the Hungarian and Romanian border where, in the early years of this century, Grand Rebbe Joel Teitelbaum molded the group into a distinct community. After World War II and the destruction of much of European Jewry, the Grand Rebbe and most of his surviving followers moved to the Williamsburg section of Brooklyn, New York. Then, 20 years ago, the Satmars purchased an approved but undeveloped subdivision in the town of Monroe and began assembling the community that has since become the Village of Kiryas Joel. When a zoning dispute arose in the course of settlement, the Satmars presented the Town Board of Monroe with a petition to form a new village within the town, a right that New York's Village Law gives almost any group of residents who satisfy certain procedural niceties. Neighbors who did not wish to secede with the Satmars objected strenuously, and after arduous negotiations the proposed boundaries of the Village of Kiryas Joel were drawn to include

From *Board of Education of Kiryas Joel Village School District v. Louis Grumet et al.,* 1994 WL 279673 (U.S. NY.). Notes and some case citations omitted.

just the 320 acres owned and inhabited entirely by Satmars. The village, incorporated in 1977, has a population of about 8,500 today. Rabbi Aaron Teitelbaum, eldest son of the current Grand Rebbe, serves as the village rov (chief rabbi) and rosh yeshivah (chief authority in the parochial schools).

The residents of Kiryas Joel are vigorously religious people who make few concessions to the modern world and go to great lengths to avoid assimilation into it. They interpret the Torah strictly; segregate the sexes outside the home; speak Yiddish as their primary language; eschew television, radio, and English-language publications; and dress in distinctive ways that include headcoverings and special garments for boys and modest dresses for girls. Children are educated in private religious schools, most boys at the United Talmudic Academy where they receive a thorough grounding in the Torah and limited exposure to secular subjects, and most girls at Bais Rochel, an affiliated school with a curriculum designed to prepare girls for their roles as wives and mothers.

These schools do not, however, offer any distinctive services to handicapped children, who are entitled under state and federal law to special education services even when enrolled in private schools. Starting in 1984 the Monroe-Woodbury Central School District provided such services for the children of Kiryas Joel at an annex to Bais Rochel, but a year later ended that arrangement in response to our decisions in *Aguilar v. Felton*, 473 U.S. 402 (1985), and *School Dist. of Grand Rapids v. Ball*, 473 U.S. 373 (1985). Children from Kiryas Joel who needed special education (including the deaf, the mentally retarded, and others suffering from a range of physical, mental, or emotional disor-

ders) were then forced to attend public schools outside the village, which their families found highly unsatisfactory. Parents of most of these children withdrew them from the Monroe-Woodbury secular schools, citing "the panic, fear and trauma [the children] suffered in leaving their own community and being with people whose ways were so different," and some sought administrative review of the public-school placements. *Board of Ed. of Monroe-Woodbury Central School Dist. v. Wieder*, 72 N.Y.2d 174, 180–181, 527 N.E.2d 767, 770 (1988).

Monroe-Woodbury, for its part, sought a declaratory judgment in state court that New York law barred the district from providing special education services outside the district's regular public schools. *Id.*, at 180, 527 N.E.2d, at 770. The New York Court of Appeals disagreed, holding that state law left Monroe-Woodbury free to establish a separate school in the village because it gives educational authorities broad discretion in fashioning an appropriate program. *Id.*, at 186–187, 527 N.E.2d, at 773. The court added, however, that the Satmars' constitutional right to exercise their religion freely did not require a separate school, since the parents had alleged emotional trauma, not inconsistency with religious practice or doctrine, as the reason for seeking separate treatment. *Id.*, at 189, 527 N.E.2d, at 775.

By 1989, only one child from Kiryas Joel was attending Monroe-Woodbury's public schools; the village's other handicapped children received privately funded special services or went without. It was then that the New York Legislature passed the statute at issue in this litigation, which provided that the Village of Kiryas Joel "is constituted a separate school district, ... and shall have and enjoy all the powers and duties of a union free school district...." 1989 N.Y. Laws, ch. 748. The statute thus empowered a locally elected board of education to take such action as opening schools and closing them, hiring teachers, prescribing textbooks, establishing disciplinary rules, and raising property taxes to fund operations. N.Y. Educ. Law § 1709 (McKinney 1988). In signing the bill into law, Governor Cuomo recognized that the residents of the new school district were "all members of the same religious sect," but said that the bill was "a good faith effort to solve th[e] unique problem" associated with providing special education services to handicapped children in the village. Memorandum filed with Assembly Bill Number 8747 (July 24, 1989), App. 40–41.

Although it enjoys plenary legal authority over the elementary and secondary education of all school-aged children in the village, the Kiryas Joel Village School District currently runs only a special education program for handicapped children. The other village children have stayed in their parochial schools, relying on the new school district only for transportation, remedial education, and health and welfare services. If any child without handicap in Kiryas Joel were to seek a public-school education, the district would pay tuition to send the child into Monroe-Woodbury or another school district nearby. Under like arrangements, several of the neighboring districts send their handicapped Hasidic children into Kiryas Joel, so that two thirds of the full-time students in the village's public school come from outside. In all, the new district serves just over 40 full-time students, and two or three times that many parochial school students on a part-time basis.

Several months before the new district began operations, the New York State School Boards Association and respondents Grumet and Hawk brought this action against the State Education Department and various state officials, challenging Chapter 748 under the national and state constitutions as an unconstitutional establishment of religion. The State Supreme Court for Albany County allowed the Kiryas Joel Village School District and the Monroe-Woodbury Central School District to intervene as parties defendant and accepted the parties' stipulation discontinuing the action against the original state defendants, although the Attorney General of New York continued to appear to defend the constitutionality of the statute. On cross-motions for summary judgment, the trial court ruled for the plaintiffs (respondents here), finding that the statute failed all three prongs of the test in *Lemon V. Kurtzman*, 403 U.S. 602 (1971), and was thus unconstitutional under both the National and State Constitutions. *Grumet v. New York State Ed. Dept.*, 151 Misc.2d 60, 579 N.Y.S.2d 1004 (1992).

A divided Appellate Division affirmed on the ground that Chapter 748 had the primary effect of advancing religion, in violation of both constitutions, 187 App. Div.2d 16, 592 N.Y.S.2d 123 (1992), and the state Court of Appeals affirmed on the federal question, while expressly reserving the state constitutional issue, 81 N.Y.2d 518, 618 N.E.2d 94 (1993). Judge Smith wrote for the court in concluding that because both the district's public school population and its school board would be exclusively Hasidic, the statute created a "symbolic union of church and state" that was "likely to be perceived by the Satmarer Hasidim as an endorsement of their religious choices, or by nonadherents as a disapproval" of their own. *Id.*, at 529, 618 N.E.2d, at 100. As a result, said the majority, the statute's primary effect was an impermissible advancement of religious belief....

We stayed the mandate of the Court of Appeals, 509 U.S. (1993), and granted certiorari, 510 U.S. (1993).

II

"A proper respect for both the Free Exercise and the Establishment Clauses compels the State to pursue a course of 'neutrality' toward religion," *Committee for Public Ed. & Religious Liberty v. Nyquist*, 413 U.S. 756, 792–793 (1973), favoring neither one religion over others nor religious adherents collectively over nonadherents. Chapter 748, the statute creating the Kiryas Joel Village School District, departs from this constitutional command by delegating the State's discretionary authority over public schools to a group defined by its character as a religious community, in a legal and historical context that gives no assurance that governmental power has been or will be exercised neutrally.

Larkin v. Grendel's Den, Inc., 459 U.S. 116 (1982), provides an instructive comparison with the litigation before us. There, the Court was requested to strike down a Massachusetts statute granting religious bodies veto power over applications for liquor licenses. Under the statute, the governing body of any church, synagogue, or school located within 500 feet of an applicant's premises could, simply by submitting written objection, prevent the Alcohol Beverage Control Commission from issuing a license. In spite of the State's valid interest in protecting churches, schools, and like institutions from " 'the hurly-burly' associated with liquor outlets," *id.*, at 123 (internal quotation marks omitted), the Court found that in two respects the statute violated

"the wholesome 'neutrality' of which this Court's cases speak," *School Dist. of Abington v. Schempp*, 374 U.S. 203, 222 (1963). The Act brought about a " 'fusion of governmental and religious functions' " by delegating "important, discretionary governmental powers" to religious bodies, thus impermissibly entangling government and religion. 459 U.S., at 126, 127 (quoting *Abington School Dist. v. Schempp, supra*, at 222); see also *Lemon v. Kurtzman, supra*, at 613. And it lacked "any 'effective means of guaranteeing' that the delegated power '[would] be used exclusively for secular, neutral, and nonideological purposes,' " 459 U.S., at 125 (quoting Committee for *Public Ed. & Religious Liberty v. Nyquist, supra*, at 780); this, along with the "significant symbolic benefit to religion" associated with "the mere appearance of a joint exercise of legislative authority by Church and State," led the Court to conclude that the statute had a " 'primary' and 'principal' effect of advancing religion," 459 U.S., at 125–126; see also *Lemon v. Kurtzman, supra*, at 612. Comparable constitutional problems inhere in the statute before us.

A

Larkin presented an example of united civic and religious authority, an establishment rarely found in such straightforward form in modern America, and a violation of "the core rationale underlying the Establishment Clause," 459 U.S., at 126....

The Establishment Clause problem presented by Chapter 748 is more subtle, but it resembles the issue raised in *Larkin* to the extent that the earlier case teaches that a State may not delegate its civic authority to a group chosen according to a religious criterion. Authority over public schools belongs to the State, N.Y. Const., Art. XI, § 1 (McKinney 1987), and cannot be delegated to a local school district defined by the State in order to grant political control to a religious group. What makes this litigation different from *Larkin* is the delegation here of civic power to the "qualified voters of the village of Kiryas Joel," 1989 N.Y. Laws, ch. 748, as distinct from a religious leader such as the village rov, or an institution of religious government like the formally constituted parish council in Larkin. In light of the circumstances of this case, however, this distinction turns out to lack constitutional significance.

It is, first, not dispositive that the recipients of state power in this case are a group of religious individuals united by common doctrine, not the group's leaders or officers. Although some school district franchise is common to all voters, the State's manipulation of the franchise for this district limited it to Satmars, giving the sect exclusive control of the political subdivision. In the circumstances of this case, the difference between thus vesting state power in the members of a religious group as such instead of the officers of its sectarian organization is one of form, not substance. . . .

It is undisputed that those who negotiated the village boundaries when applying the general village incorporation statute drew them so as to exclude all but Satmars, and that the New York Legislature was well aware that the village remained exclusively Satmar in 1989 when it adopted Chapter 748. The significance of this fact to the state legislature is indicated by the further fact that carving out the village school district ran counter to customary districting practices in the State. Indeed, the trend in New York is not toward dividing school districts but toward consolidating them. The thousands of small common school districts laid out in the early 19th century have been combined and recombined, first into union free school districts and then into larger central school districts, until only a tenth as many remain today. Most of these cover several towns, many of them cross county boundaries, and only one remains precisely coterminous with an incorporated village. The object of the State's practice of consolidation is the creation of districts large enough to provide a comprehensive education at affordable cost, which is thought to require at least 500 pupils for a combined junior-senior high school. The Kiryas Joel Village School District, in contrast, has only 13 local, full-time students in all (even including out-of-area and part-time students leaves the number under 200), and in offering only special education and remedial programs it makes no pretense to be a full-service district. . . .

Because the district's creation ran uniquely counter to state practice, following the lines of a religious community where the customary and neutral principles would not have dictated the same result, we have good reasons to treat this district as the reflection of a religious criterion for identifying the recipients of civil authority. Not even the special needs of the children in this community can explain the legislature's unusual Act, for the State could have responded to the concerns of the Satmar parents without implicating the Establishment Clause, as we explain in some detail further on. We therefore find the legislature's Act to be substantially equivalent to defining a political subdivision and hence the qualification for its franchise by a religious test, resulting in a purposeful and forbidden "fusion of governmental and religious functions." *Larkin v. Grendel's Den,* 459 U.S., at 126 (internal quotation marks and citation omitted).

B

The fact that this school district was created by a special and unusual Act of the legislature also gives reason for concern whether the benefit received by the Satmar community is one that the legislature will provide equally to other religious (and nonreligious) groups. This is the second malady the *Larkin* Court identified in the law before it, the absence of an "effective means of guaranteeing" that governmental power will be and has been neutrally employed. But whereas in *Larkin* it was religious groups the Court thought might exercise civic power to advance the interests of religion (or religious adherents), here the threat to neutrality occurs at an antecedent stage.

The fundamental source of constitutional concern here is that the legislature itself may fail to exercise governmental authority in a religiously neutral way. The anomalously case-specific nature of the legislature's exercise of state authority in creating this district for a religious community leaves the Court without any direct way to review such state action for the purpose of safeguarding a principle at the heart of the Establishment Clause, that government should not prefer one religion to another, or religion to irreligion. See *Wallace v. Jaffree,* 472 U.S., at 52–54; *Epperson v. Arkansas,* 393 U.S., at 104; *School Dist. of Abington v. Schempp,* 374 U.S., at 216–217. Because the religious community of Kiryas Joel did not receive its new governmental authority simply as one of many communities eligible for equal treatment under a general

law, we have no assurance that the next similarly situated group seeking a school district of its own will receive one; unlike an administrative agency's denial of an exemption from a generally applicable law, which "would be entitled to a judicial audience," *Olsen v. Drug Enforcement Admin.,* 878 F.2d 1458, 1461 (CADC 1989) (R. B. Ginsburg, J.), a legislature's failure to enact a special law is itself unreviewable. Nor can the historical context in this case furnish us with any reason to suppose that the Satmars are merely one in a series of communities receiving the benefit of special school district laws. Early on in the development of public education in New York, the State rejected highly localized school districts for New York City when they were promoted as a way to allow separate schooling for Roman Catholic children. R. Church & M. Sedlak, *Education in the United States* 162, 167–169 (1976). And in more recent history, the special Act in this case stands alone. The general principle that civil power must be exercised in a manner neutral to religion is one the *Larkin* Court recognized, although it did not discuss the specific possibility of legislative favoritism along religious lines because the statute before it delegated state authority to any religious group assembled near the premises of an applicant for a liquor license, as well as to a further category of institutions not identified by religion. But the principle is well grounded in our case law, as we have frequently relied explicitly on the general availability of any benefit provided religious groups or individuals in turning aside Establishment Clause challenges. In *Walz v. Tax Comm'n of New York City,* 397 U.S. 664, 673 (1970), for example, the Court sustained a property tax exemption for religious properties in part because the State had "not singled out one particular church or religious group or even churches as such," but had exempted "a broad class of property owned by non-profit, quasi-public corporations." ...

C

In finding that Chapter 748 violates the requirement of governmental neutrality by extending the benefit of a special franchise, we do not deny that the Constitution allows the state to accommodate religious needs by alleviating special burdens. Our cases leave no doubt that in commanding neutrality the Religion Clauses do not require the government to be oblivious to impositions that legitimate exercises of state power may place on religious belief and practice. Rather, there is "ample room under the Establishment Clause for 'benevolent neutrality which will permit religious exercise to exist without sponsorship and without interference,'" *Corporation of Presiding Bishop of Church of Jesus Christ of Latter-day Saints v. Amos*, 483 U.S. 327, 334 (1987) (quoting *Walz v. Tax Comm'n, supra*, at 673); "government may (and sometimes must) accommodate religious practices and ... may do so without violating the Establishment Clause." *Hobbie v. Unemployment Appeals Comm'n of Fla.*, 480 U.S. 136, 144–145 (1987). The fact that Chapter 748 facilitates the practice of religion is not what renders it an unconstitutional establishment. *Cf. Lee v. Weisman*, 505 U.S., (1992) (SOUTER, J., concurring) (*slip op.*, at 19) ("That government must remain neutral in matters of religion does not foreclose it from ever taking religion into account"); *School Dist. of Abington v. Schempp*, 374 U.S., at 299 (Brennan, J., concurring) ("[H]ostility, not neutrality, would characterize the refusal to provide chaplains and places of worship for pris-

oners and soldiers cut off by the State from all civilian opportunities for public communion").

But accommodation is not a principle without limits, and what petitioners seek is an adjustment to the Satmars' religiously grounded preferences that our cases do not countenance. Prior decisions have allowed religious communities and institutions to pursue their own interests free from governmental interference, see *Corporation of Presiding Bishop v. Amos, supra*, at 336–337 (government may allow religious organizations to favor their own adherents in hiring, even for secular employment); *Zorach v. Clauson*, 343 U.S. 306 (1952) (government may allow public schools to release students during the school day to receive off-site religious education), but we have never hinted that an otherwise unconstitutional delegation of political power to a religious group could be saved as a religious accommodation. Petitioners' proposed accommodation singles out a particular religious sect for special treatment, and whatever the limits of permissible legislative accommodations may be, compare *Texas Monthly, Inc. v. Bullock, supra* (striking down law exempting only religious publications from taxation), with *Corporation of Presiding Bishop v. Amos, supra* (upholding law exempting religious employers from Title VII), it is clear that neutrality as among religions must be honored. See *Larson v. Valente*, 456 U.S., at 244–246.

This conclusion does not, however, bring the Satmar parents, the Monroe-Woodbury school district, or the State of New York to the end of the road in seeking ways to respond to the parents' concerns. Just as the Court in *Larkin* observed that the State's interest in protecting religious meeting places could be "readily accomplished by other means," 459 U.S., at 124, there are several alternatives here for providing bilingual and bicultural special education to Satmar children. Such services can perfectly well be offered to village children through the Monroe-Woodbury Central School District. Since the Satmars do not claim that separatism is religiously mandated, their children may receive bilingual and bicultural instruction at a public school already run by the Monroe-Woodbury district. Or if the educationally appropriate offering by Monroe-Woodbury should turn out to be a separate program of bilingual and bicultural education at a neutral site near one of the village's parochial schools, this Court has already made it clear that no Establishment Clause difficulty would inhere in such a scheme, administered in accordance with neutral principles that would not necessarily confine special treatment to Satmars. See *Wolman v. Walter*, 433 U.S., at 247–248....

III

Justice Cardozo once cast the dissenter as "the gladiator making a last stand against the lions." B. Cardozo, *Law and Literature* 34 (1931). JUSTICE SCALIA's dissent is certainly the work of a gladiator, but he thrusts at lions of his own imagining. We do not disable a religiously homogeneous group from exercising political power conferred on it without regard to religion. Unlike the states of Utah and New Mexico (which were laid out according to traditional political methodologies taking account of lines of latitude and longitude and topographical features, see F. Van Zandt, *Boundaries of the United States and the Several States* 250–257 (1966)), the reference line chosen for the Kiryas Joel Village School District was one purposely drawn to separate Satmars from non-Satmars. Nor do we impugn the motives of the New York Legislature, which no doubt intended to accommodate the Satmar community without violating the Establishment Clause; we simply refuse to ignore that the method it chose is one that aids a particular religious community, rather than all groups similarly interested in separate schooling. The dissent protests [that] it is novel to insist "up front" that a statute not tailor its benefits to apply only to one religious group, but if this were so, *Texas Monthly, Inc.* would have turned out differently, see 489 U.S., at 14–15 (plurality opinion); *id.*, at 28 (BLACKMUN, J., concurring in judgment), and language in *Walz v. Tax Comm'n of New York City*, 397 U.S., at 673, and *Bowen v. Kendrick*, 487 U.S., at 608, purporting to rely on the breadth of the statutory schemes would have been mere surplusage. Indeed, under the dissent's theory, if New York were to pass a law providing school buses only for children attending Christian day schools, we would be constrained to uphold the statute against Establishment Clause attack until faced by a request from a non-Christian family for equal treatment under the patently unequal law. Cf. *Everson v. Board of Ed. of Ewing*, 330 U.S., at 17 (upholding school bus service provided all pupils). And to end on the point with which JUSTICE SCALIA begins, the license he takes in suggesting that the Court holds the Satmar sect to be New York's established church, is only one symptom of his inability to accept the fact that this Court has long held that the First Amendment reaches more than classic, 18th century establishments. See *Torcaso v. Watkins*, 367 U.S., at 492–495.

Our job, of course would be easier if the dissent's position had prevailed with the Framers and with this Court over the years. An Establishment Clause diminished to the dimensions acceptable to JUSTICE SCALIA could be enforced by a few simple rules, and our docket would never see cases requiring the application of a principle like neutrality toward religion as well as among religious sects. But that would be as blind to history as to precedent, and the difference between JUSTICE SCALIA and the Court accordingly turns on the Court's recognition that the Establishment Clause does comprehend such a principle and obligates courts to exercise the judgment necessary to apply it.

In this case we are clearly constrained to conclude that the statute before us fails the test of neutrality. It delegates a power this Court has said "ranks at the very apex of the function of a State," *Wisconsin v. Yoder,* 406 U.S. 205, 213 (1972), to an electorate defined by common religious belief and practice, in a manner that fails to foreclose religious favoritism. It therefore crosses the line from permissible accommodation to impermissible establishment. The judgment of the Court of Appeals of the State of New York is accordingly

Affirmed.

NO

Antonin Scalia

DISSENTING OPINION OF
ANTONIN SCALIA

JUSTICE SCALIA, with whom THE CHIEF JUSTICE and JUSTICE THOMAS join, dissenting.

The Court today finds that the Powers That Be, up in Albany, have conspired to effect an establishment of the Satmar Hasidim. I do not know who would be more surprised at this discovery: the Founders of our Nation or Grand Rebbe Joel Teitelbaum, founder of the Satmar. The Grand Rebbe would be astounded to learn that after escaping brutal persecution and coming to America with the modest hope of religious toleration for their ascetic form of Judaism, the Satmar had become so powerful, so closely allied with Mammon, as to have become an "establishment" of the Empire State. And the Founding Fathers would be astonished to find that the Establishment Clause —which they designed "to insure that no one powerful sect or combination of sects could use political or governmental power to punish dissenters," *Zorach v. Clauson*, 343 U.S. 306, 319 (1952) (Black, J., dissenting)—has been employed to prohibit characteristically and admirably American accommodation of the religious practices (or more precisely, cultural peculiarities) of a tiny minority sect. I, however, am not surprised. Once this Court has abandoned text and history as guides, nothing prevents it from calling religious toleration the establishment of religion.

I

Unlike most of our Establishment Clause cases involving education, these cases involve no public funding, however slight or indirect, to private religious schools. They do not involve private schools at all. The school under scrutiny is a public school specifically designed to provide a public secular education to handicapped students. The superintendent of the school, who is not Hasidic, is a 20-year veteran of the New York City public school system, with expertise in the area of bilingual, bicultural, special education. The teachers and therapists at the school all live outside the village of Kiryas Joel. While the village's private schools are profoundly religious and strictly

From *Board of Education of Kiryas Joel Village School District v. Louis Grumet et al.*, 1994 WL 279673 (U.S. NY.). Notes and some case citations omitted.

segregated by sex, classes at the public school are co-ed and the curriculum secular. The school building has the bland appearance of a public school, unadorned by religious symbols or markings; and the school complies with the laws and regulations governing all other New York State public schools. There is no suggestion, moreover, that this public school has gone too far in making special adjustments to the religious needs of its students. In sum, these cases involve only public aid to a school that is public as can be. The only thing distinctive about the school is that all the students share the same religion.

None of our cases has ever suggested that there is anything wrong with that. In fact, the Court has specifically approved the education of students of a single religion on a neutral site adjacent to a private religious school. See *Wolman v. Walter*, 433 U.S. 229, 247–248 (1977). In that case, the Court rejected the argument that "any program that isolates the sectarian pupils is impermissible," *id.*, at 246, and held that, "[t]he fact that a unit on a neutral site on occasion may serve only sectarian pupils does not provoke [constitutional] concerns," *id.*, at 247. And just last Term, the Court held that the State could permit public employees to assist students in a Catholic school. See *Zobrest v. Catalina Foothills School Dist.*, 509 U.S. (1993) (*slip op.*, at 11–12) (sign-language translator for deaf student). If a State can furnish services to a group of sectarian students on a neutral site adjacent to a private religious school, or even within such a school, how can there be any defect in educating those same students in a public school? As the Court noted in *Wolman*, the constitutional dangers of establishment arise "from the nature of the institution, not from the nature of the pupils," *Wolman, supra*, at 248. There is no danger in educating religious students in a public school.

For these very good reasons, JUSTICE SOUTER's opinion does not focus upon the school, but rather upon the school district and the New York Legislature that created it. His arguments, though sometimes intermingled, are two: that reposing governmental power in the Kiryas Joel School District is the same as reposing governmental power in a religious group; and that in enacting the statute creating the district, the New York State Legislature was discriminating on the basis of religion, i.e., favoring the Satmar Hasidim over others. I shall discuss these arguments in turn.

II

For his thesis that New York has unconstitutionally conferred governmental authority upon the Satmar sect, JUSTICE SOUTER relies extensively, and virtually exclusively, upon *Larkin v. Grendel's Den, Inc.*, 459 U.S. 116 (1982). JUSTICE SOUTER believes that the present case "resembles" *Grendel's Den* because that case "teaches that a state may not delegate its civic authority to a group chosen according to a religious criterion." That misdescribes both what that case taught (which is that a state may not delegate its civil authority to a church), and what this case involves (which is a group chosen according to cultural characteristics). The statute at issue there gave churches veto power over the State's authority to grant a liquor license to establishments in the vicinity of the church. The Court had little difficulty finding the statute unconstitutional. "The Framers did not set up a system of government in which important, discretionary governmental powers would be delegated to or shared with religious institutions." *Id.,* at 127.

JUSTICE SOUTER concedes that *Grendel's Den* "presented an example of united civic and religious authority, an establishment rarely found in such straightforward form in modern America." The uniqueness of the case stemmed from the grant of governmental power directly to a religious institution, and the Court's opinion focused on that fact, remarking that the transfer of authority was to "churches" (10 times), the "governing body of churches" (twice), "religious institutions" (twice) and "religious bodies" (once). Astonishingly, however, JUSTICE SOUTER dismisses the difference between a transfer of government power to citizens who share a common religion as opposed to "the officers of its sectarian organization"—the critical factor that made *Grendel's Den* unique and "rar[e]" —as being "one of form, not substance."

JUSTICE SOUTER's steamrolling of the difference between civil authority held by a church, and civil authority held by members of a church, is breathtaking. To accept it, one must believe that large portions of the civil authority exercised during most of our history were unconstitutional, and that much more of it than merely the Kiryas Joel School District is unconstitutional today. The history of the populating of North America is in no small measure the story of groups of people sharing a common religious and cultural heritage striking out to form their own communities. See, e.g., W. Sweet, *The Story of Religion in America* 9 (1950). It is preposterous to suggest that the civil institutions of these communities, separate from their churches, were constitutionally suspect. And if they were, surely JUSTICE SOUTER cannot mean that the inclusion of one or two nonbelievers in the community would have been enough to eliminate the constitutional vice. If the conferral of governmental power upon a religious institution as such (rather than upon American citizens who belong to the religious institution) is not the test of *Grendel's Den* invalidity, there is no reason why giving power to a body that is overwhelmingly dominated by the members of one sect would not suffice to invoke the Establishment Clause. That might have made the entire States of Utah and New Mexico unconstitutional at the time of their admission to the Union, and would undoubtedly make many units of local government unconstitutional today.

JUSTICE SOUTER's position boils down to the quite novel proposition that any group of citizens (say, the residents of Kiryas Joel) can be invested with political power, but not if they all belong to the same religion. Of course such disfavoring of religion is positively antagonistic to the purposes of the Religion Clauses, and we have rejected it before. In *McDaniel v. Paty,* 435 U.S. 618 (1978), we invalidated a state constitutional amendment that would have permitted all persons to participate in political conventions, except ministers. We adopted James Madison's view that the State could not " 'punis[h] a religious profession with the privation of a civil right.' " *Id.,* at 626 (opinion of Burger, C. J.), quoting 5 *Writings of James Madison* 288 (G. Hunt ed. 1904). Or as Justice Brennan put it in his opinion concurring in judgment: "Religionists no less than members of any other group enjoy the full measure of protection afforded speech, association, and political activity generally." *Id.,* at 641; see also *Widmar v. Vincent,* 454 U.S. 263 (1981). I see no reason why it is any less pernicious to deprive a group rather than an individual of its rights simply because of its religious beliefs.

Perhaps appreciating the startling implications for our constitutional jurisprudence of collapsing the distinction between religious institutions and their members, JUSTICE SOUTER tries to limit his "unconstitutional conferral of civil authority" holding by pointing out several features supposedly unique to the present case: that the "boundary lines of the school district divide residents according to religious affiliation"; that the school district was created by "a special act of the legislature"; and that the formation of the school district ran counter to the legislature's trend of consolidating districts in recent years. Assuming all these points to be true (and they are not), they would certainly bear upon whether the legislature had an impermissible religious motivation in creating the district (which is JUSTICE SOUTER's next point, in the discussion of which I shall reply to these arguments). But they have nothing to do with whether conferral of power upon a group of citizens can be the conferral of power upon a religious institution. It can not. Or if it can, our Establishment Clause jurisprudence has been transformed.

III

I turn, next, to JUSTICE SOUTER's second justification for finding an establishment of religion: his facile conclusion that the New York Legislature's creation of the Kiryas Joel School District was religiously motivated. But in the Land of the Free, democratically adopted laws are not so easily impeached by unelected judges. To establish the unconstitutionality of a facially neutral law on the mere basis of its asserted religiously preferential (or

discriminatory) effects—or at least to establish it in conformity with our precedents—JUSTICE SOUTER "must be able to show the absence of a neutral, secular basis" for the law. *Gillette v. United States*, 401 U.S. 437, 452 (1971); see also *Arlington Heights v. Metropolitan Housing Development Corp.*, 429 U.S. 252, 266 (1977) (facially race-neutral laws can be invalidated on the basis of their effects only if "unexplainable on grounds other than race").

There is of course no possible doubt of a secular basis here. The New York Legislature faced a unique problem in Kiryas Joel: a community in which all the non-handicapped children attend private schools, and the physically and mentally disabled children who attend public school suffer the additional handicap of cultural distinctiveness. It would be troublesome enough if these peculiarly dressed, handicapped students were sent to the next town, accompanied by their similarly clad but unimpaired classmates. But all the unimpaired children of Kiryas Joel attend private school. The handicapped children suffered sufficient emotional trauma from their predicament that their parents kept them home from school. Surely the legislature could target this problem, and provide a public education for these students, in the same way it addressed, by a similar law, the unique needs of children institutionalized in a hospital. See e.g., 1970 N.Y. Laws, ch. 843 (authorizing a union free school district for the area owned by Blythedale Children's Hospital).

Since the obvious presence of a neutral, secular basis renders the asserted preferential effect of this law inadequate to invalidate it, JUSTICE SOUTER is required to come forward with direct evidence that religious preference was the objective. His case could scarcely be weaker. It consists, briefly, of this: The People of New York created the Kiryas Joel Village School District in order to further the Satmar religion, rather than for any proper secular purpose, because (1) they created the district in an extraordinary manner —by special Act of the legislature, rather than under the State's general laws governing school-district reorganization; (2) the creation of the district ran counter to a State trend toward consolidation of school districts; and (3) the District includes only adherents of the Satmar religion. On this indictment, no jury would convict.

One difficulty with the first point is that it is not true. There was really nothing so "special" about the formation of a school district by an Act of the New York Legislature. The State has created both large school districts, see e.g., 1972 N.Y. Laws, ch. 928 (creating the Gananda School District out of land previously in two other districts), and small specialized school districts for institutionalized children, see e.g., 1972 N.Y. Laws, ch. 559 (creating a union free school district for the area owned by Abbott House), through these special Acts. But in any event all that the first point proves, and the second point as well (countering the trend toward consolidation), is that New York regarded Kiryas Joel as a special case, requiring special measures. I should think it obvious that it did, and obvious that it should have. But even if the New York Legislature had never before created a school district by special statute (which is not true), and even if it had done nothing but consolidate school districts for over a century (which is not true), how could the departure from those past

practices possibly demonstrate that the legislature had religious favoritism in mind? It could not. To be sure, when there is no special treatment there is no possibility of religious favoritism; but it is not logical to suggest that when there is special treatment there is proof of religious favoritism.

JUSTICE SOUTER's case against the statute comes down to nothing more, therefore, than his third point: the fact that all the residents of the Kiryas Joel Village School District are Satmars. But all its residents also wear unusual dress, have unusual civic customs, and have not much to do with people who are culturally different from them. (The Court recognizes that "the Satmars prefer to live together 'to facilitate individual religious observance and maintain social, cultural and religious values,' but that it is not 'against their religion' to interact with others." On what basis does JUSTICE SOUTER conclude that it is the theological distinctiveness rather than the cultural distinctiveness that was the basis for New York State's decision? The normal assumption would be that it was the latter, since it was not theology but dress, language, and cultural alienation that posed the educational problem for the children. JUSTICE SOUTER not only does not adopt the logical assumption, he does not even give the New York Legislature the benefit of the doubt. The following is the level of his analysis: "Not even the special needs of the children in this community can explain the legislature's unusual Act, for the State could have responded to the concerns of the Satmar parents [by other means]." In other words, we know the legislature must have been motivated by the desire to favor the Satmar Hasidim religion, because it could have met the needs of these children by a method that did not place the Satmar Hasidim in a separate school district. This is not a rational argument proving religious favoritism; it is rather a novel Establishment Clause principle to the effect that no secular objective may be pursued by a means that might also be used for religious favoritism if some other means is available.

I have little doubt that JUSTICE SOUTER would laud this humanitarian legislation if all of the distinctiveness of the students of Kiryas Joel were attributable to the fact that their parents were nonreligious commune-dwellers, or American Indians, or gypsies. The creation of a special, one-culture school district for the benefit of those children would pose no problem. The neutrality demanded by the Religion Clauses requires the same indulgence toward cultural characteristics that are accompanied by religious belief. "The Establishment Clause does not license government to treat religion and those who teach or practice it, simply by virtue of their status as such, as . . . subject to unique disabilities." *McDaniel v. Paty, supra,* at 641 (Brennan, J., concurring in judgment).

Even if JUSTICE SOUTER could successfully establish that the cultural distinctiveness of the Kiryas Joel students (which is the problem the New York Legislature addressed) was an essential part of their religious belief rather than merely an accompaniment of their religious belief, that would not discharge his heavy burden. In order to invalidate a facially neutral law, JUSTICE SOUTER would have to show not only that legislators were aware that religion caused the problems addressed, but also that the legislature's proposed solution was motivated by a desire to disadvantage or benefit a religious group (i.e., to disadvantage or benefit them because of their religion). For example, if the city of Hialeah, knowing of the potential health problems raised by the Santeria religious practice of animal sacrifice, were to provide by ordinance a special, more frequent, municipal garbage collection for the carcasses of dead animals, we would not strike the ordinance down just because the city council was aware that a religious practice produced the problem the ordinance addressed. See *Church of Lukumi Babalu Aye, Inc. v. Hialeah,* 508 U.S. (1993) (*slip op.,* at 15–19). Here a facially neutral statute extends an educational benefit to the one area where it was not effectively distributed. Whether or not the reason for the ineffective distribution had anything to do with religion, it is a remarkable stretch to say that the Act was motivated by a desire to favor or disfavor a particular religious group. The proper analogy to Chapter 748 is not the Court's hypothetical law providing school buses only to Christian students, but a law providing extra buses to rural school districts (which happen to be predominantly Southern Baptist).

At various times JUSTICE SOUTER intimates, though he does not precisely say, that the boundaries of the school district were intentionally drawn on the basis of religion. He refers, for example, to "[t]he State's manipulation of the franchise for this district . . . , giving the sect exclusive control of the political subdivision," *ante,* at 10—implying that the "giving" of political power to the religious sect was the object of the "manipulation." There is no evidence of that. The special district was created to meet the special educational needs of distinctive handicapped children, and the geographical boundaries selected for that district were (quite logically) those that already existed for the village. It sometimes appears as though the shady "manipulation" JUSTICE SOUTER has in mind is that which occurred when the village was formed, so that the drawing of its boundaries infected the coterminous boundaries of the district. He says, for example, that "[i]t is undisputed that those who negotiated the village boundaries when applying the general village incorporation statute drew them so as to exclude all but Satmars." It is indeed. But non-Satmars were excluded, not (as he intimates) because of their religion, but—as JUSTICE O'CONNOR clearly describes—because of their lack of desire for the high-density zoning that Satmars favored. It was a classic drawing of lines on the basis of communality of secular governmental desires, not communality of religion. What happened in the creation of the village is in fact precisely what happened in the creation of the school district, so that the former cannot possibly infect the latter, as JUSTICE SOUTER tries to suggest. Entirely secular reasons (zoning for the village, cultural alienation of students for the school district) produced a political unit whose members happened to share the same religion. There is no evidence (indeed, no plausible suspicion) of the legislature's desire to favor the Satmar religion, as opposed to meeting distinctive secular needs or desires of citizens who happened to be Satmars. If there were, JUSTICE SOUTER would say so; instead, he must merely insinuate.

IV

But even if Chapter 748 were intended to create a special arrangement for the Satmars because of their religion (not including, as I have shown in Part I, any

conferral of governmental power upon a religious entity), it would be a permissible accommodation. "This Court has long recognized that the government may (and sometimes must) accommodate religious practices and that it may do so without violating the Establishment Clause." *Hobbie v. Unemployment Appeals Comm'n of Fla.*, 480 U.S. 136, 144–145 (1987). Moreover, "there is ample room for accommodation of religion under the Establishment Clause," *Corporation for Presiding Bishop of Church of Jesus of Latter-day Saints v. Amos*, 483 U.S. 327, 338 (1987), and for "play in the joints [flexibility in interpretation] productive of a benevolent neutrality which will permit religious exercise to exist without sponsorship and without interference," *Walz v. Tax Comm'n of N. Y. City*, 397 U.S. 664, 669 (1970). Accommodation is permissible, moreover, even when the statute deals specifically with religion, see, e.g., *Zorach v. Clauson*, 343 U.S., at 312–315, and even when accommodation is not commanded by the Free Exercise Clause, see, e.g., *Walz, supra*, at 673.

When a legislature acts to accommodate religion, particularly a minority sect, "it follows the best of our traditions." *Zorach, supra*, at 314. The Constitution itself contains an accommodation of sorts. Article VI, cl. 3, prescribes that executive, legislative and judicial officers of the Federal and State Governments shall bind themselves to support the Constitution "by Oath or Affirmation." Although members of the most populous religions found no difficulty in swearing an oath to God, Quakers, Moravians, and Mennonites refused to take oaths based on Matthew 5:34's injunction "swear not at all." The option of affirmation was added to accommodate these minority religions and enable their members to serve in government. See 1 A. Stokes, *Church and State in the United States* 524–527 (1950). Congress, from its earliest sessions, passed laws accommodating religion by refunding duties paid by specific churches upon the importation of plates for the printing of Bibles, see 6 Stat. 116 (1813), vestments, 6 Stat. 346 (1816), and bells, 6 Stat. 675 (1836). Congress also exempted church property from the tax assessments it levied on residents of the District of Columbia; and all 50 States have had similar laws. See *Walz, supra,* at 676–678.

This Court has also long acknowledged the permissibility of legislative accommodation. In one of our early Establishment Clause cases, we upheld New York City's early release program, which allowed students to be released from public school during school hours to attend religious instruction or devotional exercises. See *Zorach, supra,* at 312–315. We determined that the early release program "accommodates the public service to . . . spiritual needs," and noted that finding it unconstitutional would "show a callous indifference to religious groups." 343 U.S., at 314. In *Walz, supra,* we upheld a property tax exemption for religious organizations, observing that it was part of a salutary tradition of "permissible state accommodation to religion." *Id.,* at 672–673. And in *Presiding Bishop, supra,* we upheld a section of the Civil Rights Act of 1964 exempting religious groups from the antidiscrimination provisions of Title VII. We concluded that it was "a permissible legislative purpose to alleviate significant governmental interference with the ability of religious organizations to define and carry out their religious missions." *Id.,* at 335.

In today's opinion, however, the Court seems uncomfortable with this aspect of our constitutional tradition. Although it acknowledges the concept of accommodation, it quickly points out that it is "not a principle without limits," *ante,* at 18, and then gives reasons why the present case exceeds those limits, reasons which simply do not hold water. "[W]e have never hinted," the Court says, "that an otherwise unconstitutional delegation of political power to a religious group could be saved as a religious accommodation." *Ante,* at 19. Putting aside the circularity inherent in referring to a delegation as "otherwise unconstitutional" when its constitutionality turns on whether there is an accommodation, if this statement is true, it is only because we have never hinted that delegation of political power to citizens who share a particular religion could be unconstitutional. This is simply a reply of the argument we rejected in Part II, *supra.*

The second and last reason the Court finds accommodation impermissible is, astoundingly, the mere risk that the State will not offer accommodation to a similar group in the future, and that neutrality will therefore not be preserved. Returning to the ill fitted crutch of *Grendel's Den,* the Court suggests that by acting through this special statute the New York Legislature has eliminated any " 'effective means of guaranteeing' that governmental power will be and has been neutrally employed." *Ante,* at 15, quoting *Grendel's Den,* 459 U.S., at 125. How misleading. That language in *Grendel's Den* was an expression of concern not (as the context in which it is quoted suggests) about the courts' ability to assure the legislature's future neutrality, but about the legislature's ability to assure the neutrality of the churches to which it had transferred legislative power. That concern is inapposite here; there is no doubt about the legislature's capacity to control what transpires in a public school.

At bottom, the Court's "no guarantee of neutrality" argument is an assertion of this Court's inability to control the New York Legislature's future denial of comparable accommodation. We have "no assurance," the Court says, "that the next similarly situated group seeking a school district of its own will receive one," since "a legislature's failure to enact a special law is... unreviewable." *Ante*, at 16; see also *ante*, at 6 (O'CONNOR, J., concurring in part and concurring in judgment). That is true only in the technical (and irrelevant) sense that the later group denied an accommodation may need to challenge the grant of the first accommodation in light of the later denial, rather than challenging the denial directly. But one way or another, "even if [an administrative agency is] not empowered or obliged to act, [a litigant] would be entitled to a judicial audience. Ultimately the courts cannot escape the obligation to address [a] plea that the exemption [sought] is mandated by the first amendment's religion clauses." *Olsen v. Drug Enforcement Admin.*, 878 F.2d 1458, 1461 (CADC 1989) (R. B. Ginsburg, J.).

The Court's demand for "up front" assurances of a neutral system is at war with both traditional accommodation doctrine and the judicial role. As we have described, *supra*, at 15, Congress's earliest accommodations exempted duties paid by specific churches on particular items. See, e.g., 6 Stat. 346 (1816) (exempting vestments imported by "bishop of Bardstown"). Moreover, most efforts at accommodation seek to solve a problem that applies to members of only one or a few religions. Not every religion uses wine in its sacraments, but that does not make an exemption from Prohibition for sacramental wine-use impermissible, *accord, Church of Lukumi Babalu Aye, Inc. v. Hialeah*, 508 U.S., at n. 2 (*slip op.*, at 3, n. 2) (SOUTER, J., concurring in judgment), nor does it require the State granting such an exemption to explain in advance how it will treat every other claim for dispensation from its controlled-substances laws. Likewise, not every religion uses peyote in its services, but we have suggested that legislation which exempts the sacramental use of peyote from generally applicable drug laws is not only permissible, but desirable, see *Employment Div., Ore. Dept of Human Resources v. Smith*, 494 U.S. 872, 890 (1990), without any suggestion that some "up front" legislative guarantee of equal treatment for sacramental substances used by other sects must be provided. The record is clear that the necessary guarantee can and will be provided, after the fact, by the courts. See, e.g., *Olsen v. Drug Enforcement Admin., supra*, (rejecting claim that peyote exemption requires marijuana exemption for Ethiopian Zion Coptic Church); *Olsen v. Iowa*, 808 F.2d 652 (CA8 1986) (same); *Kennedy v. Bureau of Narcotics and Dangerous Drugs*, 459 F.2d 415 (CA9 1972) (accepting claim that peyote exemption for Native American Church requires peyote exemption for other religions that use that substance in their sacraments).

Contrary to the Court's suggestion, *ante*, at 20–22, I do not think that the Establishment Clause prohibits formally established "state" churches and nothing more. I have always believed, and all my opinions are consistent with the view, that the Establishment Clause prohibits the favoring of one religion over others. In this respect, it is the Court that attacks lions of straw. What I attack is the Court's imposition of novel "up front" procedural requirements on state legislatures. Making law (and making exceptions) one case at a time, whether through adjudication or through highly particularized rulemaking or legislation, violates, *ex ante,* no principle of fairness, equal protection, or neutrality, simply because it does not announce in advance how all future cases (and all future exceptions) will be disposed of. If it did, the manner of proceeding of this Court itself would be unconstitutional. It is presumptuous for this Court to impose—out of nowhere—and unheard-of prohibition against proceeding in this manner upon the Legislature of New York State. I never heard of such a principle, nor has anyone else, nor will it ever be heard of again. Unlike what the New York Legislature has done, this is a special rule to govern only the Satmar Hasidim.

* * *

The Court's decision today is astounding. Chapter 748 involves no public aid to private schools and does not mention religion. In order to invalidate it, the Court casts aside, on the flimsiest of evidence, the strong presumption of validity that attaches to facially neutral laws, and invalidates the present accommodation because it does not trust New York to be as accommodating toward other religions (presumably those less powerful than the Satmar Hasidim) in the future. This is unprecedented—except that it continues, and takes to new extremes, a recent tendency in the opinions of this Court to turn the Establishment Clause into a repealer of our Nation's tradition of religious toleration. I dissent.

POSTSCRIPT

Are School Districts Created for Religious Reasons a Violation of the Constitution?

Why should church and state be separate? Is there any danger to be feared from public religious displays? It is probably fair to say that behind the debates over this issue and the ongoing controversy over prayer in the schools are differing interpretations of the history of religion. Does religion bring us to a higher level of existence, or is it a system that will oppress dissidents, nonbelievers, and members of minority faiths? Almost everyone has an opinion on this question, and most can find some historical support for their positions. Ironically, the same historical circumstance may even be used to support opposing points of view. For example, at a congressional hearing on school prayer, the following testimony was introduced.

> When I was educated in German public schools, they provided as part of the regular curriculum separate religious instruction for children of the three major faiths. At that time, all children in public schools from the ages of 6 to 18 were required not merely to recite a prayer at the beginning of each school session but to receive religious instruction twice a week. That system continued in the following decades. (Statement by Joachim Prinz, quoted in testimony of Nathan Dershowitz, *Hearings on Prayer in Public Schools and Buildings*, Committee on the Judiciary, House of Representatives, August 19, 1980.)

Did that program effectively teach morality to the German people? If it did, it would be difficult to explain the rise of Hitler and the total moral collapse and even depravity of the German people, which resulted in the torture and death of millions of Jews and Christians.

Yet another witness, however, testifying in support of prayer in the schools, quoted the report of the President's Commission on the Holocaust, which wrote that "the Holocaust could not have occurred without the collapse of certain religious norms; increasing secularity fueled a devaluation of the image of the human being created in the likeness of God." (Statement of Judah Glasner, *Hearings on Prayer in Public Schools and Buildings*, Committee on the Judiciary, House of Representatives, July 30, 1980.)

Relevant cases concerning religion in the public schools are *McCollum v. Board of Education*, 333 U.S. 203 (1948), about religious instruction on school property; *Zorach v. Clauson*, 343 U.S. 306 (1952), regarding free time from school for religious instruction off school property; and *Board of Education of the Westside Community Schools v. Mergens*, 110 S. Ct. 2356 (1990), regarding the use of school premises for an after-school religious club.

ISSUE 6

Is Abortion Protected by the Constitution?

YES: Sandra Day O'Connor, from Majority Opinion, *Planned Parenthood of Southeastern Pennsylvania et al. v. Robert P. Casey et al.*, U.S. Supreme Court (1992)

NO: William H. Rehnquist, from Dissenting Opinion, *Planned Parenthood of Southeastern Pennsylvania et al. v. Robert P. Casey et al.*, U.S. Supreme Court (1992)

ISSUE SUMMARY

YES: Supreme Court justice Sandra Day O'Connor upholds a woman's constitutional right to abortion under most circumstances and reaffirms the central holding of *Roe v. Wade.*

NO: Chief Justice William H. Rehnquist argues that Pennsylvania regulations on abortion should be upheld and that it is appropriate to overrule *Roe v. Wade.*

One of the strengths of the American judicial process, lawyers often claim, is that it encourages logical and objective solutions to problems and reduces the influence of emotion and whim. By proceeding slowly, by applying abstract legal rules, by relying on professional lawyers and restricting the layperson's role, it is asserted that impartiality and neutrality will be achieved and that explosive issues will be defused. The legal process works this kind of magic often, but it has clearly failed to do so with regard to the issue of abortion. Abortion remains as newsworthy and important a subject today as it was when the landmark case of *Roe v. Wade* was decided in 1973.

Perceptions of the abortion issue differ. For the courts, it is a constitutional issue, meaning that the focus is on whether or not laws restricting abortion deny a woman due process of law under the Fourteenth Amendment. Part of the reason courts have been unable to defuse the abortion issue is that they have not persuaded the public to see the subject only in these terms. How we define or categorize an issue frequently determines our conclusions about the subject.

For example, do we view abortion as an issue primarily affecting women, and thus see outlawing it as an example of sex discrimination? Or do we think firstly of the fetus, and thus conclude that abortion is murder? Do we look at abortion from a religious perspective, thinking of how the legal codes of Western religions treat the subject? Or is it a question of privacy and of preventing the state from intruding into the affairs and personal decisions of citizens? Is it a matter of health, of preventing injuries and death to women who undergo illegal abortions? Is it an issue of discrimination against the poor, who may need the state to subsidize abortions, or even racial discrimination, because a higher proportion of poor women are black? How abortion is described can be all-important. One writer, for example, has written, "The real question is not, 'How can we justify abortion?' but, 'How can we justify compulsory childbearing?' " See Cisler, "Unfinished Business: Birth Control and Women's Liberation," in Morgan, ed., *Sisterhood is Powerful: An Anthology of Writings from the Women's Movement* (Random House, 1970).

The landmark decision of *Roe v. Wade*, 410 U.S. 113 (1973) was handed down on January 23, 1973. In the majority opinion, Justice Harry A. Blackmun wrote that states may not prohibit abortions during the first trimester, that some abortions may be regulated but not prohibited during the second trimester, and that abortions may be prohibited during the last trimester.

In the years since *Roe v. Wade* there have been many attempts to circumvent, narrow, delay, or avoid the Court's ruling. In *Harris v. McCrae*, 100 S. Ct. 2671 (1980), for example, in a 5–4 decision, the Supreme Court upheld a federal law that prohibited the federal government from reimbursing states for providing Medicaid abortions to women, except under specified circumstances. The majority held that the law did not illegally discriminate against the poor, nor did it violate the doctrines of separation of church and state merely because the restrictions coincided with Roman Catholic religious beliefs. In 1991, further limits on the use of federal funds were approved by the Court in *Rust v. Sullivan*, 111 S. Ct. 1759 (1991). In that case, regulations prohibiting abortion counseling in programs receiving federal funds for family planning were upheld.

More recently, in *Webster v. Reproductive Health Services*, 109 S. Ct. 3040 (1989), the Court refused to overturn *Roe v. Wade*, but it allowed states to impose more restrictions, such as one that required doctors, when a woman is more than 20 weeks pregnant, to perform tests "to determine if the unborn child is viable." The five-member majority included four votes to overturn *Roe*. Justice Sandra Day O'Connor, the critical fifth vote, was unwilling to overturn *Roe* but felt the Missouri law was constitutional since it did not place an "undue burden" on the woman's abortion rights.

The following readings are from the most recent and, in all likelihood, the most significant abortion decision since *Roe v. Wade*. The majority refused to overturn *Roe* but was also willing to allow some Pennsylvania restrictions involving parental notification and waiting periods. It also parted ways with the trimester model of *Roe*. The decision was neither a clear victory nor a clear defeat for either the pro-choice or pro-life movements. And as you read, you should ask whether or not the Court has finally articulated a position that will be an acceptable middle ground.

YES

Sandra Day O'Connor

MAJORITY OPINION

PLANNED PARENTHOOD *v.* CASEY

JUSTICE O'CONNOR, JUSTICE KENNEDY, and JUSTICE SOUTER announced the judgment of the Court.

I

Liberty finds no refuge in a jurisprudence of doubt. Yet 19 years after our holding that the Constitution protects a woman's right to terminate her pregnancy in its early stages, *Roe v. Wade,* 410 U.S. 113 (1973), that definition of liberty is still questioned. Joining the respondents as *amicus curiae,* the United States, as it has done in five other cases in the last decade, again asks us to overrule *Roe.*

At issue in these cases are five provisions of the Pennsylvania Abortion Control Act of 1982 as amended in 1988 and 1989. 18 Pa. Cons. Stat. Sec. 3203–3220 (1990). The Act requires that a woman seeking an abortion give her informed consent prior to the abortion procedure, and specifies that she be provided with certain information at least 24 hours before the abortion is performed. For a minor to obtain an abortion, the Act requires the informed consent of one of her parents, but provides for a judicial bypass option if the minor does not wish to or cannot obtain a parent's consent. Another provision of the Act requires that, unless certain exceptions apply, a married woman seeking an abortion must sign a statement indicating that she has notified her husband of her intended abortion. The Act exempts compliance with these three requirements in the event of a "medical emergency," which is defined in Sec. 3203 of the Act. In addition to the above provisions regulating the performance of abortions, the Act imposes certain reporting requirements on facilities that provide abortion services.

Before any of these provisions took effect, the petitioners, who are five abortion clinics and one physician representing himself as well as a class of physicians who provide abortion services, brought this suit seeking declaratory and injunctive relief. Each provision was challenged as unconstitutional

From *Planned Parenthood of Southeastern Pennsylvania et al. v. Robert P. Casey et al.,* 60 L.W. 4795 (1992). Some case citations omitted.

on its face. The District Court entered a preliminary injunction against the enforcement of the regulations, and, after a 3-day bench trial, held all the provisions at issue here unconstitutional, entering a permanent injunction against Pennsylvania's enforcement of them. 744 F. Supp 1323 (ED Pa. 1990). The Court of Appeals for the Third Circuit affirmed in part and reversed in part, upholding all of the regulations except for the husband notification requirement. 947 F.2d 682 (1991). We granted certiorari.

... [A]t oral argument in this Court, the attorney for the parties challenging the statute took the position that none of the enactments can be upheld without overruling *Roe v. Wade*. We disagree with that analysis; but we acknowledge that our decisions after *Roe* cast doubt upon the meaning and reach of its holding. Further, the Chief Justice admits that he would overrule the central holding of *Roe* and adopt the rational relationship test as the sole criterion of constitutionality. State and federal courts as well as legislatures throughout the Union must have guidance as they seek to address this subject in conformance with the Constitution. Given these premises, we find it imperative to review once more the principles that define the rights of the woman and the legitimate authority of the State respecting the termination of pregnancies by abortion procedures.

After considering the fundamental constitutional questions resolved by *Roe*, principles of institutional integrity, and the rule of *stare decisis*, we are led to conclude this: the essential holding of *Roe v. Wade* should be retained and once again reaffirmed.

It must be stated at the outset and with clarity that *Roe*'s essential holding, the holding we reaffirm, has three parts.

First is a recognition of the right of the woman to choose to have an abortion before viability and to obtain it without undue interference from the State. Before viability, the State's interests are not strong enough to support a prohibition of abortion or the imposition of a substantial obstacle to the woman's effective right to elect the procedure. Second is a confirmation of the State's power to restrict abortions after fetal viability, if the law contains exceptions for pregnancies which endanger a woman's life or health. And third is the principle that the State has legitimate interests from the outset of the pregnancy in protecting the health of the woman and the life of the fetus that may become a child. These principles do not contradict one another; and we adhere to each.

II

... Men and women of good conscience can disagree, and we suppose some always shall disagree, about the profound moral and spiritual implications of terminating a pregnancy, even in its earliest stage. Some of us as individuals find abortion offensive to our most basic principles of morality, but that cannot control our decision. Our obligation is to define the liberty of all, not to mandate our own moral code. The underlying constitutional issue is whether the State can resolve these philosophic questions in such a definitive way that a woman lacks all choice in the matter, except perhaps in those rare circumstances in which the pregnancy is itself a danger to her own life or health, or is the result of rape or incest....

Our law affords constitutional protection to personal decisions relating to marriage, procreation, contraception, family relationships, child rearing, and education. *Carey v. Population Services International*, 431 U.S., at 685. Our cases recognize "the right of the *individual*, married or single, to be free from unwarranted governmental intrusion into matters so fundamentally affecting a person as the decision whether to bear or beget a child." *Eisenstadt v. Baird, supra*, at 453. Our precedents "have respected the private realm of family life which the state cannot enter." *Prince v. Massachusetts*, 321 U.S. 158, 166 (1944). These matters, involving the most intimate and personal choices a person may make in a lifetime, choices central to personal dignity and autonomy, are central to the liberty protected by the Fourteenth Amendment. At the heart of liberty is the right to define one's own concept of existence, of meaning, of the universe, and of the mystery of human life. Beliefs about these matters could not define the attributes of personhood were they formed under compulsion of the State.

These considerations begin our analysis of the woman's interest in terminating her pregnancy but cannot end it, for this reason: though the abortion decision may originate within the zone of conscience and belief, it is more than a philosophic exercise. Abortion is a unique act. It is an act fraught with consequences for others: for the woman who must live with the implications of her decision; for the persons who perform and assist in the procedure; for the spouse, family, and society which must confront the knowledge that these procedures exist, procedures some deem nothing short of an act of violence against innocent human life; and, depending on one's beliefs, for the life or potential life that is aborted. Though abortion is conduct, it does not follow that the State is entitled to proscribe it in all instances.

That is because the liberty of the woman is at stake in a sense unique to the human condition and so unique to the law. The mother who carries a child to full term is subject to anxieties, to physical constraints, to pain that only she must bear. That these sacrifices have from the beginning of the human race been endured by woman with a pride that ennobles her in the eyes of others and gives to the infant a bond of love cannot alone be grounds for the State to insist she make the sacrifice. Her suffering is too intimate and personal for the State to insist, without more, upon its own vision of the woman's role, however dominant that vision has been in the course of our history and our culture. The destiny of the woman must be shaped to a large extent on her own conception of her spiritual imperatives and her place in society.

It should be recognized, moreover, that in some critical respects the abortion decision is of the same character as the decision to use contraception, to which *Griswold v. Connecticut, Eisenstadt v. Baird,* and *Carey v. Population Services International,* afford constitutional protection. We have no doubt as to the correctness of those decisions. They support the reasoning in *Roe* relating to the woman's liberty because they involve personal decisions concerning not only the meaning of procreation but also human responsibility and respect for it. As with abortion, reasonable people will have differences of opinion about these matters. One view is based on such reverence for the wonder of creation that any pregnancy ought to be welcomed and carried to full term no matter how difficult it will be to provide for the child and ensure its well-being. Another is that the inability to provide for the nurture and care of the infant is a cruelty to the child and an anguish to the parent. These are intimate views with infinite variations, and their deep, personal character underlay our decisions in *Griswold, Eisenstadt,* and *Carey.* The same concerns are present when the woman confronts the reality that, perhaps despite her attempts to avoid it, she has become pregnant.

It was this dimension of personal liberty that *Roe* sought to protect, and its holding invoked the reasoning and the tradition of the precedents we have discussed, granting protection to substantive liberties of the person. *Roe* was, of course, an extension of those cases and, as the decision itself indicated, the separate States could act in some degree to further their own legitimate interests in protecting prenatal life. The extent to which the legislatures of the States might act to outweigh the interests of the woman in choosing to terminate her pregnancy was a subject of debate both in *Roe* itself and in decisions following it.

While we appreciate the weight of the arguments made on behalf of the State in the case before us, arguments which in their ultimate formulation conclude that *Roe* should be overruled, the reservations any of us may have in reaffirming the central holding of *Roe* are outweighed by the explication of individual liberty we have given combined with the force of *stare decisis.* We turn now to that doctrine.

III

A

... [W]hen this Court reexamines a prior holding, its judgment is customarily informed by a series of prudential and pragmatic considerations designed to test the consistency of overruling a prior decision with the ideal of the rule of law, and to gauge the respective costs of reaffirming and overruling a prior case. Thus, for example, we may ask whether the rule has proved to be intolerable simply in defying practical workability; whether the rule is subject to a kind of reliance that would lend a special hardship to the consequences of overruling and add inequity to the cost of repudiation; whether related principles of law have so far developed as to have left the old rule no more than a remnant of abandoned doctrine; or whether facts have so changed or come to be seen so differently, as to have robbed the old rule of significant application or justification.

So in this case we may inquire whether *Roe*'s central rule has been found unworkable; whether the rule's limitation on state power could be removed without serious inequity to those who have relied upon it or significant damage to the stability of the society governed by the rule in question; whether the law's growth in the intervening years has left *Roe*'s central rule a doctrinal anachronism discounted by society; and whether *Roe*'s premises of fact have so far changed in the ensuing two decades as to render its central holding somehow irrelevant or unjustifiable in dealing with the issue it addressed.

1

Although *Roe* has engendered opposition, it has in no sense proven "unworkable," see *Garcia v. San Antonio Metropolitan Transit Authority,* 469 U.S. 528, 546 (1985), representing as it does a simple limitation beyond which a state law is unenforceable. While *Roe* has, of course, required judicial assessment of state laws affecting the exercise of the choice guaranteed against government infringement, and although the need for such review will remain as a consequence of today's decision, the required determinations fall within judicial competence.

2

... [F]or two decades of economic and social developments, people have organized intimate relationships and made choices that define their views of themselves and their places in society, in reliance on the availability of abortion in the event that contraception should fail. The ability of women to participate equally in the economic and social life of the Nation has been facilitated by their ability to control their reproductive lives. See, e.g., R. Petchesky, Abortion and Woman's Choice 109, 133, n. 7 (rev. ed. 1990). The Constitution serves human values, and while the effect of reliance on *Roe* cannot be exactly measured, neither can the certain cost of overruling *Roe* for people who have ordered their thinking and living around that case be dismissed.

3

No evolution of legal principle has left *Roe*'s doctrinal footings weaker than they were in 1973. No development of constitutional law since the case was decided has implicitly or explicitly left *Roe* behind as a mere survivor of obsolete constitutional thinking.

It will be recognized, of course, that *Roe* stands at an intersection of two lines of decisions, but in whichever doctrinal category one reads the case, the result for present purposes will be the same. The *Roe* Court itself placed its holding in the succession of cases most prominently exemplified by *Griswold v. Connecticut*, 381 U.S. 479 (1965), see *Roe*, 410 U.S., at 152–153. When it is so seen, *Roe* is clearly in no jeopardy, since subsequent constitutional developments have neither disturbed, nor do they threaten to diminish, the scope of recognized protection accorded to the liberty relating to intimate relationships, the family, and decisions about whether or not to beget or bear a child. See, e.g., *Carey v. Population Services International*, 431 U.S. 678 (1977); *Moore v. East Cleveland*, 431 U.S. 678 (1977).

Roe, however, may be seen not only as an exemplar of *Griswold* liberty but as a rule (whether or not mistaken) of personal autonomy and bodily integrity, with doctrinal affinity to cases recognizing limits on governmental power to mandate medical treatment or to bar its rejection. If so, our cases since *Roe* accord with *Roe*'s view that a State's interest in the protection of life falls short of justifying any plenary override of individual liberty claims....

4

We have seen how time has overtaken some of *Roe*'s factual assumptions: advances in maternal health care allow for abortions safe to the mother later in pregnancy than was true in 1973, and advances in neonatal care have advanced viability to a point somewhat earlier. But these facts go only to the scheme of time limits on the realization of competing interests, and the divergences from the factual premises of 1973 have no bearing on the validity of *Roe*'s central holding, that viability marks the earliest point at which the State's interest in fetal life is constitutionally adequate to justify a legislative ban on nontherapeutic abortions. The soundness or unsoundness of that constitutional judgment in no sense turns on whether viability occurs at approximately 28 weeks, as was usual at the time of *Roe,* at 23 to 24 weeks, as it sometimes does today, or at some moment even slightly earlier in pregnancy, as it may if fetal respiratory capacity can somehow be enhanced in the future. Whenever it may occur, the attainment of viability may continue to serve as the critical fact, just as it has done since *Roe* was decided; which is to say that no change in *Roe's* factual underpinning has left its central holding obsolete, and none supports an argument for overruling it.

5

The sum of the precedential inquiry to this point shows *Roe's* underpinnings unweakened in any way affecting its central holding. While it has engendered disapproval, it has not been unworkable. An entire generation has come of age free to assume *Roe's* concept of liberty in defining the capacity of women to act in society, and to make reproductive decisions; no erosion of principle going to liberty or personal autonomy has left *Roe's* central holding a doctrinal remnant; *Roe* portends no developments at odds with other precedent for the analysis of personal liberty; and no changes of fact have rendered viability more or less appropriate as the point at which the balance of interests tips. Within the bounds of normal *stare decisis* analysis, then, and subject to the considerations on which it customarily turns, the stronger argument is for affirming *Roe's* central holding, with whatever degree of personal reluctance any of us may have, not for overruling it....

Our analysis would not be complete... without explaining why overruling *Roe's* central holding would not only reach an unjustifiable result under principles of *stare decisis,* but would seriously weaken the Court's capacity to exercise the judicial power and to function as the Supreme Court of a Nation dedicated to the rule of law. To understand why this would be so it is necessary to understand the source of this Court's authority, the conditions necessary for its preservation, and its relationship to the country's understanding of itself as a constitutional Republic.

The root of American governmental power is revealed most clearly in the instance of the power conferred by the Constitution upon the Judiciary of the United States and specifically upon this Court. As Americans of each succeeding generation are rightly told, the Court cannot buy support for its decisions by spending money and, except to a minor degree, it cannot independently coerce obedience to its decrees. The Court's power lies, rather, in its legitimacy, a product of substance and perception that shows itself in the people's acceptance of the Judiciary as fit to determine what the Nation's law means and to declare what it demands.

The underlying substance of this legitimacy is of course the warrant for the Court's decisions in the Constitution and the lesser sources of legal principle on which the Court draws. That substance is expressed in the Court's opinions, and our contemporary understanding is such that a decision without principled justification would be no judicial act at all. But even when justification is furnished by apposite legal principle, something more is required. Because not every conscientious claim of principled justification will be accepted as such, the justification claimed must be beyond dispute. The Court must take care to speak and act in ways that allow people to accept its decisions on the terms the Court claims for them, as grounded truly in principle, not as compromises with social and political pressures having, as such, no bearing on the principled choices that the Court is obliged to make. Thus, the Court's legitimacy depends on making legally principled decisions under circumstances in which their principled character is sufficiently plausible to be accepted by the Nation.

The need for principled action to be perceived as such is implicated to some degree whenever this, or any other appellate court, overrules a prior case. This is not to say, of course, that this Court cannot give a perfectly satisfactory explanation in most cases. People understand that some of the Constitution's language is hard to fathom and that the Court's Justices are sometimes able to perceive significant facts or to understand principles of law that eluded their predecessors and that justify departures from existing decisions. However upsetting it may be to those most directly affected when one judicially derived rule replaces another, the country can accept some correction of error without necessarily questioning the legitimacy of the Court.

In two circumstances, however, the Court would almost certainly fail to receive the benefit of the doubt in overruling prior cases. There is, first, a point beyond which frequent overruling would overtax the country's belief in the Court's good faith. Despite the variety of reasons that may inform and justify a decision to overrule, we cannot forget that such a decision is usually perceived (and perceived correctly) as, at the least, a statement that a prior decision was wrong. There is a limit to the amount of error that can plausibly be imputed to prior courts. If that limit should be exceeded, disturbance of prior rulings would be taken as evidence that justifiable reexamination of principle had given way to drives for particular results in the short term. The legitimacy of the Court would fade with the frequency of its vacillation.

That first circumstance can be described as hypothetical; the second is to the point here and now. Where, in the performance of its judicial duties, the Court decides a case in such a way as to resolve the sort of intensely divisive controversy reflected in *Roe* and those rare, comparable cases, its decision has a dimension that the resolution of the normal case does not carry. It is the dimension present whenever the Court's interpretation of the Constitution calls the contending sides of a national controversy to end their national division by accepting a common mandate rooted in the Constitution.

The Court is not asked to do this very often, having thus addressed the Nation only twice in our lifetime, in the decisions of *Brown* and *Roe*. But when the Court does act in this way, its decision requires an equally rare precedential force to counter the inevitable efforts to overturn it and to thwart its implementation. Some of those efforts may be mere unprincipled emotional reactions; others may proceed from principles worthy of profound respect. But whatever the premises of opposition may be, only the most convincing justification under accepted standards of precedent could suffice to demonstrate that a later decision overruling the first was anything but a surrender to political pressure, and an unjustified repudiation of the principle on which the Court staked its authority in the first instance. So to overrule under fire in the absence of the most compelling reason to reexamine a watershed decision would subvert the Court's legitimacy beyond any serious question. . . .

The Court's duty in the present case is clear. In 1973, it confronted the already-divisive issue of governmental power to limit personal choice to undergo abortion, for which it provided a new resolution based on the due process guaranteed by the Fourteenth Amendment. Whether or not a new social consensus is developing on that issue, its divisiveness is no less today than in 1973, and pressure to overrule the decision, like pressure to retain it, has grown only more intense. A decision to overrule *Roe's* essential holding under the existing circumstances would address error, if error there was, at the cost of both profound and unnecessary damage to the Court's legitimacy, and to the Nation's commitment to the rule of law. It is therefore imperative to adhere to the essence of Roe's original decision, and we do so today.

IV

From what we have said so far it follows that it is a constitutional liberty of the woman to have some freedom to terminate her pregnancy. We conclude that the basic decision in *Roe* was based on a constitutional analysis which we cannot now repudiate. The woman's liberty is not so unlimited, however, that from the outset the State cannot show its concern for the life of the unborn, and at a later point in fetal development the State's interest in life has sufficient force so that the right of the woman to terminate the pregnancy can be restricted.

That brings us, of course, to the point where much criticism has been directed at *Roe*, a criticism that always inheres when the Court draws a specific rule from what in the Constitution is but a general standard. We conclude, however, that the urgent claims of the woman to retain the ultimate control over her destiny and her body, claims implicit in the meaning of liberty, require us to perform that function. Liberty must not be extinguished for want of a line that is clear. And it falls to us to give some real substance to the woman's liberty to determine whether to carry her pregnancy to full term.

We conclude the line should be drawn at viability, so that before that time the woman has a right to choose to terminate her pregnancy. We adhere to this principle for two reasons. First, as we have said, is the doctrine of *stare decisis*. Any judicial act of line-drawing may seem somewhat arbitrary, but *Roe* was a reasoned statement, elaborated with great care. We have twice reaffirmed it in the face of great opposition. See *Thornburgh v. American College of Obstetricians & Gynecologists*, 476 U.S., at 759; *Akron I*, 462 U.S., at 419–420. Although we must overrule those parts of *Thornburgh* and *Akron I* which, in our view, are inconsistent with *Roe's* statement that the State has a legitimate interest in promoting the life or potential life of the unborn, the central premise of those cases represents an unbroken commitment by this Court to the essential holding of Roe. It is that premise which we reaffirm today.

The second reason is that the concept of viability, as we noted in *Roe*, is the time at which there is a realistic possibility of maintaining and nourishing a life outside the womb, so that the independent existence of the second life can in reason and all fairness be the object of state protection that now overrides the rights of the woman. See *Roe v. Wade*, 410 U.S., at

163. Consistent with other constitutional norms, legislatures may draw lines which appear arbitrary without the necessity of offering a justification. But courts may not. We must justify the lines we draw. And there is no line other than viability which is more workable. To be sure, as we have said, there may be some medical developments that affect the precise point of viability, but this is an imprecision within tolerable limits given that the medical community and all those who must apply its discoveries will continue to explore the matter. The viability line also has, as a practical matter, an element of fairness. In some broad sense it might be said that a woman who fails to act before viability has consented to the State's intervention on behalf of the developing child.

The woman's right to terminate her pregnancy before viability is the most central principle of Roe v. Wade. It is a rule of law and a component of liberty we cannot renounce.

On the other side of the equation is the interest of the State in the protection of potential life. The Roe Court recognized the State's "important and legitimate interest in protecting the potentiality of human life." Roe, supra, at 162. The weight to be given this state interest, not the strength of the woman's interest, was the difficult question faced in Roe. We do not need to say whether each of us, had we been Members of the Court when the valuation of the State interest came before it as an original matter, would have concluded, as the Roe Court did, that its weight is insufficient to justify a ban on abortions prior to viability even when it is subject to certain exceptions. The matter is not before us in the first instance, and coming as it does after nearly 20 years of litigation in Roe's wake we are satisfied that the immediate question is not the soundness of Roe's resolution of the issue, but the precedential force that must be accorded to its holding. And we have concluded that the essential holding of Roe should be reaffirmed.

Yet it must be remembered that Roe v. Wade speaks with clarity in establishing not only the woman's liberty but also the State's "important and legitimate interest in potential life." Roe, supra, at 163. That portion of the decision in Roe has been given too little acknowledgement and implementation by the Court in its subsequent cases....

Roe established a trimester framework to govern abortion regulations. Under this elaborate but rigid construct, almost no regulation at all is permitted during the first trimester of pregnancy; regulations designed to protect the woman's health, but not to further the State's interest in potential life, are permitted during the second trimester; and during the third trimester, when the fetus is viable, prohibitions are permitted provided the life or health of the mother is not at stake. Roe v. Wade, supra, at 163–166. Most of our cases since Roe have involved the application of rules derived from the trimester framework.

The trimester framework no doubt was erected to ensure that the woman's right to choose not become so subordinate to the State's interest in promoting fetal life that her choice exists in theory but not in fact. We do not agree, however, that the trimester approach is necessary to accomplish this objective. A framework of this rigidity was unnecessary and in its later interpretation sometimes contradicted the State's permissible exercise of its powers.

Though the woman has a right to choose to terminate or continue her pregnancy before viability, it does not at all follow that the State is prohibited from taking steps to ensure that this choice is thoughtful and informed. Even in the earliest stages of pregnancy, the State may enact rules and regulations designed to encourage her to know that there are philosophic and social arguments of great weight that can be brought to bear in favor of continuing the pregnancy to full term and that there are procedures and institutions to allow adoption of unwanted children as well as a certain degree of state assistance if the mother chooses to raise the child herself. " '[T]he Constitution does not forbid a State or city, pursuant to democratic processes, from expressing a preference for normal childbirth.' " *Webster v. Reproductive Health Services*, 492 U.S., at 511 (opinion of the Court) (quoting *Poelker v. Doe*, 432 U.S. 519, 521 (1977)). It follows that States are free to enact laws to provide a reasonable framework for a woman to make a decision that has such profound and lasting meaning. This, too, we find consistent with *Roe*'s central premises, and indeed the inevitable consequence of our holding that the State has an interest in protecting the life of the unborn.

We reject the trimester framework, which we do not consider to be part of the essential holding of *Roe.* Measures aimed at ensuring that a woman's choice contemplates the consequences for the fetus do not necessarily interfere with the right recognized in *Roe*, although those measures have been found to be inconsistent with the rigid trimester framework announced in that case. A logical reading of the central holding in *Roe* itself, and a necessary reconciliation of the liberty of the woman and the interest of the State in promoting prenatal life, re-

quire, in our view, that we abandon the trimester framework as a rigid prohibition on all previability regulation aimed at the protection of fetal life. The trimester framework suffers from these basic flaws: in its formulation it misconceives the nature of the pregnant woman's interest; and in practice it undervalues the State's interest in potential life, as recognized in *Roe.*

As our jurisprudence relating to all liberties save perhaps abortion has recognized, not every law which makes a right more difficult to exercise is, *ipso facto*, an infringement of that right. An example clarifies the point. We have held that not every ballot access limitation amounts to an infringement of the right to vote. Rather, the States are granted substantial flexibility in establishing the framework within which voters choose the candidates for whom they wish to vote. *Anderson v. Celebrezze*, 460 U.S. 780, 788 (1983); *Norman v. Reed*, 502 U.S. ___ (1992).

The abortion right is similar. Numerous forms of state regulation might have the incidental effect of increasing the cost or decreasing the availability of medical care, whether for abortion or any other medical procedure. The fact that a law which serves a valid purpose, one not designed to strike at the right itself, has the incidental effect of making it more difficult or more expensive to procure an abortion cannot be enough to invalidate it. Only where state regulation imposes an undue burden on a woman's ability to make this decision does the power of the State reach into the heart of the liberty protected by the Due Process Clause. . . .

A finding of an undue burden is a shorthand for the conclusion that a state regulation has the purpose or effect of placing a substantial obstacle in the path of a woman seeking an abortion of a nonviable fetus. A statute with this purpose is invalid because the means chosen by the State to further the interest in potential life must be calculated to inform the woman's free choice, not hinder it. And a statute which, while furthering the interest in potential life or some other valid state interest, has the effect of placing a substantial obstacle in the path of a woman's choice cannot be considered a permissible means of serving its legitimate ends. To the extent that the opinions of the Court or of individual Justices use the undue burden standard in a manner that is inconsistent with this analysis, we set out what in our view should be the controlling standard.... Understood another way, we answer the question, left open in previous opinions discussing the undue burden formulation, whether a law designed to further the State's interest in fetal life which imposes an undue burden on the woman's decision before fetal viability could be constitutional. The answer is no.

Some guiding principles should emerge. What is at stake is the woman's right to make the ultimate decision, not a right to be insulated from all others in doing so. Regulations which do no more than create a structural mechanism by which the State, or the parent or guardian of a minor, may express profound respect for the life of the unborn are permitted, if they are not a substantial obstacle to the woman's exercise of the right to choose. Unless it has that effect on her right of choice, a state measure designed to persuade her to choose childbirth over abortion will be upheld if reasonably related to that goal. Regulations designed to foster the health of a woman seeking an abortion are valid if they do not constitute an undue burden.

Even when jurists reason from shared premises, some disagreement is inevitable. That is to be expected in the application of any legal standard which must accommodate life's complexity. We do not expect it to be otherwise with respect to the undue burden standard. We give this summary:

1. To protect the central right recognized by *Roe v. Wade* while at the same time accommodating the State's profound interest in potential life, we will employ the undue burden analysis as explained in this opinion. An undue burden exists, and therefore a provision of law is invalid, if its purpose or effect is to place a substantial obstacle in the path of a woman seeking an abortion before the fetus attains viability.

2. We reject the rigid trimester framework of *Roe v. Wade*. To promote the State's profound interest in potential life, throughout pregnancy the State may take measures to ensure that the woman's choice is informed, and measures designed to advance this interest will not be invalidated as long as their purpose is to persuade the woman to choose childbirth over abortion. These measures must not be an undue burden on the right.

3. As with any medical procedure, the State may enact regulations to further the health or safety of a woman seeking an abortion. Unnecessary health regulations that have the purpose or effect of presenting a substantial obstacle to a woman seeking an abortion impose an undue burden on the right.

4. Our adoption of the undue burden analysis does not disturb the central holding of *Roe v. Wade*, and we reaffirm that holding. Regardless of

whether exceptions are made for particular circumstances, a State may not prohibit any woman from making the ultimate decision to terminate her pregnancy before viability.

5. We also reaffirm *Roe's* holding that "subsequent to viability, the State in promoting its interest in the potentiality of human life may, if it chooses, regulate, and even proscribe, abortion except where it is necessary, in appropriate medical judgment, for the preservation of the life or health of the mother." *Roe v. Wade*, 410 U.S., at 164–165.

NO

William H. Rehnquist

DISSENTING OPINION OF
WILLIAM H. REHNQUIST

CHIEF JUSTICE REHNQUIST, with whom JUSTICE WHITE, JUSTICE
SCALIA, and JUSTICE THOMAS join, concurring in the judgment in part
and dissenting in part.

... We believe that *Roe* was wrongly decided, and that it can and should
be overruled consistently with our traditional approach to *stare decisis* in
constitutional cases. We would adopt the approach of the plurality in *Webster
v. Reproductive Health Services*, 492 U.S. 490 (1989), and uphold the challenged
provisions of the Pennsylvania statute in their entirety.

I

... In *Roe v. Wade*, the Court recognized a "guarantee of personal privacy"
which "is broad enough to encompass a woman's decision whether or not
to terminate her pregnancy." 410 U.S., at 152–153. We are now of the view
that, in terming this right fundamental, the Court in *Roe* read the earlier
opinions upon which it based its decision much too broadly. Unlike marriage,
procreation and contraception, abortion "involves the purposeful termination
of potential life." *Harris v. McRae*, 448 U.S. 297, 325 (1980). The abortion
decision must therefore "be recognized as *sui generis*, different in kind from
the others that the Court has protected under the rubric of personal or family
privacy and autonomy." *Thornburgh v. American College of Obstetricians and
Gynecologists, supra*, at 792 (White, J., dissenting). One cannot ignore the fact
that a woman is not isolated in her pregnancy, and that the decision to abort
necessarily involves the destruction of a fetus. *See Michael H. v. Gerald D.,
supra*, at 124, n. 4 (To look "at the act which is assertedly the subject of a
liberty interest in isolation from its effect upon other people [is] like inquiring
whether there is a liberty interest in firing a gun where the case at hand
happens to involve its discharge into another person's body").

Nor do the historical traditions of the American people support the view
that the right to terminate one's pregnancy is "fundamental." The common
law which we inherited from England made abortion after "quickening" an

From *Planned Parenthood of Southeastern Pennsylvania et al. v. Robert P. Casey et al.*, 60 L.W. 4795
(1992). Notes and some case citations omitted.

offense. At the time of the adoption of the Fourteenth Amendment, statutory prohibitions or restrictions on abortion were commonplace; in 1868, at least 28 of the then-37 States and 8 Territories had statutes banning or limiting abortion. J. Mohr, Abortion in America 200 (1978). By the turn of the century virtually every State had a law prohibiting or restricting abortion on its books. By the middle of the present century, a liberalization trend had set in. But 21 of the restrictive abortion laws in effect in 1868 were still in effect in 1973 when *Roe* was decided, and an overwhelming majority of the States prohibited abortion unless necessary to preserve the life or health of the mother. *Roe v. Wade*, 410 U.S., at 139–140; *id.*, at 176–177, n. 2 (Rehnquist, J., dissenting). On this record, it can scarcely be said that any deeply rooted tradition of relatively unrestricted abortion in our history supported the classification of the right to abortion as "fundamental" under the Due Process Clause of the Fourteenth Amendment.

We think, therefore, both in view of this history and of our decided cases dealing with substantive liberty under the Due Process Clause, that the Court was mistaken in *Roe* when it classified a woman's decision to terminate her pregnancy as a "fundamental right" that could be abridged only in a manner which withstood "strict scrutiny." In so concluding, we repeat the observation made in *Bowers v. Hardwick*, 478 U.S. 186 (1986):

> "Nor are we inclined to take a more expansive view of our authority to discover new fundamental rights imbedded in the Due Process Clause. The Court is most vulnerable and comes nearest to illegitimacy when it deals with judge-made constitutional law having little or no cog-

nizable roots in the language or design of the Constitution." *Id.*, at 194.

We believe that the sort of constitutionally imposed abortion code of the type illustrated by our decisions following Roe is inconsistent "with the notion of a Constitution cast in general terms, as ours is, and usually speaking in general principles, as ours does." *Webster v. Reproductive Health Services*, 492 U.S., at 518 (plurality opinion). The Court in *Roe* reached too far when it analogized the right to abort a fetus to the rights involved in *Pierce, Meyer, Loving,* and *Griswold,* and thereby deemed the right to abortion fundamental.

II

The joint opinion of Justices O'Connor, Kennedy, and Souter cannot bring itself to say that *Roe* was correct as an original matter, but the authors are of the view that "the immediate question is not the soundness of *Roe*'s resolution of the issue, but the precedential force that must be accorded to its holding." Instead of claiming that *Roe* was correct as a matter of original constitutional interpretation, the opinion therefore contains an elaborate discussion of *stare decisis*. This discussion of the principle of *stare decisis* appears to be almost entirely dicta, because the joint opinion does not apply that principle in dealing with Roe. *Roe* decided that a woman had a fundamental right to an abortion. The joint opinion rejects that view. *Roe* decided that abortion regulations were to be subjected to "strict scrutiny" and could be justified only in the light of "compelling state interests." The joint opinion rejects that view. *Roe* analyzed abortion regulation under a rigid trimester framework, a framework which has guided this Court's decisionmaking for 19 years. The joint opinion rejects that framework.... In our view, authentic principles of *stare decisis* do not require that any portion of the reasoning in *Roe* be kept intact. "*Stare decisis* is not... a universal, inexorable command," especially in cases involving the interpretation of the Federal Constitution. *Burnet v. Coronado Oil & Gas Co.*, 285 U.S. 393, 405 (1932) (Brandeis, J., dissenting). Erroneous decisions in such constitutional cases are uniquely durable, because correction through legislative action, save for constitutional amendment, is impossible. It is therefore our duty to reconsider constitutional interpretations that "depar[t] from a proper understanding" of the Constitution.... Our constitutional watch does not cease merely because we have spoken before on an issue; when it becomes clear that a prior constitutional interpretation is unsound we are obliged to reexamine the question.

The joint opinion discusses several *stare decisis* factors which, it asserts, point toward retaining a portion of *Roe*. Two of these factors are that the main "factual underpinning" of *Roe* has remained the same, and that its doctrinal foundation is no weaker now than it was in 1973. Of course, what might be called the basic facts which gave rise to *Roe* have remained the same—women become pregnant, there is a point somewhere, depending on medical technology, where a fetus becomes viable, and women give birth to children. But this is only to say that the same facts which gave rise to *Roe* will continue to give rise to similar cases. It is not a reason, in and of itself, why those cases must be decided in the same incorrect manner as was the first case to deal with the question. And surely there is no requirement, in considering whether to depart from *stare decisis* in a constitutional case, that a decision be more wrong now than it was at the time it was rendered. If that were true, the most outlandish constitutional decision could survive forever, based simply on the fact that it was no more outlandish later than it was when originally rendered.

Nor does the joint opinion faithfully follow this alleged requirement. The opinion frankly concludes that *Roe* and its progeny were wrong in failing to recognize that the State's interests in maternal health and in the protection of unborn human life exist throughout pregnancy. But there is no indication that these components of *Roe* are any more incorrect at this juncture than they were at its inception....

The joint opinion thus turns to what can only be described as an unconventional—and unconvincing—notion of reliance, a view based on the surmise that the availability of abortion since *Roe* has led to "two decades of economic and social developments" that would be undercut if the error of *Roe* were recognized. The joint opinion's assertion of this fact is undeveloped and totally conclusory. In fact, one can not be sure to what economic and social developments the opinion is referring. Surely it is dubious to suggest that women have reached their "places in society" in reliance upon *Roe*, rather than as a result of their determination to obtain higher education and compete with men in the job market, and of society's increasing recognition of their ability to fill positions that were previously thought to be reserved only for men.

In the end, having failed to put forth any evidence to prove any true reliance, the joint opinion's argument is based solely on generalized assertions about the national psyche, on a belief that the people of this country have grown accustomed to the *Roe* decision over the last 19 years and have "ordered their thinking and living around" it. As an initial matter, one might inquire how the joint opinion can view the "central holding" of *Roe* as so deeply rooted in our constitutional culture, when it so casually uproots and disposes of that same decision's trimester framework. Furthermore, at various points in the past, the same could have been said about this Court's erroneous decisions that the Constitution allowed "separate but equal" treatment of minorities, see *Plessy v. Ferguson*, 163 U.S. 537 (1896), or that "liberty" under the Due Process Clause protected "freedom of contract." See *Adkins v. Children's Hospital of D. C.*, 261 U.S. 525 (1923); *Lochner v. New York*, 198 U.S. 45 (1905). The "separate but equal" doctrine lasted 58 years after *Plessy*, and *Lochner*'s protection of contractual freedom lasted 32 years. However, the simple fact that a generation or more had grown used to these major decisions did not prevent the Court from correcting its errors in those cases, nor should it prevent us from correctly interpreting the Constitution here.

Apparently realizing that conventional *stare decisis* principles do not support its position, the joint opinion advances a belief that retaining a portion of *Roe* is necessary to protect the "legitimacy" of this Court. Because the Court must take care to render decisions "grounded truly in principle," and not simply as political and social compromises, the joint opinion properly declares it to be this Court's duty to ignore the public criticism and protest that may arise as a result of a decision. Few would quarrel with this statement, although it may be doubted that Members of this Court, holding their

tenure as they do during constitutional "good behavior," are at all likely to be intimidated by such public protests....

The joint opinion also agrees that the Court acted properly in rejecting the doctrine of "separate but equal" in *Brown*. In fact, the opinion lauds *Brown* in comparing it to *Roe*. This is strange, in that under the opinion's "legitimacy" principle the Court would seemingly have been forced to adhere to its erroneous decision in *Plessy* because of its "intensely divisive" character. To us, adherence to *Roe* today under the guise of "legitimacy" would seem to resemble more closely adherence to *Plessy* on the same ground. Fortunately, the Court did not choose that option in *Brown*, and instead frankly repudiated *Plessy*. The joint opinion concludes that such repudiation was justified only because of newly discovered evidence that segregation had the effect of treating one race as inferior to another. But it can hardly be argued that this was not urged upon those who decided *Plessy*, as Justice Harlan observed in his dissent that the law at issue "puts the brand of servitude and degradation upon a large class of our fellow-citizens, our equals before the law." *Plessy v. Ferguson*, 163 U.S., at 562 (Harlan, J., dissenting). It is clear that the same arguments made before the Court in *Brown* were made in *Plessy* as well. The Court in *Brown* simply recognized, as Justice Harlan had recognized beforehand, that the Fourteenth Amendment does not permit racial segregation. The rule of *Brown* is not tied to popular opinion about the evils of segregation; it is a judgment that the Equal Protection Clause does not permit racial segregation, no matter whether the public might come to believe that it is beneficial. On that ground it stands, and on that ground alone the Court was justified in properly concluding that the *Plessy* Court had erred....

There are other reasons why the joint opinion's discussion of legitimacy is unconvincing as well. In assuming that the Court is perceived as "surrender[ing] to political pressure" when it overrules a controversial decision, the joint opinion forgets that there are two sides to any controversy. The joint opinion asserts that, in order to protect its legitimacy, the Court must refrain from overruling a controversial decision lest it be viewed as favoring those who oppose the decision. But a decision to *adhere* to prior precedent is subject to the same criticism, for in such a case one can easily argue that the Court is responding to those who have demonstrated in favor of the original decision. The decision in *Roe* has engendered large demonstrations, including repeated marches on this Court and on Congress, both in opposition to and in support of that opinion. A decision either way on *Roe* can therefore be perceived as favoring one group or the other. But this perceived dilemma arises only if one assumes, as the joint opinion does, that the Court should make its decisions with a view toward speculative public perceptions. If one assumes instead, as the Court surely did in both *Brown* and *West Coast Hotel*, that the Court's legitimacy is enhanced by faithful interpretation of the Constitution irrespective of public opposition, such self-engendered difficulties may be put to one side.

Roe is not this Court's only decision to generate conflict. Our decisions in some recent capital cases, and in *Bowers v. Hardwick*, 478 U.S. 186 (1986), have also engendered demonstrations in opposition. The joint opinion's message to such protesters appears to be that they must cease their activities in order to serve their cause, because their protests will only cement in place a decision which by normal standards of *stare decisis* should be reconsidered. Nearly a century ago, Justice David J. Brewer of this Court, in an article discussing criticism of its decisions, observed that "many criticisms may be, like their authors, devoid of good taste, but better all sorts of criticism than no criticism at all." Justice Brewer on "The Nation's Anchor," 57 Albany L.J. 166, 169 (1898). This was good advice to the Court then, as it is today. Strong and often misguided criticism of a decision should not render the decision immune from reconsideration, lest a fetish for legitimacy penalize freedom of expression.

The end result of the joint opinion's paeans of praise for legitimacy is the enunciation of a brand new standard for evaluating state regulation of a woman's right to abortion—the "undue burden" standard. As indicated above, *Roe v. Wade* adopted a "fundamental right" standard under which state regulations could survive only if they met the requirement of "strict scrutiny." While we disagree with that standard, it at least had a recognized basis in constitutional law at the time *Roe* was decided. The same cannot be said for the "undue burden" standard, which is created largely out of whole cloth by the authors of the joint opinion. It is a standard which even today does not command the support of a majority of this Court. And it will not, we believe, result in the sort of "simple limitation," easily applied, which the joint opinion anticipates. In sum, it is a standard which is not built to last....

The sum of the joint opinion's labors in the name of *stare decisis* and "legitimacy" is this: *Roe v. Wade* stands as a sort of judicial Potemkin Village, which may be pointed out to passers by as a monument to the importance of adhering to precedent. But behind the facade, an entirely new method of analysis, without any roots in constitutional law, is imported to decide the constitutionality of state laws regulating abortion. Neither *stare decisis* nor "legitimacy" are truly served by such an effort....

III

E

Finally, petitioners challenge the medical emergency exception provided for by the Act. The existence of a medical emergency exempts compliance with the Act's informed consent, parental consent, and spousal notice requirements. See 18 Pa. Cons. Stat. sec. 3205(a), 3206(a), 3209(c) (1990). The Act defines a "medical emergency" as

> "[t]hat condition which, on the basis of the physician's good faith clinical judgment, so complicates the medical condition of a pregnant woman as to necessitate the immediate abortion of her pregnancy to avert her death or for which a delay will create serious risk of substantial and irreversible impairment of major bodily function." sec. 3203.

Petitioners argued before the District Court that the statutory definition was inadequate because it did not cover three serious conditions that pregnant women can suffer—preeclampsia, inevitable abortion, and prematurely ruptured membrane. The District Court agreed with petitioners that the medical emergency exception was inadequate, but the Court of Appeals reversed this holding. In construing the medical emer-

gency provision, the Court of Appeals first observed that all three conditions do indeed present the risk of serious injury or death when an abortion is not performed, and noted that the medical profession's uniformly prescribed treatment for each of the three conditions is an immediate abortion. See 947 F.2d, at 700–701. Finding that "[t]he Pennsylvania legislature did not choose the wording of its medical emergency exception in a vacuum," the court read the exception as intended "to assure that compliance with its abortion regulations would not in any way pose a significant threat to the life or health of a woman." *Id.*, at 701. It thus concluded that the exception encompassed each of the three dangerous conditions pointed to by petitioners.

We observe that Pennsylvania's present definition of medical emergency is almost an exact copy of that State's definition at the time of this Court's ruling in *Thornburgh*, one which the Court made reference to with apparent approval. 476 U.S., at 771 ("It is clear that the Pennsylvania Legislature knows how to provide a medical-emergency exception when it chooses to do so"). We find that the interpretation of the Court of Appeals in this case is eminently reasonable, and that the provision thus should be upheld. When a woman is faced with any condition that poses a "significant threat to [her] life or health," she is exempted from the Act's consent and notice requirements and may proceed immediately with her abortion.

IV

For the reasons stated, we therefore would hold that each of the challenged provisions of the Pennsylvania statute is consistent with the Constitution. It bears emphasis that our conclusion in this regard does not carry with it any necessary approval of these regulations. Our task is, as always, to decide only whether the challenged provisions of a law comport with the United States Constitution. If, as we believe, these do, their wisdom as a matter of public policy is for the people of Pennsylvania to decide.

POSTSCRIPT

Is Abortion Protected by the Constitution?

In spite of the majority's refusal to overturn *Roe*, the constitutional right is still not absolutely secure. This was, after all, a 5–4 decision. In 1993 Justice Harry A. Blackmun wrote, "I am 83 years old. I cannot remain on this Court forever, and when I do step down, the confirmation process for my successor well may focus on the issue before us today." In 1994 Justice Blackmun did step down and Justice Stephen Breyer was confirmed to take his place. Justice Breyer's confirmation hearings did not focus on abortion and were relatively free of conflict. Whether or not *Roe v. Wade* is overturned is, however, still only partly a matter of legal analysis. It is also a matter of politics, of personality, of values, and of judicial philosophy.

What would be the consequences of a decision overturning *Roe*? The current state of great controversy over abortion would certainly not decline. Quite the contrary. The reason for this is that reversing *Roe* would mean that each state could permit or restrict abortion as it wished. The main contention of the justices who wish to overturn *Roe* is not necessarily that abortion should be banned but that this decision should be left to the states, and that it is not a constitutional issue. Such a position means that the political process will have to deal with the issue more than it does now, which is not likely to defuse the issue.

Even without overturning *Roe*, conflict will continue. Courts will be faced with determining whether or not state regulations constitute an "undue burden." Congress will wrestle with federal legislation that would restrict state regulations, such as the Freedom of Choice Act. New technologies, such as RU-486, the so-called abortion pill, which is approved for use in Europe but not in the United States, will raise legal challenges as will groups, such as Operation Rescue, that employ methods that are at the boundary of permissible protests.

Recent writings about abortion include Dworkin, *Life's Dominion: An Argument About Abortion, Euthanasia, and Individual Freedom* (Alfred A. Knopf, 1993); Tribe, *Abortion: The Clash of Absolutes* (W. W. Norton, 1990); Note, "Judicial Restraint and the Non-Decision in *Webster v. Reproductive Health Services*," 13 *Harvard Journal of Law and Public Policy* 263 (1990); Novick, "Justice Holmes and *Roe v. Wade*," 25 *Trial* 58 (December 1989); and Symposium on Abortion, *University of Pennsylvania Law Review* (vol. 138, 1989). The story of the *Roe* case is recounted in Faux, *Roe v. Wade: The Untold Story of the Landmark Supreme Court Decision That Made Abortion Legal* (NAL, 1988).

ISSUE 7

Should Pornography Be Protected by the First Amendment?

YES: Sarah Evans Barker, from *American Booksellers Association, Inc. v. William H. Hudnut III*, U.S. Court of Appeals for the Seventh Circuit (1984)

NO: Andrea Dworkin, from *American Booksellers Association, Inc. v. William H. Hudnut III*, U.S. Court of Appeals for the Seventh Circuit (1984)

ISSUE SUMMARY

YES: Judge Sarah Evans Barker argues that the ordinances banning pornography as a violation of the civil rights of women are unconstitutional infringements on freedom of speech.

NO: Author Andrea Dworkin maintains that pornography should not be constitutionally protected because it is destructive, abusive, and detrimental to women, and it violates their civil rights.

In April 1984, the city of Indianapolis, urged on by an unusual alliance between feminists and the conservative right, passed an ordinance banning the distribution of pornography within the city limits. Several groups in Indianapolis went to court, arguing that the new law interfered with their rights of free speech and free press as guaranteed by the First Amendment. In November 1984, Judge Sarah Evans Barker of the Federal District Court ruled that the law was indeed a violation of the Constitution. Her decision was affirmed by the Court of Appeals, 771 F.2d 323 (1984), and sustained by the Supreme Court, 106 S. Ct. 1172 (1986). The following readings contain Barker's opinion and a brief filed by Andrea Dworkin in the Court of Appeals arguing that Barker was wrong in declaring the law unconstitutional.

From a legal point of view, what is perhaps most significant about the pornography litigation is that the courts refused to recognize another exception to the First Amendment. The First Amendment does not provide absolute protection to everything that is spoken or printed. The most common example of unprotected speech is obscenity. Obscene publications have been deemed to contribute so little to society that the courts have held the First Amendment to be essentially irrelevant to obscene publications. Similarly, "fighting words," in which someone advocates illegal acts "where such advocacy is directed to inciting or producing imminent lawless action and is likely to incite or produce such action," can sometimes be punished. In general, however, constitutional theory holds that the solution to speech that someone does not like is more speech. According to the Supreme Court,

a function of speech... is to invite dispute. It may indeed best serve its high purpose when it induces a condition of unrest, creates dissatisfaction with conditions as they are, or even stirs people to anger. Speech is often provocative and challenging. It may strike at prejudices and preconceptions and have profound unsettling effects.

The main issue, in obscenity cases that are brought to court, is whether or not the material meets the standards that have been developed to define obscenity. The conclusion that obscene expression is constitutionally unprotected was affirmed more than 30 years ago. The struggle for judges since then has been to construct a precise definition of obscenity so that judges, authors, and publishers will know when a publication is legally obscene and when it is not. This has been a mighty and not particularly successful struggle, and you will see mention in the following readings of the various definitions that have been tried and then abandoned by the Supreme Court.

The legal assault on pornography, in order for it to be successful, must not only define pornography in a clear manner but must also persuade the courts that pornography is so damaging and contributes so little to our society that nothing will be lost if it is suppressed. It would have been surprising if the antipornography movement had won a complete victory in its first lawsuit. What will be worth noting is whether or not other judges, even if they reject the approach used in Indianapolis, suggest that the sale and production of pornography might be restricted in some other way.

While the courts have generally resisted attempts to restrict offensive art and expression, political pressure to combat pornography has been increasing. In 1989 and 1990, there were frequent newsworthy attempts to suppress a wide variety of forms of expression, such as the exhibit of sexually explicit photographs by the late Robert Mapplethorpe and the records of the rap music group 2 Live Crew. Efforts were made to require special warning labels on record albums that contain explicit lyrics, to prosecute some television executives for transmitting allegedly obscene films by satellite to Alabama, and to impose restrictions on artists who receive grants from the National Endowment for the Arts. These examples suggest that courts will continue to be very busy trying to distinguish protected from unprotected forms of expression.

YES

Sarah Evans Barker

PORNOGRAPHY AND FIRST AMENDMENT RIGHTS

This case comes to the Court amidst heated public and private debate over the problems of pornography and sex discrimination in American society. In apparent response to the perceived urgency and seriousness of these issues, the Indianapolis City-County Council debated and enacted an ordinance with subsequent amendments which sought to deal with both of these conditions by limiting the availability in Indianapolis of materials which depict the sexually explicit subordination of women. The Council defined pornography as the graphic depiction of the sexually explicit subordination of women and then declared pornography a discriminatory practice. By way of outlawing this practice, it then forbade most of the specific acts necessary to produce, sell, or distribute such material.

It is difficult to quarrel either with the Council's underlying concern (that pornography and sex discrimination are harmful, offensive, and inimical to and inconsistent with enlightened approaches to equality) or with its premise that some legislative controls are in order. But beyond that, it is in fact outside the rightful purview of this Court to enter the public debate over whether and to what extent these conditions constitute a real social harm. It is also beyond the purview of the Court to substitute its judgment for that of the legislative body, either in defining the acceptable community standards in these areas or in imposing appropriate sanctions for behavior which violate those standards.

Thus, the Court's duty in this circumstance is a narrow one. That duty is to assess the constitutionality of the legislative enactment: to determine whether the Ordinance, however well-motivated or otherwise meritorious it may be, unconstitutionally diminishes, violates, or otherwise derrogates our fundamental freedoms as a people.

This litigation, therefore, requires the Court to weigh and resolve the conflict between the First Amendment guarantees of free speech, on the one hand, and the Fourteenth Amendment right to be free from sex-based discrimination, on the other hand. In addition, the Court must determine whether the

From U.S. Court of Appeals for the Seventh Circuit, *American Booksellers Association, Inc. v. William H. Hudnut III*, 598 F. Supp. 1316, 106 S. Ct. 1172 (1984).

Indianapolis enactment meets the due process requirements of the Fifth and Fourteenth Amendments.

The plaintiffs in this lawsuit request the Court "to preliminarily and permanently enjoin enforcement of, and to declare facially unconstitutional, void and of no effect, City County General Ordinances No. 24 and 35, 1984 (together hereinafter referred to as the "Ordinance"), on the grounds that it is unconstitutional under the United States Constitution."...

Plaintiffs have cited numerous reasons to support their claim for relief. They first contend that the Ordinance severely restricts the availability, display and distribution of constitutionally protected, non-obscene materials, in violation of the First and Fourteenth Amendments. More specifically, they claim that the regulatory restraints of the Ordinance are not limited merely to unprotected speech, such as obscenity. As a result, plaintiffs contend that they will be forced under the Ordinance to remove from availability in Indianapolis materials which are in fact protected by the First Amendment.

Plaintiffs also contend that in seeking to ban speech directed to the general public because it is highly offensive to many, the Ordinances violate established Supreme Court precedents which preclude the banning of speech simply because its contents may be socially or politically offensive to the majority....

The defendants admit in their answer that the scope of the Ordinance goes beyond regulating obscene materials. However, they assert, such action does not violate the Constitution. Defendants deny every other allegation that the plaintiffs' rights as guaranteed by the United States Constitution are violated by this Ordinance....

FIRST AMENDMENT REQUIREMENTS

This Ordinance cannot be analyzed adequately without first recognizing this: the drafters of the Ordinance have used what appears to be a legal term of art, "pornography," but have in fact given the term a specialized meaning which differs from the meanings ordinarily assigned to that word in both legal and common parlance. In Section 16–3(v) (page 6), the Ordinance states:

> "Pornography shall mean the sexually explicit subordination of women, graphically depicted, whether in pictures or in words, that includes one or more of the following ... "

There follows at that point a listing of five specific presentations of women in various settings which serve as examples of "pornography" and as such further define and describe that term under the Ordinance.

As is generally recognized, the word "pornography" is usually associated, and sometimes synonymous, with the word, "obscenity." "Obscenity" not only has its own separate and specialized meaning in the law, but in laymen's use also, and it is a much broader meaning than the definition given the word "pornography" in the Ordinance which is at issue at this action. There is thus a considerable risk of confusion in analyzing this ordinance unless care and precision are used in that process.

The constitutional analysis of this Ordinance requires a determination of several underlying issues: first, the Court must determine whether the Ordinance imposes restraints on speech or behavior (content versus conduct); if the Ordinance is found to regulate speech, the

Court must next determine whether the subject speech is protected or not protected under the First Amendment; if the speech which is regulated by this Ordinance is protected speech under the Constitution, the Court must then decide whether the regulation is constitutionally permissible as being based on a compelling state interest justifying the removal of such speech from First Amendment protections.

Do the Ordinances Regulate Speech or Behavior (Content or Conduct)?

It appears to be central to the defense of the Ordinance by defendants that the Court accept their premise that the City-County Council has not attempted to regulate speech, let alone protected speech. Defendants repeat throughout the briefs the incantation that their Ordinance regulates conduct, not speech. They contend (one senses with a certain sleight of hand) that the production, dissemination, and use of sexually explicit words and pictures *is* the actual subordination of women and not an expression of ideas deserving of First Amendment protection....

Defendants claim support for their theory by analogy, arguing that it is an accepted and established legal distinction that has allowed other courts to find that advocacy of a racially "separate but equal" doctrine in a civil rights context is protected speech under the First Amendment though "segregation" is not constitutionally protected behavior. Accordingly, defendants characterize their Ordinance here as a civil rights measure, through which they seek to prevent the distribution, sale, and exhibition of "pornography," as defined in the Ordinance, in order to regulate and control the underlying unacceptable conduct.

The content-versus-conduct approach espoused by defendants is not persuasive, however, and is contrary to accepted First Amendment principles. Accepting as true the City-County Council's finding that pornography conditions society to subordinate women, the means by which the Ordinance attempts to combat this sex discrimination is nonetheless through the regulation of speech.

For instance, the definition of pornography, the control of which is the whole thrust of the Ordinance, states that it is "the sexually explicit subordination of women, graphically *depicted,* whether in *pictures* or in *words,* that includes one or more of the following:" (emphasis supplied) and the following five descriptive subparagraphs begin with the words, "Women are *presented* ..." (emphasis supplied).

The unlawful acts and discriminatory practices under the Ordinance are set out in Section 16–3(g):

(4) Trafficking in pornography: the production, sale, exhibition, or distribution of pornography. [Subparagraphs omitted here]

(5) Coercion into pornographic performance: coercing, intimidating or fraudulently inducing any person... into performing for pornography.... [Subparagraphs omitted here]

(6) Forcing pornography on a person:...

(7) Assault or physical attack due to pornography: the assault, physical attack, or injury of any woman, man, child or transsexual in a way that is directly caused by specific pornography....

Section (7), *supra,* goes on to provide a cause of action in damages against the perpetrators, makers, distributors, sellers and exhibitors of pornography and injunctive relief against the further exhibition, distribution or sale of pornography.

In summary, therefore, the Ordinance establishes through the legislative findings that pornography causes a tendency to commit these various harmful acts, and outlaws the pornography (that is, the "depictions"), the activities involved in the production of pornography, and the behavior caused by or resulting from pornography.

Thus, though the purpose of the Ordinance is cast in civil rights terminology—"to prevent and prohibit all discriminatory practices of sexual subordination or inequality through pornography" (Section 16–1(b)(8))—it is clearly aimed at controlling the content of the speech and ideas which the City-County Council has found harmful and offensive. Those words and pictures which depict women in sexually subordinate roles are banned legislation. Despite defendants' attempt to redefine offensive speech as harmful action, the clear wording of the Ordinance discloses that they seek to control speech, and those restrictions must be analyzed in light of applicable constitutional requirements and standards.

Is the Speech Regulated by the Ordinance Protected or Unprotected Speech Under the First Amendment?

The First Amendment provides that government shall make no law abridging the freedom of speech. However, "the First and Fourteenth Amendments have never been thought to give absolute protection to every individual to speak whenever or wherever he pleases or to use any form of address in any circumstances that he chooses." *Cohen v. California*, 403 U.S. 15, 19, 91 S.Ct. 1780, 1785, 29 L.Ed.2d 284 (1971). Courts have recognized only a "relatively few categories of instances,"

id. at 19–20, 91 S.Ct. at 1785, where the government may regulate certain forms of individual expression. The traditional categories of speech subject to permissible government regulation include "the lewd and obscene, the profane, the libelous, and the insulting or 'fighting' words—those which by their very utterance inflict injury or tend to incite an immediate breach of the peace." *Chaplinsky v. State of New Hampshire*, 315 U.S. 568, 572, 62 S.Ct. 766, 769, 86 L.Ed. 1031 (1942). In addition, the Supreme Court has recently upheld legislation prohibiting the dissemination of material depicting children engaged in sexual conduct. *New York v. Ferber*, 458 U.S. 747, 102 S.Ct. 3348, 73 L.Ed.2d 1113 (1982).

Having found that the Ordinance at issue here seeks to regulate speech (and not conduct), the next question before the Court is whether the Ordinance, which seeks to restrict the distribution, sale, and exhibition of "pornography" as a form of sex discrimination against women, falls within one of the established categories of speech subject to permissible government regulation, that is, speech deemed to be unprotected by the First Amendment.

It is clear that this case does not present issues relating to profanity, libel, or "fighting words." In searching for an analytical "peg," the plaintiffs argue that the Ordinance most closely resembles obscenity, and is, therefore, subject to the requirements set forth in *Miller v. California*, 413 U.S. 15, 93 S.Ct. 2607, 37 L.Ed.2d 419 (1973).... But the defendants admit that the scope of the Ordinance is not limited to the regulation of legally obscene material as defined in *Miller*.... In fact, defendants concede that the "pornography" they seek to control goes beyond obscenity, as defined by the

Supreme Court and excepted from First Amendment protections. Accordingly, the parties agree that the materials encompassed in the restrictions set out in the Ordinance include to some extent what have traditionally been protected materials.

The test under *Miller* for determining whether material is legal obscenity is:

"(a) whether 'the average person, applying contemporary community standards would find that the work, taken as a whole, appeals to the prurient interest, ... ; (b) whether the work depicts or describes, in a patently offensive way a sexual conduct specifically defined by the applicable state law; and (c) whether the work, taken as a whole, lacks serious literary, artistic, political, or scientific value."...

It is obvious that this three-step test is not directly applicable to the present case, because, as has been noted, the Ordinance goes beyond legally obscene material in imposing its controls. The restrictions in the Indianapolis ordinance reach what has otherwise traditionally been regarded as protected speech under the *Miller* test. Beyond that, the Ordinance does not speak in terms of a "community standard" or attempt to restrict the dissemination of material that appeals to the "prurient interest." Nor has the Ordinance been drafted in a way to limit only distributions of "patently offensive" materials. Neither does it provide for the dissemination of works which, though "pornographic," may have "serious literary, artistic, political or scientific value." Finally, the Ordinance does not limit its reach to "hard core sexual conduct," though conceivably "hard core" materials may be included in its proscriptions.

Because the Ordinance spans so much more broadly in its regulatory scope than merely "hard core" obscenity by limiting the distribution of "pornography," the proscriptions in the Ordinance intrude with defendants' explicit approval into areas of otherwise protected speech. Under ordinary constitutional analysis, that would be sufficient grounds to overturn the Ordinance, but defendants argue that this case is not governed by any direct precedent, that it raises a new issue for the Court and even though the Ordinance regulates protected speech, it does so in a constitutionally permissible fashion.

Does Established First Amendment Law Permit the Regulation Provided for in the Ordinance of Otherwise Protected Speech?

In conceding that the scope of this Ordinance extends beyond constitutional limits, it becomes clear that what defendants actually seek by enacting this legislation is a newly-defined class of constitutionally unprotected speech, labeled "pornography" and characterized as sexually discriminatory.

Defendants vigorously argue that *Miller* is not the " 'constitutional divide' separating protected from unprotected expression in this area."... Defendants point to three cases which allegedly support their proposition that *Miller* is not the exclusive guideline for disposing of pornography/obscenity cases, and that the traditional obscenity test should not be applied in the present case. *See New York v. Ferber,* 458 U.S. 747, 102 S.Ct. 3348, 73 L.Ed.2d 1113 (1982); *FCC v. Pacifica Foundation,* 438 U.S. 726, 98 S.Ct. 3026, 57 L.Ed.2d 1073 (1978); *Young v. American Mini Theatres, Inc.,* 427 U.S. 50, 96 S.Ct. 2440, 49 L.Ed.2d 310 (1976).

Defendants first argue that the Court must use the same reasoning applied by the Supreme Court in *New York v. Ferber, supra,* which upheld a New York statute prohibiting persons from promoting child pornography by distributing material which depicted such activity, and carve out another similar exception to protected speech under the First Amendment.

Defendants can properly claim some support for their position in *Ferber.* There the Supreme Court allowed the states "greater leeway" in their regulation of pornographic depictions of children in light of the State's compelling interest in protecting children who, without such protections, are extraordinarily vulnerable to exploitation and harm. The Court stated in upholding the New York statute:

"The prevention of sexual exploitation and abuse of children constitutes a government objective of surpassing importance. The legislative findings accompanying passage of the New York laws reflect this concern...."

The Supreme Court continued in *Ferber* by noting that the *Miller* standard for legal obscenity does not satisfy the unique concerns and issues posed by child pornography where children are involved; it is irrelevant, for instance, that the materials sought to be regulated contain serious literary, artistic, political or scientific value. In finding that some speech, such as that represented in depictions of child pornography, is outside First Amendment protections, the *Ferber* court stated:

"When a definable class of material, such as that covered by § 263.15, bears so heavily and pervasively on the welfare of children engaged in its production, we think the balance of competing interests is clearly struck and that it is permissible to consider these materials as without the protection of the First Amendment."...

Defendants, in the case at bar, argue that the interests of protecting women from sex-based discrimination are analogous to and every bit as compelling and fundamental as those which the Supreme Court upheld in *Ferber* for the benefit of children. But *Ferber* appears clearly distinguishable from the instant case on both the facts and law.

As has already been shown, the rationale applied by the Supreme Court in *Ferber* appears intended to apply solely to child pornography cases. In *Ferber,* the court recognized "that a state's interest in 'safeguarding the physical and psychological well-being of a minor' is 'compelling.' *Globe Newspaper v. Superior Court,* 457 U.S. 596, 607, 102 S.Ct. 2613, 2621, 73 L.Ed.2d 248 (1982)." 102 S.Ct. at 3354. *See also, FCC v. Pacifica Foundation, supra; Prince v. Massachusetts,* 321 U.S. 158, 168, 64 S.Ct. 438, 443, 88 L.Ed. 645 (1944); *Ginsberg v. New York,* 390 U.S. 629, 88 S.Ct. 1274, 20 L.Ed.2d 195 (1968). Also, the obscenity standard in *Miller* is appropriately abandoned in child pornography cases because it "[does] not reflect the State's particular and more compelling interest in prosecuting those who promote the sexual exploitations of children." *Id.* Since a state's compelling interest in preventing child pornography outweighs an individual's First Amendment rights, the Supreme Court held that "the states are entitled to greater leeway in the regulation of pornographic depictions of children." *Id.* 102 S.Ct. at 3354.

In contrast, the case at bar presents issues more far reaching than those in *Ferber.* Here, the City-County Council found that the distribution, sale, and exhibition of words and pictures depicting the subordination of women is a form of sex discrimination and as such is appropriate for governmental regulation. The state has a well-recognized interest in preventing sex discrimination, and, defendants argue, it can regulate speech to accomplish that end.

But the First Amendment gives primacy to free speech and any other state interest (such as the interest of sex based equality under law) must be so compelling as to be fundamental; only then can it be deemed to outweigh the interest of free speech. This Court finds no legal authority or public policy argument which justifies so broad an incursion into First Amendment freedoms as to allow that which defendants attempt to advance here. *Ferber* does not open the door to allow the regulation contained in the Ordinance for the reason that adult women as a group do not, as a matter of public policy or applicable law, stand in need of the same type of protection which has long been afforded children. This is true even of women who are subject to the sort of inhuman treatment defendants have described and documented to the Court in support of this Ordinance. The Supreme Court's finding in *Ferber* of the uncontroverted state interest in "safeguarding the physical and psychological well being of a minor" and its resultant characterization of that interest as "compelling," 102 S.Ct. 3348, 3354, is an interest which inheres to children and is not an interest which is readily transferrable to adult women as a class. Adult women generally have the capacity to protect themselves from participating in and being personally victimized by pornography, which makes the State's interest in safeguarding the physical and psychological well-being of women by

prohibiting "the sexually explicit subordination of women, graphically depicted, whether in pictures or in words" not so compelling as to sacrifice the guarantees of the First Amendment. ...

The second case relied upon by defendants to support their contention that *Miller* is not controlling in the present case is *FCC v. Pacifica Foundation,* 438 U.S. 726, 98 S.Ct. 3026, 57 L.Ed.2d 1073 (1978). According to defendants, *Pacifica* exemplifies the Supreme Court's refusal to make obscenity the sole legal basis for regulating sexually explicit conduct.

In *Pacifica*, the Supreme Court was faced with the question of whether a broadcast of patently offensive words dealing with sex and excretion may be regulated on the basis of their content. 438 U.S. at 745, 98 S.Ct. at 3038. The Court held that this type of speech was not entitled to absolute constitutional protection in every context. *Id.* at 747, 98 S.Ct. at 3039. Since the context of the speech in *Pacifica* was broadcasting, it was determined only to be due "the most limited First Amendment protection." *Id.* at 748, 98 S.Ct. at 3040. The reason for such treatment was twofold:

> "First, the broadcast media have established a uniquely pervasive presence in all the lives of all Americans. Patently offensive, indecent material presented over the airwaves confronts the citizen, not only in public, but also in the privacy of the home, where the individual's right to be left alone plainly outweighs the First Amendment rights of an intruder. Second, broadcasting is uniquely accessible to children, even those too young to read..."

Although the defendants correctly point out that the Supreme Court did not use the traditional obscenity test in *Pacifica*, this Court is not persuaded that the rule enunciated there is applicable to the facts of the present case. The Ordinance does not attempt to regulate the airwaves; in terms of its restrictions, it is not even remotely concerned with the broadcast media. The reasons for the rule in *Pacifica*, that speech in certain contexts should be afforded minimal First Amendment protection, are not present here, since we are not dealing with a medium that "invades" the privacy of the home. In contrast, if an individual is offended by "pornography," as defined in the Ordinance, the logical thing to do is avoid it, an option frequently not available to the public with material disseminated through broadcasting.

In addition, the Ordinance is not written to protect children from the distribution of pornography, in contrast to the challenged FCC regulation in *Pacifica*. Therefore, the peculiar state interest in protecting the "well being of its youth," *id.* at 649, 98 S.Ct. at 3040 (quoting *Ginsberg v. New York*, 390 U.S. 629, 88 S.Ct. 1274, 20 L.Ed.2d 195 (1968)), does not underlie this Ordinance and cannot be called upon to justify a decision by this Court to uphold the Ordinance.

The third case cited by defendants in support of their proposition that the traditional obscenity standard in *Miller* should not be used to overrule the Ordinance is *Young v. American Mini Theatres, Inc.*, 427 U.S. 50, 96 S.Ct. 2440, 49 L.Ed.2d 310 (1976). In *Young* the Supreme Court upheld a city ordinance that restricted the location of movie theatres featuring erotic films. The Court, in a plurality opinion, stated that "[e]ven though the First Amendment protects communication in this area from total suppression, we hold that the State may legitimately use the content of these materials as the basis for placing them in a

different classification from other motion pictures." 427 U.S. at 71–72, 96 S.Ct. at 2452. The Court concluded that the city's interest in preserving the character of its neighborhoods justified the ordinance which required that adult theaters be separated, rather than concentrated, in the same areas as it is permissible for other theaters to do without limitation. *Id.* at 71, 96 S.Ct. at 2452–53.

Young is distinguishable from the present case because we are not here dealing with an attempt by the City-County Council to restrict the time, place, and manner in which "pornography" may be distributed. Instead, the Ordinance prohibits completely the sale, distribution, or exhibition of material depicting women in a sexually subordinate role, at all times, in all places and in every manner.

The Ordinance's attempt to regulate speech beyond one of the well-defined exceptions to protected speech under the First Amendment is not supported by other Supreme Court precedents. The Court must, therefore, examine the underlying premise of the Ordinance: that the State has so compelling an interest in regulating the sort of sex discrimination imposed and perpetuated through "pornography" that it warrants an exception to free speech.

Is Sex Discrimination a Compelling State Interest Justifying an Exception to First Amendment Protections?

It is significant to note that the premise of the Ordinance is the sociological harm, *i.e.*, the discrimination, which results from "pornography" to degrade women as a class. The Ordinance does not presume or require specifically defined, identifiable victims for most of its proscriptions. The Ordinance seeks to protect adult women, as a group, from the diminution of their legal and sociological status as women, that is, from the discriminatory stigma which befalls women as *women* as a result of "pornography." On page one of the introduction to defendants' *Amicus* Brief, counsel explicitly argues that the harm which underlies this legislation is the "harm to the treatment and *status* of women... on the basis of sex."...

This is a novel theory advanced by the defendants, an issue of first impression in the courts. If this Court were to accept defendants' argument—that the State's interest in protecting women from the humiliation and degradation which comes from being depicted in a sexually subordinate context is so compelling as to warrant the regulation of otherwise free speech to accomplish that end—one wonders what would prevent the City-County Council (or any other legislative body) from enacting protections for other equally compelling claims against exploitation and discrimination as are presented here. Legislative bodies, finding support, here, could also enact legislation prohibiting other unfair expression—the publication and distribution of racist material, for instance, on the grounds that it causes racial discrimination,[1] or legislation prohibiting ethnic or religious slurs on the grounds that they cause discrimination against particular ethnic or religious groups, or legislation barring literary depictions which are uncomplimentary or oppressive to handicapped persons on the grounds that they cause discrimination against that group of people, and so on. If this Court were to extend to this case the rationale in *Ferber* to uphold the Amendment, it would signal so great a potential encroachment upon First Amendment freedoms that the precious liberties reposed within those

guarantees would not survive. The compelling state interest, which defendants claim gives constitutional life to their Ordinance, though important and valid as that interest may be in other contexts, is not so fundamental an interest as to warrant a broad intrusion into otherwise free expression.

Defendants contend that pornography is not deserving of constitutional protection because its harms victimize all women. It is argued that "pornography" not only negatively effects [sic] women who risk and suffer the direct abuse of its production,[2] but also, those on whom violent pornography is forced through such acts as compelled performances of "dangerous acts such as being hoisted upside down by ropes, bound by ropes and chains, hung from trees and scaffolds or having sex with animals...." Defendants' Memorandum In Support To Plaintiffs' Motion For Summary Judgment, pp. 3–4. It is also alleged that exposure to pornography produces a negative impact on its viewers, causing in them an increased willingness to aggress toward women, *ibid.* at p. 4, and experience self-generated rape fantasies, increases in sexual arousal and a rise in the self-reported possibility of raping. *Ibid.* at p. 6. In addition, it causes discriminatory attitudes and behavior toward all women. *Ibid.*, at pp. 11–12. The City-County Council, after considering testimony and social research studies, enacted the Ordinance in order to "combat" pornography's "concrete and tangible harms to women." *Ibid.* at p. 13.

Defendants rely on *Paris Adult Theatre I v. Slaton*, 413 U.S. 49, 93 S.Ct. 2628, 37 L.Ed.2d 446 (1973), to justify their regulation of "pornography." In that case the Supreme Court held "that there are legitimate state interests at stake in stemming the tide of commercialized obscenity... [which] include the interest of the public in the quality of life and the total community environment, the tone of commerce in the great city centers, and, possibly, the public safety itself." 413 U.S. at 57–58, 93 S.Ct. at 2635.

The Georgia Legislature had determined that in that case exposure to obscene material adversely affected men and women, that is to say, society as a whole. Although the petitioners argued in that case that there was no scientific data to conclusively prove that proposition, the Court said, "[i]t is not for us to resolve empirical uncertainties underlying state legislation, save in the exceptional case where that legislation plainly impinges upon rights protected by the constitution itself." *Id.* at 60, 93 S.Ct. at 2636–37 (footnote omitted).

In *Slaton*, the Georgia Legislature sought to regulate "obscenity," an accepted area of unprotected speech. *See Miller v. California*, 413 U.S. 15, 93 S.Ct. 2607, 37 L.Ed.2d 419 (1973). The Court specifically found that "nothing precludes the State of Georgia from the regulation of the allegedly obscene material exhibited in *Paris Adult Theatre I or II*, provided that the applicable Georgia law, as written or authoritatively interpreted by the Georgia courts, meets the First Amendment standards set forth in *Miller v. California*..." 413 U.S. at 69, 93 S.Ct. at 2642 (citations omitted).

Based on this reasoning, defendants argue that there is more than enough "empirical" evidence in the case at bar to support the City-County Council's conclusion that "pornography" harms women in the same way obscenity harms people, and, therefore, this Court should not question the legislative finding. As has already been acknowledged, it is not the Court's function to question the City-County Council's legislative finding. The Court's solitary duty is to ensure that the Ordinance accomplishes its purpose without violating constitutional standards or impinging upon constitutionally protected rights. In applying those tests, the Court finds that the Ordinance cannot withstand constitutional scrutiny.

It has already been noted that the Ordinance does not purport to regulate legal obscenity, as defined in *Miller.* Thus, although the City-County Council determined that "pornography" harms women, this Court must and does declare the Ordinance invalid without being bound by the legislative findings because "pornography," as defined and regulated in the Ordinance, is constitutionally protected speech under the First Amendment and such an exception to the First Amendment protections is constitutionally unwarranted.[3] This Court cannot legitimately embark on judicial policymaking, carving out a new exception to the First Amendment simply to uphold the Ordinance, even when there may be many good reasons to support legislative action. To permit every interest group, especially those who claim to be victimized by unfair expression, their own legislative exceptions to the First Amendment so long as they succeed in obtaining a majority of legislative votes in their favor demonstrates the potentially predatory nature of what defendants seek through this Ordinance and defend in this lawsuit.

It ought to be remembered by defendants and all others who would support such a legislative initiative that, in terms of altering sociological patterns, much as alteration may be necessary and desirable, free speech, rather than being the enemy, is a long-tested and worthy ally. To deny free speech in order to engineer social change in the name of accomplishing a greater good for one sector of our society erodes the freedoms of all and, as such, threatens tyranny and injustice for those subjected to the rule of such laws. The First Amendment protections presuppose the evil of such tyranny and prevent a finding by this Court upholding the Ordinance. . . .

SUMMARY

For the foregoing reasons, the Court finds that the Ordinance regulates speech protected by the First Amendment and is, therefore, in violation of the United States Constitution. The Ordinance's proscriptions are not limited to categories of speech, such as obscenity or child pornography, which have been excepted from First Amendment protections and permit some governmental regulation. The City-County Council, in defining and outlawing "pornography" as the graphically depicted subordination of women, which it then characterizes as sex discrimination, has sought to regulate expression, that is, to suppress speech. And although the State has a recognized interest in prohibiting sex discrimination, that interest does not outweigh the constitutionally protected interest of free speech. For these reasons the Ordinance does not withstand this constitutional challenge.

NOTES

1. In *Beauharnais v. Illinois*, 343 U.S. 250, 72 S.Ct. 725, 96 L.Ed. 919 (1952), the Supreme Court upheld an Illinois libel statute prohibiting the dissemination of materials promoting racial or religious hatred and which tended to produce a breach of the peace and riots. It has been recognized that "the rationale of that decision turns quite plainly on the strong tendency of the prohibited utterances to cause violence and disorder." *Collin v. Smith*, 578 F.2d 1197, 1204 (7th Cir. 1978). The Supreme Court has recognized breach of the peace as the traditional justification for upholding a criminal libel statute. *Beauharnais*, 343 U.S. at 254, 72 S.Ct. at 729. Therefore, a law preventing the distribution of material that causes racial discrimination, an attitude, would be upheld under this analysis. Further, the underlying reasoning of the *Beauharnais* opinion, that the punishment of libel raises no constitutional problems, has been questioned in many recent cases. *See Collin, supra,* 578 F.2d at 1205, and cases cited therein.

2. The defendants point to social research data, as well as graphic personal accounts of individuals, in support of their position that "women are recruited into all forms of sexual exploitation through physical force, psychological coercion, drugs and economic exigencies." Defendants' Memorandum In Support To Plaintiffs' Motion For Summary Judgment, p. 2.

3. Defendants again rely on *Young v. American Mini Theatres, Inc.*, 427 U.S. 50, 96 S.Ct. 2440, 49 L.Ed.2d 310 (1976), contending that since the legislation in that case was upheld upon a single affidavit of a sociologist that the location of adult movie theatres had a disruptive impact on the community, the Ordinance should be upheld because there is more than enough data to demonstrate that pornography harms women. As discussed above in subpart B, however, the legislation in *Young* sought to regulate the place where pornography could be distributed, not to completely ban its distribution. Thus *Young* is not controlling.

NO

Andrea Dworkin

THE OPPRESSION OF PORNOGRAPHY

I am co-author with Catharine A. MacKinnon of the Indianapolis legislation defining pornography as a violation of women's civil rights; the author of *Pornography: Men Possessing Women* (1981), *Woman Hating* (1974), and many articles on pornography; a lecturer at universities on pornography; a speaker at rallies protesting pornography; and an organizer involved in demonstrating against pornography. I have spent the last thirteen years analyzing the impact of pornography on women's social status and the role of pornography in sexual abuse....

PORNOGRAPHY IS A CENTRAL ELEMENT
IN THE OPPRESSION OF WOMEN

Judge Barker says that pornography as defined in the Ordinance is constitutionally protected speech. This means that the abuse of women in pornography, the trafficking in women that constitutes the bulk of pornography, the coercion of women required to make pornography, the abuses of women inevitably resulting from pornography, and the inequality created by pornography all have constitutional protection. Women cannot function as citizens in this world of social and sexual predation.

The Ordinance characterizes pornography as "a discriminatory practice based on sex." Speech and action are meshed in this discrimination, which is a system of sexual exploitation constructed on sex-based powerlessness and which generates sex-based abuse. The presence of speech cannot be used to immunize discrimination and sexual abuse from legal remedy.

When pornography is photographic, it is indisputably action. It gets perceived as speech because the woman in the photograph is effectively rendered an object or commodity by the pornography; the perception of the photograph as speech in itself denies the human status of the woman in it. The so-called speech belongs to whomever took or sold the photograph—the pornographer—not to the woman used in it, to whom things were done as if she were an object or commodity, and who indeed continues to be sold as an object or commodity. The woman is excluded from recognizably human

From U.S. Court of Appeals for the Seventh Circuit, *American Booksellers Association, Inc. v. William H. Hudnut III*, 598 F. Supp. 1316, 106 S. Ct. 1172 (1984).

dialogue by the uses to which she is put. The courts reify this injustice when they take the photograph to be real speech and do not recognize the woman in it as a real person who, by virtue of being human, is necessarily being used in ways antagonistic to full human status. The court accepts the pornographers' misogyny as its own if it holds that the pornographers' exploitation of a woman's body is an appropriate use of her: that what she is entitled to as a human being is properly expressed in these uses to which she is put.

The actions immortalized in pornography are not ideas, thoughts, or fantasies. The vocabulary of "sexual fantasy," often applied to pornography as a genre, is in fact the language of prostitution, where the act that the man wants done and pays to get done is consistently referred to as his "fantasy," as if it never happens in the real world. He goes to a prostitute and pays her money so that she will do what he tells her to do, and it is this *act* that is called "fantasy."

Similarly, in pornography, *acts* done to or by women are called "speech," even though the woman is doing an act dictated by what is required to sexually gratify men. Her body is a commodity in itself. Her body is also the literal language of the so-called publisher, who in reality is a pimp trafficking in women. Because the pimp introduces a camera into the trafficking, his whole process of exploiting the woman's body is protected as "speech."

The First Amendment predated the invention of the camera. The founding fathers could never have considered that there might be physical rights of people trampled on by rights of speech: that in protecting a photograph, for instance, one might be protecting an actual act of torture. In pornography, photographs are made with real women. These photographs are then used on real women, to get them to do the acts the real women in the photographs are doing.

The hostility and discrimination produced by written pornography is just as real. In written pornography, the vocabularies of sex and violence are inextricably combined, so that erection and orgasm are produced as pleasurable responses to sexual abuse. This behaviorally conditions men to sex as dominance over and violence against women. The nature of written pornography is definable and distinct enough from all other written material that it can be isolated as well as recognized. Sexually explicit and abusive male dominance, conveyed in repeated acts of rape, torture, and humiliation, is the entire substance of written pornography. *See* Smith, *The Social Content of Pornography*, 26 J. Communication 16 (1976). It is impossible, however, to separate the effects of written pornography from the effects of photographic pornography.

Obscenity law recognizes the incredible physical impact of this kind of sexually explicit material, written and photographic, on men—an impact so different from the impact of any known form of "speech" that the Supreme Court has repeatedly held that obscenity is not speech, even though it is words and pictures. *See,* e.g., *Roth v. United States*, 354 U.S. 476, 485 (1957). The standard of "prurient interest" suggests the kind of line that the Court wants to draw between "speech" and "not speech" even with regard to words and pictures. "Prurient" means "itch" or "itching"; it is derived from the Sanscrit "he burns." If he itches, let alone burns, the power and urgency of his response is not socially innocuous. Pornography creates the physiologically real conviction in men that women want abuse; that women are whores by nature; that women want to be raped and humiliated; that women get sexual pleasure from pain; even that women get sexual pleasure from being maimed or killed.... Obscenity law is premised on the inevitability of male sexual response to sexually explicit verbal and visual stimuli; it occurs in a world of concrete male dominance, obscenity law itself originating in a context of legalized male ownership of women.

Judicial decisions reflect and perpetuate the focus on male response, by wholly ignoring women, both in and outside the pornography. The statutory definition of pornography in the Ordinance articulates for the first time in the law how pornography both uses and impacts on women in particular, which is what distinguishes it as a uniquely destructive phenomenon. Pornography is appropriately recognized as an energetic agent of male domination over women. Pornography creates a devastating relationship between the status of some women, who are particularly powerless and vulnerable to abuse, and the status of all women. The vicious exploitation through sex of some women in pornography as entertainment establishes a sexual imperative in which forcing sex on any woman is justified. The bad treatment of some women in pornography justifies the second-class status of all women in society, because the bad treatment is presented as an appropriate response to the human worthlessness of women as such. Only *some* Christians had to be slaughtered as public entertainment in Roman circuses for all Christians and all Romans to understand who could be hurt, harassed, and persecuted with *de facto* impunity.

Pornographers draw on and benefit from particularly cruel aspects of women's vulnerability. Incest and child sexual abuse produce between two-thirds and three-quarters of the women who get exploited in pornography. *See* James and Heyerding, *Early Sexual Experiences and Prostitution*, 134 Am. J. Psychiatry 1381 (1977); Silbert and Pines, *Pornography and Sexual Abuse of Women*, 10 Sex Roles 857 (1984); Senate Committee on the Judiciary, Subcommittee on Juvenile Justice, *A Hearing to Consider the Effects of Pornography on Children and Women* (Aug. 8, 1984) (testimony of Katherine Brady). The ownership of a girl by her father or other adult male, including sexual ownership of her, is deeply implicated in the continuing vulnerability of adult women to the sexual abuse of pornography. It is not possible to draw a firm line between the uses of children in pornography, recognized in *New York v. Ferber*, 458 U.S. 747 (1982), and the uses of women in pornography, since so many of the women are habituated to sexual abuse, even first used in pornography, as children. The court must not accept the pornographers' propaganda, which insists that these women have made a career choice as free and equal adults for pornographic exploitation. The ownership of women and children by adult men is historically linked (for example, in the power of the Roman *paterfamilias*); and it is empirically and sociologically linked in the abuse of women and children in pornography.

Pornography is deeply implicated in rape, *see* Minneapolis Hearings, Sess. III (Dec. 13, 1983) at 11 (testimony of Bill Neiman), 14 (testimony of Susan Graack), 18 *et seq.* (testimony of Carol LaFavor); in battery, *see id.* at 21 (testimony of Wanda Richardson), 27 *et seq.* (testimony of Donna Dunn); in incest, *see id.* at 69 *et seq.* (testimony of Charlotte Castle); in forced prostitution, *see id.* at 75 *es seq.* (testimony of Sue Santa). Pornography is also a consistent phenomenon in the lives of serial killers. *See* S. Michaud and J. Aynesworth, *The Only Living Witness* 104, 105, 115, 118, 130 (1983) (Ted Bundy); T. Schwarz, *The Hillside Strangler* 152–153 (1982); T. Sullivan and P. Maiken, *Killer Clown: The John Wayne Gacy Murders* 28, 29, 218, 223; P. Johnson, *On Iniquity* 39, 52, 80, 81 (1967) (Moors murders); E. Williams, *Beyond Belief* 135, 143, 148–156 (1968) (Moors murders); G. Burn, '... *somebody's husband, somebody's son': The Story of Peter Sutcliffe* 113–116, 123 (1984) (Yorkshire Ripper).

Pornography presents the rape and torture of women as entertainment. This is surely the nadir of social worthlessness.

PORNOGRAPHERS' RIGHTS OF EXPRESSION ARE OUTWEIGHED BY WOMEN'S RIGHTS TO EQUALITY

The Expression of Ideas Through Injurious Acts Is Not Constitutionally Protected

It is wrong to say, as Judge Barker did, that pornography as defined in the Ordinance expresses ideas and is therefore protected speech, unless one is prepared to say that murder or rape or torture with an ideology behind it also expresses ideas and might well be protected on that account. Most acts express ideas. Most systems of exploitation or inequality express ideas. Segregation expressed an idea more eloquently than any book about the inferiority of black people ever did. Yet the Supreme Court overturned segregation—after protecting it for a very long time—because the Court

finally grasped its harm to people. The difference between the Court's view in *Plessy v. Ferguson,* 163 U.S. 537, 551 (1896), that segregation harmed blacks "solely because the colored race chooses to put that construction upon it," and its view in *Brown v. Bd. of Education of Topeka,* 347 U.S. 483, 494 (1954) that segregation "generates a feeling of inferiority as to their status in the community that may affect their hearts and minds in a way unlikely ever to be undone," is dramatic and instructive. The fact that the idea segregation expressed would suffer because the idea required the practice for much of its persuasive power did not afford segregation constitutional protection: attempts to invoke First Amendment justifications have been thoroughly repudiated.... An effort to claim that segregation was protected as first amendment "speech" because it has a point of view and an ideology would be a transparent use of the First Amendment to shield a practice of inequality; and such a claim for pornography is similarly transparent. Exploitation cannot be protected because it expresses the idea that the people being exploited are inferior or worthless as human beings or deserve to be exploited. All exploitation fundamentally expresses precisely that idea.

The Sexual Exploitation of Women Perpetuated by Pornography Negates Women's Rights to Equality

In her decision, Judge Barker says that "[a]dult women generally have the capacity to protect themselves from participating in and being personally victimized by pornography." The fault, she suggests, is with the individual who is hurt, and no legal remedy is justified. Adult men generally have the capacity to protect themselves from being murdered; yet murderers are not excused because they only succeed in murdering men who are dumb enough, weak enough, or provocative enough to get killed. Indeed, no one ever thinks of male victims of violence in those terms at all. Yet that valuation of women hurt by pornography is implicit in Judge Barker's misogynistic logic.

It is not true that women can protect ourselves from being victimized by pornography. Pornography's effect on our civil status—the way it creates attitudes and behaviors of discrimination against us—is beyond personal remedy. Pornography's role in generating sexual abuse is beyond our capacities as individuals to stop or moderate, especially with no legal recourse against its production, sale, exhibition, or distribution. Sexual abuse is endemic in this country. One-fifth to one-third of all women have an unwanted sexual encounter with an adult male as children; one woman in a hundred has had a sexual experience as a child with her father or step-father; it is estimated that 16,000 new cases of father-daughter incest are initiated each year. See J. Herman, Father-Daughter Incest 12–14 (1982). Studies and police and hospital records in different localities suggest that battery occurs in one-third to one-half of all marriages. See R. Langley and R. Levy, Wife Beating 4–11 (1977); D. Russell, Rape in Marriage 98–100 (1982). A documented forcible rape occurs every seven minutes; and rape remains one of the most under-reported violent crimes. See Federal Bureau of Investigation, Uniform Crime Reports for the United States at 5, 14 (1983). Studies continue to be done in all areas of sexual abuse, including sexual harassment, marital rape, and prostitution; and the figures showing frequency of abuse increase as the descriptions of violence become more precise and the political

efforts of feminists provide a context in which to comprehend the abuse.

The place of pornography in actually producing the scenarios and behaviors that constitute that mass of sexual abuse is increasingly documented, especially by victims. Coercion of women into pornography is expanding as the market for live women expands, especially in video pornography. Women in homes do not have the real social and economic power to keep men from using pornography on them or making them participate in it. There has been an increased use of cameras in actual rapes, with the subsequent appearance of the photographs on the commercial pornography market. Pornography itself is also being used as a form of sexual assault: the public violation of a woman—photographs made against her will or by fraud or without her knowledge, then published as public rape. Her forced exposure, like rape, is an act of hostility and humiliation. With the normalization of pornography, women who have pictures of themselves used against them as sexual abuse have no social or legal credibility to assert that rights of privacy were violated, because they appear indistinguishable from other women in similar photographs whose active compliance is presumed.

The statutory definition of pornography in the Ordinance, far from being "vague," delineates the structure of actual, concrete material produced and sold as pornography by the $8-billion-a-year pornography industry. See U.S. News and World Report, June 4, 1984, at 84–85. No adult bookstore has any problem knowing what to stock. No consumer has any problem knowing what to buy. No pornography theatre has any trouble knowing what to show. The so-called books are produced by formula, and they do not vary ever in their nature, content, or impact. They cannot be confused with the language of any writer I have ever read, including Jean Genet and Jerzy Kosinski, who are particularly graphic about rape and hate women. It may be difficult to believe that the definition is accurate and clear, because it may be difficult to believe that we are actually living in a country where the material described in the statutory definition is being produced, especially with live people. Nevertheless, we do. Or perhaps one effect of using $8 billion of pornography a year is that the basic premise of this law appears bizarre by contrast with the pornography: that women are human beings with rights of equality; and that being hurt by pornography violates those rights.

The Elimination of Sex Discrimination Is a Compelling State Interest That Is Furthered by the Ordinance

Sex discrimination keeps more than half the population from being able to enjoy the full benefits of free speech, because they are too poor to buy speech, too silenced through sexual abuse to articulate in a credible way their own experiences, too despised because of their sex to be able to achieve the public significance required to exercise speech in a technologically advanced society. The First Amendment protects speech already articulated and published from state interference. It does nothing to empower those who have been systematically excluded —especially on the bases of sex and race —from pragmatic access to the means of speech.

The First Amendment is nearly as old as this country. The eradication of sex discrimination is new as a compelling state interest, perhaps causing Judge Barker to underestimate its importance.

... Without vigorous action in behalf of equality, women will never be able to exercise the speech that the First Amendment would then protect.

State governments were not held to the proscriptions on government in the First Amendment until the Supreme Court held that the due process clause of the Fourteenth Amendment incorporated First Amendment standards. *See,* e.g., *Fiske v. Kansas,* 274 U.S. 380 (1927). Nevertheless, the simple reality is that the First Amendment and its values of free speech existed in harmony with both legal slavery and legal segregation. No effective legal challenge to those systems of racial subordination was mounted under the rubric of freedom of expression, even though in both systems reading and writing were at issue. In slavery, laws prohibited teaching slaves to read or write. *See* K. Stampp, *The Peculiar Institution* 208 (1956). In segregation, separate-but-equal education assured that blacks remained widely illiterate; then literacy tests were used to screen voters, so that blacks could not qualify to vote. *See Oregon v. Mitchell,* 400 U.S. 112, 132–33 (1970) (Black, J.); *Gaston County v. United States,* 395 U.S. 285 (1969). *Cf. Griggs v. Duke Power Company,* 401 U.S. 424, 430 (1971) (inferior segregated education hurts blacks where employer uses non-job-related educational criteria for employment decisions). Rights of speech, association, and religion (being kept out of certain churches, for instance, by state law), were simply denied blacks. The Civil War Amendments are an institutional acknowledgment that powerlessness is not cured simply by "more speech"; first amendment values alone could not fulfill constitutional ambitions for dignity and equity that reside in principles of justice not abrogated even by sadistic political institutions like slavery. The Fourteenth Amendment, however, purposefully used the word "male" in its guarantee of voting rights, U.S. Const. amend. XIV, §2, to rule out any possible application of equality rights to women's social and political condition. The right to vote, won in 1920, gave women the most mundane recognition of civil existence as citizens. U.S. Const., amend. XIX. The equality principles underlying the Fourteenth Amendment were even then not applied to women until 1971. *Reed v. Reed*, 404 U.S. 71 (1971).

The absolute, fixed, towering importance of the First Amendment and the absolute, fixed insignificance of sex discrimination and of equality of interests in Judge Barker's decision is a direct consequence of how late women came into this legal system as real citizens. Equality must be the legal priority for any group excluded from constitutional protections for so long and stigmatized as inferior. Yet the historical worthlessness of women—which is why our interests are not as old as this country—undermines any claim we make to having rights that must be taken as fundamental: equality for women is seen as trivial, faddish. The First Amendment, by contrast, is fundamental—a behemoth characterized by longevity, constancy, and familiarity. Because women have been silenced, and because women have been second-class, our equality claims are seen as intrinsically inferior. The opposite should be the case. Those whom the law has helped to keep out by enforcing conditions of inferiority, servitude, and debasement should, by virtue of that involuntary but intensely destructive exclusion, have the court's full attention when asserting any equality claim.

This must certainly be true when speech rights are asserted in behalf of pornographers, since the speech of the pornographers is exercised largely through sexual abuse and is intricately interwoven with physical assault and injury. The First Amendment here is clearly being used to shield those who are not only powerful but also cruel and cynical. The victims, targeted on the basis of sex, must ask for relief from systematic sexual predation through a recognition of equality rights, because only equality stands up against the injury of longstanding exclusion from constitutional protections. Judge Barker holds that only expression matters, even when the expression is trafficking in women; equality does not matter, and the systematic harms of inequality and abuse suffered by women on a massive scale do not matter. This view of the First Amendment relies on historical inequities to establish modern constitutional priorities.

The courts must, instead, give real weight to equality interests, because of their historical exclusion from the original Bill of Rights. The deformities of the social system caused by that exclusion destroy justice, which requires symmetry, equity, and balance. By refusing to give equality values any weight when in conflict with free speech values, Judge Barker allows speech to function as if it were a military arsenal: hoarded by men for over two centuries, it is now used to bludgeon women, who have been without it and have none in reserve; we do not even have slingshots against Goliath. If equality interests can never matter against first amendment challenges, then speech becomes a weapon used by the haves against the have-nots; and the First Amendment, not balanced against equality rights of the have-nots, becomes an intolerable instrument of dispossession, not a safeguard of human liberty.

The real exclusion of women from public discourse has allowed men to accumulate speech as a resource of power; and with that power, men have articulated values and furthered practices that have continued to debase women and to justify that debasement. The First Amendment, then, in reality, operates to the extreme detriment of those who do not have the power of socially and politically real speech. In this case, Judge Barker is saying that real people being tortured are properly not persons with rights of equality that are being violated; but, because a picture has been taken, are the abstract speech of those who exploit them. She is saying that the victim in the photograph is properly silent, even if gagged; that the victim's historical exclusion from speech need not, cannot, and should not be changed by vigorous legislative and judicial commitments to equality. She is saying that the woman's body is properly seen as the man's speech; and, in this corrupt logic, that the picture that in fact documents the abuse of a human being is to be dignified as an idea that warrants legal protection. Equality is indeed meaningless in this arrangement of power; and speech is a nightmare with a victim whose humanity is degraded by both the pornographers and the court.

The Pornographers Degrade the First Amendment

The pornographers also degrade the First Amendment by using it as a shield to protect sexual abuse and sexual trafficking. If the court allows these parasites an impenetrable shield of absolute protection because they use pictures and words as part of the sexual abuse they perpetrate and promote, there is really no end to the possible manipulations of the First Amendment to protect like forms of exploitation. All any exploiter has to do is to interject speech into any practice of exploitation, however malignant, and hide the whole practice behind the First Amendment. By isolating the speech elements in other practices of discrimination and asserting their absolute protection, the discrimination could be made to disappear. Consider, for example, a common situation in sexual harassment in employment, where a "speech" element —a sexual proposition from a supervisor —is part of a chain of events leading to an adverse employment consequence. *See*, e.g., *Tomkins v. Public Serv. Elec. & Gas Co.*, 568 F.2d 1044, 1045 (3d Cir. 1977), in which a conversation over lunch was a crucial component of the Title VII violation. No court has held that the mere presence of words in the process of discrimination turns the discrimination into protected activity. The speech is part of the discrimination. The Constitution places no value on discrimination. . . .

If the First Amendment is not to protect those who have power against the just claims of those who need equality; if pornography is sexual exploitation and produces sexual abuse and discrimination; then the Ordinance is more than justified. It saves our constitutional system from the indignity of protecting sex-based abuse. It exonerates principles of equity by allowing them vitality and potency. It shows that law can actively help the powerless and not be paralyzed by the cynical manipulations of sadists and profiteers. It is an appropriate and carefully balanced response to a social harm of staggering magnitude.

CONCLUSION

For the foregoing reasons, the judgment of the District Court should be reversed.

POSTSCRIPT

Should Pornography Be Protected by the First Amendment?

The antipornography forces have not been very successful in the courts, but they may have won at least one battle in the war. The pornography issue has attracted the attention of politicians, and attempts to regulate content seem destined to continue. It will be very interesting to follow the continuing clashes between First Amendment rights and those favoring restrictions on pornographic material to see whether or not the process of law will be influenced by the public debate.

It is also worth keeping in mind that the problem is no longer mainly one of books, magazines, and film. Pornography has always been one of the fastest growing segments of the videotape market. Should different standards apply to tapes? Should the fact that they can be viewed in the privacy of one's home make them less or more of a public concern? Congress and the Federal Communications Commission have attempted to establish penalties recently for both phone sex services and for "indecent" speech on radio and television. The ease of making and copying videotapes makes pornographic tapes a more difficult regulatory target. Even more challenging is the availability of pornographic material through computer networks. Such material may be located in a different country yet is instantaneously accessible using a computer. The relationship between obscenity, pornography, and new communications technologies is discussed in E. Katsh, *The Electronic Media and the Transformation of Law* (Oxford University Press, 1989). The Supreme Court addressed the phone sex issue in *Sable Communications of California, Inc. v. FCC*, 109 S. Ct. 2829 (1989).

The *Hudnut* case is discussed in Brest and Vandenberg, "Politics, Feminism, and the Constitution: The Anti-Pornography Movement in Minneapolis," 39 *Stanford Law Review* 607 (1987); Downs, *The New Politics of Pornography* (University of Chicago Press, 1989); and C. MacKinnon, *Feminism Unmodified: Discourses on Life and Law* (Harvard University Press, 1989). Recent writings on the problem of pornography include MacKinnon, *Only Words* (Harvard University Press, 1993); Lacombe, *Blue Politics: Pornography and the Law in the Age of Feminism* (University of Toronto Press, 1994); Sunstein, *Democracy and the Limits of Free Speech* (Free Press, 1993); Hunt, *The Invention of Pornography* (Zone Books, 1993); and Strossen, "A Feminist Critique of 'the' Feminist Critique of Pornography," 79 *Virginia Law Review* 1099 (1993). Child pornography was dealt with by the Supreme Court in *New York v. Ferber*, 458 U.S. 747. The most relevant obscenity case is *Miller v. California*, 413 U.S. 15 (1973).

ISSUE 8

Should Affirmative Action Policies Be Continued?

YES: William L. Taylor and Susan M. Liss, from "Affirmative Action in the 1990s: Staying the Course," *The Annals of the American Academy of Political and Social Science* (September 1992)

NO: Wm. Bradford Reynolds, from "Affirmative Action and Its Negative Repercussions," *The Annals of the American Academy of Political and Social Science* (September 1992)

ISSUE SUMMARY

YES: William Taylor, a lawyer specializing in civil rights, and Susan Liss, the deputy assistant attorney general of the U.S. Department of Justice, believe that affirmative action policies have been very effective in providing new opportunities for education and economic advancement.

NO: Wm. Bradford Reynolds, a senior litigation partner with a Washington, D.C., law firm, argues that any preference provided on the basis of race, gender, religion, or national origin is inconsistent with the goal and ideal of equality.

The most widely publicized Supreme Court case of the late 1970s was that of the *Regents of the University of California v. Allan Bakke* 438 US. 265 (1978). Bakke had been denied admission to the medical school of the University of California, Davis, even though he had ranked higher than some minority applicants who were admitted to the school. He sued, asserting that the affirmative action program, which reserved 16 of 100 places for minority students, discriminated against him because of his race and that "reverse discrimination" of this sort violated his constitutional right to equal protection of the laws.

In its decision, the Supreme Court held that Bakke should prevail and be admitted to the medical school. Rigid quotas, it ruled, were indeed prohibited by the Constitution. More importantly, however, the Court also indicated that affirmative action programs that did not impose quotas would be permissible. Thus, if the University of California had an admissions program that gave some preference to an ethnic or racial group and that took race or sex into account along with test scores, geographical origins, extracurricular activities, and so on, it would have been upheld. It is fair to say, therefore, that although Bakke won, the principle of affirmative action without rigid quotas also won.

The *Bakke* case, as often occurs with Supreme Court decisions, raised as many questions as it answered. *Bakke* inevitably led to cases involving the validity of affirmative action programs in a variety of contexts. In *United Steelworkers v. Weber*, 443 US. 193 (1979), the Steelworkers Union and the Kaiser Aluminum and Chemical Company negotiated a collective bargaining agreement that set aside 50 percent of trainee positions for blacks, until their low percentage (2 percent) among Kaiser craft employees rose to approximate their percentage (39 percent) in the local labor force. This case included a strict quota, but the Supreme Court upheld the program since it did not involve state action and was, according to Justice Lewis P. Powell, Jr., "adopted voluntarily" (even though it was begun in response to criticism by the Federal Office of Contract Compliance).

In 1989, in a case that did involve government, the Court ruled that a municipal public works program that allotted 30 percent of its funds for minority contractors was unconstitutional (*City of Richmond v. J. A. Croson Co.*, 109 S. Ct. 706, 1989). In the absence of some specific evidence of discrimination, such a program was held to violate the white contractors' rights to equal protection of the law. The case has been a major blow to local governmental efforts to increase minority involvement in construction, although similar programs mandated by Congress are still constitutional.

More is involved in these cases than the development of a consistent body of law, and more is involved than the determination of whether or not a particular individual should be employed or admitted to an academic institution. Affirmative action is an experiment that tests the power of the law. In his exceptional book about the 1954 school desegregation cases, *Simple Justice* (Alfred A. Knopf, 1976), Richard Kluger describes discussions that took place in 1929 about what strategies could be used to promote the legal rights of southern blacks. At that time, Roger Baldwin of the American Civil Liberties Union expressed some skepticism that the law could be used to this end "because forces that keep the Negro under subjection will find some way of accomplishing their purposes, law or no law." Such an attitude toward affirmative action programs and their real impact upon institutions might not be inappropriate today.

Affirmative action is legally required of public institutions and many private ones. Yet, it is not clear that the judges of the Supreme Court agree on standards governing affirmative action plans that differ from the ones already ruled upon.

Should the law permit otherwise equal applicants to be treated differently on the basis of sex, race, or ethnic background? The following readings come to different conclusions about the impact of and need for affirmative action programs.

YES

William L. Taylor and
Susan M. Liss

AFFIRMATIVE ACTION IN THE 1990s:
STAYING THE COURSE

The phrase "affirmative action," while capable of fairly narrow definition,[1] also serves as the line that divides people who have starkly different views on the nation's most enduring problem—how American society should treat people of color. On one side of that line are the messengers of the last 12 years who argue that discrimination is no longer to be viewed as a serious problem in this nation; what occurred in the past does not have any impact on the present. Their claim is that it is time to wipe the slate clean, to assume, in an extension of Lyndon Johnson's vivid imagery, that everyone who is now at the starting line is unburdened by any chains and has an equal chance. Government may have a continuing duty to see to it that no flagrant fouls are committed against minority competitors in the running of the race, but that is the limit of its responsibility.

On the other side of the line are those who believe that the vestiges of past discrimination are continuing barriers to the opportunities of the present generation of black people, that discrimination is still an active problem, and that substantial progress will not be made without affirmative government.

Defined in these terms, affirmative action is a touchstone for defining the role of government. Will government, acting affirmatively, extend a helping hand to those who need special assistance in order to achieve their potential, or will government, in the posture of neutrality, leave to the vagaries of the marketplace those who continue to be affected by the legacy of discrimination?

This article will assess the efficacy and fairness of affirmative action policies, review the legal standards that have guided our policymakers and courts in crafting affirmative remedies for discrimination, and conclude with a few observations about future directions for affirmative action policies.

THE LINK BETWEEN AFFIRMATIVE ACTION AND BLACK PROGRESS

A critical question about affirmative action policies is whether they have been effective, that is, whether they have worked in conjunction with other policies to provide opportunities for education and economic advancement that had previously been unavailable.

Affirmative Action Policies

Beginning with the passage of the Civil Rights Act of 1964, rules barring racial discrimination in the private sector began to be enforced, and affirmative remedies were developed to prevent or redress violations of the law. Particularly after the 1971 Supreme Court decision in *Griggs v. Duke Power*,[2] which prohibited practices that deny opportunities to minorities even when the practices are not intentionally discriminatory, courts finding the existence of pervasive patterns or practices of discrimination ordered strong affirmative remedies.[3]

Toward the end of the decade, the Supreme Court ratified lower-court interpretations of Title VII to permit employers and unions to enter into voluntary agreements that made conscious use of race to eliminate "old patterns of racial segregation and hierarchy."[4] . . .

Progress

As evidence that affirmative action policies have not been effective in addressing the needs of black Americans, critics of affirmative action like to point to the fact that in overall terms the economic progress of blacks relative to whites peaked in the early 1970s and since has stagnated or deteriorated. But no proponent of affirmative action has claimed that economic advancement for minorities can be divorced from the economic health of the nation. The issue is not whether affirmative action policies are sufficient conditions for progress but rather whether they are necessary and important conditions.

In fact, there have been a number of studies that demonstrate the effectiveness of affirmative action policies, particularly during the period of the 1970s when civil rights and affirmative action polices were being vigorously implemented.[5] Studies of the contract compliance program have indicated that companies subject to goals and timetable requirements had greater success during the 1970s in increasing minority employment in several job categories than did companies not subject to such requirements.[6] Other evidence can be gathered from examining changes in the employment patterns of companies subject to civil rights litigation. For example, studies of the huge Bell Telephone system conducted after the company entered into a Title VII consent decree in 1973 calling for the use of numerical goals and timetables showed that black workers had made substantial gains in entering managerial and skilled-craft positions.[7]

Similarly, the rapid growth in the enrollment and completion rates of black students in colleges and universities in the 1970s must be attributed in part to the application of affirmative action policies encouraging institutions of higher education to seek out minorities, as well as to the improved preparation of black students that came about through school desegregation and other improvements in educational opportunity.[8] In addition, affirmative action had an impact on the growth in minority business development that took place in skill-intensive areas of business services, finance, insurance, and real estate, areas outside the traditional realm of entrepreneurship.[9]

Mobility

Some critics of affirmative action argue that even if there are some benefits from the policy, those benefits flow largely to minorities who are already advantaged or middle class. Thus, they say, the policy is at best selective and at worse unneeded since middle-class people might advance without the aid of affirmative action.

This view is contradicted by studies showing, for example, that, of the increased enrollment of minority students in medical schools in the 1970s, significant numbers were from families of low income and job status, indicating that affirmative action policies have resulted in increased mobility, not simply in changing occupational preferences among middle-class minority families.[10] Moreover, many of the gains have come in occupations and trades not usually associated with advantaged status, such as law enforcement, fire fighting, and skilled construction work.[11]

For those seeking to achieve professional status, affirmative action has been applied at the gateway points, namely, at college and professional school admissions. Admissions policies designed to encourage minority participation in the professions may offer those who are otherwise qualified an equal chance at success in occupations with a more advantaged status. But affirmative action does not guarantee success for those who would not otherwise succeed as professionals; it merely provides the opportunity to compete.

Other critics of affirmative action have argued that there is a "creaming process" in which those most likely to seize the opportunities provided by affirmative action are apt to be the most motivated in the less advantaged group.[12] This may well be the case. Affirmative action is unlikely to be sufficient for those who are truly bereft of educational, social, and material resources. Other initiatives are called for to address the urgent needs of this group.

THE LEGAL STANDARDS GOVERNING AFFIRMATIVE ACTION

In assessing the legality of affirmative action under both the Constitution and statutes, the courts have struggled conscientiously to balance competing interests in order to meet a test of practical fairness to all parties. Cases such as *University of California Regents v. Bakke*, which invalidated an affirmative action plan for minority admissions to the medical school at the University of California,[13] and *United Steelworkers v. Weber*, which upheld a voluntary plan to remedy past discrimination in occupations traditionally closed to minorities,[14] reflect a pragmatic approach by the courts to the difficult legal and policy questions posed by affirmative action.

Using a pragmatic approach, the Supreme Court has ruled that black workers may be denied positions they would have held "but for" the discriminatory practices of an employer if awarding the positions would require the displacement of an incumbent white worker.[15] The test, as articulated in *Weber*, is whether race-conscious remedies "unnecessarily trammel the interest of the white employees." In employing this test, courts have drawn lines between actions that disappoint the expectations of whites and those that uproot them from a status that already has been vested.[16]

This practical approach to balancing competing rights may have been ushered out by a 1989 decision invalidating a minority business set-aside program adopted by the city of Richmond, *City of Richmond v. Croson*.[17] In that case, the Supreme Court, having grown more conservative and increasingly hostile to affirmative action as justices appointed by President Reagan joined the Court, applied new constitutional ground rules for state and local affirmative action programs, requiring that localities demonstrate an evidentiary predicate for affirmative action that may be nearly impossible for most state and local governments to meet.[18] During the term following the *Croson* decision, a majority of the Court in *Metro Broadcasting v. FCC*[19] rejected the applicability of the *Croson* standards to affirmative action programs mandated by Congress. Nevertheless, with the subsequent retirements of Justices Brennan and Marshall, the legal standards for assessing the validity of affirmative action are likely to be guided increasingly by ideology rather than the pragmatism of the last decade.

THE FUTURE OF AFFIRMATIVE ACTION

Affirmative action is under siege in the 1990s. The courts are no longer a friendly forum for deprived and powerless citizens who in the past were often able to find redress when it was denied in the more political arenas. The pragmatic efforts of the Supreme Court in *Bakke, Weber,* and other cases to strike a balance between the legitimate needs and expectations of white and minority workers may soon be replaced by an ideological commitment to color blindness, a cruel irony when it results in the courts' turning a blind eye to the legacy of past and continuing discrimination.

The situation also is bleak in the more explicitly political arenas. During the debate over the Civil Rights Act of 1991, the Bush administration found political gold in labeling civil rights requirements of the legislation as "quota" provisions, seeking in a flagging economy to channel the discontent of many white workers toward the scapegoating of minority workers and Democratic advocates of affirmative action. The administration was pulled back from the brink only through the efforts of moderate and conservative Republican senators concerned about the long-range consequences of their party's being seen as having made common cause with David Duke and his fellow racists. But the administration has not taken any pledge of moral sobriety, threatening even on the eve of the signing ceremony for the Civil Rights Act to dismantle long-standing federal affirmative action programs. The difficulties of defenders of affirmative action are compounded by the fact that their ability to persuade depends on reasoned explication, not easily reducible to the 30-second sound bites used effectively by their opponents.[20]

In these circumstances, some observers have suggested that goals and timetables and other effective affirmative action measures be abandoned in favor of other ameliorative approaches. Paul Starr has proposed, for example, that the response to a Supreme Court reversal of the *Weber* decision should not be a legislative struggle for restoration but a dual effort "toward the reconstruction of civil society in minority communities and toward the promotion of broad policies for economic opportunity and security that benefit low- and middle-income

Americans, black and white alike."[21] However well-intentioned the proposal to view civil rights and economic and social programs as alternatives may be, several questions need to be asked.

One is whether legislative efforts to secure such "economic opportunit[ies]" through greater public investments in education, job training, and national health and welfare reform have been stymied by continued adherence to affirmative action policies and whether affirmative action will be an impediment in the future. While there have been facile suggestions that this is the case, the evidence does not support it. Legislation to fully fund Head Start, to provide family and medical leave, and to accomplish other economic and social goals has been threatened by the same kinds of attitudinal barriers founded on race and class as undergird the resistance to affirmative action.

A second question is whether sufficient progress has been made in eliminating racial discrimination to warrant a conclusion that the forms of affirmative action that have occasioned the greatest controversy are no longer necessary. If indeed discrimination is a sporadic phenomenon that is no longer the norm, a case can be made for changing course. But here again, despite the progress that has been made, the evidence points in another direction. Studies by the Urban Institute of the treatment of black and white job seekers, by the Department of Housing and Urban Development of the treatment of black and white home seekers, by the Federal Reserve and several newspapers of the persistence of redlining by financial institutions all strongly suggest that discrimination remains a pervasive and institutional problem. Given these facts, individual lawsuits are simply inadequate;

the rationale for affirmative action policy —that it is necessary to counter the effects of past, as well as ongoing, discrimination —continues to have vitality.

Ultimately, the question is whether it is possible to develop effective measures to assure that all people will have the opportunity to develop to their full potential without confronting the nation's most entrenched social problem—racial oppression and inequality. Again, those who propose that racial issues be finessed have little evidence to suggest that such evasions will be productive.

Interestingly, the current debate over affirmative action is taking place at a time when the antigovernment binge of the Reagan era appears to be losing force. There appears to be a growing recognition that if the productivity of the private sector of the U.S. economy is to be restored, government must play an affirmative role in investing in human resources. That recognition, if coupled with a recommitment to the unredeemed national promise of racial justice, may yet yield tangible opportunity for all. Now is not the time to lose our nerve.

NOTES

1. One definition is that affirmative action encompasses "any measure, beyond simple termination of a discriminatory practice, adopted to correct or compensate for past or present discrimination or to prevent discrimination from recurring in the future." U.S., Commission on Civil Rights, *Statement on Affirmative Action*, Oct. 1977, p. 2.

2. 401 U.S. 424 (1971).

3. In particularly blatant cases of discrimination, courts restrained employers from hiring new white employees until proportionate numbers of qualified minority employees were hired. See, for example, *Boston Chapter, NAACP v. Beecher*, 504 F.2d 1017 (1st Cir. 1974), *cert. denied*, 421 U.S. 910 (1975).

4. *United Steelworkers of America v. Weber*, 443 U.S. 193 (1979).

5. See Gerald David Jaynes and Robin M. Williams, Jr., eds., *A Common Destiny: Blacks*

and *American Society* (Washington, DC: National Academy Press, 1989), pp. 269–329. See also *Affirmative Action to Open the Doors of Job Opportunity* (Washington, DC: Citizens' Commission on Civil Rights, 1984), 121–47.

6. See, for example, J. Leonard, *The Effectiveness of Equal Employment Law and Affirmative Action Regulation* (Berkeley: University of California, School of Business Administration, 1985).

7. See statement of economist Bernard Anderson in U.S., Congress, House, Committee on Education and Labor, Subcommittee on Employment Opportunities, *Oversight Hearings on Equal Employment Opportunity*, 97th Cong., 1st sess., 1981, pt. 1, pp. 219, 221. For a report on similar progress following a consent decree in the steel industry, see statement of Phyllis Wallace, in ibid., pp. 528–29.

8. See studies summarized in W. Taylor, *Brown, Equal Protection and the Isolation of the Poor, Yale Law Journal*, 95:1709-10 (1986).

9. See Jaynes and Williams, eds., *Common Destiny*, p. 314.

10. See M. Alexis, "The Effect of Admission Procedures on Minority Enrollment in Graduate and Professional Schools," in *Working Papers: Bakke, Weber and Affirmative Action* (New York: Rockefeller Foundation, 1979), pp. 52–71.

11. In law enforcement, the numbers of black police officers nearly doubled from 1970 to 1980. In Philadelphia, after the initiation of the goals and timetables program for federal contractors, the percentage of skilled minority construction workers rose from less than 1 percent to more than 12 percent of the total.

12. See William Julius Wilson, *The Truly Disadvantaged* (Chicago: University of Chicago Press, 1989), pp. 114–15.

13. 438 U.S. 265 (1978).

14. 443 U.S. 193 (1979).

15. See, for example, the statement of Justice White that even a person adversely affected by discrimination "is not automatically entitled to have a non-minority employee laid off to make room for him." *Firefighters Local Union No. 1784 v. Stotts,* 104 S.Ct. 2576, 2588 (1984). The Court in *Stotts* decided that the benefits of an affirmative action plan would have to be negated by laying off recently hired black firefighters rather than displacing more senior white workers.

16. See 443 U.S. at 208 (1979).

17. 488 U.S. 469 (1989).

18. For a comprehensive analysis of the Court's standards in the *Croson* case, see Michael Small, "The New Legal Regime: Affirmative Action after *Croson* and *Metro*," in *Lost Opportunities: The Civil Rights Record of the Bush Administration Mid-Term*, ed. S. M. Liss and W. L. Taylor (Washington, DC: Citizens' Commission on Civil Rights, 1991).

19. 110 S.Ct. 2997 (1990).

20. The problem may be illustrated by the television ad used by Senator Jesse Helms in his successful 1990 reelection campaign. The ad depicted a white worker denied a job because the employer used a quota system to hire black applicants. Of course, an alternative explanation in many situations is that the white applicant lacked the requisite qualifications. Indeed, critics of civil rights enforcement have charged that minority workers are being encouraged to think of themselves as victims rather than to examine the need to upgrade their skills and develop self-discipline. Yet, without any conscious irony, Senator Helms and other affirmative action bashers do precisely the same thing by encouraging whites to view themselves as victims. For understandable reasons, however, few politicians would seek to counter a Helms attack by suggesting that some white applicants may lack the qualifications.

21. Paul Starr, "Civil Reconstruction: What to Do without Affirmative Action," *American Prospect*, Winter 1992, p. 7.

NO
Wm. Bradford Reynolds

AFFIRMATIVE ACTION AND ITS NEGATIVE REPERCUSSIONS

The phrase "affirmative action" has been so much a part of civil rights policy over the past three decades that it rarely is defined or explained by those who use it. For the most part, the omission is calculated. Few dare to quarrel with a program offered to promote civil rights objectives and described simply as "affirmative action."

Yet it is just such programs that have energized much of the debate in the field of civil rights since the early 1960s. First introduced by President John F. Kennedy in Executive Order No. 10925,[1] "affirmative action" was originally defined in terms of active recruitment and outreach measures aimed at enhancing employment opportunities for all Americans. Its race-neutral character could not have been more clearly expressed: employers contracting with the federal government were directed to "take affirmative action to ensure that the applicants are employed, and that employees are treated during employment, without regard to race, creed, color or national origin."[2]

It should come as no surprise that in the early 1960s, measures devised to tear down racial barriers and affirmatively promote equal opportunity were required to be themselves indifferent to racial distinctions. Discrimination on account of skin color was, after all, the evil identified as constitutionally intolerable in the Supreme Court's landmark decision in *Brown v. Board of Education*.[3] "At stake," wrote Chief Justice Earl Warren for the full Court in *Brown II*, "is the personal interest of plaintiffs' admission to public schools... on a [racially] nondiscriminatory basis."[4] What the school children were seeking, their counsel Thurgood Marshall argued, was the assignment of students to the public schools "without regard to race or color."[5]

The Supreme Court's dramatic reversal of its half-century precedent of *Plessy v. Ferguson*[6] precipitated an outpouring of condemnation directed at all forms of racial segregation. During the next decade, the color line that had officially divided Americans came under stinging attack from all quarters. Racial distinctions, declared the High Court, were by their very nature "odious to a free people whose institutions are founded upon the doctrine of equality."[7]

From Wm. Bradford Reynolds, "Affirmative Action and Its Negative Repercussions," *The Annals of the American Academy of Political and Social Science* (September 1992). Copyright © 1992 by The American Academy of Political and Social Science. Reprinted by permission of Sage Publications, Inc.

Thus the visible barriers of everyday life that had for so long kept blacks out began to tumble, one by one. Water fountains, restrooms, hotels, restaurants, trolley cars, lunch counters, movie theaters, and department stores all were finally opened to blacks and whites alike throughout the 1960s and into the 1970s.

The congressional response to *Brown* was no less emphatic. With enactment of the Civil Rights Acts of 1957, 1960, and 1964,[8] the Voting Rights Act of 1965,[9] and the Fair Housing Act of 1968,[10] Congress demanded removal of the race factor in the work force, the classroom, places of public accommodation, the voting booth, and the housing market. The message was that public and private decision makers in the areas covered were to be wholly blind to color differences.

The legislative debates of that era underscored the wholesale nature of this neutrality mandate. Significantly, much of the discussion leading up to the 1964 act centered on the issue of preferential treatment, that is, whether the measure under consideration, while condemning racial discrimination, would countenance race-conscious hiring and promotion practices. Proponents of the bill's employment provisions—Title VII of the act—uniformly and unequivocally denied that the legislation should or could be so interpreted. Favoring black employees in the selection process would violate Title VII "just as much as a 'white only' employment policy," declared Senator Harrison Williams.[11] "How can the language of equality," he asked, "favor one race or one religion over another? Equality can have only one meaning, and that meaning is self-evident to reasonable men. Those who say that equality means favoritism do violence to common sense."[12]

Senator Edmund Muskie, another key supporter of the 1964 act, expressed a similar understanding of the legislation. "Every American citizen," said Muskie, "has the right to equal treatment—not favored treatment, not complete individual equality—just equal treatment."[13] Senator Hubert Humphrey agreed. The principal force behind the passage of the 1964 Civil Rights Act in the Senate, Humphrey repeatedly stated that Title VII would prohibit any consideration of race in employment matters. On one occasion he used these words:

The title does not provide that any preferential treatment in employment shall be given to Negroes or to any other persons or groups. It does not provide that any quota system may be established to maintain racial balance in employment. In fact, the title would prohibit preferential treatment for any particular group, and any person, whether or not a member of any minority group, would be permitted to file a complaint of discriminatory employment practices.[14]

The leadership of the civil rights movement echoed the same view. Appearing at congressional hearings during consideration of the 1964 civil rights laws, Roy Wilkins, executive director of the National Association for the Advancement of Colored People (NAACP), stated unabashedly, "Our association has never been in favor of a quota system."[15] "We believe the quota system is unfair whether it is used for Negroes or against Negroes," he testified.[16] "We feel people ought to be hired because of their ability, irrespective of their color.... We want equality, equality of opportunity and employment on the basis of ability."[17]

The same theme was sounded by Jack Greenberg, then director counsel of the NAACP Legal Defense Fund, in his successful 1964 argument to the Supreme Court in *Anderson v. Martin*,[18] urging that a state statute requiring the ballot designation of a candidate's race be invalidated. "The fact that this statute might operate to benefit a Negro candidate and against a white candidate... is not relevant," he insisted, "for... the state has a duty under the fifteenth amendment and the fourteenth amendment to be 'color-blind' and not to act so as to encourage racial discrimination... against any racial group."[19]

Color blindness was, in fact, the banner under which the civil rights movement marched, largely in unison, through most of the 1960s. Those who joined in—both black and white—drew legal strength from the Supreme Court's landmark decision in *Brown*, policy support from the recent acts of Congress, and moral inspiration from the words and deeds of Dr. Martin Luther King, Jr. His dream became America's dream on that summer afternoon in 1963, as he stood at the foot of the Washington Monument and, with millions of Americans watching, challenged a country to bring about the day when his children would at last be judged "by the content of their character" and measure of their abilities, not "the color of their skin."[20]

As we moved through the decade of the 1960s, there were innumerable signs of progress as the "whites only" signs were removed. The outlawing of racial discrimination in employment, coupled with the government impetus behind affirmative action recruitment and outreach efforts, introduced blacks into a significant number of workplaces previously having white employees only. With increasing regularity, the courts began issuing orders that white public schools open their doors to black students. The

message of equal opportunity had broken through.

There was, however, a growing undercurrent of discontent. Many in the civil rights movement began to express dissatisfaction over the pace of desegregation initiatives. By the early 1970s, a perception had set in that the momentum had peaked and was even slipping backward. The policymakers could have pointed out that educational and economic disparities between blacks and whites due to the long history of segregation made inevitable the sort of slowdown that followed the dramatic first-wave breakthrough. It is painfully obvious that many blacks forced into segregated classrooms in the South had been denied a quality education—some had received almost no education at all; they could hardly have been expected to compete effectively with better-educated whites for employment.

Yet, to focus on this systemwide failing and face it forthrightly was seen by many as too prolonged an effort to satisfy the political demands of the time. Instead, the policymakers sought a quick fix, without giving serious thought to its long-term repercussions or implications. The concept of racial neutrality gave way to a concept of racial balance, on the representation that the former could not be fully realized unless the latter was achieved.

In the employment arena, the principal tool used was affirmative action, not in its original race-neutral sense but now endorsing racial preference. The claim was that regulation and allocation by race were not wrong per se; rather, their validity depended upon who was being regulated, on what was being allocated, and on the purpose of the arrangement. If a racial preference would produce the desired statistical result, it was argued, its discriminatory feature could be tolerated as an unfortunate but necessary consequence of remedying the effects of past discrimination. Using race "to get beyond racism" was the way one Supreme Court Justice explained it.[21]

Once again, the use of race as a criterion for governmental classification became acceptable during the decade of the 1970s. Having been rescued in *Brown* from the insidious policy of separate but equal, the country found itself only two short decades later drifting steadily toward the policy of separate but proportional: separate avenues to school, separate employment lines, separate contract-bid procedures, all inspired by the objective of achieving proportional representation by race in the classroom, in the work force, and on the job site.

Proponents of preferential affirmative action soon discarded the precept that a race-based employment preference was constitutionally permissible only when necessary to place an individual victim of proven discrimination in a position he or she would have attained but for the discrimination. Instead they focused on entire groups of individuals said to be disadvantaged because of race.[22] Quotas, goals and timetables, and other race-conscious techniques gained increasing acceptance among federal bureaucrats and judges, and by the decade's end, racial considerations influenced public employment decisions of every kind, from hirings to layoffs.

It did not seem to matter that those favored solely because of race frequently had never been wronged by the employer or that the preferential treatment afforded them was at the expense of other employees who were themselves admittedly innocent of any discrimination or other wrongdoing. The preoccupation was on removing from the work force any racial imbalance between employees in a discrete job unit, no matter how large or small. Lost in the scramble for strictly numerical solutions was the fundamental truth that "no discrimination based on race is benign, . . . no action disadvantaging a person because of color is affirmative."[23]

By the early 1980s, the use of race in the distribution of the country's limited economic and educational resources had sadly led to the creation of a kind of racial spoils system in America, fostering competition not only between individual members of contending groups, but between the groups themselves. The color-blind ideal had largely given way to a color-conscious mentality, one that encouraged stereotyping and that invited people to view others as possessors of racial characteristics, not as unique individuals. Thus the policy of preferential affirmative action had effectively submerged the vitality of personality under the deadening prejudgments of race. The very purpose intended to be served was being defeated, for race-based preferences cut against the grain of equal opportunity. In the broadest sense, color consciousness and racial polarization pose the greatest threat to members of minority groups because it is they who are, by definition, outnumbered. As individuals, members of all racial groups suffer, because an individual's energy, ability, and dedication can take him or her no further than permitted by the group's allotment or quota.

What began as a pursuit for equality of opportunity became, therefore, through preferential affirmative action, a forfeiture of opportunity in absolute terms. Individual opportunity was diminished in order to achieve group equality, measured solely in terms of proportional representation and numerically balanced results. Yet, as Justice Powell stated in his *Bakke* concurrence, "Nothing in the Constitution supports the notion that individuals may be asked to suffer otherwise impermissible burdens in order to enhance the societal standing of their ethnic groups."[24]

Justice Powell's view was not shared by all of his colleagues on the High Court, however. Indeed, in many respects, the public debate in the late 1970s over whether use of racial preferences was affirmative or negative action was mirrored in the Supreme Court's opinions. Alan Bakke won admission to the University of California Medical School on the ground that a minority preference program designed to benefit all but Caucasian applicants excluded him unconstitutionally because of race. But the Court was sharply divided, and no single opinion could command a majority.[25]

The heart of the judicial controversy did not appear to be a difference of view as to the fundamental commitment to eradicate all forms of racial discrimination. As Justice Marshall made clear in his opinion for the Court in *McDonald v. Santa Fe Trail Transportation Co.*, color-conscious bias was condemned by law with equal force whether it operated in forward gear or reverse.[26] Rather, the break point came over whether and to what extent the antidiscrimination principle should be compromised on the strength of a promise that its equal protection guarantee would be thereby more likely to be achieved.

The signals sent by the Court were at best mixed and invariably muddled.[27] At one end of the compendium, there was the view expressed by Justice Blackmun in *Bakke* that the use of race was necessary "to get beyond racism."[28] On the other end, then Associate Justice Rehnquist argued no less forcefully that to compromise the principle of nondiscrimination, no matter how slightly, was to lose it forever to the emerging compromise.[29] Between the two was the rationale commanding the most support in *United Steelworkers v. Weber*.[30] In upholding the minority training program favoring in-plant black employees over their white counterparts for 50 percent of the openings, Justice Brennan stressed the restricted nature of the affirmative action preference that was allowed to stand: its adoption was intended to correct persistent racial exclusion from the work force; it was of limited duration; and it was tailored to remedy the identified exclusionary practices, not to maintain racial balance or skin-color proportionality.[31]

When the affirmative action issue came again to the Court two years later in a constitutional setting, the split between the justices was no less pronounced. The case was *Fullilove v. Klutznick*,[32] and, again, enough votes were pulled together to uphold a minority set-aside provision enacted by Congress. The 10 percent contracting preference survived judicial scrutiny, however, only because a majority of the justices regarded it to be (1) remedially "compelled" in order to counter persistent, industrywide discrimination and (2) "narrowly tailored" as to duration, scope, and application.[33]

If such program constraints had been endorsed by the full Court, they undoubtedly would have been taken more seriously by the lower federal courts. But, precisely because the Supreme Court spoke with many voices, a number of appellate court judges took it upon themselves to read both *Fullilove* and *Weber* expansively and assign undeserved weight to dictum in *Bakke*.[34] As a consequence, the racial preference acquired a respectability it did not justifiably deserve.[35]

Such programs, however, have been unable to sustain lasting support—a consequence that, in the final analysis, is as much a tribute to the Supreme Court as the flirtation with a racial-quota policy was one of the Court's more noticeable embarrassments. The issue of preference revisited the High Court repeatedly in the 1980s, and by the end of the decade there emerged a far clearer understanding of its acceptable use. Wholesale return to the days in the early 1960s—when "affirmative action" was a neutral phrase that demanded outreach efforts aimed at all Americans without regard to race—has not occurred.[36] But neither is it any longer the case that a racial solution can be fashioned to correct a statistical imbalance in the workplace that is attributed to discrimination in the past, not the present.[37]

Rather, in a series of decisions authorized by justices on both sides of the philosophical spectrum, affirmative action preferences have been assigned a modest, albeit not unimportant, role in the fight against discrimination. They are available not as a first-resort measure but as a remedy of last resort, to be used when—and only when—compelled by racially exclusionary practices that persist notwithstanding concerted efforts, nonracial in character, to bring them to a halt.[38] Even then, the race-conscious alternative must be narrowly tailored to the remedial purpose it is intended to serve, so as not to intrude needlessly on the rights of others who have done no wrong or last longer than necessary to correct the discrimination.[39]

Accordingly, there is good reason to believe that we are entering an era when government will no longer feel the need to rely so heavily on racial classifications. To be sure, there are those who still insist that minorities are bound to remain on the sidelines without some racial-preference measure to get them into the game. Rather than demanding rigid quotas, however, they claim to be content with goals and timetables.

But racial goals, tied to short- or long-term timetables, offer no solution to the real problems at hand. Whether racial preference is enforced by the raw racism of a quota program or guided by the more subtle hand of a flexible goal, it still confers benefits on some while denying them to others for the worst of reasons: because of skin color or ethnic origin. The unfortunate reality is that under either regime, the specter of racial inferiority is kept alive; behind every goal and timetable lurks the message that minorities cannot make it under the same rules, that they need a special set of privileges that come with being members of a particular race.

The recently concluded debates over the Civil Rights Act of 1991 reverberated around that theme. The advocates of racial preference lobbied hard for codification of a legal standard that would effectively define discrimination in terms of proportional representation—not just in terms of race and ethnicity, but also with respect to gender and religion. Any work force imbalance as to one or more of the designated groupings was, under their proposal, presumptively unlawful, and the traditional defense of merit selection would be unacceptable against any claimant minimally qualified for the job in question.

Those who opposed and ultimately defeated this measure were not far off the mark to call it a quota bill. Unless companies hired and promoted by race, gender, ethnic background, and religion, work force proportionality would simply not be achievable and therefore litigation would be a virtual certainty.[40] The most cost-effective corporate response would thus be to maintain separate lists of applicants and select new hires or promotees proportionately according to skin color, sex, ethnicity, and religious beliefs. Self-imposition of employee quotas to avoid presumptive liability was the unstated, but fully understood, objective of the offered legislation.

What finally was passed by Congress and signed by President Bush was the product of compromise and, in candor, probably eases the quota pressure on corporate America to some degree, even if it does not eliminate it altogether. The presumption of discriminatory selection procedures on a showing of work force disproportionately remained in the final bill.[41] But the employer—who, under the 1991 act, inherits the burden of proof once a *prima facie* showing of racial, gender, ethnic, or religious disparity has been made[42]—can rebut the presumption on a showing that its alleged discriminatory procedure is related to the job in question and necessary to the business.[43] In other words, proof that the selection process was designed to, and did in fact, produce the best-qualified candidates for the particular job is an acceptable defense.

To be sure, the new statute lacks definition in a number of important respects,[44] but that has become an expected character flaw in virtually all congressional legislation that is the product of extended debate and compromise. In this instance, the shortcoming probably bodes well for the forces whose understanding of civil rights continues to rest, at bottom, on the color-blind ideal of equal opportunity for all Americans and not just a preferred group or groups. For it is they who now seem to have the ear of a majority of the Supreme Court justices as well as many lower federal court judges who will be called upon to resolve definitional disputes and matters of statutory interpretation.[45]

That is the more gratifying news. An immediate legislative threat to an eventual return to race neutrality has been diverted. The new civil rights legislation at least pays symbolic deference to a principled assault on the evils of discrimination, and nothing it says provides a basis for any more expansive use of the remedy of racial—or ethnic or gender or religious—preference than has been permitted by the Supreme Court. Affirmative action measures thus are readily available as a remedial tool to respond to acts of bias and prejudice, but they must remain unconscious to color differences except as a "narrowly tailored," last-resort effort to rid a work force of persistent discrimination.[46]

This is not to suggest that the 1991 act deserves no criticism. Its new provisions on punitive damages,[47] standing,[48] limitation periods,[49] attorney and witness fees,[50] and retroactivity each raise questions that are already subject to litigation or soon will be. As a consequence, the real beneficiaries of the compromise that emerged from the prolonged legislative battle are, for now, likely to be the lawyers who will, predictably, further clog the courts' crowded dockets with numerous new lawsuits seeking to exploit the damages and fee-recovery provisions —the beneficiaries will not be the ever-expanding minority population, which is still waiting, largely in vain, for the employment opportunities promised in the Civil Rights Act of 1964. That promise has, for most, too long been thwarted by the policy of racial preference. The real disappointment is that its prospects under the new act are only marginally brighter, even on the best of assumptions that preferential affirmative action has been caged and will henceforth be available only for tailored, last-resort, remedial use.

NOTES

1. 3 CFR 1959-63, pp. 448–54.

2. Ibid.

3. 347 U.S. 483 (1954).

4. *Brown v. Board of Education*, 349 U.S. 296, 300 (1955).

5. Reprinted in *O. Brown, Argument: The Oral Argument before the Supreme Court in Brown v. Board of Education of Topeka*, 1952–55, ed. L. Friedman (New York: Walter, 1969), p. 47.

6. 163 U.S. 537 (1894). The case involved a suit by Plessy, petitioner, a "resident of the State of Louisiana, of mixed descent, in the proportion of seven-eighths Caucasian and one-eighth African blood," against the Honorable John H. Ferguson, judge of the Parish of Orleans. Ibid., p. 538. While seated in the "white race" section of an East Louisiana railway passenger train, Plessy was required by the conductor to vacate the seat and find another in a section of the train "for persons not of the white race." Ibid. Upon his refusal to move, Plessy was ejected, arrested, and charged with a criminal violation. Ibid. He was convicted and thereafter appealed the constitutionality of the Louisiana law "providing for separate railway carriage for white and colored races." Ibid., p. 539. In its now roundly criticized opinion, delivered by Justice Brown, the Court affirmed the conviction, ruling the law within the bounds of the Fourteenth Amendment. Ibid., p. 540. Laws providing for "separate but equal" public accommodations were thereby given the stamp of constitutionality. Ibid., p. 550. But see ibid., p. 559 (Harlan, J., dissenting) ("Our constitution is color-blind, and neither knows nor tolerates classes among citizens.... The law regards man as man, and takes no account of his surroundings or of his color").

7. See *Loving v. Virginia*, 388 U.S. 1, 11 (1966) (quoting *Hirabayashi v. United States*, 320 U.S. 81, 100 (1943)).

8. Civil Rights Act of 1957, Pub. L. 85-315, 71 Stat. 634 (codified as amended in scattered sections of 42 U.S.C.).

9. Pub. L. 89-110, 79 Stat. 437 (codified as amended at 42 U.S.C. §§ 1971, 1973 to 1973 bb-1 (1982)).

10. Pub. L. 90-284, 82 Stat. 81 (codified as amended at 42 U.S.C. § § 3601-19 (1982)).

11. 110 Cong. Rec. 8921 (1964).

12. Ibid.

13. Ibid., p. 12,614.

14. Ibid., p. 11,848. At another point, Senator Humphrey's exasperation with the opposition's preference argument prompted him to make the following offer: "If... in the title VII... any language [can be found] which provides that an employer will have to hire on the basis of percentage or quota related to color... I will start eating the pages [of the bill] one after another...." Ibid., p. 7,420.

15. Statement of Roy Wilkins, in U.S., Congress, House, Committee on the Judiciary, Subcommittee no. 5, *Miscellaneous Proposals Regarding the Civil Rights of Persons within the Jurisdiction of the United States, 1963: Hearings on H.R. 7152*. 88th Cong., 1st sess., 1963, p. 2,144.

16. Ibid.

17. Ibid.

18. See *Anderson v. Martin*, 375 U.S. 399 (1964), a case involving a state statute requiring that the race of each candidate for public office be accurately designated on each ballot. Noting that any governmental endorsement of racial bloc voting would tend to favor the race having a numerical majority, the Court held that the state could not constitutionally encourage racial discrimination of any kind, whether it worked to the disadvantage of blacks or whites. The state's designation of candidate's race was, according to a unanimous Court, of "no relevance" in the electoral process. Ibid., pp. 401–3.

19. Jurisdictional Statement of Appellants at 11–12, *Anderson v. Martin*, 375 U.S. 399 (1964) (No. 51).

20. M. King, Jr., "I've Got a Dream," in *Martin Luther King, Jr., A Documentary... Montgomery to Memphis*, ed. F. Schulte (New York: Norton, 1976), p. 218.

21. *Board of Regents of Univ. of Cal. v. Bakke*, 438 U.S. 265, 407 (1978) (Blackmun, J., concurring). But see *DeFunis v. Odegaard*, 416 U.S. 312, 343 (1974) (Douglas, J., dissenting) ("The Equal Protection Clause commands elimination of racial barriers, not their creation in order to satisfy our theory as to how society ought to be organized").

22. Cf. *Board of Regents of Univ. of Cal. v. Bakke*, 438 U.S. at 299 (Powell, J., concurring) ("It is the individual who is entitled to judicial protection against classifications based upon racial or ethnic background because such distinctions impinge upon personal rights, rather than the individual only because of his membership in a particular group").

23. See *United Steelworkers of America v. Weber*, 443 U.S. 193, 254 (1979) (Rehnquist, J., dissenting).

24. See *Board of Regents of Univ. of Cal. v. Bakke*, 438 U.S. at 298 (Powell, J., concurring).

25. There were four separate opinions. Chief Justice Burger, joined by Justices White, Stewart, and Rehnquist, wrote the plurality opinion, as to which Justices Blackmun, Stevens, and Powell concurred separately. Justice Brennan dissented, joined by Justice Marshall.

26. 427 U.S. 273 (1976). In *McDonald*, petitioners, two white employees of respondent company, were discharged for cause while a black employee charged with the same offense was not discharged. Petitioners filed suit alleging racial discrimination in violation of Title VII. The district court dismissed petitioners' claims on the ground that Title VII was unavailable to white people. 427 U.S. at 275. The Supreme Court reversed. Ibid., p. 296. Justice Marshall, writing for the Court, stated, "We therefore hold today that Title VII prohibits racial discrimination against white petitioners in this case upon the same standards as would be applicable were they Negroes and Jackson white." Ibid., p. 280.

27. The Court was sharply divided on the preference issue in the 1970s and for most of the 1980s, often speaking through multiple opinions without a clear majority (see *Board of Regents of Univ. of Cal. v. Bakke; Fullilove v. Klutznick; United Steelworkers of America v. Weber; Wygant v. Jackson Bd. of Educ.*, 467 U.S. 267 (1986)) or with an exceedingly narrow (5–4) margin (see *United States v. Paradise*, 480 U.S. 149 (1987); *Local 28, Sheet Metal Workers v. EEOC*, 478 U.S. 421 (1986); *Firefighters Local Union No. 1784 v. Stotts*, 467 U.S. 561 (1984); *Wards Cove Packing Co. v. Antonio*, 490 U.S. 642 (1989).

28. See fn. 21.

29. See fn. 23.

30. 443 U.S. 193 (1979).

31. Ibid., p. 208. The Court did not elaborate on how the persistent racial exclusion was to be proven or on how the tailoring and duration of the remedy must be fashioned in relation to the proof of prior exclusion.

32. 448 U.S. 448 (1980) (plurality).

33. Ibid., p. 478. In upholding a minority set-aside provision enacted by Congress, the Court's plurality—Burger, C. J., joined by Justices White and Powell—found that "Congress had abundant historical basis from which it could conclude that traditional procurement practices, when applied to minority businesses, could perpetuate the fact of past discrimination."

34. Justice Powell suggested in his separate concurrence that "in light of the countervailing constitutional interest... of the First Amendment," 438 U.S. at 313, a university could permissibly exercise its academic freedom to consider race as one factor in promoting a diverse student body. Ibid.,

pp. 311–15. Whatever force such a reading of the Fourteenth Amendment may have to accommodate First Amendment freedoms where the two come into direct conflict, there is no countervailing First Amendment interest implicated in the usual employer-employee relationship. See generally Wm. Bradford Reynolds, "The Justice Department's Enforcement of Title VII," *Labor Law Journal*, 34:259–65 (1963).

35. See, for example, *H. K. Porter Co., Inc. v. Metropolitan Dade County*, 825 F.2d 324 (11th Cir. 1987), vacated and remanded, 489 U.S. 1062 (1989); *Higgins v. City of Vallejo*, 823 F.2d 351 (9th Cir. 1987) (rejecting constitutional and Title VII challenges to award of firefighter-engineer position to third-ranked black candidate over first-ranked white candidate); *Smith v. Hennesy*, 831 F.2d 1068 (11th Cir. 1987), aff'g, 648 F.Supp 1103 (M.D. Fla. 1986) (upholding a one-for-one policy adopted by city's firefighter department over constitutional and Title VII challenges); *Kromnick v. School Dist.*, 939 F.2d 894 (3d Cir. 1984) (upholding teacher assignment program); *South Florida Chapter, Associated General Contractors of America, Inc. v. Metropolitan Dade County*, 723 F.2d 846 (11th Cir.), cert. denied, 469 U.S. 871 (1984) (upholding local set-aside program); *Bratton v. City of Detroit*, 704 F.2d 878 (6th Cir. 1983), cert. denied, 464 U.S. 1040 (1984) (upholding voluntary police quota); *Ohio Contractors Association v. Keip*, 713 F.2d 167 (6th Cir. 1983) (upholding state set-aside); *Schmidt v. Oakland Unified School Dist.*, 662 F.2d 550 (9th Cir.) (upholding local set-aside), vacated on other grounds, 457 U.S. 594 (1982); *Geier v. Alexander*, 593 F.Supp 1263 (M.D. Tenn. 1984), aff'd, 801 F.2d 799 (6th Cir. 1986) (approving special tracking of 75 black sophomores to state professional schools); *M. C. West, Inc. v. Lewis*, 522 F.Supp 338 (M.D. Tenn. 1981) (upholding U.S. Department of Transportation set-aside regulations on the basis of *Fullilove*).

36. Only Justice Scalia has insisted that the Fourteenth Amendment is truly color-blind and tolerates no racial preferences for non-victims of discrimination, even if the stated purpose is remedial. See *City of Richmond v. Croson*, 488 U.S. 469, 520-28 (Scalia, J., concurring separately).

37. A plurality of the Court in *Wygant v. Jackson Bd. of Educ.* rejected outright the proposition that racial preferences could be constitutionally justified or remedially necessary to correct "historical" or "societal" discrimination. 476 U.S. at 274-75. See also ibid., pp. 288–89 (O'Connor, J., concurring). This conclusion was adopted by five justices in *Croson*, 488 U.S. at 496–97 (O'Connor, J., joined by the Chief Justice and Justices White and Kennedy, with Scalia, J., concurring separately).

38. See, for example, *Local 28, Sheet Metal Workers v. EEOC*, 478 U.S. at 449 ("Where an employer or union has engaged in particularly long-standing or

egregious discrimination... requiring recalcitrant employers or unions to hire and to admit qualified minorities roughly in proportion to the number of qualified minorities in the work force may be the only effective way to ensure the full enjoyment of the rights protected by Title VII"); *United States v. Paradise*, 480 U.S. at 171–72 (a promotions quota was justified by a compelling governmental interest in remedying " 'long-term, open and pervasive' discrimination, including absolute exclusion of blacks from ... upper ranks [of the Alabama State Troopers]"). And see *City of Richmond v. Croson*, 488 U.S. at 509 (It is only "in the extreme case [that] some form of narrowly tailored racial preference might be necessary to break down patterns of deliberate exclusion").

39. See *City of Richmond v. Croson*, 408 U.S. at 497–98; and see *Wygant v. Jackson Bd. of Educ.*, 476 U.S. at 282–84.

40. The irony is that, under the new act, the employer is put in a catch-22 position. If the hiring is done along racial, gender, ethnic, and religious lines—so as to avoid work force disparity in any or all of the designated categories—the employer faces the prospect of a Title VII lawsuit alleging intentional discrimination on account of race, sex, national origin, or religion. Conversely, if the hiring is done without regard to race, gender, or ethnic or religious affiliation—which will invariably produce disparity on one or another basis—the employer similarly faces the prospect of a Title VII lawsuit alleging impermissible disparity.

41. Despite much debate over whether the new act was or was not a quota bill—and assurances from both proponents and opponents of the legislation that quota hiring was not permitted by the language ultimately adopted—the reality is that the Civil Rights Act of 1991 makes suspect a numerical disparity in the work force based on race, gender, national origin, or religion. Pub L. 102-166, sec. 105, 42 U.S.C. § 2000e-2 (k) (1) (A) (1991).

42. The new act shifts the burden of proof to the employer upon a showing by the complainant of a racial—or other—disparity among employee hires attributable to a particular selection practice or practices utilized by the employer. Pub. L. 102-166, sec. 105(a), 42 U.S.C. § 2000-2 (k) (1) (B) (1991).

43. See Pub. L. 102-166, sec. 105(a), 42 U.S.C. § 2000e-2(k) (1) (A) (i) (1991). In order to pass statutory muster, the challenged employment practice must be "job related for the position in question and consistent with business necessity."

44. For example, the term "business necessity" is not defined. Nor does the statute explain the appropriate comparative analysis for determining that a particular statistical imbalance creates a presumption of "disparate impact."

45. See fnn. 36–39 and accompanying text.

46. See fnn. 38–39 and accompanying text.

47. See Pub. L. 102-166, sec. 102, 42 U.S.C. § 1981 A(b) (1991).

48. See Pub. L. 102-166, secs. 108, 112, 42 U.S.C. §§ 2000e-2(n) (1) (A) and (B) (1991), 2000e-5(a) (1991).

49. See Pub. L. 102-166, sec. 112, 42 U.S.C. § 2000e-5(e) (1991).

50. See Pub. L. 102-166, sec. 103, 113, 42 U.S.C. § 1988 (1991).

POSTSCRIPT

Should Affirmative Action Policies Be Continued?

The most significant development of the last few years may not have been a court decision but a court appointment. The selection of Judge Clarence Thomas to the Supreme Court aroused controversy for many reasons, among them Judge Thomas's views on affirmative action. Judge Thomas had been an outspoken opponent of affirmative action. The justice he replaced was Justice Thurgood Marshall, who was a forceful advocate for affirmative action.

The United States is an increasingly heterogeneous society and it is likely that affirmative action claims by groups will increase rather than decrease. One law professor has observed that "the modern story of the Supreme Court has centrally been about race." Justice Harry A. Blackmun had written in a concurring opinion in *Bakke* that "in order to get beyond racism, we must first take account of race." In an era of rapid political, social, and economic change, where there is continuing competition over resources, we can expect to see frequent controversies and claims involving affirmative action.

The study of the question of affirmative action calls for an interdisciplinary approach. Beyond the legal and constitutional issues are philosophical problems of morality and justice, economic issues involving employment and the distribution of scarce resources, and sociological and psychological analyses of racism and sexism. Affirmative action programs force us to take an honest look at our own attitudes and at the nature of our society. What are the attitudes and practices of our institutions with respect to race and sex? What would we like such attitudes and practices to be in the future? What means should be employed to move us from the current state of affairs to where we would like to be?

Litigation in the affirmative action area is discussed in Devins, "Affirmative Action After Reagan," 68 *Texas Law Review* 1711 (1989); "Constitutional Scholars' Statement on Affirmative Action After *City of Richmond v. J. A. Croson Co.*," 98 *Yale Law Journal* 155 (1989); Fried, "Affirmative Action After *City of Richmond v. J. A. Croson Co.: A Response to the Scholars' Statement*," 99 *Yale Law Journal* 155 (1989); and Schwartz, "The 1986 and 1987 Affirmative Action Cases: It's All Over But the Shouting," 86 *Michigan Law Review* 524 (1987). One of the most enlightening law review articles defending affirmative action is Wasserstrom, "Racism, Sexism and Preferential Treatment: An Approach to the Topics," 24 *UCLA Law Review*, pp. 581, 622 (1977). A history of the

Bakke case is found in Dreyfuss and Lawrence, *The Bakke Case: The Politics of Inequality* (Harcourt Brace Jovanovich, 1979). Interesting recent books include Lani Guinier, *The Tyranny of the Majority* (Maxwell McMillan International, 1994); Stephen L. Carter, *Reflections of an Affirmative Action Baby* (Basic Books, 1991); and Michel Rosenfeld, *Affirmative Action and Justice* (Yale University Press, 1991).

ISSUE 9

Can States Restrict the Right to Die?

YES: William H. Rehnquist, from Majority Opinion, *Nancy Beth Cruzan v. Director, Missouri Department of Health,* U.S. Supreme Court (1990)

NO: William J. Brennan, Jr., from Dissenting Opinion, *Nancy Beth Cruzan v. Director, Missouri Department of Health,* U.S. Supreme Court (1990)

ISSUE SUMMARY

YES: Supreme Court chief justice William H. Rehnquist recognizes that a competent individual may refuse medical treatment but believes a showing of clear and convincing proof of the individual's wishes is required before allowing the termination of feeding to an incompetent person.

NO: Justice William J. Brennan, Jr., argues that the Court is erecting too high a standard for allowing an individual's wishes to be followed and that Nancy Cruzan did indeed wish to have her feeding discontinued.

> To please no one will I prescribe a deadly drug, nor give advice which may cause death.
>
> —Oath of Hippocrates

When a dispute gets to court, the issues before the court tend to be framed differently from the way they are stated in the popular press or in discussions among individuals. Legal discussions in court emphasize different issues from discussions among lay people even when the topic is the same. For example, the substantive question of what the result should be in a particular case, the kind of debate that one often finds on editorial pages of newspapers, may not be the main question in a legal case. Instead, the legal question for the court may be what is the proper procedure to follow or who has the right or authority to do something, leaving the decision of whether or not to perform the act up to the person who has won the case.

One of the most publicized cases of the 1970s involved 21-year-old Karen Ann Quinlan. Quinlan was in a coma, her doctors did not believe she would ever come out of the coma, and all believed, erroneously it turned out, that if her respirator were removed she would stop breathing. The question the court focused on was who had authority over the respirator and who should be responsible for deciding what to do with it. The court did not answer the question of whether or not the respirator should be disconnected but left this tormenting problem to the party that prevailed in the case. Soon after the decision, Quinlan's parents authorized the removal of the respirator. Contrary to what had been predicted, this did not result in her death. She survived another nine years before succumbing in 1985.

The process followed in the Quinlan case, and in the Cruzan case that follows, illustrates a basic distinction made by the law. The law prohibits active euthanasia, in which death results from some positive act, such as a lethal injection. "Mercy killings" fall into this category and can be prosecuted as acts of homicide. The law is more tolerant of passive euthanasia, in which death results from the failure to act or on the removal of life-saving equipment. As you read the following opinions, you should consider whether or not this is a reasonable distinction to make.

While modern debates about euthanasia can be traced back more than 100 years, the necessity for the legal system to become involved is more recent. Not all of these cases raise the same issues. The Quinlan case involved a person who was neither legally dead nor, according to medical opinion, ever likely to regain consciousness. She was unable to make the decision herself and the key questions were whose interests needed to be given priority and how the interests of the individual should be protected. The following case, in that it involves the termination of feeding rather than the removal of life support equipment, is more difficult. Or is it? Due to advances in medical technology, some of the traditional distinctions made in this area are not as clear as they once were. As Alexander Capron, a professor of law at the University of Southern California and a knowledgeable observer in this area, has written,

> The growing medicalization of death also meant that human interventions replaced natural processes. If pneumonia was once the old man's friend, his companion now is an antibiotic; if cardiopulmonary arrest once meant inevitable death, now the cries of 'Code Blue' echo down hospital corridors, as nurses and physicians race to the bedside to jump-start hearts with drugs and electric paddles, and to reinflate lungs with artificial pumps. We have gotten to the point... when in the age of miracle drugs and surgical derring-do, no illness can be said to have a natural course. There is no such thing as a 'natural' death. Somewhere along the way for just about every patient, death is forestalled by human choice and human action, or death is allowed to occur because of human choice. Life-support techniques make death a matter of human choice and hence a matter that provokes ethical concern. Who should make the choice? When? And on what grounds?

The *Cruzan* case that follows was probably the most discussed Supreme Court decision of the 1989–90 term. Nancy Cruzan, age 32, had been in a coma for seven years. She was one of an estimated 10,000 persons in the United States in a "vegetative state." She had left no explicit directions on whether or not she would like to continue to be fed and receive treatment if she were ever to be in such a condition. Should her parents be allowed to make this decision under such circumstances? How clear should an incompetent person's wishes be before the parents are allowed to make a decision?

YES

William H. Rehnquist

MAJORITY OPINION

CRUZAN v. MISSOURI DEPARTMENT OF HEALTH

CHIEF JUSTICE REHNQUIST delivered the opinion of the Court.

Petitioner Nancy Beth Cruzan was rendered incompetent as a result of severe injuries sustained during an automobile accident. Co-petitioners Lester and Joyce Cruzan, Nancy's parents and co-guardians, sought a court order directing the withdrawal of their daughter's artificial feeding and hydration equipment after it became apparent that she had virtually no chance of recovering her cognitive faculties. The Supreme Court of Missouri held that because there was no clear and convincing evidence of Nancy's desire to have life-sustaining treatment withdrawn under such circumstances, her parents lacked authority to effectuate such a request. We granted certiorari, and now affirm.

On the night of January 11, 1983, Nancy Cruzan lost control of her car as she traveled down Elm Road in Jasper County, Missouri. The vehicle overturned, and Cruzan was discovered lying face down in a ditch without detectable respiratory or cardiac function. Paramedics were able to restore her breathing and heartbeat at the accident site, and she was transported to a hospital in an unconscious state. An attending neurosurgeon diagnosed her as having sustained probable cerebral contusions, compounded by significant anoxia (lack of oxygen). The Missouri trial court in this case found that permanent brain damage generally results after 6 minutes in an anoxic state; it was estimated that Cruzan was deprived of oxygen from 12 to 14 minutes. She remained in a coma for approximately three weeks and then progressed to an unconscious state in which she was able to orally ingest some nutrition. In order to ease feeding and further the recovery, surgeons implanted a gastrostomy feeding and hydration tube in Cruzan with the consent of her then husband. Subsequent rehabilitative efforts proved unavailing. She now lies in a Missouri state hospital in what is commonly referred to as a persistent vegetative state: generally, a condition in which a person exhibits motor reflexes but evinces no indications of significant cognitive function.[1] The State of Missouri is bearing the cost of her care.

From *Nancy Beth Cruzan v. Director, Missouri Department of Health*, 58 L.W. 4916 (1990). Some notes and case citations omitted.

After it had become apparent that Nancy Cruzan had virtually no chance of regaining her mental faculties her parents asked hospital employees to terminate the artificial nutrition and hydration procedures. All agree that such a removal would cause her death. The employees refused to honor the request without court approval. The parents then sought and received authorization from the state trial court for termination. The court found that a person in Nancy's condition had a fundamental right under the State and Federal Constitutions to refuse or direct the withdrawal of "death prolonging procedures." The court also found that Nancy's "expressed thoughts at age twenty-five in somewhat serious conversation with a housemate friend that if sick or injured she would not wish to continue her life unless she could live at least halfway normally suggests that given her present condition she would not wish to continue on with her nutrition and hydration."

The Supreme Court of Missouri reversed by a divided vote. The court recognized a right to refuse treatment embodied in the common-law doctrine of informed consent, but expressed skepticism about the application of that doctrine in the circumstances of this case. *Cruzan v. Harmon*, 760 S. W. 2d 408, 416–417 (Mo. 1988) (en banc). The court also declined to read a broad right of privacy into the State Constitution which would "support the right of a person to refuse medical treatment in every circumstance," and expressed doubt as to whether such a right existed under the United States Constitution. *Id.*, at 417–418. It then decided that the Missouri Living Will statute, Mo. Rev. State. § 459.010 *et seq.* (1986), embodied a state policy strongly favoring the preservation of life.

760 S. W. 2d, at 419–420. The court found that Cruzan's statements to her roommate regarding her desire to live or die under certain conditions were "unreliable for the purpose of determining her intent," *id.*, at 424, "and thus insufficient to support the co-guardians claim to exercise substituted judgment on Nancy's behalf." *Id.*, at 426. It rejected the argument that Cruzan's parents were entitled to order the termination of her medical treatment, concluding that "no person can assume that choice for an incompetent in the absence of the formalities required under Missouri's Living Will statutes or the clear and convincing, inherently reliable evidence absent here." *Id.*, at 425. The court also expressed its view that "[b]road policy questions bearing on life and death are more properly addressed by representative assemblies" than judicial bodies. *Id.*, at 426.

We granted certiorari to consider the question of whether Cruzan has a right under the United States Constitution which would require the hospital to withdraw life-sustaining treatment from her under these circumstances. . . .

Before the turn of the century, this Court observed that "[n]o right is held more sacred, or is more carefully guarded, by the common law, than the right of every individual to the possession and control of his own person, free from all restraint or interference of others, unless by clear and unquestionable authority of law." *Union Pacific R. Co. v. Botsford*, 141 U.S. 250, 251 (1891). This notion of bodily integrity has been embodied in the requirement that informed consent is generally required for medical treatment. Justice Cardozo, while on the Court of Appeals of New York, aptly described this doctrine: "Every human being of adult years and sound mind has a right to determine what shall be done with his own body; and a surgeon who performs an operation without his patient's consent commits an assault, for which he is liable in damages."*Schloendorff v. Society of New York Hospital*, 211 N. Y. 125, 129–30, 105 N. E. 92, 93 (1914). The informed consent doctrine has become firmly entrenched in American tort law.

The logical corollary of the doctrine of informed consent is that the patient generally possesses the right not to consent, that is, to refuse treatment. Until about 15 years ago and the seminal decision in *In re Quinlan*, 70 N. J. 10, 355 A. 2d 647, cert. denied *sub nom., Garger v. New Jersey*, 429 U.S. 922 (1976), the number of right-to-refuse-treatment decisions were relatively few.[2] Most of the earlier cases involved patients who refused medical treatment forbidden by their religious beliefs, thus implicating First Amendment rights as well as common law rights of self-determination.[3] More recently, however, with the advance of medical technology capable of sustaining life well past the point where natural forces would have brought certain death in earlier times, cases involving the right to refuse life-sustaining treatment have burgeoned. See 760 S. W. 2d, at 412, n. 4 (collecting 54 reported decisions from 1976–1988).

In the *Quinlan* case, young Karen Quinlan suffered severe brain damage as the result of anoxia, and entered a persistent vegetative state. Karen's father sought judicial approval to disconnect his daughter's respirator. The New Jersey Supreme Court granted the relief, holding that Karen had a right of privacy grounded in the Federal Constitution to terminate treatment. *In re Quinlan*, 70 N. J., at 38–42, 355 A. 2d at 662–664. Recognizing that this right was not absolute, however, the court balanced it against asserted state interests. Noting that the State's interest "weakens and the individual's right to privacy grows as the degree of bodily invasion increases and the prognosis dims," the court concluded that the state interests had to give way in that case. *Id.*, at 41, 355 A. 2d, at 664. The court also concluded that the "only practical way" to prevent the loss of Karen's privacy right due to her incompetence was to allow her guardian and family to decide "whether she would exercise it in these circumstances." *Ibid.*

After *Quinlan*, however, most courts have based a right to refuse treatment either solely on the common law right to informed consent or on both the common law right and a constitutional privacy right. See L. Tribe, American Constitutional Law § 15–11, p. 1365 (2d ed. 1988). In *Superintendent of Belchertown State School v. Saikewicz*, 373 Mass. 728, 370 N. E. 2d 417 (1977), the Supreme Judicial Court of Massachusetts relied on both the right of privacy and the right of informed consent to permit the withholding of chemotherapy from a profoundly-retarded 67-year-old man suffering from leukemia. *Id.*, at 737–738, 370 N. E. 2d, at 424. Reasoning that an incompetent person retains the same rights as a competent individual "because the value of human dignity extends to both," the court adopted a "substituted judgment" standard whereby courts were to determine what an incompetent individual's decision would have been under the circumstances. *Id.*, at 745, 752–753, 757–758, 370 N. E. 2d, at 427, 431, 434. Distilling certain state interests from prior case law —the preservation of life, the protection of the interests of innocent third parties, the prevention of suicide, and the maintenance of the ethical integrity of the medical profession—the court recognized the first interest as paramount and noted it was greatest when an affliction was curable, "as opposed to the State interest where, as here, the issue is not whether, but when, for how long, and at what cost to the individual [a] life may be briefly extended." *Id.*, at 742, 370 N. E. 2d, at 426.

In *In re Storar* 52 N. Y. 2d 363, 420 N. E. 2d 64, cert. denied, 454 U.S. 858 (1981), the New York Court of Appeals declined to base a right to refuse treatment on a constitutional privacy right. Instead, it found such a right "adequately supported" by the informed consent doctrine. *Id.*, at 376–377, 420 N. E. 2d, at 70. In *In re Eichner* (decided with *In re Storar, supra*) an 83-year-old man who had suffered brain damage from anoxia entered a vegetative state and was thus incompetent to consent to the removal of his respirator. The court, however, found it unnecessary to reach the question of whether his rights could be exercised by others since it found the evidence clear and convincing from statements made by the patient when competent that he "did not want to be maintained in a vegetable coma by use of a respirator." *Id.*, at 380, 420 N. E. 2d, at 72. In the companion *Storar* case, a 52-year-old man suffering from bladder cancer had been profoundly retarded during most of his life. Implicitly rejecting the approach taken in *Saikewicz, supra,* the court reasoned that due to such life-long incompetency, "it is unrealistic to attempt to determine whether he would want to continue potentially life prolonging treatment if he were competent." 52 N. Y. 2d, at 380, 420 N. E. 2d, at 72. As the evidence showed that the patient's required blood transfusions did not involve excessive pain and without them his mental and physical abilities would deteriorate, the court concluded that it should not "allow an incompetent patient to bleed to death because someone, even someone as close as a parent or sibling, feels that this is best for one with an incurable disease." *Id.*, at 382, 420 N. E. 2d, at 73.

Many of the later cases build on the principles established in *Quinlan, Saikewicz* and *Storar/Eichner.* For instance, in *In re Conroy,* 98 N. J. 321, 486 A. 2d 1209 (1985), the same court that decided *Quinlan* considered whether a nasogastric feeding tube could be removed from an 84-year-old incompetent nursing-home resident suffering irreversible mental and physical ailments. While recognizing that a federal right of privacy might apply in the case, the court, contrary to its approach in *Quinlan,* decided to base its decision on the common-law right to self-determination and informed consent. 98 N. J., at 348, 486 A. 2d, at 1223. "On balance, the right to self-determination ordinarily outweighs any countervailing state interests, and competent persons generally are permitted to refuse medical treatment, even at the risk of death. Most of the cases that have held otherwise, unless they involved the interest in protecting innocent third parties, have concerned the patient's competency to make a rational and considered choice." *Id.*, at 353–354, 486 A. 2d, at 1225.

Reasoning that the right of self-determination should not be lost merely because an individual is unable to sense a violation of it, the court held that incompetent individuals retain a right to refuse treatment. It also held that such a right could be exercised by a surrogate decisionmaker using a "subjective" standard when there was clear evidence that the incompetent person would have exercised it. Where such evidence was lacking, the court held that an individual's right could still be involved in certain circumstances under objective "best interest" standards. *Id.*, at 361–368, 486 A. 2d, at 1229–1233. Thus, if some trustworthy evidence existed that the individual would have wanted to terminate treatment, but not enough to clearly establish a person's wishes for purposes of the subjective standard, and the burden of a prolonged life from the experience of pain and suffering markedly outweighed its satisfactions, treatment could be terminated under a "limited-objective" standard. Where no trustworthy evidence existed, and a person's suffering would make the administration of life-sustaining treatment inhumane, a "pure-objective" standard could be used to terminate treatment. If none of these conditions obtained, the court held it was best to err in favor of preserving life. *Id.*, at 364–368, 486 A. 2d, at 1231–1233.

The court also rejected certain categorical distinctions that had been drawn in prior refusal-of-treatment cases as lacking substance for decision purposes: the distinction between actively hastening death by terminating treatment and passively allowing a person to die of a disease; between treating individuals as an initial matter versus withdrawing treatment afterwards; between ordinary versus extraordinary treatment; and between treatment by artificial feeding versus other forms of life-sustaining medical procedures. *Id.*, at 369–374, 486 N. E. 2d, at 1233–1237. As to the last item, the court acknowledged the "emotional significance" of food, but noted that feeding by implanted tubes is a "medical procedur[e] with inherent risks and possible side effects, instituted by skilled health-care providers to compensate for impaired physical functioning" which

analytically was equivalent to artificial breathing using a respirator. *Id.*, at 373, 486 A. 2d, at 1236.[4]

In contrast to *Conroy*, the Court of Appeals of New York recently refused to accept less than the clearly expressed wishes of a patient before permitting the exercise of her right to refuse treatment by a surrogate decisionmaker. *In re Westchester County Medical Center on behalf of O'Connor*, 531 N. E. 2d 607 (1988) (*O'Connor*). There, the court, over the objection of the patient's family members, granted an order to insert a feeding tube into a 77-year-old woman rendered incompetent as a result of several strokes. While continuing to recognize a common-law right to refuse treatment, the court rejected the substituted judgment approach for asserting it "because it is inconsistent with our fundamental commitment to the notion that no person or court should substitute its judgment as to what would be an acceptable quality of life for another. Consequently, we adhere to the view that, despite its pitfalls and inevitable uncertainties, the inquiry must always be narrowed to the patient's expressed intent, with every effort made to minimize the opportunity for error." *Id.*, at 530, 531 N. E. 2d, at 613 (citation omitted). The court held that the record lacked the requisite clear and convincing evidence of the patient's expressed intent to withhold life-sustaining treatment. *Id.*, at 531–534, 531 N. E. 2d, at 613–615....

In *In re Estate of Longeway*, 123 Ill. 2d 33, 549 N. E. 2d 292 (1989), the Supreme Court of Illinois considered whether a 76-year-old woman rendered incompetent from a series of strokes had a right to the discontinuance of artificial nutrition and hydration. Noting that the boundaries of a federal right of privacy were uncertain, the court found a right to refuse treatment in the doctrine of informed consent. *Id.*, at 43–45, 549 N. E. 2d, at 296–297. The court further held that the State Probate Act impliedly authorized a guardian to exercise a ward's right to refuse artificial sustenance in the event that the ward was terminally ill and irreversibly comatose. *Id.*, at 45–47, 549 N. E. 2d, at 298. Declining to adopt a best interests standard for deciding when it would be appropriate to exercise a ward's right because it "lets another make a determination of a patient's quality of life," the court opted instead for a substituted judgment standard. *Id.*, at 49, 549 N. E. 2d, at 299. Finding the "expressed intent" standard utilized in *O'Connor, supra,* too rigid, the court noted that other clear and convincing evidence of the patient's intent could be considered. 133 Ill. 2d, at 50–51, 549 N. E. 2d, at 300. The court also adopted the "consensus opinion [that] treats artificial nutrition and hydration as medical treatment." *Id.*, at 42, 549 N. E. 2d, at 296. Cf. *McConnell v. Beverly Enterprises-Connecticut, Inc.*, 209 Conn. 692, 705, 553 A. 2d 596, 603 (1989) (right to withdraw artificial nutrition and hydration found in the Connecticut Removal of Life Support Systems Act, which "provid[es] functional guidelines for the exercise of the common law and constitutional rights of self-determination"; attending physician authorized to remove treatment after finding that patient is in a terminal condition, obtaining consent of family, and considering expressed wishes of patient).[5]

As these cases demonstrate, the common-law doctrine of informed consent is viewed as generally encompassing the right of a competent individual to refuse medical treatment. Beyond that, these decisions demonstrate both similarity and diversity in their approach to decision of what all agree is a perplexing question with unusually strong moral and ethical overtones. State courts have available to them for decision a number of sources—state constitutions, statutes, and common law—which are not available to us. In this Court, the question is simply and starkly whether the United States Constitution prohibits Missouri from choosing the rule of decision which it did. This is the first case in which we have been squarely presented with the issue of whether the United States Constitution grants what is in common parlance referred to as a "right to die." We follow the judicious counsel of our decision in *Twin City Bank v. Nebeker*, 167 U.S. 197, 202 (1897), where we said that in deciding "a question of such magnitude and importance... it is the [better] part of wisdom not to attempt, by any general statement, to cover every possible phase of the subject."

The Fourteenth Amendment provides that no State shall "deprive any person of life, liberty, or property, without due process of law." The principle that a competent person has a constitutionally protected liberty interest in refusing unwanted medical treatment may be inferred from our prior decisions. In *Jacobson v. Massachusetts*, 197 U.S. 11, 24–30 (1905), for instance, the Court balanced an individual's liberty interest in declining an unwanted smallpox vaccine against the State's interest in preventing disease....

Just this Term, in the course of holding that a State's procedures for administering antipsychotic medication to prisoners were sufficient to satisfy due process concerns, we recognized that prisoners possess "a significant liberty interest in avoiding the unwanted administration of antipsychotic drugs under the Due Process Clause of the Fourteenth Amendment." *Washington v.*

Harper, (1990) ("The forcible injection of medication into a nonconsenting person's body represents a substantial interference with that person's liberty"). Still other cases support the recognition of a general liberty interest in refusing medical treatment. *Vitek v. Jones,* 445 U.S. 480, 494 (1980) (transfer to mental hospital coupled with mandatory behavior modification treatment implicated liberty interests); *Parham v. J.R.,* 442 U.S. 584, 600 (1979) ("a child, in common with adults, has a substantial liberty interest in not being confined unnecessarily for medical treatment").

But determining that a person has a "liberty interest" under the Due Process Clause does not end the inquiry; "whether respondent's constitutional rights have been violated must be determined by balancing his liberty interests against the relevant state interests." *Youngberg v. Romeo,* 457 U.S. 307, 321 (1982). See also *Mills v. Rogers,* 457 U.S. 291, 299 (1982).

Petitioners insist that under the general holdings of our cases, the forced administration of life-sustaining medical treatment, and even of artificially-delivered food and water essential to life, would implicate a competent person's liberty interest. Although we think the logic of the cases discussed above would embrace such a liberty interest, the dramatic consequences involved in refusal of such treatment would inform the inquiry as to whether the deprivation of that interest is constitutionally permissible. But for purposes of this case, we assume that the United States Constitution would grant a competent person a constitutionally protected right to refuse lifesaving hydration and nutrition.

Petitioners go on to assert that an incompetent person should possess the same right in this respect as is possessed by a competent person. They rely primarily on our decisions in *Parham v. J. R., supra,* and *Youngberg v. Romeo,* 457 U.S. 307 (1982). In *Parham,* we held that a mentally disturbed minor child had a liberty interest in "not being confined unnecessarily for medical treatment," 442 U.S. at 600, but we certainly did not intimate that such a minor child, after commitment, would have a liberty interest in refusing treatment. In *Youngberg,* we held that a seriously retarded adult had a liberty interest in safety and freedom from bodily restraint, 457 U.S., at 320. *Youngberg,* however, did not deal with decisions to administer or withhold medical treatment.

The difficulty with petitioners' claim is that in a sense it begs the question: an incompetent person is not able to make an informed and voluntary choice to exercise hypothetical right to refuse treatment or any other right. Such a "right" must be exercised for her, if at all, by some sort of surrogate. Here, Missouri has in effect recognized that under certain circumstances a surrogate may act for the patient in electing to have hydration and nutrition withdrawn in such a way as to cause death, but it has established a procedural safeguard to assure that the action of the surrogate conforms as best it may to the wishes expressed by the patient while competent. Missouri requires that evidence of the incompetent's wishes as to the withdrawal of treatment be proved by clear and convincing evidence. The question, then, is whether the United States Constitution forbids the establishment of this procedural requirement by the State. We hold that it does not.

Whether or not Missouri's clear and convincing evidence requirement comports with the United States Constitution depends in part on what interests the State may properly seek to protect in this situation. Missouri relies on its interest in the protection and preservation of human life, and there can be no gainsaying this interest. As a general matter, the States—indeed, all civilized nations— demonstrate their commitment to life by treating homicide as serious crime. Moreover, the majority of States in this country have laws imposing criminal penalties on one who assists another to commit suicide. We do not think a State is required to remain neutral in the face of an informed and voluntary decision by a physically-able adult to starve to death.

But in the context presented here, a State has more particular interests at stake. The choice between life and death is a deeply personal decision of obvious and overwhelming finality. We believe Missouri may legitimately seek to safeguard the personal element of this choice through the imposition of heightened evidentiary requirements. It cannot be disputed that the Due Process Clause protects an interest in life as well as an interest in refusing life-sustaining medical treatment. Not all incompetent patients will have loved ones available to serve as surrogate decisionmakers. And even where family members are present, "[t]here will, of course, be some unfortunate situations in which family members will not act to protect a patient." *In re Jobes*, 108 N. J. 394, 419, 529 A. 2d 434, 477 (1987). A State is entitled to guard against potential abuses in such situations. Similarly, a State is entitled to consider that a judicial proceeding to make a determination regarding an incompetent's wishes may very well not be an adversarial one, with the added guarantee of accurate factfinding that the adversary process brings with it. Finally,

we think a State may properly decline to make judgments about the "quality" of life that a particular individual may enjoy, and simply assert an unqualified interest in the preservation of human life to be weighed against the constitutionally protected interests of the individual.

In our view, Missouri has permissibly sought to advance these interests through the adoption of a "clear and convincing" standard of proof to govern such proceedings. "The function of a standard of proof, as that concept is embodied in the Due Process Clause and in the realm of factfinding, is to 'instruct the factfinder concerning the degree of confidence our society thinks he should have in the correctness of factual conclusions for a particular type of adjudication.'" *Addington v. Texas*, 441 U.S. 418, 423 (1979) (quoting *In re Winship*, 397 U.S. 358, 370 (1970) (Harlan, J., concurring)). "This Court has mandated an intermediate standard of proof—'clear and convincing evidence' —when the individual interests at stake in a state proceeding are both 'particularly important' and 'more substantial than mere loss of money.'" *Santosky v. Kramer*, 455 U.S. 745, 756 (1982) (quoting *Addington, supra*, at 424). Thus, such a standard has been required in deportation proceedings, *Woodby v. INS*, 385 U.S. 276 (1966), in denaturalization proceedings, *Schneiderman v. United States*, 320 U.S. 118 (1943), in civil commitment proceedings, *Addington, supra*, and in proceedings for the termination of parental rights. *Santosky, supra*,[6] Further, this level of proof, "or an even higher one, has traditionally been imposed in cases involving allegations of civil fraud, and in a variety of other kinds of civil cases involving such issues as ... lost wills, oral contracts to make bequests, and the like." *Woodby, supra*, at 285, n. 18.

We think it self-evident that the interests at stake in the instant proceedings are more substantial, both on an individual and societal level, than those involved in a run-of-the-mine civil dispute. But not only does the standard of proof reflect the importance of a particular adjudication, it also serves as "a societal judgment about how the risk of error should be distributed between the litigants." *Santosky, supra*, 455 U.S. at 755; *Addington, supra*, at 423. The more stringent the burden of proof a party must bear, the more that party bears the risk of an erroneous decision. We believe that Missouri may permissibly place an increased risk of an erroneous decision on those seeking to terminate an incompetent individual's life-sustaining treatment. An erroneous decision not to terminate results in a maintenance of the status quo; the possibility of subsequent developments such as advancments in medical science, the discovery of new evidence regarding the patient's intent, changes in the law, or simply the unexpected death of the patient despite the administration of life-sustaining treatment, at least create the potential that a wrong decision will eventually be corrected or its impact mitigated. An erroneous decision to withdraw life-sustaining treatment, however, is not susceptible of correction. In *Santosky*, one of the factors which led the Court to require proof by clear and convincing evidence in a proceeding to terminate parental rights was that a decision in such a case was final and irrevocable. *Santosky, supra*, at 759. The same must be said of the decision to discontinue hydration and nutrition of a patient such as Nancy Cruzan, which all agree will result in her death.

It is also worth noting that most, if not all, States simply forbid oral testimony entirely in determining the wishes of parties in transactions which, while important, simply do not have the consequences that a decision to terminate a person's life does. At common law and by statute in most States, the parole evidence rule prevents the variations of the terms of a written contract by oral testimony. The statute of frauds makes unenforceable oral contracts to leave property by will, and statutes regulating the making of wills universally require that those instruments be in writing. See 2 A. Corbin, Contracts § 398, pp. 360–361 (1950); 2 W. Page, Law of Wills § § 19.3–19.5, pp. 61–71 (1960). There is no doubt that statutes requiring wills to be in writing, and statutes of frauds which require that a contract to make a will be in writing, on occasion frustrate the effectuation of the intent of a particular decedent, just as Missouri's requirement of proof in this case may have frustrated the effectuation of the not-fully-expressed desires of Nancy Cruzan. But the Constitution does not require general rules to work faultlessly; no general rule can.

In sum, we conclude that a State may apply a clear and convincing evidence standard in proceedings where a guardian seeks to discontinue nutrition and hydration of a person diagnosed to be in a persistent vegetative state. We note that many courts which have adopted some sort of substituted judgment procedure in situations like this, whether they limit consideration of evidence to the prior expressed wishes of the incompetent individual, or whether they allow more general proof of what the individual's decision would have been, require a clear and convincing standard of proof for such evidence.

The Supreme Court of Missouri held that in this case the testimony adduced at trial did not amount to clear and convincing proof of the patient's desire to have hydration and nutrition withdrawn. In so doing, it reversed a decision of the Missouri trial court which had found that the evidence "suggest[ed]" Nancy Cruzan would not have desired to continue such measures, but which had not adopted the standard of "clear and convincing evidence" enunciated by the Supreme Court. The testimony adduced at trial consisted primarily of Nancy Cruzan's statements made to a housemate about a year before her accident that she would not want to live should she face life as a "vegetable," and other observations to the same effect. The observations did not deal in terms with withdrawal of medical treatment or of hydration and nutrition. We cannot say that the Supreme Court of Missouri committed constitutional error in reaching the conclusion that it did.[7]

Petitioners alternatively contend that Missouri must accept the "substituted judgment" of close family members even in the absence of substantial proof that their views reflect the views of the patient. They rely primarily upon our decisions in Michael H. v. Gerald D., 491 U.S. ____ (1989), and Parham v. J. R., 442 U.S. 584 (1979). But we do not think these cases support their claim. In Michael H., we upheld the constitutionality of California's favored treatment of traditional family relationships; such a holding may not be turned around into a constitutional requirement that a State must recognize the primacy of those relationships in a situation like this. And in Parham, where the patient was a minor, we also upheld the constitutionality of a state scheme in which parents made certain decisions for mentally ill minors. Here again petitioners would seek to turn a decision which allowed a State to rely on family decisionmaking into a constitutional requirement that the State recognize such decisionmaking. But constitutional law does not work that way.

No doubt is engendered by anything in this record but that Nancy Cruzan's mother and father are loving and caring parents. If the State were required by the United States Constitution to repose a right of "substituted judgment" with anyone, the Cruzans would surely qualify. But we do not think the Due Process Clause requires the State to repose judgment on these matters with anyone but the patient herself. Close family members may have a strong feeling —a feeling not at all ignoble or unworthy, but not entirely disinterested, either —that they do not wish to witness the continuation of the life of a loved one which they regard as hopeless, meaningless, and even degrading. But there is no automatic assurance that the view of close family members will necessarily be the same as the patient's would have been had she been confronted with the prospect of her situation while competent. All of the reasons previously discussed for allowing Missouri to require clear and convincing evidence of the patient's wishes lead us to conclude that the state may choose to defer only to those wishes, rather than confide the decision to close family members.[8]

The judgment of the Supreme Court of Missouri is Affirmed.

NOTES

1. The State Supreme Court, adopting much of the trial court's findings, described Nancy Cruzan's medical condition as follows:

"...(1) [H]er respiration and circulation are not artificially maintained and are within the normal limits of a thirty-year-old female; (2) she is oblivious to her environment except for reflexive responses to sound and perhaps painful stimuli; (3) she suffered anoxia of the brain resulting in a massive enlargement of the ventricles filling with cerebrospinal fluid in the area where the brain has degenerated and [her] cerebral cortical atrophy is irreversible, permanent, progressive and ongoing; (4) her highest cognitive brain function is exhibited by her grimacing perhaps in recognition of ordinarily painful stimuli, indicating the experience of pain and apparent response to sound; (5) she is a spastic quadriplegic; (6) her four extremities are contracted with irreversible muscular and tendon damage to all extremities; (7) she has no cognitive or reflexive ability to swallow food or water to maintain her daily essential needs and ...she will never recover her ability to swallow sufficient [sic] to satisfy her needs. In sum, Nancy is diagnosed as in a persistent vegetative state. She is not dead. She is not terminally ill. Medical experts testified that she could live another thirty years." *Cruzan v. Harmon*, 760 S. W. 2d 408, 411 (Mo. 1989) (en banc) (quotations omitted; footnote omitted).

In observing that Cruzan was not dead, the court referred to the following Missouri statute:

"For all legal purposes, the occurrence of human death shall be determined in accordance with the usual and customary standards of medical practice, provided that death shall not be determined to have occurred unless the following minimal conditions have been met:

"(1) When respiration and circulation are not artificially maintained, there is an irreversible cessation of spontaneous respiration and circulation; or

"(2) When respiration and circulation are artificially maintained, and there is total irreversible cessation of all brain function, including the brain stem and that such determination is made by a licensed physician." Mo. Rev. Stat. § 194.005 (1986).

Since Cruzan's respiration and circulation were not being artificially maintained, she obviously fit within the first proviso of the statute.

Dr. Fred Plum, the creator of the term "persistent vegetative state" and a renowned expert on the subject, has described the "vegetative state" in the following terms:

" 'Vegetative state describes a body which is functioning entirely in terms of its internal controls. It maintains temperature. It maintains heart beat and pulmonary ventilation. It maintains digestive activity. It maintains reflex activity of muscles and nerves for low level conditioned responses. But there is no behavioral evidence of either self-awareness or awareness of the surroundings in a learned manner.' " *In re Jobes*, 108 N. J. 394, 403, 529 A. 2d 434, 438 (1987).

See also Brief for American Medical Association et al., as *Amici Curiae*, 6 ("The persistent vegetative state can best be understood as one of the conditions in which patients have suffered a loss of consciousness").

2. See generally Karnezis, Patient's Right to Refuse Treatment Allegedly Necessary to Sustain Life, 93 A. L. R. 3d 67 (1979) (collecting cases); Cantor, A Patient's Decision to Decline Life-Saving Medical Treatment: Bodily Integrity Versus the Preservation of Life, 26 Rutgers L. Rev. 228, 229, and n. 5 (1973) (noting paucity of cases).

3. See Chapman, The Uniform Rights of the Terminally Ill Act: Too Little, Too Late?, 42 Ark. L. Rev. 319, 324, n. 15 (1989); see also F. Rozovsky, Consent to Treatment, A Practical Guide 415–423 (2d ed. 1984).

4. In a later trilogy of cases, the New Jersey Supreme Court stressed that the analytic framework adopted in *Conroy* was limited to elderly, incompetent patients with shortened life expectancies, and established alternative approaches to deal with a different set of situations. See *In re Farrell*, 108 N. J. 335, 529 A. 2d 404 (1987) (37-year-old competent mother with terminal illness had right to removal of respirator based on common law and constitutional principles which override competing state interests); *In re Peter*, 108 N.J. 365, 529 A. 2d 419 (1987) (65-year-old woman in persistent vegetative state had right to removal of nasogastric feeding tube—under *Conroy* subjective test, power of attorney and hearsay testimony constituted clear and convincing proof of patient's intent to have treatment withdrawn); *In re Jobes*, 108 N. J. 394, 529 A. 2d 434 (1987) (31-year-old woman in persistent vegetative state entitled to removal of jejunostomy feeding tube—even though hearsay testimony regarding patient's intent insufficient to meet clear and convincing standard of proof, under *Quinlan*, family or close friends entitled to make a substituted judgment for patient).

5. Besides the Missouri Supreme Court in *Cruzan* and the courts in *McConnell, Longeway, Drabick, Bouvia, Barber, O'Connor, Conroy, Jobes,* and *Peter, supra,* appellate courts of at least four other States and one Federal District Court have specifically considered and discussed the issue of withholding

or withdrawing artificial nutrition and hydration from incompetent individuals. See *Gray v. Romeo*, 697 F. Supp. 580 (RI 1988); *In re Gardner*, 534 A. 2d 947 (Me. 1987); *In re Grant*, 109 Wash. 2d 545, 747 P. 2d 445 (Wash. 1987); *Brophy v. New England Sinai Hospital, Inc.*, 398 Mass. 417, 497 N. E. 2d 626 (1986); *Corbett v. D'Alessandro*, 487 So. 2d 368 (Fla. App. 1986). All of these courts permitted or would permit the termination of such measures based on rights grounded in the common law, or in the State or Federal Constitution.

6. We recognize that these cases involved instances where the government sought to take action against an individual. See *Price Waterhouse v. Hopkins*, 490 U.S.___, ___(1989) (plurality opinion). Here, by contrast, the government seeks to protect the interests of an individual, as well as its own institutional interests, in life. We do not see any reason why important individual interests should be afforded less protection simply because the government finds itself in the position of defending them. "[W]e find it significant that . . . the defendant rather than the plaintiff" seeks the clear and convincing standard of proof—"suggesting that this standard ordinarily serves as a shield rather than . . . a sword." *Id.*, at ___. That it is the government that has picked up the shield should be of no moment.

7. The clear and convincing standard of proof has been variously defined in this context as "proof sufficient to persuade the trier of fact that the patient held a firm and settled commitment to the termination of life supports under the circumstances like those presented," *In re Westchester County Medical Center on behalf of O'Connor*, 72 N. Y. 2d 517, 531, N. E. 2d 607, 613 (1988) *(O'Connor)*, and as evidence which "produces in the mind of the trier of

fact a firm belief or conviction as to the truth of the allegations sought to be established, evidence so clear, direct and weighty and convincing as to enable [the factfinder] to come to a clear conviction, without hesitancy, of the truth of the precise facts in issue." *In re Jobes*, 108 N. J. at 407–408, 529 A. 2d, at 441 (quotation omitted). In both of these cases the evidence of the patient's intent to refuse medical treatment was arguably stronger than that presented here. The New York Court of Appeals and the Supreme Court of New Jersey, respectively, held that the proof failed to meet a clear and convincing threshold. See *O'Connor, supra*, at 526–534, 531 N. E. 2d, at 610–615; *Jobes, supra*, at 442–443.

8. We are not faced in this case with the question of whether a State might be required to defer to the decision of a surrogate if competent and probative evidence established that the patient herself had expressed a desire that the decision to terminate life-sustaining treatment be made for her by that individual. Petitioners also adumbrate in their brief a claim based on the Equal Protection Clause of the Fourteenth Amendment to the effect that Missouri has impermissibly treated incompetent parties differently from competent ones, citing the statement in *Cleburne v. Cleburne Living Center, Inc.*, 473 U.S. 432, 439 (1985), that the clause is "essentially a direction that all persons similarly situated should be treated alike." The differences between the choice made *by* a competent person to refuse medical treatment, and the choice made *for* an incompetent person by someone else to refuse medical treatment, are so obviously different that the State is warranted in establishing rigorous procedures for the latter class of cases which do not apply to the former class.

NO

William J. Brennan, Jr.

DISSENTING OPINION OF WILLIAM J. BRENNAN, JR.

JUSTICE BRENNAN, . . . dissenting.

> "Medical technology has effectively created a twilight zone of suspended animation where death commences while life, in some form, continues. Some patients, however, want no part of a life sustained only by medical technology. Instead, they prefer a plan of medical treatment that allows nature to take its course and permits them to die with dignity."[1]

Nancy Cruzan has dwelt in that twilight zone for six years. She is oblivious to her surroundings and will remain so. Her body twitches only reflexively, without consciousness. The areas of her brain that once thought, felt, and experienced sensations have degenerated badly and are continuing to do so. The cavities remaining are filling with cerebrospinal fluid. The " 'cerebral cortical atrophy is irreversible, permanent, progressive and ongoing.' " "Nancy will never interact meaningfully with her environment again. She will remain in a persistent vegetative state until her death." Because she cannot swallow, her nutrition and hydration are delivered through a tube surgically implanted in her stomach.

A grown woman at the time of the accident, Nancy had previously expressed her wish to forgo continuing medical care under circumstances such as these. Her family and her friends are convinced that this is what she would want. A guardian ad litem appointed by the trial court is also convinced that this is what Nancy would want. See 760 S. W. 2d, at 444 (Higgins, J., dissenting from denial of rehearing). Yet the Missouri Supreme Court, alone among state courts deciding such a question, has determined that an irreversibly vegetative patient will remain a passive prisoner of medical technology—for Nancy, perhaps for the next 30 years. See *id.*, at 424, 427.

Today the Court, while tentatively accepting that there is some degree of constitutionally protected liberty interest in avoiding unwanted medical treatment, including life-sustaining medical treatment such as artificial nutrition and hydration, affirms the decision of the Missouri Supreme Court.

From *Nancy Beth Cruzan v. Director, Missouri Department of Health,* 58 L.W. 4916 (1990). Some notes and case citations omitted.

The majority opinion, as I read it, would affirm that decision on the ground that a State may require "clear and convincing" evidence of Nancy Cruzan's prior decision to forgo life-sustaining treatment under circumstances such as hers in order to ensure that her actual wishes are honored. Because I believe that Nancy Cruzan has a fundamental right to be free of unwanted artificial nutrition and hydration, which right is not outweighed by any interests of the State, and because I find that the improperly biased procedural obstacles imposed by the Missouri Supreme Court impermissibly burden that right, I respectfully dissent. Nancy Cruzan is entitled to choose to die with dignity.

I
A

"[T]he timing of death—once a matter of fate—is now a matter of human choice." Office of Technology Assessment Task Force, Life Sustaining Technologies and the Elderly 41 (1988). Of the approximately two million people who die each year, 80% die in hospitals and long-term care institutions,[2] and perhaps 70% of those after a decision to forgo life-sustaining treatment has been made.[3] Nearly every death involves a decision whether to undertake some medical procedure that could prolong the process of dying. Such decisions are difficult and personal. They must be made on the basis of individual values, informed by medical realities, yet within a framework governed by law. The role of the courts is confined to defining that framework, delineating the ways in which government may and may not participate in such decisions.

The question before this Court is a relatively narrow one: whether the Due Process Clause allows Missouri to require a now-incompetent patient in an irreversible persistent vegetative state to remain on life-support absent rigorously clear and convincing evidence that avoiding the treatment represents the patient's prior, express choice. If a fundamental right is at issue, Missouri's rule of decision must be scrutinized under the standards this Court has always applied in such circumstances. As we said in *Zablocki v. Redhail*, 434 U.S. 374, 388 (1978), if a requirement imposed by a State "significantly interferes with the exercise of a fundamental right, it cannot be upheld unless it is supported by sufficiently important state interests and is closely tailored to effectuate only those interests." ...

B

The starting point of our legal analysis must be whether a competent person has a constitutional right to avoid unwanted medical care. Earlier this Term, this Court held that the Due Process Clause of the Fourteenth Amendment confers a significant liberty interest in avoiding unwanted medical treatment. *Washington v. Harper*, (1990). Today, the Court concedes that our prior decisions "support the recognition of a general liberty interest in refusing medical treatment." The Court, however, avoids discussing either the measure of that liberty interest or its application by assuming, for purposes of this case only, that a competent person has a constitutionally protected liberty interest in being free of unwanted artificial nutrition and hydration. JUSTICE O'CONNOR's opinion is less parsimonious. She openly affirms that "the Court has often deemed state incursions into the body repugnant to the interests protected by the Due Process Clause," that there is a liberty interest in avoiding unwanted medical treatment and that it encompasses the right to be free of "artificially delivered food and water."

But if a competent person has a liberty interest to be free of unwanted medical treatment, as both the majority and JUS-TICE O'CONNOR concede, it must be fundamental. "We are dealing here with [a decision] which involves one of the basic civil rights of man." *Skinner v. Oklahoma ex rel. Williamson*, 316 U.S. 535, 541 (1942) (invalidating a statute authorizing sterilization of certain felons). Whatever other liberties protected by the Due Process Clause are fundamental, "those liberties that are 'deeply rooted in this Nation's history and tradition'" are among them. *Bowers v. Hardwick*, 478 U.S. 186, 192 (1986) (quoting *Moore v. East Cleveland, supra*, at 503 (plurality opinion).

The right to be free from medical attention without consent, to determine what shall be done with one's own body, *is* deeply rooted in this Nation's traditions, as the majority acknowledges. This right has long been "firmly entrenched in American tort law" and is securely grounded in the earliest common law. *Ibid.* See also *Mills v. Rogers*, 457 U.S. 291, 294, n. 4 (1982) ("the right to refuse any medical treatment emerged from the doctrines of trespass and battery, which were applied to unauthorized touchings of a physician"). "'Anglo-American law starts with the premise of thorough-going self determination. It follows that each man is considered to be master of his own body, and he may, if he be of sound mind, expressly prohibit the performance of lifesaving surgery, or other medical treatment.'" *Natanson v. Kline*, 186 Kan.

393, 406–407, 350 P. 2d 1093, 1104 (1960). "The inviolability of the person" has been held as "sacred" and "carefully guarded" as any common law right. *Union Pacific R. Co. v. Botsford*, 141 U.S. 250, 251–252 (1891). Thus, freedom from unwanted medical attention is unquestionably among those principles "so rooted in the traditions and conscience of our people as to be ranked as fundamental." *Snyder v. Massachusetts*, 291 U.S. 97, 105 (1934).

That there may be serious consequences involved in refusal of the medical treatment at issue here does not vitiate the right under our common law tradition of medical self-determination. It is "a well-established rule of general law ... that it is the patient, not the physician, who ultimately decides if treatment—any treatment—is to be given at all.... The rule has never been qualified in its application by either the nature or purpose of the treatment, or the gravity of the consequences of acceding to or foregoing it." *Tune v. Walter Reed Army Medical Hospital*, 602 F. Supp. 1452, 1455 (DC 1985). See also *Downer v. Veilleux*, 322 A. 2d 82, 91 (Me. 1974)....

No material distinction can be drawn between the treatment to which Nancy Cruzan continues to be subject—artificial nutrition and hydration—and any other medical treatment. The artificial delivery of nutrition and hydration is undoubtedly medical treatment. The technique to which Nancy Cruzan is subject—artificial feeding through a gastrostomy tube—involves a tube implanted surgically into her stomach through incisions in her abdominal wall. It may obstruct the intestinal tract, erode and pierce the stomach wall or cause leakage of the stomach's contents into the abdominal cavity. See Page, Andrassy, & Sandler, Techniques in Delivery of Liquid Diets, in Nutrition in Clinical Surgery 66–67 (M. Deitel 2d ed. 1985). The tube can cause pneumonia from reflux of the stomach's contents into the lung. See Bernard & Forlaw, Complications and Their Prevention, in Enteral and Tube Feeding 553 (J. Rombeau & M. Caldwell eds. 1984). Typically, and in this case, commercially prepared formulas are used, rather than fresh food. The type of formula and method of administration must be experimented with to avoid gastrointestinal problems. The patient must be monitored daily by medical personnel as to weight, fluid intake and fluid output; blood tests must be done weekly.

Artificial delivery of food and water is regarded as medical treatment by the medical profession and the Federal Government.[4] According to the American Academy of Neurology, "[t]he artificial provision of nutrition and hydration is a form of medical treatment... analogous to other forms of life-sustaining treatment, such as the use of the respirator. When a patient is unconscious, both a respirator and an artificial feeding device serve to support or replace normal bodily functions that are compromised as a result of the patient's illness." Position of the American Academy of Neurology on Certain Aspects of the Care and Management of the Persistent Vegetative State Patient, 39 Neurology 125 (Jan. 1989). See also Council on Ethical and Judicial Affairs of the American Medical Association, Current Opinions, Opinion 2.20 (1989) ("Life-prolonging medical treatment includes medication and artificially or technologically supplied respiration, nutrition or hydration"); President's Commission 88 (life-sustaining treatment includes respirators, kidney dialysis machines, special feeding procedures). The

Federal Government permits the cost of the medical devices and formulas used in enteral feeding to be reimbursed under Medicare. The formulas are regulated by the Federal Drug Administration as "medical foods," and the feeding tubes are regulated as medical devices.

Nor does the fact that Nancy Cruzan is now incompetent deprive her of her fundamental rights. See *Youngberg v. Romeo*, 457 U.S. 307, 315–316, 319 (1982) (holding that severely retarded man's liberty interests in safety, freedom from bodily restraint and reasonable training survive involuntary commitment); *Parham v. J. R.*, 442 U.S. 584, 600 (1979) (recognizing a child's substantial liberty interest in not being confined unnecessarily for medical treatment); *Jackson v. Indiana*, 406 U.S. 715, 730, 738 (1972) (holding that Indiana could not violate the due process and equal protection rights of a mentally retarded deaf mute by committing him for an indefinite amount of time simply because he was incompetent to stand trial on the criminal charges filed against him). As the majority recognizes, the question is not whether an incompetent has constitutional rights, but how such rights may be exercised. As we explained in *Thompson v. Oklahoma*, 487 U.S. 815 (1988), "[t]he law must often adjust the manner in which it affords rights to those whose status renders them unable to exercise choice freely and rationally. Children, the insane, and *those who are irreversibly ill with loss of brain function, for instance, all retain 'rights,'* to be sure, but often such rights are only meaningful as they are exercised by agents acting with the best interests of their principals in mind." *Id.*, at 825, n. 23 (emphasis added). "To deny [its] exercise because the patient is unconscious or incompetent would be to deny the right." *Foody v. Manchester Memorial*

Hospital, 40 Conn. Super. 127, 133, 482 A. 2d 713, 718 (1984)....

III

This is not to say that the State has no legitimate interests to assert here. As the majority recognizes, Missouri has a *parens patriae* interest in providing Nancy Cruzan, now incompetent, with as accurate as possible a determination of how she would exercise her rights under these circumstances. Second, if and when it is determined that Nancy Cruzan would want to continue treatment, the State may legitimately assert an interest in providing that treatment. But *until* Nancy's wishes have been determined, the only state interest that may be asserted is an interest in safeguarding the accuracy of that determination.

Accuracy, therefore, must be our touchstone. Missouri may constitutionally impose only those procedural requirements that serve to enhance the accuracy of a determination of Nancy Cruzan's wishes or are at least consistent with an accurate determination. The Missouri "safeguard" that the Court upholds today does not meet that standard. The determination needed in this context is whether the incompetent person would choose to live in a persistent vegetative state on life-support or to avoid this medical treatment. Missouri's rule of decision imposes a markedly asymmetrical evidentiary burden. Only evidence of specific statements of treatment choice made by the patient when competent is admissible to support a finding that the patient, now in a persistent vegetative state, would wish to avoid further medical treatment. Moreover, this evidence must be clear and convincing. No proof is required to support a finding that the incompetent person would wish to continue treatment.

A

The majority offers several justifications for Missouri's heightened evidentiary standard. First, the majority explains that the State may constitutionally adopt this rule to govern determinations of an incompetent's wishes in order to advance the State's substantive interests, including its unqualified interest in the preservation of human life. Missouri's evidentiary standard, however, cannot rest on the State's own interest in a particular substantive result. To be sure, courts have long erected clear and convincing evidence standards to place the greater risk of erroneous decisions on those bringing disfavored claims. In such cases, however, the choice to discourage certain claims was a legitimate, constitutional policy choice. In contrast, Missouri has not such power to disfavor a choice by Nancy Cruzan to avoid medical treatment, because Missouri has no legitimate interest in providing Nancy with treatment until it is established that this represents her choice. Just as a State may not override Nancy's choice directly, it may not do so indirectly through the imposition of a procedural rule....

The majority claims that the allocation of the risk of error is justified because it is more important not to terminate life-support for someone who would wish it continued than to honor the wishes of someone who would not. An erroneous decision to terminate life-support is irrevocable, says the majority, while an erroneous decision not to terminate "results in a maintenance of the status quo." But, from the point of view of the patient, an erroneous decision in either direction is irrevocable. An erroneous decision to terminate artificial nutrition and hydration, to be sure, will lead to failure of that last remnant of physiological life, the brain stem, and result in complete brain death. An erroneous decision not to terminate life-support, however, robs a patient of the very qualities protected by the right to avoid unwanted medical treatment. His own degraded existence is perpetuated; his family's suffering is protracted; the memory he leaves behind becomes more and more distorted.

Even a later decision to grant him his wish cannot undo the intervening harm. But a later decision is unlikely in an event. "[T]he discovery of new evidence," to which the majority refers, is more hypothetical than plausible. The majority also misconceives the relevance of the possibility of "advancements in medical science," by treating it as a reason to force someone to continue medical treatment against his will. The possibility of a medical miracle is indeed part of the calculus, but it is a part of the *patient's* calculus. If current research suggests that some hope for cure or even moderate improvement is possible within the life-span projected, this is a factor that should be and would be accorded significant weight in assessing what the patient himself would choose.[5]...

C

I do not suggest that States must sit by helplessly if the choices of incompetent patients are in danger of being ignored. Even if the Court had ruled that Missouri's rule of decision is unconstitutional, as I believe it should have, States would nevertheless remain free to fashion procedural protections to safeguard the interests of incompetents under these circumstances. The Constitution provides merely a framework here: protections must be genuinely aimed at ensuring decisions commensurate with the will of the patient, and must be reliable as instruments to that end. Of the many states which have instituted such protections, Missouri is virtually the only one to have fashioned a rule that lessens the likelihood of accurate determinations. In contrast, nothing in the Constitution prevents States from reviewing the advisability of a family decision, by requiring a court proceeding or by appointing an impartial guardian ad litem....

D

Finally, I cannot agree with the majority that when it is not possible to determine what choice an incompetent patient would make, a State's role as *parens patriae* permits the State automatically to make that choice itself.... Under fair rules of evidence, it is improbable that a court could not determine what the patient's choice would be. Under the rule of decision adopted by Missouri and upheld today by this Court, such occasions might be numerous. But in neither case does it follow that it is constitutionally acceptable for the State invariably to assume the role of deciding for the patient. A State's legitimate interest in safeguarding a patient's choice cannot be furthered by simply appropriating it.

The majority justifies its position by arguing that, while close family members may have a strong feeling about the question, "there is no automatic assurance that the view of close family members will necessarily be the same as the patient's would have been had she been confronted with the prospect of her situation while competent." I cannot quarrel with this observation. But it leads only to another question: Is there any reason to suppose that a State is *more* likely to make the choice that the patient would have made than someone who knew the patient intimately? To ask this is to answer it. As the New Jersey Supreme Court observed: "Family members are best qualified to make substituted judgments for incompetent patients not only because of their peculiar grasp of the patient's approach to life, but also because of their special bonds with him or her.... It is ... they who treat the patient as a person, rather than a symbol of a cause." *In re Jobes*, 108 N. J. 394, 416, 529 A. 2d 434, 445 (1987). The State, in contrast, is a stranger to the patient.

A State's inability to discern an incompetent patient's choice still need not mean that a State is rendered powerless to protect that choice. But I would find that the Due Process Clause prohibits a State from doing more than that. A State may ensure that the person who makes the decision on the patient's behalf is the one whom the patient himself would have selected to make that choice for him. And a State may exclude from consideration anyone having improper motives. But a State generally must either repose the choice with the person whom the patient himself would most likely have chosen as proxy or leave the decision to the patient's family.[6]

IV

As many as 10,000 patients are being maintained in persistent vegetative states in the United States, and the number is expected to increase significantly in the near future. Medical technology, developed over the past 20 or so years, is often capable of resuscitating people after they have stopped breathing or their hearts have stopped beating. Some of those people are brought fully back to life. Two decades ago, those who were not and could not swallow and digest food, died. Intravenous solutions could not provide sufficient calories to maintain people for more than a short time. Today, various forms of artificial feeding have been developed that are able to keep people metabolically alive for years, even decades. See Spencer & Palmisano, Specialized Nutritional Support of Patients—A Hospital's Legal Duty?, 11 Quality Rev. Bull. 160, 160–161 (1985). In addition, in this century, chronic or degenerative ailments have replaced communicable diseases as the primary causes of death. See R. Weir, Abating Treatment with Critically Ill Patients 12–13 (1989); President's Commission 15–16. The 80% of Americans who die in hospitals are "likely to meet their end... 'in a sedated or comatose state; betubed nasally, abdominally and intravenously; and far more like manipulated objects than like moral subjects.'"[7] A fifth of all adults surviving to age 80 will suffer a progressive dementing disorder prior to death. See Cohen & Eisdorfer, Dementing Disorders, in The Practice of Geriatrics 194 (E. Calkins, P. Davis, & A, Ford eds. 1986).

"[L]aw, equity and justice must not themselves quail and be helpless in the face of modern technological marvels presenting questions hitherto unthought of." *In re Quinlan*, 70 N. J. 10, 44, 355 A. 2d 647, 665, cert. denied, 429 U.S. 922 (1976). The new medical technology can reclaim those who would have been irretrievably lost a few decades ago and restore them to active lives. For Nancy Cruzan, it failed, and for others with wasting incurable disease it may be doomed to failure. In these unfortunate situations, the bodies and preferences and memories of the victims do not escheat to the State; nor does our Constitution permit the State or any other government to commandeer them. No singularity of feeling exists upon which such a government might confidently rely as *parens patriae*. The President's Commission, after years of research, concluded:

> "In few areas of health care are people's evaluations of their experiences so varied and uniquely personal as in their assessments of the nature and value of the processes associated with dying. For some, every moment of life is of inestimable value; for others, life without some desired level of mental or physical ability is worthless or burdensome. A moderate degree of suffering may be an important means of personal growth and religious experience to one person, but only frightening or despicable to another." President's Commission 276.

Yet Missouri and this Court have displaced Nancy's own assessment of the processes associated with dying. They have discarded evidence of her will, ignored her values, and deprived her of the right to a decision as closely approximating her own choice as humanly possible. They have done so disingenuously in her name, and openly in Missouri's own. That Missouri and this Court may truly be motivated only by concern for incompetent patients makes no matter. As one of our most prominent jurists warned us decades ago: "Experience should teach us to be most on our guard to protect liberty when the government's purposes are beneficent.... The greatest dangers to liberty lurk in insidious encroachment by men of zeal, well meaning but without understanding." *Olmstead v. United States*, 277 U.S. 438, 479 (1928) (Brandeis, J., dissenting).

I respectfully dissent.

NOTES

1. *Rasmussen v. Fleming*, 154 Arix. 207, 211, 741 P. 2d 674, 678 (1987) (en banc).

2. See President's Commission for the Study of Ethical Problems in Medicine and Biomedical and Behavioral Research, Deciding to Forego Life Sustaining Treatment 15, n. 1, and 17–18 (1983) (hereafter President's Commission).

3. See Lipton, Do-Not-Resuscitate Decisions in a Community Hospital: Incidence, Implications and Outcomes, 256 JAMA 1164, 1168 (1986).

4. The Missouri court appears to be alone among state courts to suggest otherwise, 760 S. W. 2d, at 419 and 423, although the court did not rely on a distinction between artificial feeding and other forms of medical treatment. *Id.*, at 423. See, *e. g.*, *Delio v. Westchester County Medical Center*, 129 App. Div. 2d 1, 19, 516 N. Y. S. 2d 677, 689 (1987) ("review of the decisions in other jurisdictions ... failed to uncover a single case in which a court confronted with an application to discontinue feeding by artificial means has evaluated medical procedures to provide nutrition and hydration differently from other types of life-sustaining procedures").

5. For Nancy Cruzan, no such cure or improvement is in view. So much of her brain has deteriorated and been replaced by fluid, that apparently the only medical advance that could restore consciousness to her body would be a brain transplant.

6. Only in the exceedingly rare case where the State cannot find any family member or friend who can be trusted to endeavor genuinely to make the treatment choice the patient would have made does the State become the legitimate surrogate decisionmaker.

7. Fadiman, The Liberation of Lolly and Gronky, Life Magazine, Dec. 1986, p. 72 (quoting medical ethicist Joseph Fletcher).

POSTSCRIPT

Can States Restrict the Right to Die?

Nancy Cruzan died six months after the U.S. Supreme Court's ruling on her right to die. Two months after the Court's decision, the Cruzans asked for a court hearing to present new evidence from three of their daughter's co-workers. At the hearing, the co-workers testified that they recalled her saying she would never want to live "like a vegetable." At the same hearing, Cruzan's doctor called her existence a "living hell" and recommended removal of the feeding tube. Her court-appointed guardian concurred. The judge then ruled that there was clear evidence of Cruzan's wishes and gave permission for the tube to be removed. She died on December 26, 1990.

The fundamental concern in right to die cases, indeed in most civil liberties cases, is the fear of what will happen in the next case. In other words, a judge may avoid doing what seems reasonable in one case if his ruling could be used to reach a less desirable result in a future case with slightly different facts. Lawyers refer to this as the "slippery slope." If euthanasia is justified in a case where the patient is terminally ill and in severe pain, it may be allowed in a later case where, as in *Cruzan*, the patient is in an unrecoverable state but not in pain. Perhaps euthanasia would be extended to handicapped newborns or to the senile.

Underlying the slippery slope argument in these cases, as in the abortion cases, is the fear of what might happen if life in some instances is not considered to be sacred. A member of the prosecution staff at the Nuremberg trials of Nazi doctors who participated in the killing of "incurables" and the "useless" traced the origin of Nazi policy to

> a subtle shift in emphasis in the basic attitude of the physicians. It started with the acceptance of the attitude, basic in the euthanasia movement, that there is such a thing as the life not worthy to be lived. This attitude in its early stages concerned itself merely with the severely and chronically sick. Gradually, the sphere of those to be included in this category was enlarged to encompass the socially unproductive, the ideologically unwanted, the racially unwanted and finally all non-Germans. But it is important to realize that the infinitely small wedged-in lever from which this entire trend received its impetus was the attitude toward the unrehabilitatable sick. (Kamisar, "Some Non-Religious Views Against Proposed 'Mercy Killing' Legislation," 42 *Minnesota Law Review* 969 [1958])

Considering the decisions in the *Cruzan* case, how do you feel about the slippery slope argument? Does the majority opinion, by allowing alert and competent patients to choose to remove feeding tubes, start us down the slippery slope? Does establishing a "clear and convincing" standard effectively halt the slide down the slope? Even if you feel that the slide down the slope has not begun, it is also true that there will be more cases to follow *Cruzan*. For example, what if there is disagreement between hospital and family officials about whether or not the patient's wishes are "clear and convincing"? What happens if the patient is conscious but in great pain and receiving large doses of pain medication? Which parties should be entitled to be heard if a case gets to court? What is to be done if there is disagreement among family members?

One effect of the Court's opinion is to encourage the use of living wills. Forty states and the District of Columbia have statutes permitting living wills, which allow individuals to specify in advance what treatment they would wish to receive. Most of these statutes apply only in cases of terminal illness, but the statutes are likely to be changed in the light of the *Cruzan* decision. Since less than half of the U.S. population have regular wills, the living will is unlikely to provide a total solution to the problem.

The most newsworthy recent case touching on this issue concerns Dr. Jack Kevorkian, who has assisted individuals in committing suicide. The legal issues involved in assisted suicide are covered in a symposium in the *Ohio Northern Law Review*, vol. 20, p. 559 (1994). Kevorkian's case is discussed by his attorney, Geoffrey Fieger, in "The Persecution and Prosecution of Dr. Death and His Mercy Machine," 20 *Ohio Northern Law Review* 659 (1994). Other cases involving the withdrawal of treatment are *In the Matter of Mary O'Connor*, 72 N.Y.2d 517 (1988); *Brophy v. New England Sinai Hospital*, 497 N.E.2d 626 (1986); *In re Conroy*, 486 A.2d 1209 (1985); *Bovia v. The Superior Court of Los Angeles County*, 225 Cal. 297 (1986); and *In re Quinlan*, 355 A.2d 647 (1976). Recent analyses include "The Care of the Dying: A Symposium on the Case of Betty Wright," 17 *Law, Medicine and Health Care*, pp. 207–233 (1989); Weir, *Abating Treatment With Critically Ill Patients* (Oxford University Press, 1989); Wennberg, *Terminal Choices: Euthanasia, Suicide, and the Right to Die* (Wm. B. Eerdmans, 1989); Rhoden, "Litigating Life and Death," 102 *Harvard Law Review* 375 (1988); Note, "Judicial Postponement of Death Recognition: The Tragic Case of Mary O'Connor," 15 *American Journal of Law and Medicine* 301 (1990); Glick, *The Right to Die: Policy Innovation and Its Consequences* (Columbia University Press, 1992); Misbin, ed., *Euthanasia: The Good of the Patient, The Good of Society* (University Publishing Group, 1992); and Capron, "Legal and Ethical Problems in Decisions for Death," 14 *Law, Medicine and Health Care* 141 (1987).

Further worthwhile reading on euthanasia and the right to die may be found in R. Weir, *Selective Nontreatment of Handicapped Newborns: Moral Dilemmas in Neonatal Medicine* (Oxford University Press, 1984); Note, "Physician-Assisted Suicide and the Right to Die With Assistance," 105 *Harvard Law Review* 2021 (1992); Kamisar, "When Is There a Constitutional 'Right to Die'? When Is There No Constitutional 'Right to Live'?" 25 *Georgia Law Review* 1203 (1991); Robertson, "Assessing Quality of Life: A Response to Professor Kamisar," 25 *Georgia Law Review* 1243 (1991); and A. W. Alschuler, "The Right to Die," 141 *New Law Journal* 1637 (November 29, 1991).

ISSUE 10

Should Homosexuality Bar a Parent from Being Awarded Custody of a Child?

YES: Hewitt P. Tomlin, Jr., from Concurring Opinion, *Leonard Arthur Collins v. Beverly Jo Clendenan Collins,* Court of Appeals of Tennessee (1988)

NO: Melvin P. Antell, from Majority Opinion, *M. P. v. S. P.,* Superior Court of New Jersey, Appellate Division (1979)

ISSUE SUMMARY

YES: Judge Hewitt P. Tomlin, Jr., argues that an award of child custody to a homosexual parent cannot be in the best interests of the child.

NO: Justice Melvin P. Antell refuses to allow one parent's homosexuality to be a deciding factor in the custody decision of the court.

> Parental rights are comprehensive, and they operate against the state, against third parties, and against the child. Parents have the right to custody of their child; to discipline the child; and to make decisions about education, medical treatment, and religious upbringing. Parents assign the child a name. They have a right to the child's earnings and services. They decide where the child shall live. Parents have a right to information gathered by others about the child and may exclude others from that information. They may speak for the child and may assert or waive the child's rights. Parents have the right to determine who may visit the child and to place their child in another's care.
>
> —Katharine Bartlett

In *Bowers v. Hardwick,* 478 U.S. 186 (1986), the Supreme Court upheld a Georgia law that made acts of sodomy performed by anyone in any place a crime. The 5–4 decision was one of the most controversial and widely publicized Supreme Court decisions of 1986. The Georgia law had been challenged by Michael Hardwick, a homosexual who had been arrested for acts performed in his own home. The Supreme Court refused to find that such acts, even when performed in private places, were protected by the Constitution and ruled that there was no "fundamental right to engage in homosexual sodomy."

Bowers v. Hardwick was a considerable blow to the cause of gay rights. Privacy law had been relied upon, sometimes unsuccessfully, in earlier cases that involved the legality of gay sexual activity and undoubtedly would have been used in future cases. Yet, it is also true that there are many legal protections sought by homosexuals for which privacy law is largely irrelevant.

These include conflicts involving nonsexual conduct or conduct in public—acts that involve the ability to live one's life without state interference or discrimination. As one gay rights activist has stated, "For many gay people the most important 'gay rights' issues are simply human issues—their rights to a job, a place to live, or custody of a child."

The following readings ask whether or not a person's sexual orientation should be considered in a hearing to determine which parent will be awarded custody of a child. Only one jurisdiction in the United States, the District of Columbia, prohibits a judge from making sexual orientation the sole criteria in granting custody to a father or a mother. Even this law, however, does not prohibit the court from taking sexual orientation into account.

The general standard for awarding custody of a child is "the best interests of the child." There is no single definition or set of criteria for this standard, but it typically includes all or most of the following:

1. the wishes of the child's parent or parents as to his custody;
2. the wishes of the child as to his custodian;
3. the interaction and interrelationship of the child with his parent or parents, his siblings, and any other person who may significantly affect the child's best interest;
4. the child's adjustment to his home, school, and community;
5. the mental and physical health of all individuals involved;
6. the length of time the child has lived in a stable, satisfactory environment and the desirability of maintaining continuity;
7. the permanence, as a family unit, of the existing or proposed custodial home;
8. the capacity and disposition of the parties to give the child love, affection, and guidance, and to continue educating and raising the child in the child's culture and religion or creed, if any.

As you read the following cases, try to evaluate how much weight should be given to each of the above criteria and whether or not the sexual orientation of a party relates to any of these factors.

YES

Hewitt P. Tomlin, Jr.

OPINION OF HEWITT P. TOMLIN, JR.

COLLINS *v.* COLLINS

[The parents in this case were divorced in 1978 on the grounds of irreconcilable differences. Their only child, a daughter, was less than a year old at that time. Both parties agreed that the mother would have custody of the child and the father would have reasonable visitation privileges and pay child support of $160 per month. The child was nine years old at the time of this custody hearing.

In 1984, the father filed a petition for custody. At trial he stated that he sought this change of custody solely on the basis of the mother's homosexuality.

The mother admitted that she is a practicing homosexual. She has had four serious lesbian relationships since the divorce in 1978, the first beginning when her daughter was approximately one-and-one-half years of age. The duration of these relationships ranged from eight months to three-and-one-half years. The current relationship began about one year prior to the hearing. —Ed.]

Judge P. J. Tomlin concurring:

While I agree with the results reached by my colleagues in affirming the trial court, I feel constrained to write this separate concurring opinion for the reasons that I feel that the majority did not address the issue of the homosexuality of the former custodial parent as directly as it should be addressed. It is my opinion that in the future, the courts of this state oftentimes are going to be faced with the issue of the homosexuality of a custodial parent or one desiring to be a custodial parent. For this reason adequate ground rules need to be laid down.

The majority approached the custody issue on the basis of the comparative fitness of the two parents and concluded that the father was more fit than the mother, noting that the mother was a fit parent as well. This issue was not presented to us as a matter of comparative fitness. The issue, clearly stated, is whether a child's best interests are promoted by an award of custody to a parent who carries on an active, open homosexual relationship in the family

From *Leonard Arthur Collins v. Beverly Jo Clendenan Collins,* Court of Appeals of Tennessee, Western Section (1988). Notes and some case citations omitted.

200

home. As noted in the majority opinion, the father stated at trial that he sought change of custody from the mother to himself solely on the basis of the mother's homosexuality.

The facts in the case at bar present a clear picture of a homosexual mother who has actively practiced lesbianism for the past eight years. The mother's commitment to homosexuality can best be described in her own words:

Q: Okay. In that regard, you would agree that you are a practicing homosexual?
A: Yes.
Q: All right. During the time that you have had custody of the child, and her name is J . . . , is it not?
A: Yes, it is.
Q: And she is how old?
A: Nine.
Q: Nine years old?
A: Yes.
Q: Have you had several relationships that were primary relationships with other homosexual women?
A: Yes. I've had three serious relationships and I am currently in a relationship.
Q: Okay. You are currently in a relationship?
A: Yes.
Q: By serious relationships, exactly what do you mean?
A: I mean one where someone would share my home and my life, and would actually live there. . . .
Q: Going back to that first person and to the first primary relationship that you had in your home and as a significant other person in your life; when did that person move into your home, that person being number one? . . .
A: J . . . was around two years old and I lived with that person for a year and a half. . . .

Then the second person that I was with was a short or shorter relationship because that person left me and went to Houston. That lasted for about eight months. Then when J . . . was five, I was with somebody for three and a half years. . . .

And then I was [with] the third person from the time J . . . was three until she was about eight and a half. The person that I am with now I have been seeing for about a year. . . .

Q: And you are now in a fourth relationship?
A: Yes.
Q: Does that individual, the fourth person, also reside in the house there with you and with J . . . ?
A: No.
Q: Did Lois Rainey reside there in the house with you and J . . . ?
A: Yes.
Q: Were you in love with Lois Rainey?
A: Yes. . . .
Q: Did you or do you, as a matter of practice, and this is a two-part question. Did you or do you express your affection by way of embracing these other persons?
A: Only if one or the other of us would be gone for a week or two, we might hug upon returning to each other. . . .
Q: Do you currently share the same bed with this other person, number four?
A: Yes.
Q: Did you share the same bed with number two?
A: Yes, sir.
Q: And number three?
A: Yes, sir.
Q: And number one?
A: Yes, sir.
Q: How large a home do you occupy?
A: Three bedrooms.

Q: And do you know how many square feet are in that home?

A: Fifteen hundred. ...

Q: Does Lois still see J...?

A: Yes, sir.

Q: Under what circumstances?

A: She is out of town and she has parents here and when she comes into town she often asks if she can see J... and she and J... will go over to her parents. They have adopted her as a grandchild of their own. ...

Q: Are most of your friends homosexual?

A: Yes, sir.

Q: Are they mostly female homosexuals or are they also males?

A: Mostly female.

Q: Do you ever have parties?

A: Twice a year, maybe around holidays.

Q: Are your female homosexual friends the primary core of the invited guests?

A: Yes.

Q: Would J... not be present at any of these parties?

A: I make it a strict rule with any of my friends to abide by the same values, same restrictions as I do, myself. They love J... and she is there up until her bedtime and then she goes to bed. ...

Q: You aren't around all the time that your friends are around J..., are you?

A: I am not around?

Q: That is the question. Are you around all the time that they are?

A: The entire time?

Q: Yes.

A: No, but I have trust in them.

Q: And you are not around all the time when Lois takes J... from the house, are you?

A: No, but I also trust her.

Q: Have you recently started to discuss with J... your sexual preferences and what that means to you.

A: For a long time, I put it off but knowing that this court date was going to actually occur then yes, I sat down and explained it to her.

Q: What did you tell her?

A: I told her that being gay meant that you cared and loved—gay, that you loved another woman and that love is love and there are all kinds of different loves. You know, at the same time, I also had to explain to her what her father had against that and I explained that to the best of my ability. All that I could sense from her was that I am her mother and that it doesn't matter to her whether I am gay.

Q: Have you distinguished between the love that exists between you and your friends and the kind of love that exists between a man and a woman, if any?

A: I explained to her that it is the same type of love. ...

Q: I noticed in your statements that you take J... with you when you spend the night with Barbara, and Barbara meaning number four?

A: Yes.

Q: What are the sleeping arrangements there at Barbara's house?

A: There is a downstairs bedroom. She only has two bedrooms. There's the downstairs bedroom that J... sleeps in and she and I stay upstairs in her bedroom.

In addition, the daughter's testimony sheds additional light on the nature and extent of Mother's activities. Daughter testified as follows:

Q: Do they [Mother and lesbian lover] sleep together in the same bed as well as in the same bedroom?

A: Yes.

Q: They said they love each other. As far as you know, how do they express that with each other? Do they hug each other?

A: Yes.

Q: Do they kiss each other?

A: Yes.

Q: Do they tell each other that they love each other?

A: Yes.

While we are dealing with lesbianism, there is no ground for a gender-based distinction. Therefore, I shall speak to this issue solely in terms of homosexuality. Homosexuality has been considered contrary to the morality of man for well over two thousand years. It has been and is considered to be an unnatural, immoral act. Since 1858, sexual acts connected with homosexuality have been labeled a crime. T.C.A. § 39-2-612 reads as follows:

> Crimes against nature—Crimes against nature, either with mankind or any beast, are punishable by imprisonment in the penitentiary not less than five (5) years nor more than fifteen (15) years.

There are many compelling reasons for a state to regulate homosexuality. Writing in the Cornell Law Review, J. Harvey Wilkinson and G. Edward White stated in an article entitled "Constitutional Protection for Personal Lifestyles," Vol. 62, pp. 593, 595–596 as follows:

> [S]tate interests of significant strength support a prohibition of homosexuality. First, a state may be interested in discouraging public behavior that gives widespread offense.
> ...The most threatening aspect of homosexuality is its potential to become a viable alternative to heterosexual intimacy....

This state concern, in our view, should not be minimized. The nuclear, heterosexual family is charged with several of society's most essential functions. It has served as an important means of educating the young; it has often provided economic support and psychological comfort to family members; and it has operated as the unit upon which basic governmental policies in such matters as taxation, conscription, and inheritance have been based. Family life has been a central unifying experience throughout American society. Preserving the strength of this basic, organic unit is a central and legitimate end of the police power. The state ought to be concerned that if allegiance to traditional family arrangements declines, society as a whole may well suffer....

In seeking to regulate homosexuality, the state takes as a basic premise that social and legal attitudes play an important and interdependent role in the individual's formation of his or her sexual destiny. A shift on the part of the law from opposition to neutrality arguably makes homosexuality appear a more acceptable sexual lifestyle, particularly to younger persons whose sexual preferences are as yet unformed. Young people form their sexual identity partly on the basis of models they see in society. If homosexual behavior is legalized, and thus partly legitimized, an adolescent may question whether he or she should "choose" heterosexuality. At the time their sexual feelings begin to develop many young people have more interests in common with members of their own sex; sexual attraction rather than genuine interest often first draws adolescents to members of the opposite sex. If society accorded more legitimacy to expressions of homosexual attraction, attachment to the opposite sex might be postponed or diverted for some time, perhaps until after the establishment of sexual patterns that would hamper development of traditional heterosexual family relationships. For those persons who eventually choose the heterosexual model, the existence of conflicting models might provide further sexual tension destructive to the traditional marital unit.

This writer's research has turned up only two opinions by appellate courts of this state addressing this issue. The unreported case of *Dettwiller v. Dettwiller* from the Middle Section of this Court is of little if any value for the principal reason that the *Dettwiller* opinion fails to reveal any specific homosexual activities of the mother, although she entertained male homosexuals in her home.

The sole reported Tennessee case to address the homosexual-custodial parent issue is that of *Dailey v. Dailey*, 625 S.W.2d 391 (Tenn. App. 1981), decided by the Eastern Section. While some distinctions might be made between *Dailey* and the case at bar, we characterize them as distinctions without substance. These distinctions are found on both sides of the scale. The record in *Dailey* presented a lesbian relationship that was more flagrant insofar as sexual activities were concerned than in the case at bar. However, in both *Dailey* and this case there was evidence that the two women slept together in the same bedroom in the house where the child was, and that they would hug and kiss each other and express their love for one another. On the other hand, the child in *Dailey* suffered from cerebral palsy and was described as being "somewhat handicapped physically and as mentally slow." He was only five years old at the time of trial. It was likely that with these physical and mental handicaps he would not be as aware of what was going on as the normal nine-year-old in the case at bar.

Admittedly, there was conflicting expert testimony as to the effects of a minor child being raised in a homosexual environment. In the case at bar, the only expert testimony was that offered on behalf of the lesbian mother. The expert stated essentially that the child appeared to demonstrate no harmful effects caused from living in this environment up to the time of trial, and that none was anticipated. The trial court has the privilege of passing upon the credibility of expert testimony, whether it stand unopposed or whether it be in conflict. *Gibson v. Ferguson*, 562 S.W.2d 188 (Tenn. 1976).

In affirming the action of the trial court changing custody from a lesbian mother to the father, the *Dailey* court quoted with approval from two cases from neighboring states. We quote:

> However, we think it appropriate to refer to a recent Kentucky case of *S v. S*, Ky. App., 608 S.W.2d 64 (1980) where the facts were similar to the case at bar. The court of appeals reversed the trial court for not granting a change of custody from a lesbian mother to the father. In that opinion the court said:

> "This Court would call attention to an article entitled 'Children of lesbians: their point of view' contained in the Journal of the National Association of Social Workers, Vol. 25, Number 3, May, 1980, p. 198, et seq. This article points out the fact that the lesbianism of the mother, because of the failure of the community to accept and support such a condition, forces on the child a need for secrecy and the isolation imposed by such a secret, thus separating the child from his or her peers." *Id.* at 394.

The second case was concerned with child rearing and moral values. Again we quote:

In the case of *Jarrett v. Jarrett*, 78 Ill.2d 337, 36 Ill.Dec. 1, 400 N.E.2d 421, the Supreme Court of Illinois had occasion to address the question of the adverse effects that might be had on three young children by virtue of the mother's having a "live in" boy friend. In that case the mother was awarded the custody of three small children. Shortly thereafter her boy friend moved into the home to live with the mother. The father filed a petition for a change of custody based upon a change in circumstances. The trial court denied the petition. The Supreme Court reversed, holding that such living arrangements were not in the best interest of the children. There the Court said 36 Ill. Dec. at 5, 400 N.E.2d at 425:

"At the time of this hearing, however, and even when this case was argued orally to this court, Jacqueline continued to cohabit with Wayne Hammon and had done nothing to indicate that this relationship would not continue in the future. Thus the moral values which Jacqueline currently represents to her children, and those which she may be expected to portray to them in the future, contravene statutorily declared standards of conduct and endanger the children's moral development....

"At the time of the hearing the three Jarrett children, who were then 12, 10 and 7 years old, were obviously incapable of emulating their mother's moral indiscretions. To wait until later years to determine whether Jacqueline had inculcated her moral values in the children would be to await a demonstration that the very harm which the statute seeks to avoid had occurred. Measures to safeguard the moral well-being of children, whose lives have already been disrupted by the divorce of their parents, cannot have been in-

tended to be delayed until there are tangible manifestations of damage to their character.

"While our comments have focused upon the moral hazards, we are not convinced that open cohabitation does not also affect the mental and emotional health of the children." *Id.* at 394-95.

In this writer's opinion, as a case of first impression in this state *Dailey* has erected the signpost for the direction that this Court should follow. Here we are dealing with one of our more precious, if not most precious, commodities—the life of a young child. Parents are given wide discretion in the raising of their children without state interferences. However, when they seek to dissolve the marriage relationship when children are involved, the court must assert itself as the guardian of the moral and physical welfare of these children. The rights of the children take precedence over the rights of the parents.

Other jurisdictions have reached similar conclusions. In *Roberts v. Roberts*, 489 N.E.2d 1067 (Ohio App. 1985), the Ohio Court of Appeals reversed the action of the trial court in modifying visitation rights of three minor children with their homosexual father on the ground that the modifications made did not go far enough to protect the children. The Court said:

Actually, given its concern for perpetuating the values associated with conventional marriage and the family as the basic unit of society, the state has a substantial interest in viewing homosexuality as errant sexual behavior which threatens the social fabric, and in endeavoring to protect minors from being influenced by those who advocate homosexual lifestyles. See, e.g., *Doe v. Com-*

monwealth's Attorney (E.D.Va.1975), 403 F.Supp. 1199, affirmed (1976), 425 U.S. 901, 96 S.Ct. 1489, 47 L.Ed.2d 751. See, also, *Dronenburg v. Zech* (C.A.D.C.1984), 741 F.2d 1388. *Id.* at 1170.

In the case of *S.E.G. v. R.A.G.*, 735 S.W.2d 164 (Mo. App. 1987), a lesbian mother sought to gain custody of the parties' four minor children in a divorce action wherein custody was granted to father. The record therein reflected that wife's lesbian relationship had been on-going for but six months when husband obtained a modification of the divorce decree granting custody to wife. Wife and her lover showed affection toward one another in front of the children; they slept together in the same bed at the family home; when wife and the children traveled to St. Louis to see her lover, they slept together there. Both sides presented evidence as to the effects of a parent's homosexuality on the minor children in his or her custody. In affirming the trial court, the Missouri Court of Appeals stated:

Since it is our duty to protect the moral growth and the best interests of the minor children, we find Wife's arguments lacking.... [H]omosexuality is not openly accepted or widespread. We wish to protect the children from peer pressure, teasing, and possible ostracizing they may encounter as a result of the "alternative life style" their mother has chosen....

All of these factors present an unhealthy environment for minor children. Such conduct can never be kept private enough to be a neutral factor in the development of a child's values and character. We will not ignore such conduct by a parent which may have an effect on the children's moral development. *Id.* at 166.

In *Jacobson v. Jacobson*, 314 N.W.2d 78 (N.D. 1981), the North Dakota Supreme Court reversed a judgment of the lower court awarding custody of the parties' children to the wife, who was admittedly involved in a homosexual relationship with another woman at the time of trial. In so doing, the Court stated:

[W]e cannot lightly dismiss the fact that living in the same house with their mother and her lover may well cause the children to "suffer from the slings and arrows of a disapproving society" to a much greater extent than would an arrangement wherein the children were placed in the custody of their father with visitation rights in the mother. Although we agree with the trial court that the children will be required to deal with the problem regardless of which parent has custody, it is apparent to us that requiring the children to live, day-to-day, in the same residence with the mother and her lover means that the children will have to confront the problem to a significantly greater degree than they would if living with their father. We agree with the trial court that we cannot determine whether or not the fact the custodial parent is homosexual or bisexual will result in an increased likelihood that the children will become homosexual or bisexual. There is insufficient expert testimony to make that determination. However, that issue does not control our conclusion. Rather, we believe that because of the mores of today's society, because Sandra is engaged in a homosexual relationship in the home in which she resides with the children, and because of the lack of legal recognition of the status of a homosexual relationship, the best interests of the children will be better served by placing custody of the children with Duane. *Id.* 81-82.

In *M. J. P. v. J. G. P.*, 640 P.2d 966 (Okla. 1982), the Supreme Court of Oklahoma held that an open homosexual relationship involving custodial parents was sufficient change of circumstances to warrant a modification of a child custody order giving custody of the parties' two-and-a-half-year-old son to mother. Shortly after the divorce, the mother moved in with a female lover and her twelve-year-old son. The mother admitted that she had established a homosexual relationship with her lover, and that they engaged in certain lovers' caresses in the presence of the young boy. The mother testified that she had told her lover's son that there was nothing immoral about two women being lovers and living together, and that it was not immoral for two men to have a homosexual relationship. She also told him that one day she would express those same thoughts to her own son, stating that an explanation of the strong commitment and love that she and her lover had for one another would be in her son's best welfare.

The writer is not impressed by the attempt of wife to assert a constitutional argument couched upon the Fourteenth Amendment. The cases cited by wife are not in point. Furthermore, homosexuals are not offered the constitutional protection that race, national origin and alienage have been afforded. *Anderson v. Martin,* 375 U.S. 399, 84 S.Ct. 454, 11 L.Ed.2d 430 (1964) (race); *Castaneda v. Partida,* 430 U.S. 482, 97 S.Ct. 1272, 51 L.Ed.2d 498 (1977) (national origin); and *Graham v. Richardson,* 403 U.S. 365, 91 S.Ct. 1848, 29 L.Ed.2d 534 (1971) (alienage). *Bowers v. Hardwick,*____U.S.____, 106 S.Ct. 2841, 92 L.Ed.2d 140 (1986). By the same token, I find no persuasion in wife's citation of cases from other jurisdictions that favor homosexual parental custody. *S.N.E. v. R.L.B.,* 699 P.2d 875 (Alaska 1985); *M. P. v. S. P.,* 404 A.2d 1256 (N.J. App. 1979);

D. H. v. J. H., 418 N.E.2d 286 (Ind. App. 1981).

The record before this Court presents a mother who seeks to have the courts of this state afford her the privilege of raising to adulthood the parties' nine-year-old daughter, notwithstanding the fact that during the eight years prior to trial she had been involved in not one but four ongoing homosexual relationships. Each relationship was carried on in the family home where she would hug and kiss her female lover, as well as telling her that she loved her. During the period that she had custody, Mother and her lover slept in the same bed in the same bedroom in the custodial home. In addition, Mother informed her daughter that she was a homosexual, stating that homosexual love is the same as heterosexual love. Nonetheless, the daughter has been counseled by her mother not to discuss her homosexuality with the daughter's friends.

The courts of this state have a duty to perpetuate the values and morals associated with the family and conventional marriage, inasmuch as homosexuality is and should be treated as errant and deviant social behavior. I would have this Court declare under this or a similar set of facts that a practicing homosexual parent be disqualified from obtaining legal custody of one's minor child or children. While a child the age of parties' daughter is too young to emulate her mother's conduct, to hold otherwise would be adopting a "wait and see" attitude and would endanger the child's moral development. It is too great a risk to postpone taking action to safeguard the moral well being of children until one sees tangible manifestations of harm to their characters.

In so holding, this Court would not be deciding that Mother could never obtain custody of the child. While Mother's homosexuality may be beyond her control, submitting to it and living with a person of the same sex in a sexual relationship is not. Just as an alcoholic overcomes the habit and becomes a nondrinker, so this mother should attempt to dissolve her "alternate life style" of homosexual living. Such is not too great a sacrifice to expect of a parent in order to gain or retain custody of his or her child. This Court can take judicial notice of the fact that throughout the ages, dedicated, loving parents have countless times made much greater sacrifices for their children.

NO

Melvin P. Antell

MAJORITY OPINION

M. P. *v.* S. P.

The opinion of the court was delivered by Judge Antell.

Defendant (former wife) was awarded a divorce for sexual cruelty by judgment dated September 11, 1969 after a six-year marriage from which two children were born, Franceen (fictitious name) on June 8, 1964 and Joy (fictitious name) on July 15, 1968. She received custody of the daughters, and until the determination before us for review they have always resided with their mother, a period of about seven years after the divorce.

On May 20, 1975 the Chancery Division ordered defendant to show cause why custody of the children should not be transferred to plaintiff on the ground that defendant "is an unfit mother." The order was signed on plaintiff's application, his first since the judgment of divorce. After a number of hearings, the last of which was on January 22, 1976, the trial judge, by letter opinion dated August 30, 1976, awarded custody to the father, directing that the "provision for custody shall take effect immediately and shall be explained at length in my opinion to follow as soon as possible." The judge's oral opinion was delivered September 23, 1977 and his order, transferring custody and granting defendant rights of visitation, was filed on October 3, 1977. We have not been told of any valid reason for the lengthy delays in the foregoing sequence of procedural events. Our concern is that this unexplained delay on the trial judge's part should not be the basis for denying defendant relief if she is otherwise entitled thereto. Defendant appeals on the ground that the trial judge erred in modifying the judgment and divesting her of custody.

Central to this appeal is the fact that defendant is an admitted practicing homosexual. She argues that the action below was taken because of this fact alone and is therefore not legally sustainable. Plaintiff expressly disavows any claim that defendant is an unfit mother by reason of her homosexuality. He concedes that her right to custody of the children cannot be denied, limited or restricted on the basis of her sexual orientation alone—a proposition with which we are in accord. Furthermore, compatibly with the uncontradicted

From *M. P. v. S. P.*, 169 N.J. Super. 425, 404 A.2d 1256 (1979). Notes and some case citations omitted.

expert testimony, plaintiff disclaims being concerned with "any threat that the children's sexual development will be in any way altered by the fact that defendant is a homosexual." Rather, he relies for affirmance exclusively upon a claim of changed circumstances since the date of the original custody award such that the best interests of the children dictate modification of that determination.

At the outset it is noted that the trial judge made no finding, nor in any way concerned himself with the issue, of changed circumstances.

The evidence discloses that from the beginning this marriage was afflicted by sexual discord. Although the record is burdened with detailed testimony in which each party blames the other for their disastrous relationship, much is irrelevant except to demonstrate that at least from the time of their separation in 1967 plaintiff has been aware of defendant's homosexual propensities. As he knew when they separated, defendant was involved in an affair with another woman (Barbara), one which continued through and beyond the date of the divorce.

After the divorce defendant moved into a small apartment and plaintiff exercised weekly visitation rights with respect to the older daughter, Franceen, but refused to acknowledge Joy as his child. He persisted in this refusal, failing even to visit her when she was hospitalized, until adjudicated the father and ordered to pay for her support. It was as a result of defendant's persuasion that he eventually included Joy in his visits.

On October 14, 1970 defendant voluntarily admitted herself to Ancora State Hospital to be treated for a depressive neurosis. Plaintiff made no attempt to obtain custody at that time, and the daughters were cared for by defendant's parents. After defendant left the hospital on December 17, 1970 she and the girls lived with her parents until the summer of 1974. During this time defendant worked full-time and attended counseling sessions.

In the fall of 1974 Joy developed emotional problems that impaired her learning abilities, and defendant reduced her work to a part-time basis. She observed Joy's work in school, met frequently with her teachers, met with the school psychologist and helped with remediating Joy's motor coordination skills. The child was also enrolled in a county guidance center where mother and daughter attended sessions together, and Joy was thereafter returned to regular classes.

The evidence shows that defendant has been equally concerned with the needs of Franceen.

In late 1974, upon the advice of school officials, defendant and the girls left the household where they had been residing. For three months thereafter they resided with "Joyce," defendant's lesbian companion. This arrangement was unworkable, however, since Joyce lived in a school district different from where defendant's daughters were enrolled. Therefore, in the interests of her children defendant returned to her parents' home. During the foregoing period defendant and Joyce slept apart and the children had their own room.

No specific findings were made in connection therewith, but the record is uncontradicted that defendant is an attentive mother who fed and dressed her children well, provided them with medical and dental care, and arranged for surgery, allergy tests and orthodonture.

She has done all that can be expected of a dutiful mother.

Although he determined to alter the custody arrangement, the trial judge found that defendant was "a very warm, loving mother," that she "cares for her children and generally within her means, at least at a level deemed minimally adequate, has provided for them." Recognizing, however, that plaintiff was "equally concerned" with the children, the judge decided to "examine into the question of homosexuality as a disqualifying effect on a parent."

The trial judge apparently weighed against defendant the fact that she was caught up "in an attempt to find her own identity and to deal with the problems" arising from her sexual status. However, he did not explain what problems he had in mind or in what way her problems or her quest for identity were different from those of most ordinary people; more importantly, he made no attempt to articulate a relationship between any of this and the welfare of the children. The judge also noted that defendant's ongoing liaison with her lesbian companion had "materially upset the older child and will have a slight influence in all probability, from the credible evidence, on the younger child." On an earlier occasion the judge had ordered that defendant not share Joyce's company at any time when the children were present, and this order has not been violated. Furthermore, there is nothing in the record to show any nexus between defendant's sexual companionship and the older girl's reaction.

Nowhere do we find documented in the record any specific instances of sexual misconduct by defendant or evidence that she tried in any way to inculcate the girls with her sexual attitudes. To the contrary, the evidence is affirmatively to the effect that she never displayed any sexual behavior in the presence of her children, and that she refrains from any demonstration of affection toward other women when the girls are present. Moreover, she is not a member of any homosexual organization. As we said in *De Vita v. De Vita*, 145 N.J. Super. 120 (App. Div. 1976):

> When dealing with custody the burden of proof required to show that a mother is guilty of gross sexual misconduct to the detriment of her children is a heavy one. [at 124]

It is well settled that the best interests of the child are of primary concern to the court in any matter involving the custody of minor children. Since the conditions which would satisfy the best interests of a child during all of its minority cannot be conclusively determined in a single decree, custody orders are always held to be modifiable upon a showing of changed circumstances that would affect the welfare of the child. The party seeking the modification bears the burden of showing sufficient changed circumstances so as to require modification.

In assessing a claim of changed circumstances deference is given to the length and stability of the existing custody relationship. The potential for damage which resides in removing a child from its psychological parent has been recognized in a number of cases. In *In re P, and wife*, 114 N.J. Super. 584, 592–93, 595 (App. Div. 1971), we held that although neither set of parents was obviously better fit than the other, the best interests of the child mandated that custody remain with the psychological foster parents, rather than the biological parents. So important is this factor that our Supreme Court pointedly stated in *Sorentino v. Family & Children's Soc. of Elizabeth,* 72 N.J. 127 (1976), that one seeking to change the child's custodial status quo

> ... will have the burden of proving by a preponderance of the credible evidence that the potentiality for serious psychological harm accompanying or resulting from such a move will not become a reality. [at 133]

Not only did plaintiff offer no proof to meet this formidable burden, but, as we noted earlier, the trial judge made no findings which pointed to a change of circumstances. The only conclusion to be drawn is, as defendant claims, that the custody order was modified for the sole reason that she is a homosexual and without regard to the welfare of the children. This conclusion gains added support from our further analysis of the record and the determinations before us for review.

In awarding custody to plaintiff the trial judge did so on the reasoning that plaintiff

> ... may provide a more stable atmosphere for the custody, maintenance and welfare of these children. His home is more stable. He is financially secure and is able to provide the children with the best type of care, custody, maintenance and it is in their best interest that the Court feels that custody should reside in the father.

However, absent from the record is any factual basis for the judge's belief that the father's home is more stable than the defendant's or that he is "financially secure and is able to provide the children with the best type of care, custody, maintenance...." Actually, at the time of the hearing plaintiff was in arrears on his child support obligations in the amount of almost $ 5,000, a fact which has caused defendant to apply for welfare assistance. When asked by the trial judge why he had not been making the payments, he explained only, "I imagine it is a combination of things," and stated that support would be "easier having the children with you." As to his sincerity of purpose in seeking custody, we note again that plaintiff initially denied that he was Joy's father, and in the course of the judicial proceedings which followed he admittedly testified falsely in denying that he had had sexual relations with defendant during certain critical times. The inference is at least reasonable that if defendant had not brought proceedings in aid of execution to compel plaintiff to meet his support obligations, plaintiff's custody application would not have been made.

Nor are we shown any factual support for the trial judge's evident belief that the children are being harmed or are likely to be harmed by continued custody with defendant. The only findings offered for this purpose are that defendant's homosexuality has "affected" Franceen, that it has "materially upset" her, and that it "will have a slight influence in all probability" on Joy. Against this the report of Dr. Yaskin, the psychiatrist appointed by the court at the recommendation of plaintiff's attorney, concludes that the younger child, Joy,

> ... is seriously in need of her mother's continuing emotional support. Her ongoing deep identification and dependency is with the mother and it is my clinical opinion that any attempt, at this time, to separate [Joy] from her mother will result in serious psychological consequences to the child.

Reporting on Franceen he comments that she is "rather well poised" and "that she has no ongoing emotional or behavioral problems." Further,

... [T]here is no question that she loves her mother. She states, without hesitation, that her mother has always shown an adequate concern re the nutrition and their dress. She also states her mother has always been kind to her and has never abused her. She adds, "I know she loves me." I asked her if there was anything in her ongoing relationship with her mother that she objected to and she answers, "No—Mother is a good person."

Dr. Yaskin took account of Franceen's expressed desire to live with her father, but concluded that her reasons were "puerile," i.e., that she could "go fishing and everything" with her cousins who lived nearby, that she feels sorry for her father sometimes, and that she has feelings of affection for her baby step-brother. The doctor found that Franceen had no "real ongoing concern or realistic knowledge as to what the term homosexuality connotes" and "just considers it as a type of relationship." His report left no doubt that she "has a deep maternal attachment and identification."

In dismissing this testimony the trial judge said nothing more than that he would "totally reject" the expert evidence which fully supported continued custody in defendant mother because he did "not find it credible in its postulates and conclusions." In doing so he overlooked the fact that the assistance of experts as an aid in resolving the difficult questions presented was clearly desirable. We emphasize that it was the trial judge himself who, evidently recognizing his own lack of expertise, requested the examination and report from Dr. Yaskin, whose name was recommended to him by plaintiff's own attorney. As we have noted elsewhere, the testimony of child study specialists is properly relied on by the courts. These witnesses were qualified, their opinions were unrefuted and were not inherently implausible.... [W]e see no reason why they should have been ignored in this case. See, too, *Sorentino v. Family & Children's Soc. of Elizabeth*, 74 N.J. 313, 320 (1977).

Apparently the trial judge placed greater credence in what the children told him during *in camera* hearings, some of which was recorded, some not. For example, he concluded that Franceen disliked defendant's companion, Joyce, "almost to the point of hatred," but there is nothing in Franceen's recorded testimony to support such a belief. If it was based on something he was privately told by the child, it was not memorialized in the manner suggested in *State v. Green*, 129 N.J. Super. 157, 166 (App. Div. 1974). Except for the conclusion which he drew therefrom, there is nothing to show what he was told off the record, and without some disclosure to the parties on the record it should not have been allowed to influence his decision. In effect, defendant was denied an opportunity to be heard on the facts. *Callen v. Gill*, 7 N.J. 312, 319 (1951).

In modifying custody the trial judge rejected the "tender years" doctrine as "an obsolete, untenable, antediluvian theory." We disagree that he was free to disregard in this manner the ages of the children as a factor in determining where custody should lie. Although our personal views may be contrary, the Supreme Court has still not displaced the doctrine that custody of a young child "is normally placed with the mother, if fit." *Esposito v. Esposito*, 41 N.J. 143,

154 (1963). Also see *Mayer v. Mayer*, 150 N.J. Super. 556, 563–64 (Ch. Div. 1977). That the children were still of tender years was something which should have been weighed in this case in favor of preserving the custodial arrangement, and the trial judge erred in failing to do so.

We have already noted that the trial judge made no finding of changed circumstances as a reason for modifying the custody provision. However, plaintiff argues that a change of circumstance may nevertheless be found in the fact that defendant's variant sexual orientation now causes embarrassment to the girls in the eyes of their peers. We address ourselves to this final contention.

It is first observed that the trial judge made no finding of fact which lends support to plaintiff's claim. All he said was that Franceen had been "upset" by Joyce, defendant's lesbian friend, a problem earlier resolved by banishing Joyce from the presence of the children. The only evidence of "embarrassment" is to be found in Franceen's testimony about conversations with her friends, in which she was asked why her mother dated other women. Nothing therein suggests that these were in any way traumatizing. We know of no finding by the trial judge that Franceen is "pressured by her peers," nor how such a finding could be supported by the proofs. In fact, we do not understand the sense in which this expression is used in the dissenting opinion or the weight which such a finding could be accorded within the context of this case.

Plaintiff's argument overlooks, too, the fact that the children's exposure to embarrassment is not dependent upon the identity of the parent with whom they happen to reside. Their discomfiture, if any, comes about not because of living with defendant, but because she is their mother, because she is a lesbian, and because the community will not accept her. Neither the prejudices of the small community in which they live nor the curiosity of their peers about defendant's sexual nature will be abated by a change of custody. Hard facts must be faced. These are matters which courts cannot control, and there is little to gain by creating an artificial world where the children may dream that life is different than it is.

Furthermore, the law governing grants of custody does not yield to such narrow considerations. Of overriding importance is that within the context of a loving and supportive relationship there is no reason to think that the girls will be unable to manage whatever anxieties may flow from the community's disapproval of their mother. In *Commonwealth ex rel. Lucas v. Kreischer*, 450 Pa. 352, 299 A.2d 243 (Sup. Ct. 1973), the trial court awarded custody of the children, whose mother had entered into an interracial marriage, to their father because of the "almost universal prejudice and intolerance of interracial marriage." In reversing, the Supreme Court of Pennsylvania rested its determination upon the following observation, which we deem pertinent, made by the dissenting judge of the intermediate appellate court:

"[I]n a multiracial society such as ours racial prejudice and tension are inevitable. If... children are raised in a happy and stable home, they will be able to cope with prejudice and hopefully learn that people are unique individuals who should be judged as such." [299 A.2d at 246]

Mistaken also, in our view, is plaintiff's assumption that the welfare of the children cannot be served unless they are sheltered from all the adversities that are inherent to their basic life situation. Regrettably, the decision as to where custody shall lie must be made in terms of available alternatives, and in this case neither holds out the promise of a completely unguent environment. While one is troubled by the possible problems that may arise from defendant's homosexual bent, the evidence also strongly features a disturbed and abrasive personal relationship between Joy and plaintiff's present wife which has resulted in the administration of unduly harsh discipline to this child. She also dislikes and fears plaintiff....

If defendant retains custody, it may be that because the community is intolerant of her differences these girls may sometimes have to bear themselves with greater than ordinary fortitude. But this does not necessarily portend that their moral welfare or safety will be jeopardized. It is just as reasonable to expect that they will emerge better equipped to search out their own standards of right and wrong, better able to perceive that the majority is not always correct in its moral judgments, and better able to understand the importance of conforming their beliefs to the requirements of reason and tested knowledge, not the constraints of currently popular sentiment or prejudice.

Taking the children from defendant can be done only at the cost of sacrificing those very qualities they will find most sustaining in meeting the challenges inevitably ahead. Instead of forbearance and feelings of protectiveness, it will foster in them a sense of shame for their mother. Instead of courage and the precept that people of integrity do not shrink from bigots, it counsels the easy option of shirking difficult problems and following the course of expedience. Lastly, it diminishes their regard for the rule of human behavior, everywhere accepted, that we do not forsake those to whom we are indebted for love and nurture merely because they are held in low esteem by others.

We conclude that the children's best interests will be disserved by undermining in this way their growth as mature and principled adults. Extensive evidence in the record upon which we have not commented amply confirms the trial judge's finding that defendant is a worthy mother. Nothing suggests that her homosexual preference in itself presents any threat of harm to her daughters or that in the ordinary course of their development they will be unable to deal with whatever vexation may be caused to their spirits by the community.

Careful attention has been given to the nature of the relief to be awarded. Although advantages are evident in remanding for further hearings by which the current status of the matter may be ascertained, after a thorough examination of the entire record we are satisfied that the welfare of the children will only be impaired without corresponding benefit by prolonging any further these already protracted proceedings. The order under review is therefore reversed and the custody provision contained in the judgment of divorce dated September 11, 1969 is reinstated.

POSTSCRIPT

Should Homosexuality Bar a Parent from Being Awarded Custody of a Child?

The custody issue discussed here involves both gay rights and the larger issue of what the legal definition of a family should be. Families have been changing and the law is struggling to come to grips with these changes. The proportion of American households consisting of a married couple and their own minor children, for example, declined from 44.2 percent in 1960 to 27.0 percent in 1988. In 1988 single parents with their own minor children constituted 27.3 percent of American households, more than double the number of single-parent families in 1970. More children are living with a stepparent. The number of households consisting of two unrelated adults of the opposite sex (with or without children under 15 years old) was five times greater in 1990 than 1970. Thirty percent of American children are now born to single mothers.

New living arrangements challenge the law in many areas. Unmarried couples who live together, for example, often do not receive the same health and death benefits as legally married employees receive for their spouses. The current legal definition of *family* may also deny benefits to stepfamilies, foster families, grandparents, and parents of children born through new reproductive technologies. Surrogate motherhood, for example, has been a continuously controversial and challenging legal topic since the Baby M case in 1988.

The issue at the heart of this case continues to be brought before the courts. In Illinois, a mother lost her appeal to regain custody of her daughter after a divorce in which charges were made that she was living in a lesbian relationship. In other cases, courts have struggled with whether or not laws permit a gay couple to adopt a child. Such adoptions have been granted in Massachusetts, Minnesota, California, New York, the District of Columbia, Vermont, and Washington State. But for the most part, the law has not yet addressed questions raised by the growing number of gay and lesbian couples who are creating their own families through artificial insemination, adoption, and surrogate motherhood.

The issue of redefining the family is considered in Meyers, "Gay Custody and Adoption: An Unequal Application of the Law," 14 *Whittier L. Rev.* 839 (1993); M. Minow, "Redefining Families: Who's In and Who's Out?" 62 *Colorado Law Review* 269 (1991); Note, "Looking for a Family Resemblance: The Limits of the Functional Approach to the Legal Definition of Family," 104 *Harvard Law Review* 1640 (1991); M. Glendon, *State, Law and Family: Family Law in Transition in the United States and Western Europe* (1977); and Bartlett,

"Rethinking Parenthood as an Exclusive Status: The Need for Legal Alternatives When the Promise of the Nuclear Family Has Failed," 70 *Virginia Law Review* 879 (1984). In *Braschi v. Stahl Associates*, 543 N.E.2d 49, 55 (1989), a New York court held that a homosexual partnership could be considered a "family" for purposes of New York City's rent control law. Changes in family law are discussed in "Beyond No-Fault: New Directions in Divorce Reform," in Sugarman and Kay, eds., *Divorce Reform at the Crossroads* (1990).

ISSUE 11

Can Courts Restrict the Picketing of Abortion Clinics?

YES: William H. Rehnquist, from Majority Opinion, *Judy Madsen et al. v. Women's Health Center, Inc., et al.,* U.S. Supreme Court (1994)

NO: Antonin Scalia, from Dissenting Opinion, *Judy Madsen et al. v. Women's Health Center, Inc., et al.,* U.S. Supreme Court (June 30, 1994)

ISSUE SUMMARY

YES: Chief Justice William H. Rehnquist found that a set of restrictions on persons protesting at abortion clinics were not unduly restrictive and did not violate the First Amendment.

NO: Justice Antonin Scalia, in dissent, maintains that a 36-foot buffer zone limiting how a group that had broken no laws may protest is inconsistent with the First Amendment.

If you thought that heinous crimes were being committed in a school, or department store, or other commercial building open to the public, how disturbed would you be? How far would you go to stop these crimes? And what if you believed that these crimes were the senseless murders of children and that, further, the police and courts condoned, even encouraged, these acts? What acts of civil disobedience would you participate in to try to prevent such murders? Would you join with others and protest with placards? Would you try to talk the conspirators involved out of going into these killing places? Wouldn't acts of harassment and shouting be the least of what you would do?

This is the perspective held by some antiabortion protestors in their quest to prevent patients and medical personnel from entering facilities where abortions are performed. They maintain that their chanting, whistling, yelling, and use of bullhorns, amplifiers, and pictures of fetuses are well within the scope of the protections of free speech set forth by the First Amendment. In general, they do not physically interfere with persons entering and exiting the clinic, do not obstruct the doors of the clinic, and do not prevent police from doing their job. They remain on the sidewalk, which is a public way and a place where free speech has traditionally been broadly protected.

What about the rights of the women entering the clinics for abortions? Is their right to have an abortion protected? And if it is, shouldn't they have a right to be free of harassment by protestors?

Abortion is a right guaranteed by the Fourteenth Amendment. This amendment declares that states may not deprive individuals of life, liberty, or property without due process of law. In the following case, *Madsen v. Women's Health Center*, abortion-rights protestors and abortion-rights advocates each claim that their liberties are being denied. The clinic management in this case went to court and obtained a court order forbidding the protestors from blocking the clinic's entrances and from physically abusing any persons going in or out of the clinic. The court later broadened the protection by finding that the protestors' actions, even though they did not barricade entrances or abuse anyone, impeded access to the clinic and discouraged some potential patients from entering. This amended injunction excluded protestors from a 36-foot buffer zone, restricted the verbal protestations and display of pictures, and forbade the protestors from approaching patients who do not wish to talk with them. In making this ruling, the court indicated that there is a need to protect free speech but that when that speech crosses the "invisible" fine line and becomes harassment, it is no longer acceptable behavior and is no longer protected by the First Amendment. The court extended this protection from harassment to patients, medical personnel, volunteers, and all who enter the clinic. Former employees were also protected.

The conflict then, as it was presented to the Supreme Court, is between two sets of rights: (a) freedom of speech and the right to use this speech to express convictions, and (b) the right to be free from interference in exercising one's constitutional rights. The Supreme Court's role is to interpret what the Constitution requires in such a situation.

YES

William H. Rehnquist

MAJORITY OPINION

MADSEN *v.* WOMEN'S HEALTH CENTER

CHIEF JUSTICE REHNQUIST delivered the opinion of the Court....

Petitioners challenge the constitutionality of an injunction entered by a Florida state court which prohibits antiabortion protestors from demonstrating in certain places and in various ways outside of a health clinic that performs abortions. We hold that the establishment of a 36-foot buffer zone on a public street from which demonstrators are excluded passes muster under the First Amendment, but that several other provisions of the injunction do not.

I

Respondents operate abortion clinics throughout central Florida. Petitioners and other groups and individuals are engaged in activities near the site of one such clinic in Melbourne, Florida. They picketed and demonstrated where the public street gives access to the clinic. In September 1992, a Florida state court permanently enjoined petitioners from blocking or interfering with public access to the clinic, and from physically abusing persons entering or leaving the clinic. Six months later, respondents sought to broaden the injunction, complaining that access to the clinic was still impeded by petitioners' activities and that such activities had also discouraged some potential patients from entering the clinic, and had deleterious physical effects on others. The trial court thereupon issued a broader injunction, which is challenged here.

The court found that, despite the initial injunction, protesters continued to impede access to the clinic by congregating on the paved portion of the street—Dixie Way—leading up to the clinic, and by marching in front of the clinic's driveways. It found that as vehicles heading toward the clinic slowed to allow the protesters to move out of the way, "sidewalk counselors" would approach and attempt to give the vehicle's occupants antiabortion literature. The number of people congregating varied from a handful to 400,

From *Judy Madsen et al. v. Women's Health Center, Inc., et al.*, 1994 WL 285847 (U.S. Fla.). Notes and some case citations omitted.

and the noise varied from singing and chanting to the use of loudspeakers and bullhorns.

The protests, the court found, took their toll on the clinic's patients. A clinic doctor testified that, as a result of having to run such a gauntlet to enter the clinic, the patients "manifested a higher level of anxiety and hypertension causing those patients to need a higher level of sedation to undergo the surgical procedures, thereby increasing the risk associated with such procedures." The noise produced by the protestors could be heard within the clinic, causing stress in the patients both during surgical procedures and while recuperating in the recovery rooms. And those patients who turned away because of the crowd to return at a later date, the doctor testified, increased their health risks by reason of the delay.

Doctors and clinic workers, in turn, were not immune even in their homes. Petitioners picketed in front of clinic employees' residences; shouted at passersby; rang the doorbells of neighbors and provided literature identifying the particular clinic employee as a "baby killer." Occasionally, the protestors would confront minor children of clinic employees who were home alone. This and similar testimony led the state court to conclude that its original injunction had proved insufficient "to protect the health, safety and rights of women in Brevard and Seminole County, Florida, and surrounding counties seeking access to [medical and counseling] services." The state court therefore amended its prior order, enjoining a broader array of activities. The amended injunction prohibits petitioners from engaging in the following acts:

At all times on all days, from entering the premises and property of the Aware Woman Center for Choice [the Melbourne clinic]....

At all times on all days, from blocking, impeding, inhibiting, or in any other manner obstructing or interfering with access to, ingress into and egress from any building or parking lot of the Clinic.

At all times on all days, from congregating, picketing, patrolling, demonstrating or entering that portion of public right-of-way or private property within [36] feet of the property line of the Clinic.... An exception to the 36 foot buffer zone is the area immediately adjacent to the Clinic on the east.... The [petitioners]... must remain at least [5] feet from the Clinic's east line. Another exception to the 36 foot buffer zone relates to the record title owners of the property to the north and west of the Clinic. The prohibition against entry into the 36 foot buffer zones does not apply to such persons and their invitees. The other prohibitions contained herein do apply, if such owners and their invitees are acting in concert with the [petitioners]....

During the hours of 7:30 a.m. through noon, on Mondays through Saturdays, during surgical procedures and recovery periods, from singing, chanting, whistling, shouting, yelling, use of bullhorns, auto horns, sound amplification equipment or other sounds or images observable to or within earshot of the patients inside the Clinic.

At all times on all days, in an area within [300] feet of the Clinic, from physically approaching any person seeking the services of the Clinic unless such person indicates a desire to communicate by approaching or by inquiring of the [petitioners]....

At all times on all days, from approaching, congregating, picketing, patrolling, demonstrating or using bullhorns or other sound amplification equipment within [300] feet of the residence of any of the [respondents'] employees, staff, owners or agents, or blocking or attempting to block, barricade, or in any other manner, temporarily or otherwise, obstruct the entrances, exits or driveways of the residences of any of the [respondents'] employees, staff, owners or agents. The [petitioners] and those acting in concert with them are prohibited from inhibiting or impeding or attempting to impede, temporarily or otherwise, the free ingress or egress of persons to any street that provides the sole access to the street on which those residences are located.

At all times on all days, from physically abusing, grabbing, intimidating, harassing, touching, pushing, shoving, crowding or assaulting persons entering or leaving, working at or using services at the [respondents'] Clinic or trying to gain access to, or leave, any of the homes of owners, staff or patients of the Clinic.

At all times on all days, from harassing, intimidating or physically abusing, assaulting or threatening any present or former doctor, health care professional, or other staff member, employee or volunteer who assists in providing services at the [respondents'] Clinic.

At all times on all days, from encouraging, inciting, or securing other persons to commit any of the prohibited acts listed herein." *Operation Rescue v.*

Women's Health Center, Inc., 626 So. 2d 664, 679-680 (Fla. 1993).

The Florida Supreme Court upheld the constitutionality of the trial court's amended injunction. That court recognized that the forum at issue, which consists of public streets, sidewalks, and rights-of-way, is a traditional public forum. Citing *Frisby v. Schultz*, 487 U.S. 474, 480 (1988). It then determined that the restrictions are content neutral, and it accordingly refused to apply the heightened scrutiny dictated by *Perry Education Assn. v. Perry Local Educators' Assn.*, 460 U.S. 37, 45 (1983) (To enforce a content-based exclusion the State must show that its regulation is necessary to serve a compelling state interest and that it is narrowly drawn to achieve that end). Instead, the court analyzed the injunction to determine whether the restrictions are "narrowly tailored to serve a significant government interest, and leave open ample alternative channels of communication." *Id.*, at 45. It concluded that they were.

Shortly before the Florida Supreme Court's opinion was announced, the United States Court of Appeals for the Eleventh Circuit heard a separate challenge to the same injunction. The Court of Appeals struck down the injunction, characterizing the dispute as a clash "between an actual prohibition of speech and a potential hindrance to the free exercise of abortion rights." *Cheffer v. McGregor*, 6 F. 3d 705, 711 (1993). It stated that the asserted interests in public safety and order were already protected by other applicable laws and that these interests could be protected adequately without infringing upon the First Amendment rights of others. *Ibid.* The Court of Appeals found the injunction to be content based and neither necessary to serve a compelling state interest nor narrowly drawn to achieve that end. *Ibid.*, citing *Carey v. Brown*, 447 U.S. 455, 461–462 (1980). We granted certiorari, 510 U.S. (1994), to resolve the conflict between the Florida Supreme Court and the Court of Appeals over the constitutionality of the state court's injunction.

II

We begin by addressing petitioners' contention that the state court's order, because it is an injunction that restricts only the speech of antiabortion protesters, is necessarily content or viewpoint based. Accordingly, they argue, we should examine the entire injunction under the strictest standard of scrutiny. We disagree. To accept petitioners' claim would be to classify virtually every injunction as content or viewpoint based. An injunction, by its very nature, applies only to a particular group (or individuals) and regulates the activities, and perhaps the speech, of that group. It does so, however, because of the group's past actions in the context of a specific dispute between real parties. The parties seeking the injunction assert a violation of their rights; the court hearing the action is charged with fashioning a remedy for a specific deprivation, not with the drafting of a statute addressed to the general public.

The fact that the injunction in the present case did not prohibit activities of those demonstrating in favor of abortion is justly attributable to the lack of any similar demonstrations by those in favor of abortion, and of any consequent request that their demonstrations be regulated by injunction. There is no suggestion in this record that Florida law would not equally restrain similar conduct directed at a target having

nothing to do with abortion; none of the restrictions imposed by the court were directed at the contents of petitioners' message.

Our principal inquiry in determining content neutrality is whether the government has adopted a regulation of speech "without reference to the content of the regulated speech." *Ward v. Rock Against Racism*, 491 U.S. 781, 791 (1989) (internal quotation marks omitted) (upholding noise regulations); . . . We thus look to the government's purpose as the threshold consideration. Here, the state court imposed restrictions on petitioners incidental to their antiabortion message because they repeatedly violated the court's original order. That petitioners all share the same viewpoint regarding abortion does not in itself demonstrate that some invidious content or viewpoint-based purpose motivated the issuance of the order. It suggests only that those in the group whose conduct violated the court's order happen to share the same opinion regarding abortions being performed at the clinic. In short, the fact that the injunction covered people with a particular viewpoint does not itself render the injunction content or viewpoint based. Accordingly, the injunction issued in this case does not demand the level of heightened scrutiny set forth in *Perry Education Assn.*, 460 U.S., at 45.

III

. . .The Florida Supreme Court concluded that numerous significant government interests are protected by the injunction. It noted that the State has a strong interest in protecting a woman's freedom to seek lawful medical or counseling services in connection with her pregnancy. See *Roe v. Wade*, 410 U.S. 113 (1973); In re *T. W.*,

551 So. 2d 1186, 1193 (Fla. 1989). The State also has a strong interest in ensuring the public safety and order, in promoting the free flow of traffic on public streets and sidewalks, and in protecting the property rights of all its citizens. 626 So. 2d, at 672. In addition, the court believed that the State's strong interest in residential privacy, acknowledged in *Frisby v. Schultz*, 487 U.S. 474 (1988), applied by analogy to medical privacy. 626 So. 2d, at 672. The court observed that while targeted picketing of the home threatens the psychological well-being of the "captive" resident, targeted picketing of a hospital or clinic threatens not only the psychological, but the physical well-being of the patient held "captive" by medical circumstance. *Id.*, at 673. We agree with the Supreme Court of Florida that the combination of these governmental interests is quite sufficient to justify an appropriately tailored injunction to protect them. We now examine each contested provision of the injunction to see if it burdens more speech than necessary to accomplish its goal.

1

A

We begin with the 36-foot buffer zone. The state court prohibited petitioners from "congregating, picketing, patrolling, demonstrating or entering" any portion of the public right-of-way or private property within 36 feet of the property line of the clinic as a way of ensuring access to the clinic. This speech-free buffer zone requires that petitioners move to the other side of Dixie Way and away from the driveway of the clinic, where the state court found that they repeatedly had interfered with the free access of patients and staff.... The buffer zone also applies to private property to the north and west of the clinic property. We examine each portion of the buffer zone separately.

We have noted a distinction between the type of focused picketing banned from the buffer zone and the type of generally disseminated communication that cannot be completely banned in public places, such as handbilling and solicitation.... Here the picketing is directed primarily at patients and staff of the clinic.

The 36-foot buffer zone protecting the entrances to the clinic and the parking lot is a means of protecting unfettered ingress to and egress from the clinic, and ensuring that petitioners do not block traffic on Dixie Way. The state court seems to have had few other options to protect access given the narrow confines around the clinic. As the Florida Supreme Court noted, Dixie Way is only 21 feet wide in the area of the clinic. The state court was convinced that allowing the petitioners to remain on the clinic's sidewalk and driveway was not a viable option in view of the failure of the first injunction to protect access. And allowing the petitioners to stand in the middle of Dixie Way would obviously block vehicular traffic.

The need for a complete buffer zone near the clinic entrances and driveway may be debatable, but some deference must be given to the state court's familiarity with the facts and the background of the dispute between the parties even under our heightened review. Moreover, one of petitioners' witnesses during the evidentiary hearing before the state court conceded that the buffer zone was narrow enough to place petitioners at a distance of no greater than 10 to 12 feet from cars approaching and leaving the clinic. Protesters standing across the narrow street from the clinic can still be seen and heard from the clinic parking lots. We also bear in mind the fact that the state court originally issued a much narrower injunction, providing no buffer zone, and that this order did not succeed in protecting access to the clinic. The failure of the first order to accomplish its purpose may be taken into consideration in evaluating the constitutionality of the broader order. *National Society of Professional Engineers v. United States*, 435 U.S. 679, 697–698 (1978). On balance, we hold that the 36-foot buffer zone around the clinic entrances and driveway burdens no more speech than necessary to accomplish the governmental interest at stake.

JUSTICE SCALIA's dissent argues that a videotape made of demonstrations at the clinic represents "what one must presume to be the worst of the activity justifying the injunction." This seems to us a gratuitous assumption. The videotape was indeed introduced by respondents, presumably because they thought it supported their request for the second injunction. But witnesses also testified as to relevant facts in a 3-day evidentiary hearing, and the state court was therefore not limited to JUSTICE SCALIA's rendition of what he saw on the videotape to make its findings in support of the second injunction. Indeed, petitioners themselves studiously refrained from challenging the factual basis for the injunction both in the state courts and here. Before the Florida Supreme Court, petitioners stated that "the Amended Permanent Injunction contains fundamental error on its face. The sole question presented by this appeal is a question of law, and for purposes of this appeal [petitioners] are assuming, arguendo, that

a factual basis exists to grant injunctive relief." Appellants' Motion in Response to Appellees' Motion to Require Full Transcript and Record of Proceedings in No. 93-0069 (Dist. Ct. App. Fla.), p. 2. Petitioners argued against including the factual record as an appendix in the Florida Supreme Court, and never certified a full record. We must therefore judge this case on the assumption that the evidence and testimony presented to the state court supported its findings that the presence of protesters standing, marching, and demonstrating near the clinic's entrance interfered with ingress to and egress from the clinic despite the issuance of the earlier injunction.

2

The inclusion of private property on the back and side of the clinic in the 36-foot buffer zone raises different concerns. The accepted purpose of the buffer zone is to protect access to the clinic and to facilitate the orderly flow of traffic on Dixie Way. Patients and staff wishing to reach the clinic do not have to cross the private property abutting the clinic property on the north and west, and nothing in the record indicates that petitioners' activities on the private property have obstructed access to the clinic. Nor was evidence presented that protestors located on the private property blocked vehicular traffic on Dixie Way. Absent evidence that petitioners standing on the private property have obstructed access to the clinic, blocked vehicular traffic, or otherwise unlawfully interfered with the clinic's operation, this portion of the buffer zone fails to serve the significant government interests relied on by the Florida Supreme Court. We hold that on the record before us the 36-foot buffer zone as applied to the private property to the north and west of the clinic burdens more speech than necessary to protect access to the clinic.

B

In response to high noise levels outside the clinic, the state court restrained the petitioners from "singing, chanting, whistling, shouting, yelling, use of bullhorns, auto horns, sound amplification equipment or other sounds or images observable to or within earshot of the patients inside the [c]linic" during the hours of 7:30 a.m. through noon on Mondays through Saturdays. We must, of course, take account of the place to which the regulations apply in determining whether these restrictions burden more speech than necessary. We have upheld similar noise restrictions in the past, and as we noted in upholding a local noise ordinance around public schools, "the nature of a place, 'the pattern of its normal activities, dictate the kinds of regulations...that are reasonable.'" *Grayned v. City of Rockford*, 408 U.S. 104, 116 (1972). Noise control is particularly important around hospitals and medical facilities during surgery and recovery periods, and in evaluating another injunction involving a medical facility, we stated: "'Hospitals, after all are not factories or mines or assembly plants. They are hospitals, where human ailments are treated, where patients and relatives alike often are under emotional strain and worry, where pleasing and comforting patients are principal facets of the day's activity, and where the patient and his family ... need a restful, uncluttered, relaxing, and helpful atmosphere.'" *NLRB v. Baptist Hospital, Inc.* 442 U.S. 773, 783-784, n. 12 (1979), quoting *Beth Israel Hospital v. NLRB*, 437 U.S. 483, 509 (1978) (BLACKMUN, J., concurring in judgment).

We hold that the limited noise restrictions imposed by the state court order burden no more speech than necessary to ensure the health and well-being of the patients at the clinic. The First Amendment does not demand that patients at a medical facility undertake Herculean efforts to escape the cacophony of political protests. "If overamplified loudspeakers assault the citizenry, government may turn them down." *Grayned, supra*, at 116. That is what the state court did here, and we hold that its action was proper.

C

The same, however, cannot be said for the "images observable" provision of the state court's order. Clearly, threats to patients or their families, however communicated, are proscribable under the First Amendment. But rather than prohibiting the display of signs that could be interpreted as threats or veiled threats, the state court issued a blanket ban on all "images observable." This broad prohibition on all "images observable" burdens more speech than necessary to achieve the purpose of limiting threats to clinic patients or their families. Similarly, if the blanket ban on "images observable" was intended to reduce the level of anxiety and hypertension suffered by the patients inside the clinic, it would still fail. The only plausible reason a patient would be bothered by "images observable" inside the clinic would be if the patient found the expression contained in such images disagreeable. But it is much easier for the clinic to pull its curtains than for a patient to stop up her ears, and no more is required to avoid seeing placards through the windows of the clinic. This provision of the injunction violates the First Amendment.

D

The state court ordered that petitioners refrain from physically approaching any person seeking services of the clinic "unless such person indicates a desire to communicate" in an area within 300 feet of the clinic. The state court was attempting to prevent clinic patients and staff from being "stalked" or "shadowed" by the petitioners as they approached the clinic. See *International Society for Krishna Consciousness v. Lee*, 505 U.S. (1992) (*slip op.*, at 10–11) ("face-to-face solicitation presents risks of duress that are an appropriate target of regulation. The skillful, and unprincipled, solicitor can target the most vulnerable, including those accompanying children or those suffering impairment and who cannot easily avoid the solicitation").

But it is difficult, indeed, to justify a prohibition on all uninvited approaches of persons seeking the services of the clinic, regardless of how peaceful the contact may be, without burdening more speech than necessary to prevent intimidation and to ensure access to the clinic. Absent evidence that the protesters' speech is independently proscribable (i.e., "fighting words" or threats), or is so infused with violence as to be indistinguishable from a threat of physical harm, see *Milk Wagon Drivers*, 312 U.S., at 292–293, this provision cannot stand. "As a general matter, we have indicated that in public debate our own citizens must tolerate insulting, and even outrageous, speech in order to provide adequate breathing space to the freedoms protected by the First Amendment." *Boos v. Barry*, 485 U.S., at 322 (internal quota-

tion marks omitted). The "consent" requirement alone invalidates this provision; it burdens more speech than is necessary to prevent intimidation and to ensure access to the clinic.

E

The final substantive regulation challenged by petitioners relates to a prohibition against picketing, demonstrating, or using sound amplification equipment within 300 feet of the residences of clinic staff. The prohibition also covers impeding access to streets that provide the sole access to streets on which those residences are located. The same analysis applies to the use of sound amplification equipment here as that discussed above: the government may simply demand that petitioners turn down the volume if the protests overwhelm the neighborhood. *Grayned, supra,* at 116.

As for the picketing, our prior decision upholding a law banning targeted residential picketing remarked on the unique nature of the home, as " 'the last citadel of the tired, the weary, and the sick.' " *Frisby*, 487 U.S., at 484. We stated that " '[t]he State's interest in protecting the well-being, tranquility, and privacy of the home is certainly of the highest order in a free and civilized society.' " *Ibid.*

But the 300-foot zone around the residences in this case is much larger than the zone provided for in the ordinance which we approved in *Frisby*. The ordinance at issue there made it "unlawful for any person to engage in picketing before or about the residence or dwelling of any individual." *Id.*, at 477. The prohibition was limited to "focused picketing taking place solely in front of a particular residence." *Id.*, at 483. By contrast, the 300-foot zone would ban "[g]eneral marching through residential neighborhoods, or even walking a route in front of an entire block of houses." *Ibid.* The record before us does not contain sufficient justification for this broad a ban on picketing; it appears that a limitation on the time, duration of picketing, and number of pickets outside a smaller zone could have accomplished the desired result....

V

In sum, we uphold the noise restrictions and the 36-foot buffer zone around the clinic entrances and driveway because they burden no more speech than necessary to eliminate the unlawful conduct targeted by the state court's injunction. We strike down as unconstitutional the 36-foot buffer zone as applied to the private property to the north and west of the clinic, the "images observable" provision, the 300-foot no-approach zone around the clinic, and the 300-foot buffer zone around the residences, because these provisions sweep more broadly than necessary to accomplish the permissible goals of the injunction. Accordingly, the judgment of the Florida Supreme Court is

Affirmed in part, and reversed in part.

NO

Antonin Scalia

DISSENTING OPINION OF
ANTONIN SCALIA

JUSTICE SCALIA, with whom JUSTICE KENNEDY and JUSTICE THOMAS join, concurring in the judgment in part and dissenting in part.

The judgment in today's case has an appearance of moderation and Solomonic wisdom, upholding as it does some portions of the injunction while disallowing others. That appearance is deceptive. The entire injunction in this case departs so far from the established course of our jurisprudence that in any other context it would have been regarded as a candidate for summary reversal.

But the context here is abortion. A long time ago, in dissent from another abortion-related case, JUSTICE O'CONNOR, joined by then-JUSTICE REHNQUIST, wrote: "This Court's abortion decisions have already worked a major distortion in the Court's constitutional jurisprudence. Today's decision goes further, and makes it painfully clear that no legal rule or doctrine is safe from ad hoc nullification by this Court when an occasion for its application arises in a case involving state regulation of abortion. The permissible scope of abortion regulation is not the only constitutional issue on which this Court is divided, but—except when it comes to abortion—the Court has generally refused to let such disagreements, however longstanding or deeply felt, prevent it from evenhandedly applying uncontroversial legal doctrines to cases that come before it." *Thornburgh v. American College of Obstetricians and Gynecologists*, 476 U.S. 747, 814 (1986) (citations omitted). Today the ad hoc nullification machine claims its latest, greatest, and most surprising victim: the First Amendment.

Because I believe that the judicial creation of a 36-foot zone in which only a particular group, which had broken no law, cannot exercise its rights of speech, assembly, and association, and the judicial enactment of a noise prohibition, applicable to that group and that group alone, are profoundly at odds with our First Amendment precedents and traditions, I dissent.

From *Judy Madsen et al. v. Women's Health Center, Inc., et al.*, 1994 WL 285847 (U.S. Fla.). Notes and some case citations omitted.

I

The record of this case contains a videotape, with running caption of time and date, displaying what one must presume to be the worst of the activity justifying the injunction issued by Judge McGregor and partially approved today by this Court. The tape was shot by employees of, or volunteers at, the Aware Woman Clinic on three Saturdays in February and March 1993; the camera location, for the first and third segments, appears to have been an upper floor of the clinic. The tape was edited down (from approximately 6 to 8 hours of footage to $1/2$ hour) by Ruth Arick, a management consultant employed by the clinic and by the Feminist Majority Foundation.

Anyone seriously interested in what this case was about must view that tape. And anyone doing so who is familiar with run-of-the-mine labor picketing, not to mention some other social protests, will be aghast at what it shows we have today permitted an individual judge to do. I will do my best to describe it.

On Saturday, March 6, 1993, a group of antiabortion protesters is gathered in front of the clinic, arrayed from east (camera-left) to west (camera-right) on the clinic side of Dixie Way, a small, nonartery street. Men, women, and children are also visible across the street, on the south side of Dixie Way; some hold signs and appear to be protesters, others may be just interested onlookers.

On the clinic side of the street, two groups confront each other across the line marking the south border of the clinic property—although they are so close together it is often impossible to tell them apart. On the clinic property (and with their backs to the camera) are a line of clinic and abortion-rights supporters, stretching the length of the property. Opposite them, and on the public right-of-way between the clinic property and Dixie Way itself, is a group of abortion opponents, some standing in place, others walking a picket line in an elongated oval pattern running the length of the property's south border. Melbourne police officers are visible at various times walking about in front of the clinic, and individuals can be seen crossing Dixie Way at various times.

Clinic supporters are more or less steadily chanting the following slogans: "Our right, our right, our right, to decide"; "Right to life is a lie, you don't care if women die." Then abortion opponents can be heard to sing: "Jesus loves the little children, all the children of the world, red and yellow, black and white, they are precious in His sight, Jesus loves the little children of the world." Clinic supporters respond with: Q: "What do we want?" A: "Choice." Q: "When do we want it?" A: "Now." ("Louder!") And that call and response is repeated. Later in the tape, clinic supporters chant "1-2-3-4, we won't take it anymore; 5-6-7-8, Separate the Church and State." On placards held by picketers and by stationary protesters on both sides of the line, the following slogans are visible: "Abortionists lie to women." "Choose Life: Abortion Kills." "N.O.W. Violence." "The God of Israel is Pro-life." "RU 486 Now." "She Is a Child, Not a Choice." "Abortion Kills Children." "Keep Abortion Legal." "Abortion: God Calls It Murder." Some abortion opponents wear T-shirts bearing the phrase "Choose Life."

As the abortion opponents walk the picket line, they traverse portions of the public right-of-way that are crossed by paved driveways, on each side of the clinic, connecting the clinic's parking lot to the street. At one point an automobile moves west on Dixie Way and slows to turn into the westernmost driveway. There is a 3-to-4-second delay as the picketers, and then the clinic supporters, part to allow the car to enter. The camera cuts to a shot of another, parked car with a potato jammed onto the tailpipe. There is no footage of any person putting the potato onto the tailpipe.

Later, at a point when the crowd appears to be larger and the picketers more numerous, a red car is delayed approximately 10 seconds as the picketers (and clinic supporters) move out of the driveway. Police are visible helping to clear a path for the vehicle to enter. As the car waits, two persons appearing to bear leaflets approach, respectively, the driver and front passenger doors. They appear to elicit no response from the car's occupants and the car passes safely onto clinic property. Later, a blue minivan enters the driveway and is also subject to the same delay. Still later a jeep-type vehicle leaves the clinic property and slows down slightly where the driveway crosses the public right-of-way. At no time is there any apparent effort to prevent entry or exit, or even to delay it, except for the time needed for the picketers to get out of the way. There is no sitting down, packing en masse, linking of hands or any other effort to blockade the clinic property. The persons standing but not walking the picket line include a woman with a child in a stroller, and a man shouting the Book of Daniel's account of Meshach, Shadrach, and Abednego. A woman on a stepladder holds up a sign in the direction of the clinic; a clinic supporter counters with a larger sign held up between the other and the clinic. A brief shot reveals an older man in a baseball cap—head, shoulders, and chest visible above the clinic fence—who appears to be reading silently from a small book. A man on clinic property holds a boom box out in the direction of the abortion opponents. As the crowd grows it appears at various points to have spilled over into the north-side, westbound lane of Dixie Way.

At one point, Randall Terry arrives and the press converge upon him, apparently in Dixie Way itself. A sign is held near his head reading "Randall Terry Sucks." Terry appears to be speaking to the press and at one point tears pages from a notebook of some kind. Through all of this, abortion opponents and abortion-rights supporters appear to be inches from one another on each side of the south border of the property. They exchange words, but at no time is there any violence or even any discernible jostling or physical contact between these political opponents.

The scene shifts to early afternoon of the same day. Most of the press and most of the abortion opponents appear to have departed. The camera focuses on a woman who faces the clinic and, hands cupped over her mouth, shouts the following: "Be not deceived; God is not mocked.... Ed Windle, God's judgment is on you, and if you don't repent, He will strike you dead. The baby's blood flowed over your hands, Ed Windle.... You will burn in hell, Ed Windle, if you don't repent. There were arms and legs pulled off today.... An innocent little child, a little boy, a little girl, is being destroyed right now." Cheering is audible from the clinic grounds. A second person shouts "You are responsible for the deaths of children.... You are a murderer. Shame on you." ... The first woman says "You are applauding the death of your children. We will be everywhere.... There will be no peace and no rest for the wicked.... I pray that you will give them dreams and nightmares, God."

The second segment of the videotape displays a group of approximately 40 to 50 persons walking along the side of a major highway. It is Saturday, March 13, 1993, at 9:56 a.m. The demonstrators walk in an oval pattern, carrying no signs or other visible indicators of their purpose. According to Ruth Arick, this second portion was filmed in front of the condominium where clinic owner Ed Windle lived.

A third segment begins. The date-time register indicates that it is the morning of Saturday, February 20, 1993. A teenage girl faces the clinic and exclaims: "Please don't let them kill me, Mommy. Help me, Daddy, please." Clinic supporters chant, "We won't go back." A second woman, the one who spoke at greatest length in the first segment calls, "If you [inaudible], help her through it." Off camera, a group sings "Roe, Roe, Roe v. Wade, we will never quit, Freedom of choice is the law of the land, better get used to it." The woman from the first segment appears to address specific persons on clinic property: "Do you ever wonder what your baby would have looked like? Do you wonder how old it would have been? Because I did the same thing...." Then a police officer is visible writing someone a citation. The videotape ends with a shot of an automobile moving eastbound on Dixie Way. As it slows to a stop at the intersection of U.S. 1, two leafletters approach the car and then pull back as it passes on.

The videotape and the rest of the record, including the trial court's findings, show that a great many forms of expression and conduct occurred in the vicinity of the clinic. These include singing, chanting, praying, shouting, the playing of music both from the clinic and from handheld boom boxes, speeches, peaceful picketing, communication of familiar political messages, handbilling, persuasive speech directed at opposing groups on the issue of abortion, efforts to persuade individuals not to have abortions, personal testimony, interviews with the press, and media efforts to report on the protest. What the videotape, the rest of the record, and the trial court's findings do not contain is any suggestion of violence near the clinic, nor do they establish any attempt to prevent entry or exit.

II
A

Under this Court's jurisprudence, there is no question that this public sidewalk area is a "public forum," where citizens generally have a First Amendment right to speak. *United States v. Grace*, 461 U.S. 171, 177 (1983). The parties to this case invited the Court to employ one or the other of the two well established standards applied to restrictions upon this First Amendment right. Petitioners claimed the benefit of so-called "strict scrutiny," the standard applied to content-based restrictions: the restriction must be "necessary to serve a compelling state interest and ... narrowly drawn to achieve that end." *Perry Education Assn. v. Perry Local Educators' Assn.*, 460 U.S. 37, 45 (1983). Respondents, on the other hand, contended for what has come to be known as "intermediate scrutiny" (midway between the "strict scrutiny" demanded for content-based regulation of speech, and the "rational basis" standard that is applied—under the Equal Protection Clause—to government regulation of non-speech activities). That standard, applicable to so-called "time, place and manner regulations" of speech, provides that the regulations are permissible so long as they "are content-neutral, are narrowly tailored to serve a significant government interest, and leave open ample alternative channels of communication." *Perry, supra,* at 45. The Court adopts neither of these, but creates, brand-new for this abortion-related case, an additional standard that is (supposedly) "somewhat more stringent" than intermediate scrutiny, yet not as "rigorous" as strict scrutiny. The Court does not give this new standard a name, but perhaps we could call it intermediate-intermediate scrutiny. The difference between it and intermediate scrutiny (which the Court acknowledges is inappropriate for injunctive restrictions on speech) is frankly too subtle for me to describe, so I must simply recite it: whereas intermediate scrutiny requires that the restriction be "narrowly tailored to serve a significant government interest," the new standard requires that the restriction "burden no more speech than necessary to serve a significant government interest." *Ibid.* . . .

The Court seeks to minimize the similarity between speech-restricting injunctions and content-based statutory proscriptions by observing that the fact that "petitioners all shar[ing] the same viewpoint regarding abortion does not in itself demonstrate that some invidious content or viewpoint-based purpose motivated the issuance of the order," but rather "suggests only that those in the group whose conduct violated the court's order happen to share the same opinion regarding abortions." But the Court errs in thinking that the vice of content-based

statutes is that they necessarily have the invidious purpose of suppressing particular ideas. "Our cases have consistently held that '[i]llicit legislative intent is not the sine qua non of a violation of the First Amendment.'" *Simon & Schuster v. New York Crime Victims Bd.,* 502 U.S. (1991) (*slip op.,* at 10) (quoting *Minneapolis Star & Tribune Co. v. Minnesota Comm'r of Revenue,* 460 U.S. 575, 592 (1983). The vice of content-based legislation—what renders it deserving of the high standard of strict scrutiny—is not that it is always used for invidious, thought-control purposes, but that it lends itself to use for those purposes. And, because of the unavoidable "targeting" discussed above, precisely the same is true of the speech-restricting injunction.

Finally, though I believe speech-restricting injunctions are dangerous enough to warrant strict scrutiny even when they are not technically content based, I think the injunction in the present case was content based (indeed, viewpoint based) to boot. The Court claims that it was directed, not at those who spoke certain things (anti-abortion sentiments), but at those who did certain things (violated the earlier injunction). If that were true, then the injunction's residual coverage of "all persons acting in concert or participation with [the named individuals and organizations], or on their behalf" would not include those who merely entertained the same beliefs and wished to express the same views as the named defendants. But the construction given to the injunction by the issuing judge, which is entitled to great weight, is to the contrary: all those who wish to express the same views as the named defendants are deemed to be "acting in concert or participation." Following issuance of the amended injunction, a number of persons were arrested for walking within the 36-foot speech-free zone. At an April 12, 1993, hearing before the trial judge who issued the injunction, the following exchanges occurred:

MR. LACY: "I was wondering how we can—why we were arrested and confined as being in concert with these people that we don't know, when other people weren't, that were in that same buffer zone, and it was kind of selective as to who was picked and who was arrested and who was obtained for the same buffer zone in the same public injunction."

THE COURT: "Mr. Lacy, I understand that those on the other side of the issue [abortion-rights supporters] were also in the area. If you are referring to them, the Injunction did not pertain to those on the other side of the issue, because the word in concert with means in concert with those who had taken a certain position in respect to the clinic, adverse to the clinic. If you are saying that is the selective basis that the pro-choice were not arrested when pro-life was arrested, that's the basis of the selection...."

Tr. 104–105 (Apr. 12, 1993, Appearance Hearings Held Before Judge McGregor, Eighteenth Judicial Circuit, Seminole County, Florida (emphasis added)).

AND: JOHN DOE NO. 16: "This was the first time that I was in this area myself and I had not attempted to block an entrance to a clinic in that town or anywhere else in the State of Florida in the last year or ever.

"I also understand that the reason why I was arrested was because I acted in concert with those who were demonstrating pro-life. I guess the question that I'm asking is were the beliefs in ideologies of the people that were present, were those taken into consideration when we were arrested?

"... When you issued the Injunction did you determine that it would only apply to—that it would apply only to people that were demonstrating that were pro-life?"

THE COURT: "In effect, yes." *Id.*, at 113–116 (emphasis added).

AND FINALLY: JOHN DOE NO. 31: "... How did the police determine that I was acting in concert with some organization that was named on this injunction? I again am a person who [hasn't] seen this injunction. So how did the police determine that I was acting in concert?"

THE COURT: "They observed your activities and determined in their minds whether or not what you were doing was in concert with the—I gather the pro-life position of the other, of the named Defendants." *Id.*, at 148 (emphasis added).

These colloquys leave no doubt that the revised injunction here is tailored to restrain persons distinguished, not by proscribable conduct, but by proscribable views.

B

I have discussed, in the prior subjection, the policy reasons for giving speech-restricting injunctions, even content-neutral ones, strict scrutiny. There are reasons of precedent as well, which are essentially ignored by the Court.

To begin with, an injunction against speech is the very prototype of the greatest threat to First Amendment values, the prior restraint. As THE CHIEF JUSTICE wrote for the Court last Term: "The term prior restraint is used 'to describe administrative and judicial orders forbidding certain communications when issued in advance of the time that such communications are to occur.' ... [P]ermanent injunctions, i.e.,—court orders that actually forbid speech activities—are classic examples of prior restraints." *Alexander v. United States,* 509 U.S. (1993) (*slip op.,* at 5) (quoting M. Nimmer, *Nimmer on Freedom of Speech* § 4.03, p. 4–14 (1984) (emphasis added in Alexander))....

The utter lack of support for the Court's test in our jurisprudence is demonstrated by the two cases the opinion relies upon. For the proposition that a speech restriction is valid when it "burden[s] no more speech than necessary to accomplish a significant government interest," the Court cites *NAACP v. Claiborne Hardware Co., supra,* and *Carroll v. President and Commissioners of Princess Anne,* 393 U.S., at 184. But as I shall demonstrate in some detail below, *Claiborne* applied a much more stringent test; and the very text of *Carroll* contradicts the Court. In the passage cited, Carroll says this: "An order issued in the area of First Amendment rights must be couched in the narrowest terms that will accomplish the pinpointed objective permitted by constitutional mandate and the essential needs of the public order." *Id.,* at 183. That, of course, is strict scrutiny; and it does not remotely resemble the Court's new proposal, for which it is cited as precedential support. "Significant government interest[s]" (referred to in the Court's test) are general, innumerable, and omnipresent —at least one of them will be implicated by any activity set in a public forum. "Essential needs of the public order," on the other hand, are factors of exceptional application. And that an injunction "burden no more than necessary" is not nearly as demanding as the requirement that it be couched in the "narrowest terms that will accomplish [a] pin-pointed objective." That the Court should cite this case as its principal authority is an admission that what it announces rests upon no precedent at all.

III

A

I turn now from the Court's selection of a constitutional test to its actual application of that test to the facts of the present case. Before doing that, however, it will be helpful—in order to demonstrate how far the Court has departed from past practice—to consider how we proceeded in a relatively recent case that did not involve the disfavored class of abortion protesters. *NAACP v. Claiborne Hardware Co.,* 458 U.S. 886 (1982), involved, like this case, protest demonstrations against private citizens mingling political speech with (what I will assume for the time being existed here) significant illegal behavior.

Writing for the Court, JUSTICE STEVENS summarized the events giving rise to the *Claiborne* litigation: A local chapter of the NAACP, rebuffed by public officials of Port Gibson and Claiborne County in its request for redress of various forms of racial discrimination, began a boycott of local businesses. During the boycott, a young black man was shot and killed in an encounter with Port Gibson police and "sporadic acts of violence ensued." *Id.,* at 902. The following day, boycott leader Charles Evers told a group that boycott violators would be disciplined by their own people and warned that the Sheriff "could not sleep with boycott violators at night." *Ibid.* He stated at a second gathering that "If we catch any of you going in any of them racist stores, we're gonna break your damn neck." *Ibid.* In connection with the boycott, there were marches and picketing (often by small children). "Store watchers" were posted outside boycotted stores to identify those who traded, and their names were read aloud at meetings of the Claiborne County NAACP and published in a mimeographed paper. The chancellor found that those persons were branded traitors, called demeaning names, and socially ostracized. Some had shots fired at their houses, a brick was thrown through a windshield and a garden damaged. Other evidence showed that persons refusing to observe the boycott were beaten, robbed and publicly humiliated (by spanking).

The merchants brought suit against two groups involved in organizing the boycott and numerous individuals. The trial court found tort violations, violations of a state statute prohibiting secondary boycotts, and state antitrust violations. It issued a broad permanent injunction against the boycotters, enjoining them from stationing "store watchers" at the plaintiffs' business premises; from persuading any person to withhold patronage; from using demeaning and obscene language to or about any person because of his patronage; from picketing or patrolling the premises of any of the respondents; and from using violence against any person or inflicting damage upon any real or personal property. The Mississippi Supreme Court upheld the assessment of liability and the injunction, but solely on the tort theory, saying that " '[i]f any of these factors—force, violence, or threats—is present, then the boycott is illegal regardless of whether it is primary, secondary, economical, political, social or other.' " *Id.*, at 895.

The legal analysis of this Court proceeded along the following lines: "[T]he boycott... took many forms. [It] was launched at a meeting of the local branch of the NAACP. [It] was attended by several hundred persons. Its acknowledged purpose was to secure compliance... with a lengthy list of demands for racial equality and racial justice. The boycott was supported by speeches and nonviolent picketing. Participants repeatedly encouraged others to join its cause.

"Each of these elements of the boycott is a form of speech or conduct that is ordinarily entitled to protection under the First and Fourteenth Amendments.... '[T]he practice of persons sharing common views banded together to achieve a common end is deeply embedded in the American political process.' We recognize that 'by collective effort individuals can make their views known, when, individually, their voices would be faint or lost.'" *Id.*, at 907–908 (quoting *Citizens Against Rent Control/Coalition for Fair Housing v. Berkeley*, 454 U.S. 290, 294 (1981)). We went on to say that "[t]he right to associate does not lose all constitutional protection merely because some members of the group may have participated in conduct or advocated doctrine that is not itself protected," 458 U.S., at 908, and held that the nonviolent elements of the protesters' activities were entitled to the protection of the First Amendment, *id.*, at 915.

... We said in conclusion that any characterization of a political protest movement as a violent conspiracy "must be supported by findings that adequately disclose the evidentiary basis for concluding that specific parties agreed to use unlawful means, that carefully identify the impact of such unlawful conduct, and that recognize the importance of avoiding the imposition of punishment for constitutionally protected activity." *Id.*, at 933–934. Because this careful procedure has not followed by the Mississippi courts, we set aside the entire judgment, including the injunction. *Id.*, at 924, n. 67, 934.

B

I turn now to the Court's performance in the present case. I am content to evaluate it under the lax (intermediate-intermediate scrutiny) standard that the Court has adopted, because even by that distorted light it is inadequate....

According to the Court, the state court imposed the later injunction's "restrictions on petitioner[s']...antiabortion message because they repeatedly violated the court's original order." Surprisingly, the Court accepts this reason as valid, without asking whether the court's findings of fact support it—whether, that is, the acts of which the petitioners stood convicted were violations of the original injunction.

The Court simply takes this on faith —even though violation of the original injunction is an essential part of the reasoning whereby it approves portions of the amended injunction, even though petitioners denied any violation of the original injunction, even though the utter lack of proper basis for the other challenged portions of the injunction hardly inspires confidence that the lower courts knew what they were doing, and even though close examination of the factual basis for essential conclusions is the usual practice in First Amendment cases. Let us proceed, then, to the inquiry the Court neglected. In the Amended Permanent Injunction the trial court found that "despite the injunction of September 30, 1992, there has been interference with ingress to the petitioners' facility...[in] the form of persons on the paved portions of Dixie Way, some standing without any obvious relationship to others; some moving about, again without any obvious relationship to others; some holding signs, some not; some approaching, apparently trying to communicate with the occupants of motor vehicles moving on the paved surface; some marching in a circular picket line that traversed the entrance driveways to the two parking lots of the petitioners and the short section of the sidewalk joining the two parking lots and then entering the paved portion of the north lane of Dixie Way and returning in the opposite direction.... Other persons would be standing, kneeling and sitting on the unpaved shoulders of the public right-of-way. As vehicular traffic approached the area it would, in response to the congestion, slow down. If the destination of such traffic was either of the two parking lots of the petitioners, such traffic slowed even more, sometimes having to momentarily hesitate or stop until persons in the driveway moved out of the way." Amended Permanent Injunction P A.

"As traffic slowed on Dixie Way and began to turn into the clinic's driveway, the vehicle would be approached by persons designated by the respondents as sidewalk counselors attempting to get the attention of the vehicles' occupants to give them anti-abortion literature and to urge them not to use the clinic's services. Such so-called sidewalk counselors were assisted in accomplishing their approach to the vehicle by the hesitation or momentary stopping caused by the time needed for the picket line to open up before the vehicle could enter the parking lot." Id., P E. "The...staff physician testified that on one occasion while he was attempting to enter the parking lot of the clinic, he had to stop his vehicle and remained stopped while respondent, Cadle, and others took their time to get out of the way.... This physician also testified that he witnessed the demonstrators running alongside in front of patients' vehicles, pushing pamphlets in such windows to persons who had not indicated any interest in such literature...." *Id.*, P I (emphasis added). On the basis of these findings Judge McGregor concluded that "the actions of the respondents and those in concert with them in the street and driveway approaches to the clinic of the plaintiffs continue to impede and obstruct both staff and patients from entering the clinic. The paved surfaces of the public right-of-way must be kept open for the free flow of traffic."

These are the only findings and conclusions of the court that could conceivably be considered to relate to a violation of the original injunction. They all concern behavior by the protesters causing traffic on the street in front of the abortion clinic to slow down, and causing vehicles crossing the pedestrian right-of-way, between the street and the clinic's parking lot, to slow down or even, occasionally, to stop momentarily while pedestrians got out of the way. As far as appears from the court's findings, all of these results were produced, not by anyone intentionally seeking to block oncoming traffic, but as the incidental effect of persons engaged in the activities of walking a picket line and leafletting on public property in front of the clinic. There is no factual finding that petitioners engaged in any intentional or purposeful obstruction.

Now let us compare these activities with the earlier injunction, violation of which is the asserted justification for the speech-free zone. Walking the return leg of the picket line on the paved portion of Dixie Way (instead of on the sidewalk), and congregating on the unpaved portion of that street, may, for all we know, violate some municipal ordinance (though that was not alleged,

and the municipal police evidently did not seek to prevent it); but it assuredly did not violate the earlier injunction, which made no mention of such a prohibition. Causing the traffic along Dixie Way to slow down "in response to the congestion" is also irrelevant; the injunction said nothing about slowing down traffic on public rights of way. It prohibited the doing (or urging) of only three things: 1) "physically abusing persons entering, leaving, working or using any services" of the abortion clinic (there is no allegation of that); 2) "trespassing on [or] sitting in" the abortion clinic (there is no allegation of that); and 3) "blocking, impeding or obstructing ingress into or egress from" the abortion clinic.

Only the last of these has any conceivable application here, and it seems to me that it must reasonably be read to refer to intentionally blocking, impeding or obstructing, and not to such temporary obstruction as may be the normal and incidental consequence of other protest activity. That is obvious, first of all, from the context in which the original injunction was issued—as a response to the petitioners' threatened actions of trespass and blockade, i.e., the physical shutting down of the local clinics. Secondly, if that narrow meaning of intentional blockade, impediment or obstruction was not intended, and if it covered everything up to and including the incidental and "momentary" stopping of entering vehicles by persons leafletting and picketing, the original injunction would have failed the axiomatic requirement that its terms be drawn with precision. See, e.g., *Milk Wagon Drivers*, 312 U.S., at 296; 1 D. Dobbs, *Law of Remedies* § 2.8(7), p. 219 (2d ed. 1993); 7 J. Moore, J. Lucas, & K. Sinclair, *Moore's Federal*

Practice P 65.11 (2d ed. 1994); cf. Fed. R. Civ. Proc. 65(d) ("[e]very order granting an injunction... shall be specific in terms [and] shall describe in reasonable detail... the act or acts sought to be restrained"). And finally, if the original injunction did not have that narrow meaning it would assuredly have been unconstitutional, since it would have prevented speech-related activities that were, insofar as this record shows, neither criminally or civilly unlawful nor inextricably intertwined with unlawful conduct. See *Milk Wagon Drivers, supra,* at 292, 297; *Carroll,* 393 U.S., at 183–184.

If the original injunction is read as it must be, there is nothing in the trial court's findings to suggest that it was violated. The Court today speaks of "the failure of the first injunction to protect access." But the first injunction did not broadly "protect access." It forbade particular acts that impeded access, to-wit, intentionally "blocking, impeding or obstructing." The trial court's findings identify none of these acts, but only a mild interference with access that is the incidental by-product of leafletting and picketing. There was no sitting down, no linking of arms, no packing en masse in the driveway; the most that can be alleged (and the trial court did not even make this a finding) is that on one occasion protesters "took their time to get out of the way." If that is enough to support this one-man proscription of free speech, the First Amendment is in grave peril. . . .

C

Finally, I turn to the Court's application of the second part of its test: whether the provisions of the injunction "burden no more speech than necessary" to serve the significant interest protected.

This test seems to me amply and obviously satisfied with regard to the noise restriction that the Court approves: it is only such noise as would reach the patients in the abortion clinic that is forbidden—and not even at all times, but only during certain fixed hours and "during surgical procedures and recovery periods." (The latter limitation may raise vagueness and notice problems, but that does not concern us here. Moreover, the noise restriction is invalid on other grounds.) With regard to the 36-foot speech-free zone, however, it seems to me just as obvious that the test which the Court sets for itself has not been met.

Assuming a "significant state interest" of the sort cognizable for injunction purposes (i.e., one protected by a law that has been or is threatened to be violated) in both (1) keeping pedestrians off the paved portion of Dixie Way, and (2) enabling cars to cross the public sidewalk at the clinic's driveways without having to slow down or come to even a "momentary" stop, there are surely a number of ways to protect those interests short of banishing the entire protest demonstration from the 36-foot zone. For starters, the Court could have (for the first time) ordered the demonstrators to stay out of the street (the original injunction did not remotely require that). It could have limited the number of demonstrators permitted on the clinic side of Dixie Way. And it could have forbidden the pickets to walk on the driveways. The Court's only response to these options is that "[t]he state court was convinced that [they would not work] in view of the failure of the first injunction to protect access." But must we accept that conclusion as valid—when the original injunction contained no command (or at the very least no clear command) that had been disobeyed, and contained nothing even related to staying out of the street? If the "burden no more speech than necessary" requirement can be avoided by merely opining that (for some reason) no lesser restriction than this one will be obeyed, it is not much of a requirement at all.

But I need not engage in such precise analysis, since the Court itself admits that the requirement is not to be taken seriously. "The need for a complete buffer zone," it says, "may be debatable, but some deference must be given to the state court's familiarity with the facts and the background of the dispute between the parties even under our heightened review." *Ibid.* (emphasis added). In application, in other words, the "burden no more speech than is necessary" test has become an "arguably burden no more speech than is necessary" test. This renders the Court's intermediate-intermediate scrutiny not only no more stringent than plain old intermediate scrutiny, but considerably less stringent. . . .

* * *

In his dissent in *Korematsu v. United States*, 323 U.S. 214 (1944), the case in which this Court permitted the wartime military internment of Japanese-Americans, Justice Jackson wrote the following: "A military order, however unconstitutional, is not apt to last longer than the military emergency. . . . But once a judicial opinion . . . rationalizes the Constitution to show that the Constitution sanctions such an order, the Court for all time has validated the principle of racial discrimination in criminal procedure and of transplanting American citizens. The principle then lies about like a loaded weapon ready for the hand of any authority that can bring forward a plausible claim of an urgent need." *Id.*, at 246. What was true of a misguided military order is true of a misguided trial-court injunction. And the Court has left a powerful loaded weapon lying about today.

What we have decided seems to be, and will be reported by the media as, an abortion case. But it will go down in the lawbooks, it will be cited, as a free-speech injunction case—and the damage its novel principles produce will be considerable. The proposition that injunctions against speech are subject to a standard indistinguishable from (unless perhaps more lenient in its application than) the "intermediate scrutiny" standard we have used for "time, place, and manner" legislative restrictions; the notion that injunctions against speech need not be closely tied to any violation of law, but may simply implement sound social policy; and the practice of accepting trial-court conclusions permitting injunctions without considering whether those conclusions are supported by any findings of fact— these latest by-products of our abortion jurisprudence ought to give all friends of liberty great concern.

For these reasons, I dissent from that portion of the judgment upholding parts of the injunction.

POSTSCRIPT

Can Courts Restrict the Picketing of Abortion Clinics?

While this case is primarily about peaceful protest, there is a backdrop of violence to antiabortion protests. In March 1993 Dr. David Gunn, a Pensacola, Florida, doctor who performed abortions, was murdered. In August 1993 Dr. George Tiller was shot in Wichita, Kansas, and in July 1994 Dr. John Britton, a doctor at a women's health clinic, and a security guard for the clinic were murdered in Pensacola, Florida. Since 1977, there have been more than 1,000 violent incidents reported at clinics, including 36 bombings, 81 cases of arson, 131 death threats, 84 assaults, and 2 kidnappings.

Operation Rescue, the principal organizer of abortion clinic protests, has condemned the use of violence. It has also lost members and resources in the aftermath of the violence. The possibility of future acts of violence, however, is suggested by a CNN poll taken several weeks after the July 1994 slayings. In the poll, 8 percent of all those polled indicated that using force to prevent abortions was justifiable, and 3 percent indicated that killing an abortion doctor is a justifiable act.

Abortion protest and conflict is an area of likely continuing activity, not only because of the strong feelings that are reflected in the poll but because of two areas of recent legislative activity. In May 1994 President Clinton signed into law the Freedom of Access to Clinic Entrances Act. The act makes it a federal crime, punishable by up to six months in prison, to blockade an abortion clinic or to engage in other forms of disruptive civil disobedience around clinics. Abortion has also figured prominently in the health care reform debate. In a recent poll, 49 percent of respondents said that abortion should not be included in guaranteed benefits, while 42 percent said that it should. Should major health care reform legislation be enacted any time in the next couple of years, it will, in all likelihood, be accompanied by a continuing debate over abortion.

The Supreme Court previously considered abortion clinic protests in *Bray v. Alexandria Women's Health Clinic,* 113 S. Ct. 753 (1994) and *National Organization of Women v. Scheidler,* 114 S. Ct. 798 (1994). A recent article is Randolph M. Scott-McLaughlin, "Operation Rescue Versus a Woman's Right to Choose: A Conflict Without a Federal Remedy?" 32 *Duquesne Law Review* 709 (1994).

PART 3

Law and Crime

Crime is a fact of life for many citizens in the United States, and the social, economic, and psychological costs are high for individual victims and society as a whole. Every society has to contend with those members who refuse to adhere to the established rules of behavior; how criminals are treated is often one standard for judging a society's fairness and compassion.

The debates in this section address issues concerning the treatment of criminals and the legal rights of the accused as well as the rights of citizens to be free from fear.

■ Should the Death Penalty Be Abolished?

■ Should the Exclusionary Rule Be Abolished?

■ Should "Battered Wife Syndrome" Be Barred as a Defense in a Murder Case?

■ Will Waiting Periods Control Gun Purchases?

■ Does the Clipper Chip Give the Government Too Much Control Over Citizens' Privacy?

■ Should the Insanity Defense Be Abolished?

■ Should Drug Use Be Legalized?

ISSUE 12

Should the Death Penalty Be Abolished?

YES: Harry A. Blackmun, from Dissenting Opinion, *Bruce Edwin Callins v. James A. Collins,* U.S. Supreme Court (1994)

NO: James C. Anders, from Statement Before the Committee on the Judiciary, U.S. Senate (September 19, 1989)

ISSUE SUMMARY

YES: Former Supreme Court justice Harry Blackmun argues that the application of the death penalty has been arbitrary and discriminatory.

NO: Attorney James Anders argues that the death penalty is the appropriate punishment for some crimes and that it should not be abolished even if it is not an effective deterrent.

Unlike some of the issues in this book, capital punishment has a long history. For example, in 428 B.C., Thucydides recorded the following arguments by Cleon in support of the death penalty:

> Punish them as they deserve, and teach your other allies by a striking example that the penalty of rebellion is death. Let them once understand this and you will not so often have to neglect your enemies while you are fighting with your confederates.

In response, Diodotus wrote:

> All states and individuals are alike prone to err, and there is no law that will prevent them, or why should men have exhausted the list of punishments in search of enactments to protect them from evil doers? It is probable that in early times the penalties for the greatest offenses were less severe, and that as these were disregarded, the penalty of death has been by degrees in most cases arrived at, which is itself disregarded in like manner. Either some means of terror more terrible than this must be discovered, or it must be owned that this restraint is useless....
>
> We must make up our minds to look for our protection not to legal terrors but to careful administration.... Good policy against an adversary is superior to the blind attacks of brute force.

During the last two and a half decades, the Supreme Court has been confronted with death penalty cases almost every year. The most significant decision was that of *Furman v. Georgia,* 408 U.S. 238, decided in 1972. Furman, a 26-year-old black man, had killed a homeowner during a break-in and was sentenced to death. In a 5–4 decision, the Court overturned the sentence. It held that the procedure used by Georgia (and most other states at that time) was "cruel and unusual" and therefore a violation of the Eighth Amendment of the Constitution. At the heart of the case was the fact that Georgia law left it up to the discretion of the jury to decide whether or not the death penalty was appropriate in a particular case. Two justices, Thurgood Marshall and William J. Brennan, Jr., believed that the death penalty under any circumstances violated the cruel and unusual punishment clause. The three other justices in the majority, however, felt that the death penalty was not in itself unconstitutional but that the manner in which it was applied in this case was unlawful. They felt that leaving the sentence up to the jury led it to be "wantonly" and "freakishly" imposed and "pregnant with discrimination."

Since 1972, 36 states have enacted new death penalty statutes. The following cases illustrate some of the difficulties involved in developing a consistent standard through a case-by-case approach.

1. *Gregg v. Georgia*, 428 U.S. 153 (1976) After *Furman*, Georgia enacted a new statute retaining the death penalty for murder and five other crimes. Guilt or innocence was determined at a trial and then a second hearing or trial was held for the jury to determine whether the death penalty should be applied. The law set up procedures that were intended to limit the jury's discretion and that required higher court review of the sentence with the hope that this would reduce the incidence of discrimination and prejudice. In a 7–2 decision, this law was upheld by the Supreme Court.
2. *Lockett v. Ohio*, 438 U.S. 586 (1978) Ohio law prevented the jury from considering any mitigating circumstances other than those specifically enumerated in the statute. The Supreme Court held that this law was unconstitutional.
3. *Coker v. Georgia*, 433 U.S. 584 (1977) The Supreme Court held that the death penalty may not be imposed on persons convicted of rape. The case suggests that the death penalty is unconstitutional if a death did not take place as a result of the defendant's actions.

What these cases indicate is that the death penalty is lawful and not "cruel and unusual" if the victim has been killed, if the statute provides the defendant the opportunity to present mitigating circumstances, if the statute lists aggravating circumstances that must be considered, and if it requires appellate review. These procedural requirements have been imposed mainly to reduce the possibility of discriminatory application of the death penalty.

The following reading, by recently retired Supreme Court justice Harry Blackmun, is a remarkable statement of the limits of judicial power. Blackmun does not feel that capital punishment is necessarilly unconstitutional. He concludes, however, that the Court has been unable to provide a proper framework for applying the death penalty in a nonarbitrary manner and will be unable to do so. Attorney James Anders disagrees.

YES

Harry A. Blackmun

DISSENTING OPINION OF HARRY A. BLACKMUN

CALLINS *v.* COLLINS

Justice BLACKMUN, dissenting.

On February 23, 1994, at approximately 1:00 a.m., Bruce Edwin Callins will be executed by the State of Texas. Intravenous tubes attached to his arms will carry the instrument of death, a toxic fluid designed specifically for the purpose of killing human beings. The witnesses, standing a few feet away, will behold Callins, no longer a defendant, an appellant, or a petitioner, but a man, strapped to a gurney, and seconds away from extinction.

Within days, or perhaps hours, the memory of Callins will begin to fade. The wheels of justice will churn again, and somewhere, another jury or another judge will have the unenviable task of determining whether some human being is to live or die. We hope, of course, that the defendant whose life is at risk will be represented by competent counsel—someone who is inspired by the awareness that a less-than-vigorous defense truly could have fatal consequences for the defendant. We hope that the attorney will investigate all aspects of the case, follow all evidentiary and procedural rules, and appear before a judge who is still committed to the protection of defendants' rights —even now, as the prospect of meaningful judicial oversight has diminished. In the same vein, we hope that the prosecution, in urging the penalty of death, will have exercised its discretion wisely, free from bias, prejudice, or political motive, and will be humbled, rather than emboldened, by the awesome authority conferred by the State.

But even if we can feel confident that these actors will fulfill their roles to the best of their human ability, our collective conscience will remain uneasy. Twenty years have passed since this Court declared that the death penalty must be imposed fairly, and with reasonable consistency, or not at all, see *Furman v. Georgia*, 408 U.S. 238, 92 S.Ct. 2726, 33 L.Ed.2d 346 (1972), and, despite the effort of the States and courts to devise legal formulas and procedural rules to meet this daunting challenge, the death penalty remains fraught with arbitrariness, discrimination, caprice, and mistake. This is not to say that the

From *Bruce Edwin Callins v. James A. Collins*, 114 S. Ct. 1127 (1994). Some notes and case citations omitted.

problems with the death penalty today are identical to those that were present 20 years ago. Rather, the problems that were pursued down one hole with procedural rules and verbal formulas have come to the surface somewhere else, just as virulent and pernicious as they were in their original form. Experience has taught us that the constitutional goal of eliminating arbitrariness and discrimination from the administration of death can never be achieved without compromising an equally essential component of fundamental fairness—individualized sentencing. See *Lockett v. Ohio*, 438 U.S. 586, 98 S.Ct. 2954, 57 L.Ed.2d 973 (1978).

It is tempting, when faced with conflicting constitutional commands, to sacrifice one for the other or to assume that an acceptable balance between them already has been struck. In the context of the death penalty, however, such jurisprudential maneuvers are wholly inappropriate. The death penalty must be imposed "fairly, and with reasonable consistency, or not at all." *Eddings v. Oklahoma*, 455 U.S. 104, 112, 102 S.Ct. 869, 875, 71 L.Ed.2d 1 (1982).

To be fair, a capital sentencing scheme must treat each person convicted of a capital offense with that "degree of respect due the uniqueness of the individual." *Lockett v. Ohio*, 438 U.S., at 605, 98 S.Ct., at 2964 (plurality opinion). That means affording the sentencer the power and discretion to grant mercy in a particular case, and providing avenues for the consideration of any and all relevant mitigating evidence that would justify a sentence less than death. Reasonable consistency, on the other hand, requires that the death penalty be inflicted evenhandedly, in accordance with reason and objective standards, rather than by whim, caprice, or prejudice. Finally, because human error is inevitable, and because our criminal justice system is less than perfect, searching appellate review of death sentences and their underlying convictions is a prerequisite to a constitutional death penalty scheme.

On their face, these goals of individual fairness, reasonable consistency, and absence of error appear to be attainable: Courts are in the very business of erecting procedural devices from which fair, equitable, and reliable outcomes are presumed to flow. Yet, in the death penalty area, this Court, in my view, has engaged in a futile effort to balance these constitutional demands, and now is retreating not only from the *Furman* promise of consistency and rationality, but from the requirement of individualized sentencing as well. Having virtually conceded that both fairness and rationality cannot be achieved in the administration of the death penalty, see *McCleskey v. Kemp*, 481 U.S. 279, 313, n. 37, 107 S.Ct. 1756, 1778, n. 37, 95 L.Ed.2d 262 (1987), the Court has chosen to deregulate the entire enterprise, replacing, it would seem, substantive constitutional requirements with mere aesthetics, and abdicating its statutorily and constitutionally imposed duty to provide meaningful judicial oversight to the administration of death by the States.

From this day forward, I no longer shall tinker with the machinery of death. For more than 20 years I have endeavored—indeed, I have struggled—along with a majority of this Court, to develop procedural and substantive rules that would lend more than the mere appearance of fairness to the death penalty endeavor. Rather than continue to coddle the Court's delusion that the desired level of fairness has been achieved and the need for regulation eviscerated, I feel morally and intellectually obligated simply to concede that the death penalty experiment has failed. It is virtually self-evident to me now that no combination of procedural rules or substantive regulations ever can save the death penalty from its inherent constitutional deficiencies. The basic question—does the system accurately and consistently determine which defendants "deserve" to die? —cannot be answered in the affirmative. It is not simply that this Court has allowed vague aggravating circumstances to be employed, see, e.g., *Arave v. Creech*, ___ U.S. ___ 113 S.Ct. 1534, 123 L.Ed.2d 188 (1993), relevant mitigating evidence to be disregarded, see, e.g., *Johnson v. Texas*, ___ U.S. ___, 113 S.Ct. 2658, 125 L.Ed.2d 290 (1993), and vital judicial review to be blocked, see, e.g., *Coleman v. Thompson*, 501 U.S. ___, 112 S.Ct. 1845, 119 L.Ed.2d 1 (1992). The problem is that the inevitability of factual, legal, and moral error gives us a system that we know must wrongly kill some defendants, a system that fails to deliver the fair, consistent, and reliable sentences of death required by the Constitution.[1]

I

In 1971, in an opinion which has proved partly prophetic, the second Justice Harlan, writing for the Court, observed: "Those who have come to grips with the hard task of actually attempting to draft means of channeling capital sentencing discretion have confirmed the lesson taught by the history recounted above. To identify before the fact those characteristics of criminal homicides and their perpetrators which call for the death penalty, and to express these characteristics in language which can be fairly understood and applied by the sentencing authority, appear to be tasks which are beyond present human ability.... For a court to attempt to catalog the appropriate factors in this elusive area could inhibit rather than expand the scope of consideration, for no list of circumstances would ever be really complete." *McGautha v. California*, 402 U.S. 183, 204, 208, 91 S.Ct. 1454, 1466, 1467, 28 L.Ed.2d 711 (1971). In *McGautha*, the petitioner argued that a statute which left the penalty of death entirely in the jury's discretion, without any standards to govern its imposition, violated the Fourteenth Amendment. Although the Court did not deny that serious risks were associated with a sentencer's unbounded discretion, the Court found no remedy in the Constitution for the inevitable failings of human judgment.

A year later, the Court reversed its course completely in *Furman v. Georgia*, 408 U.S. 238, 92 S.Ct. 2726, 33 L.Ed.2d 346 (1972) (*per curiam*, with each of the nine Justices writing separately). The concurring Justices argued that the glaring inequities in the administration of death, the standardless discretion wielded by judges and juries, and the pervasive racial and economic discrimination, rendered the death penalty, at least as administered, "cruel and unusual" within the meaning of the Eighth Amendment. Justice White explained that, out of the hundreds of people convicted of murder every year, only a handful were sent to their deaths, and that there was "no meaningful basis for distinguishing the few cases in which [the death penalty] is imposed from the many cases in which it is not." 408 U.S., at 313, 92 S.Ct, at 2764. If any discernible basis could be identified for the selection of those few who were chosen to die, it was "the constitutionally impermissible basis of race." *Id.*, at 310, 92 S.Ct., at 2762 (Stewart, J., concurring).

I dissented in *Furman*. Despite my intellectual, moral, and personal objections to the death penalty, I refrained from joining the majority because I found objectionable the Court's abrupt change of position in the single year that had passed since McGautha. While I agreed that the Eighth Amendment's prohibition against cruel and unusual punishments " 'may acquire meaning as public opinion becomes enlightened by a humane justice,' " 408 U.S., at 409, 92 S.Ct., at 2814, quoting *Weems v. United States*, 217 U.S. 349, 378, 30 S.Ct. 544, 553, 54 L.Ed. 793 (1910), I objected to the "suddenness of the Court's perception of progress in the human attitude since decisions of only a short while ago." 408 U.S., at 410, 92 S.Ct., at 2814. Four years after *Furman* was decided, I concurred in the judgment in *Gregg v. Georgia*, 428 U.S. 153, 96 S.Ct. 2909, 49 L.Ed.2d 859 (1976), and its companion cases which upheld death sentences rendered under statutes passed after *Furman* was decided. See *Proffitt v. Florida*, 428 U.S. 242, 261, 96 S.Ct. 2960, 2970, 49 L.Ed.2d 913 (1976), and *Jurek v. Texas*, 428 U.S. 262, 279, 96 S.Ct. 2950, 2960, 49 L.Ed.2d 929 (1976). *Cf. Woodson v. North Carolina*, 428 U.S. 280, 307, 96 S.Ct. 2978, 2992, 49 L.Ed.2d 944 (1976), and *Roberts v. Louisiana*, 428 U.S. 325, 363, 96 S.Ct. 3001, 3020, 49 L.Ed.2d 974 (1976).

A

There is little doubt now that *Furman's* essential holding was correct. Although most of the public seems to desire, and the Constitution appears to permit, the penalty of death, it surely is beyond dispute that if the death penalty cannot be administered consistently and rationally, it may not be administered at all. *Eddings v. Oklahoma*, 455 U.S., at 112, 102 S.Ct., at 875. I never have quarreled with this principle; in my mind, the real meaning of *Furman's* diverse concurring opinions did not emerge until some years after *Furman* was decided. See *Gregg v. Georgia*, 428 U.S., at 189, 96 S.Ct., at 2932 (opinion of Stewart, Powell, and STEVENS, JJ.) ("*Furman* mandates that where discretion is afforded a sentencing body on a matter so grave as the determination of whether a human life should be taken or spared, that discretion must be suitably directed and limited so as to minimize the risk of wholly arbitrary and capricious action"). Since *Gregg*, I faithfully have adhered to the *Furman* holding and have come to believe that it is indispensable to the Court's Eighth Amendment jurisprudence.

Delivering on the *Furman* promise, however, has proved to be another matter. *Furman* aspired to eliminate the vestiges of racism and the effects of poverty in capital sentencing; it deplored the "wanton" and "random" infliction of death by a government with constitutionally limited power. *Furman* demanded that the sentencer's discretion be directed and limited by procedural rules and objective standards in order to minimize the risk of arbitrary and capricious sentences of death.

In the years following *Furman*, serious efforts were made to comply with its mandate. State legislatures and appellate courts struggled to provide judges and juries with sensible and objective guidelines for determining who should live and who should die. Some States attempted to define who is "deserving" of the death penalty through the use of carefully chosen adjectives, reserving the death penalty for those who commit crimes that are "especially heinous, atrocious, or cruel," or "wantonly vile, horrible or inhuman." . . .

Unfortunately, all this experimentation and ingenuity yielded little of what *Furman* demanded. It soon became apparent that discretion could not be eliminated from capital sentencing without threatening the fundamental fairness due a defendant when life is at stake. Just as contemporary society was no longer tolerant of the random or discriminatory infliction of the penalty of death, evolving standards of decency required due consideration of the uniqueness of each individual defendant when imposing society's ultimate penalty.

This development in the American conscience would have presented no constitutional dilemma if fairness to the individual could be achieved without sacrificing the consistency and rationality promised in *Furman*. But over the past two decades, efforts to balance these competing constitutional commands have been to no avail. Experience has shown that the consistency and rationality promised in *Furman* are inversely related to the fairness owed the individual when considering a sentence of death. A step toward consistency is a step away from fairness.

B

There is a heightened need for fairness in the administration of death. This unique level of fairness is born of the appreciation that death truly is different from all other punishments a society inflicts upon its citizens. "Death, in its finality, differs more from life imprisonment than a 100-year prison term differs from one of only a year or two." *Woodson*, 428 U.S., at 305, 96 S.Ct.,

at 2991 (opinion of Stewart, Powell, and STEVENS, JJ.). Because of the qualitative difference of the death penalty, "there is a corresponding difference in the need for reliability in the determination that death is the appropriate punishment in a specific case." *Ibid.* In *Woodson*, a decision striking down mandatory death penalty statutes as unconstitutional, a plurality of the Court explained: "A process that accords no significance to relevant facets of the character and record of the individual offender or the circumstances of the particular offense excludes from consideration in fixing the ultimate punishment of death the possibility of compassionate or mitigating factors stemming from the diverse frailties of humankind." *Id.*, at 304, 96 S.Ct., at 2991.

While the risk of mistake in the determination of the appropriate penalty may be tolerated in other areas of the criminal law, "in capital cases the fundamental respect for humanity underlying the Eighth Amendment . . . requires consideration of the character and record of the individual offender and the circumstances of the particular offense as a constitutionally indispensable part of the process of inflicting the penalty of death." *Ibid.* Thus, although individualized sentencing in capital cases was not considered essential at the time the Constitution was adopted, *Woodson* recognized that American standards of decency could no longer tolerate a capital sentencing process that failed to afford a defendant individualized consideration in the determination whether he or she should live or die. *Id.*, at 301, 96 S.Ct., at 2989.

The Court elaborated on the principle of individualized sentencing in *Lockett v. Ohio*, 438 U.S. 586, 98 S.Ct. 2954, 57 L.Ed.2d 973 (1978). In that case, a plurality acknowledged that strict restraints on sentencer discretion are necessary to achieve the consistency and rationality promised in *Furman*, but held that, in the end, the sentencer must retain unbridled discretion to afford mercy. Any process or procedure that prevents the sentencer from considering "as a mitigating factor, any aspect of a defendant's character or record and any circumstances of the offense that the defendant proffers as a basis for a sentence less than death," creates the constitutionally intolerable risk that "the death penalty will be imposed in spite of factors which may call for a less severe penalty." *Id.*, at 604–605, 98 S.Ct., at 2964–2965 (emphasis in original). See also *Sumner v. Shuman*, 483 U.S. 66, 107 S.Ct. 2716, 97 L.Ed.2d 56 (1987) (invalidating a mandatory death penalty statute reserving the death penalty for life-term inmates convicted of murder). The Court's duty under the Constitution therefore is to "develop a system of capital punishment at once consistent and principled but also humane and sensible to the uniqueness of the individual." *Eddings v. Oklahoma*, 455 U.S., at 110, 102 S.Ct., at 874.

C

I believe the *Woodson-Lockett* line of cases to be fundamentally sound and rooted in American standards of decency that have evolved over time. The notion of prohibiting a sentencer from exercising its discretion "to dispense mercy on the basis of factors too intangible to write into a statute," *Gregg*, 428 U.S., at 222, 96 S.Ct., at 2947 (White, J., concurring), is offensive to our sense of fundamental fairness and respect for the uniqueness of the individual. . . .

Yet, as several Members of the Court have recognized, there is real "tension"

between the need for fairness to the individual and the consistency promised in *Furman*. On the one hand, discretion in capital sentencing must be " 'controlled by clear and objective standards so as to produce non-discriminatory [and reasoned] application.' " *Gregg*, 428 U.S., at 198, 96 S.Ct., at 2936 (opinion of Stewart, Powell, and STEVENS, JJ.), quoting *Coley v. State*, 231 Ga. 829, 834, 204 S.E.2d 612, 615 (1974). On the other hand, the Constitution also requires that the sentencer be able to consider "any relevant mitigating evidence regarding the defendant's character or background, and the circumstances of the particular offense." *California v. Brown*, 479 U.S. 538, 544, 107 S.Ct. 837, 840, 93 L.Ed.2d 934 (1987) (O'CONNOR, J., concurring). The power to consider mitigating evidence that would warrant a sentence less than death is meaningless unless the sentencer has the discretion and authority to dispense mercy based on that evidence. Thus, the Constitution, by requiring a heightened degree of fairness to the individual, and also a greater degree of equality and rationality in the administration of death, demands sentencer discretion that is at once generously expanded and severely restricted.

This dilemma was laid bare in *Penry v. Lynaugh*, 492 U.S. 302, 109 S.Ct. 2934, 106 L.Ed.2d 256 (1989). The defendant in *Penry* challenged the Texas death penalty statute, arguing that it failed to allow the sentencing jury to give full mitigating effect to his evidence of mental retardation and history of child abuse. The Texas statute required the jury, during the penalty phase, to answer three "special issues"; if the jury unanimously answered "yes" to each issue, the trial court was obligated to sentence the defendant to death. Only one of the three issues—whether the defendant posed a "continuing threat to society"—was related to the evidence Penry offered in mitigation. But Penry's evidence of mental retardation and child abuse was a two-edged sword as it related to that special issue: "it diminish[ed] his blameworthiness for his crime even as it indicate[d] that there [was] a probability that he [would] be dangerous in the future." 492 U.S., at 324, 109 S.Ct., at 2949. The Court therefore reversed Penry's death sentence, explaining that a reasonable juror could have believed that the statute prohibited a sentence less than death based upon his mitigating evidence. *Id.*, at 326, 109 S.Ct., at 2950.

After *Penry*, the paradox underlying the Court's post-*Furman* jurisprudence was undeniable. Texas had complied with *Furman* by severely limiting the sentencer's discretion, but those very limitations rendered Penry's death sentence unconstitutional.

D

The theory underlying *Penry* and *Lockett* is that an appropriate balance can be struck between the *Furman* promise of consistency and the *Lockett* requirement of individualized sentencing if the death penalty is conceptualized as consisting of two distinct stages. In the first stage of capital sentencing, the demands of *Furman* are met by "narrowing" the class of death-eligible offenders according to objective, fact-bound characteristics of the defendant or the circumstances of the offense. Once the pool of death-eligible defendants has been reduced, the sentencer retains the discretion to consider whatever relevant mitigating evidence the defendant chooses to offer. . . .

Over time, I have come to conclude that even this approach is unacceptable: It simply reduces, rather than eliminates, the number of people subject to arbitrary sentencing. It is the decision to sentence a defendant to death—not merely the decision to make a defendant eligible for death—that may not be arbitrary. While one might hope that providing the sentencer with as much relevant mitigating evidence as possible will lead to more rational and consistent sentences, experience has taught otherwise. It seems that the decision whether a human being should live or die is so inherently subjective—rife with all of life's understandings, experiences, prejudices, and passions—that it inevitably defies the rationality and consistency required by the Constitution. . . .

E

The arbitrariness inherent in the sentencer's discretion to afford mercy is exacerbated by the problem of race. Even under the most sophisticated death penalty statutes, race continues to play a major role in determining who shall live and who shall die. Perhaps it should not be surprising that the biases and prejudices that infect society generally would influence the determination of who is sentenced to death, even within the narrower pool of death-eligible defendants selected according to objective standards. No matter how narrowly the pool of death-eligible defendants is drawn according to objective standards, *Furman*'s promise still will go unfulfilled so long as the sentencer is free to exercise unbridled discretion within the smaller group and thereby to discriminate. " 'The power to be lenient [also] is the power to discriminate.' " *McCleskey v. Kemp*, 481 U.S., at

312, 107 S.Ct., at 1778 quoting K. Davis, Discretionary Justice 170 (1973).

A renowned example of racism infecting a capital-sentencing scheme is documented in *McCleskey v. Kemp*, 481 U.S. 279, 107 S.Ct. 1756, 95 L.Ed.2d 262 (1987). Warren McCleskey, an African-American, argued that the Georgia capital-sentencing scheme was administered in a racially discriminatory manner, in violation of the Eighth and Fourteenth Amendments. In support of his claim, he proffered a highly reliable statistical study (the Baldus study) which indicated that, "after taking into account some 230 nonracial factors that might legitimately influence a sentencer, the jury more likely than not would have spared McCleskey's life had his victim been black." 481 U.S., at 325, 107 S.Ct., at 1784 (emphasis in original) (Brennan, J., dissenting). The Baldus study further demonstrated that blacks who kill whites are sentenced to death "at nearly 22 times the rate of blacks who kill blacks, and more than 7 times the rate of whites who kill blacks." *Id.*, at 327, 107 S.Ct., at 1785 (emphasis in original).

Despite this staggering evidence of racial prejudice infecting Georgia's capital-sentencing scheme, the majority turned its back on McCleskey's claims, apparently troubled by the fact that Georgia had instituted more procedural and substantive safeguards than most other States since *Furman*, but was still unable to stamp out the virus of racism. Faced with the apparent failure of traditional legal devices to cure the evils identified in *Furman*, the majority wondered aloud whether the consistency and rationality demanded by the dissent could ever be achieved without sacrificing the discretion which is essential to fair treatment of individual defendants: "[I]t is difficult to imagine guidelines that would pro-

duce the predictability sought by the dissent without sacrificing the discretion essential to a humane and fair system of criminal justice.... The dissent repeatedly emphasizes the need for 'a uniquely high degree of rationality in imposing the death penalty.'... Again, no suggestion is made as to how greater 'rationality' could be achieved under any type of statute that authorizes capital punishment.... Given these safeguards already inherent in the imposition and review of capital sentences, the dissent's call for greater rationality is no less than a claim that a capital punishment system cannot be administered in accord with the Constitution." *Id.*, at 314–315, n. 37, 107 S.Ct., at 1778, n. 37.

I joined most of Justice Brennan's significant dissent which expounded McCleskey's Eighth Amendment claim, and I wrote separately, *id.*, at 345, 107 S.Ct., at 1795, to explain that McCleskey also had a solid equal protection argument under the Fourteenth Amendment. I still adhere to the views set forth in both dissents, and, as far as I know, there has been no serious effort to impeach the Baldus study. Nor, for that matter, have proponents of capital punishment provided any reason to believe that the findings of that study are unique to Georgia....

II

My belief that this Court would not enforce the death penalty (even if it could) in accordance with the Constitution is buttressed by the Court's "obvious eagerness to do away with any restriction on the States' power to execute whomever and however they please." *Herrera,* ___ U.S. ___, ___, 113 S.Ct. 853, 884, 122 L.Ed.2d 203 (BLACKMUN, J., dissenting). I have explained at length on numerous occasions that my willingness to enforce the capital punishment statutes enacted by the States and the Federal Government, "notwithstanding my own deep moral reservations... has always rested on an understanding that certain procedural safeguards, chief among them the federal judiciary's power to reach and correct claims of constitutional error on federal habeas review, would ensure that death sentences are fairly imposed." *Sawyer v. Whitley*, ___ U.S. ___, ___, 112 S.Ct. 2514, 2528, 120 L.Ed.2d 269 (1992) (BLACK-MUN, J., concurring in the judgment). See also *Herrera v. Collins*, ___ U.S., at ___, 113 S.Ct., at 880–881 (BLACKMUN, J., dissenting). In recent years, I have grown increasingly skeptical that "the death penalty really can be imposed fairly and in accordance with the requirements of the Eighth Amendment," given the now limited ability of the federal courts to remedy constitutional errors. *Sawyer*, ___ U.S., at ___, 112 S.Ct., at 2525 (BLACK-MUN, J., concurring in the judgment).

Federal courts are required by statute to entertain petitions from state prisoners who allege that they are held "in violation of the Constitution or the treaties of the United States." 28 U.S.C. §2254(a). Serious review of these claims helps to ensure that government does not secure the penalty of death by depriving a defendant of his or her constitutional rights. At the time I voted with the majority to uphold the constitutionality of the death penalty in *Gregg v. Georgia*, 428 U.S. 153, 227, 96 S.Ct. 2909, 2950 49 L.Ed.2d 859 (1976), federal courts possessed much broader authority than they do today to address claims of constitutional error on habeas review. In 1976, there were few procedural barriers to the federal judiciary's review of a State's capital sentencing scheme, or the fairness and reliability of a State's decision to impose death in a particular case. Since then, however, the Court has "erected unprecedented and unwarranted barriers" to the federal judiciary's review of the constitutional claims of capital defendants.

The Court's refusal last term to afford Leonel Torres Herrera an evidentiary hearing, despite his colorable showing of actual innocence, demonstrates just how far afield the Court has strayed from its statutorily and constitutionally imposed obligations. See *Herrera v. Collins, supra.* In *Herrera*, only a bare majority of this Court could bring itself to state forthrightly that the execution of an actually innocent person violates the Eighth Amendment. This concession was made only in the course of erecting nearly insurmountable barriers to a defendant's ability to get a hearing on a claim of actual innocence. *Ibid.* Certainly there will be individuals who are actually innocent who will be unable to make a better showing than what was made by Herrera without the benefit of an evidentiary hearing. The Court is unmoved by this dilemma, however; it prefers "finality" in death sentences to reliable determinations of a capital defendant's guilt. Because I no longer can state with any confidence that this Court is able to reconcile the Eighth Amendment's competing constitutional commands, or that the federal judiciary will provide meaningful oversight to the state courts as they exercise their authority to inflict the penalty of death, I believe that the death penalty, as currently administered, is unconstitutional....

III

Perhaps one day this Court will develop procedural rules or verbal formulas that actually will provide consistency, fairness, and reliability in a capital-sentencing scheme. I am not optimistic that such a day will come. I am more optimistic, though, that this Court eventually will conclude that the effort to eliminate arbitrariness while preserving fairness "in the infliction of [death] is so plainly doomed to failure that it—and the death penalty—must be abandoned altogether." *Godfrey v. Georgia*, 446 U.S. 420, 442, 100 S.Ct. 1759, 1772, 64 L.Ed.2d 398 (1980) (Marshall, J., concurring in the judgment). I may not live to see that day, but I have faith that eventually it will arrive. The path the Court has chosen lessens us all. I dissent.

NOTES

1. Because I conclude that no sentence of death may be constitutionally imposed under our death penalty scheme, I do not address Callins' individual claims of error. I note, though, that the Court has stripped "state prisoners of virtually any meaningful federal review of the constitutionality of their incarceration." *Butler v. McKellar*, 494 U.S. 407, 417, 110 S.Ct. 1212, 1219, 108 L.Ed.2d 347 (1990) (Brennan, J., dissenting) (emphasis in original). Even if Callins had a legitimate claim of constitutional error, this Court would be deaf to it on federal habeas unless "the state court's rejection of the constitutional challenge was so clearly invalid under then-prevailing legal standards that the decision could not be defended by any reasonable jurist." *Id.*, at 417–418, 110 S.Ct., at 1219 (emphasis in original). That a capital defendant facing imminent execution is required to meet such a standard before the Court will remedy constitutional violations is indefensible.

NO

STATEMENT OF JAMES C. ANDERS

There are in this world a number of extremely wicked people, disposed to get what they want by force or fraud, with complete indifference to the interests of others, and in ways which are totally inconsistent with the existence of civilized society.

— James Fitzjames Stephen

What is society to do with these people? I believe that in certain cases, the death penalty can be shown to be the only rational and realistic punishment for an unspeakable crime. But before embarking on a discussion on the merits of the death penalty, a fundamental philosophical question must be answered. What is the purpose of punishment? Harmonious coexistence among people in any society is dependent upon the advancement of mutually agreed upon goals for the good of the whole society. Obviously, the most basic right a citizen has is the right to be secure in his person, the right to be safe from physical or economic harm from another. Laws to protect citizens and advance the harmony of society are founded upon these principles. To enforce these laws, created in the best interest of society as a whole, there has to be a deterrent for a breach of the law. Therefore, deterrence is the first aim of a system of punishment.

Deterrence is only one side of the punishment coin, however. An equally fundamental reason to punish lies in society's compelling desire to see justice done. Punishment expresses the emotions of the society wronged, the anger and outrage felt, and it solidifies and reinforces the goals, values and norms of acceptable behavior in the society. Punishment is justified purely on the ground that wrongdoing merits punishment, and that it is morally fitting that one who does wrong suffers, and suffers in proportion to his wrongdoing.

Consider the facts of a 1977 case from my jurisdiction. Codefendants Shaw, Roach and Mahaffey spent the morning of October 29th drinking and shooting up drugs. That afternoon the three decided to, in Mahaffey's words, "see if we could find a girl to rape." They drove to a nearby baseball field where they spotted a car parked with two teenagers inside. They robbed and killed the young man on the spot. The girl was carried to a dirt road a short

From U.S. Senate. Committee on the Judiciary. *The Death Penalty*. Hearing, September 19, 1989. Washington, DC: Government Printing Office, 1989.

distance away where she was repeatedly raped and sodomized over a period of hours. When they finished with her, they forced her to place her head in a circle they had drawn in the dirt, and they executed her. Later that evening, Shaw returned by himself and sexually mutilated the girl's body.

The deterrent effect of the death penalty is the favorite criticism of the opponents of capital punishment. The social scientists' studies have been mixed at best and there is no authoritative consensus on whether or not the death penalty deters anyone from committing a crime. Threats of punishment cannot and are not meant to deter everybody all of the time. They are meant to deter most people most of the time.

The threatened punishment must be carried out—otherwise the threats are reduced to bluffs and become incredible and therefore ineffective.

— Ernest van den Haag

Therefore, the death penalty can only be a deterrent if it is meted out with a reasonable degree of consistency. The deterrent effect lies in the knowledge of the citizenry that it will more likely than not be carried out if the named crime is committed.

Even if one is not fully convinced of the deterrent effect of the death penalty, he or she would surely choose the certainty of the convicted criminal's death by execution over the possibility of the deaths of new victims. These new deaths could either be deterred by the execution, or prevented by the executed criminal's obvious incapacity. Simply put, one should opt to execute a man convicted of having caused the death of others than to put the lives

of innocents at risk if there is a chance their deaths could be prevented by the deterrent effect.

Death penalty opponents argue that if life is sacred (as, presumably, we all believe) then the murderer's life, too, is sacred and for the State to punish him by execution is barbaric and causes the State to bend to the murderer's level. The only similarity between the unjustified taking of an innocent life and the carrying out of a convicted murderer's execution is the end result —death. The death penalty is a legal sentence, enacted by the legislatures of various states which presumably reflect their constituents' desires. It is a penalty that can finally be carried out only after a trial where the defendant is afforded all of his constitutional rights, and the lengthy appellate process has been exhausted. It is a penalty that has been sanctioned by the United States Supreme Court, a majority of whose members have said, regardless of their personal feelings, that the death penalty is a constitutionally valid punishment. How then can its invocation be compared to the senseless, irrational murder of an innocent victim who is afforded no rights, and is tried and convicted by his murderer for the crime of being in the wrong place at the wrong time? Legal execution and murder are no more comparable than driving a car and knowingly driving a stolen car. Although the physical act of driving either is the same, the two acts are separated by the crime involved in the latter, and that makes all the difference.

Death penalty opponents are also troubled by the studies that purport to show that the death penalty is applied capriciously, that it discriminates racially and economically. They cite these studies as justification for eliminating the penalty. Notice that they are not claiming that some innocent person may be executed, but, rather, that not all the guilty are executed. Assuming that premise for the sake of argument, is that a rational reason to abolish the death penalty? Is the fact that some guilty persons escape punishment sufficient to let all guilty persons escape it? If it is then, in practice, penalties never could be applied if we insisted that they cannot be inflicted on any guilty persons unless we are able to make sure that they are equally applied to all other guilty persons. There is no more merit in persuading the courts to let all capital defendants go because some escaped penalties than it is to say let all burglars go because some have escaped detection and imprisonment. If discrimination exists in the application of the death penalty, then the remedy is statutory reform to minimize or abolish the discrimination, not the abolition of the penalty itself.

The capricious/discriminatory complaint seems by and large to be an abolitionist sham. The abolitionists would oppose the death penalty if it could be meted out without any discretion, if it were mandatory under certain conditions. They would oppose it in a homogeneous country without racial discrimination. It is the death penalty itself, not its possible maldistribution that the abolitionists oppose. Opponents rarely raise the objection that an innocent person might be sent to the electric chair. With the sophistication of the criminal justice system today, the likelihood of convicting, let alone executing, an innocent man is all but nil. But there is another more subtle reason abolitionists no longer advance the "innocent man proposition" as a justification for their opposition to the penalty and that is because this argument

too would be a sham. Death penalty opponents would rid the world of the death penalty for everyone, including the admittedly guilty.

To defend the death penalty should not lead to one's being labeled "cold", "blood-thirsty" or "barbaric". A person who commits capital murder simply cannot and should not expect to be given a pat on the back and told to "go and sin no more." If the death penalty can deter one murder of an innocent life or if it can make a statement to the community about what will and will not be tolerated, then it is justified.

Opponents of the death penalty advocate the life sentence in prison as a viable alternative to execution. My experiences lead me to believe that life imprisonment is not a satisfactory means of dealing with the most horrid of criminals. Early release programs, furloughs, and escapes combine to place a shockingly high number of convicted murderers back on the streets in record time. Hardly a day goes by when one cannot pick up a newspaper and read a gruesome account of the crimes committed by a now liberated "lifer". But that is not the worst of it. Consider the plight of the victims' families, forced to relive the nightmare again and again each time a parole hearing is scheduled. Year after year they endure the uncertainty and agony while waiting on the decision of the parole board. Will this be the year the man who turned their lives upside down will be released to live out his life, perhaps to put another family through the same nightmare?

The life without parole sentence is no solution either. First the possibility of escape cannot be completely eliminated, even in the most secure of institutions. For example, convicted triple murderer and death row inmate Fred Kornahrens escaped with a ploy so simple it caught prison officials completely by surprise. During a body search prior to being transported to court, Kornahrens concealed a key between his index and middle fingers. When handcuffed, he simply uncuffed himself and made good his escape. Given enough time, I am certain Fred Kornahrens could escape again. Second, the life without parole sentence places a tremendous burden on prison administrators. Faced with controlling inmates who have already received the worst punishment society can mete out, they can only throw their hands up in frustration. Lastly, the true lifer is not only capable of continuing to murder, but may actually be more likely to do so. Every prison in the country has its own stories of the lifer who killed another inmate over a cigarette or a piece of chicken. In my home state this scenario was taken one step further when disenchanted crime victim Tony Cimo hired convicted mass murderer Donald "Pee Wee" Gaskins to kill another convicted murderer Rudolph Tyner, the slayer of Cimo's parents. Pee Wee Gaskins is a perfect example of why life imprisonment is never going to be an acceptable alternative to the death penalty and why the death penalty for murder by a federal prisoner serving a life term is a viable proposal.

I recently prosecuted a capital case involving the murder of a state highway patrolman. Trooper George Radford was brutally beaten and executed with his own weapon over a $218 ticket. All Trooper Radford did was show his murderer the same consideration and courtesy he exhibited to all every day on duty. Rather than handcuffing the defendant, Warren Manning, whom he had ticketed for driving under suspension, Trooper Radford allowed him to remain unhandcuffed for the twenty minute ride to the police station so that he would be more comfortable. Manning surprised Trooper Radford halfway there and callously murdered him. Law enforcement personnel deserve the additional protection and security the death penalty affords them. The scores of highway patrolmen who travelled to Camden, South Carolina, for the sentencing of Warren Manning show exactly how important the death penalty issue is to them.

Based on the foregoing analysis, the death penalty takes on special significance in deterrence and punishment of federal law violations. Serious problems exist in American society on a large scale basis or threaten to grow to such a basis. As discussed above, the benefits of deterrence and social justice on crimes such as murder, murder for hire and attempts to assassinate the President are obvious under the death penalty.

Drug-related murders are on the rise and the death penalty could be particularly effective in combatting this murder-for-profit trend. Law enforcement officers who are often required to work undercover in the drug community would be protected to a degree under the deterrence effect of the death penalty. In order to support President Bush's plan to combat the drug problem nationally and internationally, it seems obvious that drug kingpins should know that they are subject to the death penalty. What group of individuals create more chaos and death than these?

Other heinous crimes which pose a threat of great magnitude are those of terrorism. Crimes such as explosions, air piracy, mailing bombs and taking hostages, all where death results, very simply and obviously demand the strongest punishment and deterrent the law can impose. The effects of terrorism are so potentially great and devastating that the death penalty is the only conceivable punishment. The death penalty is not merely an alternative but a necessity for dealing with these large scale national problems.

One leading proponent of the death penalty, E. van den Haag, wrote "never to execute a wrongdoer, regardless of how depraved his acts, is to proclaim that no act can be so irredeemably vicious as to deserve death." In the question of deterrence this principle is exacerbated by a special group of sane murderers who, knowing that they will not be executed, will not hesitate to kill again. If opponents of the death penalty admit that there is a reasonable probability that such wrongdoers will murder again and/or attempt to murder again, and still insist they would never approve of capital punishment, I would conclude that they are indifferent to the lives of the human beings doomed to be the victims of the unexecuted criminals. "Charity for all human beings must not deprive us of our common sense." Hugo Adam Bedau. To those who could not impose the death penalty under any circumstances, van den Haag attributed what he called "a failure of nerve," a feeling that they themselves are incapable of rationally and justly making a life and death decision and that, therefore, everyone else is equally unqualified to decide life or death.

Such a view grossly and tragically underestimates our system of justice. I have always been impressed with the intelligence, compassion and common sense jurors display. Jurors really are the "conscience of the community." That is more than just a phrase lawyers bandy about in closing arguments. I have seen how seriously jurors take their oath to decide the issues, based on the law, regardless of their personal prejudices, and biases. The juries and the courts can evade decisions on life and death only by giving up paramount duties: those of serving justice, securing the lives of citizens and vindicating the norms that society holds inviolable. Justice requires that the punishment be proportional to the gravity of the crime. The death penalty comes closest to meeting this supreme standard while still falling short because those criminals sentenced to execution still had the luxury of choosing their fate when their victims did not.

POSTSCRIPT

Should the Death Penalty Be Abolished?

We are in a new era in the history of capital punishment. The death penalty is constitutional, and almost 3,000 persons are on death row, a larger number than at any time since a national count was begun. In the first edition of this book, published in 1982, I wrote, "Although only four persons have been executed in the past fifteen years, this situation seems certain to change in the next two years as appeals in many cases are exhausted." There has indeed been an increase in executions, although the rise has not been as fast as some had predicted. One hundred and eighty-eight persons had been executed through the end of 1992.

Appeals are still time-consuming, a situation that some Supreme Court justices have complained about. As a result of the appeals process, the number of persons on death row is still growing by about 200 a year. In 1982 there were more than 1,000 people on death row, approximately a third of the number today. The increase in the death row population means that there are more people sentenced to death each year than there are executions. The slow pace of executions has been a source of great frustration to some Supreme Court justices and, as a result, the Court has restricted some appeals.

The Supreme Court has made several notable decisions in recent years involving the death penalty. These include *Penry v. Lyunaugh,* 109 S. Ct. 2934 (1989), in which the Court ruled that murderers with mental retardation may be executed, and *Stanford v. Kentucky,* 109 S. Ct. 2969 (1989), in which the Court ruled that persons as young as 16 years of age may be executed.

Interesting works on capital punishment include M. Tushnet, *The Death Penalty* (1993); G. Russell, *The Death Penalty and Racial Bias* (1994); F. Zimring and G. Hawkins, *Capital Punishment and the American Agenda* (Cambridge University Press, 1989); Brown and Adler, *Public Justice, Private Mercy: A Governor's Education on Death Row* (Weidenfeld & Nicolson, 1989); H. Bedau, *Death Is Different: Studies in the Morality, Law, and Politics of Capital Punishment* (Northeastern University Press, 1987); E. van den Haag and J. P. Conrad, *The Death Penalty: A Debate* (Plenum, 1983); Bright, "Counsel for the Poor: The Death Sentence Not for the Worst Crime but for the Worst Lawyer," 103 *Yale Law Journal* 1835 (1994); J. M. Giarrantano, "To the Best of Our Knowledge, We Have Never Been Wrong: Fallibility vs. Finality in Capital Punishment," 100 *Yale Law Journal* 1005 (1991); W. S. White, "The Death Penalty in the Nineties: An Examination of the Modern System of Capital Punishment," 53 *University of Pittsburgh Law Review* 251 (1991); and Note, "The Madness of the Method: The Use of Electrocution and the Death Penalty," 70 *Texas Law Review* 1039 (1992).

ISSUE 13

Should the Exclusionary Rule Be Abolished?

YES: Malcolm Richard Wilkey, from "The Exclusionary Rule: Why Suppress Valid Evidence?" *Judicature* (November 1978)

NO: Yale Kamisar, from "The Exclusionary Rule in Historical Perspective: The Struggle to Make the Fourth Amendment More Than 'an Empty Blessing,' " *Judicature* (February 1979)

ISSUE SUMMARY

YES: U.S. Court of Appeals judge Malcolm Richard Wilkey raises objections to the exclusionary rule on the grounds that it may suppress evidence and allow the guilty to go free.

NO: Professor of law Yale Kamisar argues that the exclusionary rule is necessary to prevent abuses by police and to protect citizens' rights.

The Fourth Amendment to the Constitution provides that "the right of the people to be secure in their persons, houses, papers, and effects against unreasonable searches and seizures, shall not be violated, and no Warrants shall issue, but upon probable cause." Thus, if the police wish to search someone's property, they must first persuade a judge that probable cause exists that a crime has been committed and that the evidence sought will be found in the place to be searched. The warrant requirement is the key constitutional element restricting the power of the police to decide unilaterally to invade the privacy of someone's home.

What should happen if the police conduct an illegal search and, as a result, discover incriminating evidence? According to the exclusionary rule, such evidence may not be introduced at a trial or be considered by a jury in considering guilt or innocence. If no other evidence of guilt exists, therefore, the defendant will go free. If there is enough other evidence of the defendant's guilt, he may still be convicted.

The exclusionary rule is over 70 years old. It is not required by the Constitution nor mentioned in it. Rather, courts have imposed it because they felt it was the most workable and feasible way to deter illegal police conduct and maintain an honest system of law enforcement. In the following articles, Judge Malcolm Richard Wilkey asserts that society can no longer bear the costs that the rule brings, that guilty persons escape prosecution because of it, and that illegal police conduct is not deterred. Yale Kamisar, a noted criminal law scholar, argues that the rule's rationale is still valid and that the rule should be maintained.

The articles mention a number of legal cases that should be understood since they describe the historical development of the rule:

1. *Weeks v. United States,* 232 U.S. 383 (1914) The U.S. Supreme Court imposed the exclusionary rule for the first time and ruled that illegally seized evidence could not be used in the federal courts. Such evidence, however, could still be used in criminal cases in state courts unless the state decided on its own to require the exclusionary rule in its courts. Although a few states did impose the exclusionary rule, most did not. The New York Court of Appeals, for example, rejected the rule, with Judge Benjamin N. Cardozo refusing to accept the proposition that "the criminal is to go free because the constable has blundered" (*People v. Defore,* 150 N.E. 585, 1926).

2. *Wolf v. Colorado,* 338 U.S. 25 (1949) The Supreme Court ruled that due process of law under the Fourteenth Amendment is denied individuals who are illegally searched. But the Court refused to require state courts to impose or apply the exclusionary rule. Thus, the Court held that "in a prosecution in a State court for a State crime the Fourteenth Amendment does not forbid the admission of evidence obtained by an unreasonable search and seizure."

3. *Rochin v. California,* 342 U.S. 165 (1952) and *Irvine v. California,* 347 U.S. 128 (1954) These two cases involved particularly blatant Fourth Amendment violations by the police. The defendants were convicted, but the Supreme Court refused, as in *Wolf,* to require states to follow the exclusionary rule. Rochin's conviction, however, was reversed because the police action was "shocking to the conscience."

4. *Mapp v. Ohio,* 367 U.S. 643 (1961) Dollree Mapp was convicted of possession of obscene materials after the police conducted a search of her home without a search warrant. The Supreme Court decided to overrule the *Wolf* decision and require state courts to apply the exclusionary rule. The Court cited a well-known statement by Justice Louis D. Brandeis that "if the government becomes a lawbreaker, it breeds contempt for the law; it invites every man to become a law unto himself; it invites anarchy." As you read the following articles, consider whether Justice Brandeis's statement is still valid. (A fascinating description of the facts of the *Mapp* case is contained in Friendly and Elliot's *The Constitution: That Delicate Balance* [Random House, 1984].)

YES

Malcolm Richard Wilkey

WHY SUPPRESS VALID EVIDENCE?

America is now ready to confront frankly and to examine realistically both the achievements and social costs of the policies which have been so hopefully enacted in the past 40 years. That reappraisal has made the most headlines in regard to economic and fiscal matters. It is imperative that this honest reappraisal include the huge social costs which American society—alone in the civilized world—pays as a result of our unique exclusionary rule of evidence in criminal cases.

We can see that huge social cost most clearly in the distressing rate of street crimes—assaults and robberies with deadly weapons, narcotics trafficking, gambling and prostitution—which flourish in no small degree simply because of the exclusionary rule of evidence. To this high price we can rightfully add specific, pernicious police conduct and lack of discipline—the very opposite of the objectives of the rule itself....

Though scholars have been shedding more and more light on this problem, few people have considered the enormous social cost of the exclusionary rule, and fewer still have thought about possible alternatives to the rule. I propose to do both those things in this article.

THE RULE'S MYSTIQUE

What is the exclusionary rule? It is a judge-made rule of evidence, originated in 1914 by the Supreme Court in *Weeks v. United States*, which bars "the use of evidence secured through an illegal search and seizure." It is not a rule required by the Constitution. No Supreme Court has ever held that it was. As Justice Black once said,

> [T]he Fourth Amendment does not itself contain any provision expressly precluding the use of such evidence and I am extremely doubtful that such a provision could properly be inferred from nothing more than the basic command against unreasonable searches and seizures.

The greatest obstacle to replacing the exclusionary rule with a rational process, which will both protect the citizenry by controlling the police and avoid rewarding the criminal, is the powerful, unthinking emotional attachment

From Malcolm Richard Wilkey, "The Exclusionary Rule: Why Suppress Valid Evidence?" *Judicature* (November 1978). Copyright © 1978 by Malcolm Richard Wilkey. Reprinted by permission.

to the rule. The mystique and misunderstanding of the rule causes not only many ordinary citizens but also judges and lawyers to feel (not think) that the exclusionary rule was enshrined in the Constitution by the Founding Fathers, and that to abolish it would do violence to the whole sacred Bill of Rights. They appear totally unaware that the rule was not employed in U.S. courts during the first 125 years of the Fourth Amendment, that it was devised by the judiciary in the assumed absence of any other method of controlling the police, and that no other country in the civilized world has adopted such a rule.

Realistically, the exclusionary rule can probably never be abolished until both the public and the Supreme Court are satisfied that there is available in our legal system a reasonably workable alternative. Unfortunately, the converse may also be true—we will never have any alternative in operation until the rule is abolished. So long as we keep the rule, the police are not going to investigate and discipline their own men, and thus sabotage prosecutions by invalidating the admissibility of vital evidence.

HOW THE RULE WORKS

The impact of the exclusionary rule may not be immediately apparent from the simple phrase of the *Wolf* decision that it bars "the use of evidence seized through an illegal search and seizure." It may help to consider three examples to see how the exclusionary rule needlessly frustrates police and prosecutors trying to do a very difficult job on the streets of our cities.

In *U.S. v. Montgomery*, two police officers on auto patrol in a residential neighborhood at 6 P.M. on a winter day saw Montgomery driving his car in a way that suggested he was "sizing up" the area. When they stopped and identified him, they learned by radio that an arrest warrant was outstanding against him. Before taking him into custody, the officers searched him for weapons and found a .38 caliber bullet in his pants pocket, a magnum revolver loaded with six rounds and an unregistered, sawed-off shotgun with shells in the car.

A trial court convicted him of illegal possession of firearms, but the Court of Appeals (2–1) reversed, holding that no probable cause existed for stopping Montgomery in the first place, and that all evidence discovered thereafter was the product of an illegal search and seizure. Applying the exclusionary rule, the court suppressed as evidence the revolver and the sawed-off shotgun, which made it impossible to convict Montgomery or to retry the case.

Montgomery is an example of typical routine police work, which many citizens would think of as needed reasonable effort to prevent crime. But now look at *U.S. v. Willie Robinson*, a similar case with a different result. A policeman stopped Robinson for a minor traffic violation and discovered that license bureau records indicated his license was probably a forgery. Four days later, the same officer spotted Robinson about 2 A.M. and arrested him for driving with a forged credential.

Since police regulations required him to take Robinson into custody, the officer began a pat down or frisk for dangerous weapons. Close inspection of the cigarette package in the outer pocket of the man's jacket revealed heroin. Robinson was convicted of heroin possession but the Court of Appeals held 5–4 that, in light of the exclusionary rule, the search of Robinson was illegal and the heroin evidence must be suppressed. The Supreme Court reversed, holding that probable cause existed for the search, the evidence was legally obtained, and it could be offered in evidence. The High Court reinstated the original conviction.

This is one search and seizure case which turned out, in my view, correctly. But it took a U.S. District Court suppression hearing, a 2–1 panel decision in the Court of Appeals, a 5–4 decision in the court *en banc*, and a 6–3 decision of the Supreme Court to confirm the validity of the on-the-spot judgment of a lone police officer exercised at 2 A.M. on a Washington Street—five years and eight months earlier.

In *Coolidge v. New Hampshire*, a 14-year-old girl was found with her throat slit and a bullet in her head eight days after she had disappeared. Police contacted the wife of a suspect whose car was like one seen near the crime, and she gave them her husband's guns. Tests proved that one of the weapons had fired the fatal bullet.

Invoking his statutory authority, the attorney general of the state issued a warrant for the arrest of the suspect and the seizure of his car. Coolidge was captured and convicted. But the Supreme Court reversed the conviction on the grounds that the warrant was defective, the search of the auto unreasonable and vacuum sweepings from the auto (which matched the victim's clothing) were inadmissible. Why? Because the attorney general who issued the warrant had personally assumed direction of the investigation and thus was not a "neutral and detached magistrate."

Observe that here the conviction was reversed because of a defect in the warrant, not because of any blunder. Errors of law by either the attorney preparing the affidavit and application for the warrant or the magistrate in issuing the warrant frequently invalidate the entire search that the police officers make, relying in good faith on the warrant; those errors cause the suppression of the evidence and the reversal of the conviction. How does the exclusionary rule improve police conduct in such cases?

THE COURT'S RATIONALE

Deterrence: During the rule's development, the Supreme Court has offered three main reasons for the rule. The principal and almost sole theory today is that excluding the evidence will punish the police officers who made the illegal search and seizure or otherwise violated the constitutional rights of the defendant, and thus deter policemen from committing the same violation again. The flaw in this theory is that there is absolutely no empirical data that excluding evidence against a defendant has anything to do with either punishing police officers or thereby deterring them from future violations.

Chief Justice Burger has flatly asserted "...there is no empirical evidence to support the claim that the rule actually deters illegal conduct of law enforcement officials," and the Supreme Court has never sought to adduce such empirical evidence in support of the rule. Probably such a connection can never be proved, for as a matter of logical analysis "the exclusionary rule is well tailored to deter the prosecutor from illegal conduct. But the prosecutor is not the guilty party in an illegal arrest or search and seizure, and he rarely has any measure of control over the police who are responsible."

Privacy: From *Weeks* (1914) to *Mapp* (1961) the rule was also justified as protecting the privacy of the individual against illegal searches and seizures as guaranteed by the Fourth Amendment. The Supreme Court later downgraded the protection of privacy rationale, perhaps because of the obvious defect that the rule purports to do nothing to recompense innocent victims of Fourth Amendment violations, and the gnawing doubt as to just what right of privacy guilty individuals have in illegal firearms, contraband narcotics and policy betting slips— the frequent objects of search and seizure.

Judicial integrity: A third theme of the Supreme Court's justifying rationale, now somewhat muted, is that the use of illegally obtained evidence brings the court system into disrepute. In *Mapp* Justice Clark referred to "that judicial integrity so necessary in the true administration of justice," which was reminiscent of Justice Brandeis dissenting in *Burdeau v. McDowell*, " ... respect for law will not be advanced by resort, in its enforcement, to means which shock the common man's sense of decency and fair play."

THE IMPACT OF THE RULE

It is undeniable that, as a result of the rule, the most valid, conclusive, and irrefutable factual evidence is excluded from the knowledge of the jury or consideration by the judge. As Justice Cardozo predicted in 1926, in describing the complete irrationality of the exclusionary rule:

> The criminal is to go free because the constable has blundered.... A room is searched against the law, and the body of a murdered man is found.... The privacy

of the home has been infringed, and the murderer goes free.

Fifty years later Justice Powell wrote for the Court:

> The costs of applying the exclusionary rule even at trial and on direct review are well known: ...the physical evidence sought to be excluded is typically reliable and often the most probative evidence bearing on the guilt or innocence of the defendant.... Application of the rule thus deflects the truthfinding process and often frees the guilty. The disparity in particular cases between the error committed by the police officer and the windfall afforded the guilty defendant by application of the rule is contrary to the idea of proportionality that is essential to the concept of justice.

I submit that justice is, or should be, a truth-seeking process. The court has a duty to the accused to see that he receives a fair trial; the court also has a duty to society to see that all the truth is brought out; only if all the truth is brought out can there be a fair trial. The exclusionary rule results in a complete distortion of the truth. Undeniable facts, of the greatest importance, are forever barred—facts such as Robinson's heroin, Montgomery's sawed-off shotgun and pistol, the bullet fired from Coolidge's gun and the sweepings from his car which contained items from the dead girl's clothes.

If justice is a truth-seeking process, it is all important that *there is never any question of reliability* in exclusionary rule cases involving material evidence, as the three examples illustrate. We rightly exclude evidence whenever its reliability is questionable—a coerced or induced confession, for example, or a faulty line-up for identification of the suspect. We exclude it because it is inherently unreliable, not because of the illegality of obtaining it. An illegal search in no way reduces the reliability of the evidence.

There have been several empirical studies on the effects of the exclusionary rule in five major American cities—Boston, Chicago, Cincinnati, New York and Washington, D.C.—during the period from 1950 to 1971. These have been recently collected and analyzed, along with other aspects of the exclusionary rule and its alternatives, by Professor Steven Schlesinger in his book *Exclusionary Injustice: The Problem of Illegally Obtained Evidence.*

Three of these studies concluded that the exclusionary rule was a total failure in its primary task of deterring illegal police activity and that it also produced other highly undesirable side effects. The fourth study, which said the first three were too harsh in concluding that the rule was totally ineffective, still said: "Nonetheless, the inconclusiveness of our findings is real enough; they do not nail down an argument that the exclusionary rule has accomplished its task."

Schlesinger and others regard the study by Dallin Oakes as perhaps the most comprehensive ever undertaken, both in terms of data and the breadth of analysis of the rule's effects. Oakes concluded:

As a device for directly deterring illegal searches and seizures by the police, the exclusionary rule is a failure.... The harshest criticism of the rule is that it is ineffective. It is the sole means of enforcing the essential guarantees of freedom from unreasonable arrests and searches and seizures by law enforcement officers, and it is a failure in that vital task.

Spiotto made a comparative study of both the American exclusionary rule and the existing Canadian tort alternative, taking Chicago and Toronto as comparable metropolitan areas. He found that an

empirical study [of narcotics and weapons cases] indicates that, over a 20-year period in Chicago, the proportion of cases in which there were motions to suppress evidence allegedly obtained illegally increased significantly. This is the opposite result of what would be expected if the rule had been efficacious in deterring police misconduct.

Three studies conducted between 1950 and 1971 show a substantial increase in motions to suppress in both narcotics and gun offenses. The increase from 1950 to 1971 can fairly be attributed to the impact of *Mapp* (1961) on search and seizure in the state courts.

CRITICISMS OF THE RULE

By this point, we should be able to see that the exclusionary rule actually produces many effects opposite from those that the Court intended to produce. No matter what rationale we consider, the rule in its indiscriminate workings does far more harm than good and, in many respects, it actually prevents us from dealing with the real problems of Fourth Amendment violations in the course of criminal investigations.

In the eyes of the Supreme Court, the first and primary rationale of the exclusionary rule is deterrence. I submit that all available facts and logic show that excluding the most reliable evidence does absolutely nothing to punish and thus deter the official wrongdoer, but the inevitable and certain result is that the guilty criminal defendant goes free.

The second—now rather distant second—rationale in the eyes of the Court has been the protection of privacy. I submit a policy of excluding incriminating evidence can never protect an innocent victim of an illegal search against whom no incriminating evidence is discovered. The only persons protected by the rule are the guilty against whom the most serious reliable evidence should be offered. It cannot be separately argued that the innocent person is protected *in the future* by excluding evidence against the criminal *now*, for this is only the deterrent argument all over again.

The third rationale found in the past opinions of the Court is that the use of illegally obtained evidence brings our court system into disrepute. I submit that the exclusion of valid, probative, undeniably truthful evidence undermines the reputation of and destroys the respect for the entire judicial system.

Ask any group of laymen if they can understand why a pistol found on a man when he is searched by an officer should not be received in evidence when the man is charged with illegal possession of a weapon, or why a heroin package found under similar circumstances should not be always received in evidence when he is prosecuted for a narcotics possession, and I believe you will receive a lecture that these are outrageous technicalities of the law which the American people should not tolerate. If you put the same issue to a representative group of lawyers and judges, I predict you would receive a strong preponderance of opinions supporting the lay view, although from those heavily imbued with a mystique of the exclusionary rule as of almost divine origin you would doubtless hear some support.

The rationale of protecting judicial integrity is also inconsistent with the behavior of the courts in other areas of the criminal law. For example, it is well settled that courts will try defendants who have been illegally seized and brought before them. In *Ker v. Illinois*, a defendant kidnapped in Peru was brought by force to Illinois for trial; in *Mahon v. Justice* the accused was forcibly abducted from West Virginia for trial in Kentucky; and in *Frisbie v. Collins*, the defendant was forcibly seized in Illinois for trial in Michigan.

Said the *Frisbie* court:

> This court has never departed from the rule announced in *Ker v. Illinois* ... that the power of the court to try a person for crime is not impaired by the fact that he had been brought within the court's jurisdiction by reason of 'forcible abduction.'

Why should there be an exclusionary rule for illegally seized evidence when there is no such exclusionary rule for illegally seized people? Why should a court be concerned about the circumstances under which the murder weapon has been obtained, while it remains unconcerned about the circumstances under which the murderer himself has been apprehended? It makes no sense to argue that the admission of illegally seized evidence somehow signals the judiciary's condonation of the violation of rights when the judiciary's trial of an illegally-seized *person* is not perceived as signaling such condonation.

OTHER DEFECTS OF THE RULE

The rule does not simply fail to meet its declared objectives; it suffers from five other defects, too. One of those defects is that it uses an undiscriminating, meat-ax approach in the most sensitive areas of the administration of justice. It totally fails to discriminate between the degrees of culpability of the officer or the degrees of harm to the victim of the illegal search and seizure.

It does not matter whether the action of the officer was grossly willful and flagrant or whether he was conscientiously using his very best judgment under difficult circumstances; the result is the same: the evidence is out. The rule likewise fails to distinguish errors of judgment which cause no harm or inconvenience to the individual whose person or premises are searched, except for the discovery of valid incriminating evidence, from flagrant violations of the Fourth Amendment as in *Mapp* or *Rochin*. Chief Justice Burger's point in *Bivens* is undeniable:

> ... society has at least as much right to expect rationally graded responses from judges in place of the universal 'capital punishment' we inflict on all evidence when police error is shown in its acquisition.

Another defect is that the rule makes no distinction between minor offenses and more serious crimes. The teenage runner caught with policy slips in his pocket and the syndicate hit man accused of first degree murder are each automatically set free by operation of the exclusionary rule, without any consideration of the impact on the community. Customarily, however, we apply different standards to crimes which vary as to seriousness, both in granting bail before trial and in imposing sentence afterwards.

A third problem is that, strangely, a rule which is supposed to discipline and improve police conduct actually results in encouraging highly pernicious police behavior. A policeman is supposed to tell the truth, but when he knows that describing the search truthfully will taint the evidence and free the suspect, the policeman is apt to feel that he has a "higher duty" than the truth. He may perjure himself to convict the defendant.

Similarly, knowing that evidence of gambling, narcotics or prostitution is hard to obtain under the present rules of search and seizure, the policeman may feel that he can best enforce the law by stepping up the incidence of searches and seizures, making them frequent enough to be harassing, with no idea of ultimate prosecution. Or, for those policemen inclined *ab initio* to corruption, the exclusionary rule provides a fine opportunity to make phony raids on establishments, deliberately violating the standards of the Fourth Amendment and immunizing the persons and premises raided—while making good newspaper headlines for active law enforcement.

Fourth, the rule discourages internal disciplinary action by the police themselves. Even if police officials know that an officer violated Fourth Amendment standards in a particular case, few of them will charge the erring officer with a Fourth Amendment violation: it would sabotage the case for the prosecution before it even begins. The prosecutor hopes the defendant will plea bargain and thus receive some punishment, even if the full rigor of the law cannot be imposed because of the dubious validity of the search. Even after the defendant has been convicted or has pleaded guilty, it would be dangerous to discipline the officer—months or years later—because the offender might come back seeking one of the now popular post-conviction remedies.

Finally, the existence of the federally imposed exclusionary rule makes it virtually impossible for any state, not only the federal government, to experiment with any other methods of controlling police. One unfortunate consequence of *Mapp* was that it removed from the states both the incentive and the opportunity to deal with illegal search and seizure by means other than suppression. Justice Harlan, in commenting on the evil impact of the federal imposition of the exclusionary rule on the states, observed:

> Another [state], though equally solicitous of constitutional rights, may choose to pursue one purpose at a time, allowing all evidence relevant to guilt to be brought into a criminal trial, and dealing with constitutional infractions by other means.

ALTERNATIVES TO THE RULE

The excuse given for the persistence of the exclusionary rule in this country is that there is no effective alternative to make the police obey the law in regard to unreasonable searches and seizures. If this excuse did not come from such respected sources, one would be tempted to term it an expression of intellectual bankruptcy.

"No effective alternative"? How do all the other civilized countries control their police? By disciplinary measures against the erring policeman, by effective civil damage action against both the policeman and the government—not by freeing the criminal. Judging by police conduct in England, Canada and other nations, these measures work very well. Why does the United States alone rely upon the irrational exclusionary rule?

It isn't necessary. Justice Frankfurter in *Wolf* (1949) noted that none of the 10 jurisdictions in the British Commonwealth had held evidence obtained by an illegal search and seizure inadmissible, and "the jurisdictions which have rejected the *Weeks* doctrine have not left the right to privacy without other means of protection...." Justice Harlan in his dissent in *Mapp* noted the wisdom of allowing all evidence to be brought in and "dealing with constitutional infractions by other means." Justice Black, concurring in *Mapp*, noted that the Fourth Amendment did not itself preclude the use of illegally obtained evidence.

In his dissent in *Bivens*, Chief Justice Burger suggested that Congress provide that Fourth Amendment violations be made actionable under the Federal Tort Claims Act, or something similar. Senator Lloyd Bentsen and other members of Congress have put forward proposals to abolish the rule and substitute the liability of the federal government toward the victims of illegal searches and seizures, both those innocent and those guilty of crimes.

THE PURPOSES OF AN ALTERNATIVE

Before examining what mechanism we might adopt in place of the exclusionary rule as a tool for enforcing the rights guaranteed by the Fourth Amendment, let us see clearly what objectives we desire to achieve by such alternatives.

The *first* objective, in sequence and perhaps in the public consciousness of those who are aware of the shortcomings of the rule, is to prevent the unquestionably guilty from going free from all punishment for their crime—to put an end to the ridiculous situation that the murderer goes free because the constable has blundered. Let me reiterate: the exclusionary rule, as applied to tangible evidence, has never prevented an innocent person from being convicted.

Second, the system should provide effective guidance to the police as to proper conduct under the Fourth Amendment. When appellate courts rule several years after the violation, their decisions are not only years too late, but usually far too obscure for the average policeman to understand. They are remote in both time and impact on the policeman at fault. Immediate guidance to the policeman as to his error, with an appropriate penalty, is obviously more effective, in contrast to simply rewarding the criminal.

Third sequentially, but first in value, the mechanism should protect citizens from Fourth Amendment violations by law enforcement officers. (I say sequentially, because it is necessary first to abolish the exclusionary rule and then to provide guidance to the police.) If police receive immediate and meaningful rulings, accompanied by prompt disciplinary penalties, they will be effectively deterred from future wrongful action and citizens will thus be effectively protected.

Fourth, the procedure should provide effective and meaningful compensation to those citizens, particularly innocent victims of illegal searches and seizures. This the present exclusionary rule totally fails to do. Only the guilty person who has suffered an illegal search and seizure receives some form of compensation—an acquittal, which is usually in gross disproportion to the injury inflicted on him by an illegal search and seizure. Thus, under the present irrational exclusionary rule system, the guilty are over-rewarded by a commutation of all penalties for crimes they did commit and the innocent are never compensated for the injuries they suffered.

THE MAGNITUDE OF THE OFFENSE

Fifth, it should be an objective of any substitute for the exclusionary rule to introduce comparative values into what is now a totally arbitrary process and inflexible penalty. Under the exclusionary rule, the "penalty" is the same irrespective of the offense. If an officer barely oversteps the line on probable cause and seizes five ounces of heroin from a peddler on the street corner, or an officer without a warrant and without probable cause barges into a home and seizes private papers, the result is automatic—the evidence is barred, the accused is freed, and this is all the "punishment" the officer receives.

Surely the societal values involved in the two incidents are of a totally different magnitude. The error of the officer in dealing with narcotics peddlers should not be overlooked, his misapprehension of the requirement of probable cause should be called to his attention quickly in a way which he will remember, but actual punishment should be relatively minimal. In the instance of an invalid seizure of private papers in the home, the officer should be severely punished for such a gross infraction of Fourth Amendment rights.

The exclusionary rule is applied automatically now when there is no illegal action by investigative officers and hence no possible deterrence to future police misconduct. For example, where government agents have dutifully applied to a judge or magistrate for a search warrant, and executed the warrant in strict conformity with its terms, a warrant which later proves defective will force the judge later to exclude the evidence illegally seized. All that is involved in these instances is a legal error on the part of the judge, magistrate, or perhaps the attorney who drew the papers. It is absurd to say that the court subsequently is "punishing" or attempting to "deter" the judge, magistrate, or attorney who made the legal error by suppressing the evidence and letting the accused go free, but this is what happens now.

If these are valid objectives in seeking a substitute procedure for the exclusionary rule as a method of enforcing Fourth Amendment rights, there seem to be two general approaches which might well be combined in one statute—internal discipline by the law enforcement authorities themselves, and external control by the courts or an independent review board.

INTERNAL DISCIPLINE

Disciplinary action against the offending law enforcement officer could be initiated by the law enforcement organization itself or by the person whose Fourth Amendment rights had been allegedly violated. The police could initiate action either within the regular command structure or by an overall disciplinary board outside the hierarchy of command. Many law enforcement organizations have such disciplinary boards now and they could be made mandatory by statute in all federal law enforcement agencies. Wherever they may be located, the organization would require action to be taken following the seizure of material evidence, if the criminal trial or an independent investigation showed a violation of the Fourth Amendment standards.

The person injured could also initiate action leading to internal discipline of the offending officer by complaint to the agency disciplinary board. Each enforcement agency or department could establish a process to hear and decide the complaint, providing both a penalty for the offending officer (if the violation were proved) and government compensation to the injured party.

This procedure would cover numerous cases in which citizens suffer violations of Fourth Amendment rights, but in which no court action results. The injured party could choose this administrative remedy in lieu of court action, but any award in the administrative proceedings would be taken into account by a court later if a citizen, dissatisfied with the award, instituted further legal action.

The penalty against the officer would be tailored to fit his own culpability; it might be a reprimand, a fine, a delay in promotion, a suspension, or discharge. Factors bearing upon the extent of the penalty would include the extent to which the violation was willful, the manner in which it deviated from approved conduct, the degree to which it invaded the privacy of the injured party, and the extent to which human dignity and societal values were breached.

Providing compensation to the injured party from the government is necessary, for it is simply realistic to make the government liable for the wrongful acts of its agent in order to make the prospect of compensation meaningful. Policemen traditionally are not wealthy and the government has a deep purse. Moreover, higher administrative officials and irate taxpayers may be expected to react adversely to losses resulting from the misconduct of policemen and to do something about their training and exercise of responsibilities.

EXTERNAL CONTROL

When a prosecutor tries a defendant in the wake of a violation of Fourth

Amendment rights, the court could conduct a mini-trial of the offending officer after the violation is alleged and proof outlined in the principal criminal case. This mini-trial would be similar to a hearing on a motion to suppress now, but it would be conducted after the main criminal case. The burden would be on the injured party to prove, by preponderance of the evidence, that the officer violated his Fourth Amendment rights. The policeman could submit his case to either the judge or the jury who heard the main criminal case.

By initiating the "trial" of the officer immediately following the criminal case in which he was charged with misconduct, the court could determine the question of his violation speedily and economically. Presumably both the judge and jury have been thoroughly familiarized with the facts of the main case and are able to put the conduct of the officer in perspective.

Such a mini-trial would provide an outside disciplinary force that the injured party could utilize in lieu of internal discipline by the agency. Any previous administrative action taken against the officer would be considered by the judge and jury, if a penalty were to be assessed as a result of the mini-trial. The same factors bearing on the penalty to the officer and compensation to the injured party as discussed under the administrative remedy would be relevant in the mini-trial.

In those instances where police violate Fourth Amendment rights but the prosecutor does not bring charges against the suspect, the wronged party should be able to bring a statutory civil action against the government and the officer. Both would be named as defendants: the officer to defend against any individual penalty, the government to be able to respond adequately in damages to the injured party if such were found. Many instances of Fourth Amendment violation now go unnoticed because no criminal charge is brought and the injured party is not in position to bring a *Bivens*-type suit for the alleged constitutional violation. The burden of proof on the factors in regard to penalty and compensation would be the same as in a mini-trial following the principal criminal case, as discussed above.

The creation of this civil remedy could be accomplished by simple amendment to the present Federal Tort Claims Act. This is the procedure followed in many other countries, among them Canada.

> ... the remedy in tort has proved reasonably effective; Canadian juries are quick to resent illegal activity on the part of the police and to express that resentment by a proportionate judgment for damages.

Disciplinary punishment and civil penalties directly against the erring officer involved would certainly provide a far more effective deterrent than the Supreme Court has created in the exclusionary rule. The creation of a civil remedy for violations of privacy, whether or not the invasion resulted in a criminal prosecution, would provide a remedy for the innocent victims of Fourth Amendment violations which the exclusionary rule has never pretended to give. And the rationale that the "government should not 'profit' from its own agent's misconduct" would disappear completely if erring officers were punished and injured parties compensated when there was a Fourth Amendment violation. If such a law and procedure were enforced, there would be no remaining objection to the subject of search and seizure still receiving his appropriate punishment for his crime.

CONCLUSION

All of the above was written before I read Professor Kamisar's ["Is the exclusionary rule an 'illogical' or 'unnatural' interpretation of the Fourth Amendment?" 62 Judicature 66.] It is apparent that our respective positions are widely divergent. After pondering his statement, I believe it fair to say that he must attempt to defend his position on one of two grounds, and that on analysis neither is defensible.

First, if Professor Kamisar believes that the Fourth Amendment necessarily mandates the exclusionary rule, then he ought to cite Supreme Court authority for this position. Nowhere in his article does he do so. It is undeniable that at no time in the Court's history has a majority in any case ever so held, and I do not believe that any more than two individual justices in the Court's history have so expressed themselves. In contrast, numerous justices, both favoring and opposing the rule, have stated that the rule itself is *not* mandated by the Fourth Amendment.

Second, if Professor Kamisar's article is intended only to say that under the Constitution we have a choice of methods to enforce the ban against "unreasonable searches and seizures," and that the exclusionary rule is a good choice only because of "the imperative of judicial integrity," then I submit both logic and experience in this country and all other countries refutes this. If the Supreme Court or the Congress has a choice of methods under the Constitution, then it simply will not do to rest the choice of exclusionary rule solely on the high principle of "judicial integrity" and to ignore the pragmatic result, the failure to achieve the objective of enforcement and the other pernicious side effects discussed above, which themselves strongly discredit judicial integrity.

If we have a choice, to attempt to justify the continuation of the exclusionary rule on this basis is to be stubbornly blind to 65 years of experience. If we have a choice, to insist on continuing a method of enforcement with as many demonstrated faults as the exclusionary rule is to be blindly stubborn. If we have a choice, let us calmly and carefully consider the available alternatives, draw upon the experience of other nations with systems of justice similar to our own, and by abolishing the rule permit in the laboratories of our 51 jurisdictions the experimentation with various possible alternatives promising far more than the now discredited exclusionary rule.

NO

Yale Kamisar

THE STRUGGLE TO MAKE
THE FOURTH AMENDMENT
MORE THAN "AN EMPTY BLESSING"

In the 65 years since the Supreme Court adopted the exclusionary rule, few critics have attacked it with as much vigor and on as many fronts as did Judge Malcolm Wilkey in his recent *Judicature* article, "The exclusionary rule: why suppress valid evidence?" (November 1978).

According to Judge Wilkey, there is virtually nothing good about the rule and a great deal bad about it. He thinks the rule is partly to blame for "the distressing rate of street crimes." He tells us that it "discourages internal disciplinary action by the police themselves"; actually results in "encouraging highly pernicious police behavior" (e.g., perjury, harassment and corruption); "makes it virtually impossible for any state, not only the federal government, to experiment with any methods of controlling police"; and "undermines the reputation of and destroys the respect for the entire judicial system."

Judge Wilkey claims, too, that the rule "dooms" "every scheme of gun control . . . to be totally ineffective in preventing the habitual use of weapons in street crimes." Until we rid ourselves of this rule, he argues, "the criminal can parade in the street with a great bulge in his pocket or a submachine gun in a blanket under his arm" and "laugh in the face of the officer who might wish to search him for it."

UNTHINKING, EMOTIONAL ATTACHMENT?

Why, then, has the rule survived? "The greatest obstacle to replacing the exclusionary rule with a rational process," Judge Wilkey maintains, is "the powerful, unthinking emotional attachment" to the rule. If you put the issue to a representative group of lawyers and judges, he concedes, "you would doubtless hear some support" for the rule, but only from those "heavily imbued with a mystique of the exclusionary rule as of almost divine origin."

It is hard to believe that nothing more substantial than "unthinking emotional attachment" or mystical veneration accounts for support for the rule by Justices Holmes and Brandeis [and,] more recently, by such battlescarred veterans as Roger Traynor, Earl Warren and Tom Clark.

In the beginning, Judge Traynor was not attached to the rule, emotionally or otherwise. Indeed, in 1942 he wrote the opinion of the California Supreme Court reaffirming the admissibility of illegally seized evidence. But by 1955, it became apparent to Traynor that illegally seized evidence "was being offered and admitted as a routine procedure" and "it became impossible to ignore the corollary that illegal searches and seizures were also a routine procedure, subject to no effective deterrent."

> [W]ithout fear of criminal punishment or other discipline, law enforcement officers... casually regard [illegal searches and seizures] as nothing more than the performance of their ordinary duties for which the City employs and pays them.

In light of these circumstances, Traynor overruled the court's earlier decision.

And consider Earl Warren. During the 24 years he spent in state law enforcement work in California (as deputy district attorney, district attorney and attorney general), California admitted illegally seized evidence. Indeed, Warren was the California Attorney General who successfully urged Judge Traynor and his brethren to reaffirm that rule in 1942. In 1954, during his first year as Chief Justice of the United States, he heard a case involving police misconduct so outrageous as to be "almost incredible if it were not admitted" (the infamous *Irvine* case), but he resisted the temptation to impose the exclusionary rule on the states, even in such extreme cases. It was not until 1961 that he joined in the opinion

for the Court in *Mapp*, which imposed the rule on the states.

Chief Justice Warren knew the exclusionary rule's limitations as a tool of judicial control, but at the end of an extraordinary public career—in which he had served more years as a prosecutor than any other person who has ascended to the Supreme Court—Warren observed:

> [I]n our system, evidentiary rulings provide the context in which the judicial process of inclusion and exclusion approves some conduct as comporting with constitutional guarantees and disapproves other actions by state agents. A ruling admitting evidence in a criminal trial, we recognize, has the necessary effect of legitimizing the conduct which produced the evidence, while an application of the exclusionary rule withholds the constitutional imprimatur.

The author of the *Mapp* opinion, Tom Clark, was, of course, U.S. Attorney General for four years before he became a Supreme Court justice and he was assistant attorney general in charge of the criminal division before that. Evidently, nothing in his experience gave Clark reason to believe that the rule had "handcuffed" federal officials or would cripple state law enforcement. And he never changed his views about the need for the exclusionary rule during his 18 years on the Court or the 10 years he spent in the administration of justice following his retirement. Indeed, shortly before his death, he warmly defended *Mapp* and *Weeks*.

Moreover, nothing in Justice Clark's career suggests that he endorsed *Mapp* out of "sentimentality" or in awe of the "divine origins" of the exclusionary rule. More likely, he was impressed with the failure of *Wolf* and *Irvine* to stimulate any meaningful alternative to the exclusionary rule in the more than 20 states that still admitted illegally seized evidence at the time of *Mapp*.

I do not mean to suggest that Judge Wilkey's views on the exclusionary rule are aberrational among lawyers and judges; many members of the bench and bar share his deep distress with the rule. Indeed, when Judge Wilkey asks us to abolish the exclusionary rule now—without waiting for a meaningful alternative to emerge—he but follows the lead of Chief Justice Burger, who recently maintained:

> [T]he continued existence of the rule, as presently implemented, inhibits the development of rational alternatives.... It can no longer be assumed that other branches of government will act while judges cling to this Draconian, discredited device in its present absolutist form.

Because so many share Judge Wilkey's hostility to the exclusionary rule, it is important to examine and to evaluate Wilkey's arguments at some length. Only then can we determine whether the rule is as irrational and pernicious as he and other critics maintain—and whether we can abolish it before we have developed an alternative.

CRIME AND THE RULE

A year before the California Supreme Court adopted the exclusionary rule on its own—and years before the "revolution" in American criminal procedure began—William H. Parker, the Chief of the Los Angeles Police Department, said:

> [O]ur most accurate crime statistics indicate that crime rates rise and fall on the tides of economic, social, and political cycles with embarrassingly

little attention to the most determined efforts of our police.

Almost as soon as the California Supreme Court adopted the exclusionary rule, though, Chief Parker began blaming the rule for the high rate of crime in Los Angeles, calling it "catastrophic as far as efficient law enforcement is concerned," and insisting "that the imposition of the exclusionary rule has rendered the people powerless to adequately protect themselves against the criminal army."

Such criticism of the *Cahan* rule was only a preview of the attack on *Mapp*. Chief Justice Traynor, speaking about the debate following the *Mapp* decision, rightly observed that: "Articulate comment about [*Mapp*]...was drowned out in the din about handcuffing the police."

Thus, it is not surprising that Judge Wilkey would claim on his very first page that "[w]e can see [the] huge social cost [of *Weeks* and *Mapp*] most clearly in the distressing rate of street crimes...which flourish in no small degree simply because of the exclusionary rule." Nevertheless, it is disappointing to hear a critic repeat this charge, because after 65 years of debate, there was reason to hope that this criticism, at least, would no longer be made. As Professor James Vorenberg pointed out, shortly after he completed his two years of service as Executive Director of the President's Commission on Law Enforcement and Administration of Justice:

> What the Supreme Court does has practically no effect on the amount of crime in this country, and what the police do has far less effect than is generally realized.

Even Professor Dallin Oaks (now a university president), upon whose work

Judge Wilkey relies so heavily, advised a decade ago:

> The whole argument about the exclusionary rule 'handcuffing' the police should be abandoned. If this is a negative effect, then it is an effect of the constitutional rules, not an effect of the exclusionary rule as the means chosen for their enforcement.
>
> Police officials and prosecutors should stop claiming that the exclusionary rule prevents effective law enforcement. In doing so they attribute far greater effect to the exclusionary rule than the evidence warrants, and they are also in the untenable position of urging that the sanction be abolished so that they can continue to violate the [constitutional] rules with impunity.

A WEAK LINK

Over the years, I have written about the impact of *Cahan, Mapp* and other decisions on crime rates and police-prosecution efficiency. I will not restate my findings again, especially since Judge Wilkey has presented no statistical support for his assertion. I would, however, like to summarize a few points:

- Long before the exclusionary rule became law in the states—indeed, long before any of the procedural safeguards in the federal Constitution was held applicable to the states —invidious comparisons were made between the rate of crime in our nation and the incidence of crime in others.

Thus, in 1911, the distinguished ex-president of Cornell University, Andrew D. White, pointed out that, although London's population was two million larger than New York's, there were 10 times more murders in New York. And in 1920, Edwin W. Sims, the first head of the Chicago Crime Commission, pointed out that "[d]uring 1919 there were more murders in Chicago (with a population of three million) than in the entire British Isles (with a population of forty million)." This history ought to raise some doubts about the alleged causal link between the high rate of crime in America and the exclusionary rule.

- England and Wales have not experienced anything like the "revolution" in American criminal procedure which began at least as early as the 1961 *Mapp* case. Nevertheless, from 1955–65 (a decade which happened to be subjected to a most intensive study), the number of indictable offenses against the person in England and Wales increased 162 percent. How do opponents of the exclusionary rule explain such increases in countries which did not suffer from the wounds the Warren Court supposedly inflicted upon America?

- In the decade before *Mapp*, Maryland admitted illegally seized evidence in all felony prosecutions; Virginia, in all cases. District of Columbia police, on the other hand, were subject to both the exclusionary rule and the *McNabb-Mallory* rule, a rule which "hampered" no other police department during this period. Nevertheless, during this decade the felony rate per 100,000 population increased much more in the three Virginia and Maryland suburbs of the District (69 percent) than in the District itself (a puny one percent).

- The predictions and descriptions of near-disaster in California law enforcement which greeted the 1955 *Cahan* decision find precious little empirical support. The percentage of narcotics convictions did drop almost 10 points (to 77 percent), but only posses- sion cases were significantly affected. Meanwhile, both the rate of arrests and felony complaints filed for narcotics offenses actually increased! Thus, in 1959–60, 20 percent more persons were convicted of narcotics offenses in Cal- ifornia superior courts than in the record conviction percentage years be- fore *Cahan.*

The overall felony conviction rate was 84.5 percent for the three years before *Cahan*, 85.4 percent for the *Cahan* year and 86.4 percent in the three years after *Cahan* (even including the low narcotic percentages). Conviction rates for murder, manslaughter, felony assault, rape, robbery and burglary remained almost the same, though the number of convicted felons rose steadily.

The exclusionary rule, to be sure, does free some "guilty criminals" (as would an effective tort remedy that inhibited the police from making illegal searches and seizures in the first place), but very rarely are they robbers or murderers. Rather they are "offenders caught in the everyday world of police initiated vice and narcotics enforcement...."

Though critics of the exclusionary rule sometimes sound as though it constitutes the main loophole in the administration of justice, the fact is that it is only a minor escape route in a system that filters out far more offenders through police, prosecutorial, and judicial discretion than it tries, convicts and sentences....

Moreover, the critics' concentration on the formal issue of conviction tends to overlook the very real sanctions that are imposed even on defendants who 'escape' via the suppression of evidence [e.g., among the poor, most suffer at least several days of imprisonment, regardless of the ultimate verdict; many lose their jobs as a result and have a hard time finding another]....

When one considers that many con- victions in the courts that deal with large numbers of motions to suppress often amount to small fines, suspended sen- tences, and probation, the distinction be- tween conviction and escape becomes even more blurred.

AN UNDEMONSTRATED CONNECTION

... Judge Wilkey hints darkly that there is a "connection" between America's high crime rate and its "unique" exclusionary rule. So far as I am aware, no one has been able to demonstrate such a connection on the basis of the annual *Uniform Crime Reports* or any other statistical data. In Michigan, for example, the rate of violent crime seems to have fluctuated without regard to the life and death of the state's "anti-exclusionary" proviso.

From 1960–64, the robbery rate in- creased only slightly in the Detroit Metropolitan Statistical Area but it quadrupled from 1964 to 1970 (from 152.5 per 100,000 to 648.5). When the Michigan Supreme Court struck down the state's "anti-exclusionary" proviso in 1970, the robbery rate fell (to 470.3 per 100,000 in 1973), climbed (to 604.2 in 1975), then dropped again (to 454.3 in 1977, the low- est it has been since the 1960's).

From 1960–64, the murder and non- negligent manslaughter rate remained almost the same in the Detroit area, but it rose extraordinarily the next six years (5.0 in 1964 to 14.7 in 1970). In the next four years it continued to climb (but less sharply) to 20.2 in 1974. Then it dropped to 14.1 in 1977, the lowest it has been since the 1960's.

Finally, I must take issue with Judge Wilkey's case of the criminal who "parade[s] in the streets with a great bulge in his pocket or a submachine gun in a blanket under his arm," "laugh[ing] in the face of the officer who might wish to search him for it." If American criminals "know the difficulties of the police in making a valid search," as Judge Wilkey tells us, they know, too, that the exclusionary rule has "virtually no applicability" in "large areas of police activity which do not result in criminal prosecutions" and that confiscation of weapons is one of them. (The criminal might get back his blanket, but not the submachine gun).

Moreover, it is not at all clear that an officer who notices a "great bulge" in a person's pocket or, as in the recent *Mimms* case, a "large bulge" under a person's sports jacket, lacks lawful authority to conduct a limited search for weapons. Indeed, *Mimms* seems to say that a policeman *does* have the authority under such circumstances. Even if I am wrong, however, even if the Fourth Amendment does not permit an officer to make such a limited search for weapons, *abolishing the exclusionary rule wouldn't change that.* If an officer now lacks the lawful authority to conduct a "frisk" under these circumstances, he would still lack the lawful authority to do so if the rule were abolished. This is a basic point, one that I shall focus on in the next section.

A BASIC CONFUSION

In my earlier *Judicature* article, I pointed out how police and prosecutors have treated the exclusionary rule as if it were itself the guaranty against unreasonable search and seizure (which is one good

reason for retaining the rule). At several places Judge Wilkey's article reflects the same confusion.

He complains, for example, that if a search or frisk turns up a deadly weapon, that weapon cannot be used in evidence if the officer lacked the constitutionally required cause for making the search or frisk in the first place. But this is really an attack on the constitutional guaranty itself, not the exclusionary rule. Prohibiting the use of illegally seized evidence may be poor "public relations" because by then we know who the criminal is, but an *after-the-fact* prohibition

> prevents convictions in no greater degree than would effective prior direction to police to search only by legal means...[T]he maintenance of existing standards by means of exclusion is not open to attack unless it can be doubted whether the standards themselves are necessary.

If we replace the exclusionary rule with "disciplinary punishment and civil penalties directly against the erring officer involved," as Judge Wilkey proposes, and if these alternatives "would certainly provide a far more effective deterrent than...the exclusionary rule," as the judge assures us, the weapon still would not be brought in as evidence in the case he poses because the officer would not *make* the search or frisk if he lacked the requisite cause to do so.

Judge Wilkey points enviously to England, where "the criminals know that the police have a right to search them *on the slightest suspicion,* and they know that if a weapon is found they will be prosecuted" (emphasis added). But what is the relevance of this point in an article discussing the exclusionary rule and its alternatives? Abolishing the rule would not confer a *right* on our police to search "on the slightest suspicion"; it would not affect lawful police practices in any way. Only a change in the substantive law of search and seizure can do that.... And replacing the exclusionary rule with a statutory remedy against the government would not bring about an increase in unlawful police activity if the alternative were equally effective—and Judge Wilkey expects it to be "a far more effective deterrent."

I venture to say that Judge Wilkey has confused the *content* of the law of search seizure (which proponents of the exclusionary rule need not, and have not always, defended) with the *exclusionary rule*—which "merely states the consequences of a breach of whatever principles might be adopted to control law enforcement officers." The confusion was pointed out more than 50 years ago by one who had the temerity to reply to the great Wigmore's famous criticism of the rule. Every student of the problem knows Wigmore's views on this subject, but very few are familiar with Connor Hall's reply. It is worth recalling:

> When it is proposed to secure the citizen his constitutional rights by the direct punishment of the violating officer, we must assume that the proposer is honest, and that he would have such consistent prosecution and such heavy punishment of the offending officer as would cause violations to cease and thus put a stop to the seizure of papers and other tangible evidence through unlawful search.
>
> If this, then, is to be the result, no evidence in any appreciable number of cases would be obtained through unlawful searches, and the result would be the same, so far as the conviction of criminals goes, as if the constitutional right was enforced by a return of the evidence.

Then why such anger in celestial breasts? Justice can be rendered inefficient and the criminal classes coddled by the rule laid down in *Weeks* only upon the assumption that the officer will not be directly punished, but that the court will receive the fruits of his lawful acts, will do no more than denounce and threaten him with jail or the penitentiary and, at the same time, with its tongue in its cheek, give him to understand how fearful a thing it is to violate the Constitution. This has been the result previous to the rule adopted by the Supreme Court, and that is what the courts are asked to continue.

... If punishment of the officer is effective to prevent unlawful searches, then equally by this is justice rendered inefficient and criminals coddled. It is only by violations that the great god Efficiency can thrive.

WAITING FOR ALTERNATIVES

Judge Wilkey makes plain his agreement with Chief Justice Burger that "the continued existence of [the exclusionary rule] ... inhibits the development of rational alternatives" and that "incentives for developing new procedures or remedies will remain minimal or nonexistent so long as the exclusionary rule is retained in its present form."

Thus, Judge Wilkey warns that "we will never have any alternative in operation until the rule is abolished. So long as we keep the rule, the police are not going to investigate and discipline their men, and thus sabotage prosecutions by invalidating the admissibility of vital evidence...." He argues that *Mapp* "removed from the states both the incentive and the opportunity to deal with illegal search and seizure by means other than suppression." And he concludes his first article with these words:

> [L]et us ... by abolishing the rule permit in the laboratories of our 51 jurisdictions the experimentation with the various possible alternatives promising far more than the now discredited exclusionary rule.

In light of our history, these comments (both the Chief Justice's and Judge Wilkey's) are simply baffling. First, the fear of "sabotaging" prosecutions has never inhibited law enforcement administrators from disciplining officers for committing the "many unlawful searches of homes and automobiles of innocent people which turn up nothing incriminating, in which no arrest is made, about which courts do nothing, and about which we never hear."

Second, both defenders of the rule and its critics recognize that

> there are large areas of police activity which do not result in criminal prosecutions [e.g., arrest or confiscation as a punitive sanction (common in gambling and liquor law violations), illegal detentions which do not result in the acquisition of evidence, unnecessary destruction of property]—hence the rule has virtually no applicability and no effect in such situations.

Whatever the reason for the failure to discipline officers for "mistakes" in these "large areas of police activities," it cannot be the existence of the exclusionary rule.

Finally, and most importantly, *for many decades* a majority of the states had no exclusionary rule but *none of them* developed any meaningful alternative. Thirty-five years passed between the time the federal courts adopted the exclusionary rule and the time *Wolf* was decided in 1949, but none of the 31 states which still admitted illegally seized evidence had established an alternative method of controlling the police. Twelve more years passed before *Mapp* imposed the rule on the state courts, but none of the 24 states which still rejected the exclusionary rule had instituted an alternative remedy. This half-century of post-*Weeks* "freedom to experiment" did not produce any meaningful alternative to the exclusionary rule anywhere.

DISPARITY BETWEEN FACT AND THEORY

Of course, few critics of the exclusionary rule have failed to suggest alternative remedies that *might be devised* or that *warranted study*. None of them has become a reality.

In 1922, for example, Dean Wigmore maintained that "the natural way to do justice" would be to enforce the Fourth Amendment directly "by sending for the high-handed, overzealous marshal who had searched without a warrant, imposing a 30-day imprisonment for his contempt of the Constitution, and then proceeding to affirm the sentence of the convicted criminal." Nothing ever came of that proposal. Another critic of the rule suggested that a civil rights office be established, independent of the regular prosecutor, "charged solely with the responsibility of investigating and prosecuting alleged violations of the Constitution by law-enforcement officials." Nothing came of that proposal either.

Judge Wilkey recognizes that "policemen traditionally are not wealthy," but "[t]he government has a deep purse." Thus, as did Chief Justice Burger in his *Bivens* dissent, Judge Wilkey proposes that in lieu of the exclusion of illegally seized evidence there be a statutory remedy against the government itself to afford meaningful compensation and restitution for the victims of police illegality. Two leading commentators, Caleb Foote and Edward Barrett, Jr., made the same suggestion 20 years ago, but none of the many states that admitted illegally seized evidence at the time seemed interested in experimenting along these lines.

Indeed, the need for, and the desirability of, a statutory remedy against the government itself was pointed out at least as long ago as 1936. In a famous article published that year, Jerome Hall noted that the prospects of satisfying a judgment against a police officer were so poor that the tort remedy in the books "collapses at its initial application to fact." Said Hall:

> [W]here there is liability (as in the case of the policeman), the fact of financial irresponsibility is operative and, presumably, conclusive; while, where financial responsibility exists (as in the case of a city), there is no liability.

"This disparity between theory and fact, between an empty shell of relief and substantial compensation," observed Professor Hall—43 years ago—"could not remain unnoticed."

This disparity—no longer unnoticed, but still uncorrected—has troubled even the strongest critics of the rule. Thus, more than 35 years ago, J. A. C. Grant suggested "implement[ing] the law covering actions for trespass, even going so far as to hold the government liable in damages for the torts of its agents." And William Plumb, Jr., accompanied his powerful attack on the rule with a similar suggestion.

MAPP'S TRAUMATIC EFFECTS

At the time of Plumb's article, the admissibility of illegally seized evidence had "once more become a burning question in New York." Delegates to the 1938 constitutional convention had defeated an effort to write the exclusionary rule into the constitution, but only after a long and bitter debate. The battle then moved to the legislature, where bills were pending to exclude illegally obtained, or at least illegally wiretapped, evidence.

Against this background, Plumb offered a whole basketful of alternatives to the rule and he said the state legislature "should make a thorough study of the problem of devising effective direct remedies [such as those he had outlined] to make the constitutional guarantee 'a real, not an empty blessing.'" But nothing happened.

Otherwise why would a New York City Police Commissioner say of *Mapp* some 20 years later:

> I can think of no decision in recent times in the field of law enforcement which had such a dramatic effect as this.... I was immediately caught up in the entire problem of reevaluating our procedures which had followed the *Defore* rule, and modifying, amending, and creating new policies and new instructions for the implementation of *Mapp*. The problems were manifold. [Supreme Court decisions such as *Mapp*] create tidal waves and earthquakes which require rebuilding of our institutions sometimes from their very foundations upward. Retraining sessions had to be held from the very top administrators down to each of the thousands of foot patrolmen....

In theory, *Defore*, which rejected the exclusionary rule in New York, had not expanded lawful police powers one iota.

Nor, in theory, had *Mapp* reduced these powers. What was an illegal search before *Defore* was still an illegal search. What was an unlawful arrest before *Mapp* was still an unlawful arrest.

The *Defore* rule, of course, was based largely upon the premise that New York did not need to adopt the exclusionary rule because existing remedies were adequate to effectuate the guaranty against illegal search and seizure. Cardozo said that:

> The officer might have been resisted[!], or sued for damages or even prosecuted for oppression. He was subject to removal or other discipline at the hands of his superiors.

Why, then, did *Mapp* have such a "dramatic" and "traumatic" effect? Why did it necessitate "creating new policies"? What were the old policies like? Why did it necessitate retraining sessions from top to bottom? What was the *old* training like? What did the commissioner mean when he said that before *Mapp* his department had "followed the *Defore* rule"?

> On behalf of the New York City Police Department as well as law enforcement in general, I state unequivocally that every effort was directed and is still being directed at compliance with and implementation of *Mapp*....

Isn't it peculiar to talk about police "compliance with" and "implementation of" a *remedy* for a violation of a body of law the police were supposed to be complying with and implementing all along? Why did the police have to make such strenuous efforts to comply with *Mapp* unless they had not been complying with the Fourth Amendment?

> Flowing from the *Mapp* case is the issue of defining probable cause to constitute a lawful arrest and subsequent search and seizure.

Doesn't this issue flow from the Fourth Amendment itself? Isn't that what the Fourth Amendment is all about?

The police reaction to *Mapp* demonstrates the unsoundness of the underlying premise of *Defore*. Otherwise why, at a post-*Mapp* training session on the law of search and seizure, would Leonard Reisman, then the New York Deputy Police Commissioner in charge of legal matters, comment:

> The *Mapp* case was a shock to us. We had to reorganize our thinking, frankly. Before this, nobody bothered to take out search warrants. Although the U.S. Constitution requires warrants in most cases, the U.S. Supreme Court had ruled [until 1961] that evidence obtained without a warrant—illegally if you will —was admissible in state courts. So the feeling was, why bother?

NO INCENTIVE FOR CHANGE

As I have already indicated, critics of the exclusionary rule have often made proposals for effectuating the Fourth Amendment by means other than the exclusionary rule—but almost always as a *quid pro quo* for rejecting or repealing the rule. Who has ever heard of a police-prosecution spokesman urging— or a law enforcement group supporting —an effective "direct remedy" for illegal searches and seizures in a jurisdiction which *admitted* illegally seized evidence? Abandoning the exclusionary rule without waiting for a meaningful alternative (as Judge Wilkey and Chief Justice Burger would have us do) will not furnish an incentive for devising an alternative, but *re-*

lieve whatever pressure there now exists for doing so.

I spoke in my earlier article of the great symbolic value of the exclusionary rule. Abolition of the exclusionary rule, after the long, bitter struggle to attain it, would be even more important as a symbol.

During the 12-year reign of *Wolf*, some state judges

remained mindful of the cogent reasons for the admission of illegally obtained evidence and clung to the fragile hope that the very brazenness of lawless police methods would bring on effective deterrents other than the exclusionary rule.

Their hope proved to be in vain. *Wolf* established the "underlying constitutional doctrine" that "the Federal Constitution, by virtue of the Fourteenth Amendment, prohibits unreasonable searches and seizures by state officers" (though it did not require exclusion of the resulting evidence); *Irvine* warned that if the state "defaulted and there were no demonstrably effective deterrents to unreasonable searches and seizures in lieu of the exclusionary rule, the Supreme Court might yet decide that they had not complied with 'minimal standards' of due process." But neither *Wolf* nor *Irvine* stimulated a single state legislature or a single law enforcement agency to demonstrate that the problem could be handled in other ways.

The disappointing 12 years between *Wolf* and *Mapp* give added weight to Francis Allen's thoughtful commentary on the *Wolf* case at the time it was handed down:

This deference to local authority revealed in the *Wolf* case stands in marked contrast to the position of the court in other cases arising within the last decade involving rights 'basic to a free society.' It seems safe to assert that in no other area of civil liberties litigation is there evidence that the court has construed the obligations of federalism to require so high a degree of judicial self-abnegation.
... [I]n no other area in the civil liberties has the court felt justified in trusting to public protest for protection of basic personal rights. Indeed, since the rights of privacy are usually asserted by those charged with crime and since the demands of efficient law enforcement are so insistent, it would seem that reliance on public opinion in these cases can be less justified than in almost any other....

Now Judge Wilkey asks us to believe that the resurrection of *Wolf* (and evidently the overruling of the 65-year-old *Weeks* case as well) will permit "the laboratories of our 51 jurisdictions" to produce meaningful alternatives to the exclusionary rule. His ideological ally, Chief Justice Burger, is even more optimistic. He asks us to believe that a return to the pre-exclusionary rule days "would inspire a surge of activity toward providing some kind of statutory remedy for persons injured by police mistakes or misconduct."

And to think that Judge Wilkey accuses *defenders* of the exclusionary rule of being "stubbornly blind to 65 years of experience"!

POSTSCRIPT

Should the Exclusionary Rule Be Abolished?

Wilkey is not the only federal judge to have opposed the exclusionary rule. The most famous judicial critic was former Supreme Court chief justice Warren E. Burger. Burger's opposition to the rule, however, did not lead to an overturning of *Mapp* or *Weeks*. But during the past several decades, there have been a substantial number of cases in which the Court considered the rule and restricted its scope. Thus, while the rule can still be invoked by a defendant at a criminal trial, it cannot be used at a grand jury proceeding (see *United States v. Calandra*, 414 U.S. 338, 1974), in a *habeas corpus* proceeding by a state prisoner (see *Stone v. Powell*, 428 U.S. 465, 1976), when the illegal search is conducted on someone other than the defendant (see *United States v. Payner*, 447 U.S. 727, 1980), or when the illegal search was conducted outside the United States (see *U.S. v. Verdugo-Urguidez*, 110 S. Ct. 1056, 1990).

The Court has approved a good faith exception to the rule in cases where the police officer believed that he was acting lawfully, even though the warrant may have been defective or procured illegally (*Massachusetts v. Sheppard*, 104 S. Ct. 3424, 1984). It has also ruled that search warrants are not required for school officials to search school lockers if there are reasonable grounds for believing the search will reveal evidence of criminal behavior (*New Jersey v. T. L. O., A Juvenile*, 105 S. Ct. 733, 1985). The Burger and Rehnquist courts have generally been lenient in upholding police law enforcement practices and the policy of limiting the defendant's opportunities for invoking the exclusionary rule seems likely to continue.

In part, the resistance to the exclusionary rule is based on a belief that it does not deter illegal police conduct. An interesting debate on the subject, which examines many of the relevant research studies, is found in a series of articles in *Judicature*: B. Canon, "The Exclusionary Rule: Have Critics Proven That It Doesn't Deter Police?" (March 1979) and S. S. Schlesinger, "The Exclusionary Rule: Have Proponents Proven That It Is a Deterrent to Police?" (March 1979). Other articles about the exclusionary rule include Crocker, "Can the Exclusionary Rule Be Saved?" 84 *Journal of Criminal Law and Criminology* 310 (1993); Nelson, "The Paradox of the Exclusionary Rule," *The Public Interest* (Summer 1989); LaFave, "Pinguitudinous Police, Pachydermatous Prey: Whence Fourth Amendment 'Seizures'?" 1991 *University of Illinois Law Review* 729 (1991); C. Slobogin, "The World Without A Fourth Amendment," 39 *UCLA Law Review* 1 (1991); and Note, "Cameras in Teddy Bears: Electronic Visual Surveillance and the Fourth Amendment," 58 *University of Chicago Law Review* 1045 (1991).

ISSUE 14

Should "Battered Wife Syndrome" Be Barred as a Defense in a Murder Case?

YES: Burley B. Mitchell, Jr., from Majority Opinion, *State of North Carolina v. Judy Ann Laws Norman,* Supreme Court of North Carolina (1989)

NO: Harry C. Martin, from Dissenting Opinion, *State of North Carolina v. Judy Ann Laws Norman,* Supreme Court of North Carolina (1989)

ISSUE SUMMARY

YES: Justice Burley B. Mitchell, Jr., is unwilling to recognize "battered wife syndrome" as meeting the standards of immediacy and necessity needed for a self-defense claim in a homicide case.

NO: Justice Harry C. Martin, dissenting in the same case, believes that, given the actions of the husband, the wife's behavior can be viewed in such a way as to meet the standards of self-defense.

The statistics are quite startling. In the United States, one in every five women involved in an intimate relationship with a man is beaten repeatedly by that man. In at least half the cases in which women are battered, children are also battered. Of the children who witness domestic violence, 60 percent of the boys eventually become batterers, and 50 percent of the girls become victims. Battery is the single major cause of injury to women, exceeding even muggings and automobile accidents. Four women, on average, are beaten to death every day in the United States.

As the following readings reveal, the law is having considerable difficulty with this issue. The case involves a woman on trial for killing her husband. Should the trial judge recognize the fact that she was beaten repeatedly, that she suffered from "battered wife syndrome," as constituting a claim of self-defense?

The issue discussed here does not put forward a solution to the problem of spouse abuse. The legal issue is focused quite narrowly on what kind of evidence the trial court may hear and consider. You might reasonably ask whether the legal system's struggle to develop an approach to the condition of "battered wife syndrome" itself suggests failure on the part of the legal system. That such a syndrome exists implies, at least, that the woman has not been protected from repeated battering, and that the legal authorities have failed to intervene effectively.

Spouse abuse is an issue that can be traced back to antiquity. The law in this country has dealt with it for hundreds of years. In the mid-1800s, for example, a North Carolina judge wrote:

> the wife must be subject to the husband. Every man must govern his household, and if by reason of an unruly temper, or an unbridled tongue, the wife persistently treats her husband with disrespect, and he submits to it, he not only loses all sense of self-respect, but loses the respect of other members of his family, without which he cannot expect to govern them, and forfeits the respect of his neighbors. Such have been the incidents of the marriage relation from the beginning of the human race. Unto the woman it is said: 'Thy desire shall be to thy husband, and he shall rule over thee': Gen. iii, 16. It follows that the law gives the husband the power to use such a degree of force as is necessary to make the wife behave herself and know her place. (*Joyner v. Joyner,* 59 N.C. 322, 1862)

Interestingly, a little more than a decade later, the same court considered the issue again and reached a different conclusion:

> We may assume that the old doctrine that a husband had a right to whip his wife, provided he used a switch no larger than his thumb, is not law in North Carolina. Indeed, the Courts have advanced from that barbarism until they have reached the position that the husband has no right to chastise his wife under any circumstances. (*State v. Oliver,* 70 N.C. 60, 1874)

It was not until 1883 that Maryland became the first state to outlaw wife beating by legislation. As you read the following opinions, ask yourself what might account for the rather ineffective response of governmental institutions to enforcing the law and coming to terms with the problem of spousal abuse.

YES

Burley B. Mitchell, Jr.

MAJORITY OPINION

NORTH CAROLINA *v.* NORMAN

Opinion by Justice Mitchell:

The defendant was tried at the 16 February 1987 Criminal Session of Superior Court for Rutherford County upon a proper indictment charging her with the first degree murder of her husband. The jury found the defendant guilty of voluntary manslaughter. The defendant appealed from the trial court's judgment sentencing her to six years imprisonment.

The Court of Appeals granted a new trial, citing as error the trial court's refusal to submit a possible verdict of acquittal by reason of perfect self-defense. Notwithstanding the uncontroverted evidence that the defendant shot her husband three times in the back of the head as he lay sleeping in his bed, the Court of Appeals held that the defendant's evidence that she exhibited what has come to be called "the battered wife syndrome" entitled her to have the jury consider whether the homicide was an act of perfect self-defense and, thus, not a legal wrong.

We conclude that the evidence introduced in this case would not support a finding that the defendant killed her husband due to a reasonable fear of imminent death or great bodily harm, as is required before a defendant is entitled to jury instructions concerning either perfect or imperfect self-defense. Therefore, the trial court properly declined to instruct the jury on the law relating to self-defense. Accordingly, we reverse the Court of Appeals.

At trial, the State presented the testimony of Deputy Sheriff R. H. Epley of the Rutherford County Sheriff's Department, who was called to the Norman residence on the night of 12 June 1985. Inside the home, Epley found the defendant's husband, John Thomas Norman, lying on a bed in a rear bedroom with his face toward the wall and his back toward the middle of the room. He was dead, but blood was still coming from wounds to the back of his head. A later autopsy revealed three gunshot wounds to the head, two of which caused fatal brain injury. The autopsy also revealed a .12 percent blood alcohol level in the victim's body.

From *State of North Carolina v. Judy Ann Laws Norman*, 324 N.C. 253, 378 S.E.2d 8 (1989). Notes and some case citations omitted.

Later that night, the defendant related an account of the events leading to the killing, after Epley had advised her of her constitutional rights and she had waived her right to remain silent. The defendant told Epley that her husband had been beating her all day and had made her lie down on the floor while he slept on the bed. After her husband fell asleep, the defendant carried her grandchild to the defendant's mother's house. The defendant took a pistol from her mother's purse and walked the short distance back to her home. She pointed the pistol at the back of her sleeping husband's head, but it jammed the first time she tried to shoot him. She fixed the gun and then shot her husband in the back of the head as he lay sleeping. After one shot, she felt her husband's chest and determined that he was still breathing and making sounds. She then shot him twice more in the back of the head. The defendant told Epley that she killed her husband because "she took all she was going to take from him so she shot him."

The defendant presented evidence tending to show a long history of physical and mental abuse by her husband due to his alcoholism. At the time of the killing, the thirty-nine-year-old defendant and her husband had been married almost twenty-five years and had several children. The defendant testified that her husband had started drinking and abusing her about five years after they were married. His physical abuse of her consisted of frequent assaults that included slapping, punching and kicking her, striking her with various objects, and throwing glasses, beer bottles and other objects at her. The defendant described other specific incidents of abuse, such as her husband putting her cigarettes out on her, throwing hot coffee on her, breaking glass against her face and crushing food on her face. Although the defendant did not present evidence of ever having received medical treatment for any physical injuries inflicted by her husband, she displayed several scars about her face which she attributed to her husband's assaults.

The defendant's evidence also tended to show other indignities inflicted upon her by her husband. Her evidence tended to show that her husband did not work and forced her to make money by prostitution, and that he made humor of that fact to family and friends. He would beat her if she resisted going out to prostitute herself or if he was unsatisfied with the amounts of money she made. He routinely called the defendant "dog," "bitch" and "whore," and on a few occasions made her eat pet food out of the pets' bowls and bark like a dog. He often made her sleep on the floor. At times, he deprived her of food and refused to let her get food for the family. During those years of abuse, the defendant's husband threatened numerous times to kill her and to maim her in various ways.

The defendant said her husband's abuse occurred only when he was intoxicated, but that he would not give up drinking. She said she and her husband "got along very well when he was sober," and that he was "a good guy" when he was not drunk. She had accompanied her husband to the local mental health center for sporadic counseling sessions for his problem, but he continued to drink.

In the early morning hours on the day before his death, the defendant's husband, who was intoxicated, went to a rest area off I-85 near Kings Mountain where the defendant was engaging in prostitution and assaulted her. While driving home, he was stopped by a patrolman and jailed on a charge of driving while impaired. After the defendant's mother got him out of jail at the defendant's request later that morning, he resumed his drinking and abuse of the defendant.

The defendant's evidence also tended to show that her husband seemed angrier than ever after he was released from jail and that his abuse of the defendant was more frequent. That evening, sheriff's deputies were called to the Norman residence, and the defendant complained that her husband had been beating her all day and she could not take it anymore. The defendant was advised to file a complaint, but she said she was afraid her husband would kill her if she had him arrested. The deputies told her they needed a warrant before they could arrest her husband, and they left the scene.

The deputies were called back less than an hour later after the defendant had taken a bottle of pills. The defendant's husband cursed her and called her names as she was attended by paramedics, and he told them to let her die. A sheriff's deputy finally chased him back into his house as the defendant was put into an ambulance. The defendant's stomach was pumped at the local hospital, and she was sent home with her mother.

While in the hospital, the defendant was visited by a therapist with whom she discussed filing charges against her husband and having him committed for treatment. Before the therapist left, the defendant agreed to go to the mental health center the next day to discuss those possibilities. The therapist testified at trial that the defendant seemed depressed in the hospital, and that she expressed considerable anger toward her husband. He testified that the defendant threatened a number of times that night to kill her husband and that she said she should kill

him "because of the things he had done to her."

The next day, the day she shot her husband, the defendant went to the mental health center to talk about charges and possible commitment, and she confronted her husband with that possibility. She testified that she told her husband later that day: "J. T., straighten up. Quit drinking. I'm going to have you committed to help you." She said her husband then told her he would "see them coming" and would cut her throat before they got to him.

The defendant also went to the social services office that day to seek welfare benefits, but her husband followed her there, interrupted her interview and made her go home with him. He continued his abuse of her, threatening to kill and to maim her, slapping her, kicking her, and throwing objects at her. At one point, he took her cigarette and put it out on her, causing a small burn on her upper torso. He would not let her eat or bring food into the house for their children.

That evening, the defendant and her husband went into their bedroom to lie down, and he called her a "dog" and made her lie on the floor when he lay down on the bed. Their daughter brought in her baby to leave with the defendant, and the defendant's husband agreed to let her baby-sit. After the defendant's husband fell asleep, the baby started crying and the defendant took it to her mother's house so it would not wake up her husband. She returned shortly with the pistol and killed her husband.

The defendant testified at trial that she was too afraid of her husband to press charges against him or to leave him. She said that she had temporarily left their home on several previous occasions, but he had always found her, brought her home and beaten her. Asked why she killed her husband, the defendant replied: "Because I was scared of him and I knowed when he woke up, it was going to be the same thing, and I was scared when he took me to the truck stop that night it was going to be worse than he had ever been. I just couldn't take it no more. There ain't no way, even if it means going to prison. It's better than living in that. That's worse hell than anything."

The defendant and other witnesses testified that for years her husband had frequently threatened to kill her and to maim her. When asked if she believed those threats, the defendant replied: "Yes. I believed him he would, he would kill me if he got a chance. If he thought he wouldn't a had to went to jail, he would a done it."

Two expert witnesses in forensic psychology and psychiatry who examined the defendant after the shooting, Dr. William Tyson and Dr. Robert Rollins, testified that the defendant fit the profile of battered wife syndrome. This condition, they testified, is characterized by such abuse and degradation that the battered wife comes to believe she is unable to help herself and cannot expect help from anyone else. She believes that she cannot escape the complete control of her husband and that he is invulnerable to law enforcement and other sources of help.

Dr. Tyson, a psychologist, was asked his opinion as to whether, on 12 June 1985, "it appeared reasonably necessary for Judy Norman to shoot J. T. Norman?" He replied: "I believe that... Mrs. Norman believed herself to be doomed... to a life of the worst kind of torture and abuse, degradation that she had experienced over the years in a progressive way that it would only get worse, and that death was inevitable...." Dr. Tyson later added:

"I think Judy Norman felt that she had no choice, both in the protection of herself and her family, but to engage, exhibit deadly force against Mr. Norman, and that in so doing, she was sacrificing herself, both for herself and for her family."

Dr. Rollins, who was the defendant's attending physician at Dorothea Dix Hospital when she was sent there for evaluation, testified that in his opinion the defendant was a typical abused spouse and that "[s]he saw herself as powerless to deal with the situation, that there was no alternative, no way she could escape it." Dr. Rollins was asked his opinion as to whether "on June 12th, 1985, it appeared reasonably necessary that Judy Norman would take the life of J. T. Norman?" Dr. Rollins replied that in his opinion, "that course of action did appear necessary to Mrs. Norman."

Based on the evidence that the defendant exhibited battered wife syndrome, that she believed she could not escape her husband nor expect help from others, that her husband had threatened her, and that her husband's abuse of her had worsened in the two days preceding his death, the Court of Appeals concluded that a jury reasonably could have found that her killing of her husband was justified as an act of perfect self-defense. The Court of Appeals reasoned that the nature of battered wife syndrome is such that a jury could not be precluded from finding the defendant killed her husband lawfully in perfect self-defense, even though he was asleep when she killed him. We disagree.

The right to kill in self-defense is based on the necessity, real or reasonably apparent, of killing an unlawful aggressor to save oneself from imminent death or great bodily harm at his hands. *State v. Gappins*, 320 N.C. 64, 357 S.E. 2d 654

(1987). Our law has recognized that self-preservation under such circumstances springs from a primal impulse and is an inherent right of natural law. *State v. Holland*, 193 N.C. 713, 718, 138 S.E. 8, 10 (1927).

In North Carolina, a defendant is entitled to have the jury consider acquittal by reason of perfect self-defense when the evidence, viewed in the light most favorable to the defendant, tends to show that at the time of the killing it appeared to the defendant and she believed it to be necessary to kill the decedent to save herself from imminent death or great bodily harm. *State v. Gappins*, 320 N.C. at 71, 357 S.E. 2d at 659. That belief must be reasonable, however, in that the circumstances as they appeared to the defendant would create such a belief in the mind of a person of ordinary firmness. Further, the defendant must not have been the initial aggressor provoking the fatal confrontation. A killing in the proper exercise of the right of perfect self-defense is always completely justified in law and constitutes no legal wrong.

Our law also recognizes an imperfect right of self-defense in certain circumstances, including, for example, when the defendant is the initial aggressor, but without intent to kill or to seriously injure the decedent, and the decedent escalates the confrontation to a point where it reasonably appears to the defendant to be necessary to kill the decedent to save herself from imminent death or great bodily harm. *State v. Mize*, 316 N.C. 48, 340 S.E. 2d 439 (1986); *State v. Wilson*, 304 N.C. 689, 285 S.E. 2d 804 (1982). Although the culpability of a defendant who kills in the exercise of imperfect self-defense is reduced, such a defendant is not justified in the killing so as to be entitled to acquittal, but is guilty at least of voluntary manslaughter. *State v. Mize*, 316 N.C. at 52, 340 S.E. 2d at 441.

The defendant in the present case was not entitled to a jury instruction on either perfect or imperfect self-defense. The trial court was not required to instruct on either form of self-defense unless evidence was introduced tending to show that at the time of the killing the defendant reasonably believed herself to be confronted by circumstances which necessitated her killing her husband to save herself from imminent death or great bodily harm. No such evidence was introduced in this case, and it would have been error for the trial court to instruct the jury on either perfect or imperfect self-defense.

The jury found the defendant guilty only of voluntary manslaughter in the present case. As we have indicated, an instruction on imperfect self-defense would have entitled the defendant to nothing more, since one who kills in the exercise of imperfect self-defense is guilty at least of voluntary manslaughter. Therefore, even if it is assumed *arguendo* that the defendant was entitled to an instruction on imperfect self-defense—a notion we have specifically rejected—the failure to give such an instruction was harmless in this case. Accordingly, although we recognize that the imminence requirement applies to both types of self-defense for almost identical reasons, we limit our consideration in the remainder of this opinion to the issue of whether the trial court erred in failing to instruct the jury to consider acquittal on the ground that the killing was justified and, thus, lawful as an act of perfect self-defense.

The killing of another human being is the most extreme recourse to our inherent right of self-preservation and can be justified in law only by the utmost real or apparent necessity brought about by the decedent. For that reason, our law of self-defense has required that a defendant claiming that a homicide was justified and, as a result, inherently lawful by reason of perfect self-defense must establish that she reasonably believed at the time of the killing she otherwise would have immediately suffered death or great bodily harm. Only if defendants are required to show that they killed due to a reasonable belief that death or great bodily harm was imminent can the justification for homicide remain clearly and firmly rooted in necessity. The imminence requirement ensures that deadly force will be used only where it is necessary as a last resort in the exercise of the inherent right of self-preservation. It also ensures that before a homicide is justified and, as a result, not a legal wrong, it will be reliably determined that the defendant reasonably believed that absent the use of deadly force, not only would an unlawful attack have occurred, but also that the attack would have caused death or great bodily harm. The law does not sanction the use of deadly force to repel simple assaults.

The term "imminent," as used to describe such perceived threats of death or great bodily harm as will justify a homicide by reason of perfect self-defense, has been defined as "immediate danger, such as must be instantly met, such as cannot be guarded against by calling for the assistance of others or the protection of the law." Black's Law Dictionary 676 (5th ed. 1979). Our cases have sometimes used the phrase "about to suffer" interchangeably with "imminent" to describe the immediacy of threat that is required to justify killing in self-defense.

The evidence in this case did not tend to show that the defendant reasonably believed that she was confronted by a threat of imminent death or great bodily harm. The evidence tended to show that no harm was "imminent" or about to happen to the defendant when she shot her husband. The uncontroverted evidence was that her husband had been asleep for some time when she walked to her mother's house, returned with the pistol, fixed the pistol after it jammed and then shot her husband three times in the back of the head. The defendant was not faced with an instantaneous choice between killing her husband or being killed or seriously injured. Instead, all of the evidence tended to show that the defendant had ample time and opportunity to resort to other means of preventing further abuse by her husband. There was no action underway by the decedent from which the jury could have found that the defendant had reasonable grounds to believe either that a felonious assault was imminent or that it might result in her death or great bodily injury. Additionally, no such action by the decedent had been underway immediately prior to his falling asleep.

Faced with somewhat similar facts, we have previously held that a defendant who believed himself to be threatened by the decedent was not entitled to a jury instruction on either perfect or imperfect self-defense when it was the defendant who went to the decedent and initiated the final, fatal confrontation. *State v. Mize*, 316 N.C. 48, 340 S.E. 2d 439 (1986). In *Mize*, the decedent Joe McDonald was reported to be looking for the defendant George Mize to get revenge for Mize's alleged rape of McDonald's girl friend, which had exacerbated existing animosity between Mize and McDonald. After hiding from McDonald for most of the day, Mize finally went to McDonald's residence, woke him up and then shot and killed him. Mize claimed that he feared McDonald was going to kill him and that his killing of McDonald was in self-defense. Rejecting Mize's argument that his jury should have been instructed on self-defense, we stated:

Here, although the victim had pursued defendant during the day approximately eight hours before the killing, defendant Mize was in no imminent danger while McDonald was at home asleep. When Mize went to McDonald's trailer with his shotgun, it was a new confrontation. Therefore, even if Mize believed it was necessary to kill McDonald to avoid his own imminent death, that belief was unreasonable.

The same reasoning applies in the present case.

Additionally, the lack of any belief by the defendant—reasonable or otherwise —that she faced a threat of imminent death or great bodily harm from the drunk and sleeping victim in the present case was illustrated by the defendant and her own expert witnesses when testifying about her subjective assessment of her situation at the time of the killing. The psychologist and psychiatrist replied affirmatively when asked their opinions of whether killing her husband "appeared reasonably necessary" to the defendant at the time of the homicide. That testimony spoke of no imminent threat nor of any fear by the defendant of death or great bodily harm, imminent or otherwise. Testimony in the form of a conclusion that a killing "appeared reasonably necessary" to a defendant does not tend to show all that must be shown to establish self-defense. More specifically, for a killing to be in self-defense, the perceived necessity must arise from a reasonable fear of imminent death or great bodily harm.

Dr. Tyson additionally testified that the defendant "believed herself to be doomed... to a life of the worst kind of torture and abuse, degradation that she had experienced over the years in a progressive way that it would only get worse, and that death was inevitable." Such evidence of the defendant's speculative beliefs concerning her remote and indefinite future, while indicating she had felt generally threatened, did not tend to show that she killed in the belief—reasonable or otherwise—that her husband presented a threat of imminent death or great bodily harm. Under our law of self-defense, a defendant's subjective belief of what might be "inevitable" at some indefinite point in the future does not equate to what she believes to be "imminent." Dr. Tyson's opinion that the defendant believed it was necessary to kill her husband for "the protection of herself and her family" was similarly indefinite and devoid of time frame and did not tend to show a threat or fear of imminent harm.

The defendant testified that, "I knowed when he woke up, it was going to be the same thing, and I was scared when he took me to the truck stop that night it was going to be worse than he had ever been." She also testified, when asked if she believed her husband's threats: "Yes.... [H]e would kill me if he got a chance. If he thought he wouldn't a had to went to jail, he would a done it." Testimony about such indefinite fears concerning what her sleeping husband might do at some time in the future did not tend to establish a fear—reasonable or otherwise—of imminent death or great bodily harm at the time of the killing.

We are not persuaded by the reasoning of our Court of Appeals in this case that when there is evidence of battered wife syndrome, neither an actual attack nor threat of attack by the husband at the moment the wife uses deadly force is required to justify the wife's killing of him in perfect self-defense. The Court of Appeals concluded that to impose such requirements would ignore the "learned helplessness," meekness and other realities of battered wife syndrome and would effectively preclude such women from exercising their right of self-defense. 89 N.C. App. 384, 392–393, 366 S.E. 2d 586, 591–592 (1988). See Mather, The Skeleton in the Closet: The Battered Woman Syndrome, Self-Defense, and Expert Testimony, 39 Mercer L. Rev. 545 (1988); Eber, The Battered Wife's Dilemma: To Kill Or To Be Killed, 32 Hastings L.J. 895 (1981). Other jurisdictions which have addressed this question under similar facts are divided in their views, and we can discern no clear majority position on facts closely similar to those of this case.

The reasoning of our Court of Appeals in this case proposes to change the established law of self-defense by giving the term "imminent" a meaning substantially more indefinite and all-encompassing than its present meaning. This would result in a substantial relaxation of the requirement of real or apparent necessity to justify homicide. Such reasoning proposes justifying the taking of human life not upon the reasonable belief it is necessary to prevent death or great bodily harm—which the imminence requirement ensures—but upon purely subjective speculation that the decedent probably would present a threat to life at a future time and that the defendant would not be able to avoid the predicted threat.

The Court of Appeals suggests that such speculation would have been particularly reliable in the present case be-cause the jury, based on the evidence of the decedent's intensified abuse during the thirty-six hours preceding his death, could have found that the decedent's passive state at the time of his death was "but a momentary hiatus in a continuous reign of terror by the decedent [and] the defendant merely took advantage of her first opportunity to protect herself." 89 N.C. App. at 394, 366 S.E. 2d at 592. Requiring jury instructions on perfect self-defense in such situations, however, would still tend to make opportune homicide lawful as a result of mere subjective predictions of indefinite future assaults and circumstances. Such predictions of future assaults to justify the defendant's use of deadly force in this case would be entirely speculative, because there was no evidence that her husband had ever inflicted any harm upon her that approached life-threatening injury, even during the "reign of terror." It is far from clear in the defendant's poignant evidence that any abuse by the decedent had ever involved the degree of physical threat required to justify the defendant in using deadly force, even when those threats were imminent. The use of deadly force in self-defense to prevent harm other than death or great bodily harm is excessive as a matter of law. State v. Hunter, 315 N.C. 371, 338 S.E. 2d 99 (1986).

As we have stated, stretching the law of self-defense to fit the facts of this case would require changing the "imminent death or great bodily harm" requirement to something substantially more indefinite than previously required and would weaken our assurances that justification for the taking of human life remains firmly rooted in real or apparent necessity. That result in principle could not be limited to a few cases decided on evidence as poignant as this.

The relaxed requirements for perfect self-defense proposed by our Court of Appeals would tend to categorically legalize the opportune killing of abusive husbands by their wives solely on the basis of the wives' testimony concerning their subjective speculation as to the probability of future felonious assaults by their husbands. Homicidal self-help would then become a lawful solution, and perhaps the easiest and most effective solution, to this problem. See generally Rosen, The Excuse of Self-Defense: Correcting A Historical Accident on Behalf of Battered Women Who Kill, 36 Am. U.L. Rev. 11 (1986) (advocating changing the basis of self-defense acquittals to excuse rather than justification, so that excusing battered women's killing of their husbands under circumstances not fitting within the traditional requirements of self-defense would not be seen as justifying and therefore encouraging such self-help killing); Mitchell, Does Wife Abuse Justify Homicide?, 24 Wayne L. Rev. 1705 (1978) (advocating institutional rather than self-help solutions to wife abuse and citing case studies at the trial level where traditional defenses to homicide appeared stretched to accommodate poignant facts, resulting in justifications of some killings which appeared to be motivated by revenge rather than protection from death or great bodily harm).

It has even been suggested that the relaxed requirements of self-defense found in what is often called the "battered woman's defense" could be extended in principle to any type of case in which a defendant testified that he or she subjectively believed that killing was necessary and proportionate to any perceived threat. Rosen, The Excuse of Self-Defense: Correcting A Historical Accident on Behalf of Battered Women Who Kill, 36 Am. U.L. Rev. 11, 44 (1986).

In conclusion, we decline to expand our law of self-defense beyond the limits of immediacy and necessity which have heretofore provided an appropriately narrow but firm basis upon which homicide may be justified and, thus, lawful by reason of perfect self-defense or upon which a defendant's culpability may be reduced by reason of imperfect self-defense. As we have shown, the evidence in this case did not entitle the defendant to jury instructions on either perfect or imperfect self-defense.

For the foregoing reasons, we conclude that the defendant's conviction for voluntary manslaughter and the trial court's judgment sentencing her to a six-year term of imprisonment were without error. Therefore, we must reverse the decision of the Court of Appeals which awarded the defendant a new trial.

Reversed.

NO

Harry C. Martin

DISSENTING OPINION OF HARRY C. MARTIN

Justice Martin dissenting.

At the outset it is to be noted that the peril of fabricated evidence is not unique to the trials of battered wives who kill. The possibility of invented evidence arises in all cases in which a party is seeking the benefit of self-defense. Moreover, in this case there were a number of witnesses other than defendant who testified as to the actual presence of circumstances supporting a claim of self-defense. This record contains no reasonable basis to attack the credibility of evidence for the defendant.

Likewise, the difficulty of rebutting defendant's evidence because the only other witness to many of the events is deceased is not unique to this type of case. This situation is also commonplace in cases in which self-defense is raised, although, again, in the case *sub judice* there was more than one surviving witness to such events. In considering the argument that the state is faced with a difficult burden in attempting to rebut evidence of which defendant is the only surviving witness, one must not overlook the law: the burden is always on the state to prove that the killing was intentional beyond a reasonable doubt. "Defendant may always rest ultimately on the weakness of the state's case and the state's failure to carry its burden of proof." *State v. Patterson*, 297 N.C. 247, 256, 254 S.E. 2d 604, 610 (1979).

At the heart of the majority's reasoning is its unsubstantiated concern that to find that the evidence presented by defendant would support an instruction on self-defense would "expand our law of self-defense beyond the limits of immediacy and necessity." Defendant does not seek to expand or relax the requirements of self-defense and thereby "legalize the opportune killing of allegedly abusive husbands by their wives," as the majority overstates. Rather, defendant contends that the evidence as gauged by the existing laws of self-defense is sufficient to require the submission of a self-defense instruction to the jury. The proper issue for this Court is to determine whether the evidence, viewed in the light most favorable to the defendant, was sufficient to require the trial court to instruct on the law of self-defense. I conclude that it was.

From *State of North Carolina v. Judy Ann Laws Norman*, 324 N.C. 253, 378 S.E.2d 8 (1989). Notes and some case citations omitted.

In every jury trial, it is the duty of the court to charge the jury on all substantial features of the case arising on the evidence, whether or not such instructions have been requested. All defenses presented by the defendant's evidence are substantial features of the case, even if that evidence contains discrepancies or is contradicted by evidence from the state. This rule reflects the principle in our jurisprudence that it is the jury, not the judge, that weighs the evidence.

A defendant is entitled to an instruction on self-defense when there is evidence, viewed in the light most favorable to the defendant, that these four elements existed at the time of the killing:

1. it appeared to defendant and he believed it to be necessary to kill the deceased in order to save himself from death or great bodily harm and
2. defendant's belief was reasonable in that the circumstances as they appeared to him at the time were sufficient to create such a belief in the mind of a person of ordinary firmness and
3. defendant was not the aggressor in bringing on the affray, i.e., he did not aggressively and willingly enter into the fight without legal excuse or provocation and
4. defendant did not use excessive force, i.e., did not use more force than was necessary or reasonably appeared to him to be necessary under the circumstances to protect himself from death or great bodily harm.

The first element requires that there be evidence that the defendant believed it was necessary to kill in order to protect herself from serious bodily harm or death; the second requires that the circumstances as defendant perceived

them were sufficient to create such a belief in the mind of a person of ordinary firmness. Both elements were supported by evidence at defendant's trial.

Evidence presented by defendant described a twenty-year history of beatings and other dehumanizing and degrading treatment by her husband. In his expert testimony a clinical psychologist concluded that defendant fit "and exceed[ed]" the profile of an abused or battered spouse, analogizing this treatment to the dehumanization process suffered by prisoners of war under the Nazis during the Second World War and the brainwashing techniques of the Korean War. The psychologist described the defendant as a woman incarcerated by abuse, by fear, and by her conviction that her husband was invincible and inescapable:

> Mrs. Norman didn't leave because she believed, fully believed that escape was totally impossible. There was no place to go. He, she had left before he had come and gotten her. She had gone to the Department of Social Services. He had come and gotten her. The law, she believed the law could not protect her no one could protect her, and I must admit, looking over the records, that there was nothing done that would contradict that belief. She fully believed that he was invulnerable to the law and to all social agencies that were available that nobody could withstand his power. As a result, there was no such thing as escape.

When asked if he had an opinion whether it appeared reasonably necessary for Judy Norman to shoot her husband, this witness responded:

> Yes.... I believe that in examining the facts of this case and examining the psychological data, that Mrs. Norman believed herself to be doomed ... to a life of the worst kind of torture and abuse,

degradation that she had experienced over the years in a progressive way that it would only get worse, and that death was inevitable death of herself, which was not such, I don't think was such an issue for her, as she had attempted to commit suicide, and in her continuing conviction of J. T. Norman's power over her, and even failed at that form of escape. I believe she also came to the point of beginning to fear for family members and her children, that were she to commit suicide that the abuse and the treatment that was heaped on her would be transferred onto them.

This testimony describes defendant's perception of circumstances in which she was held hostage to her husband's abuse for two decades and which ultimately compelled her to kill him. This testimony alone is evidence amply indicating the first two elements required for entitlement to an instruction on self-defense.

In addition to the testimony of the clinical psychologist, defendant presented the testimony of witnesses who had actually seen defendant's husband abuse her. These witnesses described circumstances that caused not only defendant to believe escape was impossible, but that also convinced them of its impossibility. Defendant's isolation and helplessness were evident in testimony that her family was intimidated by her husband into acquiescing in his torture of her. Witnesses also described defendant's experience with social service agencies and the law, which had contributed to her sense of futility and abandonment through the inefficacy of their protection and the strength of her husband's wrath when they failed. Where torture appears interminable and escape impossible, the belief that only the death of the oppressor can provide relief is reasonable in the mind of a person of

ordinary firmness, let alone in the mind of the defendant, who, like a prisoner of war of some years, has been deprived of her humanity and is held hostage by fear.

In *State v. Mize*, 316 N.C. 48, 53, 340 S.E. 2d 439, 442 (1986), this Court noted that if the defendant was in "no imminent danger" at the time of the killing, then his belief that it was necessary to kill the man who had pursued him eight hours before was unreasonable. The second element of self-defense was therefore not satisfied. In the context of the doctrine of self-defense, the definition of "imminent" must be informed by the defendant's perceptions. It is not bounded merely by measurable time, but by all of the facts and circumstances. Its meaning depends upon the assessment of the facts by one of "ordinary firmness" with regard to whether the defendant's perception of impending death or injury was so pressing as to render reasonable her belief that it was necessary to kill.

Evidence presented in the case *sub judice* revealed no letup of tension or fear, no moment in which the defendant felt released from impending serious harm, even while the decedent slept. This, in fact, is a state of mind common to the battered spouse, and one that dramatically distinguishes Judy Norman's belief in the imminence of serious harm from that asserted by the defendant in *Mize*. Psychologists have observed and commentators have described a "constant state of fear" brought on by the cyclical nature of battering as well as the battered spouse's perception that her abuser is both "omnipotent and unstoppable." See Comment, The Admissibility of Expert Testimony on the Battered Woman Syndrome in Support of a Claim of Self-Defense, 15 Conn. L. Rev. 121, 131 (1982). Constant fear means a perpetual anticipation of the next blow, a perpetual expectation that the next blow will kill. "[T]he battered wife is constantly in a heightened state of terror because she is certain that one day her husband will kill her during the course of a beating.... Thus from the perspective of the battered wife, the danger is constantly 'immediate.'" Eber, The Battered Wife's Dilemma: To Kill or To Be Killed, 32 Hastings L.J. 895, 928–29 (1981). For the battered wife, if there is no escape, if there is no window of relief or momentary sense of safety, then the next attack, which could be the fatal one, is imminent. In the context of the doctrine of self-defense, "imminent" is a term the meaning of which must be grasped from the defendant's point of view. Properly stated, the second prong of the question is not whether the threat was in fact imminent, but whether defendant's belief in the impending nature of the threat, given the circumstances as she saw them, was reasonable in the mind of a person of ordinary firmness.

Defendant's intense fear, based on her belief that her husband intended not only to maim or deface her, as he had in the past, but to kill her, was evident in the testimony of witnesses who recounted events of the last three days of the decedent's life. This testimony could have led a juror to conclude that defendant reasonably perceived a threat to her life as "imminent," even while her husband slept. Over these three days, her husband's anger was exhibited in an unprecedented crescendo of violence. The evidence showed defendant's fear and sense of hopelessness similarly intensifying, leading to an unsuccessful attempt to escape through suicide and culminating in her belief that escape would be possible only through her husband's death.

Defendant testified that on 10 June, two days before her husband's death, he had again forced her to go to a rest stop near Kings Mountain to make money by prostitution. Her daughter Phyllis and Phyllis's boyfriend Mark Navarra accompanied her on this occasion because, defendant said, whenever her husband took her there, he would beat her. Phyllis corroborated this account. She testified that her father had arrived some time later and had begun beating her mother, asking how much money she had. Defendant said they all then drove off. Shortly afterwards an officer arrested defendant's husband for driving under the influence. He spent the night in jail and was released the next morning on bond paid by defendant's mother.

Defendant testified that her husband was argumentative and abusive all through the next day, 11 June. Mark Navarra testified that at one point defendant's husband threw a sandwich that defendant had made for him on the floor. She made another; he threw it on the floor, as well, then insisted she prepare one without touching it. Defendant's husband had then taken the third sandwich, which defendant had wrapped in paper towels, and smeared it on her face. Both Navarra and Phyllis testified that they had later watched defendant's husband seize defendant's cigarette and put it out on her neck, the scars from which defendant displayed to the jury.

A police officer testified that he arrived at defendant's home at 8:00 that evening in response to a call reporting a domestic quarrel. Defendant, whose face was bruised, was crying, and she told the officer that her husband had beaten her all day long and that she could not take it any longer. The officer told her that he could do nothing for her unless she took out a warrant on her husband. She responded that if she did, her husband would kill her. The officer left but was soon radioed to return because defendant had taken an overdose of pills. The officer testified that defendant's husband was interfering with ambulance attendants, saying "Let the bitch die." When he refused to respond to the officer's warning that if he continued to hinder the attendants, he would be arrested, the officer was compelled to chase him into the house.

Defendant's mother testified that her son-in-law had reacted to the discovery that her daughter had taken the pills with cursing and obscenities and threats such as, "Now, you're going to pay for taking those pills," and "I'll kill you, your mother and your grandmother." His rage was such that defendant's mother feared he might kill the whole family, and knowing defendant's sister had a gun in her purse, she took the gun and placed it in her own.

Defendant was taken to the hospital, treated, and released at 2:30 a.m. She spent the remainder of the night at her grandmother's house. Defendant testified that the next day, 12 June, she felt dazed all day long. She went in the morning to the county mental health center for guidance on domestic abuse. When she returned home, she tried to talk to her husband, telling him to "straighten up. Quit drinking.... I'm going to have you committed to help you." Her husband responded, "If you do, I'll see them coming and before they get here, I'll cut your throat."

Later, her husband made her drive him and his friend to Spartanburg to pick up the friend's paycheck. On the way, the friend testified, defendant's husband "started slapping on her" when she was following a truck too closely, and he periodically poured his beer into a glass, then reached over and poured it on defendant's head. At one point defendant's husband lay down on the front seat with his head on the arm rest, "like he was going to go to sleep," and kicked defendant, who was still driving, in the side of the head.

Mark Navarra testified that in the year and a half he had lived with the Normans, he had never seen defendant's husband madder than he was on 12 June, opining that it was the DUI arrest two days before that had ignited J.T.'s fury. Phyllis testified that her father had beaten her mother "all day long." She testified that this was the third day defendant's husband had forbidden her to eat any food. Phyllis said defendant's family tried to get her to eat, but defendant, fearing a beating, would not. Although Phyllis's grandmother had sent over a bag of groceries that day, defendant's husband had made defendant put them back in the bag and would not let anyone eat them.

Early in the evening of 12 June, defendant's husband told defendant, "Let's go to bed." Phyllis testified that although there were two beds in the room, her father had forbidden defendant from sleeping on either. Instead, he had made her lie down on the concrete floor between the two beds, saying, "Dogs don't lay in the bed. They lay in the floor." Shortly afterward, defendant testified, Phyllis came in and asked her father if defendant could take care of her baby while she went to the store. He assented and eventually went to sleep. Defendant was still on the floor, the baby on the small bed. The baby started to cry and defendant "snuck up and took him out there to [her] mother's [house]." She asked her mother to watch the baby, then asked if her mother had anything for a headache, as her head was "busting." Her mother responded that she had some pain pills in her purse. Defendant went in to get the pills, "and the gun was in there, and I don't know, I just seen the gun, and I took it out, and I went back there and shot him."

From this evidence of the exacerbated nature of the last three days of twenty years of provocation, a juror could conclude that defendant believed that her husband's threats to her life were viable, that serious bodily harm was imminent, and that it was necessary to kill her husband to escape that harm. And from this evidence a juror could find defendant's belief in the necessity to kill her husband not merely reasonable but compelling.

The third element for entitlement to an instruction on self-defense requires that there be evidence that the defendant was not the aggressor in bringing on the affray. If the defendant was the aggressor and killed with murderous intent, that is, the intent to kill or inflict serious bodily harm, then she is not entitled to an instruction on self-defense. *State v. Mize*, 316 N.C. 48, 340 S.E. 2d 439. A hiatus between provocation by the decedent and the killing can mark the initiation of a new confrontation between the defendant and the decedent, such that the defendant's earlier perception of imminent danger no longer appears reasonable and the defendant becomes the aggressor.

For example, in *Mize*, the defendant, who had been told the day before that the decedent was "out to get" him, went to the decedent's trailer with a shotgun, knocked on the front door, and hid under the steps when the decedent opened the door and asked who was there.

Defendant then went to the back door, knocked again, and shot the decedent. When the defendant went with his shotgun to the decedent's trailer, this Court said, it was a new confrontation, and if the defendant still believed that it was necessary to kill the decedent to avoid his own imminent death, that belief was unreasonable.

Where the defendant is a battered wife, there is no analogue to the victim-turned-aggressor, who, as in *Mize*, turns the tables on the decedent in a fresh confrontation. Where the defendant is a battered wife, the affray out of which the killing arises can be a continuing assault. There was evidence before the jury that it had not been defendant but her husband who had initiated "the affray," which the jury could have regarded as lasting twenty years, three days, or any number of hours preceding his death. And there was evidence from which the jury could infer that in defendant's mind the affray reached beyond the moment at which her husband fell asleep. Like the ongoing threats of death or great bodily harm, which she might reasonably have perceived as imminent, her husband continued to be the aggressor and she the victim.

Finally, the fourth element of self-defense poses the question of whether there was any evidence tending to show that the force used by defendant to repel her husband was not excessive, that is, more than reasonably appeared to be necessary under the circumstances. This question is answered in part by abundant testimony describing defendant's immobilization by fear caused by abuse by her husband. Three witnesses, including the decedent's best friend, all recounted incidents in which defendant passively accepted beatings, kicks, commands, or humiliating affronts without striking back. From such evidence that she was paralyzed by her husband's presence, a jury could infer that it reasonably appeared to defendant to be necessary to kill her husband in order ultimately to protect herself from the death he had threatened and from severe bodily injury, a foretaste of which she had already experienced.

In *State v. Wingler*, 184 N.C. 747, 115 S.E. 59 (1922), in which the defendant was found guilty for the murder of his wife, Justice (later Chief Justice) Stacy recognized the pain and oppression under which a woman suffers at the hands of an abusive husband: "The supreme tragedy of life is the immolation of woman. With a heavy hand, nature exacts from her a high tax of blood and tears." at 751, 115 S.E. at 61. By his barbaric conduct over the course of twenty years, J. T. Norman reduced the quality of the defendant's life to such an abysmal state that, given the opportunity to do so, the jury might well have found that she was justified in acting in self-defense for the preservation of her tragic life.

It is to be remembered that defendant does not have the burden of persuasion as to self-defense; the burden remains with the state to prove beyond a reasonable doubt that defendant intentionally killed decedent without excuse or justification. If the evidence in support of self-defense is sufficient to create a reasonable doubt in the mind of a rational juror whether the state has proved an intentional killing without justification or excuse, self-defense must be submitted to the jury. This is such a case.

POSTSCRIPT

Should "Battered Wife Syndrome" Be Barred as a Defense in a Murder Case?

This case presents not only a disagreement by the two judges, but a very graphic and disturbing description of a particular woman's plight over time. The Court focuses on whether a particular psychological condition, "battered wife syndrome," can be raised at trial to prove self-defense. The Court does not see its role as requiring it to get into the issue of what the authorities were doing during the years when the defendant was being battered.

Who is responsible for the lack of attention paid to this issue? One obvious answer is that sexism has colored the attitudes of many of those who are responsible for enforcing the law. It has been written, for example, that the seeds of wife beating lie in the subordination of females to male authority and control. This relationship between women and men has been institutionalized in the structure of the patriarchal family and is supported by economic, political, and religious systems that make such relationships seem natural, morally just, even sacred (Susan Brooks Thistlewaite, "Battered Women of the Bible: From Subjection to Liberation," *Christianity and Crisis,* p. 308 [November 2, 1981]).

The case you just read makes it clear that the law does not enforce itself. The police exercise a great deal of discretion in how to respond to a "domestic disturbance" and in whether or not to make an arrest. District attorneys have some discretion in what charges to file. Judges have discretion in what sentences to hand out. There are, in other words, numerous opportunities for biases and prejudices to creep into the enforcement process and shape it.

There is a long tradition of legal noninvolvement in "family matters." There is also a longstanding tendency among many to view victims as somehow deserving of their beatings and many have difficulty comprehending how it is possible for someone who has been beaten many times to continue to stay with their spouse. You might ask whether or not the following perspective is reflected in the first reading in this issue:

> They [are] both beaten and blamed for not ending their beatings. Told they have the freedom to leave a violent situation, they are blamed for the destruction of their family life. Free to live alone, they cannot expect equal pay for equal work. Encouraged to express their feelings, they are beaten when they express anger. They have the same inalienable right to the pursuit of happiness as men do, but they must make sure that their men's and children's rights are met first. They are blamed for not seeking help, yet when they do, they are advised to go home and stop the inappropriate behavior which causes their mate to hurt them. (Lenore Walker, *The Battered Woman,* p. 15 [1979])

Recommended readings on the issue of family violence include the following: Boland, "Battered Women Who Act Under Duress," 28 *New England Law Review* 603 (1994); M. Mahoney, "Legal Images of Battered Women: Redefining the Issue of Separation," 90 *Michigan Law Review* 1 (1990); F. McNulty, *The Burning Bed* (Bantam Books, 1980); A. Browne, *When Battered Women Kill* (Free Press, 1987); G. Walker, *Family Violence and the Women's Movement* (University of Toronto Press, 1990); E. Pleck, *The Making of American Social Policy Against Family Violence from Colonial Times to the Present* (Oxford University Press, 1987); L. Walker, *The Battered Woman* (Harper & Row, 1979); L. Dickstein and C. Nadelson, eds., *Family Violence: Emerging Issues of a National Crisis* (American Psychiatric Press, 1989); and L. Okun, *Woman Abuse: Facts Replacing Myth* (State University of New York Press, 1986).

ISSUE 15

Will Waiting Periods Control Gun Purchases?

YES: Sarah Brady, from Statement Before the Subcommittee on Crime, Committee on the Judiciary, U.S. House of Representatives (February 24, 1988)

NO: James Jay Baker, from Statement Before the Subcommittee on Crime and Criminal Justice, Committee on the Judiciary, U.S. House of Representatives (March 21, 1991)

ISSUE SUMMARY

YES: Sarah Brady, head of a citizens' lobby for gun control, argues that a waiting period for purchasing a weapon does not change who is lawfully allowed to buy a gun, that it would not impose an undue burden on law enforcement agencies, and that it would prevent many crimes.

NO: James Jay Baker, director of federal affairs for the National Rifle Association, claims that waiting periods do not work, that criminals would still be able to obtain weapons, and that an additional burden would be placed on law enforcement authorities.

Unlike previous assassinations or attempted assassinations, the attempt on former president Ronald Reagan's life in 1981 did not lead to a widespread debate about gun control. The issue that captured public discussion was the insanity defense raised by his would-be assassin, John Hinckley. Probably because Reagan opposed gun control legislation, Hinckley's act did little, at least at first, to further the cause of gun control on the federal level.

Much more seriously injured than Reagan was his press secretary, James Brady. As a result of the attempted assassination, gun control became a major concern of James and Sarah Brady. For many years, the Bradys lobbied in Congress for stronger gun control measures. Finally, in 1993, the Brady Bill was passed and went into effect in early 1994. The Bill provides for a mandatory waiting period before one can purchase a gun.

Can a measure such as the Brady Bill reduce illegal gun use and the violence associated with guns? Are more restrictive measures desirable, such as the regulation of the manufacture of weapons or a complete ban?

Both proponents and opponents of gun control come "armed" with statistics. Proponents point out that in Great Britain, where gun owners must be certified and their weapons stored at gun clubs, handguns killed only 22 people in 1990. In Australia, which requires a background check and a license to buy a handgun, they killed 10. In Japan, which bans most private ownership of handguns, they took 87 lives. In the United States, they killed 10,567. Yet, there are already over 200 million guns held by citizens, and regulation of sales will not really affect these weapons or their owners.

One of the most frequently mentioned legal justifications for permitting individuals to possess handguns is the Second Amendment to the Constitution. This amendment states, "A well regulated Militia, being necessary to the security of a free State, the right of the people to keep and bear Arms, shall not be infringed." Yet, due to court interpretations of the meaning of these words, the amendment has become almost irrelevant to the issue of gun control. Certainly, one convicted of violating a firearms statute is unlikely to win his or her case by relying on the Second Amendment.

Although many people are familiar with the last half of the amendment, the crucial words are contained in the first part. The right to bear arms is not absolute. Rather, it is a right related to the need for a state militia. This was the ruling of the Supreme Court in the case of *United States v. Miller*, 307 U.S. 174 (1939), the only case interpreting the Second Amendment as it relates to the federal government. In that case, two men were charged in federal court with transporting an unregistered sawed-off shotgun and violating the National Firearms Act. The defendants claimed that they were protected by the Second Amendment and won in the trial court. The Supreme Court, however, interpreted the rights granted by the Second Amendment differently. Justice James C. McReynolds wrote,

> In the absence of any evidence tending to show that possession or use of a "shotgun having a barrel of less than eighteen inches in length" at this time has some reasonable relationship to the preservation or efficiency of a well regulated militia, we cannot say that the Second Amendment guarantees the right to keep and bear such an instrument....
>
> The Constitution as originally adopted granted to the Congress power—"To provide for calling forth the Militia to execute the Laws of the Union, suppress Insurrections and repel Invasions."... With obvious purpose to assure the continuation and render possible the effectiveness of [the Militia] the declaration and guarantee of the Second Amendment were made. It must be interpreted and applied with that end in view.

In the following selections, Sarah Brady, wife of James Brady and a gun control lobbyist, argues for legislation to institute a waiting period for the purchase of guns. James Jay Baker, of the National Rifle Association, opposes such legislation and contends that waiting periods are ineffective in achieving their stated purposes and are not a good idea.

YES

Sarah Brady

STATEMENT OF SARAH BRADY

Thank you for the opportunity to testify once again before this distinguished Subcommittee. My name is Sarah Brady. I am Vice-Chair of Handgun Control, Inc., a national citizens organization working to keep handguns out of the wrong hands. I am here today in strong support of H.R. 975, introduced by Representative Edward Feighan.... This legislation establishes a seven-day waiting period and allows for a background check on handgun purchasers.

Having previously testified before this Subcommittee, I know many of you are familiar with my personal experience and my involvement with this issue. It seems odd to me that it is in question whether we should act to keep handguns out of the wrong hands. For that is what this debate is about —whether we allow convicted felons to simply walk into gun stores and immediately walk out with handguns.

We already have a federal law prohibiting convicted felons, minors, people who have been adjudicated mentally ill, illegal aliens, and drug addicts from acquiring handguns. But what does that mean if we do not have the tools to enforce that law? And so I ask you today, do you believe that a convicted felon should be able to walk into a gun store and get a handgun instantly? I cannot believe that anyone could sanction that. Yet as long as we do not have a reasonable waiting period and give police the opportunity to run background checks, a convicted felon will have our seal of approval. That is why I am here today. I am making a very personal appeal to you because I believe you have a responsibility to act to keep handguns out of the hands which would misuse them. Handguns in the wrong hands result in tragedy. I do not say that theoretically. I speak from experience.

I know that you are familiar with what happened on March 30, 1981. At 2:30 P.M. that day, my husband, Jim Brady, was shot through the head by a deranged young man. Jim nearly died. The President nearly died, and two of his security men were seriously wounded.

It has been almost seven years now. March 30th marks the anniversary of the shooting. I often think about the other handgun tragedies which have taken place in these seven years that could have been prevented if there were a national waiting period. We must not wait another seven years for other

From U.S. House of Representatives. Committee on the Judiciary. Subcommittee on Crime. *In Support of H.R. 975*. Hearing, February 24, 1988. Washington, DC: Government Printing Office, 1988.

tragedies to occur. We must not wait any longer. We need a national waiting period now.

John Hinckley's handguns were confiscated in October 1980 as he tried to board an airplane in Tennessee, where he was stalking President Jimmy Carter. Hinckley, a drifter, then gunless, needed to replenish his arsenal. In possession of a Texas driver's license and knowing that Texas had no waiting period or background check, Hinckley made the trip to Dallas to purchase the handgun he used to shoot my husband and the President of the United States. Hinckley no longer lived at the address he listed on the federal form he was required to complete. A simple check might have stopped him. Had police been given an opportunity to discover that Hinckley lied on the federal form, Hinckley might well have been in jail instead of on his way to Washington. Now Jim lives daily with the consequence of Hinckley's easy access to a handgun.

This bill does not change who is legally permitted to purchase a handgun. Nor does it impose a major burden on law-abiding citizens. This legislation also provides that if an individual has a legitimate, immediate need for a handgun, the waiting period can be waived by local law enforcement. Is seven days too much to ask a responsible citizen to wait when we know that so many lives are at stake? I don't think so.

Public support for a waiting period and background check is strong. A 1981 Gallup Poll found that more than 90% of Americans want such a law. This legislation is supported by every major law enforcement organization in the nation, many representatives of which are here today to testify in support of this bill. The American Bar Association, the American Medical Association, the AFL-CIO, and other organizations too numerous to mention, all support a federal seven-day waiting period. The 1981 Reagan Administration Task Force on Violent Crime recommended such a law. A 1985 Justice Department report states that "at minimum, the acquisition of a firearm by a felon should be somewhat more complicated than just walking into a gun shop and buying one."

While the National Rifle Association opposes this bill, it is important to note that several years ago in its own publication, the NRA stated that a waiting period would be effective as a means of "reducing crimes of passion and in preventing people with criminal records or dangerous mental illness from acquiring guns."

The NRA has flip-flopped on waiting periods and recently taken extreme positions on machine guns, cop-killer bullets, and plastic guns. Considering these extreme positions, I find it incomprehensible that any Member of Congress could trust the judgment of the NRA on a national waiting period or any legislation affecting American lives and public safety, especially when the NRA is in direct opposition to America's law enforcement community which is charged with the responsibility of protecting us.

The NRA argues that proscribed persons do not purchase their handguns over the counter and certainly will not do so if they have to submit to a waiting period. Yet, a 1985 Department of Justice study entitled "The Armed Criminal in America" found that over 20 percent of criminals obtain their handguns through gun dealers. In fact, in states with waiting period laws, many criminals and others disqualified from buying handguns have been caught trying to purchase their handguns over the counter. Law enforcement officials from across the nation report tremendous success where waiting periods are in effect.

For example, according to a police official in Memphis, Tennessee, the state's fifteen-day waiting period screens out about 50 applicants a month, most of whom have criminal records.

According to the California Department of Justice, the state's fifteen-day waiting period screened out more than 1500 prohibited handgun purchasers in 1986. In that same year, Maryland's seven-day waiting period caught more than 700 prohibited handgun buyers.

States with waiting periods have been effective in stopping criminals before tragedy occurs, but it is unfortunate that in states without waiting periods or background checks, police do not have the same tools to prevent such tragedy.

One of the most shocking and disturbing cases of 1987 occurred in Florida in the wake of the October stock market crash. Arthur Kane purchased a handgun only forty-five minutes before murdering his Florida stock broker and wounding another. If police had been able to conduct a background check, they could have discovered that Kane was a convicted felon.

In another well-publicized event, Dwain Wallace, who had a history of mental illness, was able to instantly purchase a handgun from a Youngstown, Ohio pawnshop. Just two days later, he brandished the handgun in the Pentagon and was immediately gunned down by a Pentagon guard.

A convicted felon, Larry Dale, purchased a handgun at a Tulsa, Oklahoma gun shop, and within 24 hours opened fire at a grocery store, killing one customer and wounding another.

I have described a few of the many well-known cases of proscribed persons who instantly purchased their handguns over the counter without having to undergo a waiting period or background check. But for each well-known case, there are many, many more which never make the front page.

While I am not suggesting that a waiting period will stop all crime, it is obvious from these examples that we can save many lives if we want to.

The NRA claims that waiting periods do not prevent criminals from obtaining handguns because criminals will get them from other sources. But in reality, it is the states without waiting periods that are a significant source of handguns for criminals.

The Treasury's Bureau of Alcohol, Tobacco and Firearms' study of handguns used in crime found that of all the handguns used in crime in New York City, only four percent were purchased in New York State which requires a background check. Virtually all the rest were from states without waiting periods or background checks. In addition, the study found that in states without waiting periods or background checks, an overwhelming majority of handguns used in crime were purchased within the same state. For example, of all the handguns used in crime in Dallas, almost 90 percent were purchased in Texas which has no waiting period.

The NRA argues that waiting periods should be left up to the states, not the federal government. While individual states, many counties and municipalities have passed local waiting periods, a national law is critical because it will ensure that handguns are not purchased over the counter in states without waiting periods and then sold on the street in states requiring waiting periods and/or background checks.

I am ashamed that my own state of Virginia, which has no waiting period or background check, is a major source of handguns used in crime elsewhere. Just a few weeks ago, police arrested one Richmond man who reportedly purchased more than seventy guns in Virginia and then brought them into Washington, D.C. to sell on the street. Another man from the District was charged with using false identification, purchasing more than two dozen semi-automatic handguns in Virginia and selling them to District drug dealers. Unfortunately, these examples represent only the tip of the iceberg of this criminal traffic in handguns.

We can prevent needless tragedy. We can make it more difficult for criminals to get handguns. I hope that the day will come when no American family has to go through what my family has suffered. Again I ask, do you really believe that a convicted felon should be able to walk into a gun store and instantly purchase a handgun? The American people do not believe that. But until action is taken on this bill, a convicted felon purchasing a handgun will have our seal of approval.

The NRA would like to turn back the clock to the days before passage of the 1968 Gun Control Act, which has served our nation well for nearly two decades....

I ask that you stand with our law enforcement community and provide the leadership that will save lives by keeping handguns out of the wrong hands.

NO

STATEMENT OF JAMES JAY BAKER

Mr. Chairman, I am here today as the Representative of the National Rifle Association of America to comment on H.R. 7, the "Brady Handgun Violence Prevention Act." H.R. 7 is virtually identical to legislation the NRA opposed in the 101st Congress. The reason for our opposition is based on an objective analysis of the facts, which when stripped of the emotionalism and sentimentality which has almost completely overshadowed the reality of this issue, indicate that imposing further restrictions on the firearms ownership rights of law-abiding citizens will not only be ineffective, but counter-productive to the stated goals of its proponents. We firmly believe the need for H.R. 7 to be unsubstantiated by circumstance, logic, or the form and factual content of the debate between responsible and criminal firearms ownership and is antithetical to the rights of every law-abiding citizen under the Bill of Rights.

Before proceeding to a more specific discussion of our substantive disagreements with the issues surrounding H.R. 7, the National Rifle Association Institute for Legislative Action (NRA-ILA) would like to, once again, attempt to lay to rest one of the linchpin myths used to argue in favor of a national waiting period and background check before purchase of a pistol or revolver. It is unfortunate that we must spend so much time belaboring this point; it is equally unfortunate that advocates of "gun control" continue to misrepresent the facts concerning the tragic assassination attempt on President Ronald Reagan.

In much of the propaganda produced in support of waiting periods, the allegation is made that, if such a waiting period/background check system had been in place, "John Hinckley would have been caught" because "he lied on a federal form" when he purchased the revolver used in his attack on President Reagan. It is further claimed that Hinckley "would have been in jail, instead of on his way to Washington, D.C." had such a background check been conducted. These allegations are irrefutably false.

John Hinckley purchased a total of eight firearms—two .38 cal. and four .22 cal. revolvers, as well as two rifles—from August 1979 to January 1981. The .22 cal. revolver used in his assault on President Reagan was one of two he purchased in October 1980, more than six months before he left for

From U.S. House of Representatives. Committee on the Judiciary. Subcommittee on Crime and Criminal Justice. Hearing, March 21, 1991. Washington, DC: Government Printing Office, 1991.

Washington, D.C. Federal law was so diligently complied with in this case by the seller that multiple purchase forms were quickly filed with the regional office of ATF after the purchase.

Indeed, this purchase, and all previous purchases, were legal. And they would have been legal under this or any other "waiting period" scheme ever devised. At the time of his purchase, and until his attack on the President, John Hinckley had no felony record, he had no recorded history of mental illness or commitment, (as no check currently involves police inspection of private conversations with a psychiatrist) and he was using a *valid* Texas driver's license issued May 23, 1979, to make this firearms purchases. The contention that a background check would have "uncovered" the fact that he did not physically reside at the address listed on his license is a willful distortion of the criminal record check made by local police. To the contrary, had a check been run and all criminal records been thorough and completely available, they would have confirmed that Hinckley was not a prohibited person and that his last known address was in Lubbock, Texas.

Simply put, no detection system ever proposed or ever devised has mindreading capabilities. Advocates of the waiting period do a gross disservice to the nation by asserting that the tragic assassination attempt on President Reagan would have been prevented by the imposition of any regulatory "gun control" scheme. I urge this Committee to look carefully at other arguments made by those who continue to make that claim citing the case of John Hinckley as evidence.

The long history of waiting period schemes points up the failure of those systems in other criminal justice areas, as well. Waiting periods, permit-to-

purchase laws, and police background checks have been instituted around the country for most of the century. After the 1911 Sullivan law in New York, many were enacted in the 1920's and 1930's, about the same time that Uniform Crime Reporting system was implemented to facilitate the collection of crime data from cities and states throughout the nation. Thus, criminologists and other scholars have had ample time and abundant evidence with which to study and document the effectiveness of a waiting period in deterring violent crime. The results are a damning indictment of those who propose to control crime by regulating the behavior of law-abiding members of the community.

In October 1975, Douglas R. Murray of the University of Wisconsin published "Handguns, Gun Control Laws and Firearms Violence." Using the standard statistical methods—a multiple regression statistical framework—he compared the various state firearms laws —including purchase permit, waiting period, police notification, retail license, minimum age, permit to carry openly, and permit to carry concealed—to crime rates, while considering socio-economic conditions. Murray found that "gun control laws have no significant effect on rates of violence beyond what can be attributed to background social conditions." Secondly, he found that such laws do not effectively limit access to guns by the violence-prone; and, finally, accessibility to handguns "seems to have no effect on rates of violent crime and firearms accidents, another reason why gun control laws are ineffective."

Murray summarized: "On the basis of these data, the conclusion is, inevitably, that gun control laws have no individual or collective effect in reducing the rates of violent crime."

Murray's study was replicated by a self-proclaimed "gun control" advocate, Professor Matthew DeZee at Florida State University. His conclusion? "The results indicate that not a single gun control law, and not all the gun control laws added together, had a significant impact... in determining gun violence. It appears, then, that present legislation created to reduce the level of violence in society falls far short of its goals... Gun laws do not appear to affect gun crimes." Keep in mind that the types of laws studied by these scholars were identical to the legislation before you today.

Another study was conducted by two professors at the California State University at Long Beach. Professors Joseph Maggaddino and Marshall Medoff studied "waiting periods" and "cooling-off" periods and found them to be totally useless in curbing crime. They found no relationship between a waiting period or cooling-off period and any type of violent crime, except that they noted a slightly higher homicide rate and a slightly higher robbery rate in places with such laws.

Currently, there are twenty-four states with waiting periods or permit to purchase regulations required for the purchase of a pistol or revolver. Additionally, there are scores of cities and counties that have their own restrictive systems of this type. Again, the majority of these systems have been in place for decades, giving criminologists such as Murray, DeZee, Maggaddino and Medoff ample opportunity to unearth any supposed efficacy these systems have. Likewise, there has existed more than sufficient data for evaluation by those who are represented by Handgun Control Incorporated (HCI).

We find that, despite a great deal of sympathy, albeit short-lived, in the academic community for the idea of restrictive waiting periods scholars have failed to discern any benefits of the waiting period concept. A few, notably Massachusetts Professor James D. Wright, have been honest enough to change their position on this issue after their research revealed the facts.

In keeping with this criminological evaluation, which actually served to confirm common sense, the trend in this nation has been more towards rolling back or repealing existing waiting periods for handguns at the state and local level. Some states with handgun waiting periods have confirmed gun owners fears, not to mention their initial predictions, by increasing the length of waiting periods and including rifles and shotguns under waiting period strictures. In fact, voters in many states and cities have chosen to defeat attempts at imposing or lengthening existing waiting periods. The story at the state level in the recent past is of pro-gun initiatives, such as preemption and constitutional right to keep and bear arms amendments, passing overwhelmingly in reflection of the public's support of lawful, private firearms ownership. Waiting period proponents may quote as many simplistic polls as they choose, but it is these votes by duly elected state legislators, that should be viewed as the turn gauge of public opinion. Clearly, public opinion reflected at the ballot box is running strong and hard *against* restrictive gun laws.

Preemption represents an implicit rejection of waiting periods and justifiable claim for supremacy of the state legislative process in setting firearms regulatory law. Currently, forty states have preempted the field in firearms legislation, claiming for the state legislature the sole responsibility over the regulation of firearms. In Representative Feighan's own state of Ohio, Mr. Chairman, waiting periods have died in the 114th, 115th, 116th, 117th, and 118th, General Assemblies.

One of the more glaring deficiencies of H.R. 7 is that it would impose an additional burden of liability on law enforcement, if not de jure than de facto, without addressing the major problem in conducting a nation wide felon check—namely the lack of accurate [information]. The Attorney Generals Task Force on Felon Identification indicates that given the current state of criminal record keeping among the fifty states it is simply impossible to conduct a thorough and accurate background check on an individual on a state level. More to the point, Attorney General Thornburgh has said that to the extent criminal records are available for checking, the information is available on virtually an instantaneous basis, and that nothing is gained from the imposition of a seven-day waiting period.

Given this information we believe it is appropriate to restate our strong support for the implementation of a National Instantaneous Felon Identification system as embodied in H.R. 1412, the "Felon Handgun Purchase Prevention Act". H.R. 1412 was recently introduced by Representative Staggers, a member of the Judiciary Committee. Modeled on the very successful Virginia Firearms Transaction Program, H.R. 1412 addresses several key points which H.R. 7 either does not address, or worse, exacerbates rather than resolves.

First, it must be noted that H.R. 7 specifically exempts those states from the seven day waiting period which have in place, or implement an instantaneous

check system. While we hardly consider this a definitive endorsement for H.R. 1412, it certainly obviates any argument that the proponents of H.R. 7 might make that such a system is ineffectual. To the contrary, an explicit endorsement of the superiority of H.R. 1412 has already been given by Handgun Control Inc. and Sarah Brady when testifying in support of the Virginia system. That same testimony indicated that they believe it is legislation which could be used as a "model" for the nation. We agree. Moreover, based on the experience that Virginia has had, an instantaneous check system could be put into place in a relatively short period of time and at a reasonable cost. A strong argument can be made that a national felon identification system accessed directly by firearms dealers would be significantly cheaper than H.R. 7. At the very least, it will help to free law enforcement departments from the increasingly onerous burden of paperwork which so sorely impacts crime-fighting abilities. Then, too, the spillover benefits of upgrading the current national records keeping system are obviously applicable to many other areas in which certifying the lack of a criminal background may be a prerequisite for employment suitability. These include, but are not limited to" child care functions, banking, the securities and exchange industry, transportation, and the private security industry.

We are certainly not suggesting that this information should be widely accessible. To the contrary, we believe that the release of any information whatsoever must be strictly regulated and conveyed only on a legitimate need to know basis. We further believe that the penalties for the unlawful use or dispersal of such information should be clearly defined, and sufficiently stringent to discourage abuse. However, there are obvious advantages for implementing a system which encourages the respective states to comply with felon record keeping and conveyance systems which are already in place but are either deficient or misutilized. . . .

One of the more obvious shortcomings of H.R. 7 is that it essentially mandates police compliance without enhancing capabilities. Although H.R. 7 does not specifically mandate a background check it does require law enforcement to sign off on all handgun purchases. Handgun Control Inc. has raised the threat of litigation against any law enforcement agency which approves the sale of a handgun on the basis of an incomplete or inaccurate background check from which subsequent harm would arise. In fact, in one of HCI's mass mailings they specifically cite a case in which a widow sued the City of Philadelphia and was awarded $350,000 as a result of a handgun sale which should not have been allowed. If H.R. 7 is enacted you can expect, at a minimum, that there will be a proliferation of litigation against law enforcement, regardless of the circumstances of the approval. As a result not only will there by every incentive to do an extensive background check on every individual when possible, there will also be every incentive for police departments to delay or deny a purchase for as long as possible when available information is incomplete. Again, the result of this will be that numerous suits will, no doubt, be brought against law enforcement agencies by those individuals who are denied lawful possession of their firearm after the seven day period has elapsed.

. . . [O]ne of the oft repeated questions asked in some form to most members of this Committee at some time or another,

is "Why can't an individual wait seven days to purchase a handgun?" The obvious response is another question, "Why should a law-abiding citizen be denied a constitutional right?" There is no comparable waiting restriction levied on any of the other amendments, nor an unsupported invalidation or restriction placed on any other right based on an unsubstantiated presumption of guilt. By accepting other than the minimum criteria necessary to insure that those whom society has judged to be, by circumstances or behavior, unsuitable or in forfeiture of the legitimate exercise of the rights ordained by our Constitution, the American people will have adulterated and diminished not only their Second Amendment rights, but all other Constitutional protection in turn. Because H.R. 1412 provides for, essentially, the instant exercise of a constitutional right in keeping with the overall philosophy of the Founding Fathers, there is little question that it most clearly satisfies both the spirit and the letter of the Constitution. H.R. 7 fulfills neither criteria.

However, to specifically address the suitability of giving law enforcement the means to preclude an individual from taking possession of a handgun for a period of seven days, even were such a period necessary or desirable, highlights perhaps the most egregious, and in isolation, fatal flaw in H.R. 7. H.R. 7 specifically requires a firearms dealer to convey to local law enforcement the purchase request filled out by the customer within 24 hours. Yet, nowhere in H.R. 7 is there a similar mandate defined for law enforcement to return a purchaser's application to the gun store owner within the seven day time period the bill's supporters suppose to be reasonable, or penalty if law enforcement fails to do so. It takes but a small exercise of the imagination to envision the scenarios under which unreasonable delays well in excess of the seven day period could occur. Regardless, the effect will be that a law-abiding citizen will be precluded from taking possession of the firearm which he is lawfully entitled to own, and for which he may have imminent necessity or practical need.

H.R. 1412 is value neutral and specifically defines the rights of an individual and the responsibilities of the system. And, unlike H.R. 7, H.R. 1412 entails no needless infringement or proscription of individual constitutional rights based on the false assumption that firearms, and those who desire to possess them, are inherently deserving of societal suspicion. H.R. 1412 eliminates bias from the equation, H.R. 7 reinforces the circumstances under which biases can be exercised.

Perhaps the main reason there is no mandatory criminal records check by local law enforcement agencies is that those who support the concept embodied in H.R. 7 wish to have law enforcement support for the bill. Yet, a federal law which imposed duties on state and local law enforcement plainly might not be supported by state and local law enforcement; indeed, it might be actively opposed by them. Thus, the result is a bill which, by its express terms, "shall [not] be interpreted to require any action by a chief law enforcement officer which is not otherwise required." This places those in the law enforcement community who are supportive of any effort to prevent private acquisition and possession of firearms in a position where they can support legislation which appears to involve them in the acquisition process but which, in reality, requires them to do nothing.

Throughout its material, HCI misuses the word "caught" in reference to individuals denied lawful access to a handgun, for example, in saying that Columbus, Georgia or New Jersey police "catch" X number of convicted criminals under their system, or that Hinckley would "have been in jail instead of on his way to Washington." Rejection under the system does not equate with indictment, conviction, or incarceration for violation of firearms laws. In fact, our contacts with law enforcement around the country confirm that most individuals are not prosecuted, much less imprisoned, for violations of restrictive gun laws detected by background checks.

HCI's reference to New Jersey is especially interesting, in so far as it makes a stronger case against institution of their scheme than for its implementation. HCI alleged that New Jersey officials denied applications of "33,000 criminals." NRA-ILA and many others pointed out that, in fact, a majority of those rejections were not based on previous criminals records; that the system in question included applications for permits to carry a concealed firearm which are frequently denied solely because the issuing authority determines the "need" is insufficient; and that the system allowed denial based on the arbitrary and subjective standard that issuance would "not be in the interest of the public health, safety or welfare."

HCI has now apparently adopted a lower number of "rejections of criminals," by citing 10,000 most recently. But, according to the New Jersey State Police Firearm Licensing Division, this number is also misleading. The fact is that the "10,000" includes applicants rejected as drug addicts, for medical reasons: as alcoholics, for falsifying records and for the following three completely arbitrary reasons: "public health, safety and welfare; insufficient need, and, of course, other." The police officers we spoke with have completely rejected HCI's characterization of the denials, saying, "we don't keep records that way." This is hardly evidence of an efficient system weeding out criminals while protecting the rights of the law-abiding. And in the face of data showing that the level of firearms-related violent crime in New Jersey, has been rapidly rising, relative to the U.S. as a whole, it is obvious that the system is not preventing the criminal acquisition of firearms.

HCI then claims that the Chief of Police in Columbus, Georgia, believes their waiting period system to be working. NRA-ILA staff has followed up on this assertion and has found that the officers responsible for the waiting period system in Columbus do not share the Chief's view, as reported by HCI. In fact, HCI and/or the Chief appear to expand the level of rejections by more than four-fold. And again, denial does not necessarily indicate prevention of criminal acquisition of a firearm, nor does it relate to the level of violent crime in a community.

HCI also approvingly cites Memphis, Tennessee, and Atlanta, Georgia, as communities where restrictive gun laws are "working." They neglect to point out that those communities are two of the most crime-ridden within their respective states, and indeed within the South as a whole.

California's Attorney General may have been correct in his assessment of the effectiveness of their system in denying a constitutional right with frequency—even though the number of rejections which ultimately result from the California system given represents less than $1/2\%$ of the applicants—but that assertion is unrelated to any crime reductive effect. It should be noted that the homicide rate in California increased 126% as the state increased the length of its waiting period from 48 hours to 5 days to 15 days, even as the national rate rose by less than half as much.

HCI also misrepresents the Wright-Rossi felon study, conducted under a grant from the U.S. Department of Justice. That study found no difference in the methods of firearms acquisition by criminals regardless of the type of state "gun control" laws in place. Wright notes that criminals "obtain guns in hard-to-regulate sources... Swaps, purchases, and trades among private parties (friends and family members) represent the dominant pattern of acquisition within the illicit firearms market." HCI would have us believe that these private networks would suddenly dry up, or that they would suddenly participate in a law enforcement effort aimed at them.

Finally, it is instructive to once again note that waiting periods, police background checks, and permit-to-purchase systems have been in existence at the state and local level for most of this century. HCI alleges that these laws work, and contend that they have examples in x number of states and dozens, if not hundreds, of cities and counties. Yet when called upon to produce evidence of this efficacy, all that they can muster are three states and a few localities. And, upon further examination, even this scant "evidence" is usually found to be completely lacking, outright deceitful, or distorted beyond the recognition of truth.

Mr. Chairman, and members of the Subcommittee, I thank you once again for the opportunity to present the views of millions of NRA members on the legislation proposed here today, H.R. 7. The timely disposal of this proposal would free this Congress to address issues providing hope for real reductions in our nation's rate of violent crime, such as the implementation of the instantaneous handgun check system proposed by H.R. 1412, the streamlining of our criminal justice system and the imposition of swift and certain punishment for criminal offenders. Above all else we need to abandon the skewed logic of H.R. 7 and its ilk which mistakenly targets not the criminal elements in our society, but rather those who already obey the law. This is the wrong approach in the short term, and a long-term prescription for disaster. The Founding Fathers of our Nation sought to create a structure of government not to rule the individual, but rather that the individual might to the fullest extent possible be free to rule his own action. This is exactly why they were careful to specifically describe the inviolate rights of the first Ten Amendments to the U.S. Constitution apart from the restrictions which might be lawfully imposed under the general rubric of the preamble and body of the U.S. Constitution. H.R. 7 is inimical to these protections. Thank you.

POSTSCRIPT

Will Waiting Periods Control Gun Purchases?

The United States has about 20,000 gun control laws, the vast majority of which are state or local ordinances. There is considerable variation, therefore, from place to place. There have been several federal statutes enacted to control firearms in addition to the Brady Bill. The Federal Firearms Act of 1934 regulated possession of submachine guns, silencers, and several other weapons. In 1938 the National Firearms Act was passed, requiring the licensing of firearms manufacturers and dealers. As a result, all new weapons sold in the United States since 1938 have been registered and can be traced. The most important federal action was taken with the passage of the Gun Control Act of 1968. The act prohibited the interstate retailing of all firearms. Its purpose was to prevent individuals who cannot legally own a gun from ordering guns by mail under phony names.

There has been renewed attention to the issue of gun control lately as a result of rising drug-related violence and fear of violent crime generally. Is the Brady Bill merely a first step in a plan for a more comprehensive model of gun control? Or, if the Brady Bill does not have an impact on violent crime, will gun control legislation generally be perceived as unworkable?

Public opinion polls suggest that a majority of the public wants more regulation. Yet, membership in the National Rifle Association is also growing, and gun purchases are increasing. It is highly likely that gun control will continue to be an area of intense political conflict.

The power and influence of the National Rifle Association was recently examined in O. G. Davidson, *Under Fire: The NRA and the Battle for Gun Control* (1993). The meaning and history of the Second Amendment is discussed in Levinson, "The Embarrassing Second Amendment," 99 *Yale Law Journal* 637 (1989); Brown, "Guns, Cowboys, Philadelphia Mayors, and Civic Republicanism: On S. Levinson's 'The Embarrassing Second Amendment,'" 99 *Yale Law Journal* 661 (1989); Hardy, "Armed Citizens, Citizen Armies: Toward A Jurisprudence of the Second Amendment," 9 *Harvard Journal of Law and Public Policy* 559 (1986); and S. Halbrook, *That Every Man Be Armed* (University of New Mexico Press, 1984). Recent discussions of handgun regulation are contained in F. Zimring and G. Hawkins, *The Citizen's Guide to Gun Control* (Macmillan, 1987); J. Wright and P. Rossi, *Armed and Considered Dangerous* (Aldine De Gruyter, 1986); D. Kates, ed., *Firearms and Violence* (Pacific Institute for Public Policy Research, 1984); and Symposium, "Gun Control," *Law and Contemporary Problems* (vol. 46, 1986).

ISSUE 16

Does the Clipper Chip Give the Government Too Much Control Over Citizens' Privacy?

YES: Whitfield Diffie, from Statement Before the Subcommittee on Technology and the Law, Committee on the Judiciary, U.S. Senate (May 6, 1994)

NO: Stewart A. Baker, from "Why Clipper Is Good for You," *Wired* (June 1994)

ISSUE SUMMARY

YES: Computer scientist Whitfield Diffie argues that a governmental program to permit government to unlock encrypted communications will violate privacy and damage the ability of American businesses to compete in the international marketplace.

NO: Attorney Stewart Baker believes that the Clipper Chip proposal contains adequate safeguards to protect privacy and that the proposal does no more than preserve the power that law enforcement agencies have today.

New technologies have presented us with devices that appear to have come out of the literature of science fiction. We do not yet travel routinely in outer space, but computers are, in a sense, space machines, in that they allow us to acquire information from anywhere. We cannot "beam" individuals between home and office, but we do "beam" information between machines located in different parts of the globe. We cannot shrink people or objects but we can shrink information, in the sense that all of the words in this book can easily fit on an ordinary disk and an entire encyclopedia can be placed on a single CD-ROM (compact disk–read only memory). When computer networks move millions of bits of data in a second and when computers perform millions of operations per second, we find it possible to act, in a sense, as if we have been transported from one place to another.

Concern over privacy has existed since the early days of computers. The image of Big Brother in control of technology invading everyone's life has been with us since the 1948 publication of George Orwell's classic novel *1984*. (Orwell chose the year 1984 for the book's title by transposing the last two numbers in 1948.) Some of our fears about computers have come true. Others have not. For example, computers do not appear to support Orwellian-type political regimes. There is even reason to believe that the new communications technologies were instrumental in the collapse of the Soviet Union. States and many other large institutions are finding information more difficult to control than before, not less difficult. Our opportunities for expression have increased, and attempts by government to censor communication are often futile.

As will be explained in the following readings, the Clipper Chip and more recent proposals about digital communications arise out of a governmental concern that it is losing one of its weapons of law enforcement. Digital communications can be encrypted and, as a result, cannot be wiretapped. The Clipper Chip proposal requires that a computer chip be placed inside every digital communications device produced. The chip would encrypt all communications but the government would also have a key that could unlock the communication. The key would have two parts and would be held by two different organizations. This would ensure that no single individual could take the key and use it to invade privacy. Under the proposal, a court order, similar to the order the government must obtain for a wiretap, would be required. In addition, the Clinton administration's proposal would permit individuals to continue to use other encryption devices, if they chose to do so. This would guarantee that individuals could ensure that eavesdropping could not occur.

Privacy has been defined as the control of information about oneself. It is not surprising, therefore, that maintaining and protecting one's privacy has become difficult in an age when new technologies make it possible to obtain and process information in new ways, and when collecting data has become big business. Information about each of us is not simply stored somewhere but is often communicated to others who claim a need for such information. Encryption devices provide a means to ensure privacy in a world where privacy is increasingly difficult to achieve. Should government be trusted with the keys to our conversations? In the following readings, Whitfield Diffie and Stewart Baker take two very different positions on this.

YES

Whitfield Diffie

STATEMENT OF WHITFIELD DIFFIE

Just over a year ago, the Administration revealed plans for a program of key escrow technology best known by the name of its flagship product the Clipper chip. The program's objective is to promote the use of cryptographic equipment incorporating a special back door or trap door mechanism that will permit the Federal Government to decrypt communications without the knowledge or consent of the communicating parties when it considers this necessary for law enforcement or intelligence purposes. In effect, the privacy of these communications will be placed in escrow with the Federal Government.

The committee has asked me to address myself to this proposal and in particular to consider three issues:

- Problems with key escrow, particularly in the area of privacy.
- The impact of the key escrow proposal on American business both at home and abroad.
- Alternatives to key escrow.

SCOPE

In the course of discussing the key escrow program over the past year, I have often encountered a piecemeal viewpoint that seeks to take each individual program at face value and treat it independently of the others. I believe, on the contrary, that it is appropriate to take a broad view of the issues. The problem confronting us is to assess the advisability of key escrow and its impact on our society. This requires examining the effect of private, commercial, and possibly criminal use of cryptography and the advisability and effect of the use of communications intelligence techniques by law enforcement....

PRIVACY PROBLEMS OF KEY ESCROW

When the First Amendment became part of our constitution in 1791, speech took place in the streets, the market, the fields, the office, the bar room, the bedroom, etc. It could be used to express intimacy, conduct business,

From U.S. Senate. Committee on the Judiciary. Subcommittee on Technology and the Law. Hearing, May 3, 1994. Washington, DC: Government Printing Office, 1994.

or discuss politics and it must have been recognized that privacy was an indispensable component of the character of many of these conversations. It seems that the right—in the case of some expressions of intimacy even the obligation—of the participants to take measures to guarantee the privacy of their conversations can hardly have been in doubt, despite the fact that the right to speak privately could be abused in the service of crime.

Today, telephone conversations stand on an equal footing with the venues available in the past. In particular, a lot of political speech—from friends discussing how to vote to candidates planning strategy with their aides—occurs over the phone. And, of all the forms of speech protected by the first amendment, political speech is foremost. The legitimacy of the laws in a democracy grows out of the democratic process. Unless the people are free to discuss the issues—and privacy is an essential component of many of these discussions—that process cannot take place.

There has been a very important change in two hundred years, however. In the seventeen-nineties two ordinary people could achieve a high degree of security in conversation merely by the exercise of a little prudence and common sense. Giving the ordinary person comparable access to privacy in the normal actions of the world today requires the ready availability of complex technical equipment. It has been thoughtlessly said, in discussions of cryptographic policy, that cryptography brings the unprecedented promise of absolute privacy. In fact, it only goes a short way to make up for the loss of an assurance of privacy that can never be regained.

As is widely noted, there is a fundamental similarity between the power of the government to intercept communications and its ability to search premises. Recognizing this power, the fourth amendment places controls on the government's power of search and similar controls have placed by law on the use of wiretaps. There is, however, no suggestion in the fourth amendment of a guarantee that the government will find what it seeks in a search. Just as people have been free to protect the things they considered private, by hiding them or storing them with friends, they have been free to protect their conversations from being overheard.

The ill ease that most people feel in contemplating police use of wiretaps is rooted in awareness of the abuses to which wiretapping can be put. Unlike a search, it is so unintrusive as to be invisible to its victim and this inherently undermines accountability. Totalitarian regimes have given us abundant evidence that the use of wiretaps and even the fear of their use can stifle free speech. Nor is the political use of electronic surveillance a strictly foreign problem. We have precedent in contemporary American history for its use by the party in power in its attempts to stay in power.

The essence of the key escrow program is an attempt to use the buying power and export control authority of government to promote standards that will deny ordinary people ready options for true protection of their conversations. In a world where more and more communications take place between people who frequently can not meet face to face, this is a dangerous course of action.

The objections raised so far apply to the principle of key escrow. Objections can also be raised to details of the present proposal. These deal with the secrecy of the algorithm, the impact on security of the escrow mechanism, and the way in which the proposal has been put into effect....

SECURITY PROBLEMS WITH KEY ESCROW

From the viewpoint of a user, any key escrow system diminishes security. It puts potential for access to the user's communications in the hands of an escrow agent whose intentions, policies, security capabilities, and future cannot be entirely known. In the context of modern secure telephone systems, the contrast between escrowed and unescrowed communications is particularly stark. In the process of setting up a secure call, modern secure telephones manufacture cryptographic keys that will be used for the protection of one and only one call and will be erased after the call is complete. Public key cryptography has made it possible to do this in such a way that these keys, once erased, can never be recovered. This gives the users a degree of privacy similar to that in a face to face meeting. The effect of key escrow is much like having a tape recorder on throughout the meeting. Even if the tapes are very carefully protected, the people whose words they hold can never be certain that they will not someday be played to a much wider audience....

IMPACT ON BUSINESS

Business today is characterized by an unprecedented freedom and volume of travel by both people and goods. Ease of communication, both physical and electronic, has ushered in an era of international markets and multinational corporations. No country is large enough that its industries can concentrate on the domestic market to the exclusion of all others. When foreign sales rival or exceed domestic ones, the structure of the corporation follows suit with new divisions placed in proximity to markets, materials, or labor.

Security of electronic communication is as essential in this environment as security of transportation and storage have been to businesses throughout history. The communication system must ensure that orders for goods and services are genuine, guarantee that payments are credited to the proper accounts, and protect the privacy of business plans and personal information.

Two new factors are making security both more essential and more difficult to achieve. The first is the rise in importance of intellectual property. Since much of what is now bought and sold is information varying from computer programs to surveys of customer buying habits, information security has become an end in itself rather than just a means for ensuring the security of people and property. The second is the rising demand for mobility in communications. Traveling corporate computer users sit down at workstations they have never seen before and expect the same environment that is on the desks in their offices. They carry cellular telephones and communicate constantly by radio. They haul out portable PCs [personal computers] and dial their home computers from locations around the globe. With each such action they expose their information to threats of eavesdropping and falsification barely known a decade ago.

Because this information economy is relentlessly global, no nation can successfully isolate itself from international competition. The communication systems we build will have to be interoperable with those of other nations. A standard based on a secret American technology and designed to give American intelligence access to the communications it protects seems an unlikely candidate for widespread acceptance. If we are to maintain our leading position in the information market places, we must give our full support to the development of open international security standards that protect the interests of all parties fairly.

POTENTIAL FOR EXCESSIVE REGULATION

The key escrow program also presents the specter of increased regulation of the design and production of new computer and communications products. FIPS185 [Escrowed Encryption Standard] states that "Approved implementations may be procured by authorized organizations for integration into security equipment." This raises the question of what organizations will be authorized and what requirements will be placed upon them? Is it likely that people prepared to require that surveillance be built into communication switches would shrink from requiring that equipment make pre-encryption difficult as a condition for getting "approved implementations"? Such requirements have been imposed as conditions of export approval for security equipment. Should industry's need to acquire tamper resistant parts force it to submit to such requirements, key escrow will usher in an era of unprecedented regulation of American development and manufacturing.

ALTERNATIVES TO KEY ESCROW

It is impossible to address the issue of alternatives to key escrow without asking whether there is a problem, what the problem is and what solution, if any, the problem requires.

In recent testimony before this committee, the FBI has portrayed communications interception as an indispensable tool of police work and complained that the utility of this tool is threatened by developments in modern communications. This testimony, however, uses the broader term "electronic surveillance" almost exclusively and appears to include some cases in which the electronic surveillance consisted of bugs rather than wiretaps. Although the FBI testimony speaks of numerous convictions, it names not a single defendant, court, case, or docket number. This imprecision makes adequate study of the testimony impossible and leaves open two issues: the effectiveness of communications interception in particular and that of electronic surveillance in general.

On balance, it appears more likely that the investigative and evidential utility of wiretaps is rising than that it is falling. This is partly because criminals, like law abiding citizens, do more talking on the phone these days. It is partly because modern communication systems, like ISDN [Integrated Services Digital Network] provide much more information about each call, revealing where it came from in real time even when it originated a long way away. This detailed information about who called whom, when, and for how long, that modern switches provide, improves the... trap and trace techniques that police use to map the extent of criminal conspiracies. It is unaffected by any encryption that the callers may apply.

With respect to other kinds of electronic surveillance, the picture for law enforcement looks even brighter. Miniaturization of electronics and improvements in digital signal processing are making bugs smaller, improving their fidelity, making them harder to detect, and making them more reliable. Forms of electronic surveillance for which no warrant is held to be necessary, particularly TV cameras in public places, have become widespread. This creates a base of information that was, for example, used in two distinct ways in the Tylenol poisoning case of the mid-1980s.

Broadening the consideration of high tech crime fighting tools to include vehicle tracking, DNA fingerprinting, individual recognition by infrared tracing of the veins in the face, and database profiling makes it seem unlikely that the failures of law enforcement are due to the inadequacy of its technical tools.

If we turn our attention to foreign intelligence, we see a similar picture. Communications intelligence today is enjoying a golden age. The steady migration of communications from older, less accessible, media, both physical and electronic, has been the dominant factor. The loss of information resulting from improvements in security has been consistently outweighed by the increased volume and quality of information available. As a result, the communications intelligence product has been improving for more than fifty years, with no end in sight. The rising importance of telecommunications in the life of industrialized countries, coupled with the rising importance of wireless communications, can be expected to give rise to an intelligence bonanza in the decades to come.

Mobile communication is one of the fastest growing areas of the telecommunications industry and the advantages of cellular phones, wireless local area networks, and direct satellite communica-

tion systems are such that they are often installed even in applications where mobility is not required. Satellite communications are in extensive use, particularly in equatorial regions and cellular telephone systems are being widely deployed in rural areas throughout the world in preference to undertaking the substantial expense of subscriber access wiring.

New technologies are also opening up new possibilities. Advances in emitter identification, network penetration techniques, and the implementation of cryptanalytic or crypto-diagnostic operations within intercept equipment are likely to provide more new sources of intelligence than are lost as a result of commercial use of cryptography.

It should also be noted that changing circumstances change appropriate behavior. Although intelligence continues to play a vital role in the post cold war world, the techniques that were appropriate against an opponent capable of destroying the United States within hours may not be appropriate against merely economic rivals.

If, however, we accept that some measure of control over the deployment of cryptography is needed, we must distinguish two cases:

- The use of cryptography to protect communications and
- The use of cryptography to protect stored information.

It is good security practice in protecting communications to keep any keys that can be used to decipher the communications for as short a time as possible. Discoveries in cryptography in the past two decades have made it possible to have secure telephones in which the keys last only for the duration of the call and can never be recreated thereafter. A key escrow proposal surrenders this advantage by creating a new set of escrowed keys that are stored indefinitely and can always be used to read earlier traffic.

With regard to protection of stored information, the situation is quite different. The keys for decrypting information in storage must be kept for the entire lifetime of the stored information; if they are lost, the information is lost. An individual might consider encrypting files and trusting the keys to memory, but no organization of any size could risk the bulk of its files in this fashion. Some form of key archiving, backup, or escrow is thus inherent in the use of cryptography for storage. Such procedures will guarantee that encrypted files on disks are accessible to subpoena in much the same way that files on paper are today.

Many business communications, such as electronic funds transfers, fall into an intermediate category. Although the primary purpose is communication rather than storage, the transactions are of a formal nature. In these cases, an escrow mechanism much like those in current commercial use may be appropriate. In a high value transaction, where the buyer and the seller do not have an established business relationship, either party may demand the use of a mutually trusted escrow agent who will take temporary custody of both the goods and the payment. In a similar fashion, either party to an encrypted transaction might demand that only keys escrowed with a mutually acceptable escrow agent be used.

What is most important here is that the laws, customs, and practices governing electronic commerce and, in a broader context, electronic society are just beginning to develop. It is likely that escrow mechanisms will be among the tools employed. It is, however, too early to say what form they should take. They will need to be worked out as society gets more experience with the new communications media. They should not be imposed by government before society's real needs have been determined.

CONDUCT OF THE KEY ESCROW INITIATIVE

In my experience, the people who support the key escrow initiative are inclined to express substantial trust in the government. I find it ironic therefore that in its conduct of this program, the administration has followed a course that could hardly have been better designed to provoke distrust. The introduction of mechanisms designed to assure the government's ability to conduct electronic surveillance on its citizens and limit the ability of the citizens to protect themselves against such surveillance is a major policy decision of the information age. It has been presented, however, as a technicality, buried in an obscure series of regulations. In so doing, it has avoided congressional consideration of either its objectives or its budget. The underlying secrecy of the technology has been used as a tool for doling out information piecemeal and making a timely understanding of the issues difficult to achieve.

SUPPOSE WE MAKE A MISTAKE

In closing, I would like to ask a question. Suppose we make a mistake?

- Suppose we fail to adopt a key escrow system and later decide that one is needed?
- Suppose we adopt a key escrow system now when none is needed?

Which would be the more serious error?

It is generally accepted that rights are not absolute. If private access to high-grade encryption presented a clear and present danger to society, there would be little political opposition to controlling it. The reason there is so much disagreement is that there is so little evidence of a problem.

If allowing or even encouraging wide dissemination of high-grade cryptogra-phy proves to be a mistake, it will be a correctable mistake. Generations of electronic equipment follow one another very quickly. If cryptography comes to present such a problem that there is popular consensus for regulating it, this will be just as possible in a decade as it is today. If on the other hand, we set the precedent of building government surveillance capabilities into our security equipment we risk entrenching a bureaucracy that will not easily surrender the power this gives.

NO

Stewart A. Baker

WHY CLIPPER IS GOOD FOR YOU

With all the enthusiasm of Baptist ministers turning their Sunday pulpits over to the Devil, the editors of *Wired* have offered me the opportunity to respond to some of the urban folklore that has grown up around key escrow encryption—also known as the Clipper Chip.

Recently the Clinton administration has announced that federal agencies will be able to buy a new kind of encryption hardware that is sixteen million times stronger than the existing federal standard known as DES. But this new potency comes with a caveat. If one of these new encryption devices is used, for example, to encode a phone conversation that is subject to a lawful government wiretap, the government can get access to that device's encryption keys. Separate parts of each key are held by two independent "escrow agents," who will release keys only to authorized agencies under safeguards approved by the attorney general. Private use of the new encryption hardware is welcome but not required. That's a pretty modest proposal. Its critics, though, have generated at least seven myths about key escrow encryption that deserve answers.

Myth Number One: Key escrow encryption will create a brave new world of government intrusion into the privacy of Americans.

Opponents of key escrow encryption usually begin by talking about government invading the privacy of American citizens. None of us likes the idea of the government intruding willy-nilly on communications that are meant to be private.

But the key escrow proposal is not about increasing government's authority to invade the privacy of its citizens. All that key escrow does is preserve the government's current ability to conduct wiretaps under existing authorities. Even if key escrow were the only form of encryption available, the world would look only a little different from the one we live in now.

In fact, it's the proponents of widespread unbreakable encryption who want to create a brave new world, one in which all of us—crooks included —have a guarantee that the government can't tap our phones. Yet these

From Stewart A. Baker, "Why Clipper Is Good for You," *Wired* (June 1994).

proponents have done nothing to show us that the new world they seek will really be a better one.

In fact, even a civil libertarian might prefer a world where wiretaps are possible. If we want to catch and convict the leaders of criminal organizations, there are usually only two good ways to do it. We can "turn" a gang member—get him to testify against his leaders. Or we can wiretap the leaders as they plan the crime.

I once did a human rights report on the criminal justice system in El Salvador. I didn't expect the Salvadorans to teach me much about human rights. But I learned that, unlike the US, El Salvador greatly restricts the testimony of "turned" co-conspirators. Why? Because the co-conspirator is usually "turned" either by a threat of mistreatment or by an offer to reduce his punishment. Either way, the process raises moral questions—and creates an incentive for false accusations.

Wiretaps have no such potential for coercive use. The defendant is convicted or freed on the basis of his own, unarguable words.

In addition, the world will be a safer place if criminals cannot take advantage of a ubiquitous, standardized encryption infrastructure that is immune from any conceivable law enforcement wiretap. Even if you're worried about illegal government taps, key escrow reinforces the existing requirement that every wiretap and every decryption must be lawfully authorized. The key escrow system means that proof of authority to tap must be certified and audited, so that illegal wiretapping by a rogue prosecutor or police officer is, as a practical matter, impossible.

Myth Number Two: Unreadable encryption is the key to our future liberty.

Of course there are people who aren't prepared to trust the escrow agents, or the courts that issue warrants, or the officials who oversee the system, or anybody else for that matter. Rather than rely on laws to protect us, they say, let's make wiretapping impossible; then we'll be safe no matter who gets elected.

This sort of reasoning is the long-delayed revenge of people who couldn't go to Woodstock because they had too much trig homework. It reflects a wide—and kind of endearing—streak of romantic high-tech anarchism that crops up throughout the computer world.

The problem with all this romanticism is that its most likely beneficiaries are predators. Take for example the campaign to distribute PGP ("Pretty Good Privacy") encryption on the Internet. Some argue that widespread availability of this encryption will help Latvian freedom fighters today and American freedom fighters tomorrow. Well, not quite. Rather, one of the earliest users of PGP was a high-tech pedophile in Santa Clara, California. He used PGP to encrypt files that, police suspect, include a diary of his contacts with susceptible young boys using computer bulletin boards all over the country. "What really bothers me," says Detective Brian Kennedy of the Sacramento, California, Sheriff's Department, "is that there could be kids out there who need help badly, but thanks to this encryption, we'll never reach them."

If unescrowed encryption becomes ubiquitous, there will be many more stories like this. We can't afford as a society to protect pedophiles and criminals today just to keep alive the far-fetched notion that some future tyrant will be brought down by guerrillas wearing bandoleers and pocket protectors and sending PGP-encrypted messages to each other across cyberspace.

Myth Number Three: Encryption is the key to preserving privacy in a digital world.

Even people who don't believe that they are likely to be part of future resistance movements have nonetheless been persuaded that encryption is the key to preserving privacy in a networked, wireless world, and that we need strong encryption for this reason. This isn't completely wrong, but it is not an argument against Clipper.

If you want to keep your neighbors from listening in on your cordless phone, if you want to keep unscrupulous competitors from stealing your secrets, even if you want to keep foreign governments from knowing your business plans, key escrow encryption will provide all the security you need, and more.

But I can't help pointing out that encryption has been vastly oversold as a privacy protector. The biggest threats to our privacy in a digital world come not from what we keep secret but from what we reveal willingly. We lose privacy in a digital world because it becomes cheap and easy to collate and transmit data, so that information you willingly gave a bank to get a mortgage suddenly ends up in the hands of a business rival or your ex-spouse's lawyer. Restricting these invasions of privacy is a challenge, but it isn't a job for encryption. Encryption can't protect you from the misuse of data you surrendered willingly.

What about the rise of networks? Surely encryption can help prevent password attacks like the recent Internet virus, or the interception of credit card numbers as they're sent from one digital assistant to another? Well, maybe. In fact, encryption is, at best, a small part of network security.

The real key to network security is making sure that only the right people get access to particular data. That's why a digital signature is so much more important to future network security than encryption. If everyone on a net has a unique identifier that others cannot forge, there's no need to send credit card numbers—and so nothing to intercept. And if everyone has a digital signature, stealing passwords off the Net is pointless. That's why the Clinton administration is determined to put digital signature technology in the public domain. It's part of a strategy to improve the security of the information infrastructure in ways that don't endanger government's ability to enforce the law.

Myth Number Four: Key escrow will never work. Crooks won't use it if it's voluntary. There must be a secret plan to make key escrow encryption mandatory.

This is probably the most common and frustrating of all the myths that abound about key escrow. The administration has said time and again that it will not force key escrow on manufacturers and companies in the private sector. In a Catch-22 response, critics then insist that if key escrow isn't mandated it won't work.

That misunderstands the nature of the problem we are trying to solve. Encryption is available today. But it isn't easy for criminals to use; especially in telecommunications. Why? Because as long as encryption is not standardized and ubiquitous, using encryption means buying and distributing expensive gear to all the key members of the conspiracy. Up to now only a few criminals have had the resources, sophistication, and discipline to use specialized encryption systems.

What worries law enforcement agencies—what should worry them—is a world where encryption is standardized and ubiquitous: a world where anyone who buys an US$80 phone gets an "encrypt" button that interoperates with everyone else's; a world where every fax machine and every modem automatically encodes its transmissions without asking whether that is necessary. In such a world, every criminal will gain a guaranteed refuge from the police without lifting a finger.

The purpose of the key escrow initiative is to provide an alternative form of encryption that can meet legitimate security concerns without building a web of standardized encryption that shuts law enforcement agencies out. If banks and corporations and government agencies buy key escrow encryption, criminals won't get a free ride. They'll have to build their own systems—as they do now. And their devices won't interact with the devices that much of the rest of society uses. As one of my friends in the FBI puts it, "Nobody will build secure phones just to sell to the Gambino family."

In short, as long as legitimate businesses use key escrow, we can stave off a future in which acts of terror and organized crime are planned with impunity on the public telecommunications system. Of course, whenever we say that, the critics of key escrow trot out their fifth myth:

Myth Number Five: The government is interfering with the free market by forcing key escrow on the private sector. Industry should be left alone to develop and sell whatever form of encryption succeeds in the market.

In fact, opponents of key escrow fear that businesses may actually prefer key escrow encryption. Why? Because the brave new world that unreadable encryption buffs want to create isn't just a world with communications immunity for crooks. It's a world of uncharted liability. What if a company supplies unreadable encryption to all its employees, and a couple of them use it to steal from customers or to encrypt customer data and hold it hostage? As a lawyer, I can say it's almost certain that the customers will sue the company that supplied the encryption to its employees. And that company in turn will sue the software and hardware firms that built a "security" system without safeguards against such an obvious abuse. The only encryption system that doesn't conjure up images of a lawyers' feeding frenzy is key escrow.

But there's a second and even more compelling reason why the key escrow initiative can't fairly be characterized as interfering with private enterprise: The encryption market has been more or less created and sustained by government. Much of the market for encryption devices is in the public sector, and much of the encryption technology now in widespread use in the private sector was funded, perfected, or endorsed by the federal government.

And not by accident, either. Good encryption is expensive. It isn't just a matter of coming up with a strong algorithm, although testing the strength of an algorithm can be enormously time-consuming. The entire system must be checked for bugs and weaknesses, a laborious and unglamorous process. Generally, only the federal government has been willing to pay what it costs to develop secure communications gear. That's because we can't afford to have our adversaries reading our military and diplomatic communications.

That's led to a common pattern. First, the government develops, tests, or perfects encryption systems for itself. Then the private sector drafts along behind the government, adopting government standards on the assumption that if it's good enough for the government's information, it's good enough to protect industry's.

As encryption technology gets cheaper and more common, though, we face the real prospect that the federal government's own research, its own standards, its own purchases will help create the future I described earlier—one in which criminals use ubiquitous encryption to hide their activities. How can anyone expect the standard-setting arms of government to use their power to destroy the capabilities of law enforcement—especially at a time when the threat of crime and terror seems to be rising dramatically?

By adopting key escrow encryption instead, the federal government has simply made the reasonable judgment that its own purchases will reflect all of society's values, not just the single-minded pursuit of total privacy.

So where does this leave industry, especially those companies that don't like either the 1970s-vintage DES or key escrow? It leaves them where they ought to be—standing on their own two feet. Companies that want to develop and sell new forms of unescrowed encryption won't be able to sell products that bear the federal seal of approval. They won't be able to ride piggyback on federal research efforts. And they won't be able to sell a single unreadable encryption product to both private and government customers.

POSTSCRIPT

Does the Clipper Chip Give the Government Too Much Control Over Citizens' Privacy?

The building of an information superhighway has been one of the major goals of the Clinton administration. It is hoped that the "development of the NII (National Information Infrastructure) can unleash an information revolution that will change forever the way people live, work, and interact with each other." The Clipper Chip initiative has been welcomed by law enforcement agencies but vehemently opposed by many users of computer networks. Forty thousand electronic mail messages were collected by one organization opposed to the use of the Clipper Chip.

Benjamin Franklin once wrote that "they that give up essential liberty to obtain a little temporary safety deserve neither liberty nor safety." The Clipper Chip has aroused considerable passion and emotion but it is worth remembering that it is one of the first controversies to arise out of our electronically interconnected world. As the selections in this issue note, we live in an age in which business and commerce are international activities. It is an age in which individuals have opportunities to acquire and distribute information previously available only to large corporations. It is an era in which working with information is the core economic activity.

The Clipper Chip controversy is important in itself but it also suggests that the age of cyberspace will not necessarily be a tranquil period. Control over information and communication has always been a source of power. Since this is a period in which information is both valuable and difficult to control, we can expect further conflicts of this nature as power is sought and resisted.

An analysis of this controversy is contained in Jaleen Nelson, "Sledge Hammers and Scalpels: The FBI Digital Wiretap Bill and Its Effect on Free Flow of Information and Privacy," 41 *UCLA Law Review* 1139 (1994). Those with access to the Internet can find a great deal of information about the Clipper Chip at the archives of the Electronic Frontier Foundation (www.eff.org) and of *Wired Magazine* (www.wired.com).

ISSUE 17

Should the Insanity Defense Be Abolished?

YES: Jonathan Rowe, from "Why Liberals Should Hate the Insanity Defense," *The Washington Monthly* (May 1984)

NO: Richard Bonnie, from Statement Before the Committee on the Judiciary, U.S. Senate (August 2, 1982)

ISSUE SUMMARY

YES: Editor Jonathan Rowe examines the insanity defense as it is now administered and finds that it is most likely to be used by white middle- or upper-class defendants and that its application is unfair and leads to unjust results.

NO: Professor of law Richard Bonnie argues that the abolition of the insanity defense would be immoral and would leave no alternative for those who are not responsible for their actions.

The verdict in the 1982 trial of John Hinckley, accused of shooting former president Ronald Reagan, brought the insanity defense out of the pages of legal journals and onto the front pages of newspapers and popular magazines. What had been a subject of considerable scholarly and judicial debate during the previous 20 years became a newsworthy topic as well. That an attempted assassination of a political figure led to calls for abolishing the insanity defense is somewhat ironic, since the modern standard for the insanity defense originated in a similar incident about 150 years ago.

In 1843, Daniel McNaughtan, suffering from delusions of persecution, fired a shot at a man he believed was British prime minister Robert Peel. Actually, the victim was the prime minister's secretary and the bullet killed him. Englishmen were outraged, since three other attempted assassinations of political officials had recently taken place, and Queen Victoria was prompted to send her husband, Prince Albert, to the trial as an observer. When McNaughtan was found not guilty by reason of insanity, Victoria sent a letter to the House of Lords, complaining that McNaughtan and the other assassins were "perfectly conscious and aware of what they did." The Lords summoned 15 judges who, after considering the matter, pronounced the McNaughtan rule (commonly referred to as the M'Naghten rule) as the most appropriate formulation of the insanity defense. This test requires that a jury must find that the defendant, when the act was committed, did not know the nature and quality of his act or that he could not tell right from wrong.

One of the problems with the insanity defense is in defining insanity. If one argues in favor of the defense, one should be able to define insanity with reasonable precision and in a way that can be applied consistently. The great difficulty in providing a definition is the basic argument against the insanity defense. The insanity defense issue has caused great controversy between lawyers and psychiatrists over the meaning of insanity and mental illness and over the ability of psychiatrists reliably to diagnose the problems of defendants.

A frequent objection to the M'Naghten rule was that there were persons who could distinguish between good and evil but still could not control their behavior. One response to this critique was the "irresistible impulse" test. Using this standard, a defendant would be relieved of responsibility for his or her actions even if he or she could distinguish right from wrong but, because of mental disease, could not avoid the action in question. A somewhat broader and more flexible version of the combined M'Naghten–irresistible impulse test was recommended by the American Law Institute in 1962. Under this formulation, people are not responsible for criminal conduct if they lack *substantial capacity* to appreciate the criminality of their conduct or to conform their conduct to the requirements of the law.

The most noteworthy and radical experiment with the reformulation of the insanity defense occurred in *Durham v. United States,* 214 F.2d 862 (1954). The District of Columbia Court of Appeals ruled that an accused was not criminally responsible if his act was the product of mental disease or defect. The effect of this rule was to increase the amount of expert psychiatric testimony presented in court about whether or not mental disease was present and whether or not the act was a product of the disease. While welcomed by many since it allowed for a more complete psychiatric picture to be presented to the jury, the rule proved to be too vague and led to too much power being given to psychiatric experts. As a result, in *United States v. Brawner,* 471 F.2d 969 (1972), the Durham experiment was abandoned.

Examination of the insanity defense opens up some extremely important issues of law. For example, what are the purposes of punishment? What assumptions does the law make about human nature, free will, and personal responsibility? What should be the role of the jury and what authority should be given medical and psychiatric experts in evaluating deviant behavior? How should we deal with the often competing goals of rehabilitation, retribution, and deterrence? These are among the questions raised in the following arguments presented by Jonathan Rowe and Richard Bonnie on the need for reforming or abolishing the insanity defense.

YES
Jonathan Rowe

WHY LIBERALS SHOULD HATE THE INSANITY DEFENSE

"It's the fallacy of your legal system," said Gary Trapnell, a bank robber who not long afterwards would hijack a TWA 707 flying from Los Angeles to New York. "Either the man falls under this antiquated psychiatric scheme of things, or he doesn't." Trapnell was talking about the insanity defense, which he had used with great acumen to avoid jail for his innumerable crimes over the years. "I have no right to be on the streets," he added.

The insanity defense has been much in the news of late. We read cases such as that of the Michigan ex-convict who pleaded insanity after seven killings, won an acquittal, but returned to the streets two months later when he was declared sane. In a month, he was charged with murdering his wife. Or take the 23-year-old Connecticut man who left the state hospital three months after an insanity acquittal for stabbing a man. The acquittee's mother pleaded to have him recommitted, but to no avail. Shortly thereafter, he repeatedly stabbed a man whose home he was burglarizing. Once again he was declared not guilty by reason of insanity.

It sounds like the warmup for a right-wing tirade against the coddlers of criminals. But the much publicized trials of John Hinckley and others have cast the issue in a somewhat different light. In a strange way, by jumbling liberal and conservative loyalties, these have made debate on the subject not only necessary, but possible as well. Take the "Twinkie Defense," which enabled former San Francisco City Supervisor Dan White to get off with a light eight-year sentence after shooting, with obvious deliberation, San Francisco Mayor George Moscone and his city administrator, Harvey Milk. As Milk was both liberal and openly homosexual, thousands who probably never before identified with the cause of law and order were outraged that this brutal act of (at least symbolic) homophobia should go lightly punished. John Hinckley, for his part, was the son of a wealthy upper-middle-class family, and not the sort of fellow who evoked sympathies usually reserved for the downtrodden. His trial prompted even *The Nation*, which rarely concedes the cops an inch, to suggest some mild reforms in the insanity defense.

From Jonathan Rowe, "Why Liberals Should Hate the Insanity Defense," *The Washington Monthly*, vol. 16, no. 4 (May 1984). Copyright © 1984 by The Washington Monthly Company, 1611 Connecticut Avenue, NW, Washington, DC 20009; (202) 462–0128. Reprinted by permission of *The Washington Monthly*.

In the wake of the Hinckley trial, a number of reforms have been suggested. *The Nation*, along with many others, advocates that we put the burden of proof upon the defendant. (In the Hinckley case, the prosecutors actually had to prove him sane, which is no mean feat.) Others have called for a tighter legal definition of insanity itself. Such changes might be helpful, but they amount to fiddling. The only way to resolve the injustices of the insanity defense is to do away with it entirely. This may sound cruel, but it is not. Nor is it a proposal to "lock 'em up and throw away the key." To the contrary, the injustices of this defense go much deeper than a few criminals getting off the hook. They go close to the core of our current practices regarding punishment and correction. Getting rid of the insanity defense would help to make us confront the need for humane reform in the way we sentence and confine those who break the law.

SUCH A DEAL

The insanity defense looms a good deal larger in our minds than it does in actual life. Somewhere between 1,000 and 2,000 criminals make use of it each year, or about 1 percent to 2 percent of felonies that go to trial (over 90 percent in many jurisdictions are plea-bargained before trial). The issue is important not because it arises frequently, but because it tends to arise in the most serious crimes: think of Son of Sam, for example, or the Hillside Strangler. Such people tend to be dangerous, and their trials attract so much publicity that they put our entire system of justice to a test. What single event of the last two years affected your view of the criminal justice system more than the Hinckley trial did?

It is hard to read about such trials without getting the impression that something is fundamentally wrong. Take the case of Robert H. Torsney, the New York City policeman who shot a 15-year-old black youth in the head from two feet away in November of 1978. In an article in the *Journal of Legal Medicine*, Abraham Halpern, director of psychiatry at the United Hospital, Port Chester, New York, tells the case in salient detail.

At first, Torsney's lawyer resisted any suggestion of psychological observation or treatment for his client. Such treatment for an officer who was only acting in the line of duty was "worse than putting him in the electric chair," the attorney said. As public indignation rose, however, and acquittal became more and more unlikely, the attorney decided that Torsney might have deep-seated psychological problems after all. At a hearing on Torsney's insanity defense, his paid psychiatrist explained the policeman's errant account of the incident, which was contradicted by other witnesses as an "involuntary retrospective falsification." Not a lie, mind you. The psychiatrist went on to explain that Torsney shot the kid because of an "organic psychomotor seizure" arising from a "mental defect."

The jury found Torsney not guilty by reason of insanity. After a year, however, the staff at the mental hospital recommended that he be released because they could find nothing wrong with him. When the lower court balked—such hasty releases are unseemly if nothing else—Torsney's attorney indignantly filed an appeal. "It can't be seriously argued," he wrote, "that the record in this case establishes that Mr. Torsney is either seriously mentally ill or presently dangerous. At most he may be said to have a personality flaw, which certainly does not distinguish him from the rest of society."

What really distinguished Torsney, it seemed, was that he had shot somebody and deserved to be punished. That such simple observations can become so obscured is largely the result of the wholesale invasion of psychiatry into the courtroom that has been underway since the 1950s. Back then, the stars of psychiatry and psychoactive drugs were shining bright. To many, we were on the threshold of a new age, in which psychiatrists could measure such things as responsibility and mental disease down to minute calibrations and effect cures with the precision of engineers. If only we could let these new wizards into the courtroom, to bring their expertise to bear upon the processes of justice.

The main opening came in 1954, when federal appeals Judge David Bazelon, of the Washington, D.C., District Court, declared the so-called "Durham Rule." Under the old "M'Naghten Rule," a criminal could be judged insane only if he or she didn't know right from wrong. This crimped the psychiatrists somewhat, since they tend to shrug their shoulders on questions of values. In the *Durham* case Judge Bazelon set them free, declaring that henceforth in the District of Columbia an accused was not criminally responsible "if his unlawful act was the product of mental disease or defect." Bazelon received a special award from the American Psychiatric Association, but not everyone was that enthused. The American Law Institute (ALI) produced a sort of compromise, declaring that a person wouldn't be responsible for a misdeed if he couldn't appreciate the wrongfulness of it or if he "lacked a substantial capacity...to conform his conduct to the requirements of the law." Though somewhat stiffer on paper, this ALI rule didn't vary from the Durham Rule in practice all that much. Adopted by a majority of the states, its various permutations have given the psychiatrists virtual free rein in the courtroom ever since.

The Hinckley trial demonstrated what the heavenly city of courtroom psychiatry has become. Three teams of psychiatrists—11 in all—picked over Hinckley's mind for hours in an exercise that 200 years from now will no doubt seem much the way that the heated debates over the medieval heresies seem to us today. The resulting trial dragged on for 52 excruciating days. One defense psychiatrist, Thomas C. Goldman, told the jury with a straight face that Hinckley saw actress Jody Foster as an "idealized mother who is all-giving and endowed with magical power," while President Reagan was an "all evil prohibitive figure who hates him, seeks to destroy him, and deny access to the idealized mother figure." No wonder he tried to shoot the man.

Or take the comments of Richard Delman, a psychiatrist who testified for the defense in the Dan White trial. As Lee Coleman, also a psychiatrist, tells it in his new book, *The Reign of Error*, Delman concluded on the basis of inkblot and other tests that it was White's deep concern for others that led him to sneak into San Francisco City Hall through a window rather than walk in through the front door. "He didn't want to embarrass the officer who was operating the metal detector [and would have discovered his gun]," Delman said.

On at least one occasion this kind of analysis has been more than even the defendant could take. Coleman cites the case of Inez Garcia, who was raped by two men in Soledad, California;

afterwards, she went home, got a rifle, and shot one of her attackers. At her trial she sat listening to defense psychiatrist Jane Olden go on and on about her "reactive formations" and her self-image as a "saint-like idealized virgin." "If you trigger her negative feelings, which would be provoked by such an act as rape," Olden explained, "being a hysterical person who was striving always to express this sensuality and aggression, then you could indeed throw her into a state where she is emotionally relating to her own conflict."

Garcia stood up and yelled at the judge, "I killed [him] because I was raped and I'd kill him again."

If you smell a fish in such psychologizing, it is with good reason. There is a cadre of so-called "forensic psychiatrists," who show up in these insanity trials again and again, plying their offensive or defensive specialties. Dr. Alan Stone of Harvard, former head of the American Psychiatric Association, describes the kind of trial that results as a "three-ring circus, in which lawyers are the ringmasters and the psychiatric witnesses are the clowns, and if they are carefully trained, then they will be trained clowns." Another Harvard psychiatrist, David Baer, was a defense witness in the Hinckley trial but does not regularly participate in these affairs, and he revealed some of the details to a reporter from *Harper's*. He spent, he said, at least 20 to 25 hours rehearsing his testimony with the lawyers, who admonished him, among other things, not to "weaken your answers with all the qualifications you think you ought to make." They said, "Oh, don't mention the exploding bullets. My God, that's so damaging to the case," he recalls. Baer, who was paid $35,000 for his efforts, added

that he was "determined never to tell a lie."

That may be. But what happens to most psychiatrists who resist the "training" of the defense lawyers? "If a man doesn't testify the right way, he is not rehired," said one defense attorney in a study published in the *Rutgers Law Journal*. (Section 6 of the "Principles of Medical Ethics" of the American Psychiatric Association, by the way, reads: "A physician should not dispose of his services under terms or conditions which tend to interfere with or impair the free and complete exercise of his medical judgment.")

DID YOU HEAR VOICES?

The theory behind our "adversary" system is that when you pit one group of experts like these against another the truth will somehow emerge. When the hired-gun psychiatrists do their act, however, the result is not information, but confusion. "None of them had the same conclusion," complained Nathalia Brown, a shop mechanic at the local electric utility and a Hinckley juror. "All of them said he had this illness, that illness, so how are we to know what illness he has? I felt on the brink of insanity myself going through this, you know."

This, of course, is precisely what defense lawyers seek. As far back as 1945, Julian Carroll, the New York attorney who handled poet Ezra Pound's famous insanity defense against treason charges, wrote a friend that insanity trials are a "farce" in which the "learned medicos for each side squarely contradict each other and completely befuddle the jury." What was true then is even more true today, and all it took was confusion and nagging doubts in the minds of the jurors to gain Hinckley's acquittal.

In the nation's prisons, fooling the shrinks is getting to be a science. Inkblot tests offer fertile ground for displays of psychosis, and inmates who have successfully pleaded insanity have instructed their cohorts on what to see—sexual acts, genitalia, and the like. Ken Bianchi, the Hillside Strangler, studied books on psychology and hypnosis before convincing a number of psychiatrists he had a dual personality, and only an especially alert one found him out. An experiment at Stanford University suggested that conning these psychiatrists may not be all that hard. Eight subjects, all without any record of mental illness, feigned hearing voices and thereby gained admission to 12 different mental hospitals. They did not falsify any details of their lives other than that they heard voices. Eleven of the 12 were diagnosed as "schizophrenic" while the 12th was diagnosed "manic depressive."

"I probably know more about psychiatry ... than your average resident psychiatrist," boasted Gary Trapnell, who had some justification for his claim. "I can bullshit the hell out of one in ten minutes."

It's not that psychiatry has nothing to tell us, nor that many of its practitioners are not dedicated to helping others. The problem is the way this specialty is used in insanity trials: the endeavor itself is in many ways absurd. These psychiatrists are interviewing criminals who know that if they come off seeming a little bananas, they might get off the hook. The notion that something resembling scientific data will always result from such subjective encounters is, well, a little bananas itself. On top of that, the courtroom psychiatrists are not purporting to inform us of a defendant's *present* mental state, though even that can be elusive enough. They are claiming to divine the defendant's mental state when he committed the crime, which probably was months before. "I can't even tell you what *I* was thinking about a week ago, or a year ago, let alone what someone else was thinking," says criminal psychologist Stanton Samenow, author of *Inside the Criminal Mind*, whose eight years working at St. Elizabeths hospital in Washington made him deeply skeptical of traditional attempts to understand and catalogue criminals according to Freudian concepts. Indeed, how would you begin to *prove* an assertion such as the one that John Hinckley tried to shoot Reagan because he saw the president as an "all evil prohibitive figure"? This is not evidence. It is vaporizing. Coleman testifies at criminal trials with delightful iconoclasm that psychiatrists such as himself have no more ability than anyone else to inform the jury as to what was going on in a criminal's mind at any given time.

POOR RELATIONS

But one should not conclude that the only thing wrong with the insanity defense is that it lets the felons free on the basis of recondite psychiatric excuses. The injustice goes much deeper. Some psychiatrists, for example, lend their courtroom aura and mantle of expertise to the prosecution. Jim Grigson, the so-called "Hanging Shrink" of Texas, will tell a jury after a 90-minute interview with a defendant that this individual "has complete disregard for another human being's life" and that "no treatment, no medicine, nothing is going to change this behavior." Psychiatric opinionizing can cut both ways.

There's the further problem that psychiatrists, the gatekeepers of this defense, have their greatest rapport with the problems of those closest to their own social status. A few years ago, Dr. Daniel Irving, a psychiatrist in Washington, demonstrated this attitude in an article Blain Harden wrote for *The Washington Post*. "I hate to say this," Irving confided, "but I don't like to work with poor people.... They are talking about stuff that doesn't interest me particularly. They are the kind of people who don't interest me." Over 95 percent of all psychiatric patients are white, and James Collins, a black psychiatrist who is chairman of the Howard University Medical School Department of Psychiatry, told Harden that "[the] biggest problem is that many psychiatrists cannot relate to poor people."

In fact, the insanity defense itself can be weighted heavily towards those who are well-off. This is not just because a Hinckley family can muster upwards of a million dollars to mount a prodigious legal and psychiatric defense. On a subtler level, someone from a "nice" upper-middle-class background who commits a heinous crime is more readily seen as off his rocker than is someone from a poorer background in which crime is closer to the norm (or is at least perceived to be). During the Hinckley trial the jury witnessed his family sitting behind him, the "perfect couple," as one observer said later. "Hinckley's father was sitting there with a pondering look on his face; his mother was wearing red, white, and blue outfits; and his sister was a former cheerleader and homecoming queen. Real Americans." Surely there must be something wrong with a young man who could enjoy such advantages and still go out and shoot a president. It was the sort of tableau that a black felon from, say, East St. Louis, might have some trouble assembling.

Such, considerations may help explain why Henry Steadman of the New York State Department of Mental Hygiene found that while whites account for only 31 percent of the prison population in his state, they were a full 65 percent of those found not guilty by reason of insanity. "Racial discrimination favoring whites in successful insanity defenses is strongly suggested by these figures," writes Abraham Halpern.

This in turn points to something even more fundamentally unjust about the insanity defense: the way it draws arbitrary and culture-bound distinctions between defendants with different kinds of life burdens and afflictions. A John Hinckley may well harbor anger against his parents and anguish at his unrequited love for actress Jody Foster. Such problems can be very real for those who go through them. But they are no *more* real, no *more* inclined to affect behavior, than are the problems of a teenager of lesser means, who may be ugly, or kept back in school two or three times, or whose parents may not love him and who may have been "passed around" among relatives and older siblings for as long as he can remember, or who may find doors closed to him because he is not blond and blue-eyed the way Hinckley is. If a Hinckley merits our compassion, then surely those with hard life circumstances do also. Under the insanity defense, we absolve Hinckley totally of responsibility, while we label his hypothetical counterpart a bad person and send him to jail.

So arbitrary is the line that the insanity defense invites us to draw that all sorts of prejudices and vagaries can enter, of which racial and class bias are just two. "The actual psychological state of the defendant may be a rather minor factor" in the decision even to use the insanity defense, writes C. R. Jeffrey in his book, *Criminal Responsibility and Mental Disease*. Rather, this decision is based on such factors as "the economic position of the defendant, the nature of the criminal charges, the medical facilities in the community," and the like.

BIG DIFFERENCE

This is not to say that you won't find any poor people or non-Caucasians in the maximum-security hospitals in which insanity acquittees are kept. You will, but it's important to understand how they got there. It probably wasn't through the kind of circus trial that John Hinckley could afford. Very likely, it was a plea bargain, in which a prosecutor decided it was better to put a dangerous person away, even if just for a short time, than to devote scarce resources to a trial that he or she might lose. One study, published in the *Rutgers Law Review,* found at least two jurisdictions in which the prosecutors actually raised the insanity defense more frequently than the defense attorney did. "Clearly the prosecutor saw the [insanity] defense as a means to lock defendants up without having their guilt proved beyond a reasonable doubt," the study concludes.

Given such realities, it should not be surprising that there is often not much difference between those who end up in maximum security mental hospitals and those who end up in their penal counterparts. "Lots of people could have ended up in either one or the other," says E. Fuller Torrey, a psychiatrist at St. Elizabeths mental hospital in Washington. Samenow goes further. On the basis of his own experience studying insanity acquittees at St. Elizabeths, he declares flatly that "neither [his colleague Dr. Samuel] Yochelson nor I found that any of the men we evaluated were insane unless one took tremendous liberties with that word."

That may be a bit of an exaggeration. But the similarities between criminals we call "insane," and those we call simply "criminals," cannot be dismissed. Take recidivism. There is evidence that criminals released from mental hospitals tend to repeat their crimes with about the same frequency as their counterparts released from prison. This point is crucial because the purpose of a criminal justice system is not just to punish offenders; it is to protect the rest of us from dangerous people as well. Through the insanity defense, we go to lengths that are often ridiculous to make a distinction that in many cases is without a difference.

Sometimes the experts are the last to see what needs to be done. Listen to Lawrence Coffey, one of the Hinckley jurors who was unhappy with the verdict for which he himself voted. "I think it [the law] should be changed," he told a Senate hearing, "in some way where the defendant gets mental help enough that where he's not harmful to himself and society, and then be punished for what he has done wrong." Maryland Copelin, also one of the jurors, agreed. "I think they [defendants] should get the help they need and also punishment for the act they did." In other words, Hinckley needed treatment, but he deserved punishment, too. Who could argue with that? Well, the law, for one. It said that Hinckley was either guilty or not guilty by reason of insanity. "We could not do any better than what we did," Copelin said, "on account of your forms," which gave the jury only these two options.

In short, the insanity defense cuts the deck the wrong way. I makes no provision for the vast middle ground in which offenders have problems but should bear responsibility too. Instead of persisting in making this artificial distinction between "normal" criminals (whatever that means) and "insane" ones, we should ask first a very simple question: did the individual commit the crime? That established in a trial, we should then, in a sentencing phase, take all relevant factors into account in deciding what combination of punishment and treatment is appropriate. "Either you did it or you didn't do it," says Samenow, who supports the abolition of the insanity defense. "I think we should try the criminal first, and then worry about treatment." In other words, don't expect the jury to make Talmudic distinctions on which even the experts cannot agree. Get the psychiatrists out of the courtroom, where they cause confusion, and put them into the sentencing and treatment process, where they may be able to help.

In this sentencing phase, which would take on a new importance, Hinckley's infatuation with Jody Foster, and Dan White's overindulgence in junk food, would be given due regard. So too would the incapacity of one who was totally deranged. The crucial difference from current practice is that the examination would be done by court-appointed psychiatrists (or other professionals) instead of by hired guns proffered by either side. Since psychiatrists are as human as the rest of us, this system would not be perfect. It would, however, be better than what we have today.

In almost all cases, some punishment would be in order. You don't have to believe that retribution is the whole purpose of the law to acknowledge that something very basic in us requires that when someone causes serious harm to someone else, he should pay. This approach would eliminate perhaps the most dangerous absurdity of the present insanity defense. When a criminal wins acquittal on this ground, the criminal justice system has no more claim on him. The only way he can be kept in confinement is if he is declared insane and committed to a mental institution through a totally separate procedure. (Some states require an automatic confinement for one or two months, ostensibly to "observe" the acquittee.) No Problem, you say. They've just been declared insane. The problem is, *that* insanity was at the time of the crime, which may have been a year or more before. By the time of the commitment hearing, the old problem may have miraculously cleared up. The commitment authorities are then faced with two bad options. Either they tell the truth and let a dangerous person out or they fill a bed in a crowded mental hospital with someone who will be there not for treatment, but only to be kept off the streets. Eliminating the insanity defense would eliminate such charades.

Once punishment is completed, the question of danger to society would come to the fore. First offenders committing nonviolent crimes generally pose little such threat, and in most cases could be safely paroled. At the other extreme, violent repeat offenders would be locked up for a very long time. While reform is always possible, the sad fact is that most repeat offenders will keep on repeating until they reach a "burn-out" period sometime after they reach age 40. Since the recidivism rates cut across the categories we call "normal" and "insane" criminality, the insanity defense simply doesn't help us deal with reality in this regard.

Hot-blooded crimes, such as the Dan White shooting, should be seen for what they are. Such people generally don't pose a great threat because the circumstances of their crime are not likely to happen again. It costs between $10,000 and $20,000 a year to keep a prisoner in jail, and that money would be better spent on those for whom it's really needed. In other words, White's eight-year sentence was not necessarily wrong. The wrong was in the psychiatric speculation through which that result was justified. We can achieve justice in such cases through simpler and more honest means.

WHAT A TIME

But isn't the insanity defense necessary to protect the infirm? "People who are mentally ill deserve treatment," says Flora Rheta Schreiber, whose book *The Shoemaker* details the sad story of a troubled murderer. "They don't deserve to be locked up in prison."

Fair enough. The trouble is, virtually all criminals have mental problems. The difference between a bank robber and yourself is not in your shirt size or the shape of your hands. Is there any such thing as a "sane" rape or a "sane" axe murder? If anyone did such deeds with calm and rational deliberation, would that individual not be the most insane—and dangerous—of all? Samenow, moreover, says that for the vast majority of criminals, the kind of treatment that might be effective is pretty much the same. The secret scandal of the insanity defense is the way it justifies our atrocious penal system by purporting to show kindness for one group that is selected arbitrarily in the first place. We deny treatment to the many under the pretext of providing it for a few.

And a pretext it often is. Talk to someone who has visited a maximum-security hospital for the criminally insane. To be sure, there are good ones here and there. But in his book *Beating the Rap*, Henry Steadman describes a reality that is probably more common than not. Such hospitals in his state are "prisonlike," he writes, with "locked wards, security officers, and barbed wire fences. . . . There is a substantial level of patient-patient assault; homosexuality, both consenting and nonconsenting, is common, and guards *are sometimes unnecessarily brutal...It is simply doing time in a different setting.*" (Emphasis added.) Barbara Weiner, who heads a special outpatient program for insanity acquittees in Chicago—one of the few programs of its kind in the country—told a Senate hearing that "few states have specialized programs for treating mentally ill offenders." (Those of means, of course, can often arrange a transfer to private facilities at which conditions are more genteel.)

So averse are American psychiatrists to helping people in life's lower stations that over half the staffs of this country's public mental hospitals are graduates of foreign medical schools, where standards may not be awfully high. In 11 states, including Illinois and Ohio, the figure is over 70 percent. Just try to imagine a psychiatrist from, say, India, trying to understand a felon from the South Bronx. Torrey cites a psychiatrist who left the Illinois state hospital system telling of a colleague in charge of prescribing drugs who did not know that .8 and .80 were the same number.

Much of the problem is that most of us prefer to keep a comfortable arm's length from such realities. The people who run our criminal justice system are no exception. After observing a year's worth of mental incompetency hearings in New York, Steadman observed that "of about 35 judges, 12 attorneys, six district attorneys, and 12 psychiatrists, not one had ever seen or been inside either of the two facilities to which incompetent defendants are committed." A former public defender in Washington, D.C., who had pleaded before the Supreme Court the case of an insanity-acquittee who was trying to get out of St. Elizabeths, told me he had never met the individual for whose release he was pleading.

Getting rid of the insanity defense would help to break the spell and make us confront the deficiencies in our correctional systems. No longer could we congratulate ourselves that we are being humane and just when we are being neither. If eliminating the defense would help get a few dangerous felons off the street, so much the better. But a great deal more is at stake.

NO

Richard Bonnie

STATEMENT OF RICHARD BONNIE

The effect of most of the proposals now before you would be to abolish the insanity defense as it has existed for centuries in Anglo-American criminal law. I urge you to reject these sweeping proposals. The insanity defense should be retained, in modified form, because some defendants afflicted by severe mental disorder cannot justly be blamed for their criminal conduct and do not, therefore, deserve to be punished. The defense, in short, is essential to the moral integrity of the criminal law.

I realize that the figure of John Hinckley looms before us today. Doubts about the moral accuracy of the jurors' verdict in this sad case have now been turned on the insanity defense itself. I do not want to second guess the verdict in the Hinckley case, but I do urge you to keep the case in proper perspective.

The highly visible insanity claim, pitting the experts in courtroom battle, is the aberrational case. The plea is raised in no more than 2% of felony cases and the defense is rarely successful when the question is contested in a jury trial. Most psychiatric dispositions in the criminal process are arranged without fanfare, without disagreement among the experts, and without dissent by the prosecution. In short, the exhaustive media coverage of cases like Hinckley's gives the public a distorted picture of the relative insignificance of the insanity defense in the day-to-day administration of justice.

In another way, however, the public debate about the aberrant case is highly to be desired because the trial of insanity claims keeps the community in touch with the moral premises of the criminal law. The legitimacy of the institution of punishment rests on the moral belief that we are all capable of rational choice and therefore deserve to be punished if we choose to do wrong. By acknowledging the exception, we reaffirm the rule. I have no doubt that the Hinckley trial and verdict have exposed the fundamental moral postulates of the criminal law to vigorous debate in every living room in the Nation. Thus, in a sense, whether John Hinckley was or was not legally insane may be less important than the fact that the question was asked at all.

These are the reasons I do not favor abolition of the insanity defense. However, I do not discount or dismiss the possibility that the defense occasionally may be successfully invoked in questionable cases. There is, in fact, some

From U.S. Senate. Committee on the Judiciary. *Insanity Defense*. Hearing, August 2, 1982. Washington, DC: Government Printing Office, 1982. (Y4.J89/2:J–97–126.)

evidence that insanity acquittals have increased in recent years. However, I am persuaded that the possibility of moral mistakes in the administration of the insanity defense can be adequately reduced by narrowing the defense and by placing the burden of proof on the defendant.

THE OPTIONS

You have basically three options before you.

The Existing (Model Penal Code) Law

One option is to leave the law as it now stands, by judicial ruling, in all of the federal courts (and, parenthetically, as it now stands in a majority of the states). Apart from technical variations, this means the test proposed by the American Law Institute in its Model Penal Code. Under this approach, a person whose perceptual capacities were sufficiently intact that he had the criminal "intent" required in the definition of the offense can nonetheless be found "not guilty by reason of insanity" if, by virtue of mental disease or defect, he lacked substantial capacity *either* to understand or appreciate the legal or moral significance of his actions, *or* to conform his conduct to the requirements of law. In other words, a person may be excused if his thinking was severely disordered—this is the so-called volitional prong of the defense.

Revival of M'Naghten

The second option is to retain the insanity defense as an independent exculpatory doctrine—independent, that is, of mens rea—but to restrict its scope by eliminating the volitional prong. This is the approach that I favor, for reasons I will outline below. Basically, this option is to restore the *M'Naghten* test—although I do not think you should be bound by the language used by the House of Lords in 1843—as the sole basis for exculpation or ground of insanity. Although this is now distinctly the minority position in this country—it is used in less than one third of the states—it is still the law in England.

Abolition: The Mens Rea Approach

The third option is the one I have characterized as abolition of the defense. Technically, this characterization is accurate because the essential substantive effect of the so-called "mens rea" approach (or "elements" approach) would be to eliminate any criterion of exculpation, based on mental disease, which is independent of the elements of particular crimes. To put it another way, the bills taking this approach would eliminate any separate exculpatory doctrine based on proof of mental disease; instead mentally ill (or retarded) defendants would be treated just like everyone else. A normal person cannot escape liability by proving that he did not know or appreciate the fact that his conduct was wrong, and—under the mens rea approach—neither could a psychotic person.

THE CASE AGAINST THE MENS REA APPROACH

Most of the bills now before you would adopt the mens rea option, the approach recently enacted in Montana and Idaho. As I have already noted, this change, abolishing the insanity defense, would constitute an abrupt and unfortunate departure from the Anglo-American legal tradition.

If the insanity defense were abolished, the law would not take adequate account of the incapacitating effects of severe mental illness. Some mentally ill defendants may be said to have "intended" to do what they did—that is, their technical guilt can be established—but they nonetheless may have been so severely disturbed that they were unable to appreciate the significance of their actions. These cases do not frequently arise, but when they do, a criminal conviction—signifying the societal judgment that the defendant *deserves* punishment—would offend the basic moral intuitions of the community. Judges and juries would then be forced either to return a verdict which they regard as morally obtuse or to acquit the defendant in defiance of the law. They should be spared such moral embarrassment.

Let me illustrate this point with a real case evaluated at our Institute's Forensic Clinic in 1975. Ms. Joy Baker, a thirty-one-year-old woman, admitted killing her aunt. She had no previous history of mental illness, although her mother was mentally ill and had spent all of Ms. Baker's early years in mental hospitals. Ms. Baker was raised by her grandparents and her aunt in a rural area of the state. After high school graduation Ms. Baker married and had two children. The marriage ended in divorce six years later and Ms. Baker remarried. This second marriage was stressful from the outset. Mr. Baker was a heavy drinker and abusive to his wife. He also was extremely jealous and repeatedly accused his wife of seeing other men.

The night before the shooting Mr. Baker took his wife on a ride in his truck. He kept a gun on the seat between them and stopped repeatedly. At each place he told listeners that his wife was an adultress. He insisted his wife throw her wedding ring from the car, which she did because she was afraid of her husband's anger. The Bakers didn't return home until three in the morning. At that time Ms. Baker woke her children and fed them, then stayed up while her husband slept because she was afraid "something terrible would happen."

During this time and for the three days prior to the day of the shooting Ms. Baker had become increasingly agitated and fearful. Her condition rapidly deteriorated and she began to lose contact with reality. She felt that her dogs were going to attack her and she also believed her children and the neighbors had been possessed by the devil.

On the morning of the shooting, Ms. Baker asked her husband not to leave and told him that something horrible was about to happen. When he left anyway she locked the doors. She ran frantically around the house holding the gun. She made her children sit on the sofa and read the Twenty-Third Psalm over and over. She was both afraid of what they might do and of what she might do but felt that reading the Bible would protect them. Shortly afterwards, Ms. Baker's aunt made an unexpected visit. Ms. Baker told her to go away but the aunt persisted and went to the back door. Ms. Baker was afraid of the dog which was out on the back porch and repeatedly urged her aunt to leave. At this time the aunt seemed to Ms. Baker to be sneering at her.

When her aunt suddenly reached through the screening to unlock the door Ms. Baker said, "I had my aunt over there and this black dog over here, and both of them were bothering me.... And then I had that black dog in front of me and she turned around and I was trying to kick the dog and my aunt was coming in the door and I just—took my hands I just went like this—right through the screen.... I shot her."

Ms. Baker's aunt fell backward into the mud behind the porch. Although she was bleeding profusely from her chest, she did not die immediately. "Why, Joy?" she asked. "Because you're the devil, and you came to hurt me," Joy answered. Her aunt said, "Honey, no, I came to help you." At this point, Ms. Baker said, she saw that her aunt was hurting and became very confused. Then, according to her statement, "I took the gun and shot her again just to relieve the pain she was having because she said she was hurt." Her aunt died after the second shot.

All the psychiatrists who examined Ms. Baker concluded that she was acutely psychotic and out of touch with reality at the time she shot her aunt. The police who arrested her and others in the small rural community concluded that she must have been crazy because there was no other explanation for her conduct. After Ms. Baker was stabilized on antipsychotic medication, she was permitted to leave the state to live with relatives in a neighboring state. Eventually the case against her was dismissed by the court, with the consent of the prosecution, after a preliminary hearing at which the examining psychiatrists testified. She was never indicted or brought to trial.

It seems clear, even to a layman, that Ms. Baker was so delusional and regressed at the time of the shooting that she did not understand or appreciate the wrongfulness of her conduct. It would be morally obtuse to condemn and punish her. Yet, Ms. Baker had the state of mind required for some form of criminal homicide. If there were no insanity defense, she could be acquitted only in defiance of the law.

Let me explain. The "states of mind" which are required for homicide and other criminal offenses refer to various aspects of conscious awareness. They do not have any qualitative dimension. There is good reason for this, of course. The exclusive focus on conscious perceptions and beliefs enhances predictability, precision and equality in the penal law. If the law tried to take into account degrees of psychological aberration in the definition of offenses, the result would be a debilitating individualization of the standards of criminal liability.

At the time of the first shot, it could be argued that Ms. Baker lacked the "state of mind" required for murder because she did not intend to shoot a "human being" but rather intended to shoot a person whom she believed to be possessed by the devil. At common law, this claim would probably be characterized as a mistake of fact. Since the mistake was, by definition, an unreasonable one—i.e., one that only a crazy person would make—she would most likely be guilty of some form of homicide (at least manslaughter) if ordinary mens rea principles were applied. Even under the modern criminal codes, . . . , she would be guilty of negligent homicide since an ordinary person in her situation would have been aware of the risk that her aunt was a human being. And she possibly could be found guilty of manslaughter since she was probably aware of the risk that her aunt was a human being even though she was so regressed that she disregarded the risk.

It might also be argued that Ms. Baker's first shot would have been justified if her delusional beliefs had been true since she would have been defending herself against imminent annihilation at the hands of the devil. Again, however, the application of ordinary common-law principles of justification... would indicate that she was unreasonably mistaken as to the existence of justificatory facts (the necessity for killing to protect one-self) and her defense would fail, although the grade of the offense would probably be reduced to manslaughter on the basis of her "imperfect" justification.

At the time of the second shot, Ms. Baker was in somewhat better contact with reality. At a very superficial level she "knew" that she was shooting her aunt and did so for the non-delusional purpose of relieving her aunt's pain. But euthanasia is no justification for homicide. Thus, if we look only at her legally relevant "state of mind" at the time of the second shot, and we do not take into account her highly regressed and disorganized emotional condition, she is technically guilty of murder.

I believe that Joy Baker's case convincingly demonstrates why, in theoretical terms, the mens rea approach does not take sufficient account of the morally significant aberrations of mental functioning associated with severe mental disorder. I readily concede, however, that these technical points may make little practical difference in the courtroom. If the expert testimony in Joy Baker's case and others like it were admitted to disprove the existence of mens rea, juries may behave as many observers believe they do now—they may ignore the technical aspects of the law and decide, very bluntly, whether the defendant was too crazy to be convicted. However, I do not believe that rational criminal law reform is served by designing rules of law in the expectation that they will be ignored or nullified when they appear unjust in individual cases.

IMPROVING THE QUALITY OF EXPERT TESTIMONY

I have tried to show that perpetuation of the insanity defense is essential to the moral integrity of the criminal law. Yet an abstract commitment to the moral relevance of claims of psychological aberration may have to bend to the need for reliability in the administration of the law.

I fully recognize that the litigation of insanity claims is occasionally imperfect. The defense is sometimes difficult to administer reliably and fairly. In particular, I recognize that we cannot calibrate the severity of a person's mental disability, and it is sometimes hard to know whether the disability was profound enough to establish irresponsibility. Nor can we be confident that every fabricated claim will be recognized. Yet these concerns are not unlike those presented by traditional defenses such as mistake, duress and other excuses which no one is seeking to abolish. Indeed, problems in sorting valid from invalid defensive claims are best seen as part of the price of a humane and just penal law. Thus, to the extent that the abolitionists would eradicate the insanity defense in response to imperfections in its administration, I would reply that a decent respect for the moral integrity of the criminal law sometimes requires us to ask questions that can be answered only by approximation. Rather than abolishing the defense we should focus our attention on ways in which its administration can be improved.

Some of the abolitionist sentiment among lawyers seems to be responsive to doubts about the competence—and, unfortunately, the ethics—of expert witnesses. The cry for abolition is also raised by psychiatrists and psychologists who believe that the law forces experts to "take sides" and to offer opinions on issues outside their sphere of expertise. These are all legitimate concerns and I have no doubt that the current controversy about the insanity defense accurately reflects a rising level of mutual professional irritation about its administration. However, the correct solution is not to abolish the insanity defense but rather to clarify the roles and obligations of expert witnesses in the criminal process. Some assistance in this effort can be expected from the American Bar Association's Criminal Justice-Mental Health Standards now being drafted by interdisciplinary panels of experts in the field.

A properly trained expert can help the judge or jury to understand aberrations of the human mind. However, training in psychiatry or psychology does not, by itself, qualify a person to be an expert witness in criminal cases. Specialized training in forensic evaluation is necessary, and a major aim of such special training must be to assure that the expert is sensitive to the limits of his or her knowledge.

THE CASE FOR TIGHTENING THE DEFENSE

I do not favor abolition of the "cognitive" prong of the insanity defense. However, I do agree with those critics who believe the risks of fabrication and "moral mistakes" in administering the defense are greatest when the experts and the jury are asked to speculate whether the defendant had the capacity to "control" himself or whether he could have "resisted" the criminal impulse.

Few would dispute the moral predicate for the control test—that a person who "cannot help" doing what he did is not blameworthy. Unfortunately, however, there is no scientific basis for measuring a person's capacity for self-control or for calibrating the impairment of such capacity. There is, in short, no objective basis for distinguishing between offend-

ers who were undeterrable and those who were merely undeterred, between the impulse that was irresistible and the impulse not resisted, or between substantial impairment of capacity and some lesser impairment. Whatever the precise terms of the volitional test, the question is unanswerable—or can be answered only by "moral guesses." To ask it at all, in my opinion, invites fabricated claims, undermines equal administration of the penal law, and compromises its deterrent effect....

The sole test of legal insanity should be whether the defendant, as a result of mental disease, lacked "substantial capacity to appreciate the wrongfulness of his conduct." This language, drawn from the Model Penal Code, uses clinically meaningful terms to ask the same question posed by the House of Lords in *M'Naghten* 150 years ago. During the past ten years, I have not seen a single case at our Clinic involving a claim of irresponsibility that I personally thought was morally compelling which would not be comprehended by this formulation. Thus, I am convinced that this test is fully compatible with the ethical premises of the penal law, and that results reached by judges and juries in particular cases ordinarily would be congruent with the community's moral sense. In sum, then, I believe that the insanity defense, as I have defined it, should be narrowed, not abandoned, and that the burden of persuasion may properly be shifted to the defendant. Like the mens rea proposal, this approach adequately responds to public concern about possible misuse of the insanity defense. Unlike the mens rea proposal, however, I believe this approach is compatible with the basic doctrines and principles of Anglo-American penal law.

POSTSCRIPT

Should the Insanity Defense Be Abolished?

The furor over the Hinckley case led to some changes in the federal insanity defense standard. As part of a major anticrime bill passed in 1984, Congress has required the defendant to have the burden of proving that he or she was insane. In the Hinckley trial, the prosecution was required to prove beyond a reasonable doubt that Hinckley was sane. The defendant in such a case must now persuade a jury that, as a result of a severe mental disease or defect, he or she was unable to appreciate the nature and wrongfulness of the act.

In addition to raising questions about the diagnosis of mental illness, the insanity defense also requires consideration of treatment, of sentencing, and of institutionalization. Those advocating its retention argue not only that blameless people should not be punished but also that such individuals need care and treatment for their problems. The fact that many mental institutions have failed to provide adequate treatment or are, by their nature, inappropriate places for some individuals who need help but not institutionalization has been recognized recently in various lawsuits. As a result, the number of people in institutions has been declining. The ineffectiveness of prisons and mental institutions in reducing recidivism or promoting treatment should be considered in the debate over the insanity defense, since even those who wish to abolish the defense are willing to take the mental state of the defendant into account at the time of sentencing. There is, in addition, a possible relationship between the increase in the number of defendants invoking the insanity defense and the deinstitutionalization trend. The reason for this is that the insanity defense becomes more appealing as the expectation of a long stay in a mental institution decreases.

Recommended readings on the insanity defense and mental health law include Appelbaum, *Almost a Revolution: Mental Health Law and the Limits of Change* (1994); Steadman, *Before and After Hinckley: Evaluating Insanity Defense Reform* (1993); Smith and Meyer, *Law, Behavior, and Mental Health* (New York University Press, 1987); Eisner, "Returning the Not Guilty By Reason of Insanity to the Community: A New Scale to Determine Readiness," 17 *The Bulletin of the American Academy of Psychiatry and the Law* 401 (1989); Klofas and Yandrasits, " 'Guilty But Mentally Ill' and the Jury Trial: A Case Study," 24 *Criminal Law Bulletin* 424 (1988); Symposium, "The Insanity Defense," *The Annals* (January 1985); and Moran, *Knowing Right from Wrong: The Insanity*

Defense of Daniel McNaughtan (Free Press, 1981), which provides an interesting look at McNaughtan's trial and at the central figure in the history of the insanity defense. Other books about particular cases include Kaplan and Waltz, *The Trial of Jack Ruby* (Macmillan, 1965); Gaylin, *The Killing of Bonnie Garland* (Simon & Schuster, 1982); and Caplan, *The Insanity Defense and the Trial of John W. Hinckley, Jr.* (David Godine, 1983).

ISSUE 18

Should Drug Use Be Legalized?

YES: James Ostrowski, from "The Moral and Practical Case for Drug Legalization," *Hofstra Law Review* (vol. 18, 1990)

NO: Steven Brill, from "Should We Give Up?" *The American Lawyer* (March 1990)

ISSUE SUMMARY

YES: James Ostrowski, a policy analyst, asserts that drug prohibition increases crime, raises medical and economic costs, and fails to deter people from using illicit drugs.

NO: Steven Brill, lawyer and founder of *The American Lawyer* magazine, maintains that government should not abdicate its responsibility, that legalization would make the drug problem worse, and that some segments of the population would be devastated if enforcement were stopped.

One can hardly miss the impact of illegal drugs on the fabric of American life. If you watch the local evening news, you will notice that there is a continuing link between drugs and violent crime in urban neighborhoods and that most of the victims of violence are young. The lure of the "get very rich quick" lifestyle of drug dealers has tempted many poor teenagers into a life of violence, even against their own families. It may be hard to believe that a child would turn the family apartment into a "shooting gallery" or sell all the family possessions for money to purchase drugs, but it happens.

According to the article you will read by Steven Brill, one-fifth of 3,000 babies born in New York City's Harlem Hospital in 1990 were born to addicted mothers. That is a staggering figure, particularly because those 600 children were among thousands of other similarly afflicted children born in other urban hospitals across the nation. The statistics are not improving.

What is even more harrowing is the description of the crack-addicted mothers in Brill's article. Fifty percent of the children of these mothers go into foster care. But 100 percent need to go to school, and many of these children are now entering the public education systems around the nation. What educators are facing are children who exhibit serious neurological and learning problems that may condemn them to a lifelong struggle to attain any learning. How much can be hoped for a child who is part of the foster care system, who is from a desperately poor family, who cannot attend to task for any length of time?

The drug problem touches everyone. One poll indicated that Americans are far more worried about the impact of drugs on their lives than about problems of international peace or terrorism abroad. And so they should be, because the drug problem is not just the problem of the poor teenager in Detroit or Philadelphia. In Massachusetts recently, a mother was tried for leaving her two small children alone in an apartment, which they set on fire and in which they died. Her defense was astonishing—she asked for leniency because she was an addict and had to leave her home to get a fix.

What is the solution to this situation that is ripping apart our society? Should we legalize drugs, or should we continue with the traditional approach of criminalizing drug use? James Ostrowski, in "The Moral and Practical Case for Drug Legalization," argues that we only have an illusion of prohibition and that only through legalization of drugs can we get a grip on the situation. Present approaches—relying heavily on the police and court systems—are not putting much of a dent in either the rate of use or the supply of drugs. In fact, the prices of drugs are declining while the potency of street drugs is increasing. Furthermore, our present system is draining the government coffers of billions of dollars while urban street crime increases.

Steven Brill, an attorney and journalist, in "Should We Give Up?" argues for continuing the illegal status and consequent punishments attached to using and selling drugs. He cites some chilling evidence on the results of drug addiction and argues for more money and more effort going to treat addiction, thereby reducing the demand for drugs and the devastating effects that addiction has not only on the addict but on everyone else in the addict's life.

YES

James Ostrowski

THE MORAL AND PRACTICAL CASE FOR DRUG LEGALIZATION

INTRODUCTION

This article presents a comprehensive argument for the legalization of con-
sciousness-altering drugs....

The paradox of prohibition is that it fails to deter those who need it most
—the hard core users. The "protection" it provides the rest of the population
is redundant; they do not need it. The illusion of prohibition is that it takes
from us the responsibility to make the choice to use or not to use. But in
fact, the drugs are there if we want them and the media is constantly and
inadvertently advertising them. Technology is continually creating new and
potent mind-altering drugs. As individuals, we must exercise responsible
choice in these matters—with or without drug laws. We must awaken out of
our child-like slumber and accept the fact that one of the difficult tasks adult
human beings must perform is to decide the role that drugs will play in their
lives.

Wars against drugs fail because drugs and drug profits are more powerful motivators than drug laws. Drug dealers usually prevail because they
are ruthless entrepreneurs fighting government bureaucrats who are paid
whether they stop drug dealing or not. While the police struggle with the
paperwork from the last bust, the dealers busily market new drugs produced
by the latest technology.

Policy alternatives to prohibition are diverse, ranging from the medical
model of Great Britain to the alcohol model. If the goal of reform is elimination
of the black market in drugs, the best option for reform is non-prescription
adult availability which leaves very little room for a black market. If we
repeal prohibition, the benefits would be immediate and substantial: streets
would become safer, law enforcement would become unburdened, and the
black market in drugs, together with its many ill effects, would be destroyed.
The risk of legalization is significantly less than the risk of continuing the
availability of cigarettes, alcohol and cholesterol. Many innocent victims of

prohibition—including many drug abstainers—would no longer be sacrificed in the futile attempt to protect self-destructive people from themselves....

THE COST-BENEFIT ANALYSIS

Introduction

On Thursday, March 17, 1988, at 10:45 p.m. in the Bronx, Vernia Brown was killed by stray bullets fired in a dispute over illegal drugs. The 19-year-old mother of one was not involved in the dispute, yet her death was a direct consequence of the "war on drugs."

There can be little doubt that most, if not all, "drug-related murders" are the result of drug prohibition. The same type of violence came with the eighteenth amendment's ban of alcohol in 1920. The murder rate rose with the start of Prohibition, remained high during Prohibition, then declined for eleven consecutive years when Prohibition ended. The rate of assaults with a firearm rose with Prohibition and declined for ten consecutive years after Prohibition. In 1933, the last year of Prohibition, there were 12,124 homicides; 7,863 resulted from assaults with firearms and explosives. By 1941 these figures had declined to 8,048 and 4,525 respectively.

Vernia Brown died because of the policy of drug prohibition. If her death is a "cost" of that policy, what did the "expenditure" of her life "buy"? What benefits has society derived from the policy of prohibition that led to her death? To find the answer, it was necessary to turn to the experts and to the supporters of drug prohibition.

In 1988, I wrote to then–Vice President George Bush, the head of the South Florida Drug Task Force, then–Education Secretary William Bennett, Assistant Secretary of State for Drug Policy Ann Wrobleski, White House drug policy adviser Dr. Donald I. McDonald, and the public information directors of the Federal Bureau of Investigation, Drug Enforcement Administration, General Accounting Office, National Institute of Justice, and National Institute on Drug Abuse. None of these officials were able to cite any study that demonstrated the beneficial effects of drug prohibition when weighed against its costs. The leaders of the war on drugs are apparently unable to defend on rational cost-benefit grounds their 70-year-old policy, which costs nearly $10 billion per year, imprisons nearly 75,000 persons, and fills our cities with violent crime. It would seem that Vernia Brown and many others like her have died for nothing.

Some supporters of drug prohibition claim that its benefits are undeniable and self-evident. Their main assumption is that without prohibition, drug use would skyrocket with disastrous results. There is precious little evidence for this commonly held belief. The few cases of empirical evidence lend little support to the prediction of soaring drug use. For example, in the Netherlands and Alaska, two places in the Western world where use of small amounts of marijuana is legal, the rate of marijuana consumption is arguably lower than in the continental United States where marijuana is banned. In 1982, 6.3 percent of American high school seniors smoked marijuana daily, but only 4 percent did so in Alaska. In 1983, 5.5 percent of American high school seniors used marijuana daily, but in the Netherlands in 1985 only 0.5 percent of high school seniors used marijuana daily. These are not controlled comparisons; no such comparisons exist. However, the numbers that are available do not bear out the drastic scenario portrayed by supporters of continued prohibition.

Finally, there is at least some evidence that the "forbidden fruit" aspects of prohibition may lead to increased use of, or experimentation with, drugs, particularly among the young. This phenomenon apparently occurred with marijuana, LSD, and glue-sniffing. The case for legalization does not rely on such an argument, but those who believe prohibition needs no defense should consider this possibility.

Legalizers and prohibitionists agree that the status quo is intolerable. Change is demanded by all concerned. Yet, we have only two options: escalate the war on drugs or legalize them. Once we grasp the consequences of still further escalation, the legalization option may win by default.

Escalating the war on drugs is doomed to fail. First, past escalations by Richard M. Nixon, Nelson Rockefeller, and Ronald Reagan have failed. Second, there are the seemingly intractable problems of lack of funds, lack of prison space, lack of political will to put middle-class drug users in jail, and the simple impossibility of preventing consenting adults in a free society from engaging in extremely profitable transactions involving tiny amounts of illegal drugs.

However, none of these factors ultimately explain why escalating the war on drugs will fail. Failure is guaranteed because the black market thrives on the war on drugs and benefits from its intensification. At best, intensified law enforcement simply boosts the black market price of drugs, encouraging more drug suppliers to supply more drugs. The publicized conviction of a drug dealer, which instantly creates a vacancy in the lucrative drug business, has the same effect as hanging up a help-wanted sign which says, "Drug dealer needed—$5,000 a week—exciting work."

While escalating the war on drugs cannot succeed, there is a real danger that an intensified war on drugs will squander much of our nation's wealth and freedom and cause enormous social disruption. As of yet, there is no limit in sight to the amount of money and new enforcement powers that committed advocates of prohibition will demand before giving up.

It is instructive to note the parallel between the current debate over the drug problem and the debate over the alcohol problem in the twenties and thirties. In the alcohol debate, one side called for intensified enforcement efforts, while the other called for outright repeal. The prohibitionists won all the battles: enforcement efforts escalated throughout the duration of Prohibition. Convictions under the National Prohibition Act rose from approximately 18,000 in 1921 to approximately 61,000 in 1932. Prison terms grew longer and were meted out with greater frequency in the latter years of Prohibition. The enforcement budget rose from $7 million in 1921 to $15 million in 1930. The number of stills seized rose from 32,000 in 1920 to nearly 282,000 in 1930. In 1926, the Senate Judiciary Committee produced a 1,650-page report evaluating enforcement efforts and proposing reforms. In 1927, the Bureau of Prohibition was created to streamline enforcement efforts, and agents were brought under civil service protection to eliminate corruption and improve professionalism. In 1929, the penalties for violating the National Prohibition Act were increased. ...

Proponents of legalization won the war. In 1933, two years later, Prohibition was dead. In light of this history, it should not be at all surprising that increasing support for drug legalization is coming at the same time as the war on drugs is intensifying. There is nothing incongruous about a highly respected big-city mayor, Kurt Schmoke of Baltimore, Maryland, endorsing legalization at the same time that the first "drug czar" is appointed. Rather, it means that the nation may be ready for a major change in its policy toward drugs.

This Article does not suggest that legalization would solve the drug problem in its entirety. Legalization is offered as a solution only to the "drug problem problem," that is, the problems such as the crime, corruption, and AIDS caused not by the pharmacological effects of illegal drugs but by the attempt to fight drug use with the criminal justice system. The repeal of alcohol prohibition provides the appropriate analogy. Repeal did not end alcoholism—as indeed Prohibition did not—but it did solve many of the problems created by Prohibition, such as corruption, murder, and poisoned alcohol. We can expect no more and no less from drug legalization today.

The Costs of Prohibition

Street Crime by Drug Users

Drug laws greatly increase the price of illegal drugs, often forcing users to steal to get the money to obtain them. Although difficult to estimate, the black market prices of heroin and cocaine appear to be about 50 to 100 times greater than their anticipated market price under legalization. It is frequently estimated that at least forty percent of all property crime in the United States is committed by drug users so that they can maintain their expensive habits. That amounts to about eight million crimes

per year and $6 billion in stolen property. In addition, many victims of property crime are beaten and severely injured an estimated 1,200 are murdered each year.

Supporters of prohibition have traditionally used drug-related crime as a simplistic argument for enforcement: stop drug use to stop drug-related crime. They have even exaggerated the amount of such crime in the hopes of demonstrating a need for larger budgets and greater powers. In recent years, the more astute prohibitionists have noticed that drug-related crime is drug-law-related. Thus, in many cases they have begun to argue that even if drugs were legal and thus relatively inexpensive, drug users would still commit crime simply because they are criminals at heart.

While some researchers have questioned the causal connection between illegal drugs and street crime, many studies over a long period have confirmed what every inner-city dweller already knows: drug users steal to get the money to buy expensive illegal drugs.

Moreover, in addition to causing street crime and drug-related violence, prohibition also stimulates crime by:

- criminalizing users of illegal drugs, creating disrespect for the law;
- forcing users into daily contact with professional criminals, which often leads to arrest and prison records that make legitimate employment difficult to obtain;
- discouraging legitimate employment because of the need to "hustle" for drug money;
- encouraging young people to become criminals by creating an extremely lucrative black market in drugs;
- destroying, through drug crime, the economic viability of low-income

neighborhoods, leaving young people fewer alternatives to working in the black market; and

- removing the settling of drug-related disputes from the legal process, creating a context of violence for the buying and selling of drugs.

Black Market Violence

Prohibition also causes what the media and police misname "drug-related violence." This prohibition-related violence includes all of the random shootings and murders associated with black market drug transactions: ripoffs, eliminating the competition, killing informers and suspected informers.

Those who doubt that prohibition is responsible for this violence need only note the absence of violence in the legal drug market. For example, there is no violence associated with the production, distribution, and sale of alcohol. Such violence was ended by the repeal of Prohibition.

The President's Commission on Organized Crime estimates a total of about 70 drug-market murders yearly in Miami alone. Based on that figure and FBI data, a reasonable nationwide estimate would be that at least 825 murders each year are drug-market murders. Recent estimates from New York City and Washington, D.C. suggest an even higher figure. In addition, many law enforcement officers are killed enforcing drug laws each year.

Do Drugs Cause Crime?

It is often thought that illegal drugs cause crime through their pharmacological effects on the mind. Marijuana laws were originally justified on that basis. Today, the notion that marijuana causes crime "is no longer taken seriously by even the most ardent anti-marijuana propagan-

dists." Even heroin use "is a neutral act in terms of its potential criminogenic effect upon an individual's behavior. . . . [T]here is nothing in the pharmacology, or physical or psychological impact, of the drug that would propel a user to crime." Cocaine, like other stimulants such as nicotine and caffeine, can stimulate aggressive behavior. However, Grinspoon and Bakalar argue:

> [P]ersonality and setting as usual make all the difference. . . . Jared Tinkelberg, commenting on [a DEA] study and in general on the relation between cocaine and violence, expresses some surprise that it seems to produce "amphetamine-like paranoid assaultiveness" so seldom and concludes that at present it is not a serious crime problem.
>
> . . . [M]ost violence in the illicit cocaine trade, like the violence in the illicit heroin traffic today and in the alcohol business during Prohibition, is of course not necessarily related to the psychopharmacological properties of the drug. Al Capone did not order murders because he was drunk, and the cocaine dealer "Jimmy" does not threaten his debtors or fear the police because of cocaine-induced paranoia. . . .

Drugs Made More Dangerous

Because there is no quality control in the black market, prohibition also kills by making drug use more dangerous. Illegal drugs contain poisons, are of uncertain potency, and are injected with dirty needles. Many deaths are caused by infections, accidental overdoses, and poisoning.

At least 3,500 people will die from AIDS each year as a result of the use of unsterile needles, a greater number than the combined death toll from cocaine and heroin. These casualties include the sexual partners and children of intravenous drug users. Drug-related AIDS is almost exclusively the result of drug prohibition. Users inject drugs rather than taking them in tablet form because tablets are expensive. They go to "shooting galleries" to avoid arrests for possessing drugs and needles. They share needles because possession of needles is illegal and they are difficult to obtain. In Hong Kong, where needles are legal, there are no cases of drug-related AIDS. Legalization would fight AIDS in three ways:

- by making clean needles cheaply available;
- by making drugs in tablet form less expensive;
- by helping to break up the drug subculture, with its "shooting galleries" and needle-sharing.

The number of deaths caused by illnesses other than AIDS spread through the use of unsterile needles is unknown.

As many as 2,400 of the 3,000 deaths attributed to heroin and cocaine use each year—80 percent—are actually caused by black market factors. For example, many heroin deaths are caused by an allergic reaction to the street mixture of the drug, while 30 percent are caused by infections.

In summary, the attempt to protect users from themselves has backfired, as it did during Prohibition. The drug laws have succeeded only in making drug use much more dangerous by driving it underground and out of the reach of moderating social and medical influences....

An implicit point throughout this Article is made explicit here; drug users do not benefit from drug prohibition. Users die of overdoses caused by the uncertain quality of illegal drugs, and of AIDS contracted through dirty needles. They are murdered in remarkable numbers while buying or selling drugs. They are led into a criminal lifestyle by the need to raise large sums of money quickly, and must constantly associate with professional criminals to secure a drug supply. Many users have long records of convictions for drug offenses, making it difficult for them to secure legitimate employment. "It is difficult to overestimate the harm caused by forcing drug users into a life of crime. Once this threshold is crossed, there is often no return."

Yet, isn't the point of drug prohibition the salvaging of the welfare of those who, for whatever reasons, are unable to resist the lure of drugs? The 250,000 drug users infected with the AIDS virus are a grim reminder of the failure of prohibition to do so.

Economic Impact of Prohibition

What about the economic impact of prohibition? First, take a common estimate of annual black market drug sales which in 1980 was $79 billion. Because the black market price of drugs is inflated at least ten-fold over the probable legal price, 90 percent of this figure, or about $70 billion, constitutes an economic loss caused by prohibition. The drug user (and his dependents) is deprived of the purchasing power of 90 percent of the money he spends on illegal drugs without any net benefit accruing to the economy as a whole.

The added expenditure to the drug user under prohibition pays for the dramatically increased costs of producing and selling illegal drugs. Large amounts of land, labor and capital, not required in the legal drug market, are utilized in the illegal drug market. The high prices drug users pay for illegal drugs compensate drug dealers for their expenditure:

in acquiring the drugs, as well as for the risks of violence and imprisonment.

The economic loss to drug users is evident in such phenomena as wealthy users squandering hundreds of thousands of dollars on drugs, middle-class users losing their houses and cars to drug expenditures, and poor users going without food or shelter because the bulk of their funds is spent on purchasing expensive illegal drugs. Ironically, this economic loss to drug users under prohibition is frequently cited as a justification for prohibition. However, this harm is a major cost of prohibition and should be held against it in the legalization debate.

The total cost of drug-related law enforcement—courts, police, prisons, on all levels of government—is about [a] billion each year. Each dollar spent on drug enforcement yields seven dollars in economic loss. Prohibition takes $10 billion from taxpayers and uses it to raise billion[s] for organized crime and drug dealers, impoverishing many drug users in the process. To pay for expensive black market drugs, poor drug users then victimize the taxpayers by stealing $7.5 billion from them. Thus, the total economic cost of prohibition is about $80 billion each year (excluding the $7.5 billion in thefts).

Even this $80 billion figure does not include a number of other negative economic consequences of prohibition that are difficult to estimate. These include:

- the lost productivity of those who die as a result of prohibition;
- the lost productivity of those in prison on drug convictions or drug users who must "hustle" all day to pay for their drugs;
- the costs imposed by organized crime activities funded by drug profits;
- government and private funds spent on prohibition-created illnesses such as AIDS, hepatitis, and accidental overdose; and
- the funds spent on private security to fight drug-related crime.

Another difficult-to-measure economic cost of prohibition merits special mention: the negative impact of prohibition on the economic viability of inner cities and their inhabitants. Prohibition-related violence and property crime raise costs, make loans and insurance difficult or impossible to secure, and make it difficult to attract skilled workers. Prohibition lures some workers away from legitimate businesses and into the black market, where salaries are astronomically higher. As long as a black market in illegal drugs thrives in the inner cities, it is difficult to see how inner cities can ever become economically viable.

Economic Costs of Drug Use
If prohibition causes at least $80 billion in economic loss each year, what are the economic costs of illegal drug use per se? What costs of drug use would remain the same despite legalization? The author is unaware of any studies that attempt to directly measure these costs. However, an examination of the various components of economic cost indicates that the costs of legal drug use would be less than the costs of legal alcohol and tobacco use.

Crime
As noted above, the pharmacological effects of cocaine, heroin, and marijuana on violent crime are slight. The drug most frequently associated with crime and violence is alcohol.

Accidents

The primary drug associated with accidents is, again, alcohol. Large numbers of drunk drivers have killed themselves and others on the nation's roads. In a study of 440 fatally injured drivers, "[a]lcohol was by far the drug found most frequently, and the crash responsibility analysis provided evidence of its causal role in crashes," but the role of marijuana and other illegal drugs could not be determined. Heroin was present in very few of the victims. Cocaine, a stimulant, is unlikely to constitute a major accident problem. The Research Triangle Institute study was unable to find evidence to show that illegal drugs play a major role in causing auto accidents. The point is not that legalization would not have an impact on accidents, but that the impact will be far less than the impact of alcohol consumption on the number of fatal accidents.

Health Care Costs

Tobacco and alcohol are more lethal on a per capita basis than illegal drugs. In addition, since the pernicious effects of tobacco and alcohol are primarily chronic and long-term, there can be little doubt that users of these drugs do and will consume greater health care resources than the users of the illegal drugs.

Productivity

Some legal drugs, such as caffeine, seem to make people more productive. Others, such as alcohol, seem to make them less productive. Many illegal drugs could impair productivity if used on the job. As with alcohol, however, on-the-job use of a drug is no reason to make a drug illegal. . . .

Clogged Courts and Prisons

Each dollar spent enforcing drug laws and fighting the violent crimes stimulated by those laws is a dollar that cannot be spent fighting other violent crimes. Incarceration is one law enforcement technique that works in deterring violent crime. Put a violent career criminal in prison for five years and that person simply will not commit his usual quota of over 100 serious crimes per year during the period of his incarceration.

Currently, there are not enough judges and prosecutors to try cases or enough prison cells to house convicts. In 1987, the federal prison system had 44,000 inmates; 16,000 were drug offenders. Official capacity in federal prisons was only 28,000. In addition, many prisons are operating under court orders due to overcrowding or poor conditions. Because of the lack of prison space, violent criminals frequently are given deals, probation, and shorter terms than they deserve. Then they are back on the streets, and often back to serious crime.

Corruption

Drug money corrupts law enforcement officials. Corruption is a major problem in drug enforcement because drug agents are given tremendous power over desperate persons in possession of large amounts of cash. Drug corruption charges have been leveled against FBI agents, policemen, prison guards, U.S. Customs inspectors, even prosecutors. In 1986, in New York City's 77th Precinct, 12 police officers were arrested for stealing and selling drugs. Miami's problem is worse. In June 1986, seven officers there were indicted for using their jobs to run a drug operation that used murders, threats, and bribery. Add to that two dozen other cases of corruption in Miami in the last few years.

We must question a policy that so frequently turns policemen into organized criminals. There are two solutions to drug corruption: hire morally perfect policemen or eliminate the black market in drugs.

Assault on Civil Liberties

Drug war hysteria has created an atmosphere in which long-cherished rights are discarded wherever drugs are concerned. Suspected drug users are subject to urine testing, roadblocks, routine strip searches, school locker searches without probable cause, abuses of the good faith exception to the exclusionary rule, preventive detention, and nonjudicial forfeiture.

These governmental intrusions into our most personal activities are the natural and necessary consequence of drug prohibition. It is no accident that a law review article entitled "Crackdown: The Emerging 'Drug Exception' to the Bill of Rights" was published in 1987. In explaining why drug prohibition, by its very nature, threatens civil liberties, law professor Randy Barnett notes that drug offenses differ from violent crimes in that there is rarely a complaining witness to a drug transaction. Drug transactions are hidden from police view because the transactions are illegal, but the participants in the crime are willing. Thus, to be effective, drug agents must intrude into the innermost private lives of suspected drug criminals....

The same principle operates in enforcement efforts seemingly far removed from the invasive practice of body searches. Roadblocks, used with greater frequency in the war on drugs, impose an inconvenience on all citizens for the sake of allowing the police to ferret out a few drug suspects. One of the main purposes of currency reporting laws is to allow government agents to trace cash from drug transactions that is being "laundered" [transferred to conceal the money's source]. Currently, most cash transactions involving more than $10,000 must be reported to the government. Thus, the financial privacy of all must be sacrificed to allow government agents to search for a relatively small number of drug criminals. This intrusion is simply another cost of criminalizing an activity in which all the participants are willing.

The dangerous precedents used in the war on drugs represent a permanent increase in government power for all purposes. The tragedy is how cheaply our rights have been sold. Our society was once one in which the very thought of men and women being strip-searched and forced to urinate in the presence of witnesses was revolting. Furthermore, this degradation of our individual rights is in furtherance of a policy that does not work. It does not work because prohibition is the cause of the problems that make these extreme measures appear necessary.

Destruction of Community

Drug prohibition has had devastating effects on inner-city minority communities. A poorly educated young person in the inner city now has three choices: welfare, a low-wage job, or the glamorous, high-profit drug business. It is no wonder that large numbers of ghetto youth have gone into drug dealing, some of them as young as 10 years old. When the most successful people in a community are those engaged in illegal activities, the natural order of the community is destroyed. How can a mother maintain authority over a 16-

year-old son who pays the rent out of his petty cash? How can a teacher persuade students to study hard when dropouts drive BMWs? The profits from prohibition make a mockery of the work ethic and of family authority.

A related problem with prohibition is that it forces drug users to come into contact with people of real criminal intent. For all the harm that alcohol and tobacco cause, one does not have to deal with criminals to use those drugs. Prohibition drags the drug user into a criminal culture.

Once familiar with breaking the law by using drugs and dealing with criminals, it is difficult for the drug user, and especially the drug dealer, to maintain respect for other laws. Honesty, respect for private property, and other aspects of a law-abiding community are further casualties of the drug laws. When the huge illegal profits and violence of the illegal-drug business permeate a neighborhood, it ceases to be a functioning community. The natural tendency of people to help each other and to maintain standards of decency and order is undermined. In the communities where drug dealing is most prevalent, this has many consequences. For example, legitimate businesses are discouraged from opening or remaining in business, education is disdained, and the resulting violence makes mail carriers and ambulance drivers afraid to enter housing complexes. The destruction of inner-city communities is one of the major evils of prohibition....

Would Drug Use Increase?

Would there be any substantial increase in drug use under decriminalization? Long-term trends in legal drug use suggest not. As a society, we are gradually moving away from the harmful use of alcohol and tobacco.

> In 1956, 42 percent of adults smoked; in 1980 only 33 percent. In 1977, 29 percent of high school seniors smoked; in 1981, 20 percent.... We did not declare a war on tobacco. We did not make it illegal.... We did seek to convince our citizens not to smoke through persuasion, objective information, and education.

The consumption of alcohol, and deaths caused by alcohol, have also been gradually declining as people switch from hard liquors to less potent formulations. Finally, users of marijuana—now a de facto [actual] legal drug in some states—declined from 18 million in 1985 to 12 million in 1988 according to the National Institute on Drug Abuse (NIDA).

As our society grows increasingly health and fitness conscious, heavy drug use will lose its appeal. Many are trading in the tavern for the health club and choosing vitamins over martinis. This process of bringing legal drug use under the influence of positive social values such as health and moderation has less influence on the illegal drug scene. There, hard-core drug users form subcultures that reinforce the values of heavy, reckless drug use....

The fatal flaw in the policy of prohibition is that those who need to be protected most from drug use—hard-core users—are those who will not be deterred by laws against drugs. These individuals consider drug use to be one of their highest values in life. They will take great risks, pay high prices, and violate the law to achieve this value. The remainder of the population consists of moderate drug users and non-drug users. These are people who have developed the individual or social resources which allow them to avoid harmful legal drug use.

Even when it comes to illegal drugs, it is naive to think that prohibition relieves moderate drug users of having to make responsible choices regarding these substances. Regardless of the expense of long-term use, obtaining the first batch of "crack" or heroin is not expensive and opportunities abound—on the street, in broad daylight, illegal drugs are there. Thus, the level of illegal drug use is strongly influenced by individual choices and values. For example, individual preference—not law enforcement—is the likely explanation for the existence of 20,000,000 marijuana smokers, but a mere 500,000 heroin users. If 20,000,000 people demanded heroin, the black market would meet that demand, just as it met the enormous demand for alcohol in the 1920s. Thus, prohibition is at best a comforting illusion.

The ideal test of the effectiveness of our drug laws is whether they have reduced overall drug use since their enactment. In fact, they have not. On a per capita basis, the use of narcotics was no greater before prohibition than it is today and the use of cocaine is far greater today than it was when cocaine was legally available. In 1915, the year the first national control laws became effective, there were about 200,000 regular narcotics users and only 20,000 regular cocaine users. Today, there are about 500,000 regular heroin users and nearly three million regular cocaine users. Since the population is more than twice what it was in 1915, it is apparent that the percentage of the population using narcotics has remained about the same, while cocaine use has increased astronomically.... Seventy years of intensive law enforcement efforts

have failed to measurably reduce drug use....

The Failure of Enforcement

Common sense tells us that illegal drugs will always be readily available. Prison wardens cannot keep drugs out of their own institutions—an important lesson for those who would turn this country into a prison to stop drug use. Even the Soviet Union has admitted to having a serious illegal drug problem. In this country, police officers are regularly caught using drugs, selling drugs and even stealing drugs. How are these people going to lead a drug war?...

A General Accounting Office (GAO) report released at the White House Conference for a Drug Free America in 1988 contains overwhelming evidence of the failure of President Reagan's war on drugs. Contrary to the claims of some critics, the Reagan war on drugs did not fail for lack of trying. The federal drug control budget increased from $1.2 billion in 1981 to nearly $4 billion in 1987. The FBI and the military were brought into drug enforcement. Two major pieces of legislation were passed to toughen penalties and give enforcers more powers —the Comprehensive Crime Control Act of 1984 and the Anti-Drug Abuse Act of 1986. Arrests rose 58 percent and federal prisons became filled with convicted drug dealers. Drug seizures greatly increased—362 percent in the case of cocaine from 1982 to 1986.

The GAO reported the results:

- Drug abuse in the United States has persisted at a very high level throughout the 1980s.
- Cocaine: The amount of cocaine consumed more than doubled. The price declined about 30 percent. The aver-

age purity doubled. Cocaine-related deaths rose substantially.

- Heroin: The price [of] heroin declined 20 percent. The average purity rose 33 percent. Heroin-related deaths rose substantially.
- Marijuana: While use declined, "[m]arijuana continues to be readily available in most areas of the country, with a trend toward increased potency levels." Marijuana is now grown in all fifty states and "[t]o avoid detection, marijuana growers are moving their operations indoors and are growing smaller and more scattered plots outdoors." ...

CONCLUSION

Drug prohibition is immoral because it violates the individual right of self-ownership. Drug prohibition is also a practical failure. The moral and practical arguments come together since prohibition fails precisely because it violates the right of self-ownership. Prohibition relies on force as opposed to persuasion to achieve its goal. Tens of millions of Americans who have not been rationally persuaded to avoid drug use are using illegal drugs in spite of the law whenever the force of law is absent. In a free society, it is in the nature of law enforcement to be absent most of the time.

While prohibition fails to deter millions of individual drug users whose main risk of arrest occurs only when purchases are made, prohibition does absolutely deter legitimate businesses from entering the drug market. Since businesses would have to establish fixed locations for production, distribution and sale, drug enforcement would put them out of business within hours. Thus, prohibition, by violating the rights of legitimate busi-

nessmen and women to produce and sell drugs to willing buyers, destroys any possibility of a drug market which would produce drugs designed to reduce the chances of death by overdose and other maladies, and to sell drugs at a low enough price so that consumers would not have to impoverish themselves to buy them.

Prohibition, by mandating that the conditions of drug production, distribution, and sale will be secrecy, violence, and risk, puts the drug industry in the hands of professionals in the art of engaging in clandestine action and systematic violence; avoiding arrest, conviction, and imprisonment and tolerating the same if necessary. Since the risks of engaging in clandestine activities and systematic violence, and facing long prison terms are very high, illegal drug users pay very high prices to compensate drug dealers for the cost of these risks.

Violence between dealers is common because it is their primary mode of resolving disputes since they are denied access to the courts. Further, to be a dealer means that one is more willing to use violence and incur the risk of violence than the average person. Thus, dealers use this "skill" to enhance the profitability of their businesses by murdering their competitors.

In sum, each of the problems caused by prohibition is ultimately traceable to the fact that individuals are prevented from acting on their own judgment by the initiation of force by the state. It is not that prohibition violates individual rights to liberty and also happens not to work. Rather, prohibition does not work because it violates the individual right to liberty.

NO   Steven Brill

SHOULD WE GIVE UP?

On the Lower East Side of Manhattan Benito Sanchez is panhandling for drug money while wheeling his girlfriend's 3-year-old in a stroller. According to subsequent police reports, passersby notice that the motionless little girl isn't napping. She's stiff. Dead. Sanchez had beaten her the night before because she wouldn't stop crying. A police investigation reveals that Sanchez was high on crack at the time. (After plea bargaining to manslaughter he is sentenced to eight-and-a-third to twenty-five years in prison.)

In midtown, Earl Caple brings his one-month-old baby to the emergency room at Bellevue Hospital because her vagina is bleeding. He later tells police he raped her while he was high on crack because she wouldn't stop crying. (He pleads guilty to assault in the first degree and gets five to fifteen years.)

Uptown, in the neonatal care ward on the fourth floor of Harlem Hospital, David Bateman, the doctor who runs the unit, talks almost drearily about the crack mothers who, he says, "have no maternal instinct.... They smoke the stuff while they're pregnant," which typically makes the babies underdeveloped at birth. "Then," he adds, "when we have to keep the babies here in the unit because they've got some sort of problem, the mothers leave and often don't come back. Or you'll see them once in thirty or forty days come in at midnight with sunglasses on, giggling, looking for their baby.... With the poorest, most desperate mothers in this area who have babies who have to remain here, you don't see that kind of neglect. Unless they're on crack."

Across the country, ... illegal drugs, particularly crack, are poisoning us in so many ways, in so many places, and with such nightmarish results that it's as if Frankenstein, or Muammar Qaddafi, had broken into our water supply.

Whether we can fight back and enforce the laws against these drugs would seem, therefore, to be a pivotal test for what we have always thought was the sturdiest, surest legal system on earth.

Yet Dr. Bateman, the man who treats the premature babies of the cracked-out mothers with the sunglasses, isn't so sure we should spend our time worrying about enforcing the law.

And as I listened over the last several weeks to people like him and to others who favor legalization more strongly, I almost joined their side. Almost.

From Steven Brill, "Should We Give Up?" *The American Lawyer* (March 1990). Copyright © 1990 by *The American Lawyer.* Reprinted by permission.

"Sure, I hate the people who sell this stuff," Bateman says. "But so what? I'm not sure that even if we hang them all up by their toes and pelt them with tomatoes, it will do any good. There will just be someone else to take their place.... This is a medical and social problem, not a legal problem, but it's become caught up in politics.... And so we have the rhetoric of a war on drugs and drug dealers, when we should probably legalize it and focus on the medical and social problems."

Bateman has been at Harlem Hospital for nine years. He is anything but cavalier about drugs and what drug abuse has wrought in America's most famous center of the underclass. He sees the horror of it all every day.

"Crack has produced social devastation," he says. "What you see is shockingly abnormal maternal behavior. The complete absence of a maternal instinct.... Mothers who have no thought of taking their babies home when they leave."

A good percentage of those crack babies can't go home, anyway, because of what their mothers' drug habit has done to them in the womb. Bateman says that before 1985 approximately 3 percent of the babies born at Harlem Hospital had mothers who were using addictive illegal drugs. By 1986, when crack—which because it is smoked is more popular with women than injectable heroin—had begun its full sweep through the ghetto, the number had risen to 15 percent. By 1988 it was 20 percent.

Which is where it is now: One fifth of the 3,000 babies born in Harlem Hospital this year will be born of mothers addicted to drugs, usually crack.

Crack babies, explains Bateman, are often premature and almost always physically smaller—in everything from bone size to weight to brain size—than normal babies. "And the evidence so far," he adds, "is spotty, but the ones we've watched so far don't seem to catch up as they get older," meaning that they will probably stay smaller, with less fully developed brains and other faculties.

Bateman says that nationally the birth rate of "small, premature babies," which are defined as babies weighing three pounds, four ounces or less at birth is about 1 percent. At Harlem Hospital it is now 3.5 percent.

Nationally, about 7 percent of all babies require intensive hospital care after birth; according to Bateman, the rate at Harlem Hospital in the nine years he has been there has jumped from 13 percent to 24 percent, an increase he attributes almost exclusively to crack.

The mothers of these crack babies—mothers who traditionally have formed the core of the nuclear family in the ghetto—have been so robbed of maternal instinct, or their living situations are so unsustainable, that 50 percent of all the babies Bateman treats in the neonatal unit go into foster care, where they typically become wards of the state.

The ones who do go home are likely to be shell-shocked by mothers whose moods swing from euphoria to violent paranoia and whose promiscuity is a predictable side effect of the addiction. These children are the faces behind the avalanche of child abuse cases reported in New York and other urban areas. According to New York Court of Appeals chief judge Sol Wachtler's 1989 annual report on the state of the judiciary, child abuse cases have exploded by 232 percent in the last four years in New York City. "Those numbers are the cost of crack, pure and simple," says Wachtler. "It's as if this drug's effects were designed by the devil."

Bateman asserts that "much of what you've read in the newspapers about crack babies suffering the shakes or other pain is garbage, part of the drug war rhetoric." But he says he is "willing to concede" the bona fides of recent studies at the National Institute on Drug Abuse in Washington, D.C., that have asserted that prenatal exposure to crack interferes with babies' emotional development in a way that may leave them permanently handicapped in developing basic employment skills and close human relationships— "flat moods and emotional poverty," *The New York Times* called it in a September 1989 article. "That wouldn't surprise me." Bateman says. "It's an awful drug."

Across the country, the best data is that there are now 30,000–50,000 crack babies born every year. Almost 1,000 a week. More than 100 a day. Parentless, or living with an addicted mother. Underdeveloped. Probably less capable of normal emotional attachments. Future zombies.

Nonetheless, Bateman argues that "spending all this money and energy and rhetoric on putting people in jail just hasn't worked.... You can go right around the corner from this hospital and buy crack," he adds (an assertion I found to be true when I left him that afternoon), "and you always will be able to until we treat the social causes and the medical causes of addiction."

"When I talk about legalization, people tell me I should go visit the crack babies in Harlem Hospital," says federal district court judge Robert Sweet, who lately has assumed a leading public role among a growing group of public figures who favor legalization. "Well, what I tell them is that those crack babies are there *now*

with the present system. What we have now just doesn't work."

Sweet, 67, is a former federal prosecutor, deputy mayor of New York under John Lindsay, and partner at Skadden, Arps, Slate, Meagher & Flom. He's a serious, thoughtful man, and a highly regarded judge (and no bleeding heart) near the end of his career. As such he is above the suspicion one might harbor about a politician who might be eager to ride this issue to greater glory. In fact, Sweet's first public pronouncement on legalization was in what he thought was a private dinner speech; only when his remarks generated a story in *The New York Times* did he allow himself to be nudged into the limelight enough to defend his position.

But he does defend it, and persuasively.

"The other day," he begins, "I had to sentence a kid about twenty years old to the five-year mandatory minimum that this new statute requires ... because he was caught steering someone to a sale of a few hundred dollars' worth of crack.... The kid was an addict.... And I felt like leaning over the bench and saying to him. 'Why didn't you just get high off of alcohol.' ...

"It's the profit from the stuff being illegal that drives the whole market.... This kid was encouraged to be an addict because some pusher could make money off of him.... He was a gofer, who was swept up in this....

"Why did he get into it? Because he saw a way to make some easy dollars. He saw the only way for him to make some easy dollars....

"We need to deal with the problem of desperation that these people face, but first we have to take the economics and the corruption out of it. Treat it like a disease."

"But don't you hate the idea of people being allowed to sell something that kills other people?" I asked. "How can you make that legal? How would you feel about our society and our rule of law if you could walk up to someone at a cocktail party and ask him what he did for a living and he said matter-of-factly, 'Oh, I sell crack in Harlem'?"

"Well, how do you feel if you see Edgar Bronfman at a cocktail party... or Larry Tisch," Sweet replied, referring, respectively, to the chairman of Joseph E. Seagram & Sons, Inc., and to the chairman of the Loews Corporation (in addition to CBS), which owns the Lorillard Tobacco Company. "Alcohol and tobacco kill more people, but we don't outlaw it because we are willing to let people be responsible for their own conduct. . . .

"It's all a question of responsibility," Sweet adds. "We tend to want to push responsibility up, from the individual to society as a whole, or to government. But it doesn't work. . . .

"How many times do you hear of someone being indicted for attempted suicide? What we do is try to treat people who attempt to commit suicide, just as we try to treat alcoholics."

As I said, he is persuasive.

In fact, Sweet's point could be carried further: We attempt to persuade and treat people who abuse alcohol and tobacco because these people are as often as not white and middle-class. But heroin and crack are mostly the province of the nonwhite underclass. And because this kind of suicidal drug abuse is a symptom of their desperation —desperation for which the rest of us are arguably responsible—we need to criminalize it rather than face it and treat it: If we call it criminal conduct, then it's not our fault. And if we call it criminal

conduct we can send in the police rather than the more expensive doctors and other therapists.

Similarly, it could be argued (and Sweet, in fact, seems to be arguing) that criminalization amounts to nothing less than the worst kind of racist paternalism: People in the ghetto are incapable of being responsible for themselves; they need the long arm of our law to help them save themselves.

One of Sweet's key allies on the legalization side is Ethan Nadelmann, a 32-year-old Harvard-trained lawyer and an assistant professor of politics and public affairs at Princeton's Woodrow Wilson School. . . . Nadelmann's writing is credited with persuading many of the recent enlistees to the legalization side, such as former Secretary of State George Schulz and Baltimore Mayor Kurt Schmoke.

In a compelling September 1989 article in *Science* magazine the professor— who, unlike Sweet, does seem eager to have this issue be his ticket to regular appearances on ABC's *Nightline*—notes that, despite all of our law enforcement efforts against cocaine, the price has actually come down in the last decade even as the purity of a typical gram of the stuff has quintupled.

Worse, crack is a particularly cheap but potent form of cocaine. (Indeed, the development of this cheap, smokeable, baking soda-based "junk food" form of cocaine in the mid-1980s was a seminal breakthrough for the drug marketers, equivalent to the development of the microchip for information processing.) Thus, there is almost no hope of putting its price beyond the reach of a potential addict.

Nor is there much hope for eradicating it at its source in South America;

Nadelmann says that only 700 square miles of the roughly 2.5 million square miles of farmland in South America that are arid enough to grow cocaine are now used for that crop, which means there is lots of room for the growers to move around.

Meanwhile, at home we are spending what Nadelmann says is more than $10 billion a year to enforce laws that fill our prisons, clog our courts with arrests that are mostly for possession, preoccupy our police, and do little to curb drug abuse, while enriching and encouraging a $10–50 billion black market that, says Nadelmann, would be devastated by legalization.

And we do all of that, Nadelmann points out, while we allow the sale of cigarettes, when "an estimated 320,000 people die prematurely each year as a consequence of their consumption of tobacco." Similarly, we tolerate alcohol, despite the fact that booze is a "contributing factor in ... 40 percent of suicide attempts and about 40 percent of the 46,000 ... traffic deaths in 1983," and that "no illicit drug ... is as strongly associated with violent behavior as is alcohol. According to Justice Department statistics, 54 percent of all jail [sic] inmates convicted of violent crimes in 1983 reported having used alcohol just prior to committing their offense."

("We're not sure yet of what crack does to babies," adds Bateman of Harlem Hospital. "But there is one drug we are certain of, and that's alcohol. We have identified a clear fetal syndrome associated with babies whose mothers are alcoholics; the babies are often retarded.")

"All of the health costs of marijuana, cocaine, and heroin combined amount to only a small fraction of those caused by either of these two licit substances," Nadelmann adds, referring to tobacco and alcohol.

"Legalization of drugs," Nadelmann concludes, "would yield its greatest benefit in the ghettos, where it would sever much of the drug-crime connection, seize the market away from the criminals, deglorify involvement in the illicit drug business, help redirect the work ethic from illegitimate to legitimate employment opportunities, help stem the transmission of AIDS in I.V. drug users, and significantly improve the safety, health, and well-being of those who do use and abuse drugs" because "billions in new revenues" from taxes on the newly legal drugs would fund treatment programs, and because the drugs would be dispensed in a setting that would guarantee their purity and safety.

But what kind of setting?

Nadelmann's article seems to be missing a page in this regard; he tells us nothing of how the legalization scheme would work.

But Sweet says, "Addicts would go into a government-licensed store, maybe a pharmacy. They would have to register, and they'd get their drugs [which would be manufactured by legitimate drug companies] at the same time that they would be encouraged to enroll in treatment."

The more one ponders Sweet's scenario, the easier it is to see why Nadelmann chose to avoid the issue of how legalization would work. For it's here that the whole appealing, facile argument begins to crumble.

Let's remember that crack is a particularly fiendish drug.

"Two or three hits can turn many people into addicts," says Dr. Mitchell Rosenthal, who helped pioneer the Phoenix

House drug treatment centers in New York in the late 1960s, and who now treats 1,400 addicts as inpatients and 300 more as outpatients at ten treatment centers in New York and California.

Adds Rosenthal: "When you take one hit, you want to binge. You want five or ten more hits. You have to keep going until you drop with exhaustion, because the high is so quick—straight to the brain—but so short—maybe a few minutes—and the down is so terrible that you have to keep going.... And when you're on crack you will do all kinds of violent, antisocial things. It is not like heroin, where you nod off."

So, will our friendly government dispensary keep giving out hits?

If not, won't the black market be out there ready and willing to help the binging crack addict?

"Bars don't serve drunks," says Sweet. Sure, but many drunks don't usually feel compelled, physically, to keep drinking, or if they do they can go home and raid their own bars. Are we going to sell crack addicts large enough amounts for them to store at home? Besides, do we really want to hold up our "success" in controlling binging drunks as our standard for crack addicts?

Asked about that, Nadelmann says, "I haven't really worked out the details, but there could be two scenarios.... One idea might be just to sell cocaine in powder form to see if snorting it will satisfy crack addicts."

Which, of course, it won't. And which will allow the purchasers to buy some baking soda and go into the black market crack business for themselves—good perhaps for our balance of trade (with Colombia) but absurd as a way of controlling the problem.

"Another alternative," the professor continues, "would be, yes, to sell them unlimited quantities of crack. At least that would drive out the black market.... Look at it this way: Suppose to get crack you had to walk up to the counter at a government store and there was a sign that says, 'You have a sixty percent chance of becoming addicted, and a one in two thousand chance of dying from one dose.' Wouldn't that setting send a different message than what we now have, where kids are pushed into it for fast money?"

Speaking of kids, what about minors? Will they be allowed, or will the black market serve them, too?

Sweet, again, points to liquor. But do we want today's teenage alcohol problem to be matched by a teenage crack problem?

Nadelmann says, "Sure, there would be a black market for kids, but it would be less than what we have now." Really? With everyone else allowed to buy unlimited quantities from the neighborhood dispensary, everyone else could be a black marketeer.

What about pregnant women? Will we serve them? Will we force them to have abortions? "Those are tough questions," Nadelmann says.

And who's going to come in and register at these dispensaries, anyway, rather than go to the black market? If the lure for signing up (and being fingerprinted, too, says Sweet) will be that they'll save money, then what will happen to Nadelmann's "billions" in tax revenue? How much below the current price of $5 per hit can the government go and still collect its taxes?

Asked about that, Nadelmann says that he still hasn't "worked out all the details of sale and price, or location."

But it's all in the details, a reality that seemed to dawn on Nadelmann as I questioned him further and he backpedaled, asserting that "at this point I'm probably only arguing that we *experiment* with legalization, beginning, probably, just with marijuana... or just in one isolated community."

In short, it is impossible to imagine any legalization scheme that would eliminate, or even make a dent in, the black market. All that legalization is likely to do is make crack more available and less forbidding to the vast majority of people, including ghetto residents, who are now deterred by the stigma and the relative inaccessibility that results from its being illegal, and who might experiment with it if they could walk into a store and get it.

"To me it seems horrible to contemplate selling heroin or cocaine over the counter," says "Steve," a former big-firm lawyer-addict.... "Sure, some people try drugs because they are illegal and there's a thrill in that," he continues. "But a lot more would be tempted if it were legal. You have to assume that."

In that regard, Nadelmann and Sweet can be hoisted on their own liquor and tobacco analogies and all the accompanying statistics. Maybe the reason that the death and illness numbers attached to tobacco and the death, sickness, and violence numbers attached to alcohol are so high is because they *are* legal. Do we want to find out how many more people would try crack if it were legal?

"I wouldn't let crack be sold at seven cents a piece in vending machines," says Nadelmann. "And we shouldn't do that with cigarettes either." Fine, but should we take it from the back alleys of the ghetto to the friendly neighborhood dispensary? Won't the increased availability and the elimination of the stigma of illegality create thousands, even millions, of new addicts who will now be free to try it?

Nadelmann attempts to deal with this point in his article by noting that studies show that most people who tried cocaine and marijuana in the 1960s and 1970s did not become addicted. But that was before crack cocaine. It was when cocaine was snorted and therefore far less potent, addictive, and dangerous, an obvious point that Nadelmann ignores, and which he dismissed in our conversation by saying that "we shouldn't let one drug like crack" that is "temporarily popular" dictate our whole drug policy.

Yet the overriding reality of drug abuse in the 1990s is that with scientific advances there are likely to be more types of fiendish drugs like crack coming on line. "Ice," now in vogue on the West Coast and in Hawaii, is the latest example. Crack and ice and the drugs we haven't heard of yet are the realities we have to assume when we consider legalization.

"Brian," a lawyer-addict from Skadden, Arps..., says he is "torn" by the question of legalization, but on balance favors it, because "the stigma of it being illegal makes people like me afraid to seek help. There was a time when a partner asked me what was wrong with me and I so wanted to tell him, but was afraid because I was breaking the law."

Perhaps, but he did ultimately seek treatment, and many more of his colleagues today are alcohol abusers, in part because the barriers to initial use aren't there.

Leaving aside the question of whether Nadelmann's numbers make a good case for making alcohol and tobacco illegal rather than making crack legal, it seems clear that there are differences between alcohol and tobacco that compel the conclusion that at least crack should be illegal.

First, to the extent that tobacco has victims other than the user, we can control that victimization, as we are now starting to do, by prohibiting smoking in places where nonsmokers will have their lungs polluted. Second, not all smokers automatically die or have their lives ruined, the way almost all crack users do. Third, while tobacco is addictive, cigarette addicts and potential addicts are far more capable of being persuaded to end their habits, as we know from all the data showing recent declines in smoking.

As for alcohol, we can't claim to be very good at controlling victimization of others, but there is some evidence that tougher enforcement of drunk driving laws is helping in at least that area. (Similarly, although the fetal alcohol syndrome cited by Bateman of Harlem Hospital is horrendous, he concedes that pregnant women apparently give up their drinking enough and that the syndrome is rare enough that he sees "fewer than ten babies a year" with that problem.)

Also, we can agree that not all drinkers become alcohol addicts, let alone die or ruin their lives as a result of their drinking. And as with tobacco, there is some evidence that people are being weaned off alcohol as its dangers become clearer and more clearly articulated.

So it may not make sense—indeed, it may be emblematic of the bankruptcy of our principles as a nation—that beer and cigarette maker Philip Morris Companies, Inc., was listed last month in a *Fortune* poll of the business community as the second-most-admired corporation in America, or that a man like cigarette

peddler Henry Kravis, whose LBO partnership owns RJR/Nabisco, is one of the darlings of New York society. But alcohol and tobacco aren't crack.

The point is that when Judge Sweet says, "Are we going to ban red meat because it causes heart attacks?" we ought to say that there is not one all-encompassing principle at work in our society that says we allow everything or we allow nothing. Rather, there is a continuum, a line, and a place where we draw the line. We will draw the line between products we will tolerate freely and leave for people to make their own decisions about (like red meat), products we will tolerate with some controls on who can buy them and how they can be marketed (cigarettes, prescription drugs, cars, and guns someday, one hopes), and products we won't tolerate at all, with the line-drawing based on weighing the costs and the benefits of that product and how likely it is that those using the product will be able to make rational decisions about it and will not victimize others if they make the wrong decision.

Sweet argues that the purpose of law is to direct itself to those areas where people hurt others, not themselves. Even on that basis, the case for the current legal prohibition against crack is clear. Selling it clearly hurts others. That's easy. But buying it hurts others too, because it sustains the marketplace for the sellers. And just possessing it—the most difficult legal prohibition to rationalize on Sweet's theoretically reasonable terms—also hurts others because its use so predictably makes the user uncontrollably antisocial, be it in terms of child abuse, fetal abuse, or random violent crime.

Rosenthal of Phoenix House is a lot less theoretical about it, and for good reason: "Comparing crack to alcohol or tobacco is like comparing a BB gun to a shotgun," he says. "Adding another chemical to what's already legal out there that is by many magnitudes more potent would be mindless....

"Nadelmann and Sweet think that if we give these drugs to people they'll achieve some kind of equilibrium," Rosenthal continues heatedly. "That they won't be criminals. That they won't be antisocial. That their crime is because of the money they need for drugs. Well, I've seen people with unlimited money come in here who had enough to buy all the drugs they wanted and they didn't stabilize. They weren't in that social equilibrium that Sweet and Nadelmann think they'll find....

"They figure that maybe we can't solve the problem, but that if we just give the addict what he's asking for, he'll settle down and be a nice fella and won't bother us. Well, he won't be a nice fella, and he will bother us. He'll be violent. He'll be paranoid. He'll binge. He'll need twenty or thirty crack vials a day, and he'll never reach that equilibrium."

A young black woman from Brooklyn named Kelly, who is being treated for crack addiction at Phoenix House, puts it this way: "When you have one vial, you scheme to get the second. If you have ten, when you get to the ninth you think about what you can sell—your body, the TV set, anything—to get the eleventh. You look at a TV set and say, 'The TV, who needs it? I'll sell it.' The next day ... after you've passed out, you get up and say, 'What happened to the TV?' ... Legalize crack and let me be able to buy it anytime, and I'd have a home with no furniture, and I'd die."

"I feel so bad about this legalization theory," adds Rosenthal, whose program claims a 60 percent success rate for its patients, who include all varieties of addicts. "I have never met a drug user who's untreatable. But I have met plenty who don't want treatment. And one way you get them to want it is to say, 'You can't have drugs.'"

Conversely, Rosenthal notes that "you can't treat people for addiction and give them drugs."

Kelly adds, "Legalize it, and this place would be empty. You'd be telling me, 'It's okay to do crack. It's legal.' So why be here?"

The fact is that for all the talk about current enforcement not working, it may, in fact, be working. "We've clearly made progress with mainstream America," says Rosenthal. "Drug use is down in mainstream America."

And Bateman of Harlem Hospital concedes that the rate of drug abusing mothers has "leveled off at twenty percent since last year and may even be dropping a bit," an assessment that echoes an observation by noted criminologist James Q. Wilson in a recent article in *Commentary* that despite the argument for legalization of heroin in the 1970s—that law enforcement wasn't working—heroin addiction in fact has leveled off since 1972, while it has escalated in England, where the drug is legally administered to addicts.

But the more important point is that we haven't really tried to do what we need to do to bring that percentage of addicted mothers below 20 percent. As Manhattan district attorney Robert Morgenthau puts it, "We haven't tried enforcement, so how do we know if it will work?"

Morgenthau points out that despite President Bush's drug war rhetoric, the entire federal Drug Enforcement Agency consists of 2,600 agents across the country —roughly half of the police force in the

Bronx—and that the new money in the President's drug war chest totals $39 million, to be spread among the 50 states.

"There are two cheap answers to drugs," says Morgenthau. "Legalization and the death penalty. The real answer is the expensive answer: real money for real enforcement and real treatment programs."

"People can be treated, if they want to be treated," adds Rosenthal. "And one of the ways you get them to want to be treated is to have the foot of the law up their ass, to have them facing prosecution if they don't go into treatment.... If we weren't so wimpy about this, we could make progress."

What's the way to be unwimpy?

"Well, we know from studies that seventy to eighty percent of all those arrested have a drug problem," Rosenthal says. "Right now, we have eight thousand people a week arraigned in New York, and seventy percent of them are addicts. And it's the same in every city across the country. But do we test them? No. We should test them, and then make treatment a condition of their release."

That, of course, means billions for new treatment facilities, but, as Rosenthal notes, "We're putting them in prison anyway. It wouldn't cost more to treat them."

On this front, too, there is progress. For example, in New York, Governor Mario Cuomo has started a program whereby 2,450 of the state's 52,000 prison beds in the next year will be converted to drug treatment beds.

But the real progress will only come when efforts like this aren't an exception. If we discovered that Muammar Qaddafi was contaminating our water supply with a poison that made millions of us paranoid, violent, and incapable of fulfilling any obligations to loved ones, we would post police and national guardsmen everywhere necessary. And we would treat all the victims.

We wouldn't write off the victims, let alone set up dispensaries for the poisoned water.

"If Bob Sweet found out that his fourteen-year-old daughter was using crack, he wouldn't want the government to help her get it," says Rosenthal. "He'd be knocking on my door to get her into a drug-free program, and he'd do whatever he had to do to force her into it. Why should he have a different solution for someone else's fourteen-year-old daughter?"

Rosenthal is right. We can't write off anyone's daughter. We can't just write off those communities where the desperation is highest and, therefore, the reach for an escape the most frequent. This is one instance where the politicians' rhetoric would actually match reality. For this would be the genocide that many black political leaders have labeled it to be. And in the process we would also encourage the poisoning among those not in the underclass who are now more likely to be deterred by the illegality of drugs like crack.

Nor as a society should we commit the most destabilizing act in a system built on the rule of law—the abandonment of a law because it takes too much resolve to enforce it.

If for a year or two it takes cops on half the street corners of America, let's do it.... Let's put cops, or troops, on that block next to Dr. Bateman's hospital. And if it takes investments in treatment equal to 20 or 30 percent of what we're paying to bail out the Charlie Keatings of the world, let's do that, too. If it takes another 30 or 40 percent of what we're spending to bail out the S&Ls to provide real educational and job opportunity for the people whose desperation drove them to crack in the first place, let's do that too.

Or, at least, let's try.

In the coming months the arguments for legalization, supported by an eye-catching coalition of respected thinkers from the right and left, are going to be increasingly in vogue. For the liberals, the lure will be the notion of enlightened treatment taking the place of a storm-trooper police effort that features wire-taps and stool pigeons and the incarceration of desperate people "swept up," to use Sweet's words, in this activity. For conservatives the lure will be a Chicago School kind of argument, that we should let people decide for themselves in the great marketplace out there what they want to do to themselves.

But liberals should understand that legalization represents the ultimate abdication of governmental responsibility, a decision to give the underclass (and ultimately everyone else) whatever drugs they want, with whatever consequences to themselves and their families, as long as they won't bother us with crime. (Indeed, liberals should understand that the fact that addicts commit crimes against the mainstream is probably the only reason there is any broad-based constituency at all today for providing drug treatment.)

And conservatives should know that legalization represents the ultimate throwing in of the towel, the ultimate abandonment of the notion that we're serious about being a society based on the rule of law. For we'd be getting rid of the law simply because we've found that it's hard to enforce.

"You don't solve this by saying, 'There's nothing I can do, so let's put a government label on crack and give it out at the government crack house,'" says Rosenthal. "If you do, there will be more instability, more violence, more child abuse. And the addicts will stand there at the crack house and take the stuff until they drop dead."

POSTSCRIPT

Should Drug Use Be Legalized?

The question of whether or not illicit drugs should be legalized is an extremely difficult one and one that will continue to confront us. Current public opinion surveys find that the "legalizing" option has insignificant public support. But another few years of drug-related violence and complaints by judges and court administrators that drug cases are clogging the courts could bring about a shift in public attitudes. (Drug cases account for 4 percent of criminal trials and 50 percent of criminal appeals in the federal courts.) See Martin, "Drugs, Crime, and Urban Trial Court Management: The Unintended Consequences of the War on Drugs," 8 *Law and Policy Review* 117 (1990).

It should be emphasized that one choice is not necessarily the easy one and the other the hard one. The "legalizers" are occasionally depicted as advocates of a free market of drugs, of letting individuals make decisions about personal use of drugs, and of letting the market regulate the price of a product that now has an artificially elevated price. But most "legalizers" are, in fact, asking that government involvement in dealing with the drug problem continue. To suggest a noncriminal approach to drugs is not to advocate a hands-off approach. Treatment is needed and education is needed. It is not all that clear that this would be cheaper than the current approach.

It would also not necessarily be easier. Other than complete legalization, where drugs might be as readily available as aspirin, most approaches call for some regulation by the state. Choices would have to be made among these alternatives, ranging from outlawing sales to minors, to requiring medical prescriptions for some drugs, to establishing clinics that would distribute the drugs. Each of these alternatives would raise questions about free access and about effects on the black market for drugs.

Recent writings on the legalization question include Duke, *America's Longest War: Rethinking Our Tragic Crusade Against Drugs* (1993); Bayer and Oppenheimer, *Confronting Drug Policy: Illicit Drugs in a Free Society* (1993); Trebach, *Legalize It? Debating American Drug Policy* (1993); Moire, "Drugs: Getting a Fix on the Problem and the Solution," 8 *Yale Law and Policy Review* 8 (1990); and Wilson, "Against the Legalization of Drugs," *Commentary* (February 1990), p. 21. Cloud, "Cocaine, Demand, and the Addiction: A Study of the Possible Convergence of Rational Theory and National Policy," 42 *Vanderbilt Law Review* 725 (1989) contains a discussion of the legislative history of prevention and treatment programs. The myths and realities of the Prohibition era are examined in Clark, *Deliver Us From Evil* (1976) and Kyvig, ed., *Law, Alcohol and Order: Perspective on National Prohibition* (1985).

CONTRIBUTORS
TO THIS VOLUME

EDITOR

M. ETHAN KATSH, a graduate of Yale Law School, is a professor of legal studies at the University of Massachusetts–Amherst. He has served as the chair of the legal studies department at the University of Massachusetts and as the president of the American Legal Studies Association. His articles have appeared in scholarly journals as well as such popular publications as the *Wall Street Journal, TV Guide,* and *Saturday Review.* He is the coauthor of *Before the Law,* 2d ed. (Houghton Mifflin) and the author of *The Electronic Media and the Transformation of the Law* (Oxford University Press, 1989). Professor Katsh has also produced simulation games on plea bargaining and mediation, and he is a codesigner of Rock 'n' Roll LEXIS, multimedia software that teaches electronic legal research.

STAFF

Mimi Egan   Publisher
Brenda S. Filley   Production Manager
Libra Ann Cusack   Typesetting Supervisor
Juliana Arbo   Typesetter
Lara Johnson   Graphics
Diane Barker   Proofreader
David Brackley   Copy Editor
David Dean   Administrative Editor
Richard Tietjen   Systems Manager

AUTHORS

JAMES C. ANDERS is the solicitor of the Fifth Judicial Circuit of the State of South Carolina.

MELVIN P. ANTELL is the presiding justice of the Superior Court of New Jersey, Appellate Division, Part A.

JAMES JAY BAKER is the director of federal affairs for the National Rifle Association of America, an association of firearm enthusiasts headquartered in Washington, D.C., that promotes firearm safety, marksmanship, hunting, and collecting.

STEWART A. BAKER is an international law attorney for the Washington, D.C., law firm of Steptoe and Johnson. He is also a former general counsel for the National Security Agency, and he worked briefly as deputy general counsel for the U.S. Department of Education during the Carter administration.

SARAH EVANS BARKER is a judge in Indiana's U.S. District Court (south district). She is on the board of directors of the New Hope of Indiana and a member of the Indianapolis Bar Association.

HARRY A. BLACKMUN is a former associate justice of the U.S. Supreme Court. He received an LL.B. from Harvard Law School in 1932 and worked in a law firm in Minneapolis, Minnesota, where he specialized in taxation, litigation, wills, trusts, and estate planning. He was nominated to the U.S. Court of Appeals by President Dwight Eisenhower in 1959, and he served in that capacity until he was nominated to associate justice of the Supreme Court by President Richard Nixon in 1970. He served as an associate justice of the Supreme Court for 24 years until his retirement in 1994.

RICHARD BONNIE is the John S. Battle Professor of Law at the University of Virginia School of Law and the director of the university's Institute of Law, Psychiatry, and Public Policy. He has written extensively on the legal aspects of mental disability and behavioral health, and he was elected to the National Academy of Sciences Institute of Medicine.

SARAH BRADY is the vice chair of Handgun Control, Inc., in Washington, D.C., a public citizens' lobby working for legislative controls and government regulations on the manufacture, importation, sale, and civilian possession of handguns.

WILLIAM J. BRENNAN, JR., is a former associate justice of the U.S. Supreme Court. He served on the Supreme Court from 1956 to 1990, when he retired at the age of 84.

STEVEN BRILL is the founder and editor in chief of *The American Lawyer* magazine. He received the 1977 John Hancock Award for excellence in business reporting, and he is the author of *The Teamsters* (Simon & Schuster, 1978).

PENELOPE E. BRYAN is a professor in the School of Law at the University of Denver in Denver, Colorado.

WHITFIELD DIFFIE is the Distinguished Engineer for Sun Microsystems, Inc.

ANDREA DWORKIN, a coauthor of the Indianapolis legislation that defines *pornography* as a violation of women's civil rights, is an American nonfiction writer, essayist, novelist, and short story writer. She is best known for her controversial nonfiction works that examine the status of women in modern society, including *Letters from a War Zone: Writings 1976–1989* (E. P. Dutton, 1989).

STEPHEN K. ERICKSON is a mediator for and the director of the Erickson Mediation Institute in Minneapolis, Minnesota, an institute where lawyers and therapists train to be mediators. A founding board member of the Academy of Family Mediators, he was one of the first individuals in the United States to begin practicing as a divorce mediator.

YALE KAMISAR is a lawyer and a professor of law at the University of Michigan Law School. He is the author of *Police Interrogation and Confessions: Essays in Law and Policy* (University of Michigan Press, 1980).

KENNETH KIPNIS is a professor of philosophy at the University of Hawaii at Manoa. He is the the editor of several volumes on legal, social, and political philosophy and the author of *Legal Ethics* (Prentice Hall, 1986).

SUSAN M. LISS is the deputy assistant attorney general of the U.S. Department of Justice and a former director and counsel of the Citizens' Commission on Civil Rights.

HARRY C. MARTIN is an associate justice of the Supreme Court of North Carolina. He has served in a judicial capacity in North Carolina for 30 years, first as a judge in its superior court and its court of appeals and then in its supreme court, beginning in 1982.

BURLEY B. MITCHELL, JR., is an associate justice in the Supreme Court of North Carolina. He has served as an assistant attorney general for North Carolina, a district attorney for Raleigh, and a judge in the North Carolina Court of Appeals.

JOHN B. MITCHELL is a clinical professor of law at the University of Puget Sound School of Law in Tacoma, Washington. He has authored or coauthored numerous articles on lawyer's ethics, and he is a coauthor, with Marilyn J. Berger and Ronald H. Clark, of *Trial Advocacy: Planning, Analysis, and Strategy* (Little, Brown, 1989).

SANDRA DAY O'CONNOR is an associate justice of the U.S. Supreme Court. She worked in various legal capacities both in the United States and in Germany until she was appointed to the Arizona state senate in 1969. She served as a state senator for four years and served in the Arizona judiciary for six years before she was nominated to the Supreme Court by President Ronald Reagan in 1981.

JAMES OSTROWSKI is a former policy analyst for the Cato Institute in Washington, D.C., a public policy research foundation.

WILLIAM H. REHNQUIST became the 16th chief justice of the U.S. Supreme Court in 1986. He engaged in a general practice of law with primary emphasis on civil litigation for 16 years before being appointed assistant attorney general, Office of Legal Counsel, by President Richard Nixon in 1969. He was nominated by Nixon to the Supreme Court in 1972.

WM. BRADFORD REYNOLDS is a senior litigation partner with the Washington, D.C., law firm of Collier, Shannon, Rill, and Scott. He served as the assistant attorney general, Civil Rights Division, for the Reagan administration's Department of Justice, and he was a counsellor to former attorney general Edwin Meese from 1987 to 1988. He has been in private practice for 17 years.

JONATHAN ROWE is a contributing editor for *The Washington Monthly.*

ANTONIN SCALIA is an associate justice of the U.S. Supreme Court. He taught law at the University of Virginia, the American Enterprise Institute, Georgetown University, and the University of Chicago before being nominated to the U.S. Court of Appeals by President Ronald Reagan in 1982. He served in that capacity until he was nominated by Reagan to the Supreme Court in 1986.

NICK SCHWEITZER is an assistant district attorney for Rock County, Wisconsin. He has been a member of the Wisconsin Bar Association since 1985.

DAVID H. SOUTER is an associate justice of the U.S. Supreme Court and a former judge for the U.S. Court of Appeals for the First Circuit in Boston, Massachusetts. He was nominated by President George Bush to the Supreme Court in 1990.

JOHN PAUL STEVENS is an associate justice of the U.S. Supreme Court. He worked in law firms in Chicago, Illinois,

for 20 years before being nominated by President Richard Nixon to the U.S. Court of Appeals in 1970. He served in that capacity until he was nominated to the Supreme Court by President Gerald Ford in 1975.

HARRY I. SUBIN is a professor of law in the School of Law at New York University in New York City. He is the author of *Criminal Justice in Metropolitan Court* (Da Capo, 1973).

WILLIAM L. TAYLOR is a lawyer specializing in civil rights and education issues and an adjunct professor of law at the Georgetown University Law Center in Washington, D.C. He is also the vice chair of the Citizen's Commission on Civil Rights and a former staff director of the U.S. Commission on Civil Rights.

HEWITT P. TOMLIN, JR., is the presiding judge in the Tennessee Court of Appeals, Western Section.

MALCOLM RICHARD WILKEY, a former judge for the District of Columbia Circuit, served as special counsel in the House of Representative's bank scandal investigations. He is a fellow of the American Bar Foundation and a member of the American Bar Association.

INDEX